CENSUS OF INDIA 1931

Census of India 1871-1951, 9 Sets In 384 Bindings (9788121258876) Rs. 700000

Census of India 1931, 28 Vols. In 52 Bindings (9788121271233) Rs. 102000

1. India - Report (9788121276153) Rs. 2820 (Vol. I, Pt. 1)
2. India - Imperial Tables (9788121276139) Rs. 3210 (Vol. I, Pt. 2)
3. India - Ethnographical and Administration Report (9788121276115) Rs. 2900 (Vol. I, Pt. 3 & 5)
4. The Andaman And Nicobar Islands - Report, Tables (9788121276078) Rs. 720 (Vol. II, Pt. 1, Pt. 2)
5. Assam - Report (9788121276054) Rs. 1340 (Vol. III, Pt. 1)
6. Assam - Tables and Administrative Report (9788121276030) Rs. 1830 (Vol. III, Pt. 2 & 3)
7. Baluchistan - Report, Imeprial and Provincial Tables and Administrative Report (9788121276016) Rs. 2320 (Vol. IV, Pt. 1 & 2 & 3)
8. Bengal & Sikkim - Report (9788121275972) Rs. 2860 (Vol. V, Pt. 1)
9. Bengal & Sikkim - Tables (9788121275958) Rs. 1660 (Vol. V, Pt. 2)
10. Calcutta (9788121275910) Rs. 960 (Vol. VI, Pt. 1 & 2)
11. Bengal, Sikkim And Calcutta - Administrative Report (9788121275934) Rs. 580 (Vol. V & VI, Pt. 3)
12. Bihar And Orissa - Report (9788121275897) Rs. 1780 (Vol. VII, Pt. 1)
13. Bihar And Orissa - Tables and Administrative Report (9788121275873) Rs. 1190 (Vol. VII, Pt. 2 & 3)
14. Bombay Presidency - General Report (9788121275835) Rs. 3620 (Vol. VIII, Pt. 1)
15. Bombay - Statistical tables (9788121275811) Rs. 3060 (Vol. VIII, Pt. 2)
16. Bombay Presidency Aden - report and tables and Administrative report (9788121275798) Rs. 520 (Vol. VIII, Pt. 3 & 4)
17. Cities of the Bombay Presidency Report & Statistical tables (9788121275750) Rs. 2020 (Vol. IX, Pt. 1 & 2)
18. The Western India States Agency, In Two Parts - The Report & The Statistical Tables (9788121275736) Rs. 2560 (Vol. X, Pt. 1 & 2)
19. Burma - Report (9788121275712) Rs. 1860 (Vol. XI, Pt. 1)
20. Burma - Tables and Administrative Report (9788121275699) Rs. 1690 (Vol. XI, Pt. 2 & 3)
21. Central Provinces & Berar - Report (9788121275651) Rs. 2340 (Vol. XII, Pt. 1)
22. Central Provinces & Berar - Tables and Administrative Report (9788121275637) Rs. 3120 (Vol. XII, Pt. 2 & 3)
23. Coorg - Report And Tables and Madras - Report (9788121275613) Rs. 2680 (Vol. XIV, Pt. 1)
24. Madras - Imperial And Provincial Tables and The Administration Report (9788121275576) Rs. 1950 (Vol. XIV, Pt. 2 & 4)
25. North - West Frontier Province - Report & Tables (9788121275538) Rs. 2300 (Vol. XV, Pt. 1 & 2)
26. Delhi - Report & Tables (9788121275514) Rs. 1180 (Vol. XVI, Pt. 1 & 2)
27. Punjab - Report (9788121275491) Rs. 2070 (Vol. XVII, Pt. 1)
28. Punjab - Tables (9788121275477) Rs. 1690 (Vol. XVII, Pt. 2)
29. United Provinces of Agra And Oudh - Report (9788121275453) Rs. 3380 (Vol. XVIII, Pt. 1)
30. United Provinces of Agra And Oudh - Imperial And Provincial Tables and Administrative (9788121275439) Rs. 3600 (Vol. XVIII, Pt. 2 & 3)
31. Baroda - Report (9788121275415) Rs. 2800 (Vol. XIX, Pt. 1)
32. Baroda - Tables (9788121275392) Rs. 730 (Vol. XIX, Pt. 2)
33. Baroda - Administrative (9788121275378) Rs. 780 (Vol. XIX, Pt. 3)
34. Central India Agency - Report (9788121275354) Rs. 1690 (Vol. XX, Pt. 1)
35. Central India Agency - Tables and Administrative Volume (9788121275330) Rs. 2260 (Vol. XX, Pt. 2 & 3)
36. Cochin - Report & Tables (9788121275293) Rs. 2460 (Vol. XXI, Pt. 1 & 2 - A & B.)
37. Gwalior - Report (9788121275279) Rs. 1470 (Vol. XXII, Pt. 1)
38. Gwalior - Tables (9788121275255) Rs. 980 (Vol. XXII, Pt. 2)
39. H. E. H. The Nizam's Dominions (Hyderabad State) - Report (9788121275231) Rs. 1540 (Vol. XXIII, Pt. 1)
40. H. E. H. The Nizam's Dominions (Hyderabad State) - Tables (9788121275217) Rs. 1510 (Vol. XXIII, Pt. 2)
41. Jammu & Kashmir State - Report (9788121275194) Rs. 2060 (Vol. XXIV, Pt. 1)
42. Jammu & Kashmir State - Imperial & State Tables (9788121275170) Rs. 1940 (Vol. XXIV, Pt. 2 & 3)
43. Mysore - Report (9788121275156) Rs. 1950 (Vol. XXV, Pt. 1)
44. Mysore - Tables (9788121275132) Rs. 1380 (Vol. XXV, Pt. 2)
45. Ajmer-Merwara - Report And Tables (9788121275118) Rs. 780 (Vol. XXVI)
46. Rajputana Agency And Ajmer-Merwara - Report and Tables and Administrative (9788121275095) Rs. 2380 (Vol. XXVII, Pt. 1 & 2)
47. Travancore - Report (9788121276092) Rs. 2960 (Vol. XXVIII, Pt. 1)
48. Travancore - Tables & Administrative (9788121275996) Rs. 1360 (Vol. XXVIII, Pt. 2 & 4)
49. Jaipur State- Report (9788121275859) Rs. 1280 (Pt. 1)
50. Jaipur State- Tables (9788121275774) Rs. 2030 (Pt. 2)
51. Mayurbhanj state- Report (9788121275675) Rs. 3180 (Pt. 1)
52. Mayurbhanj state- Tables (9788121275552) Rs. 3070 (Pt. 2)

Owing to the antiquity and rarity of this book, certain pages are regrettably absent, and readability is compromised due to the blurring of the original text. If you possess any insights regarding the availability of these missing sections, kindly inform us. Your assistance is crucial in ensuring the completion of this significant work for the benefit of future generations.

CENSUS OF INDIA, 1931

BOOK - 7: VOLUME - IV

BALUCHISTAN

PART I - REPORT
PART II - IMEPRIAL AND PROVINCIAL TABLES
PART III - ADMINISTRATIVE REPORT

GUL MUHAMMAD KHAN

GYAN

Published by

Gyan Publishing House
5, Ansari Road
Daryaganj, New Delhi-110002
Phone: 011-47034999, 9811692060
E-mail: books@gyanbooks.com

Distribution Network
gyanbooks.com
India, USA, Canada, UK, Australia

ISBN: 978-81-212-7123-3 (Set) 28 Vols. In 52 Bindings

ISBN: 978-81-212-7601-6 (PB) Vol. IV, Pt. I, II, III

First Published, 1934

2nd Impression 2024

Printed at: Gyan Press, Delhi.

CENSUS OF INDIA 1931

Census of India, 1931

VOLUME IV

BALUCHISTAN

PARTS I & II.

PART I.—Report.
PART II.—Imperial and Provincial Tables.

BY

GUL MUHAMMAD KHAN,
SUPERINTENDENT OF CENSUS OPERATIONS
IN BALUCHISTAN.

1934
PRINTED AT THE "CIVIL AND MILITARY GAZETTE" LTD.,
Lahore.

Agents for the Sale of Books published by the Superintendent of Government Printing, India, Calcutta.

IN EUROPE.

Constable & Co., 10, Orange Street, Leicester Square, London, W.C.

Kegan Paul, Trench, Trubner & Co., 68-74, Carter Lane, E.C., and 25, Museum Street, London, W.C.

Bernard Quaritch, 11, Grafton Street, New Board Street, London, W.

P. S. King & Sons, 2 & 4, Great Smith Street, Westminster, London, S.W.

H. S. King & Co., 65, Cornhill, E.C., and 9, Pall Mal London, W.

Grindlay & Co., 54, Parliament Street, London, S.W.

Luzac & Co., 46, Great Russell Street, London, W.C.

W. Thacker & Co., 2, Creed Lane, London, E.C.

T. Fisher Unwin, Ltd., 1, Adelphi Terrace, London, W.C.

Wheldon & Wesley, Ltd., 2, 3, & 4, Arthur Street, New Oxford Street, London, W.C. 2.

Messrs. East and West, Ltd., 3, Victoria St., London, S.W. 1.

B. H. Blackwell, 50 & 51, Broad Street, Oxford.

Deighton Bell & Co., Ltd., Cambridge.

Oliver and Boyd, Tweeddale Court, Edinburgh.

E. Ponsonby, Ltd., 116, Grafton Street, Dublin.

Ernest Leroux, 28, Rue Bonaparte, Paris.

Martinus Nijhoff, The Hague, Holland.

Friedländer and Sohn, Berlin.

Otto Harrassowitz, Leipzig.

IN INDIA AND CEYLON.

Thacker, Spink & Co., Calcutta and Simla.

Newman & Co., Ltd., Calcutta.

R. Cambray & Co., Calcutta.

S. K. Lahiri & Co., Calcutta.

B. Banerjee & Co., Calcutta.

The Indian School Supply Depot, 309, Bow Bazar Street, Calcutta, and 226, Nawabpur, Dacca.

Butterworth & Co. (India), Ltd., Calcutta.

Rai M. C. Sarcar Bahadur & Sons, 90-2A, Harrison Road, Calcutta.

The Weldon Library, 57, Park Street, West Calcutta.

Standard Literature Company, Limited, Calcutta.

Lal Chand & Sons, Calcutta.

Association Press, Calcutta.

The International Buddhist Book Depôt, 4, Chandney Chowk, 1st Lane, Calcutta.

Higginbotham & Co., Madras.

V. Kalyanarama Iyer & Co., Madras.

G. A. Natesan & Co., Madras.

S. Murthy & Co., Madras.

Thompson & Co., Madras.

Temple & Co., Madras.

P. R. Rama Iyer & Co., Madras.

Vas & Co., Madras.

E. M. Gopalakrishna Kone, Madura.

Thacker & Co., Ltd., Bombay.

D. B. Taraporevala, Sons & Co., Bombay.

Mrs. Radhabai Atmaram Sagoon, Bombay.

Sunder Pandurang, Bombay.

Gopal Narayan & Co., Bombay.

Ram Chandra Govind & Son, Kalbadevi, Bombay.

Proprietor, New Kitabkhana, Poona.

The Standard Bookstall, Karachi, Rawalpindi and Murree.

Mangaldas Karishandas, Surat.

Karsandas Narandas & Sons, Surat.

A. H. Wheeler & Co., Allahabad, Calcutta and Bombay.

N. B. Mathur, Supdt., Nazir Kanun Hind Press, Allahabad.

Munshi Seetaram, Managing Proprietor, Indian Army Book Depôt, Juhi, Cawnpore.

Rai Sahib M. Gulab Singh & Sons, Mufid-i-Am Press, Lahore and Allahabad.

Rama Krishna & Sons, Lahore.

Oxford Book and Stationery Company, Delhi.

Supdt., American Baptist Mission Press, Rangoon.

Proprietor, Rangoon Times Press, Rangoon.

The Modern Publishing House, Ltd., 70, Sparks Street, Rangoon.

Manager, the "Hitavada," Nagpur.

S. C. Talukdar, Proprietor, Students & Company, Cooch Behar.

A. M. & J. Ferguson, Ceylon.

Manager, Educational Book Depôts, Nagpur and Jubbulpore.*

Manager of the Imperial Book Depôt, 63, Chandney Chauk Street, Delhi.*

Manager, "The Agra Medical Hall and Co-operative Association, Ltd." (Successors to A. John & Co., Agra.)*

Supdt., Basel Mission Book and Tract Depository, Mangalore.*

P. Varadachary & Co., Madras.*

Ram Dayal Agarwala, 184, Katra, Allahabad.*

D. C. Anand & Sons, Peshawar.*

Manager, Newal Kishore Press, Lucknow.*

Maung Lu Gale, Proprietor, Law Book Depôt, Mandalay.*

Times of Ceylon Co., Ltd.†

*Agents for the sale of Legislative Department publications only.
† Agents for the sale of Archæological publications only.

General Table of Contents.

Census of India, 1931

VOLUME IV—BALUCHISTAN.

CONSISTING OF THREE PARTS.

Part I.—Report	Bound together in this Volume.
Part II.—Imperial and Provincial Tables	
Part III.—Administrative Report	Issued separately.

PART I.

The Report.

DETAILED TABLE OF CONTENTS

OF

Volume IV.

Part I.—Report.

CHAPTER VIII.—OCCUPATION.

LIST OF MAPS AND DIAGRAMS.

INTRODUCTION.

CENSUS HISTORY.

This report deals with the results of the 1931 census of Baluchistan which was technically the fifth but in reality the third complete enumeration of the whole province.

Previous Censuses. The first attempt at a census of this province was made in 1891. The enumeration was fragmentary, covering an area of only 20,568 square miles out of a total area of 134,638, and consisted of a synchronous enumeration on the Standard Schedule of only the alien settlements in towns and cantonments and railway premises and a rough non-synchronous estimate of the population of the Quetta-Pishin District and of parts of the Sibi, Loralai and Zhob Districts. The second census was taken in 1901. It covered an area of 82,950 square miles, Makran, Kharan and Western Sanjrani country being left out of the count. The third census took place in 1911. This was the first real census in view of the fact that for the first time it embraced the whole province on a comprehensive schedule. The operations of the two succeeding censuses were identical with those of 1911 in respect of area and procedure.

The population is so thin and widely scattered that a synchronous census of the whole province in the present state of its advancement is physically impracticable. An enumeration within a reasonable time limit is rendered possible only by splitting the province into Regular and Tribal Areas. The former consisting of towns and cantonments, railway premises and head-quarters stations are subjected to a synchronous census while the Tribal Areas comprising the rest of the province are enumerated non-synchronously. In the Regular Areas the census has been taken from its inception on the Standard Indian Schedule. The dates on which the various synchronous censuses were taken are given below :—

February 26, 1891.
March 1, 1901.
March 10, 1911.
March 18, 1921.
February 26, 1931.

Forms of Schedule. In the Tribal Areas the Schedule has undergone gradual change. It began in 1891 with merely an estimate of human heads, for, complete figures even for each sex were not recorded, children of both sexes being entered as females. In 1901 the scope of the enquiry was enlarged so as to include tribe, sex, religion and occupation, the record of age being confined to a distinction between under 12 and over 12 years of age. The enumeration was conducted not by individuals but by families in British and Administered territory, the numbers in the States and Tribal Areas being based on estimates for each section and sub-section arrived at with the help of Tribal Chiefs and headmen. Similarly the occupation of the head of the family in British and Administered territory and of the head of the tribal group in the States and Tribal Areas was assumed to be the occupation of all members of the family or group concerned. No information was collected in respect of subsidiary occupations, birth-place, language, literacy, infirmities and civil condition. In 1911, however, a more comprehensive schedule was introduced in the Tribal Areas. It fell short of the standard schedule only in regard to the record of individual ages and civil condition while on the other hand it went a step further in adding a column for bilingualism.

Census of 1931.

The Censuses of 1921 and 1931 followed the model of their predecessor of 1911. A special feature of the Census of 1931, however, was that a beginning was made successfully to break tribal prejudice against the searching inquiries of the standard schedule by enumerating the whole of Kharan in full detail of the standard schedule. At the same time the principal and subsidiary occupations as well as mother-tongues and secondary languages were, for the first time in the census history of the province, recorded for each individual throughout the Tribal Areas as distinguished from the Regular Areas. Special statistics were also compiled in 1931 for educated unemployment while fertility and mortality statistics were collected for 39,744 families against 6,641 and 3,582 families at the two preceding censuses respectively.

HOW THE CENSUS WAS TAKEN IN 1931.

Census Divisions and Census officers.

For purposes of taking the census the whole province was divided into census districts which were conterminous with the civil administrative divisions. With the exception of the Bolan and Chagai Districts where the Extra Assistant Commissioners were appointed District Census Officers under their respective Political Agents, the Assistant Political Agent for each district and State was appointed as District Census Officer under the control of his Political Agent who was relieved of all routine census work. All instructions and orders were, however, forwarded through him to the District Census Officer who was instructed to keep his Political Agent informed of progress of work or other important questions relating to census operations.

Railway Census Officer.

A separate Railway Census Officer was appointed for the census of railway premises within the limits of the province. He was made responsible for the organisation and conduct of census operations within railway limits and had instructions to work in direct communication with the Provincial Census Superintendent in regard to instructions and the supply of forms, etc., and to co-operate and work in consultation with the District Census Officer concerned for delimitation of boundaries and submission of provisional totals.

Military Census Officers.

Similarly the census of Strictly Military Areas, which actually comprised persons subject to military law, was placed in the case of each cantonment or outpost in the Quetta Military District under the charge of a Military Census Officer who received instructions and forms, etc., direct from the Provincial Census Superintendent but worked, for purposes of delimitation of boundaries and advice, in co-operation and direct consultation with the local Civil District Census Officer and Charge Superintendent of each station. In the Zhob Independent Military Area the Officer Commanding each station or outpost or an officer nominated by him was appointed the Charge Superintendent. The census of the population not comprised in the Strictly Military Area was taken by the Excutive Officer of the Cantonment or the person appointed by him, under and in accordance with the direction of the Civil Census Authority. This distinction between Strictly Military and Non-Strictly Military Areas proved extremely inconvenient to the officers in charge of both areas owing to overlapping of charges and the procedure needs improvement at future censuses.

Duties of Census officers.

The first thing that a District Census Officer was required to do was to prepare a village register showing all towns and inhabited and uninhabited villages and hamlets as well as all inhabited or uninhabited camping grounds of nomads. After delimitation of boundaries in consultation with the Military and Railway Census Officers he proceeded with the division of his census district into Charges and selection of Charge Superintendents who in turn were required to subdivide their Charges into Circles and Blocks and prepare lists of officials and non-officials whom it was proposed to appoint Supervisors of Circles and Enumerators in charge of Blocks. The indents for forms were based on these lists and the forms were obtained from the Provincial Census Superintendent. The same procedure was followed by the Military and Railway Census Officers.

In the Regular Areas a Charge usually corresponded to a town or cantonment or a headquarters station. A Circle was a compact block of 10 to 15 Enumerators' Blocks while a Block consisted usually of 30 to 50 houses. In the Tribal Areas, a Charge usually corresponded with a recognised administrative division such as the Tahsil in British territory, or a whole State or a Division of a State. A Circle was usually conterminous with the Kanungo's jurisdiction or a Niabat etc., while a Block coincided with a Patwari's circle or other recognised administrative or tribal unit. The division of the province into Census Districts and Sub-Divisions was made with the advice of the Provincial Census Superintendent in each and every case.

As soon as forms were received from the Provincial Census Superintendent, steps were taken by District and other Census Officers to give a thorough coaching to the enumerating and supervising staff at meetings held at central places. Then followed the numbering of houses in the Regular Areas and the preparation of House Lists. Houses were not numbered in the Tribal Areas where lists of families living in villages and its hamlets were prepared at a meeting in which all headmen and the majority of the heads of families were required to be present at a place and time previously notified. House-numbering was commenced and completed in some places in January 1931. In a few places it was put off till the last moment in order to prevent damage by winter rains but experience has shown that winter rains cause but little damage and it is, therefore, advisable to finish house-numbering as early in the summer as possible.

Census Staff.

Altogether a staff of over 82 Charge Superintendents, 443 Supervisors and 2,784 Enumerators was employed for the Census of 1931. Of these, 58 Charge Superintendents, 300 Supervisors and 1,347 Enumerators were employed in the Regular Areas, and 24 Charge Superintendents, 143 Supervisors and 1,437 Enumerators in the Tribal Areas or altogether 1,604 men including supervising officers for an area covering 134,438 square miles of country which was subjected to a non-synchronous census extending over nearly three months. All this staff was drawn from amongst officials of all departments and private individuals including school-boys.

Preliminary record. Tribal Areas.

In the tracts not subject to inter-provincial migration, the enumeration was commenced about the end of August 1930. In the greater part of the province subject to autumn migration, however, enumeration was not started until after the close of the seasonal migration. It was commenced about the middle of November 1930, and completed by January 15th, 1931. The enumeration books with summaries giving totals for Blocks, Circles and Charges in each District were forwarded to the Central Tabulation office at Quetta where the entries were checked and the totals incorporated in a statement, a copy of which was supplied to each Political Agent before the date of final census.

Preliminary Record-Regular Areas.

As elsewhere in India, the operation was divided into two processes, the preliminary record and the final census. The preliminary record commenced three to six weeks before the date of the final census, and was completed one to two weeks before the census night. The schedules were filled up for each person ordinarily residing in each house. Between the date of the commencement of the preliminary enumeration and the final census the record was checked and corrected where necessary by all grades of supervising officers. At sunset on February 26, the night of the final census, the enumerators revisited each house in order to bring the record up-to-date by striking out all persons who had left the house and entering those who had newly arrived, omitting residents of Tribal Areas who happened to be unavoidably present within the Regular Areas on the census night. All supervising officers remained on duty till after midnight inspecting and checking the results of the enumerators' second visit to each house.

Railway trains and platform enumeration.

For the persons in trains on the census night and for platform enumeration detailed instructions were issued by the Railway Census Officer in consultation with the Provincial Census Superintendent. Six up and down trains expected to run within the limits of the province were enumerated on the night intervening February 26 and 27, 1931. Two female enumerators were detailed by the Railway authorities to enumerate the females in these trains. A couple of trained clerks were also deputed by the Provincial Census Superintendent to help in enumeration work. For the enumeration of ballast trains the guards in charge were held responsible. The Station Masters at all railway stations were instructed to enumerate all passengers who bought tickets at their stations after 7 p.m. on February 26 and before 6 a.m. on February 27, and to give them enumeration passes supplied by the census office to show that they had been enumerated. For platform enumeration of the Sibi Railway Station additional instructions were issued in consultation with the Extra Assistant Commissioner, Sibi, for the enumeration of the passengers who alighted or entrained at Sibi.

Provisional totals.

On the morning following the final check on the night between February 26 and 27, 1931, all enumerators of a Circle met in a central place and under the supervision of the Supervisor checked the number of enumeration books due from each Circle and the household schedules due from each Block, and examined every entry in each enumeration book to correct obvious mistakes and supply omissions. Two enumerators then made totals of males and females in each enumeration book and filled up the enumerator's abstract from which the Circle Summary was prepared and handed over to the Charge Superintendent together with the enumeration books. The same procedure was followed in the Charge Superintendent's office who compiled the Charge Summary giving the number of occupied houses and of males and females and forwarded it to the District Census Officer, the books with copies of Charge and Circle summaries being forwarded direct to the Central Tabulation office at Quetta. The District Census officer consolidated the figures for each Civil District including the Military and Railway premises and the totals for the Tribal Areas previously supplied to him, and telegraphed the figures to the Census Commissioner for India and the Provincial Census Superintendent by the 4th of March 1931. The only exception was the Kalat State whose totals were delayed till the 8th of March owing to the alleged return from Sind on the last day of a large number of Jhalawan nomads. The provisional totals for the province thus telegraphed disclosed a variation from the final figures by 0·1 per cent. which was due to the omission of a whole tribe by the Kalat State enumerators. The mistake was discovered by the Central Census office and the tribe was enumerated a few days after the provisional totals had been telegraphed.

TABULATION OF THE RESULTS.

The second phase of the operations opened with the tabulation of the results of enumeration. This consisted of three stages namely Slip-Copying, Sorting and Compilation. All enumeration books were forwarded by the various Charge Superintendents direct to the Central Tabulation office at Quetta immediately after reporting the provisional totals. Full details of the procedure followed in the Tabulation office have been preserved in the Census Administration Report. It will suffice to give here merely an outline of the process. On receipt in the Tabulation Office the books were examined and after carrying out corrections where necessary were passed on to the Slip-Copying Branch of the Tabulation office where all entries were copied on to slips, a separate slip being used for each individual for the Regular Areas. A special slip was devised for the Tribal Areas where the basis of enumeration was the family. After entries on the slips had been compared and corrected by the Checking Branch, they were passed on to the Sorting Branch where they were sorted according to the requirements of the various Imperial or Provincial Tables and for purposes of revision of the B. Volumes of District Gazetteers. The results were entered in the Sorter's tickets which after being checked by the Checking Branch were handed over to the Compilation Branch to compile the statistics in the prescribed forms of tables. Tabulation.

CATTLE CENSUS AND REVISION OF GAZETTEERS.

The census of cattle and the compilation of material for the revision of the B. Volumes of District Gazetteers were carried out *pari passu* with the population census. Owing to financial stringency, however, the Gazetteer work was discontinued. The results of the cattle census were tabulated and the information was supplied to the Director of Statistics in accordance with the orders of the Government of India.

COST.

The total expenditure in connection with the census of 1931 amounted to Rs. 1,37,271 against Rs. 1,28,111 for the census of 1921 showing an increase of Rs. 9,160 or 7 per cent. The increase would have been greater but for the fact that the allotments were cut down considerably as an economy measure in view of financial stringency, which entailed considerable hard work on all concerned in the Central office. Several causes contributed to the increase, the principal ones being the increase in wages varying from 18 to 34 per cent. since 1921, the larger size of the report including the addition of two large scale maps, 11 smaller maps, 24 diagrams, and the printing of the Administrative Volume which was not printed in 1921. In 1921 the report was printed at the Government of India Press free of all over-head charges. In 1931, it was printed at a private press and all charges for printing the two reports and preparing and printing the maps had to be debited to the census grant besides the additional expenditure thrown on the census by a change in the method of accounting.

Excluding the additional expenditure thus debited against the census budget, the cost of the operations in 1931 was decidedly lower than in 1921 in spite of the increase in wages.

THE REPORT.

This brings me to the last phase of the operations, namely, the analysis of the statistics which appear in the form of this report. Unluckily I was not so fortunate here as I had been during the first two stages. I took over charge as a temporary measure on March 1, 1930, when I was acting as Assistant Political Agent, Kalat, pending the arrival of Captain Burnett of the Political Department who had been nominated as Census Superintendent. I was relieved of the additional duties of Assistant Political Agent, Kalat, on June 4, 1930, and it was only on November 20, 1930, that I was informed that Captain Burnett's services could not be spared and that I had been appointed Provincial Census Superintendent for the duration of the operations. I thus had the misfortune to lose, marking time, nearly nine months during which I could have done a great deal to prepare the frame-work of my report. All Imperial, Provincial and Subsidiary Tables had been completed and the Tables Volume had been printed off by the end of February, 1932, and I had been able to complete only the first three chapters of the report when on March 1, 1932, I was appointed Wazir-i-Azam, Kalat State. In spite of the Local Administration's representation to relieve me of census work, it was decided by Government that I should complete the report in preference to a new officer. I did my best, but the multifarious duties of Wazir-i-Azam which had multiplied with the inauguration of the new regime in Kalat accompanied by the activities of the new generation left me but little time to devote to census work which needed continuous and concentrated attention to study and translate masses of dull, deceptive figures into facts. This was not all. The two fat Jail Manuals for the Province which I had been compiling since 1929 still needed my attention and I was grateful to the Hon'ble Sir Norman Cater who not only relieved me of this duty when the time came to send the volumes to the press but also, through his timely intervention as Revenue Commssioner, prevented a possible failure of the census operations at an early stage in the Kalat State owing to some misapprehension on the part of the State authorities. At the same time His late Highness's prolonged tours followed by his prolonged illness kept me fully occupied so that I was able to complete altogether three more chapters. Thus the rest of the seven chapters including the Introduction, besides the Census Administration Report, were written by me after my official demise both as Wazir-i-Azam and a paid servant of Government.

Acknowledgments. So much for an explanation for this rather belated report which I close with apologies to the friendly critic who I doubt will, excepting a few, ever read this dry discussion of statistics bereft of that fascinating fund of ethnographical and other valuable information that is contained in the 1911 report. Standing as it does shoulders high above census reports with reputation as the best report ever written, the report for 1911 has been my guiding star with its wide range of illuminating information, its searching enquiries and unassailable prophetic conclusions, and its perfect diagnosis and infallible prescriptions for social, economic and political ailments. I owe its author, the Rt. Hon. Sir Denys Bray, P.C., K.C.I.E., K.C.V.O., both my apologies and my grateful acknowledgments.

I now turn to my duty of recording my obligations to those whose efforts and co-operation were instrumental in bringing the first phase of the operations to a successful issue. First and foremost are the Political Officers. Although they were relieved of all routine census work, the responsibility for the successful conduct of the operations continued to rest on their shoulders and it was due entirely to their personal influence, co-operation and constant vigilance that the enumeration was completed so smoothly and well without a single untoward incident throughout the province. The actual duties of organisation, selection and training of the staff, complete and correct enumeration, the prompt collection from all Departments and from all parts of their Districts of the provisional totals and their compilation and timely submission fell to the lot of the District Census Officers. 87 per cent. of the population lives in widely isolated villages and nomadic encampments constantly shifting from place to place. Most of it is subject to inconvenient waves of seasonal migration so that an accurate census is rendered extremely difficult. Thanks to the zeal and intelligent interest taken by the whole revenue staff that the results proved to be as satisfactory as could be expected in such adverse circumstances and I do not hesitate to place on record the fact that the lion's share of the obligations under which the census department is placed at each successive census goes to the District Census Officer and his staff who have to bear the heaviest burden. While speaking of the census of the Tribal Areas, I cannot help singling out a couple of individual cases. Sardar Bahadur Nawab Habibullah Khan, Chief of Kharan, realising the benefits of the census inquiry, voluntarily undertook to census the whole of Kharan on the Standard Schedule. He came to Quetta to receive personally practical instruction in filling up the various census forms. On return to Kharan he sent for the enumerating staff from distant parts of the country, gave them practical instruction at his headquarters and personally supervised and checked their work from start to finish. He has set an admirable example for tribal Chiefs in the rest of the Province who will, it is to be hoped, benefit by his example at future censuses.

The Jam Sahib of Las Bela evinced similar personal interest in the operations and under his keen and constant guidance the Wazir of Las Bela—K. S. Mir Yakub Shah and the Tahsildar, M. Ahmadali Khan, did everything in their power to make the operations a success. And I should be failing in my duty of expressing my acknowledgments if I did not place on record the valuable assistance rendered by the Mari and Bugti Chiefs, K.B. Nawab Mehrulla Khan Mari and K. B. Nawab Mehrab Khan Bugti, C.I.E., C.B.E., in whose tribal territories a census of the population is still beset with peculiar difficulties. The successful termination of the operations in the rest of the Tribal Areas speaks highly of the public spirit shown by all Sardars and headmen who have now come to look on this inquiry with amusement instead of resentment. Without the good humour infused by them into this inconveniently searching inquiry, the tribesmen would not have entered into the spirit of this periodical stock-taking with alacrity.

Speaking of the Regular Areas here, the census, though covering only about 13 per cent. of the population, is by no means less difficult than that of the Tribal Areas. In fact it is more confusing in some aspects and needs greater intelligence and care for both organisers and the enumerating and supervising staff. Quetta with its continual encroachments on surrounding villages will soon have to be treated as a City with a separate set of tables and a report. The

Census work for the Municipality with its suburbs which formed the largest and most difficult charge throughout the synchronously censused area was entrusted to K. B. Sardar Mir Ahmad Khan, City Magistrate. His task was rendered more trying owing to the inclusion in the regular census of the Kasi and Nichari villages inhabited by local tribesmen who resented the questionnaire of the standard schedule. He had to work hard in the rains and severe cold of January and February to complete the house-numbering and the preliminary and final census. Ably assisted by Wazirzada Abdul Ahad Khan, Assistant Municipal Secretary, and Arbab Mohammad Umar Khan in Kasi and tactfully securing the co-operation of all communities, he acquitted himself creditably and I am indebted to them all for the successful conduct of work in this area.

In the synchronous operations however the Military Department has placed the census authorities under a special debt of gratitude. The courtesy shown by the highest local Military Authorities and their rank and file, their willing co-operation and the manner in which they entered into the spirit of the inquiry were most admirable. If a Census Superintendent could be assured from all parts of the province of efficiency and accuracy such as that displayed by the Military Department he could confidently say that the enumeration of his province was accurate to a man. Captain D. E. Murray in charge of all Military census arrangements in the Quetta Military District who displayed extraordinary ability in respect of organisation and enviable energy, efficiency and keenness all through the operations deserves special mention. Captain Davis, Charge Superintendent of the Non-Strictly Military Area, had a difficult task in his limited area in consequence of the confusing distinction between Strictly Military and Non-Strictly Military Areas introduced at the census of 1931. He spared no pains to overcome his difficulties and personally to train his staff and to check their work.

The Railway Census Officer, Captain K. N. Simner, R.E., had difficulties of his own. At the most critical moment in the operations, a portion of his charge became snow-bound while another was rendered inpassable by breaches caused by floods rendering enumeration and check at out-stations and outlying gang huts extremely difficult. Thanks to the energetic action taken by him and his European and Indian colleagues, the situation was handled quite successfully. I am grateful to Captain Simner and his staff for all the trouble they took to make the Railway Census a success over a wide area which passed through a large number of administrative units and rendered the work of organisation and allocation of duties so perplexing.

It now remains for me to acknowledge my obligations to those who have actively helped me in connection with my Report. I am specially indebted to Dewan Bahadur Dewan Jamiat Rai, C. I. E., who with his previous experience of census work and his wide and intimate knowledge of the country and its people came to my help at a time when his ripe experience was most needed. He very kindly examined the whole Report within the shortest space of time and made valuable suggestions for which I am deeply grateful. Mr. C. P. Skrine, Political Agent, Kalat, with all his preoccupations, very kindly gave finishing touches to my draft of Chapter I. Doctor H. T. Holland, C.I.E., M.B., was kind enough to examine the Chapter on Infirmities. Major J. E. Lidierth, M.B.E., Assistant Secretary to the Local Government and Major H. J. Ford of the Grammar School, examined the proofs of the Report for which they have earned my sincere gratitude. I am also indebted to

Sheikh Abdul Samad, B.A., Superintendent of Education, for examining the Chapter on Literacy and to K. B. Maulvi Najmud-din for his note on educational progress which is printed as an appendix to Chapter IX. K. B. Mirza Sher Muhammad Khan, my Deputy Superintendent and colleague in three censuses, and Lala Choith Ram, my Assistant for gazetteer work, helped me whole-heartedly and I acknowledge with great pleasure their loyal co-operation and devotion to duty. But my special debt of gratitude is due to L. Sunder Dass Johar of the Revenue Commissioner's Office who was in charge of the Tabulation work. He was selected by me for his general experience of office routine and for his previous experience of census and revenue work both in the Punjab and Baluchistan. He worked as Head Clerk for one year when the work of drafting and translating the instructions was heavy. Later on he was appointed as Assistant Superintendent in charge of Tabulation which is the most intricate and tedious stage in the Census Operations requiring technical knowledge of the processes of Slip-Copying, Sorting and Compilation which in this province keep changing at every census owing to the dual system of enumeration. The Officer in charge has to control a large low-paid temporary establishment not easily amenable to discipline and is expected to get the maximum amount of work out of every one under him. L. Sunder Dass not only discharged his arduous personal duties with remarkable diligence and ability but also continued to help me without remuneration, while on leave, in completing the Report for about six months. Of my Ministerial Staff I have specially to thank my painstaking Head Clerk, Sheikh Bashir Ahmed, for running the office smoothly throughout the period. He lightened my task appreciably by rendering valuable assistance in preparing a large number of difficult maps and diagrams to illustrate my Report.

In conclusion I must express my indebtedness to the Civil and Military Gazette Press, Lahore, where the Report has been printed, for the excellence of this difficult work. Many of the tables were most unwieldy and difficult to compress into suitable sizes. They were rearranged in the press, and the clear and compact forms in which they have been finally printed are due entirely to the keen personal interest taken in the work by Mr. Wollen, the Works Manager, and the intelligent manner in which his instructions were carried out by his painstaking Foreman, Shaikh Mohammad Ashraff.

GUL MUHAMAD.

MAP SHOWING THE GEOGRAPHICAL SITUATION OF BALUCHISTAN

MAP NO 1

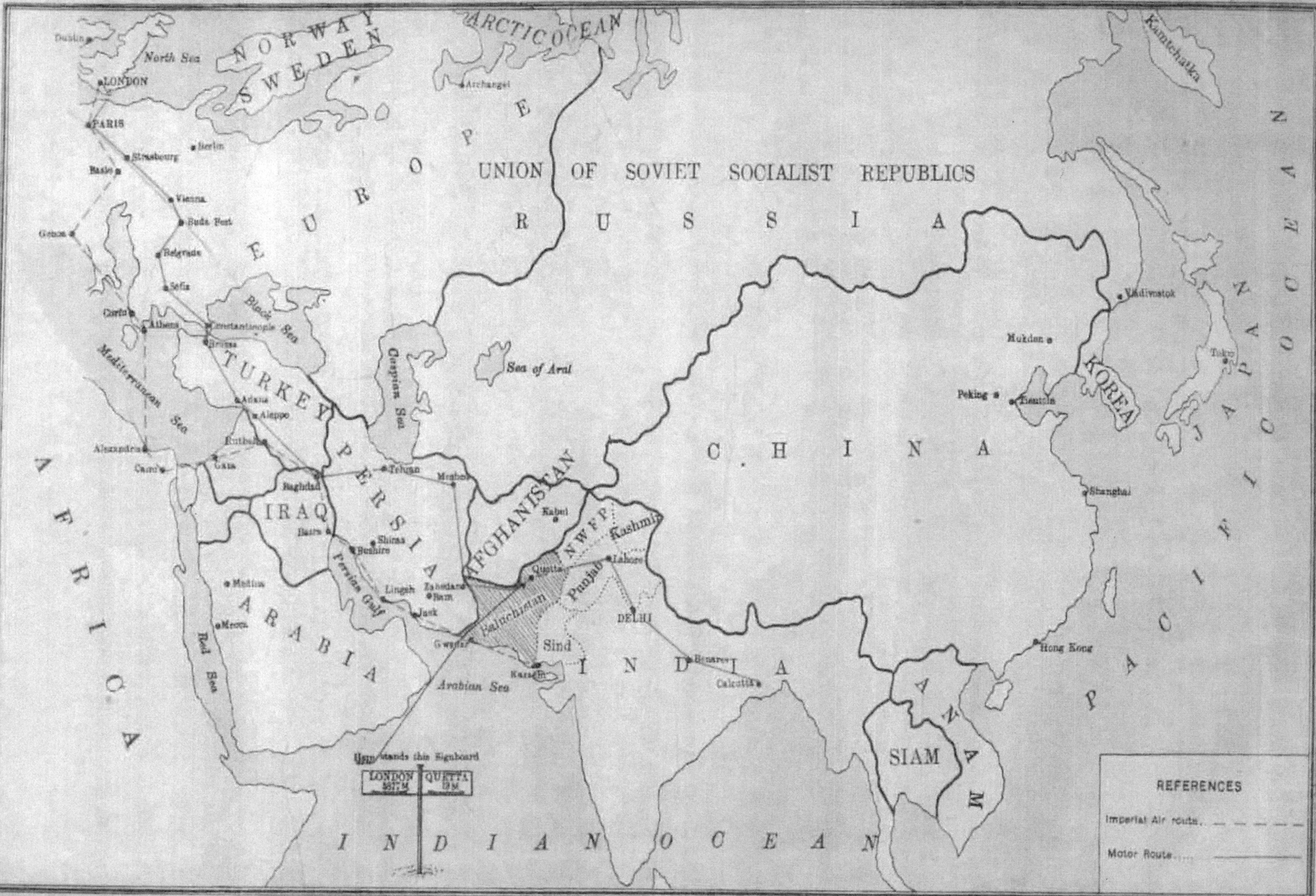

Reg No 73 EDE Copy 1853 '34o.

REPORT

ON THE

CENSUS OF BALUCHISTAN

1931.

CHAPTER I.

DISTRIBUTION AND MOVEMENT OF THE POPULATION.

Total Area of Baluchistan .. .. 134,638 square miles.
Total Population .. .. 868,617 persons.

1. The statistical data will be found in the following tables :— **Reference to statistics.**

Particulars.	Table.	Part I of this Report. Page	Part II. Page
Area, Houses and population ..	Imperial Table I ..	..	1
Variation in population ..	Imperial Table II ..	..	3
Race, Tribe or Caste ..	Imperial Table XVII ..	..	107
Population by Political Agencies and Tahsils.	Provincial Tables I and II	..	125 & 127
Density, Water Supply and Crops ..	Subsidiary Table 1 ..	18	..
Density ..	Subsidiary Tables 2 and 4 ..	18 & 20	..
Variation in Indigenous population by Districts and States.	Subsidiary Table 3 ..	19	..
Vital Statistics for Quetta Town ..	Subsidiary Table 5 ..	20	..
Racial Variation ..	Subsidiary Table 6 ..	21	..
House Population in Regular and Tribal Areas.	Subsidiary Tables 7 and 9 ..	22 & 23	..
Distribution of Indigenous and Alien Population in Regular and Tribal Areas.	Subsidiary Table 8 ..	22	..

2. Map No. 1 on the opposite page shows the geographical situation of Baluchistan excluding the small inlet of territory round Gwadur which is at present in the possession of the Sultan of Muscat but to which the Khans of Kalat have never waived claim. It also excludes, as at previous censuses, the interesting little Island, Haptalar, known to the Arabs as Astalo, to the Meds **Geographical.**

as Astalu and to the Hindus as Satadep. It is situated in the Arabian Sea about 16 miles off the Makran coast and 26 from the Pasni Port. It is about three miles long and one mile broad. An atmosphere of mystery and legend has always surrounded Haptalar. It has been identified with the Nosala of Arrian the weird accounts of which frightened the superstitious seamen of Niarchus. In Hindu mythology it is believed to be the abode of the goddess Kalidevi who is said to remain there for seven out of eight periods into which the day and night are divided. Only in the morning is she believed to leave it to take her bath at Hinglaj some 100 miles away in the Lasbela State of Baluchistan. The place is held in extreme veneration by the Hindus, and pilgrims from all parts visit it in small numbers. The island has never figured before in the census returns evidently owing to its isolated situation. It nearly met the same fate at the Census of 1931 and only came to notice through a Bengali mendicant whom I met in Pasni in the course of my tours when it was too late to include him in the census returns. He assured me, however, that he had been in the island for a year all by himself and that there were no pilgrims or other visible human beings there on the Census night. An interesting account of this little island is given in Mr. Hughes-Buller's Gazetteer of Makran.

3. With these two exceptions the province includes the whole of the remaining area within the boundaries indicated on the map and consists of British Baluchistan and British-administered territory, Tribal Areas and the States of (1) Kalat including Kharan, and (2) Las Bela. Its geographical and physical features are described in previous Census Reports and Imperial and Provincial Gazetteers. With a frontier of 520 miles with Persia, 723 miles with Afghanistan, 38 with what was formerly no-man's-land in the extreme North, 471 miles of coast line, several miles of the Imperial Airways route and finally a long and important link in the Calcutta-London Motor road which in the near future promises to become the high road to the Hedjaz and beyond, Baluchistan enjoys a pride of place which justly entitles it to high rank among Indian provinces as India's sentinel on the most gigantic historical gateway to India.

Political Divisions.

4. The province is composed of the following political divisions :—

I. British Baluchistan (including British-administered territory).
II. Tribal Areas.
III. Baluchistan States, namely (*i*) Kalat including Kharan and (*ii*) Las Bela.

Legally, only two divisions are recognised under British Baluchistan, namely, British Baluchistan and Agency Territories. The smaller units included in each category are shown in the subjoined table with their respective areas and population.

Administrative Divisions.	Total.		Parts in British Baluchistan.			Parts in Agency Territories.		
	Area. (Square miles.)	Population.	Divisions.	Area (square miles.)	Population.	Divisions.	Area (square miles.)	Population.
BALUCHISTAN ..	134,638	868,617	..	9,084	136,793	..	37,864	271,491
I.—British Baluchistan.	54,228	463,508	..	9,084	136,793	..	37,864	271,491
DISTRICTS. 1. Quetta-Pishin District.	4,806	147,541	Pishin-Tahsil ..	3,052	53,375	Quetta-Tahsil ..	548	76,649
			Chaman Sub-Division	1,206	17,517	..	..	..
				4,258	70,892			
2. Loralai District.	7,525	86,087	Duki-Tahsil ..	1,688	17,998	Bori Tahsil ..	1,671	18,532
						Barkhan Tahsil ..	1,309	20,434
						Musakhel Tahsil ..	2,181	22,810
						Sanjawi Sub-Tahsil	676	6,313
							5,837	68,089

MAP NO. 2

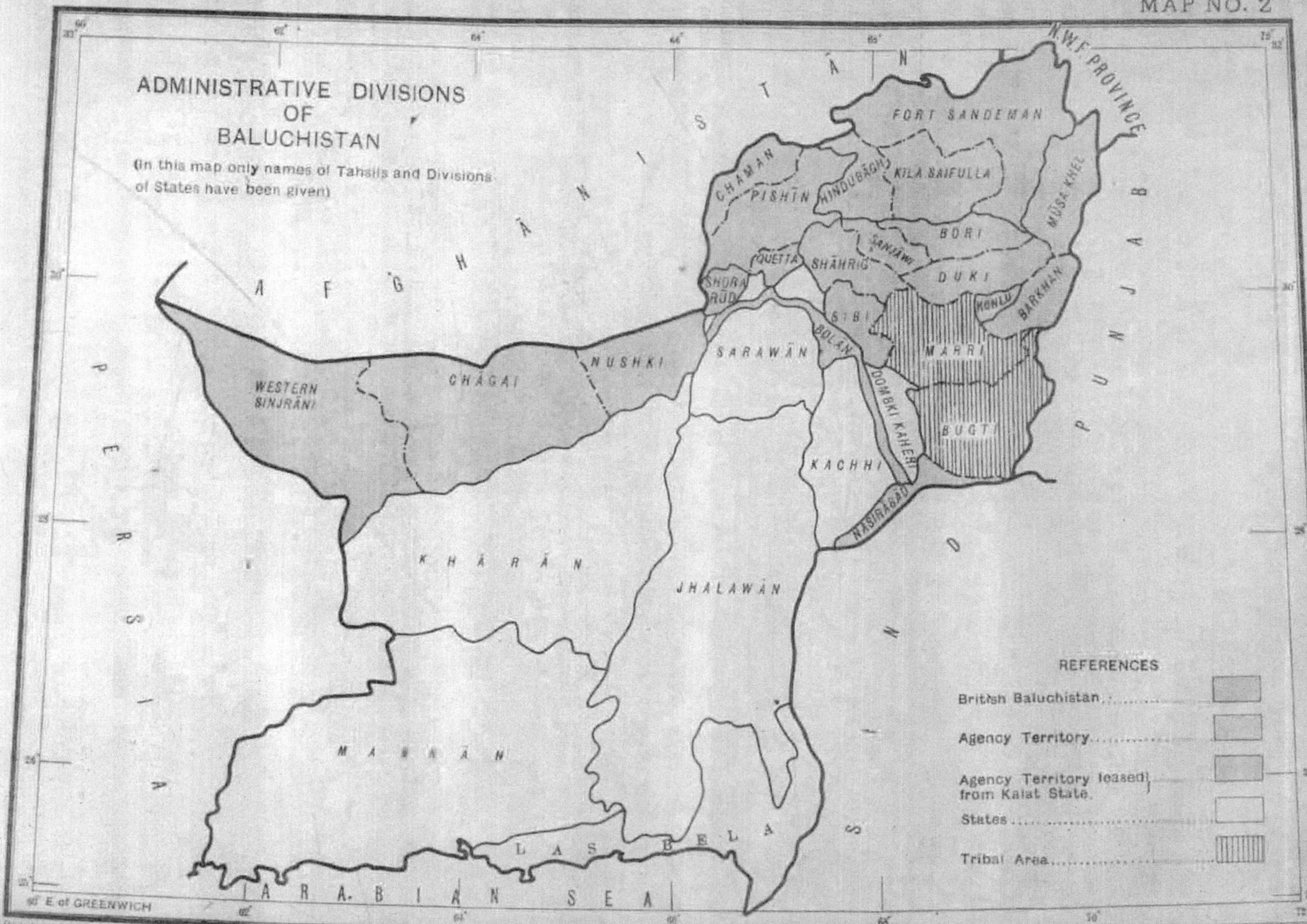

Reproduced by E Company Survey of India Quetta

Administrative Divisions.	Total.		Parts in British Baluchistan.			Parts in Agency Territories.		
	Area. (Square miles.)	Population.	Divisions.	Area. (Square miles)	Population.	Divisions.	Area. (Square miles.)	Population.
3. Zhob-District	10,315	57,963	..	..	..	Fort Sandeman Tahsil.	6,458	32,989
						Hindubagh-Tahsil	1,459	11,580
						Killa Saifullah Tahsil.	2,398	13,394
							10,315	57,963
4. Chagai-District.	20,036	24,224	Shorarud Sub-Tahsil	414	2,219	Nushki-Tahsil ..	2,361	10,820
						Dalbandin Tahsil	17,261	11,185
							19,622	22,005
5. Bolan and Kachhi Railway District.	359	4,688	..	..	..	..	359	4,688
6. Sibi-District	11,187	143,005	..	..	..	..	..	..
Administered area.	3,907	87,781	Sibi-Tahsil ..	1,148	27,507	Nasirabad Tahsil..	821	36,634
			Shahrig-Tahsil	1,576	18,177	Kohlu Sub-Tahsil	362	5,463
				2,724	45,684		1,183	42,097
II.—Tribal Areas.	7,280	55,224						*
Mari ,, ..	3,404	24,860						
Bugti ,, ..	3,876	30,364						
III.—States ..	80,410	405,109	..	..	..	..	..	..
1. Kalat ..	73,278	342,101	..	..	..	..	..	..
Sarawan ..	5,230	28,464	..	..	..	..	..	..
Jhalawan ..	20,795	88,978	..	..	..	..	..	..
Kachhi ..	4,060	105,886	..	..	..	..	..	..
Dombki-Kaheri country.	1,359	26,953	..	..	..	..	..	..
Makran ..	23,269	68,462	..	..	..	..	..	..
Kharan ..	18,565	23,358	..	..	..	..	..	..
2. Las Bela ..	7,132	63,008	..	..	..	..	..	..

* For administrative purposes these form part of Sibi District.

The distinction between British Baluchistan and Agency Territories is however only nominal. For practical purposes they are one and the same. Chagai was the only tract in which administration was carried on by executive order on the lines of Agency Territories until 1924 when it was declared to be Agency Territory and formally included in that category.

5. The Tribal Areas consist of the Mari and Bugti countries which are administered by the tribal Chiefs under the political control of the Political Agent, Sibi. It may be mentioned that the term "Agency Territories" includes the tracts named in the margin which are held on lease from Kalat and are shown in green in Map No. 2 facing this page.

Tahsil.	*Area.*	*Population*
Total ..	4,089	128,791
Quetta Tahsil ..	548	76,649
Nushki Tahsil ..	2,361	10,820
Nasirabad Tahsil ..	821	36,634
Bolan Tahsil ..	359	4,688

6. British Baluchistan proper represents 7 per cent. of the total area and 16 per cent of the total population of the Province. Including Agency Territories, Tribal Areas and areas leased from Kalat the figures rise to 40 and 53 respectively but excluding Tribal Areas and areas leased from Kalat the percentage of both area and population falls to 32.

Administrative Divisions.

7. The administrative divisions of the province including States with their respective areas and population are shown in the subjoined table :—

	Area.	Population.
BALUCHISTAN	134,638	868,617
DISTRICTS	54,228	463,508
Quetta-Pishin	4,806	147,541
Loralai	7,525	86,087
Zhob	10,315	57,963
Bolan	359	4,688
Chagai	20,036	24,224
Sibi	11,187	143,005
(*a*) Administered area	3,907	87,781
(*b*) Mari and Bugti Tribal Areas ..	7,280	55,224
STATES	80,410	405,109
Kalat	73,278	342,101
Sarawan	5,230	28,464
Jhalawan	20,795	88,978
Kachhi	4,060	105,886
Dombki-Kaheri country	1,359	26,953
Makran	23,269	68,462
Kharan	18,565	23,358
Las Bela	7,132	63,008

8. The total area of the province covered by the Census of 1931 was 134,638 square miles which is the same as in 1921 and 1911. The areas and population of Districts and States are given in Imperial Table I. Those of minor divisions will be found in Provincial Table I. The external boundaries of the province remained unchanged but the following inter-district transfers of area and population took place during the decade 1921-1931.

Name of unit or area transferred.	Area transferred.	Population (1921).	Unit from which transferred.	Unit to which transferred.
Shorarud Sub-tahsil ..	414	1,273	Quetta-Pishin District ..	Chagai District.
Kachhi Railway line between Jhatpat and Pirak Railway stations.	6	1,256	Sibi District ..	Bolan District.
Quat-Mandai Valley ..	12	935	Sibi District, Administered area.	Sibi District, Mari Tribal country.

Internal changes of area within a unit are confined to the Sibi and Chagai districts. In the former the Pur Valley covering an area of 9 square miles with a population of 1,652 and forming part of the Sibi Tahsil in the Sibi District, was transferred to the Shahrig Tahsil of the same district. The Quat Mandai Valley with an area of 12 miles and a population of 935 was transferred from the Sibi Tahsil to the Mari Tribal area. The Western Sanjrani country, a part of the Chagai District which had formerly been treated as a separate unit, was amalgamated with the Chagai (Dalbandin) Tahsil in the same district and declared as Agency Territory.

Population. Definition.

9. The term population as used in this report means all persons who were present within the limits of the province on the night of February 26, 1931, the date of the final Census—whether in houses or tents, in trains or in boats or on the march. The statistics collected at the Census thus represent the *de facto* population which the Indian Census aims at and not the *de jure* population. Every effort was made to ascertain the correct numbers but this is no easy task in a province covering a vast area with a surprisingly small population living in scattered villages and hamlets or constantly wandering over difficult mountains and through deserts grazing their flocks or looking for means of livelihood. A synchronous census of the whole area in such conditions is a physical impossibility

This is particularly so because the average distance to be covered by an enumerator ranges from 50 to over 150 miles while private literate enumerating agencies are practically non-existent owing to educational backwardness.

10. To overcome these difficulties the province was divided for purposes of Census into (*a*) Regular Areas and (*b*) Tribal Areas. In the Regular Areas the Census was taken synchronously on the Standard Schedule. This category covered only 200 square miles. The inhabitants of this region are almost entirely aliens with a negligible admixture of local tribesmen. On the other hand, the Tribal Areas inhabited practically exclusively by indigenous tribesmen extend over 134,438 square miles. These divisions are shown in Map No. 6. The tracts shown in black on the map represent the Regular Areas in which the Census was taken synchronously on the Standard Schedule excepting Kharan which though censused on the Standard Schedule for the first time, had, for reasons explained above, to be subjected to a non-synchronous enumeration. The map indicates plainly the manifold dangers to which a synchronous census is exposed. In the first place the synchronous and non-synchronous areas are inter-mixed and great care has to be exercised to prevent double enumeration. In the second place the population keeps constantly shifting in considerable numbers from one part of the country to another, in search of work and pasturage. Again in the autumn, a regular exodus of the local population takes place towards India and the plains of Kachhi and Sibi as well as towards Afghanistan, and to a small extent to Persia, while in winter an enormous wave of migration sets in from Afghanistan bringing down large caravans of nomads some of whom winter in Baluchistan and some drift into Sind, the Derajat and beyond. The chances of double-counting in Sind and other adjoining provinces were further increased at the Census of 1931 owing to the fact that the final date of the Census was fixed about three weeks earlier than in 1921. The emigrants to Sind and other Indian provinces do not begin to return before the beginning or middle of March and it was certain that if enumerated in Baluchistan they would also be included in the census of Indian provinces in which they were present on the Census night (26th February 1931). **Enumeration Procedure.**

11. To prevent duplication and omissions, various methods were employed. In the Regular Areas censused synchronously, the enumerators were instructed to enumerate only such tribesmen as were actually employed and were living within synchronous areas. All tribesmen not living within these areas were prohibited from entering them on the Census night. Where their presence was unavoidable they were scrupulously excluded. On the other hand enumerators in non-synchronous areas were told to exclude from their papers tribesmen and others who were employed in the synchronous areas and were actually living there. The local shifting population was enumerated wherever found. The heads of families were supplied with enumeration passes. To prevent double-counting, copies of these passes were supplied to the enumerating staff of the areas which they were likely to visit before the Census night.

12. The prevention of duplication due to seasonal migration was, however, a more difficult matter. This disturbance sets in motion at the fall of the year. To enumerate these migrants within the province would have resulted in double-counting both in the plains as well as in Indian provinces for the reasons already explained. The best way out of this difficult position was found in putting off their enumeration until after the shifting part of the population had filtered through the passes to settle down in their winter quarters within or outside Baluchistan. The actual enumeration for these reasons was commenced in areas subject to this disturbance as late as the first week of December 1930 and was completed by February 26, 1931.

13. A different method was employed in respect of nomads from Afghan territory passing through Baluchistan on their annual winter excursions into Sind and the Derajat. The enumerators were instructed to ignore them altogether. Such families or individuals however as were actually wintering in the province or were found within the limits of the province on the Census night on their way back to their homes in Afghanistan were included in the census of the population

of Baluchistan. Such of these nomads as were sure to cross the border before the Census night were not taken into account. Under instructions from the Census Commissioner for India, a separate modified schedule for their census was issued to all enumerators at the outposts through which these nomads commonly known as Powindahs cross into India. The statistics thus collected will be dealt with separately. Another factor which affects the accuracy of the figures in non-synchronous areas is the number of births and deaths that occur during the interval between the commencement of enumeration and the final census. In order to reduce the loss from this source to a minimum, instructions were issued to all enumerators in non-synchronous areas to call upon the headmen to collect and report figures of births and deaths a few days before the Census night. The results I am afraid are not very satisfactory but the resultant loss is insignificant.

14. On the whole, the instructions mentioned were faithfully carried out to the best of the enumerators' ability and I am satisfied that the results presented in Part II of this volume are normally accurate. The enumerators' work was subjected to a variety of tests by a number of supervising officers. These tests need not be discussed in detail. One of them is however, noteworthy. In the course of our tours to check non-synchronous enumeration my assistants and myself as well as the supervising staff encountered travellers and flock-owners and questioned them at random. All particulars relating to them, the heads of their families and other details as to tribe, religion and occupation in respect of themselves and the other members of their families were noted. On arrival at the enumerator's headquarters the enumeration book concerned was examined and in almost every case the entries were found to tally.

***De Facto* Population.**

15. The total *de facto* population in 1931 was 868,617 persons. This consists of the following :—

(1) Indigenous resident population (760,125).

(2) Semi-indigenous population (21,922).

(3) Aliens from India and all other orientals and foreigners (86,570).

(4) Seasonal nomads from Afghanistan who winter in Baluchistan and were present in the province on the Census night (included in (2)).

The population thus excludes :—

(1) The permanent indigenous and semi-indigenous residents away in India and beyond on the Census night.

(2) The permanent indigenous and semi-indigenous residents away in Afghanistan or Persia for the winter months.

(3) Aliens or their families ordinarily residing in the province but away on the Census night to escape the winter.

(4) Temporary spring and summer visitors from Sind and elsewhere.

The statistics, actual and estimated, for each of these classes are given in the subjoined table.

1.	Indigenous population ..	760,125
2.	Semi-indigenous	6,969
3.	Aliens	86,570
4.	Seasonal Afghan nomads	14,953
5.	Temporary emigrants to India	42,594
6.	Temporary emigrants to Foreign countries ..	Not known.
7.	Seasonal emigrants to Afghanistan (estimated)	1,000

By adding the emigrants (43,594) to the total (868,617) and subtracting the Afghan seasonal nomads (14,953) we get a total of 897,258 which, based on the ordinary methods of gauging the normal population, represents the normal population of the province. Again, if the alien population (86,570) were deducted from the balance the actual resident population would fall to 810,688 which represents,

DIAGRAM NO. 1

Diagram showing ratio of area of each district and division to total area of province

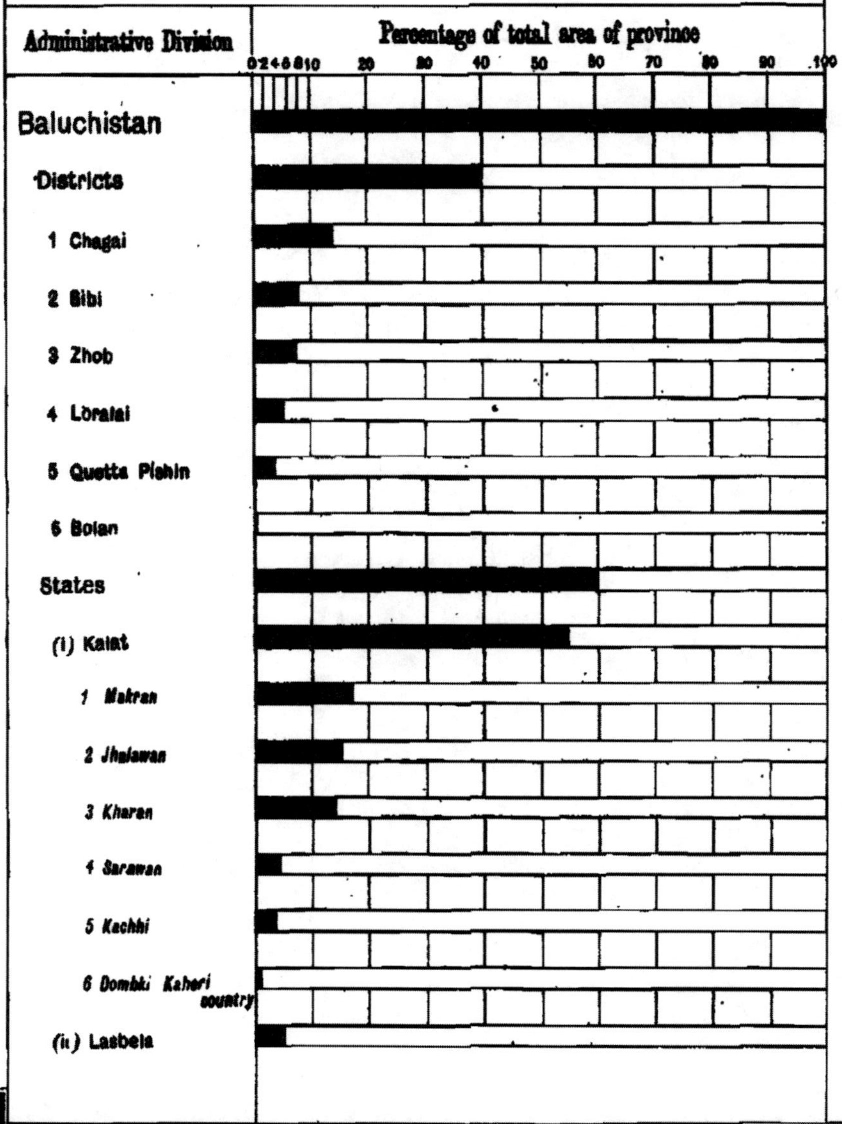

Diagram showing ratio of population of each district and division to total population of province

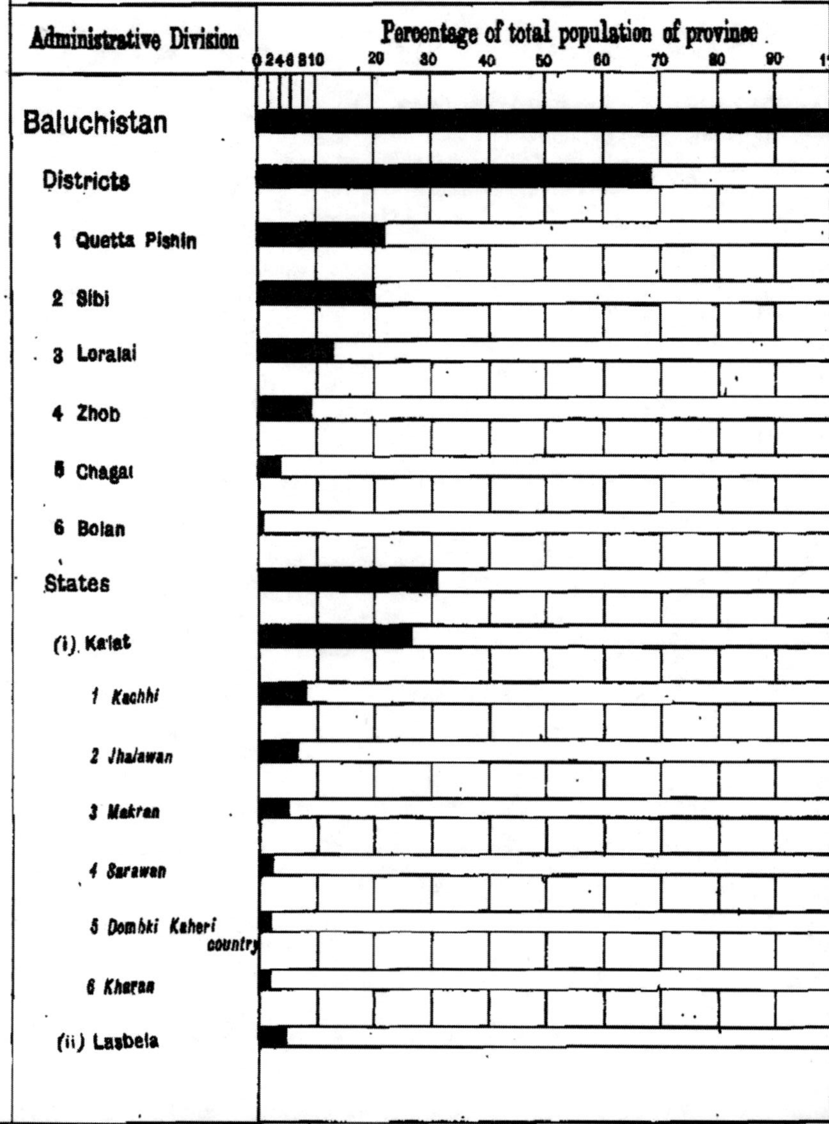

Reg. No. E.O.(E Coy) 1933.

Reproduced by E Coy Survey of India Quetta

DIAGRAM NO. 2

DIAGRAM COMPARING THE AREA AND POPULATION OF BALUCHISTAN WITH OTHER COUNTRIES AND PROVINCES

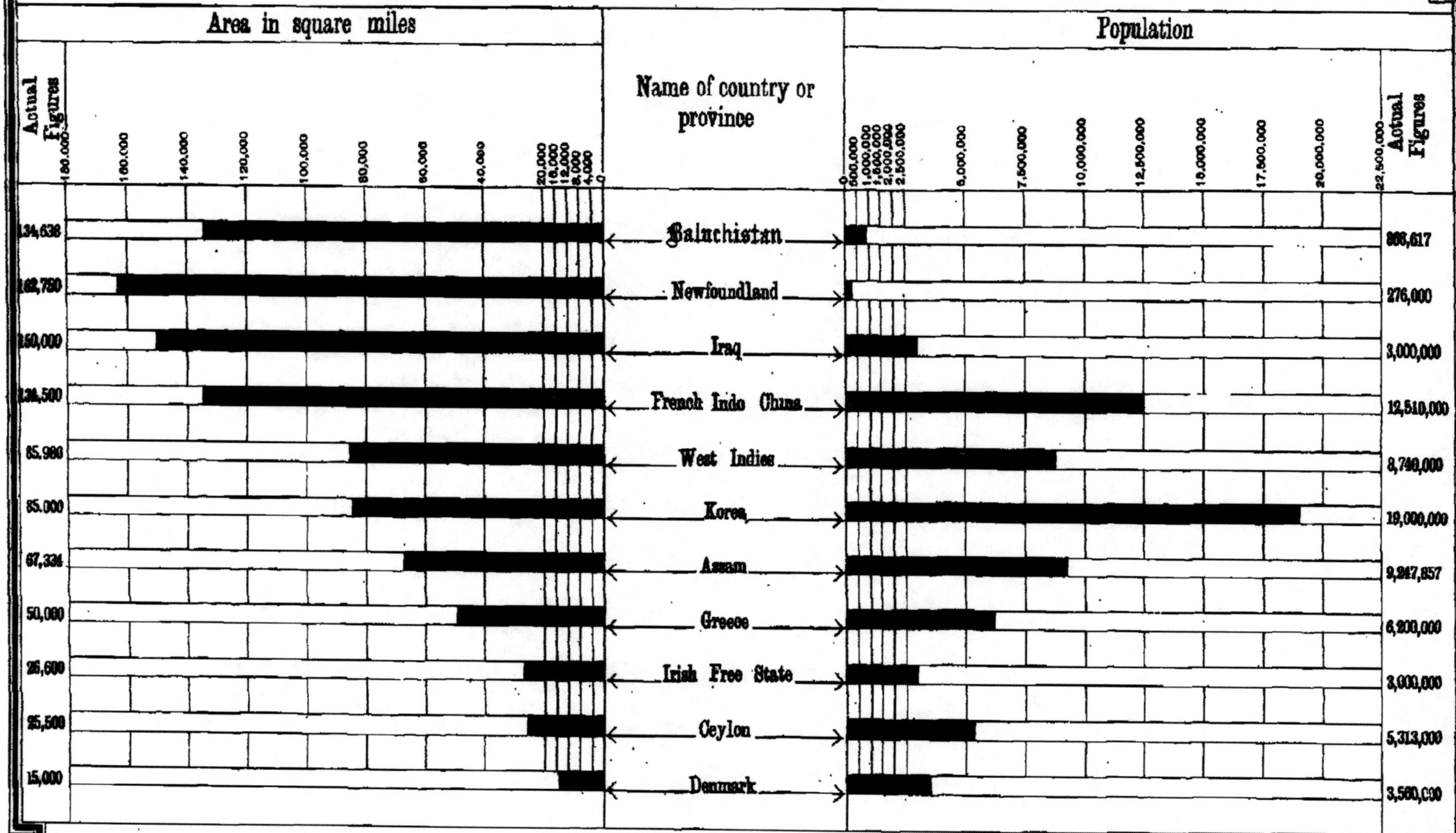

Reg. No. 795 D ('E' Coy.) 1933:-

Reproduced by 'E' Company Survey of India Quetta

with the exception of 6,969 semi-indigenous residents, the purely resident indigenous population of the province. The birthplace statistics supplied by the Indian provinces, however, are not very encouraging as pointed out in the Census Report for 1911. On the one hand they include children of parents from Indian provinces and foreign countries who happened to be temporarily sojourning in Baluchistan at the time of the birth of their children. And these are not few, for Quetta has become a summer health resort especially for Sind from where large numbers visit the province to escape the heat of the plains, for health, and for the sake of expectant mothers. On the other hand, questions as to birthplace are difficult for the ignorant indigenous inhabitants of Baluchistan to answer and more difficult to record for the enumerator of Sind and elsewhere owing to lack of detailed geographical knowledge. A resident of Makran found in India would call himself a Makrani, and that of Las Bela, a Lasi. Similarly a resident of Jhalawan would either give only the name of his country or of his village which are difficult for the enumerator to locate. Baluchistan thus loses many of the indigenous inhabitants which it should rightly claim as its own. The gain from the source first named is comparatively small but the loss from the second is considerable, amounting I believe to several thousands. Another source of error which is inseparable from birthplace statistics is that large numbers of Makranis from Makran, Lasis from Las Bela, Brahui, Baloch and Jatts from Jhalawan and Kachhi have migrated into Sind and settled down there temporarily or semi-permanently. The birthplace record automatically gives births in these families to Sind which means a corresponding loss to Baluchistan.

Normal Population.

16. In framing estimates of the normal population of Baluchistan the fact should not however be lost sight of that the population has been subject to a regular winter migration ever since the restoration of peace and prosperity with British occupation. This emigration will not cease so long as economic conditions in the Kalat State do not change for the better. In the winter the population moves down *en masse* to the plains and into Sind to escape the winter in the highlands, and to find grazing and more lucrative employment. In the spring the tide turns and it flows back through the old channels into its summer quarters. So long as the process continues the *de facto* population as disclosed by a winter census must be taken to be the normal *winter* population. The normal population for the summer, however, would be considerably larger. To arrive at an approximately correct estimate of the normal summer population we should include not only the emigrants but also the large crowds of summer visitors from Sind and elsewhere who have been causing so much anxiety every year to the local authorities of Quetta owing to pressure on the limited accommodation available and an inadequate supply of drinking water. The marginal calculations put the normal summer population at close upon one million souls. Unless the water difficulty proves insurmountable, this is likely to continue to grow rapidly in future years, for, Quetta has acquired considerable popularity as a sanitorium amongst residents of Sind and other adjoining districts.

De facto population including 86,570 aliens ..	868,617
Deduct—Afghan nomads who return to Afghanistan in the summer ..	14,953
Balance ..	853,664
Add—	
1. Emigrants who return in the summer ..	42,594
2. Omissions due to mistakes in birthplace return of other provinces and due to emigration to Afghanistan and Persia, etc. (estimated) ..	32,742
3. Summer visitors from India, etc., and seasonal immigrants in Regular Areas approximately ..	45,000
Total ..	974,000

Area and Population.

17. The administrative divisions of the province with their respective areas and population, in 1931 have been given in paragraph 7. Diagram No. 1 illustrates the proportions per cent. of each unit to the total area and population of the province. The population and area of Baluchistan are compared with some of the other Indian provinces and foreign countries, etc., in the marginal table and are illustrated in a more convenient form in Diagram No. 2. Taking the area and population of Baluchistan as 100, the proportions which these provinces and countries bear to Baluchistan in point of area and population are exhibited in the subjoined table.

Name of Country or Province.	Area.	Population.
1. Assam ..	67,334	9,247,857
2. Baluchistan ..	134,638	868,617
3. Ceylon ..	25,500	5,313,000
4. Denmark ..	15,000	3,560,000
5. French Indo-China ..	134,500	12,500,000
6. Greece ..	50,000	6,200,000
7. Iraq ..	150,000	3,000,000
8. Korea ..	85,000	19,000,000
9. Newfoundland ..	162,750	276,000
10. West Indics ..	85,980	8,740,000

	Area.	*Population.*
Baluchistan	100	100
Assam	50	1,067
Bengal	62	5,881
Bombay	113	3,024
Central Provinces and Berar	74	1,785
North-West Frontier Province	27	539
Punjab	101	3,280
Sind	34	448
Ceylon	19	612
Denmark	11	410
French Indo-China	100	1,554
Greece	37	714
Iraq	111	345
Korea	63	2,187
Newfoundland	122	32
West Indies	64	1,006

Density.

18. In the marginal table are set forth statistics of density for Baluchistan and its main political divisions as well as some of the Indian provinces and States and a few foreign countries with approximately corresponding dimensions. Strange to say, Baluchistan can beat in density of population two countries at least namely Nejd and Hedjaz, and Tibet which have only two and four persons respectively to the square mile. A glance at the list of Indian provinces and States will show that Baluchistan stands at the lowest rung. Looking from another angle one can clearly see that density is comparatively higher in almost all areas under direct British control where the magnetic charm of European civilisation, safety of life and property, medical facilities, industrial and agricultural improvements, more lucrative employment and other amenities are attracting people from all directions and are slowly but surely breaking down the walls of that traditional insularity which has been a characteristic of the people of this province.

District, State, Province or Country.	*Area.*	*Population.*	*Density per square mile.*
I.—BALUCHISTAN ..	134,638	868,617	6
DISTRICTS ..	54,228	463,508	9
Quetta-Pishin ..	4,806	147,541	31
Loralai ..	7,525	86,087	11
Zhob ..	10,315	57,963	6
Bolan ..	359	4,688	13
Chagai ..	20,036	24,224	1
Sibi ..	11,187	143,005	13
Administered area ..	3,907	87,781	22
Mari-Bugti country ..	7,280	55,224	8
STATES ..	80,410	405,109	5
Kalat ..	73,278	342,101	5
Las Bela ..	7,132	63,008	9
II.—INDIAN PROVINCES AND STATES.			
(a) *Provinces.*			
1. North-West Frontier Province ..	36,356	4,684,364	129
2. Punjab ..	135,496	28,490,857	210
3. Bombay ..	151,593	26,271,784	173
4. Bengal ..	82,955	51,087,338	616
5. Assam ..	67,334	9,247,857	137
6. Central Provinces and Berar ..	99,920	15,507,723	155
(b) *States.*			
1. Travancore ..	7,625	5,095,973	668
2. Gwalior ..	26,367	3,523,070	134
3. Hyderabad ..	82,698	14,436,114	175
4. Baroda ..	8,164	2,443,007	299
5. Mysore ..	29,326	6,557,302	224
6. Cochin ..	1,480	1,205,016	814
7. Central India Agency ..	51,597	6,632,790	129
III.—FOREIGN COUNTRIES.			
1. China ..	3,100,000	340,000,000	97
2. Nejd and Hedjaz ..	1,000,000	1,500,000	2
3. Tibet ..	750,000	3,000,000	4
4. Persia ..	630,000	10,000,000	16
5. Egypt ..	360,000	14,000,000	31
6. Afghanistan ..	245,000	6,400,000	21
7. Iraq ..	150,000	3,000,000	20

19. The mean density for Baluchistan is 6 persons to the square mile. Excluding alien settlements it falls to 5. Taking the political divisions separately, British Baluchistan including British Administered territory as well as Tribal Areas has a density of 9. In the States it is only 5. Splitting the province again into the three main natural divisions—the uplands, the plains and the barren sandy deserts, the most densely populated part in the highlands is the Quetta tahsil with 140 persons to the square mile. This is largely due to the presence of the Military garrison in the Quetta Cantonment, and the alien population of all classes in the Quetta town, the largest business and industrial centre of the province which is continually attracting additional population from all quarters of the Baluchistan as well as adjoining Indian provinces and from across the Afghan and Persian borders. Without the Quetta town and cantonment the density of the Quetta tahsil falls to 30.

HOW THE CENSUS WAS TAKEN IN BALUCHISTAN

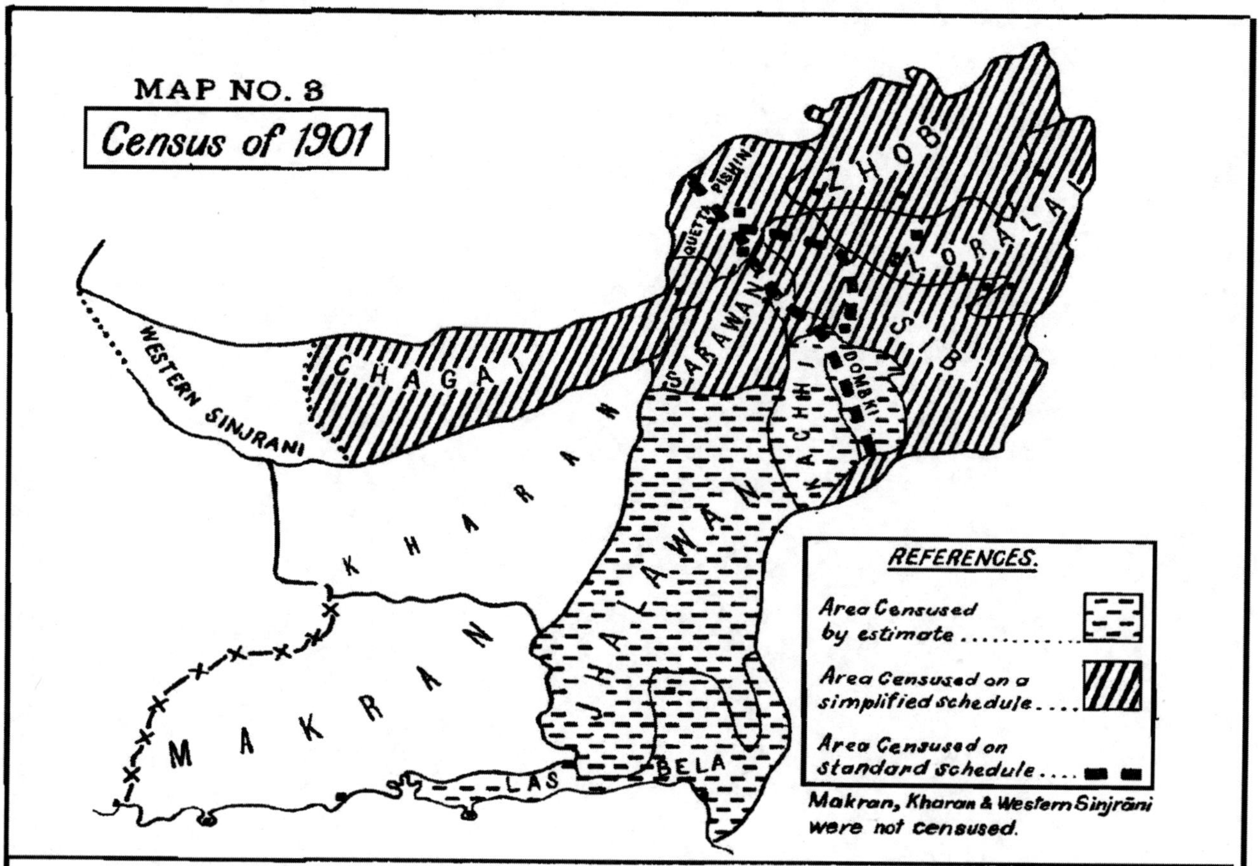

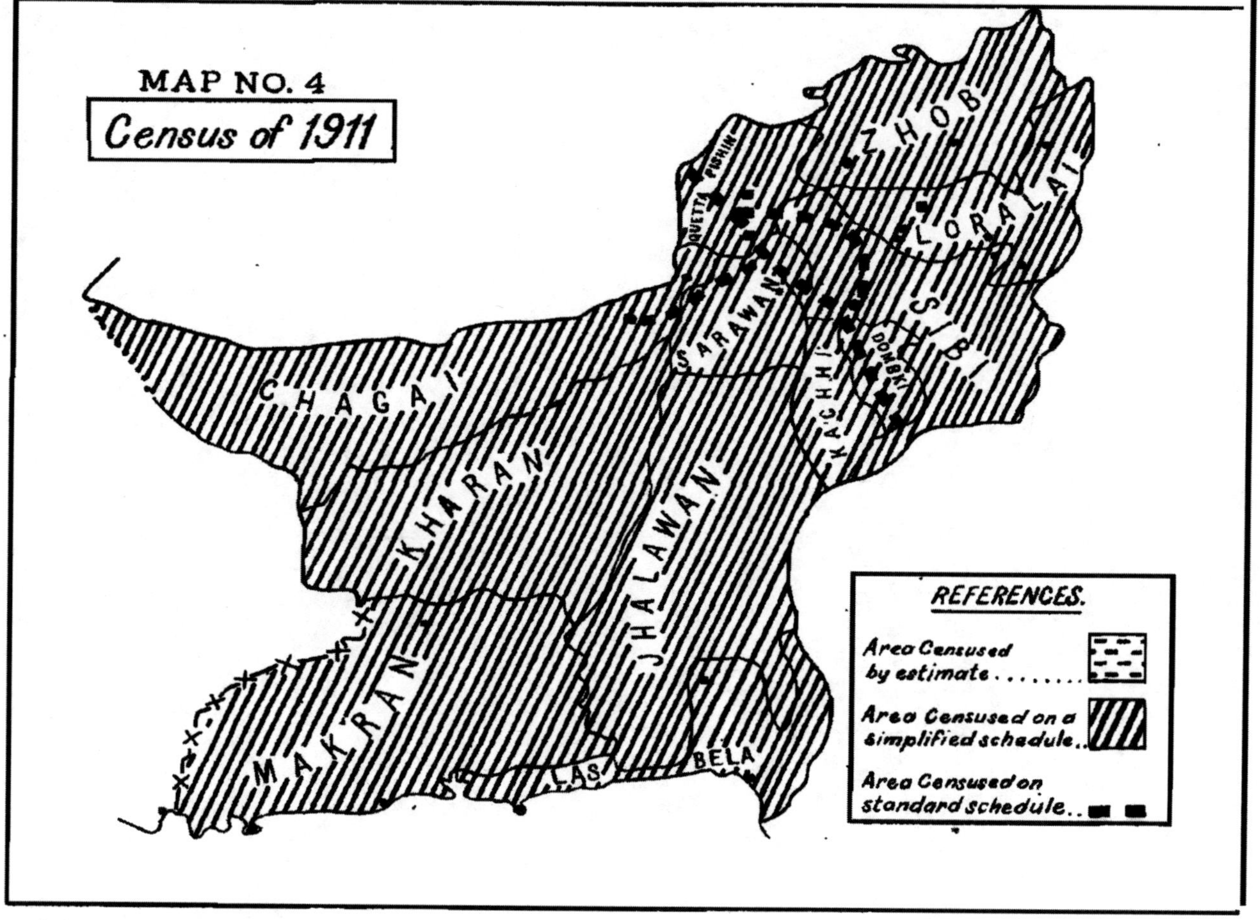

Reg No.76.E D (E Coy) 1933-540.

IN 1901, 1911, 1921, AND 1931.

MAP NO. 5

Census of 1921

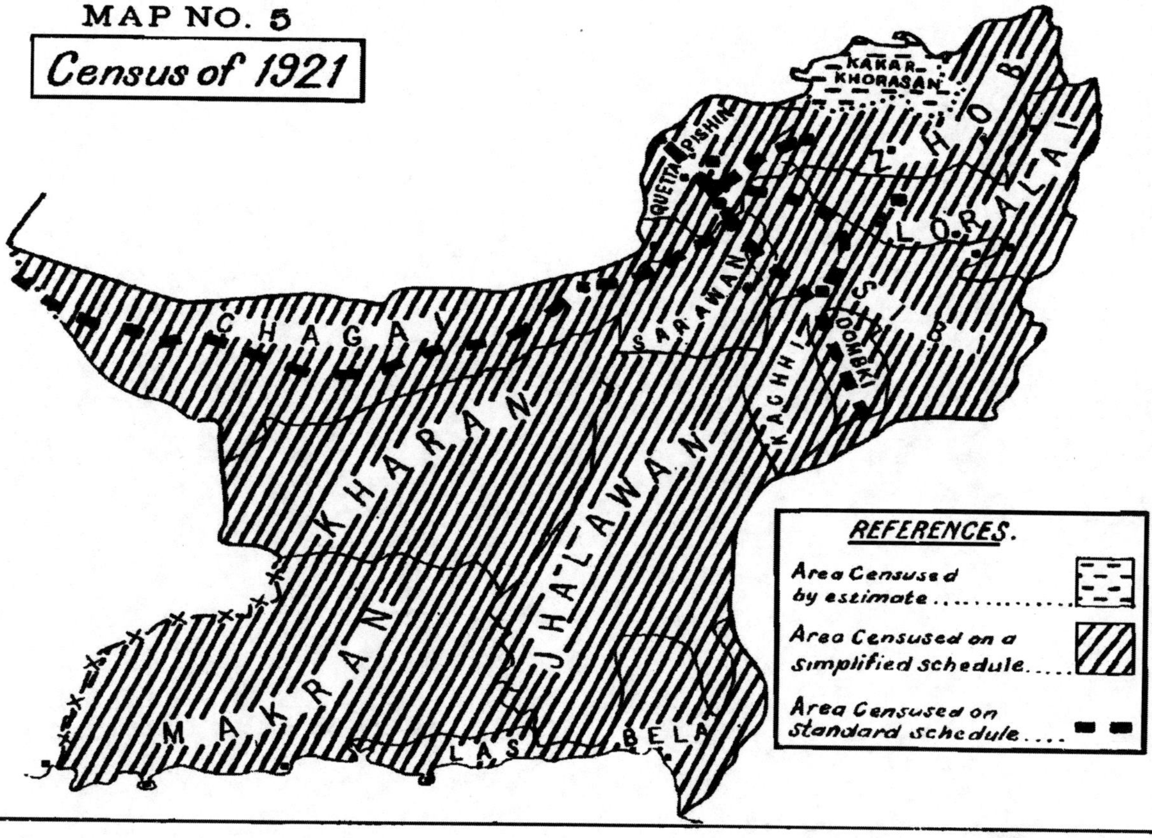

MAP NO. 6

Census of 1931

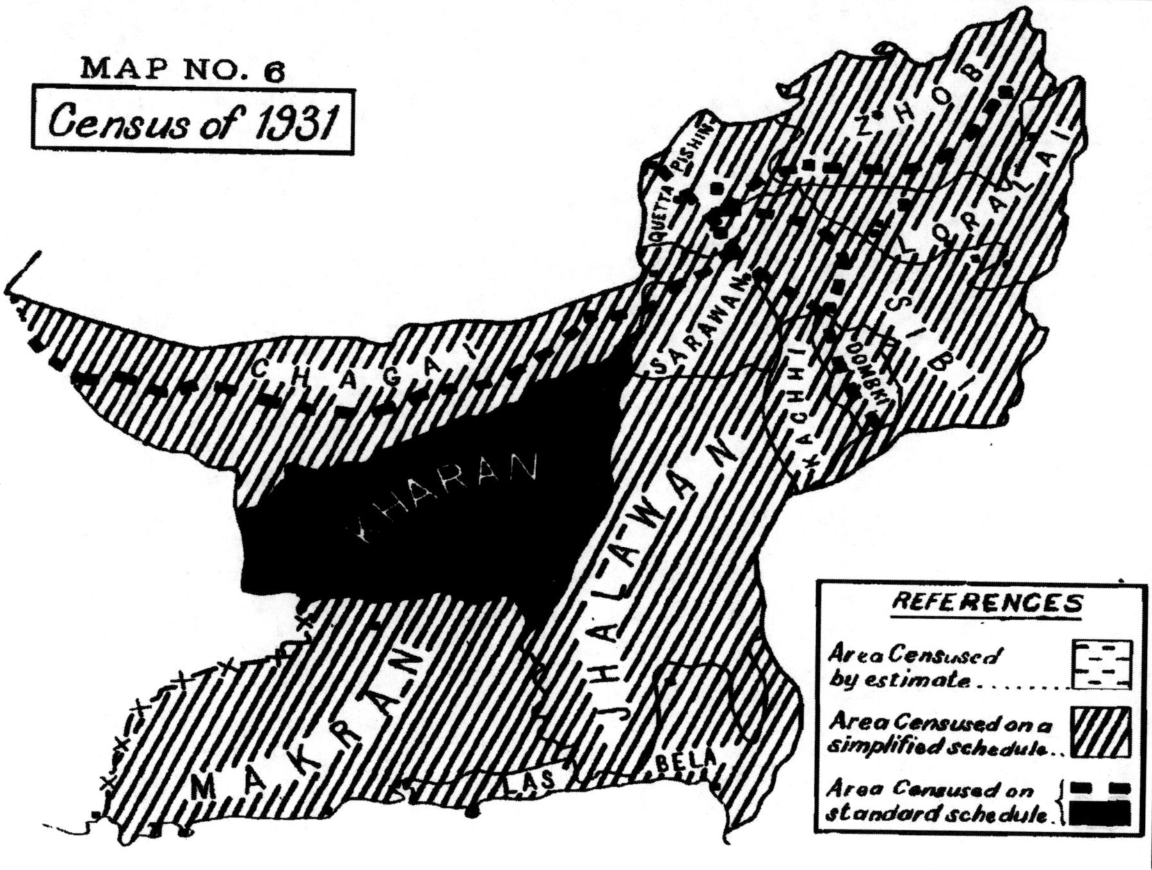

Reproduced by 'E Company Survey of India, Quetta

20. In the plains which include the Sibi and Nasirabad tahsils of the Sibi district and the Kachhi division of the Kalat State the most densely populated area lies in the Nasirabad tahsil with 45, followed by Kachhi 26, and the Sibi tahsil with 24 persons to the square mile. The figures for Kachhi and Sibi fluctuate chiefly owing to seasonal immigration of Brahuis from the highlands, and Powindahs from Afghanistan. The numbers would have been considerably smaller had the Census been taken in the summer. In Nasirabad, however, the density is mainly permanent. This is the only part of the province which possesses canal irrigation from the Indus and where agricultural facilities are largely responsible for the comparatively higher density. In the third natural division which in the main comprises the Chagai district and Kharan, the density is only 1.

Variation in Population, Census of 1891.

21. The first attempt at a Census was made in 1891. A regular Census was taken synchronously in all cantonments, railway stations, railway gang-huts and the town and cantonment of Quetta. A rough estimate of the resident population was made in the remaining parts of the Quetta-Pishin district in 1890 and checked in 1891. A similar estimate was prepared for the old Thal Chotiali district which has since been truncated and formed into the Sibi and Loralai districts. In the Zhob district, estimates were framed for only Bori which now forms the headquarters tahsil of the Loralai district. There was no Census Superintendent. No report was written and no records are available.

22. The total area covered was 20,568 square miles against 134,638 in 1931. The population was 171,752 against 868,617 in 1931. The Census was too fragmentary and the estimates were incomplete in as much as they included estimates of the resident population only and ignored nomads. Moreover children of both sexes were classed as females. Comparisons in these circumstances with statistics collected at subsequent censuses will only yield misleading results and have therefore been avoided. Maps Nos. 3, 4, 5 and 6 show the various methods, standard and modified, synchronous and non-synchronous by which the Census was taken between 1901 and 1931. Figures of area and population for each of these categories are shown in the marginal table.

Year of Census.	Area in square miles dealt with.	Population enumerated.			
		On a modified schedule.	On the Standard Schedule.	Estimated.	Total.
1901 ..	82,950	302,311	48,707	459,728	810,746
1911 ..	134,638	771,696	63,007	..	834,703
1921 ..	134,638	702,558	94,836	2,231	799,625
1931 ..	134,638	757,768	110,849	..	868,617

Census of 1901.

23. The Census of 1901 went far beyond its predecessor. It embraced the whole province excepting Makran and Kharan, and the Western Sanjrani country in the Chagai district. The alien population living in towns and cantonments, in railway limits, at District and other headquarters stations and in all alien settlements was censused synchronously by regular methods on the Standard Schedule. The indigenous population in British and British-administered districts was enumerated non-synchronously on a simple family schedule. The population of the States was estimated still more roughly on a tribal basis. Age, marriage, subsidiary occupation, means of subsistence of dependents, birthplace, language, literacy, knowledge of English and infirmities were not recorded in respect of the indigenous population both in the Districts and in the States.

Census of 1911.

24. The Census of 1911 was the first real Census and covered the whole province. It was taken by actual enumeration. In the Regular Areas inhabited practically entirely by aliens, the census was carried out synchronously by actual enumeration of individuals on the Standard Schedule. Elsewhere the enumeration was conducted on a modified schedule adopted to suit local susceptibilities. The schedule together with supplementary enquiries fell short of the Standard Schedule in so far as the record of Civil condition and age was omitted. Civil condition was omitted on political grounds, age on account of ignorance of individuals or headmen to furnish even approximate ages. The 1911 Census, however, went a step further in collecting a mass of statistics of considerable administrative value for the very wide range of clans, sections and sub-sections of all indigenous tribes while it stole a march on the Indian Census in respect of bilingualism. Sir Denys Bray, my far-seeing predecessor of 1911, brought within the range of enumeration statistics of bilingualism which in subsequent decades attracted considerable attention of scientists and eventually in 1931 figured in the Standard Indian Schedule at the special request of European scientists.

25. Comparing like with like, that is to say, excluding from the population of 1911 the areas not censused in 1901, the decennium ending with 1911 disclosed a decrease of 72,268 persons, or 10 per cent. of the total population. This decline was not due to any pestilence nor to any other unusual disturbing influences, for, conditions during the decade were on the whole normal. It was due chiefly to over-estimates in 1901. In his report on the Census of 1901, Mr. Hughes Buller remarked that the Extra Assistant Commissioner who was in original charge of the operations in the enumeration stage thought that the numbers of the Brahui tribes were excessive and that those for the Jhalawan country should be received with special caution. "The numbers in Jhalawan," as subsequently pointed out in the 1911 Report, "were generally felt to be pitched too high." The idea that there was a tendency among tribal chiefs to exaggerate numbers of their tribesmen cannot be brushed aside without giving it due weight. The larger the number of followers, the greater was the importance of the Chief according to the criterion of strength of those backward days. The secret of tribal prowess was being exposed to the public eye for the first time, so the temptation not to look small among rival chiefs was irresistible. The real strength was thus possibly magnified. And in doing so they evidently not only included in their estimates the numbers present but also all those families which had migrated to Sind permanently or to both Sind and Kachhi for the winter season.

Census of 1921.

26. In 1921 the final Census was taken on the 18th March. The division of the province into synchronous and non-synchronous areas, the forms of the Standard and Local Schedules and the procedure adopted for enumeration were identical with those of 1911. The Census was carried out by actual enumeration as in 1911 excepting a small portion of the Fort Sandeman Tahsil (Kakar Khurasan) where owing to the disturbed condition of the borderland after the rising of 1919, statistics were collected by estimates. Thus, for practical purposes, the operations covered the whole province. The total population as shown in the margin revealed a drop of 35,078 persons in the decade ending with 1921. This was largely due to the influenza epidemic of 1918 followed by a serious outbreak of cholera, scarcity and famine in 1920 and 1921. The influenza epidemic alone claimed 61,452 victims which is believed to be exclusive of a considerable number of unrecorded deaths in outlying areas. All told, the total loss from this cause was not less than 70,000. The death roll from cholera and famine and scarcity was not very large but famine and scarcity induced temporary emigration on an extensive scale and large numbers escaped enumeration within the province.

	1911.	1921.
Baluchistan ..	834,703	799,625

But for the presence of large numbers of alien immigrants composed of troops and followers, railway gangmen and other employees, traders and immigrants from Afghan territory in consequence of the Great world war and subsequently the Afghan war, the decline disclosed by the Census of 1921, would have been considerably greater.

Immigrants in 1911 ..	42,309
,, in 1921 ..	66,166

Census of 1931. Conditions of the Decade.

27. The past decennium (1921-31) opened under unfavourable conditions. The Sheranis and other tribesmen of Zhob who had been driven across the border into Afghanistan and the Waziri country during the troubles of 1919 had not all returned to their homes before the end of the last decennium. In subsequent years some of them gradually came in and settled down again. The drought of 1920-21 resulted in scarcity which culminated in famine in 1921-22. In 1922-23 the rainfall was generally timely and well distributed and conditions on the whole were better. The years 1923-24 and 1924-25 were comparatively prosperous ones except that grazing was scarce in the Mari-Bugti country in 1924-25. In 1925-26 the rainfall was below the average, and the winter rains were deficient and untimely. The crops were damaged by severe cold. Parts of the province, especially the Mari and Bugti tribal areas and the Chagai district were threatened with scarcity. In 1926-27 rainfall was above the average. Crops were better and grazing and fodder facilities were generally adequate. Locusts appeared about the end of the year and did some damage to crops. In 1927-28 and 1928-29, the rainfall was below the average. In some parts locusts did some damage in 1927-28 and there was scarcity in the Mari and Bugti country. Elsewhere agricultural conditions were unfavourable. Spring crops were below the average owing to damage caused by locusts and cold winds and grazing was poor. 1929-30 and 1930-31 were years of fitful rain-

DIAGRAM NO. 3

Diagram showing variation in wages during the decades 1911-20 and 1921-30

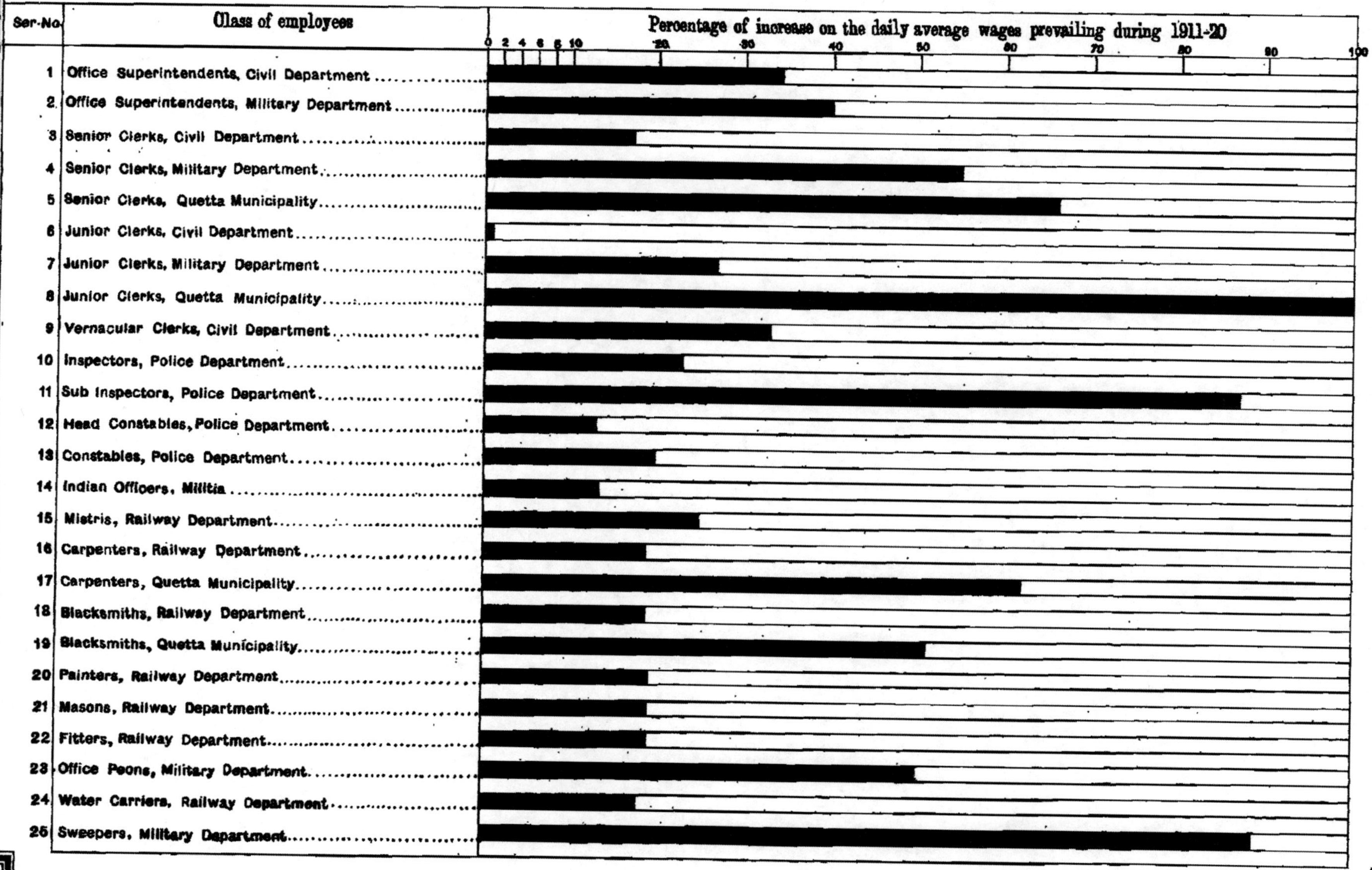

Reg. No. 77. ED (E Coy) 1933-540.

Reproduced by E Company Survey of India Quetta

fall. In some parts it was above, in others below the average where it adversely affected the autumn crops. Conditions were bad in Chagai where both autumn and spring crops failed. The Sibi district, however, suffered most from deficient rainfall and ravages of locusts. In other parts of the country agricultural conditions were on the whole normal.

28. Thus the unfavourable conditions under which the decennium commenced continued more or less unmitigated, though in a milder form, throughout the period in one part or the other. The scarcity and famine which prevailed throughout the province in 1920-21 and 1921-22 and partly in 1922-23 caused serious devastation among the flocks. Emigration naturally set in, as always happens, and scattered large numbers in all directions across the provincial frontiers. Shifting sands brought in from the deserts of Chagai by clouds of sand-storms laid waste a considerable area of arable lands in the Mastung Valley and closed down a large number of perennial sources of irrigation. Down in the plains of Kachhi, many villages were deserted owing to the inability of cultivators to utilise flood water on which the population mainly depends. It is difficult to estimate the numbers that left their homes to save their lives outside the province, but there is no doubt that they amounted to several thousands.

29. Several parts of the province were declared famine-stricken areas during the earlier years of the decennium. Relief works were opened in British territory which cost over Rs. 2,16,000. Gratuitous relief amounted to over Rs. 1,37,000. Special Takavis to the extent of over a million rupees were also distributed in cash and kind, in addition to the ordinary Takavi loans, amounting to Rs. 23,62,000. A considerable portion of the special Takavi loans was eventually written off besides remissions of revenue amounting to over Rs. 1,50,000, a sure proof of the fact that economic conditions during the decade were bad enough for the natural growth of population.

30. Diagram No. 3 shows the rise per cent. on the wages prevailing at the end of the preceding decade. It seems that the rise was the lowest in the case of the Civil Junior Clerks but this is not the case, for, this class of employees had received their due share just before the commencement of the decennium under review. Prices ruled high during 1921-22 and 1922-23. There was a sudden drop during the following two years. They began to rise again in 1925-26 and remained practically stationary when in 1930-31 they fell to a level which had never been reached before.

Public Health.

31. Except in the urban areas which are well supplied with means of medical relief, the standard of health was generally low in consequence of scarcity and famine and the general economic conditions after the famine years. To make matters worse, before the rural population had time to show signs of recovery, another serious visitation of cholera coupled with outbreaks of small-pox and measles caused considerable loss of life in the beginning of the decade. In the latter part of the decennium, however, public health regained normal proportions.

Communications.

32. During the decade under review, motor traffic almost completely displaced wheeled traffic and pack animals in the Districts except in remote areas. In the States, motor traffic continued to increase. All headquarters stations both in British territory and the States were connected by metalled or fair weather roads fit for motor traffic. Mechanical transport is becoming more popular for transport of passengers, agricultural produce, and trade goods in rural areas and is causing some anxiety to the Railway Department. By the extension of the Zhob Valley railway from Hindubagh to Fort Sandeman, 132 miles of rail-road were added during the decennium.

Movement of Population.

33. As has been explained, the conditions of the past decennium were not very favourable to the normal growth of population. Yet the Census of 1931 discloses an increase of 68,992 persons since 1921. The actual and percentage increases are exhibited below :—

	Actual population.				Actual increase or decrease.			Percentage increase or decrease.		
	1901.	1911.	1921.	1931.	1901-1931.	1911-1931.	1921-1931.	1901-1931.	1911-1931.	1921-1931.
Balnchistan ..	810,746	834,703	799,625	868,617	+57,871	+33,914	+68,992	+7	+4	+9
Districts ..	382,106	414,412	420,648	463,508	+81,402	+49,096	+42,860	+21	+12	+10
States ..	428,640	420,291	378,977	405,109	−23,531	−15,182	+26,132	−5	−4	+7

The main causes which can contribute to an increase are threefold, namely, double-counting, balance of immigration, and natural growth. In a province which is subject to constant waves of migration, double counting is inevitable. Special measures were taken in 1931 to reduce errors from this source to a minimum and I have no doubt that the numbers have not been inflated to an extent which would vitiate the results. The various tests to which the statistics have been subjected tend to confirm this conclusion. We have thus to look to balance of immigration and natural growth as the two main causes of increase.

34. Eliminating the gain by immigration and adding the loss by emigration, we find that the increase in the past decennium due to natural growth was 39,505 but that compared to the previous decade (1911) there has been a decline amounting to 31,318. Details are shown below :—

	Actual numbers.			Variation per cent.		
	1911.	1921.	1931.	1911-21.	1921-31.	1911-1931
Total Census population	834,703	799,625	868,617	—4	+9	+4
Add—Loss by emigration	76,273	60,415	42,594	—21	—29	—44
Total	910,976	860,040	911,211	—6	+6	..
Deduct—Gain by immigration.. ..	58,500	78,387	90,053	+34	+15	+54
Balance—Natural population ..	852,476	781,653	821,158	—8	+5	— 4

It will be seen that the rate of natural growth between the intercensal period 1921-31 was 5 per cent. but compared to the population of 1911, there was a decline of about 4 per cent. These figures do not disclose the true state of affairs. The natural population of Baluchistan in 1911 was 852,476. If we add to our natural population for 1931 the 70,000 lives which Baluchistan lost in its recorded and unrecorded victims of the influenza epidemic we get a total of 891,158 which means an increase of 4·5 per cent. instead of a decrease of 4 per cent. since 1911 as shown above. The fact is, it is not safe to commit oneself to any definite conclusions in view of the serious disturbance which is caused by migration at each successive census. We have no record of vital statistics to measure the growth of population. The only locality where registration of vital statistics is supposed to be compulsory is the town of Quetta, statistics for which are given in Subsidiary Table 5. This record is hardly of any use owing to the shifting nature of the population which is almost entirely alien. An attempt was made in 1911 to collect statistics of births and deaths for 6,641 families from all parts of the country. In 1921, figures were collected for 3,582 families but, in 1931, a more elaborate form was used for this purpose, and the number of families examined for fertility and mortality was 39,744. The results are exhibited in the subjoined table :—

Census Year.		*Families examined.*	*Survivals per thousand children born.*
1911	..	6,641	613
1921	..	3,582	622
1931	..	39,744	669

Though the rate of survivals is fairly high and shows a steady increase yet it hardly serves any useful purpose for any definite deductions. Again, we have no means of ascertaining the number of emigrants into Afghanistan and Persia which have a frontier of 1,281 miles with Baluchistan. Similarly we lose all our fishermen, traders and others from the Makran coast who may be on the high seas on the Census night carrying on business outside Baluchistan waters. And lastly I am convinced that our loss of population is considerable owing to incomplete record of birthplace, for, emigrants who are mostly ignorant cannot give correct answers and enumerators in foreign lands cannot classify them accurately. This is proved by the statistics of Baluchistan emigrants, and of Brahuis, and Brahui-

	Baluchistan emigrants.	*Brahuis by caste.*	*Brahui language speakers.*
1881 ..	..	..	24,310
1891 ..	..	29,907	28,984
1901 ..	..	47,758	47,898
1911 ..	69,373	60,389	28,930
1921 ..	54,352	54,391	45,000
1931 ..	35,440	71,827	79,361

speakers censused in the Bombay Presidency shown in the marginal table. While the number of emigrants from Baluchistan censused in Bombay has fallen by 35 per cent., the number of Brahuis and Brahui-speakers has risen by 32 and 77 per cent. in ten years. This enormous increase cannot possibly be attributed to natural growth without additions by immigration, and the anomally only serves to strengthen the suspicion that emigration statistics are unreliable as a guide.

35. With so many disturbing elements which influence the movement of population of this province, it is hopeless to draw any definite conclusions and I cannot do better, after a fruitless struggle, than leave the subject by repeating the opinion formed by Sir Denys Bray after a laborious research in 1911 that "the more clearly the nature of the problem is realised, the more hopeless it appears to attempt to measure the increase or decrease that has occurred in the population of Baluchistan during the past ten years."

Variation by Districts and States and their Divisions.

36. The historical, physical and economic factors influencing the distribution of population have been fully discussed in the 1911 Report. Here I shall confine the discussion to a brief analysis of the more important factors concerning the variations in respect of each district and the states.

Districts.

Sibi.

37. Statistics of variation in population and density for districts since 1921 are shown in the marginal table. The Sibi district tops the list with an increase of 24,797 persons or 21 per cent. The Mari-Bugti tribal area of the Sibi district shows the highest increase of 17,265 or 45 per cent. Taking the two areas separately, the Mari country alone accounts for an increase of 71 per cent. This high rate of increase is discounted partly by a decrease of 24 per cent. in the adjoining tahsil (Kohlu). which is inhabited chiefly by Maris who step across into the Mari country in winter in search of pasture. The Bugti area has been content with a more digestible increase of only 29 per cent. Both Maris and Bugtis are pastoral tribes. Both lost large numbers in 1921 by emigration due to famine and scarcity, the Maris perhaps in a much larger measure, and recovered their emigrants with the return of normal conditions in the decennium under review. Both are turbulent rival tribes with an historic record of insatiable jealousies which year in, year out end in the spilling of valuable Baloch blood. Their jealousies have so overgrown normal proportions that, despite the evident disadvantages of exaggeration or suppression of numbers, a rival section is liable to succumb to the temptation of looking large by its numerical strength. I suspected the accuracy of the figures and personally interviewed the Mari Chief. I was assured that the numbers at the previous Censuses had been understated and that at the Census of 1921, they were necessarily low owing to the causes stated above. Amongst the Maris, as amongst some other tribes, the periodical division of agricultural land is based on the number of males of all ages. Similarly, in criminal cases compensation is assessed on the numerical strength of sections or clans or even on the whole tribe. The Mari Chief assured me that only in the year preceding the Census he had an opportunity of estimating the strength of the tribe which was very near that disclosed by the Census. The argument, I am inclined to admit, deserves consideration. Nevertheless, the recovery appears surprisingly rapid for both tribes.

Districts.	Population.		Variation.	Density.	
	1921.	1931.		1921.	1931.
DISTRICTS ..	420,648	463,508	+42,860	8	9
Quetta-Pishin ..	135,809	147,541	+11,732	28	31
Loralai ..	82,473	86,087	+3,614	11	11
Zhob ..	56,668	57,963	+1,295	[illegible]	6
Bolan ..	4,874	4,688	−186	14	13
Chagai ..	22,616	24,224	+1,608	1	1
Sibi ..	118,208	143,005	+24,797	11	13
Administered Area	80,249	87,781	+7,532	21	22
Mari-Bugti Country	37,959	55,224	+17,265	5	8
(a) Mari Country ..	14,501	24,860	+10,359	4	7
(b) Bugti Country	23,458	30,364	+6,906	6	8

38. The administered area of the Sibi district as distinguished from the Mari and Bugti tribal area shows a gain of 7,532 persons or 9 per cent. to which the Sibi tahsil contributed 5,067 persons. This was due to temporary immigration on a larger scale consisting mostly of Brahuis from the Sarawan and

Jhalawan divisions of Kalat and the enumeration of the train population which, had the train not been late on the Census night, would have been enumerated in Bolan. The Nasirabad tahsil shows the next higher increase, namely, 6,178 persons or 20 per cent. Here, as elsewhere, the increase is not entirely natural, for, numbers were swelled to a small extent by alien gangmen working on irrigation works and by indigenous labourers from adjoining areas who move down to the plains to escape the winter in the highlands or from the plains of Kachhi to earn a living. The decrease in the Kohlu and Shahrig tahsils is due entirely to the annual winter migration.

Quetta-Pishin.

39. Next among the districts stands Quetta-Pishin with an increase of 11,732 or 9 per cent. followed by Loralai and Zhob with 3,614 and 1,295 persons or 4 and 2 per cent., respectively. The Quetta tahsil accounts for an increase of 8,426 persons or 12 per cent. The actual increase, however, in the rural population which is the natural resident population is only 3. The Quetta town alone, which has a floating population, contributes an increase of 9 per cent. The Pishin tahsil shows an increase of 7 per cent. The loss to Chaman of 5 per cent. should have been actually greater, for, the Achakzais were censused after some of the families who winter in Afghan limits had left British territory, but this loss was nearly counterbalanced by immigration due to the expansion of the town which shows an increase of 1,824 since 1921.

Bolan.

40. Bolan, in spite of gain of population by the opening of a Central Jail at Mach and the increase in the number of indigenous inhabitants amounting in all nearly to 2,500 persons, shows a decrease of 186. This is entirely due to the absence of temporary workmen on roads and railway gangmen and employees who were discharged after the close of the Afghan war.

Loralai.

41. In the Loralai district which, as a whole, shows an increase of 3,614 or 4 per cent. the Duki tahsil contributes the highest percentage increase of 14. Barkhan with 13 follows next, the increase being due largely to Afghan nomads. Bori and Musakhel have an increase of 4 each. These two tahsils are subject to least disturbance from migration and the increase in their cases represents approximately the normal rate of growth. The increase in Duki is due partly to internal migration from Sanjawi as well as a larger number of Afghan nomads. The absence of Afghan Powindahs at the Census of 1931, as well as the winter emigration of its permanent summer population account for the decrease of 17 per cent. in the Sanjawi tahsil.

Zhob and Chagai.

42. In Zhob, with an increase of 2 per cent. only, Killa Saifullah shows an increase of 13 per cent., Hindubagh a decrease of 12 per cent. and Fort Sandeman an increase of 4 per cent. Here also winter migration is mainly responsible. The same remarks apply to Chagai which shows an increase of 7 per cent.

States. Kalat.

43. Variations in the population and density of States are exhibited in the marginal table. Kalat, including Kharan, has contributed a modest 4 per cent. during the ten years 1921-31. Taking the divisions individually, Kachhi accounts for an increase of 41, Dombki and Kaheri 39 and Jhalawan 12 per cent. while Sarawan heads the list with a fall of 48 followed by Kharan and Makran with decreases of 16 and 5 per cent., respectively. The loss of Sarawan is the gain of Kachhi and the Dombki-Kaheri country where Brahuis from Sarawan and Jhalawan own agricultural lands and find grazing for their flocks in winter. Not only do the land-owning Brahuis, their satellites the Loris and other labouring classes find shelter in the plains but also nomads from Shorawak and other parts of Afghanistan and from the Chagai Agency follow suit in considerable numbers, thus causing an abnormal rise in the resident population of the plains. The increase would have been larger but for the fact that about 20,000 Brahuis returned much earlier to Jhalawan from the plains of Kachhi and Sind owing to timely rains which accounts for the increase of 12 per cent.

States and Divisions.	Population.		Variation.	Density.	
	1921.	1931.		1921.	1931.
STATES ..	378,977	405,109	+26,132	5	5
Kalat ..	328,281	342,101	+13,820	5	5
Sarawan ..	54,262	28,464	−25,798	10	5
Jhalawan ..	70,710	88,978	+9,268	4	4
Kachhi ..	75,153	105,886	+30,733	19	26
Dombki-Kaheri Country ..	19,558	26,953	+7,395	14	20
Makran ..	71,860	68,462	−3,398	3	3
Kharan ..	27,738	23,358	−4,380	2	1
Las Bela ..	50,696	63,008	+12,312	7	9

MAP NO. 7

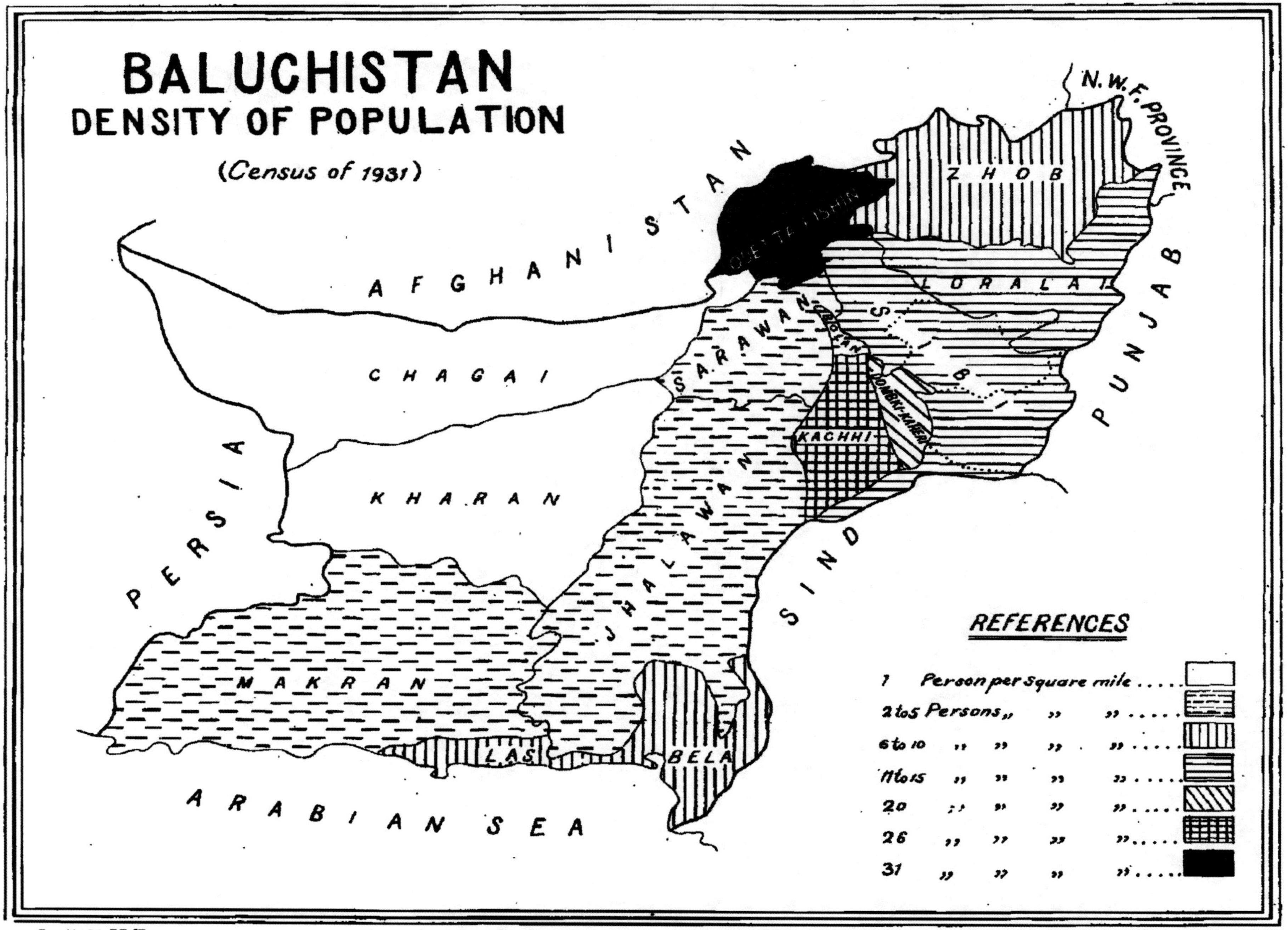

Reg No.74.ED (E

The decreases in Kharan and Makran are due to the annual winter migration into Sind and elsewhere.

44. Las Bela shows an increase of 24 per cent. against 4 of Kalat. An increase of 12,312 persons in ten years in a total population of 50,696 in 1921 is remarkable. The principal contributions by indigenous races to this apparently abnormal increase are shown in the margin. The increase (1,874 persons) among the Baloch is contributed mainly by the Sangur tribe and is due either to a change of classification or the emigration in 1921 of a large number of members of this tribe to Sind. The increases among the Brahuis are due to seasonal migration which vary from year to year. It is difficult, however, to trace the causes of the abnormal increase among the Lasis which amounts to 7,823 or 34 per cent. The marginal table gives the strength of each of the Lasi tribes in 1921 and 1931. The classification of tribes no doubt underwent some change in 1931 owing to the separation of some of the minor tribes and their amalgamation with the five main tribes called the Panj Raj but it is difficult to account for the large increase of 34 per cent. unless the decline in 1921 is attributed to their wholesale emigration to Sind owing to scarcity and subsequent famine in 1920 and 1921 which is most probable in view of their close proximity to Karachi. **Las Bela.**

Race.	Population. 1921.	Population. 1931	Variation.
Baloch ..	4,293	6,497	+2,204
Brahui ..	7,292	8,277	+985
Lasi ..	23,052	30,875	+7,823
Jatt ..	2,475	4,323	+1,848
Angaria ..	3,363	3,962	+599
Burra ..	4,279	3,307	—882
Jamot ..	6,658	5,104	—1,554
Runjha ..	5,027	4,617	—410
Sheikh ..	3,725	4,261	+536
Mangia ..	..	2,555	+2,555
Shahok ..	..	1,305	+1,305
Mondra ..	..	3,231	+3,231
Gonga ..	..	2,443	+2,443

45. Map No. 7 illustrates the density of districts and states for 1931. In the marginal table are given statistics of density for three censuses. These figures do not represent the actual state of density in the countryside ; for miles and miles outside town areas and railway premises not a soul, not even a bird is to be seen over many parts of the province while in some tracts there are more grave-yards than inhabited villages. Excluding the Regular Areas occupied by the shifting population living in towns and cantonments, railway premises, headquarters stations, etc., the figures of density for 1931 shown in the following table will be found to be interesting :— **Density.**

Districts and States.	*Persons per square mile in* 1911.	1921.	1931.
DISTRICTS ..	8	8	9
Quetta-Pishin	26	28	31
Loralai ..	11	11	11
Zhob ..	7	5	6
Bolan ..	8	14	13
Chagai ..	1	1	1
Sibi ..	10	11	13
STATES ..	5	5	5
Kalat ..	5	5	5
Las Bela ..	9	7	9

	Persons per square mile excluding Regular Areas (1931).	*Persons per square mile including Regular Areas* (1931).		*Persons per square mile excluding Regular Areas* (1931).	*Persons per square mile including Regular Areas* (1931).
DISTRICTS ..	7	9	Chagai ..	1	1
Quetta-Pishin ..	16	31	Sibi ..	12	13
Loralai ..	11	11	STATES ..	5	5
Zhob ..	5	6	Kalat ..	5	5
Bolan ..	1	13	Las Bela ..	9	9

The Chagai district is the most sparsely populated with a density of 1. The Quetta-Pishin district is the most densely populated tract in the province with 31 persons to the square mile. Compared with districts of adjoining provinces these figures present an interesting contrast. The most thinly populated district of Sind, Thar Parkar, has 3 more persons to the square mile than the most densely populated district (Quetta-Pishin) in Baluchistan. In the Punjab, the minimum density is 56 in the Dera Ghazi Khan district. In the North-West Frontier Province, Dera Ismail Khan, the most thinly populated district, has 79 persons to the square mile against 31 of Quetta-Pishin.

46. In the Regular Areas " House " was defined as the dwelling place of a commensal family including its resident dependents such as widows, servants, guests, etc. This term also included hotels, serais, cooley lines, encampments, religious places, mosques, temples, etc., shops, godowns and garages where, in the majority of cases, a single person was found sleeping on the Census night. In the Tribal Areas censused on a modified schedule, the termhad a much wider application. It included not only the houses made of sun-dried and baked bricks **Houses.**

as defined in the Regular Areas but also mud huts of a primitive type, the Kizhdi or Gidan (the common goat-hair blanket-tent of the nomad and semi-nomad tribesmen), shelters made of dwarf-palm mats, dug-outs covered with conical roofs of juniper bark and branches, Jhuggis and Bhungis or mat-hut shelters, and even caves in hill-sides.

47. The marginal table shows that there is a strong tendency towards settled life. The purely nomadic population fell from 33 in 1911 to 22 per cent. in 1921. It rose to 25 per cent. in 1931 but, if the Afghan nomads censused in the province in 1931 were excluded, the percentage would fall to 16. Semi-nomads fell from 13 in 1911 to 12 in 1931 while the proportion of settled inhabitants rose from 54 in 1911 and 60 in 1921 to 63 in 1931.

	Tribal Census.			Variation.			Percentage of each class to Total Population		
	1911.	1921.	1931.	1911 to 1921.	1921 to 1931.	1911 to 1931.	1911.	1921.	1931.
TOTAL ..	771,696	704,789	757,768	−66,907	+52,979	−13,928	100	100	100
Nomad ..	255,338	157,744	191,647	−97,594	+33,903	−63,691	33	22	25
Semi-nomad ..	96,995	125,025	90,434	+28,030	−34,591	−6,561	13	18	12
Settled ..	419,363	422,020	475,687	+2,657	+53,667	+56,324	54	60	63

Families. 48. The number of persons per house or family as shown in the marginal table is the same as it was at the last census except in the case of the Mari-Bugti tribal country where it dropped to 7 from 9 in 1921, and Chagai which shows a decrease of one person per house.

Districts and States.	Persons per house or family on total population.		Districts and States.	Persons per house or family on total population.	
	1931.	1921.		1931	1921
BALUCHISTAN	5	5	Sibi ..	6	6
DISTRICTS	5	5	Administered area..	5	5
Quetta-Pishin	5	5	Mari-Bugti country	7	9
Loralai	5	5			
Zhob ..	5	5	STATES ..	5	5
Bolan ..	3	3	Kalat ..	5	5
Chagai ..	4	5	Las Bela ..	5	5

49. Subsidiary Table 9 and the figures in the margin show that the number of inhabited houses per square mile for the province is 1. It is 2 in the districts of Loralai and Sibi and the Las Bela State. The Quetta-Pishin district being densely populated has 6 houses per square mile and goes at the top. Turning to Chagai District, the area is so vast and the number of houses so small that there is only one house to two square miles. The most densely populated tahsils are Quetta in the Quetta-Pishin District and Nasirabad in the Sibi District where the number of houses per square mile works out to 26 and 8, respectively. In the Quetta tahsil the number in 1921 was 29. The decrease of 3 in 1931 is due mainly to the exclusion of houses for the Strictly Military Areas. In Nasirabad, however, the increase of two is real owing to increase of population due to greater irrigation facilities. The two sub-divisions of Kalat State (Kachhi and Dombki Kaheri country) though densely populated have 4 and 3 houses, respectively, per square mile.

Districts and States.	Houses per square mile in the Province.	Districts and States.	Houses per square mile in the Province
BALUCHISTAN	1	Chagai	..
DISTRICTS ..	2	Sibi	2
Quetta-Pishin	6		
Loralai ..	2	STATES	1
Zhob ..	1	Kalat ..	1
Bolan ..	5	Las Bela	2

Summary. 50. It has been shown in the foregoing paragraphs that the population of Baluchistan has increased by 68,992 or about 9 per cent. between 1921 and 1931. Splitting up the population into the three main groups, namely indigenous, semi-indigenous and alien, according to the classification first introduced in the 1911 report, we find that the contribution of the indigenous group towards the total increase amounts to 7 while that of the other two groups together represents only about 2 per cent. Before proceeding further it appears necessary to give a brief description of what is actually meant by this threefold classification.

The indigenous group represents the true indigenous inhabitants of pre-British days who are, broadly speaking, united by bonds of common weal and woe, who are subject to the system of tribal responsibility and who possess a share in tribal lands, together with the dependent occupational groups that have been attached to the various indigenous tribes from the earliest times as their cultivating classes or as their artizans, or as musicians or domestic servants. The second group, semi-indigenous, consists of the Buzdar Baloch and the Durrani and Ghilzai Pathan and Hazaras. The Buzdars who were at one time indigenous to Baluchistan emigrated to Dera Ghazi Khan. About 1,800 Buzdar were censused within the Province in 1931. With the exception of only a few, these are now settled inhabitants of Baluchistan. In the same way the Durranis who are Afghan immigrants are now permanently settled in the Province. Of the 14,000 odd Ghilzais, over two-thirds are Afghan nomads whose numbers fluctuate from year to year. The Hazaras who are mostly employed in the army still look to Afghanistan as their home and are strictly speaking all aliens. The third group, the aliens, includes all other foreigners—Europeans, Anglo-Indians, and all other orientals whether domiciled or not.

It will be observed that the grouping is, on the whole, only a rough one. Its correctness was questioned at the Census of 1931 in alien circles on the ground that the grouping is an arbitrary one in so far as it makes no distinction between the purely nomad and aliens on the one hand and on the other the domiciled semi-indigenous and aliens who now claim to be permanent residents entitled by domicile to be included among the indigenous inhabitants. The objection appears to be more in the nature of a shadow of the changing future. Whatever view may be taken of this psychological manifestation, the fact remains that so far as the ordinary scope of a census is concerned the separation of the numbers of indigenous inhabitants from the rest of the population is essential in order correctly to measure the movement of population and its progress in various other directions. And unless special circumstances necessitate a different change of classification or grouping at the next census, I venture to suggest that the population be divided up into two groups only, *i.e.*, Indigenous and Alien, all persons not covered by the former category being lumped under the latter. The labour and expense involved in the threefold classification are out of all proportion to the results obtained. It is extremely difficult to maintain the distinction throughout the report and the simplification of the classification will accelerate work without sacrificing essential detail.

Reverting to the question of the increase it will be seen that the highest increase is disclosed by the semi-indigenous who have improved by 17 per cent. followed by the aliens who have gone up by 12 per cent. since 1921. The increase is lowest among the indigenous group whose rate of increase is only 8 per cent.

51. The chief interest must, however, centre round the true indigenous inhabitants. Unluckily here also migration causes such a serious disturbance that the increase cannot safely be put down wholly to the credit of natural growth. On the whole the facts and figures given in the foregoing paragraphs indicate that Baluchistan is not lagging behind in contributing its normal share in normal conditions to the ever-increasing population of the world. Where birth-rate is fairly high and the rate of survivals 669 per thousand births, it is difficult to believe that the population is stationary. The fact is that poverty, lack of capital and failure of means of irrigation at home, higher wages and a more congenial winter climate in Sind for the Brahui, Baloch and Jatt, Lasi and Makrani, and high profits with compound interest on trade goods and cash loans for the Pathan, have attracted into Sind and beyond during the past 50 years or so large numbers of Baluchistan tribesmen not only from Kalat and Las Bela States but also from the districts, particularly Pishin. The marginal figures extracted from the Bombay tables for 1931 and partly arrived at by estimates based on personal enquiries from tribesmen have an interesting tale to tell. The 135,519 Pathans do not wholly belong to Baluchistan but there is no doubt that they include a certain number of emigrants from this Province.

Censused in Sind.		1931.
1. Brahui language speakers	..	79,561
2. Makranis	..	16,906
3. Pathans	..	135,519
4. Baloch } 5. Jatt } 6. Lasi }	roughly	70,000
		301,986

52. This large emigration which is continually though slowly swelling the ranks of emigrants who have settled down in the Bombay Presidency is naturally responsible for the low rate of increase. It is, however, a far cry yet to talk of pressure on the existing means of livelihood. There is plenty of land and irrigation water for the extension of cultivation ; the means to this end have alone been lacking. Large sums of money have been spent on improving the means of irrigation during the past ten years while several schemes estimated to cost several lakhs of rupees are under consideration for the District areas. A new era has dawned in Kalat. Barring natural calamities, the next decennium gives good promise of increase of prosperity as well as numbers.

SUBSIDIARY TABLES.

1. Density, Water Supply and Crops (1930-31).

District and Tahsil.	Mean density per square mile.	Rainfal	Total Area (acres).				Area under crop (acres).										
							Total.		Wheat.		Juar.		Palezat.		Minor crops.		
			Total.	Unculti-vable.	Culti-vable.	Irri-gated.	Flood and dry crop.	Irri-gated.	Flood and dry crop.	Irri-gated.	Flood and dry crop.	Irri-gated.	Flood and dry crop.	Irri-gated.	Flood and dry crop.	Irri-gated.	Flood and dry crop.
1	2	3	4	5	6	7	8	9	10	11	12	13	14	15	16	17	18
I. Quetta-Pishin District.	**31**	**7·67**	**599,315**	**351,001**	**248,314**	**136,365**	**111,949**	**43,251**	**38,378**	**29,718**	**33,909**	**354**	**510**	**2,439**	**1,103**	**10,740**	**2,858**
1. Quetta ..	140	8·02	104,745	60,452	44,293	28,519	15,774	13,371	2,280	8,099	1,312	339	508	1,026	342	3,907	118
2. Pishin ..	17	8·23	494,570	290,549	201,021	107,846	96,175	29,880	36,098	21,619	32,597	15	2	1,413	761	6,833	2,738
II. Sibi District ..	**13**	**8·00**	**843,284**	**152,325**	**695,959**	**595,907**	**100,052**	**123,105**	**101,140**	**22,253**	**15,720**	**37,042**	**22,278**	**388**	**1**	**63,422**	**63,141**
1. Sibi ..	24	4·76	260,891	99,595	161,296	89,966	71,330	20,170	26,775	12,297	2,918	5,713	15,447	31	..	2,129	8,410
2. Shahrig ..	12	10·72	50,777	29,786	20,991	12,588	8,403	8,660	3,029	4,693	2,561	13	836	22	..	3,932	532
3. Nasirabad ..	45	4·13	500,006	7,539	492,467	402,467	..	94,159	*64,749	5,177	5,239	31,315	5,538	326	1	57,341	53,971
4. Kohlu ..	15	10·56	36,610	15,405	21,205	886	20,319	116	5,687	86	5,002	1	457	9	..	20	228
III. Loralai District	**11**	**8·85**	**728,910**	**485,775**	**238,135**	**94,976**	**143,159**	**21,262**	**52,491**	**33,606**	**61,915**	**450**	**10,205**	**1,026**	**99**	**13,924**	**4,421**
1. Sanjawi ..	9	7·56	52,785	36,554	16,231	8,570	7,661	3,823	2,746	1,892	2,689	1	2	44	..	1,886	55
2. Duki ..	11	8·23	260,741	179,923	80,818	34,448	46,370	5,172	17,812	3,490	14,002	155	3,052	222	60	1,305	698
3. Bori ..	11	7·97	145,027	87,131	57,896	40,728	17,168	9,248	8,050	25,463	26,650	273	2,509	711	16	10,545	2,934
4. Barkhan ..	16	13·70	265,357	182,167	83,190	11,230	71,960	3,019	23,883	2,761	18,574	21	4,552	49	23	188	734
IV. Zhob District ..	**6**	**9·01**	**64,537**	**20,494**	**44,043**	**42,431**	**1,612**	**9,505**	**10,653**	**6,297**	**9,678**	**529**	**518**	**134**	**2**	**2,545**	**455**
1. Killa-Saifullah	6	5·56	31,100	8,163	22,937	22,230	707	5,465	10,635	4,367	9,660	49	518	55	2	994	455
2. Hindubagh ..	8	6·86	33,437	12,331	21,106	20,201	905	4,040	18	1,930	18	480	..	79	..	1,551	..

* Irrigated area cultivated as flood and dry crop area.

2. Distribution of the Population Classified according to Density.

Districts and States.	Tahsils, etc., with a population per square mile of																			
	Under 5.		5—10.		10—15.		15—20.		20—25.		25—40.		40—45.		45—50.		50—100.		100—150.	
	Area.	Population.	Area.	Population.	Area.	Population.	Area.	Population.	Area.	Population.	Area.	Population.	Area.	Population.	Area.	Population.	Area.	Population.	Area.	Population.
1	2	3	4	5	6	7	8	9	10	11	12	13	14	15	16	17	18	19	20	21
BALUCHISTAN ..	**79,890**	**191,983**	**33,408**	**224,011**	**7,475**	**82,205**	**5,929**	**96,789**	**2,507**	**54,460**	**4,060**	**105,886**	..	..	**821**	**36,634**	..	..	**548**	**76,649**
	*59·3	22·1	24·8	25·8	5·6	9·5	4·4	11·1	1·9	6·3	3·0	12·2	..	..	·6	4·2	..	..	·4	8·1
Districts ..	**17,261**	**11,185**	**21,046**	**132,539**	**7,475**	**82,205**	**5,929**	**96,789**	**1,148**	**27,507**	..	..	..	..	**821**	**36,634**	..	..	**548**	**76,649**
Quetta-Pishin ..	..	..	..	..	..	..	4,258	70,892	..	..	..	..	..	..	..	..	..	..	548	76,649
Loralai ..	..	..	676	6,313	5,540	59,340	1,309	20,434	..	..	..	..	..	..	..	..	..	..	..	..
Zhob ..	..	..	10,315	57,963	..	..	..	..	..	..	..	..	..	..	..	..	..	..	..	..
Bolan ..	..	..	..	..	359	4,688	..	..	..	..	..	..	..	..	..	..	..	..	..	..
Chagai ..	17,261	11,185	2,775	13,039	..	..	..	..	..	..	..	..	..	..	..	..	..	..	..	..
Sibi ..	..	..	7,280	55,224	1,576	18,177	362	5,463	1,148	27,507	..	..	..	..	821	36,634	..	..	..	..
Administered area ..	..	..	..	..	*1,576*	*18,177*	*362*	*5,463*	*1,148*	*27,507*	..	..	..	..	*821*	*36,634*	..	..	..	..
Mari-Bugti country	..	..	*7,280*	*55,224*	..	..	..	..	..	..	..	..	..	..	..	..	..	..	..	..
States ..	**62,629**	**180,798**	**12,362**	**91,472**	..	..	..	..	**1,359**	**26,953**	**4,060**	**105,886**	..	..	..	..	..	..	..	
Kalat ..	62,629	180,798	5,230	28,464	..	..	..	..	1,359	26,953	4,060	105,886	..	..	..	..	..	..	..	..
Sarawan ..	..	..	*5,230*	*28,461*	..	..	..	..	..	..	..	..	..	..	..	..	..	..	..	..
Jhalawan ..	*20,795*	*88,978*	..	..	..	..	..	..	..	..	..	..	..	..	..	..	..	..	..	..
Kachhi ..	..	..	..	..	..	..	..	..	..	..	*4,060*	*105,886*	..	..	..	..	..	..	..	..
Dombki-Kaheri country.	..	..	..	..	..	..	..	..	*1,359*	*26,953*	..	..	..	..	..	..	..	..	..	..
Makran ..	*23,269*	*68,462*	..	..	..	..	..	..	..	..	..	..	..	..	..	..	..	..	..	..
Kharan ..	*18,565*	*23,358*	..	..	..	..	..	..	..	..	..	..	..	..	..	..	..	..	..	..
Las Bela ..	..	..	7,132	63,008	..	..	..	..	..	..	..	..	..	..	..	..	..	..	..	..

*The figures in leaded *italics* denote the proportion per cent. which the area and population of each density group bear to the total area and population of the Province.

3. Variation in Indigenous Population by Districts and States.

Districts and States.	Total.				Indigenous.				Semi-Indigenous.				Aliens.			
	1901—11.	1911—21.	1921—31.	1901—31.	1901—11.	1911—21.	1921—31.	1901—31.	1901—11.	1911—21.	1921—31.	1901—31.	1901—11.	1911—21.	1921—31.	1901—31.
1	2	3	4	5	6	7	8	9	10	11	12	13	14	15	16	17
BALUCHISTAN ..	**+23,957**	**−35,078**	**+68,992**	**+57,871**	**+6,550**	**−48,450**	**+56,181**	**+14,281**	**+10,851**	**−9,207**	**+3,264**	**+4,908**	**+6,556**	**+22,579**	**+9,547**	**+38,682**
Districts ..	**+32,306**	**+6,236**	**+42,860**	**+81,402**	**+17,081**	**−9,119**	**+30,238**	**+38,200**	**+9,877**	**−8,601**	**+3,409**	**+4,685**	**+5,348**	**+23,956**	**+9,213**	**+38,517**
Quetta-Pishin ..	+13,561	+9,434	+10,459	+33,454	+4,174	−5,530	+618	−538	+4,529	−1,398	+871	+4,002	+4,858	+10,162	+8,970	+29,990
Loralai ..	+12,437	+1,704	+3,614	..	..	+3,167	+985	..	..	−1,984	+1,213	..	..	+521	+1,416	..
Zhob ..	+648	−13,698	+1,295	..	..	−12,899	+1,176	..	..	−4,496	+615	..	..	+3,697	−496	..
Sibi ..	+4,845	+2,275	+23,541	+36,661	+12,813	+3,474	+22,432	+31,148	+4,859	−834	+248	−379	+258	−365	+861	+5,892
Administered area ..	*+4,436*	*+17*	*+5,341*	..	..	*+1,154*	*+4,691*	..	..	−844	*+281*	..	..	*−293*	*+369*	..
Mari-Bugti country ..	*+409*	*+2,258*	*+18,200*	..	..	*+2,320*	*+17,741*	..	..	*+10*	*−33*	..	..	*−72*	*+492*	..
Bolan ..	+160	+1,522	+1,070	+2,752	+142	+653	+896	+1,691	−167	+137	−19	−49	+185	+732	+193	+1,110
Chagai ..	+655	+4,999	+2,881	+8,535	−48	+1,816	+4,131	+5,899	+656	−26	+481	+1,111	+47	+3,209	−1,731	+1,525
States ..	**−8,349**	**−41,314**	**+26,132**	**−23,531**	**−10,531**	**−39,331**	**+25,948**	**−23,919**	**+974**	**−606**	**−145**	**+223**	**+1,208**	**−1,377**	**+334**	**+165**
Kalat ..	−13,445	−30,805	+13,820	−30,430	−16,611	−28,975	+13,569	−32,017	+1,082	−638	−119	+335	+2,084	−1,192	+360	+1,252
Sarawan ..	*−1,768*	*−9,519*	*−25,798*	..	..	*−9,597*	*−25,647*	..	..	*+100*	*−51*	..	..	*−22*	*−100*	..
Jhalawan ..	*−1,39,675*	*−4,688*	*+9,268*	..	..	*−4,609*	*+9,108*	..	..	*+62*	*−42*	..	..	*−141*	*+204*	..
Kachhi ..	*+29,392*	*−17,606*	*+30,733*	..	..	*−16,982*	*+30,361*	..	..	*−234*	*+28*	..	..	*−390*	*+344*	..
Dombki-Kaheri country ..	*+4,001*	*−3,985*	*+7,395*	*−30,130*	*−16,611*	*−3,359*	*+7,402*	*−32,017*	*+1,082*	*−127*	*+10*	*+335*	*+2,084*	*−499*	*−17*	*+1,252*
Makran ..	*+71,942*	*−82*	*−3,398*	..	..	*+426*	*−3,323*	..	..	*−371*	*−6*	..	..	*−137*	*−66*	..
Kharan ..	*+22,663*	*+5,075*	*−4,380*	..	..	*+5,146*	*−4,327*	..	..	*−68*	*−48*	..	..	*−3*	*−5*	..
Las Bela ..	+5,096	+10,509	+12,312	+6,899	+6,080	−10,356	+12,374	+8,098	−108	+32	−36	−112	−876	−185	−26	−1,087

The figures in columns (2—5) against districts have not been adjusted according to inter-district transfers owing to the classification of the transferred units by Indigenous, Semi-Indigenous and Aliens not being available for the previous Censuses.

4. Variation in relation to density.

District or State.	Mean density per square mile.			Percentage of variation Increase (+) Decrease (—).		
	1931.	1921.	1911.	1911-21.	1921-31.	1911-31.
1	2	3	4	5	6	7
BALUCHISTAN ..	6	6	6	—4·2	+8·6	+4·1
Districts ..	9	8	8	+1·5	+10·2	+11·8
Quetta-Pishin ..	31	28	26	+8·2	+8·6	+17·5
Loralai ..	11	11	11	+2·1	+4·4	+6·6
Zhob ..	6	5	7	—19·5	+2·3	—17·6
Bolan ..	13	14	8	+69·2	—3·8	+62·7
Chagai ..	1	1	1	+22·7	+7·1	+31·5
Sibi ..	13	11	10	+1·5	+21·0	+22·9
Administered area ..	22	21	21	—0·5	+9·4	+8·8
Mari-Bugti country ..	8	5	5	+6·3	+45·5	+54·6
States ..	5	5	5	—9·8	+6·9	—3·6
Kalat ..	5	5	5	—8·6	+4·2	—4·7
Las Bela ..	9	7	9	—17·2	+24·3	+2·9

5. Vital Statistics for the Town of Quetta.

Serial No.	Year.	Births.		Deaths.		Remarks.
		Males.	Females.	Males.	Females.	
TOTAL ..	1911—1920	2,281	1,856	3,169	1,851	
TOTAL ..	1921—1930	*2,380	*2,081	*4,836	*2,384	*The registration of births is incomplete and the birth figures therefore do not supply correct and adequate information for statistical purposes.
1 ..	1911 1921	169 188	134 184	160 495	93 228	
2 ..	1912 1922	257 166	226 138	167 675	227 223	
3 ..	1913 1923	258 162	210 129	197 390	123 142	
4 ..	1914 1924	238 138	192 139	243 395	177 192	
5 ..	1915 1925	268 498	199 450	319 412	172 231	
6 ..	1916 1926	262 442	230 440	249 413	187 224	
7 ..	1917 1927	241 237	194 190	380 525	264 319	
8 ..	1918 1928	217 329	176 252	564 484	269 269	
9 ..	1919 1929	194 100	155 71	461 530	258 299	
10 ..	1920 1930	177 120	140 88	429 517	181 257	

Note.—Outside the Quetta Town there is no registration of births and deaths.

6. Racial Variation.

Race.	1931. Regular Census. Persons.	Males.	Females.	1931. Tribal Census. Persons.	Males.	Females.	1921. Regular Census. Persons.	Males.	Females.	1921. Tribal Census. Persons.	Males.	Females.	Variation. 1911-21.	1921-31.	1911-31.
1	2	3	4	5	6	7	8	9	10	11	12	13	14	15	16
BALUCHISTAN ..	**110,849**	**80,197**	**30,652**	**757,768**	**408,217**	**349,551**	**94,836**	**77,149**	**17,687**	**704,789**	**383,851**	**320,938**	**−35,078**	**+68,992**	**+33,914**
Indigenous ..	**22,824**	**15,315**	**7,509**	**737,301**	**396,626**	**340,675**	**13,239**	**10,173**	**3,066**	**690,705**	**375,826**	**314,879**	**−48,450**	**+56,181**	**+7,731**
Baloch ..	4,366	2,794	1,572	221,675	120,066	101,609	1,446	1,094	352	171,949	94,469	77,480	+4,205	+52,646	+56,851
Brahui ..	5,554	3,784	1,770	147,034	79,744	67,290	2,738	2,270	468	156,996	86,691	70,305	−8,053	−7,146	−15,199
Pathan ..	7,342	5,274	2,068	168,665	90,198	78,467	4,349	3,705	644	169,712	92,184	77,528	−14,032	+1,946	−12,086
Lasi ..	13	13	..	31,799	16,622	15,177	..	..	..	23,212	12,365	10,847	−4,567	+8,600	+4,033
Jatt ..	977	685	292	76,180	41,542	34,638	1,105	797	308	62,086	34,298	27,788	−15,206	+13,966	−1,240
Sayyid ..	831	551	280	21,145	10,576	10,569	567	417	150	19,698	10,150	9,548	−1,031	+1,711	+680
Other Muslims ..	1,362	803	559	56,229	30,079	26,150	878	576	302	70,888	36,787	34,101	−10,302	−14,175	−24,477
Hindu ..	2,375	1,408	967	14,530	7,767	6,763	2,049	1,243	806	15,430	8,420	7,010	+2,494	−574	+1,920
Sikh ..	4	3	1	44	32	12	107	71	36	734	462	272	−1,958	−793	−2,751
Semi-Indigenous	**6,805**	**4,839**	**1,966**	**15,117**	**8,367**	**6,750**	**5,986**	**4,758**	**1,228**	**12,672**	**7,047**	**5,625**	**−10,857**	**+3,264**	**−7,593**
Baloch ..	100	77	23	1,705	915	790	198	160	38	2,380	1,337	1,043	−516	−773	−1,289
Pathan ..	3,696	2,571	1,125	13,322	7,401	5,921	3,446	2,934	512	10,021	5,543	4,478	−8,850	+3,551	−5,299
Others ..	3,009	2,191	818	90	51	39	2,342	1,664	678	271	167	104	−1,491	+486	−1,005
Aliens ..	**81,220**	**60,043**	**21,177**	**5,350**	**3,224**	**2,126**	**75,611**	**62,218**	**13,393**	**1,412**	**978**	**434**	**+24,229**	**+9,547**	**+33,776**
Europeans ..	5,024	3,802	1,222	..	..	..	4,751	3,966	785	..	..	..	+541	+273	+814
Anglo-Indians ..	379	200	179	..	..	..	234	129	105	..	..	..	+111	+145	+256
Orientals ..	75,817	56,041	19,776	5,350	3,221	2,126	70,626	58,123	12,503	1,412	978	434	+23,577	+9,129	+32,706

7. Persons per house and houses per square mile.

Tahsil, etc.	Area in square miles.	Number of houses.	Population Total.	Population per family.	Population per square mile.	Houses per square mile. 1931	Houses per square mile. 1921.
1	2	3	4	5	6	7	8
BALUCHISTAN	**134,638**	***166,644**	**868,617**	**5**	**6**	**1**	**1**
I.—Districts	**54,228**	**90,116**	**463,508**	**5**	**9**	**2**	**2**
(i) Quetta-Pishin District ..	*4,806*	*28,172*	*147,541*	*5*	*31*	*6*	*6*
1. Pishin	3,052	11,055	53,375	5	17	4	3
2. Chaman	1,206	3,137	17,517	6	15	3	2
3. Quetta	548	13,980	76,649	5	140	26	29
(ii) Loralai District	*7,525*	*16,402*	*86,087*	*5*	*11*	*2*	*2*
1. Duki	1,688	3,415	17,998	5	11	2	2
2. Bori	1,671	3,598	18,532	5	11	2	2
3. Sanjawi	676	1,260	6,313	5	9	2	3
4. Barkhan	1,309	3,661	20,434	6	16	3	3
5. Musakhel	2,181	4,468	22,810	5	10	2	2
(iii) Zhob District	*10,315*	*12,675*	*57,963*	*5*	*6*	*1*	*1*
1. Fort Sandeman	6,458	6,543	32,989	5	5	1	1
2. Hindubagh	1,459	2,573	11,580	4	8	2	2
3. Killa Saifullah	2,398	3,559	13,394	4	6	1	1
(iv) Bolan District	*359*	*1,635*	*4,688*	*3*	*13*	*5*	*4*
(v) Chagai District	*20,036*	*6,187*	*24,224*	*4*	*1*	..	..
1. Nushki	2,361	2,665	10,820	4	5	1	1
2. Dalbandin including Western Sanjrani	17,261	3,019	11,183	4	1	--	..
3. Shorarud	414	503	2,219	4	5	1	1
(vi) Sibi District	*11,187*	*25,045*	*143,005*	*6*	*13*	*2*	*2*
(a) Administered area	*3,907*	*17,550*	*87,731*	*5*	*22*	*5*	*4*
1. Sibi	1,148	6,138	27,507	4	24	5	4
2. Shahrig	1,576	3,852	18,177	5	12	2	3
3. Kohlu	362	1,006	5,463	5	15	3	3
4. Nasirabad	821	6,554	36,634	6	45	8	6
(b) Mari-Bugti Country	*7,280*	*7,495*	*55,224*	*7*	*8*	*1*	*1*
1. Mari Country	3,404	3,235	24,860	8	7	1	..
2. Bugti Country	3,876	4,260	30,364	7	8	1	1
II.—STATES	**80,410**	**76,528**	**405,109**	**5**	**5**	**1**	**1**
(i) Kalat	*73,278*	*65,007*	*342,101*	*5*	*5*	*1*	*1*
1. Sarawan	*5,230*	*6,281*	*28,464*	*5*	*5*	*1*	*2*
2. Jhalawan	*20,795*	*14,139*	*88,978*	*6*	*4*	*1*	*1*
3. Kachhi	*4,060*	*18,255*	*105,886*	*6*	*26*	*4*	*3*
4. Dombki-Kaheri Country ..	*1,359*	*4,592*	*26,953*	*6*	*20*	*3*	*2*
5. Makran	*23,269*	*15,464*	*68,462*	*4*	*3*	*1*	*1*
6. Kharan	*18,565*	*6,276*	*23,358*	*4*	*1*	..	..
(ii) Las Bela	7,132	11,521	63,008	5	9	2	1

*Excludes houses in the Strictly Military Areas.

8. Distribution of Indigenous and Alien Population in the Regular and Tribal Areas.

District or State.	Indigenous. Regular Area. Males.	Females.	Indigenous. Tribal Area. Males.	Females.	Semi-Indigenous. Regular Area. Males.	Females.	Semi-Indigenous. Tribal Area. Males.	Females.	Aliens. Regular Area. Males.	Females.	Aliens. Tribal Area. Males.	Females.	Year of Census
1	2	3	4	5	6	7	8	9	10	11	12	13	14
BALUCHISTAN ..	**10,173**	**3,066**	**375,826**	**314,879**	**4,758**	**1,228**	**7,047**	**5,625**	**62,218**	**18,893**	**978**	**434**	**1921**
	15,315	*7,509*	*396,626*	*340,675*	*4,839*	*1,966*	*8,367*	*6,750*	*60,043*	*21,177*	*3,224*	*2,126*	*1931*
Districts ..	**10,141**	**3,058**	**171,087**	**142,445**	**4,750**	**1,228**	**6,740**	**5,420**	**61,888**	**18,315**	**508**	**178**	**1921**
	14,601	*7,153*	*180,187*	*154,973*	*4,829*	*1,964*	*8,151*	*6,600*	*59,701*	*21,102*	*2,532*	*1,712*	*1931*
Quetta-Pishin ..	3,473	1,326	41,292	36,115	2,900	1,034	1,218	944	37,993	10,478	225	84	1921
	5,862	*3,143*	*38,171*	*35,618*	*3,217*	*1,520*	*1,231*	*969*	*41,639*	*15,888*	*152*	*71*	*1931*
Loralai ..	642	128	36,577	31,005	686	69	4,047	3,750	4,249	497	172	42	1921
	574	*270*	*36,964*	*31,529*	*384*	*125*	*5,324*	*4,541*	*3,825*	*1,125*	*865*	*561*	*1931*
Zhob ..	938	77	25,924	21,266	415	28	72	47	7,782	115	4	..	1921
	1,234	*215*	*26,040*	*21,802*	*689*	*103*	*250*	*135*	*6,364*	*1,013*	*19*	*9*	*1931*
Bolan ..	819	139	309	238	143	2	..	..	1,631	328	8	1	1921
	1,429	*484*	*279*	*209*	*99*	*26*	*7*	..	*1,642*	*494*	*16*	*9*	*1931*
Chagai ..	964	272	8,450	7,305	107	29	266	239	3,361	338	8	4	1921
	1,723	*1,014*	*9,863*	*8,522*	*107*	*52*	*624*	*339*	*1,318*	*494*	*86*	*82*	*1931*
Sibi ..	3,305	1,111	58,485	46,516	499	66	637	431	6,822	1,559	91	42	1921
	3,779	*2,027*	*68,870*	*57,173*	*303*	*138*	*724*	*616*	*4,913*	*2,088*	*1,394*	*980*	*1931*
Administered Area ..	*3,305*	*1,111*	*37,429*	*30,599*	*499*	*66*	*511*	*419*	*6,822*	*1,559*	*81*	*39*	*1921*
	3,779	2,027	38,617	32,712	303	138	720	615	4,913	2,088	1,115	754	1931
Mari-Bugti Country ..	..	..	*21,056*	*15,917*	..	..	*26*	*12*	..	..	*10*	*3*	*1921*
	..	..	30,253	24,461	..	..	4	1	..	..	279	226	1931
States ..	**32**	**13**	**204,789**	**172,434**	**8**	..	**307**	**205**	**380**	**78**	**470**	**261**	**1921**
	714	*350*	*216,439*	*185,702*	*10*	*2*	*213*	*150*	*342*	*75*	*692*	*414*	*1931*
Kalat ..	32	13	178,004	148,832	7	..	291	185	372	78	297	170	1921
	714	*356*	*183,100*	*156,230*	*10*	*2*	*212*	*150*	*342*	*75*	*537*	*323*	*1931*
Sarawan ..	*22*	*1*	*29,940*	*23,649*	*2*	..	*156*	*77*	*178*	*38*	*124*	*75*	*1921*
	47	24	15,152	12,742	6	..	116	62	88	14	136	77	1931
Jhalawan ..	..	..	*43,609*	*35,977*	..	..	*40*	*35*	..	..	*38*	*11*	*1921*
	..	..	47,758	40,934	..	..	18	15	62	..	149	42	1931
Kachhi ..	..	..	*41,269*	*33,750*	..	..	*16*	*8*	..	..	*64*	*46*	*1921*
	16	1	57,520	47,843	..	..	24	28	64	..	220	170	1931
Dombki-Kaheri Country	..	..	*10,602*	*8,912*	..	..	..	..	..	..	*26*	*18*	*1921*
	..	..	14,536	12,380	..	..	5	5	..	..	12	15	1931
Makran ..	*10*	*12*	*37,555*	*33,948*	*5*	..	*21*	*15*	*194*	*40*	*41*	*19*	*1921*
	651	331	35,660	31,557	4	2	20	9	128	61	20	19	1931
Kharan ..	..	..	*15,029*	*12,595*	..	..	*58*	*50*	..	..	*4*	*1*	*1921*
	..	..	12,474	10,824	..	..	29	31	..	..	..	..	1931
Las-Bela ..	..	..	26,785	23,602	1	..	16	20	8	..	173	91	1921
	..	..	*33,339*	*29,422*	..	..	*1*	..	..	..	*155*	*91*	*1931*

9. Area and Population of the Tribal and Regular Areas by Tahsils and Political Agencies.

District and Tahsil.	Tribal Areas.					Regular Areas.					Total.					In Tribal Areas.			In Regular Areas.		
	Area in square miles.	Population. Occupied Houses.	Persons.	Males.	Females.	Area in square miles.	Population. Occupied Houses.	Persons.	Males.	Females.	Area in square miles.	Population. Occupied Houses.	Persons.	Males.	Females.	No. of persons per sq. mile.	No. of persons per house.	No. of houses per sq. mile.	No. of persons per sq. mile.	No. of persons per house.	No. of houses per sq. mile.
1	2	3	4	5	6	7	8	9	10	11	12	13	14	15	16	17	18	19	20	21	22
BALUCHISTAN	**134,438**	**143,735**	**757,768**	**408,217**	**349,551**	**200**	**22,909**	**110,849**	**80,197**	**30,652**	**134,638**	**†166,644**	**868,617**	**488,414**	**380,203**	**6**	**5**	**1**	**554**	**5**	**115**
I.—Districts	**54,037**	**67,542**	**354,158**	**190,873**	**163,285**	**191**	**22,574**	**109,350**	**79,131**	**30,219**	**54,228**	**90,116**	**463,508**	**270,004**	**193,504**	**7**	**5**	**1**	**573**	**5**	**118**
(i) Quetta-Pishin	*4,756*	*15,386*	*76,242*	*39,554*	*36,688*	*50*	*12,786*	*71,299*	*50,748*	*20,551*	*4,806*	*28,172*	*147,541*	*90,302*	*57,239*	*16*	*5*	*3*	*1,426*	*6*	*256*
Pishin	3,048·2	9,874	49,131	24,614	24,517	3·8	1,181	4,244	3,206	1,038	3,052	11,055	53,375	27,820	25,555	16	5	3	1,117	4	311
Chaman	1,198·9	2,122	11,121	6,161	4,960	7·1	1,015	6,396	4,794	1,602	1,206	3,137	17,517	10,955	6,562	9	5	2	901	6	143
Quetta	508·9	3,390	15,990	8,779	7,211	39·1	10,590	60,659	42,748	17,911	548	13,980	76,649	51,527	25,122	31	5	7	1,551	6	271
(ii) Loralai	*7,521*	*15,287*	*79,784*	*43,153*	*36,631*	*4*	*1,115*	*6,303*	*4,783*	*1,520*	*7,525*	*16,402*	*86,087*	*47,936*	*38,151*	*11*	*5*	*2*	*1,576*	*6*	*279*
Duki	1,686·238	3,309	17,621	9,489	8,132	1·767	106	377	282	95	1,688	3,415	17,998	9,771	8,227	10	5	2	213	3	60
Bori	1,669·017	2,812	13,203	7,387	5,816	1·983	786	5,329	4,077	1,252	1,671	3,598	18,532	11,464	7,068	8	5	2	2,687	7	396
Sanjavi	675·983	1,200	6,147	3,381	2,766	·017	60	166	120	46	676	1,260	6,313	3,501	2,812	9	5	2	9,765	3	3,529
Barkhan	1,308·8	3,568	20,124	10,692	9,432	·2	93	310	209	101	1,309	3,661	20,434	10,901	9,533	15	6	3	1,550	3	465
Musakhel'	2,180,967	4,398	22,689	12,204	10,485	·033	70	121	95	26	2,181	4,468	22,810	12,299	10,511	10	5	2	3,667	2	2,121
(iii) Zhob District	*10,225*	*10,741*	*48,345*	*26,309*	*22,036*	*90*	*1,934*	*9,618*	*8,287*	*1,331*	*10,315*	*12,675*	*57,963*	*34,596*	*23,367*	*5*	*5*	*1*	*107*	*5*	*21*
Fort Sandeman	6,448·9	5,415	25,754	13,896	11,858	9·1	1,128	7,235	6,215	1,020	6,458	6,543	32,989	20,111	12,878	4	5	1	795	7	124
Hindubagh	1,379·6	2,158	10,112	5,433	4,679	79·4	415	1,468	1,291	177	1,459	2,573	11,580	6,724	4,856	7	5	2	18	4	5
Killa Saifullah	2,396·5	3,168	12,479	6,980	5,499	1·5	391	915	781	134	2,398	3,559	13,394	7,761	5,633	5	4	1	610	2	261
(iv) Bolan District	*344*	*162*	*514*	*296*	*218*	*15*	*1,473*	*4,174*	*3,170*	*1,004*	*359*	*1,635*	*4,688*	*3,466*	*1,222*	*1*	*3*	..	*278*	*3*	*98*
(v) Chagai, District	*20,016*	*4,579*	*19,516*	*10,573*	*8,943*	*20*	*1,608*	*4,708*	*3,148*	*1,560*	*20,036*	*6,187*	*24,224*	*13,721*	*10,503*	*1*	*4*	..	*235*	*3*	*80*
Nushki	2,355·3	2,218	9,154	4,908	4,246	5·7	447	1,666	1,108	558	2,361	2,665	10,820	6,016	4,804	4	4	1	292	4	78
Dalbandin including Western Sanjrani.	17,248·3	1,889	8,251	4,423	3,828	12·7	1,130	2,934	1,951	983	17,261	3,019	11,185	6,374	4,811	..	4	..	231	3	89
Shorarud	412·4	472	2,111	1,242	869	1·6	31	108	89	19	414	503	2,219	1,331	888	5	4	1	68	3	19
(vi) Sibi District	*11,175*	*21,387*	*129,757*	*70,988*	*58,769*	*12*	*3,658*	*13,248*	*8,995*	*4,253*	*11,187*	*25,045*	*143,005*	*79,983*	*63,022*	*12*	*6*	*2*	*1,104*	*4*	*305*
Sibi	1,141·5	3,526	17,742	9,535	8,207	6·5	2,612	9,765	6,288	3,477	1,148	6,138	27,507	15,823	11,684	16	5	3	1,502	4	402
Shahrig	1,572·6	3,148	16,137	8,629	7,508	3·4	704	2,040	1,564	476	1,576	3,852	18,177	10,193	7,984	10	5	2	600	3	207
Nasirabad	818·9	6,237	35,260	19,322	15,938	2·1	317	1,374	1,093	281	821	6,554	36,634	20,415	16,219	43	6	8	654	4	151
*Kohlu	362	981	5,394	2,966	2,428	..	25	69	50	19	362	1,006	5,463	3,016	2,447	15	5	3	..	3	..
Mari Country	3,404	3,235	24,860	13,880	10,980	..	..	..	..	..	3,404	3,235	24,860	13,880	10,980	7	8	1	..	..	..
Bugti Country	3,876	4,260	30,364	16,656	13,708	..	..	..	..	..	3,876	4,260	30,364	16,656	13,708	8	7	1	..	..	..
II.—States	**80,401**	**76,193**	**403,610**	**217,344**	**186,266**	**9**	**335**	**1,499**	**1,066**	**433**	**80,410**	**76,528**	**405,109**	**218,410**	**186,699**	**5**	**5**	**1**	**167**	**4**	**37**
(i) Kalat	73,269	64,672	340,602	183,849	156,753	9	335	1,499	1,066	433	73,278	65,007	342,101	184,915	157,186	5	5	1	167	4	37
Sarawan	*5,229*	*6,226*	*28,285*	*15,404*	*12,881*	*1*	*55*	*179*	*141*	*38*	*5,230*	*6,281*	*28,464*	*15,545*	*12,919*	*5*	*5*	*1*	*179*	*3*	*55*
*Jhalawan	*20,795*	*14,119*	*88,916*	*47,925*	*40,991*	..	*20*	*62*	*62*	..	*20,795*	*14,139*	*88,978*	*47,987*	*40,991*	*4*	*6*	*1*	..	*3*	..
*Kachhi	*4,060*	*18,252*	*105,805*	*57,764*	*48,041*	..	*3*	*81*	*80*	*1*	*4,060*	*18,255*	*105,886*	*57,844*	*48,042*	*26*	*6*	*4*	..	*27*	..
Dombki-Kaheri Country	*1,359*	*4,592*	*26,953*	*14,553*	*12,400*	..	..	..	..	..	*1,359*	*4,592*	*26,953*	*14,553*	*12,400*	20	6	3	..	..	..
Makran	*23,261*	*15,207*	*67,285*	*35,700*	*31,585*	*8*	*257*	*1,177*	*783*	*394*	*23,269*	*15,464*	*68,462*	*36,483*	*31,979*	3	*4*	*1*	*147*	5	*32*
Kharan	*18,565*	*6,276*	*23,358*	*12,503*	*10,855*	..	..	..	..	..	*18,565*	*6,276*	*23,358*	*12,503*	*10,855*	*1*	*4*	..	..	..	..
(ii) Las Bela	7,132	11,521	63,008	33,495	29,513	..	..	..	..	..	7,132	11,521	63,008	33,495	29,513	9	5	2	..	..	..

* 1. In column 7 against Kohlu, Jhalawan and Kachhi, the figures of area being negligible have not been shown as the population in columns 9—11 consisted of establishments at Tahsil headquarters and small camps of Survey parties, respectively, found on the night of the census.

† 2. Excludes houses in the strictly Military areas.

CHAPTER II.

THE POPULATION OF CITIES, TOWNS AND VILLAGES.

Reference to statistics.

53. This chapter deals with the population of towns and villages in Baluchistan. The statistics are contained in the following tables :—

Particulars.	Table.	Part I of this Report—page.	Part II of this Report—page.
Towns and Villages	Imperial Table III	..	5
Urban variation	Imperial Table IV ..	..	7
Urban population by religion ..	Imperial Table V ..	..	11
Distribution of the Population between Towns and Villages	Subsidiary Table 10	28	..
Number *per mille* of total population and of each main religion who live in towns ..	Subsidiary Table 11	29	..
Towns classified by population	Subsidiary Table 12	29	..
Tables compiled for the Quetta Municipality (printed in a separate volume).			

Definitions. City.

54. A city for Census purposes means every town containing not less than 100,000 inhabitants.

Town.

55. A town includes every Municipality, all civil lines not falling within Municipal limits, every cantonment and other continuous collection of houses inhabited by not less than 5,000 persons treated as a town by the Provincial Census Superintendent.

56. The Census of all towns and cantonments was taken synchronously on the Standard Schedule with the exception of Bela, Pasni, Kalat and the suburbs of Mastung which were censused non-synchronously on the local modified schedule. The cantonments of Quetta, and all Military stations, which are not recognised cantonments, have for the first time been treated as towns and shown separately in the Census tables. With the exception of Quetta and Sibi Towns, all the places treated as towns have a population of less than 5,000 in each case. They have been treated as towns because they are either headquarters stations or have urban characteristics.

Village.

57. In the districts, a village means a revenue *mauza* with all its attached hamlets. In the States, a village means not only the revenue *mauza* with its hamlets but also residential villages as well as localities which often containing no permanent dwellings are regularly occupied at certain seasons of the year by semi-nomadic population in the course of migration. A village also includes nomadic and semi-nomadic encampments outside recognised village limits. In such cases the encampment has been treated as a separate village under the name of the headman of the encampment.

58. All Railway gang-huts and roadside gang encampments have been treated as unclassed population.

DIAGRAM NO. 4

DIAGRAM SHOWING PERCENTAGE OF URBAN AND RURAL POPULATION OF BALUCHISTAN, 1931.

District or Divisions of States.	Total Population		Urban Population		Rural Population	
	Persons	Percentage to total Population	Persons	Percentage to total Population	Persons	Percentage to total Population
BALUCHISTAN	868,617	100	102,602	12	766,015	88
DISTRICTS	463,508	53	92,025	11	371,483	42
Quetta-Pishin	147,541	17	68,757	8	78,784	9
Loralai	86,087	10	5,321	1	80,766	9
Zhob	57,963	7	6,581	1	51,382	6
Bolan	4,668	·5	1,834	·2	2,854	·3
Chagai	24,224	3	—	—	24,224	3
Sibi	143,005	15.6	9,532	·8	133,473	14.7
STATES	405,109	47	10,577	1	394,532	46
KALAT	342,109	39	7,237	·8	334,864	38·2
Sarawan	28,464	3	4,816	·6	23,648	2·4
Jhalawan	88,978	10	—	—	88,978	10
Kachhi	105,886	12	—	—	105,886	12
Dombki-Kaheri	26,953	3	—	—	26,953	3
Makran	68,462	8	2,421	·2	66,041	7·8
Kharan	23,358	3	—	—	23,358	3
LASBELA	63,008	8	3,340	·2	59,668	7·8

Percentage of Urban and Rural Population to total Population.

Urban Population shown thus:- ■ Rural Population shown thus:- ▒

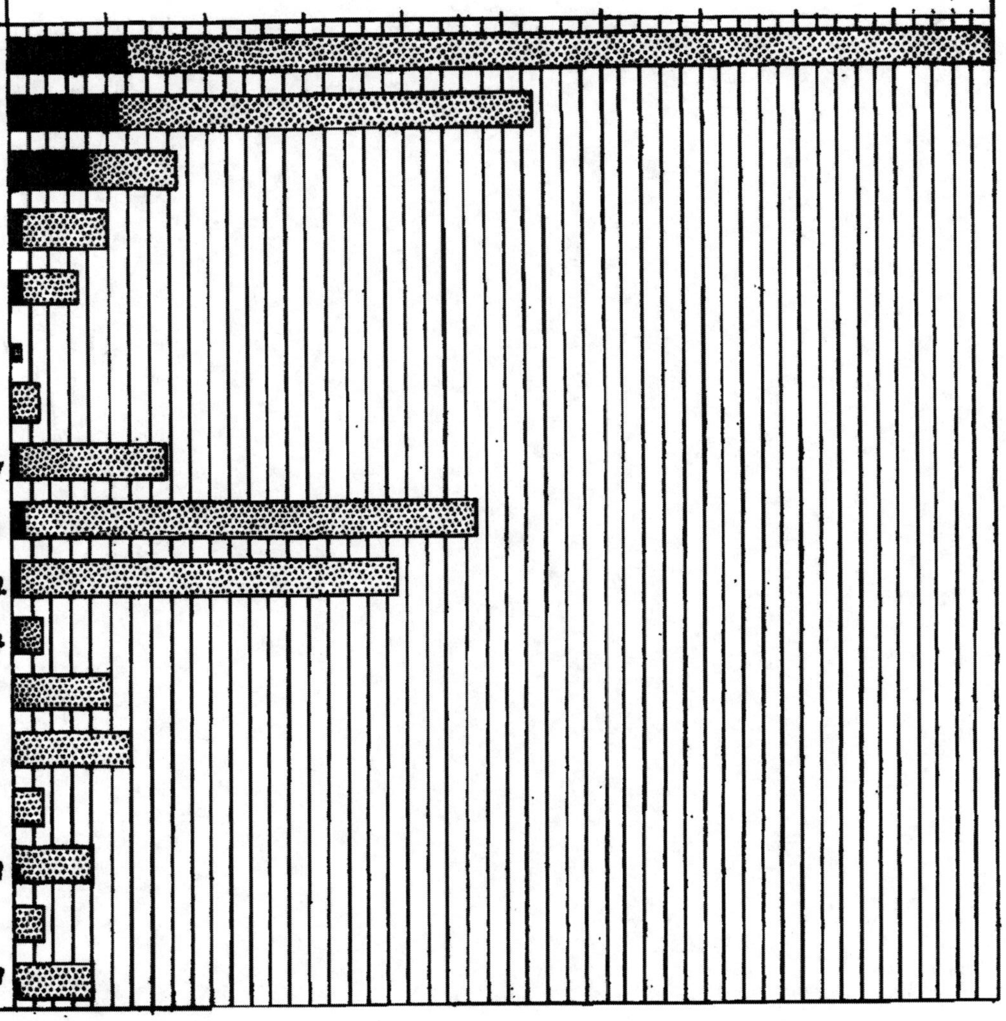

Reg No. 22 E. D. (E Coy) 1933.

Sibi	142,005	15·6	9,532	·8	133,473	14·7
STATES	405,109	47	10,577	1	394,532	46
KALAT	342,109	39	7,237	·8	334,864	38·2
Sarawan	28,464	3	4,816	·6	23,648	2·4
Jhalawan	88,978	10	—	—	88,978	10
Kachhi	105,886	12	—	—	105,886	12
Dombki-Kaheri	26,953	3	—	—	26,953	3
Makran	68,462	8	2,421	·2	66,041	7·8
Kharan	23,368	3	—	—	23,368	3
LASBELA	63,008	8	3,340	·2	59,668	7·8

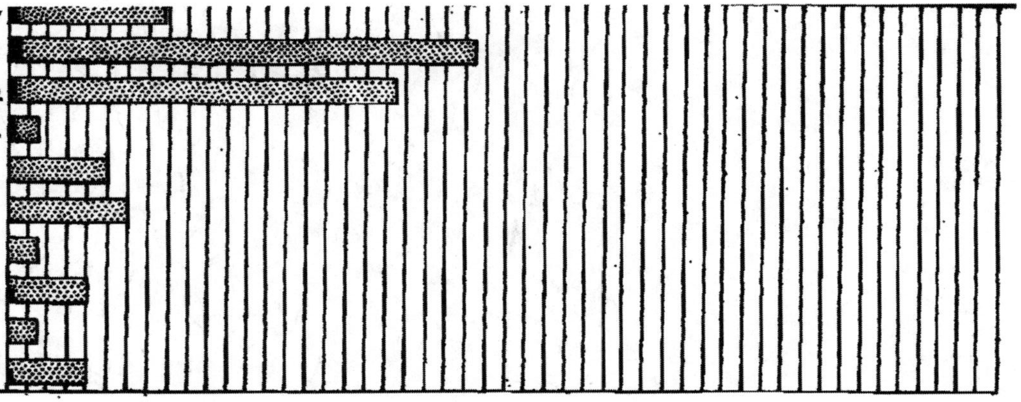

DIAGRAM NO. 5

URBAN AND RURAL POPULATION OF BALUCHISTAN AND OF ADJOINING PROVINCES

Percentage of Urban population shown thus ■

Percentage of Rural population shown thus ▨

Provinces	Population: Urban	Population: Rural	Percentage of Urban population	Percentage of Rural population
Baluchistan	102,602	766,015	12	88
Punjab	3,521,449	24,969,406	12	88
Sind	699,307	3,187,763	18	82
Bombay	6,444,602	23,953,645	21	79
N.W.F.Province	386,177	4,298,187	8	92

Percentage of Urban and Rural population

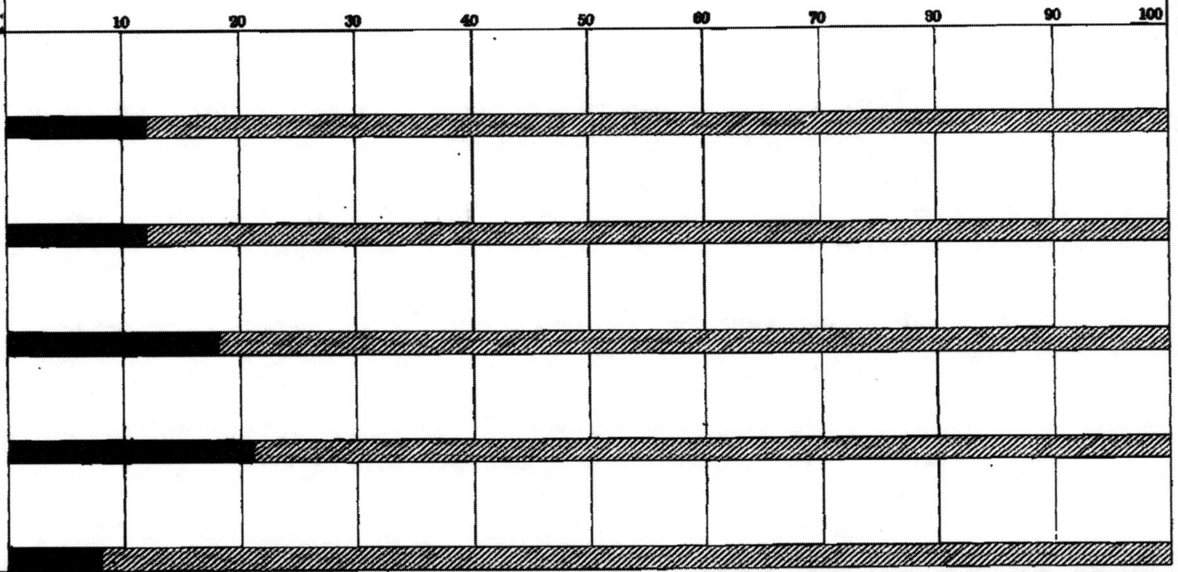

Reg No. 28. ED (E' Coy.) 1933-

Distribution of Urban and Rural population.

59. Statistics of urban and rural population for the past four censuses are compared in the margin with those for 1931. The figures for 1891 and 1901 are not comparable with those for subsequent years as the former did not embrace the whole province. A comparison can only be made between the urban population of 1891 and that of 1931 for such towns as existed at both these censuses. In 1891 there were only four towns namely, Quetta, Sibi, Loralai and Pishin.

Year of Census.	*Urban.*	*Rural.*
1891	25,952	145,800
1901	40,033	770,713
1911	59,593	775,110
1921	70,063	720,562
1931	102,602	766,015

Town.	Population.				
	1891.	1901.	1911.	1921.	1931.
TOTAL ..	25,952	34,248	44,209	61,494	77,560
Quetta ..	18,802	24,584	33,922	49,001	60,272
Sibi ..	2,944	4,551	6,597	6,386	9,532
Loralai ..	3,674	3,561	2,936	4,303	5,321
Pishin ..	532	1,552	754	1,804	2,435

The marginal figures will show that the total population of these four stations was only 25,952 in 1891. It rose to 34,248 in 1901, 44,209 in 1911, 61,494 in 1921 and 77,560 in 1931 showing a total increase of 51,608 persons in a period of 40 years. This increase represents the actual increase in the urban population except in so far as it includes 4,963 persons censused in the Kasi and Nichari villages which in 1931 were transferred from the rural to urban areas owing to the extension of the boundaries of the Quetta Town. The net actual increase, therefore, is 46,645 which means an increase of 180 per cent. in 40 years and of 18 per cent. during the ten years ending with 1931.

60. Taking, however, the three censal periods which embraced the whole province, *i.e.*, 1911, 1921 and 1931, we find that the total urban population has increased from 59,593 in 1911 to 102,602 in 1931, showing an increase of 72 per cent. in 20 years. On the other hand during this period the rural population has decreased by 9,095 or 1 per cent. The transfer of 9,218 persons from rural areas representing the population of villages which were treated as towns for the first time in 1931 and the inclusion of Kasi and Nichari in the town of Quetta as well as the loss of over 60,000 persons from the influenza epidemic during the preceding inter-censal period are responsible for this decrease. The decennium under review has however more than made up the loss, for, the rural population of 1931 shows an increase since 1921 of 45,453 persons or 6 per cent. Diagram No. 4 facing this page illustrates the ratio of urban to rural population in Baluchistan.

61. Of every hundred persons in Baluchistan twelve live in towns. This ratio is inclusive of the alien population numbering 86,570 who are—as is generally the case with all aliens—town dwellers almost to a man. If we exclude the aliens the ratio of town-dwellers among the indigenous population dwindles down to 2 per cent. The proportions of urban to rural population in the various provinces of India adjoining Baluchistan are compared in the margin and are illustrated in Diagram No. 5.

Province.	Population.		Proportion per cent.	
	Urban.	Rural.	Urban.	Rural.
Baluchistan ..	102,602	766,015	12	88
Punjab ..	3,521,449	24,969,408	12	88
North-West Frontier Province ..	386,177	4,298,187	8	92
Bombay ..	6,444,602	23,953,645	21	79
Sind ..	699,307	3,187,763	18	82

62. The distribution of population by Administrative divisions is shown below:—

Divisions.	1911.		1921.		1931.	
	Urban.	Rural.	Urban.	Rural.	Urban.	Rural.
BALUCHISTAN ..	**59,559**	**775,144**	**79,063**	**720,562**	**102,602**	**766,015**
DISTRICTS ..	**49,609**	**364,808**	**69,948**	**350,700**	**92,025**	**371,483**
Quetta-Pishin ..	36,685	90,963	55,031	82,051	68,757	78,784
Loralai ..	2,936	77,833	4,303	78,170	5,321	80,766
Zhob ..	3,391	66,975	4,228	52,440	6,581	51,382
Bolan ..	..	2,096	..	3,618	1,834	2,854
Chagai ..	..	16,344	..	21,343	..	24,224
Sibi ..	6,597	110,592	6,386	113,078	9,532	133,473
STATES ..	**9,984**	**410,307**	**9,115**	**369,862**	**10,577**	**394,582**
Kalat ..	6,978	352,108	6,403	321,878	7,237	334,864
Las Bela ..	3,006	58,199	2,712	47,984	3,340	59,668

It will be seen that the progress of urbanisation has been fairly satisfactory for a backward province like Baluchistan where industrial life is still in its infancy. Of the total urban population for the whole province (102,602), 90 per cent. live in the District areas while only 10 per cent. are found in the States. To the population of the districts, the Quetta-Pishin District alone contributes 73 per cent. Sibi follows next with 13. Percentage figures for all districts are given in the margin.

Districts.	*Percentage of urban population*, 1931.
DISTRICTS ..	100
Quetta-Pishin ..	73
Loralai ..	5
Zhob ..	7
Bolan ..	2
Chagai ..	0
Sibi ..	13

Distribution of Urban population by religion.

63. Of their respective total numbers, there are 66 *per mille* Muslims in towns, 642 Hindus, 834 Sikhs, 983 Christians and 886 Others. These figures indicate that the Christian, Sikh, Hindu and Other religions mainly live in towns, while 934 *per mille* of the Muslim population reside in rural areas. Further particulars are contained in Subsidiary Table 11.

The main attractions for the growth of urban population are industrial and transport employment, and trade. The province possesses practically no artisan class of its own—not even sweepers—and masons and carpenters, blacksmiths, goldsmiths, painters, tailors, potters, boot and shoe-makers and skilled labourers, etc., are all drawn from the Indian provinces principally from the Punjab. The marginal table shows how the population of urban areas has increased in each religion since 1921.

Census Year.	*Population (both sexes.)*	*Males.*	*Females.*
Total Urban—			
1931 ..	102,602	71,561	31,041
1921 ..	79,063	60,099	18,964
Hindu—			
1931 ..	34,484	24,850	9,634
1921 ..	25,759	19,765	5,994
Sikh—			
1931 ..	7,029	5,194	1,835
1921 ..	5,844	4,842	1,002
Muslim—			
1931 ..	52,853	35,776	17,077
1921 ..	39,011	29,111	9,900
Christian—			
1931 ..	7,918	5,537	2,381
1921 ..	6,404	4,978	1,426

Growth of Towns.

64. According to the Census of 1931, there was no city in Baluchistan, the population of even the largest station in the province namely Quetta including its cantonment and suburbs being only 60,272. There were 17 towns in 1931 against 9 in 1921. The 8 new towns include 2 cantonments and 3 Military stations namely Quetta, Pishin, Chaman, Loralai and Fort Sandeman which at previous censuses were amalgamated with their respective towns and have been classed as separate towns in 1931. The actual increase thus amounts to 3 due to classification as towns of three places namely Pasni, Panjgur and Mach which were treated as villages at previous censuses.

Towns in Baluchistan.

65. The whole of the urban population of 1931 is distributed over the following 17 towns namely :—

Towns.	Population.	
	1921.	1931.
1. Quetta	49,001	60,272
(*a*) Town and Suburbs	27,220	34,881
(*b*) Cantonment	21,781	25,391
2. Sibi	6,386	9,532
3. Fort Sandeman	4,228	6,581
(*a*) Town	..	3,944
(*b*) Cantonment		2,637
4. Chaman	4,226	6,050
(*a*) Town	..	36,96
(*b*) Cantonment	..	2,354
5. Mastung	4,569	3,372
6. Bela	2,712	3,340
7. Loralai	4,303	5,321
(*a*) Town	..	2,695
(*b*) Cantonment	..	2,626
8. Pasni	1,446	1,989
9. Mach	794	1,834
10. Pishin	1,804	2,435
(*a*) Town	..	1,625
(*b*) Cantonment	..	810
11. Kalat	1,834	1,444
12. Panjgur	530	432

Quetta.

66. All these excepting Quetta are towns by courtesy for they have been treated as such owing partly to their being headquarters or Military stations and partly owing to their urban characteristics. Quetta still remains the only unimpeachable township. A detailed account of Quetta's past history is given in Mr. Hughes-Buller's Gazetteer of the Quetta-Pishin District. An interesting description of its geographical situation and strategic importance was published in the *Statesman* of Calcutta in its issue of October 11, 1931. The following is an extract from this article :—

" Far off the beaten track of India's tourist routes, lonely guardian of the Khojak Pass " and tunnel from Chaman and of the Bolan rail and road passage to India, Quetta stands as " a typical outpost of Empire, ready for the day it hopes will never come * * * " Among Indian Military stations, Quetta, so lately the tragic scene of a terrific seismic dis- " turbance is an outstanding example of an outpost of Empire which is in but not of the coun- " try. Unlike many other cantonments, it boasts no teeming surrounding districts, its his- " torical associations are few, no magnificent ruins exist to remind the curious passer-by of the " glories of other days. But for Nature's action, countless centuries ago, in splitting the face " of those barren bluffs of India's western boundary, so providing a tortuous, inhospitable " route as an alternative, albeit distant, route to that of the Khyber, there would probably " be no Quetta."

Quetta is situated at an altitude of 5,500 feet and is 536 miles from Karachi, 700 miles from Lahore and 143 miles from Kandahar. Prior to 1868, little existed beyond a few mud huts occupied by Hindus which clustered round the mound (now the Fort) under the domination of the Khan of Kalat. The Khan's Naib or Governor occupied the Miri or Fort which was garrisoned by two companies of Kalat infantry and a troop of cavalry. There was little cultivation in the valley. In 1828, Masson, the first European traveller, found that the town comprised about 300 houses. In 1839 Quetta was described by General Havelock as a most miserable mud town with a small castle on a mound having one small gun on a rickety carriage.

The Quetta of 1931, however, presents quite a different picture. The number of its houses has risen to over 14,000. Its population including its cantonment now stands at 60,272, The miserable mud town of 1839 has been described by visitors as a well planned and cleaner station than most Indian cities while its peaches, apricots, melons and grapes have been praised both by Indians and foreigners. Quetta is gradually growing into a summer resort for people from the plains chiefly from Sind and the Punjab.

The population of Quetta town itself (34,881) as revealed by the Census of 1931, represents its winter population as at previous censuses. According to the Special Census taken in September 1929, Quetta's normal population in the summer should be at least 50 per cent. more than its winter population

The subjoined table shows the racial composition for 1921 and 1931 of the indigenous element in the population of Quetta.

		Persons.	Males.	Females.			Persons.	Males.	Females.
Total Indigenous ..	1931	6,206	3,814	2,392	Hazara ..	1931	2,412	1,667	745
	1921	2,730	1,849	881		1921	1,541	1,091	450
Hindus ..	1931	794	450	344	Indian Christian ..	1931	2,090	1,271	819
	1921	551	307	244		1921	1,475	931	544
Muslim ..	1931	5,412	3,364	2,048	*Total Aliens* ..	1931	50,082	35,935	14,147
	1921	2,087	1,481	606		1921	42,906	33,141	9,765
Brahui ..	1931	1,584	1,009	575	Alien Muslim ..	1931	16,685	12,142	4,543
	1921	754	510	244		1921	14,007	10,998	3,009
Pathan ..	1931	2,709	1,662	1,047	Sikh ..	1931	4,786	3,399	1,387
	1921	793	595	198		1921	4,417	3,595	822
Baloch ..	1931	498	320	178	Christians ..	1931	7,012	4,948	2,064
	1921	141	101	40		1921	6,042	4,699	1,343
Semi-Indigenous ..	1931	3,984	2,678	1,306	Hindu ..	1931	21,350	15,307	6,043
	1921	3,365	2,419	946		1921	18,102	13,584	4,518

The increase since 1921 in the proportion of females to males among the indigenous inhabitants is remarkable. It is due mainly to the amalgamation with the Quetta town of the Kasi and Nichari villages which are inhabited almost entirely by the indigenous races. There are indications, however, that the influx into urban areas is rapidly changing from individual to family migration of a permanent nature.

Rural Areas.

67. In Baluchistan, 118 persons *per mille* reside in towns while 882 live in rural areas. The total rural population of the province is 766,015 residing in 3,501 villages and encampments scattered over an area of 134,584 square miles. Thus on an average, Baluchistan possesses only one village over an area of 38 square miles. In rural areas, 532 *per mille* live in villages and encampments with a population of less than 500; 220 in villages with population ranging between 500 to 1,000; 143 in villages with a population of 1,000 to 2,000; 74 in villages with population 2,000 to 5,000 and 27 in villages with a population of 5,000 to 10,000. Four *per mille* represent unclassed population. Details by Districts and States are given in Subsidiary Table 10.

SUBSIDIARY TABLES.

10. Distribution of the population between Towns and Villages.

Districts and States.	*Average population per*		*Number per mille residing in*		*Number per mille of urban population residing in towns with a population of*						*Number per mille of rural population residing in villages with a population of*					
	Town.	Village	Towns.	Villages.	1,000 and under	1,000 to 2,000	2,000 to 3,000	3,000 to 4,000	9,000 to 10,000	20,000 to 50,000	500 and under	500 to 1,000	1,000 to 2,000	2,000 to 5,000	5,000 to 10,000	Un-classed
1	2	3	4	5	6	7	8	9	10	11	12	13	14	15	16	17
BALUCHISTAN ..	**6,035**	**219**	**118**	**882**	**12**	**67**	**101**	**140**	**93**	**587**	**532**	**220**	**143**	**74**	**27**	**4**
DISTRICTS ..	**7,669**	**261**	**199**	**801**	**9**	**38**	**112**	**83**	**103**	**655**	**435**	**250**	**166**	**86**	**56**	**7**
Quetta-Pishin ..	11,460	210	466	534	12	24	34	54	..	876	482	273	175	65	..	5
Loralai ..	2,661	188	62	938	..	..	1,000	..	..	..	587	285	127	..	..	1
Zhob ..	3,291	205	114	886	..	-	400	600	..	..	606	211	172	..	..	11
Bolan ..	1,834	102	391	609		1,000	..	..	..	..	847	..	..	..	..	153
Chagai ..	..	336	..	1,000	..	..	..	..	..	..	347	272	348	..	..	33
Sibi ..	9,532	496	67	933	..	..	..	..	1,000	..	255	233	153	200	157	2
Administered Area	9,532	323	109	791	..	..	..	..	1,000	..	410	370	189	28	..	3
Mari-Bugti Country	..	2,045	..	1,000	..	..	..	..	..	..	36	40	102	444	378	..
STATES ..	**2,115**	**190**	**26**	**974**	**40**	**325**	..	**635**	..	..	**624**	**192**	**123**	**61**	..	..
Kalat ..	1,809	186	21	979	60	474	..	466	..	..	631	177	127	65	..	..
Sarawan ..	2,408	127	169	831	..	300	..	700	..	..	790	81	129	..	..	..
Jhalawan ..	..	187	..	1,000	..	..	..	..	..	..	536	212	84	168	..	..
Kachhi ..	..	180	..	1,000	..	..	..	..	..	..	656	131	183	30	..	..
Dombki-Kaheri-Country	..	219	..	1,000	..	..	..	..	..	..	478	156	198	168	..	..
Makran ..	1,211	217	35	965	178	822	..	..	..	..	661	264	75	..	..	..
Kharan ..	..	196	..	1,000	..	..	..	..	..	..	816	131	53	..	..	..
Las-Bela ..	3,340	214	53	947	..	..	..	1,000	..	..	585	273	100	42	..	..

11. Number *per mille* of the total population and of each main Religion who live in Towns.

Districts and States.	Number *per mille*, who live in Towns. Total population.	Muslim.	Hindu.	Sikh.	Christian.	Others.
1	2	3	4	5	6	7
BALUCHISTAN	**118**	**66**	**642**	**834**	**963**	**886**
DISTRICTS	**196**	**106**	**805**	**837**	**983**	**890**
Quetta-Pishin	466	269	930	981	999	1,000
Loralai	62	32	579	900	847	..
Zhob	114	62	819	694	722	871
Bolan	391	355	390	787	725	933
Chagai	..	..	..	..	..	..
Sibi	67	45	463	373	910	195
STATES	**26**	**24**	**89**	**474**	**937**	**1,000**
Kalat	21	19	68	286	937	1,000
Sarawan	168	151	829	1,000	1,000	..
Jhalawan	..	..	..	..	..	..
Kachhi	..	..	..	..	..	..
Dombki-Kaheri Country ..	..	..	..	..	..	..
Makran	35	33	597	567	1,000	1,000
Kharan	..	..	..	..	..	..
Las Bela	53	48	245	1,000	..	..

12. Towns classified by Population.

Class of Town.	Number of towns of each class 1931.	Proportion of total urban population.	Number of females to 1,000 males.	*Increase or decrease per cent. in the population of towns at different Censuses.* 1901-11.	1911-21.	1921-31.	1901-31.
1	2	3	4	5	6	7	8
TOTAL ..	17	100	434	+49	+33	+30	+156
1,000 and under ..	2	1	178	..	+139	..	..
1,000 to 2,000 ..	4	7	810	—51	—7	—15	+5
2,000 to 3,000 ..	4	10	200	—10	+72	+23	+66
3,000 to 4,000 ..	4	14	569	—11	+8	..	—7
4,000 to 5,000 ..	..	..	..	+45	..	—21	+109
5,000 to 6,000 ..	..	..	..	..	—9	..	..
6,000 to 7,000 ..	..	..	..	..	—3	+49	..
7,000 to 8,000 ..	..	..	..	..	..	..	..
8,000 to 9,000 ..	..	..	..	..	..	..	..
9,000 to 10,000 ..	1	9	366	..	..	..	..
10,000 to 50,000 ..	2	59	421	+38	+44	+23	+145

CHAPTER III.

BIRTHPLACE AND MIGRATION.

Reference to statistics.

68. The birthplace statistics discussed in this chapter are contained in the following tables :—

Particulars.	Table.	Page No. Part I.	Page No. Part II.
Birthplace	Imperial Table VI ..	..	13
Race, Tribe or Caste	Imperial Table XVII ..	..	107
Immigrants	Subsidiary Table 13 ..	38	..
Emigrants	Subsidiary Table 14 ..	38	..
Migration between Districts	Subsidiary Table 15 ..	39	..
Migration between Baluchistan and other parts of India	Subsidiary Table 16 ..	39	..
Nomadism among selected tribes ..	Subsidiary Table 17 ..	40	..

How the statistics were collected.

69. These statistics are based on column 13 of the Standard Schedule which was confined to synchronous areas and Kharan with a population of 134,207. For every person born within the province in the synchronous areas as well as the few aliens, officials or traders who were enumerated in non-synchronous areas, the enumerator was required to enter the District or State only in which he or she was born. In the case of births in India beyond Baluchistan, the name of the province was added; for persons born outside India, only the name of the country was recorded. The statistics thus collected are as accurate as can possibly be expected.

The method of registration adopted in respect of the non-synchronous areas with a population of 734,410 was however, arbitrary. In these tracts it was assumed that all indigenous tribesmen censused within the District or State of their permanent residence were born in that District or State. All exceptions to this general rule, which are not inconsiderable, for instance births in the course of wanderings in adjoining Districts or States of Baluchistan or births in India and adjoining countries or abroad among tribesmen of Baluchistan temporarily absent from the province, were ignored. In order, however, to ascertain the extent of growth of the resident population of each administrative unit as well as the volume of inter-district migration within the province at the time of enumeration, an attempt was made to record in the remarks column of the local schedule the District or State of permanent residence of all indigenous families censused within the province but outside the district of their permanent residence.

The statistics of Baluchistan emigrants censused in India were supplied for purposes of this chapter by the Provincial and State Superintendents concerned.

Main Results.

70. It must be confessed that the birthplace statistics thus collected fail to serve the double purpose for which they are intended, namely, as a means of gauging the growth of population of different parts of the province, and the extent to which the people move from one part of the country to another. The reasons for this have been explained at great length in paragraph 69 of the Census Report for 1911 and it is hardly necessary to recapitulate them here. Taking the figures at their face value we find that against the actual population

DIAGRAM NO. 6

PROPORTION OF POPULATION OF BALUCHISTAN BORN WITHIN THE PROVINCE TO THAT BORN ELSEWHERE

Born in Baluchistan shown thus.... Born in India and Indian States shown thus..... Born elsewhere shown thus.........

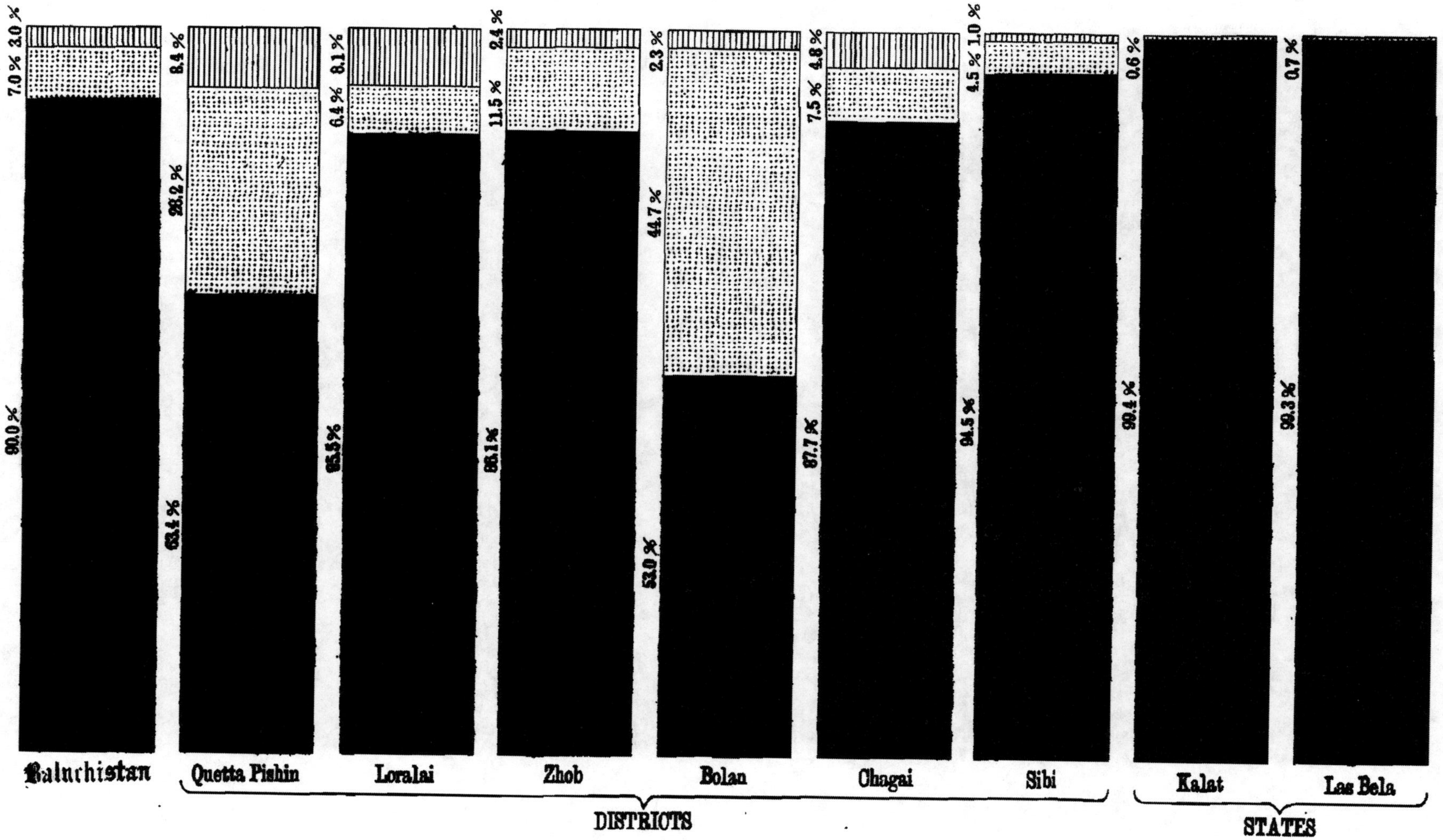

of Baluchistan as disclosed by the Census of 1931 (868,617 persons) we have a natural population amounting to 821,158 as shown in the margin. The question of accuracy of the latter figure has been discussed in Chapter I of this report. Here I shall confine the discussion to bare figures relating to the tracts which supply the immigrants or support our emigrants. Out of the total Census population of 868,617 persons, 778,564 were assumed to have been born within the province as explained above. The rest 90,053 were immigrants who came from India and foreign countries while 42,594 persons born within the province were censused outside provincial boundaries. In other words, of the total census population of the province, 900 *per mille* were born within the province, 70 elsewhere in India and 30 abroad. Thus the gain *per mille* to the province by immigration was 100 while the loss by emigration amounted to 49.

Total Census population	868,617
Add—Traceable emigrants	42,594
Total	911,211
Deduct—Immigrants	90,053
Balance Natural population	821,158

71. The following table shows the numbers of foreign born as well as those born within the Province per 1,000 of population of each District or State :—

District or State.	Born in India.			Born outside India.
	Total born in Baluchistan.	Contiguous areas.	Non-contiguous areas.	
DISTRICTS	811	100	38	51
Quetta-Pishin	634	200	82	84
Loralai	855	47	17	81
Zhob	861	93	22	24
Bolan	530	317	130	23
Chagai	877	48	27	48
Sibi	945	35	10	10
STATES	994	5	1	..
Kalat	994	5	1	..
Las Bela	993	6	1	..

Diagram No. 6 on the opposite page shows the proportions of population by birthplace.

72. Five types of migration are generally recognised, namely :— **Types of Migration.**

(*a*) *Casual*, which comprises minor movements between neighbouring villages, which may be of a permanent or temporary character and come into our records only when the persons cross the borders of two birthplace units ;

(*b*) *Temporary*, due usually to the migration of coolies to meet the demand for labour on canals, railways and so forth and to journeys on business or in connection with pilgrimage, marriage ceremonies and the like ;

(*c*) *Periodic*, due to seasonal demands for labour, generally for the harvests;

(*d*) *Semi-permanent*, where the inhabitants of one place earn their living in another but maintain connection with their own homes and ultimately return there ;

(*e*) *Permanent*, usually in the nature of colonisation.

To this may be added :—

(*f*) *Daily Migration* of recent birth, and

(*g*) *Transit Migration* which is a special feature of Baluchistan. It covers those nomads from Afghanistan (known as the Powindahs) and travellers from Persia who pass through Baluchistan in the winter on their way to India and back in the spring to escape the severity of winter and to earn a living in more congenial climes, or for purposes of trade.

73. The *casual* form of migration is at present of no importance. The daily migration is growing rapidly. Large numbers of villagers visit the headquarters stations every day for business, to work as coolies, to attend Courts of Law and various other purposes, and return to their homes in the evenings on

bicycles or by hired lorries of which latter regular services have been established between trade centres and outlying villages. The other types affect both immigrants and emigrants and will be dealt with later.

Immigration.

74. The total number of immigrants recorded at the Census of 1931 was 90,053. Of these 66,542 (50,061 males and 16,481 females) were born in Indian Provinces and States, 19,344 (12,959 males and 6,385 females) in other Asiatic countries; 4,082 (3,298 males and 784 females) in Europe; 29 (18 males and 11 females) in Africa; 41 (26 males and 15 females) in America; and 15 (12 males and 3 females) in Australasia. Details of immigrants from the principal Asiatic countries and other continents are shown below :—

Where born.	1931.			1921.			1911.		
	Persons.	Males.	Females.	Persons.	Males.	Females.	Persons.	Males.	Females.
A. Born in Baluchistan ..	778,564	422,040	356,524	721,238	395,362	325,876	776,203	420,697	355,506
B. Born in Indian Provinces and States ..	66,542	50,061	16,481	66,166	55,232	10,934	42,309	33,302	9,007
C. Born in other Asiatic countries ..	19,344	12,959	6,385	8,014	6,716	1,298	12,801	9,444	3,357
(a) Afghanistan ..	14,953	9,572	5,381	5,285	4,436	849	10,625	7,694	2,931
(b) Nepal ..	3,868	3,120	748	2,455	2,085	370	1,677	1,439	238
(c) Persia ..	417	189	228	210	149	61	214	148	66
(d) China ..	34	24	10	14	9	5	8	5	3
(e) Other Asiatic countries	72	54	18	50	37	13	277	158	119
D. Born in Europe ..	4,082	3,298	784	4,141	3,640	501	3,323	2,926	397
(a) United Kingdom ..	4,041	3,277	764	4,109	3,620	489	3,287	2,908	379
(b) Other European countries ..	41	21	20	32	20	12	36	18	18
E. Born in Africa ..	29	18	11	18	13	5	8	6	2
F. Born in America ..	41	26	15	32	24	8	37	27	10
G. Born in Australasia ..	15	12	3	16	13	3	19	15	4
H. Born at sea ..	..	..	..	..	..	..	3	2	1

75. The number of immigrants has risen by 31,553 or 54 per cent. since 1911 and by 11,666 or 15 per cent. since 1921. Between 1911 and 1931, Indian Provinces and States alone have contributed 41 per cent. of the total increase. Since 1921, the numbers of the Indian born have been practically stationary being 66,166 in 1921 and 66,542 in 1931. The next chief contributor is Afghanistan which supplied seasonal nomads numbering 10,625 in 1911, 5,285 in 1921 and 14,953 in 1931. The immigrants from India comprise temporary immigrants, periodic immigrants as well as semi-permanent and permanent immigrants. Exact numbers of each class are not available. Roughly, the temporary element represents about 40 per cent. of the total consisting mainly of troops and their followers and families, civil Government employees and their families, and artisans and coolies. The semi-permanent class represents about 50 per cent. consisting mainly of traders and artisans. The remainder 10 per cent. are permanent immigrants, consisting of traders, artisans and retired Government servants who have permanently settled down in the Province. The marginal table gives the distribution of Indian immigrants by principal Provinces and States. The subjoined

Immigrants from.	Persons.	Males.	Females.
TOTAL ..	**66,542**	**50,061**	**16,481**
(a) Indian Provinces ..	61,112	45,656	15,456
Punjab ..	36,329	26,490	9,839
United Provinces ..	11,876	9,644	2,232
North-West Frontier Province ..	6,148	4,742	1,406
Bombay ..	4,805	3,502	1,303
Other Provinces, etc	1,954	1,278	676
(b) Indian States ..	5,430	4,405	1,025
Kashmir States ..	2,081	1,793	288
Rajputana-Ajmere	914	713	201
Other States ..	2,435	1,899	536

DIAGRAM NO. 7

PROPORTION OF NOMAD TO SEMI-NOMAD AND SETTLED POPULATION IN 1911, 1921 AND 1931.

Settled population shown thus..........

Semi-nomad population shown thus..

Nomad population shown thus..........

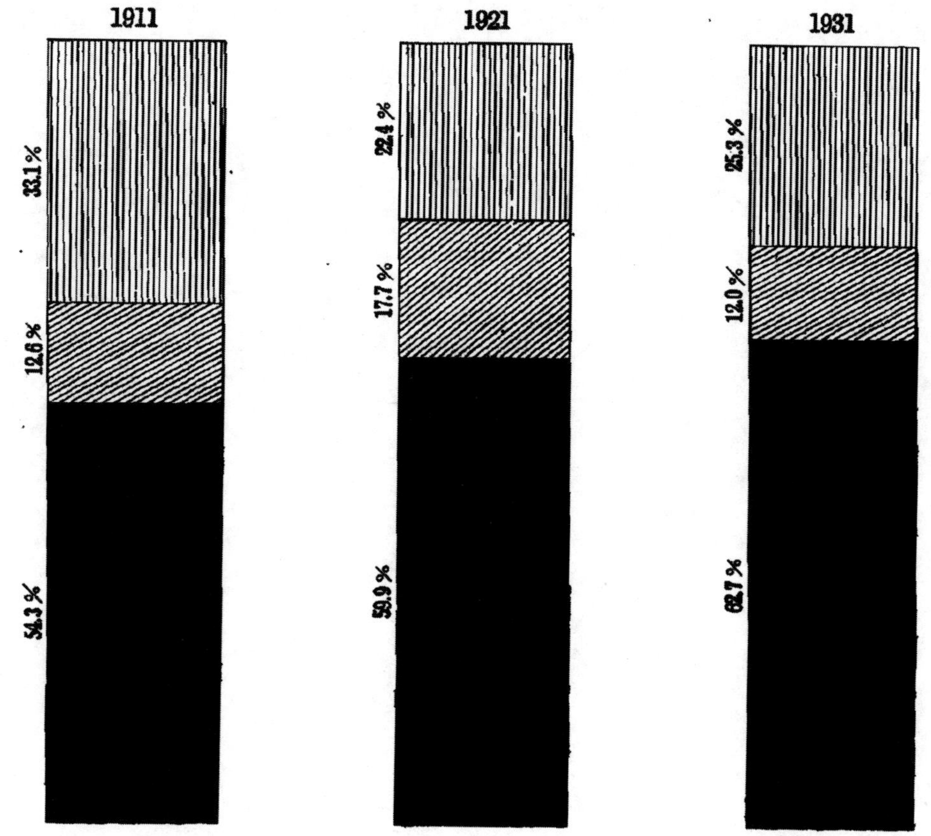

Reg No. 20 E.D.(E Coy)1933-545.

table shows the distribution by religion for these five provinces including their States :—

Religion.	Bombay. Males.	Bombay. Females.	N.-W. Frontier Province. Males.	N.-W. Frontier Province. Females.	Punjab. Males.	Punjab. Females.	United Provinces. Males.	United Provinces. Females.	Delhi. Males.	Delhi. Females.
ALL RELIGIONS	**3,898**	**1,366**	**4,762**	**1,421**	**27,322**	**10,023**	**9,668**	**2,239**	**536**	**216**
Muslim ..	414	186	4,230	1,140	12,469	3,863	2,949	890	101	57
Hindu ..	3,290	1,052	396	214	10,103	4,581	6,447	1,211	399	144
Sikh ..	36	8	83	41	3,846	1,072	61	16	3	1
Christian ..	100	87	53	26	865	507	203	118	33	14
Others ..	58	33	..	..	39	..	8	4	..	..

76. The immigrants from Asiatic countries other than India numbered 19,344 in 1931 :—

Afghanistan	14,953
Persia	417
Nepal	3,868
Other Asiatic countries	106

66 per cent. of the Afghans were seasonal nomads who pass the winter in Baluchistan. Their numbers vary from year to year according to nature of the season and the time of year at which the Census is taken. The immigrants from Persia are temporary migrants chiefly engaged in trade. The rest, Nepalese and others, are almost wholly Military employees with their families who come and go with the regiments to which they belong. The immigrants from Europe and other continents are likewise practically wholly Military and Civil employees with a few members of the trading community.

Internal Migration.

77. Internal migration from one District or State to another exists on an extensive scale. Large numbers of indigenous inhabitants keep on continually shifting from place to place in search of pasture for their flocks and for work at harvest times according to seasons and altitudes of the localities which provide grazing and field work. As actual birthplace was not recorded in the non-synchronous areas it is not possible to gauge the extent of this migration with the help of numbers. Though the permanent abode of all persons who were enumerated outside their own district was recorded (Subsidiary Table 15) the record I am afraid is not complete inasmuch as the numbers are much below the mark in several cases. But they serve to show that the population is of a very fluid nature. It will however be noticed from the marginal figures that there are indications of a progressive preference for settled life. The number of persons leading a purely nomadic life has fallen since 1911 from 33 to 25.

	Tribal Census. 1911.	Tribal Census. 1921.	Tribal Census. 1931.	Variation. 1911 to 1921.	Variation. 1921 to 1931.	Variation. 1911 to 1931.
TOTAL ..	**771,696**	**704,789**	**757,768**	**—66,907**	**+52,979**	**—13,928**
Nomad ..	255,338	157,744	191,647	—97,594	+33,903	—63,691
Semi-Nomad ..	96,995	125,025	90,434	+28,030	—34,591	—6,561
Settled ..	419,363	422,020	475,687	+2,657	+53,667	+56,324

Those who are leading a semi-nomadic life represented 12 in 1931 against 13 per cent. in 1911. On the other hand the percentage of settled inhabitants rose from 54 in 1911 to 63 in 1931. The change that has taken place between 1911 and 1931 is graphically shown in Diagram No. 7.

78. Analysing these figures by races, we find that the Baloch race as a whole shows a rise of 3 per cent. in the number of nomads during the past 20 years, *i.e.*, from 1911 to 1931, while the number of semi-nomad and settled inhabitants has decreased by 2 and 1 per cent. respectively. This decrease is entirely among the Eastern Baloch and is attributed to the return in 1931 of a

considerable number of nomads who had temporarily migrated to Sind and the Punjab in consequence of drought and famine. The number of those who are gradually taking to settled life is steadily on the increase among the Western Baloch. Taking the Brahuis and Pathans as individual races, the number of their settled inhabitants has risen by 19 and 9 per cent. respectively. Percentage variations for the three principal races and their main sub-divisions between 1911 and 1931 are shown in the following table and illustrated in Diagram No. 8.

TRIBAL CENSUS.

Race and Tribes.	Percentage of Population that is								
	Nomad.			*Semi-nomad.*			*Settled.*		
	1911.	1921.	1931.	1911.	1921.	1931.	1911.	1921.	1931.
BALOCH ..	**37**	**34**	**40**	**5**	**10**	**3**	**58**	**56**	**57**
Eastern ..	39	42	43	4	6	2	57	52	55
Western ..	36	20	33	6	19	4	58	61	63
BRAHUI ..	**60**	**38**	**47**	**13**	**19**	**7**	**27**	**43**	**46**
Original Nucleus ..	67	54	50	5	12	5	28	34	45
Sarawan ..	34	28	20	29	21	13	37	51	67
Jhalawan ..	75	42	59	5	18	4	20	40	37
Miscellaneous ..	30	10	24	35	67	2	35	23	74
PATHAN ..	**24**	**3**	**6**	**33**	**39**	**42**	**43**	**58**	**52**
Kakar ..	18	5	5	37	46	55	45	49	40
Pani ..	13	1	7	56	34	31	31	65	62
Tarin ..	56	1	7	7	16	28	37	83	65
Others ..	8	4	9	26	52	7	66	44	84

If further proof were needed of this tendency towards settled life it would be found in the figures in the subjoined table :—

REGULAR AREAS.

Year.	Baloch.		Brahui.		Pathan.	
	Males.	Females.	Males.	Females.	Males.	Females.
1931	2,794	1,572	3,784	1,770	5,274	2,068
1921	1,094	352	296	153	3,705	644
1911	889	269	458	113	2,938	561

The number of Baloch tribesmen living in the urban areas and along the Railway line was 889 males and 269 females in 1911. In 1931 the numbers rose to 2,794 and 1,572 respectively. The Brahuis numbered only 458 males and 113 females in 1911. In 1931, the numbers rose to 3,784 males and 1,770 females. The Pathans show a similar increase, the numbers having risen from 2,938 males and 561 females in 1911 to 5,274 and 2,068 respectively in 1931. The causes for this migration, which is gradually becoming permanent, as is apparent from the numbers of females at each of the two periods, are more lucrative and continuous employment and better amenities of life.

Periodic Immigration.

79. Statistics of periodic immigration are not included in the Census of 1931 as the movement of this form of migration did not coincide with the Census date. Thousands of residents of Sind and fairly large numbers from the Punjab and elsewhere visit the capital of the province during the summer to escape the oppressive heat of the plains. Quetta in particular has become a summer health resort for people from Sind and elsewhere who cause considerable congestion owing to deficient accommodation and drinking water supply. In spite of these obstacles and the set back brought about by the severe earthquakes of 1931 when the visitors fled in a panic, the summer influx is likely to continue in increasing numbers.

DIAGRAM NO. 8

PROPORTION OF NOMAD, SEMI-NOMAD AND SETTLED POPULATION AMONG THE PRINCIPAL INDIGENOUS TRIBES OF BALUCHISTAN

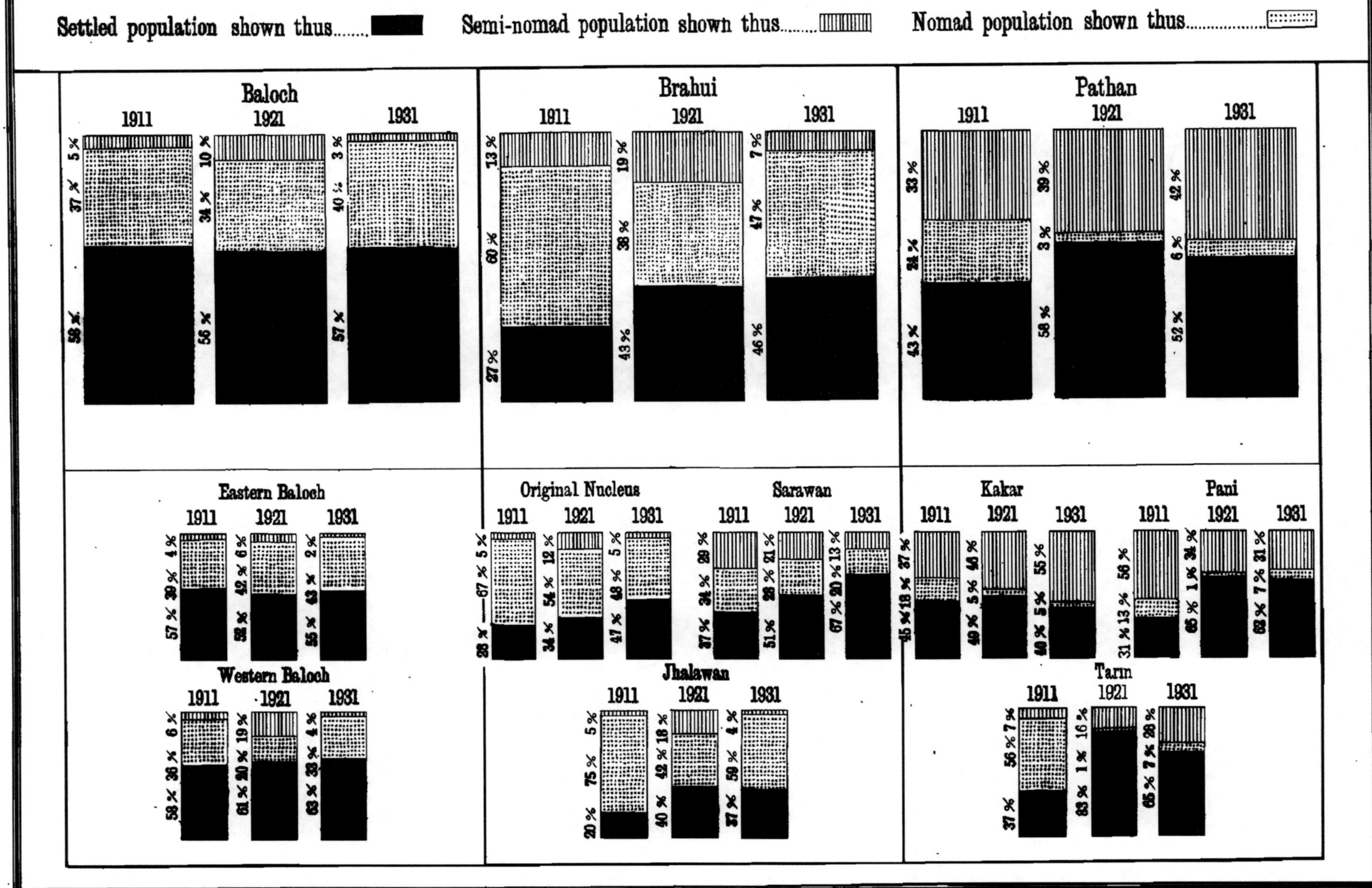

Reg No. 21 E.D. (E Cov) 1933-545.

80. The total number of Baluchistan emigrants in 1931 was 42,594 against 60,415 in 1921 and 76,031 in 1911. These figures included not only permanent residents of Baluchistan born in Baluchistan but enumerated in India on the Census night, but also those censused in India who happened to be born in Baluchistan of alien parents but have been classed as Baluchistan emigrants owing to birth in that province. These numbers, however, exclude emigrants to the adjoining countries—Afghanistan and Persia—and emigrants on the high seas or other Asiatic and foreign countries for whom statistics are not available. Estimated very roughly, the number of those who emigrate into Afghanistan and Persia in the course of their seasonal winter migration do not exceed a few thousands. But the numbers of those who emigrate into India are comparatively speaking very large indeed although the statistics of birthplace supplied by Sind fail to prove this. **Emigration.**

81. In the marginal table are given available statistics for four censuses, for the principal Indian Provinces and States which give shelter to Baluchistan emigrants. Bombay (Sind) absorbs by far the largest number of our emigrants: the number of such emigrants in 1931 according to the figures supplied by the Census Superintendent for Bombay and Sind being 35,449 out of a total of 42,594. Next comes the Punjab with 4,065. The rest (3,080) are scattered all over India. These latter may be called Baluchistan emigrants by courtesy for although a few Makranis may be found in the Bengal mines and in Assam and Baroda, a few Pathan traders in Bengal, Hyderabad, Bombay and a few other localities, the large majority of these 3,080 are classed as emigrants only on the strength of birthplace which is a mere matter of accidental birth in the course of temporary sojourn in Baluchistan of Indian parents engaged in trade or in Military or Civil employ. True migration is confined to Sind and it was in respect of this exodus that Baluchistan received its first warning note in 1911 from Sir Denys Bray who said "Conscious though I was that Sind was luring Brahuis away from their own country, I little thought that Jhalawan was veritably draining into Sind." Yet the numbers of Baluchistan emigrants into Sind as disclosed by the Bombay Census of 1931 only tend to disprove this apparently alarming statement, for, the number of such emigrants in 1931 as supplied by Bombay was only 35,449. The corresponding figures for the past three censuses show that between 1901 and 1911 the emigrants increased by 3,704. Between 1911 and 1921 they fell by 15,021 and between 1921 and 1931 there was a further decline of 18,903 persons. These figures appear to indicate that Baluchistan has no cause to apprehend that Sind has been lu ng away its population. This is decidedly not the case. The Sind figures are manifestly far below the mark for they cannot stand the tests that lie in our power to apply. Take for instance, the Bombay Birth place table. The Baluchistan emigrants censused in Sind in 1931 numbered 35,449 all told. The Bombay "Caste" Table for 1931 however shows that the Brahuis censused in Sind in that year numbered 71,827, while there were according to the 1931 Bombay Language table 79,561 speakers of Brahui—a language which admittedly is not enlisting new recruits but is losing ground even at home in Kalat. Add to these latter 16,906 Makranis censused in Sind. This brings the total to 96,467. To this must be added the thousands of Baloch and Jatt from Kachhi, from the Mari and Bugti countries, and from the Dombki-Kaheri country which are all situated on the borders of Sind; some thousands of Rakhshanis and Mengals and other miscellaneous tribesmen from Kharan and Chagai, and the crowd of freed slaves who have been sent adrift to find new homes in Sind. Again let us take into account the fairly large numbers of Lasis from Las Bela who have most probably been lumped with the Soma, Sumra and other Sind castes. Taking all these figures into consideration the number of Baluchistan emigrants who have found their way into Sind must be very considerably larger than the paltry figure of 35,449 and I am constrained to repeat the warning that

Emigrants in	Census of 1931.	1921.	1911.	1901.
TOTAL ..	**42,594**	**60,415**	**76,031**	**70,267**
(a) Indian Provinces	41,957	59,667	75,537	70,174
Bombay ..	35,449	54,352	69,373	65,669
Punjab ..	4,065	3,567	3,704	3,445
Other Provinces	2,443	1,748	2,460	1,060
(b) Indian States ..	637	674	494	93
(c) Foreign countries	..	74	..	..

	1931.	1921.	1911.	1901.
Baluchistan emigrants censused in Sind ..	35,449	54,352	69,373	65,669

Baluchistan particularly the Jhalawan, Makran and Kachhi divisions of the Kalat State as well as Kharan and Chagai are being continually drained off by Sind. The influences at work have been so completely analysed in paragraph 79 of the report for 1911 that it hardly leaves room for further enlightenment. Land and irrigation water exist in plenty judging by the standards of a country which has been described by Sir Charles Napier as the place where, after the creation of the World, the spare rubbish was shot down. It is the means—the capital and organisation to utilise them—that are lacking and, as pointed out in 1911, the only thing that is likely to bring about a wholesale change in the mode of life of the tribesmen is government irrigation on a large scale. In the districts areas, large sums of money have been laid out and earmarked for several expensive and useful schemes sanctioned and carried out or in hand or under consideration since the remedy was suggested in 1911. The parts of Kalat however which are mainly affected by this extensive emigration stand where they were twenty years ago. Of the causes enumerated in the 1911 report, I quote one which appears to be the most important in respect of the Kalat tribesman. "It is," says Sir Denys Bray, "not only the slothful ease and the fine food and fair clothes that he misses; crushed by the demands of his tribal chief (for unlike his brother of Sarawan he usually has to pay revenue to his Chief—no one seems to know why) he yearns for his untroubled life in Sind where he was free to go his own way so long as he kept on the windy side of the law." The tribesman's reluctance to return home is further accentuated by the inability of the Sardar to afford any financial help for his agricultural needs. The hope lies in the new regime in Kalat. It is also not unlikely that the tide may turn with the opening of the Sukkur Barrage which has given to this Province an additional irrigation canal—the Khirtar— and Baluchistan may be able to bring back into its fold a part of its lost inhabitants. One thing appears to be certain. Although the present winter exodus from the highlands to Sind and the plains is never likely to cease, for it takes place both as a winter holiday as well as a matter of necessity, it is most likely to cease in the course of time as emigration of a permanent nature.

Transit Migration. Afghan Powindahs.

82. The Afghan Powindahs or nomads who winter in Baluchistan were enumerated on the local schedule with the rest of the population. The Powindahs transiting Baluchistan on their way to India were censused on a special schedule under the special orders of the Census Commissioner for India. Map No. 8 facing this page shows the various routes taken by them. The instructions issued for their enumeration have been preserved in the Administrative Volume. The main statistics relating to these nomads are given in the following table :—

Place where enumerated.			Number of Families.	Number of Persons.									Number of Animals.								
				Persons.			*Males.*			*Females.*											
District.	Tahsil.	Villages.		Total.	Males.	Females.	Total.	Adult.	Non-Adult.	Total.	Adul.	Non-Adult.	Bullocks.	Cows.	Calves.	Goats.	Horses and Ponies.	Mares.	Donkeys.	Camels.	She-Camels.
Loralai ..	Barkhan	Basti Rahmatan.	241	1,303	700	603	700	460	240	603	427	176	25	18	17	31	2	..	23	693	1,664
Bolan ..	Bolan ..	Dasht Thana.	1,463	2,318	2,310	8	2,310	1,794	516	8	5	3	3	..	..	30	7	11	8,829	..	..
Sibi ..	Sibi ..	Sibi Railway Station.	616	5,092	5,087	5	5,087	5,071	16	5	4	1	..	..	..	..	..	..	..	..	..
		TOTAL ..	2,320	8,713	8,097	616	8,097	7,325	772	616	436	180	28	18	17	61	9	11	8,852	693	1,664

It will be seen that 8,713 Powindahs (8,097 males and 616 females) passed through the Province in addition to the 10,000 who spent the winter within Baluchistan. The numbers I am afraid are not quite correct, for, Zhob does not appear at all in the above statement. There is no doubt that a considerable number of these Powindahs cross into Dera Ismail Khan through Zhob. Unfortunately the instructions were misunderstood by the enumerators and no record was kept of these nomads on their way down to India and back.

MAP NO. 8

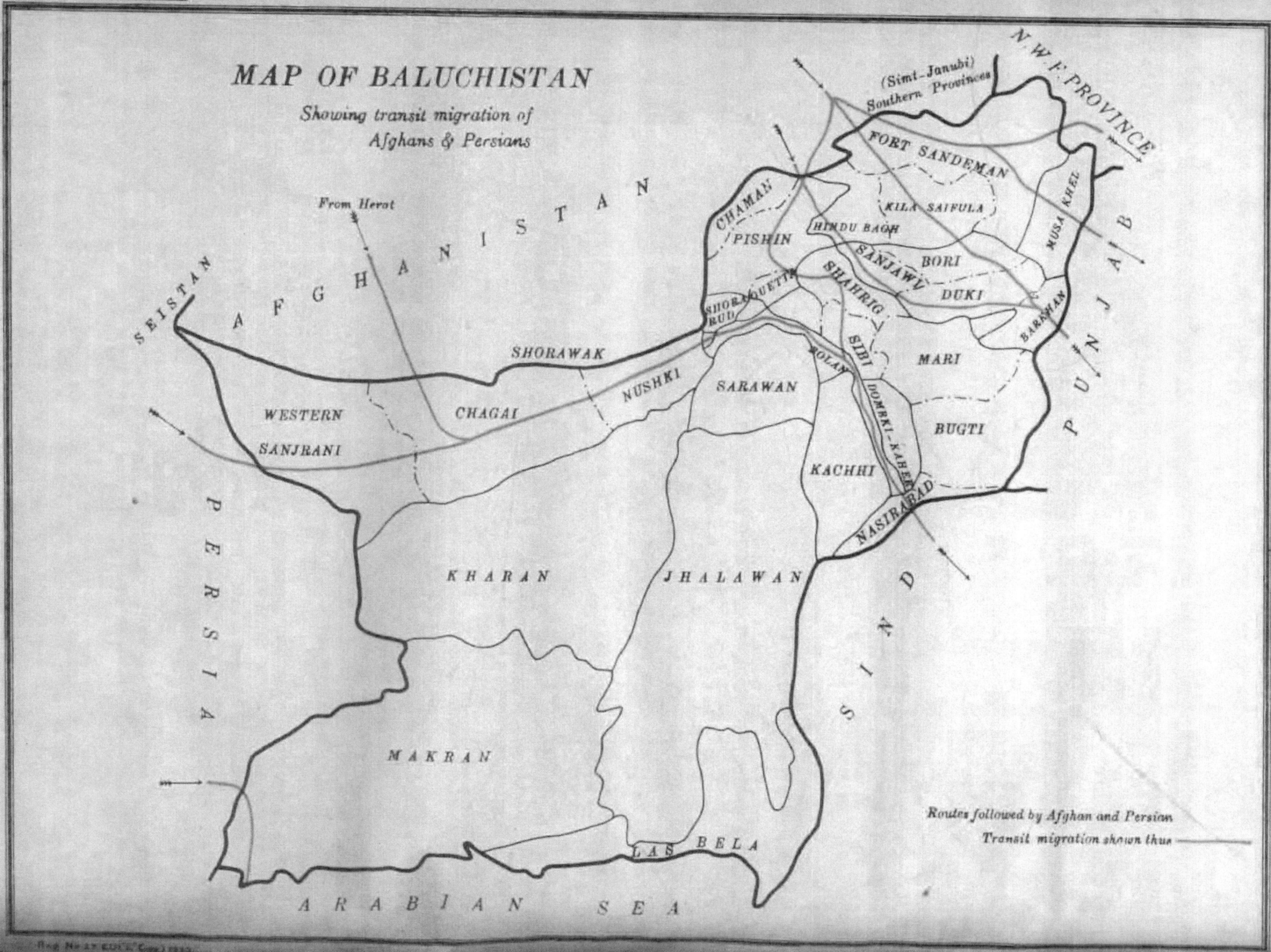

MAP OF BALUCHISTAN
Showing transit migration of
Afghans & Persians
From Herat
SEISTAN
AFGHANISTAN
PERSIA
ARABIAN SEA
SIND
PUNJAB
N.W.F. PROVINCE
(Simt-Janubi)
Southern Provinces
FORT SANDEMAN
KILA SAIFULA
MUSA KHEL
CHAMAN
PISHIN
HINDU BAGH
SANJAWI
BORI
DUKI
SHAHRIG
QUETTA
SHORARUD
BARKHAN
SHORAWAK
NUSHKI
SARAWAN
BOLAN
SIBI
MARI
DOMBKI-KAHERI
BUGTI
WESTERN
SANJRANI
CHAGAI
KACHHI
NASIRABAD
KHARAN
JHALAWAN
MAKRAN
LAS BELA
Routes followed by Afghan and Persian
Transit migration shown thus

Afghan powindahs.

These Powindahs are mostly Ghilzais including a few families of Tajaks, Sayyids and Durranis. Their distribution by permanent residence in Afghanistan is shown in the margin. About half of these nomads hail from Ghazni and Kandahar while the rest come from other parts of Afghanistan especially from the tract known as Khurasan. Seventy-six per cent spent the winter in Sind, 22 per cent. in the Punjab, and one per cent. in Bengal. The rest were scattered in various other places. Their distribution in India by Provinces and States is given in the marginal table. Their main occupations in the Punjab were trade in cloth, cattle and dry fruit supplemented by miscellaneous labour in a few cases. In Bombay city three men were engaged in trade in cloth while the fourth worked as a tailor. In Sind their principal occupations were :—

Permanent residence in Afghanistan.	Persons.	Males.	Females.
TOTAL ..	8,713	8,097	616
Ghazni ..	4,185	4,176	9
Kandahar ..	429	426	3
Khurasan ..	1,066	1,065	1
Mukar ..	606	606	..
Nawa ..	760	760	..
Other places ..	1,667	1,064	603

Province or State.	Persons.	Males.	Females.
TOTAL ..	8,713	8,097	616
Ajmer ..	2	2	..
Bikaner State ..	15	15	..
Calcutta (Bengal) ..	109	109	..
Delhi ..	7	7	..
Punjab ..	1,921	1,317	604
North-West Frontier Province ..	11	11	..
Bombay (Sind) ..	6,629	6,617	12
Unspecified ..	19	19	..

	Males.	Females.
(*i*) Canal digging and cleaning	4,155	8
(*ii*) Earthwork (donkey driving)	755	..
(*iii*) Miscellaneous labour	1,487	2
(*iv*) Trade unspecified	105	..
(*v*) Stone breaking	14	..
(*vi*) Trade in cloth	13	..
(*vii*) Bricklayers	4	..
(*viii*) Other miscellaneous jobs such as Baker, Barber, Beggar, Shopkeeper, Contractor, etc. ..	80	2
	6,613	12

Arranged by occupations their numbers stand as shown below :—

	Males.	Females.
Canal digging and cleaning	4,174	8
Miscellaneous labour	2,010	2
Trade in cloth	692	537
Trade in carpets	5	..
Trade in cattle	41	36
Trade in dry fruit	30	30
Asafoetida sellers	2	..
Trade unspecified	262	2
Donkey drivers	771	..
Camel driver	1	..
Tailor	1	..
Barbers	3	..
Bakers	2	..
Brick-layers	4	..
Stone-breakers	20	..
Rosary sellers	3	..
(Patients for eye treatment)	8	..
Priests	4	..
Receivers of religious instruction	5	..
Pilgrims to Mecca	44	1
Pilgrims to shrines	4	..
Contractors	2	..
Field labourers	2	..
Physicians	3	..
Musician	1	..
Beggars	3	..
Total ..	8,097	616

SUBSIDIARY TABLES.

13. Immigration (Actual figures).

District where enumerated.	Born in											
	Baluchistan.			*Contiguous parts of other provinces, etc.*			*Non-Contiguous parts of other Provinces, etc.*			*Outside India.*		
	Total.	Males.	Females.	Total.	Males.	Females.	Total.	Males.	Females.	Total.	Males.	Females.
1	2	3	4	5	6	7	8	9	10	11	12	13
BALUCHISTAN ..	**778,564**	**422,040**	**356,524**	**48,792**	**35,982**	**12,810**	**17,750**	**14,079**	**3,671**	**23,511**	**16,313**	**7,198**
DISTRICTS ..	**376,010**	**205,226**	**170,784**	**46,576**	**34,630**	**11,946**	**17,558**	**13,920**	**3,638**	**23,364**	**16,228**	**7,136**
Quetta-Pishin ..	93,564	49,881	43,683	29,558	21,653	7,905	12,149	9,490	2,659	12,270	9,278	2,992
Loralai ..	73,681	39,894	33,787	4,034	2,980	1,054	1,457	1,167	290	6,915	3,895	3,020
Zhob ..	49,904	27,559	22,345	5,366	4,506	860	1,306	1,227	79	1,387	1,304	83
Bolan ..	2,483	1,770	713	1,488	1,119	369	610	484	126	107	93	14
Chagai ..	21,256	11,627	9,629	1,132	817	315	659	522	137	1,177	755	422
Sibi ..	135,122	74,495	60,627	4,998	3,555	1,443	1,377	1,030	347	1,508	903	605
STATES ..	**402,554**	**216,814**	**185,740**	**2,216**	**1,352**	**864**	**192**	**159**	**33**	**147**	**85**	**62**
Kalat ..	340,011	183,644	156,367	1,813	1,068	745	140	123	17	137	80	57
Las Bela ..	62,543	33,170	29,373	403	284	119	52	36	16	10	5	5

14. Emigrants born in Baluchistan and enumerated in other Provinces.

Provinces or State where Enumerated.	1931.		1921.		1911.		1901.		Variation.							
									1901-1911.		1911-1921.		1921-1931.		1901-1931.	
	Males.	Females.	Males.	Females.	Males.	Females.	Males.	Females.	Males.	Females.	Males.	Females.	Males.	Females.	Males.	Females.
1	2	3	4	5	6	7	8	9	10	11	12	13	14	15	16	17
GRAND TOTAL ..	**26,113**	**16,481**	**36,045**	**24,370**	**44,266**	**31,765**	**41,364**	**28,903**	**+2,902**	**+2,862**	**−8,221**	**−7,395**	**+9,783**	**+7,887**	**−15,102**	**−12,420**
A.—PROVINCES ..	**25,623**	**16,334**	**35,511**	**24,156**	**43,874**	**31,663**	**41,286**	**28,888**	**+2,588**	**+2,775**	**−8,363**	**−7,507**	**−9,739**	**−7,820**	**−15,514**	**−12,552**
Ajmer-Merwara	54	4	18	6	13	10	11	2	+2	+8	+5	−4	+36	−2	+43	+2
Andamans and Nicobars ..	20	..	67	..	39	..	..	..	+39	..	+28	..	−47	..	+20	..
Assam ..	212	33	155	33	180	30	644	11	−464	+19	−25	+3	+57	..	−432	+22
Bengal ..	152	40	75	17	75	38	25	11	+50	+27	..	−21	+77	+23	+127	+29
Bihar and Orissa	11	5	32	17	18	1	..	..	+18	+1	+14	+16	−21	−12	+11	+5
Bombay ..	21,188	14,261	31,911	22,441	39,385	29,988	38,141	27,528	+1,244	+2,460	−7,474	−7,547	−10,574	−8,178	−16,804	−13,265
Burma ..	103	12	24	7	27	3	6	2	+21	+1	−3	+4	+79	+5	+97	+10
Central Provinces and Berar ..	399	110	366	69	971	93	173	4	+798	+889	−405	−24	+33	+41	+426	+106
Ceylon ..	..	..	99	6	..	..	..	..	..	..	+99	+6	−99	−6	..	..
Madras ..	..	..	135	12	116	10	16	7	+100	+3	+19	+2	−135	−12	−16	−7
North-West Frontier Province..	226	218	4	7	226	43	..	..	..	..	−222	−36	+222	+211	..	..
Punjab ..	2,578	1,487	2,190	1,377	2,395	1,309	2,137	1,308	+484	+44	−205	+68	+388	+110	..	..
Delhi ..	128	61	26	8	..	..	..	..	..	..	+26	+8	+102	+53	+795	+458
United Provinces	352	103	209	156	429	138	133	15	+296	+123	−220	+18	+143	−53	+219	+88
B.—STATES ..	**490**	**147**	**499**	**175**	**392**	**102**	**78**	**15**	**+314**	**+87**	**+107**	**+73**	**−9**	**−28**	**+412**	**+132**
Baroda ..	181	19	206	26	31	10	..	..	+31	+10	+175	+16	−25	−7	+181	+19
Central India Agency.	117	45	131	27	25	5	..	..	+25	+5	+106	+22	−14	+18	+117	+15
Cochin State ..	4	4	..	..	..	..	..	..	..	..	..	..	+4	+4	+4	+4
Gwalior ..	6	1	20	5	..	..	..	..	..	..	+20	+5	−14	−4	+6	+1
Hyderabad ..	17	4	34	12	171	10	13	..	+158	+10	−137	+2	−17	−8	+4	+4
Jammu and Kashmir.	54	39	20	74	17	3	15	1	+2	+2	+3	+71	+34	−35	+39	+38
Mysore	68	27	47	16	8	3	2	5	+6	−2	+39	+13	+21	+11	+66	+22
Rajputana Agency	43	8	40	15	140	70	48	9	+92	+61	−100	−55	+3	−7	−5	−1
Sikkim ..	..	..	..	..	..	1	..	..	..	+1	..	−1	..	..	..	..
Travancore ..	..	..	1	..	..	..	..	..	..	..	+1	..	−1	..	..	..
C.—FOREIGN COUNTRIES.	..	..	**35**	**39**	..	..	..	..	..	..	**+35**	**+39**	**−35**	**−39**	..	..
Africa ..	..	..	35	39	..	..	..	..	..	..	+35	+39	−35	−39	..	..
(i) Kenya ..	..	..	24	38	..	..	..	..	..	..	+24	+38	−24	−38	..	..
(ii) Nayasa Land ..	..	..	3	1	..	..	..	..	..	..	+8	+1	−8	−1	..	..
(iii) Tanganyika ..	..	..	3	..	..	..	..	..	..	..	+3	..	−3	..	..	..

15. Migration between Districts (actual figures) according to the Census of 1931.

District or State in which born.	Number enumerated in the District or State of															
	Quetta-Pishin.		Loralai.		Zhob.		Bolan.		Chagai.		Sibi.		Kalat.		Las Bela.	
	1931.	1921.	1931.	1921.	1931.	1921.	1931.	1921.	1931.	1921.	1931.	1921.	1931.	1921.	1931.	1921.
1	2	3	4	5	6	7	8	9	10	11	12	13	14	15	16	17
Quetta-Pishin	90,808	87,002	203	169	335	161	234	244	53	81	1,995	769	400	12	1	..
Loralai ..	90	41	72,155	76,412	109	9	44	1	2	3	520	96	..	1	..	..
Zhob ..	228	105	300	153	49,234	48,030	50	20	2	6	21	28	2	14	..	..
Bolan ..	19	3	..	..	..	1	594	599	..	..	6	4	..	..	..	..
Chagai ..	297	77	89	3	12	2	23	14	20,302	16,934	46	25	584	..	..	..
Sibi ..	243	247	475	68	67	62	320	85	33	20	129,665	108,067	38	2	..	..
Kalat ..	1,875	1,016	459	122	147	94	1,218	544	864	363	2,865	1,750	338,978	327,345	..	..
Las Bela ..	4	6	..	..	..	..	..	..	..	..	4	4	9	..	62,542	50,423
Outside the Province (in India, etc.).	53,977	48,585	12,406	5,546	8,059	8,309	2,205	2,111	2,968	3,936	7,883	8,721	2,090	907	465	273

16. Migration between Baluchistan and other parts of India, etc.

Province or State.	Immigrants to Baluchistan.			Emigrants from Baluchistan.			Excess (+) Deficiency (—) of immigrants over emigrants.	
	1931.	1921.	Variation.	1931.	1921.	Variation.	1931.	1921.
1	2	3	4	5	6	7	8	9
TOTAL	**66,542**	**66,166**	+376	**42,594**	**60,415**	**—17,821**	**+23,948**	**+5,751**
(A) INDIAN PROVINCES ..	**62,896**	**61,292**	**+1,604**	**41,957**	**59,667**	**—17,710**	**+20,939**	**+1,625**
Ajmere-Merwara	117	257	—140	58	24	+34	+59	+233
Andamans and Nicobars	2	..	+2	20	67	—47	—18	—67
Assam	17	22	—5	245	188	+57	—228	—166
Bengal	578	456	+122	192	92	+100	+386	+364
Bihar and Orissa	44	150	—106	16	49	—33	+28	+101
Bombay	5,264	5,371	—107	35,449	54,352	—18,903	—30,185	—48,981
Burma	60	208	—148	115	31	+84	—55	+177
Central Provinces and Berar ..	203	128	+75	709	635	+74	—506	—507
Ceylon	..	..	..	..	105	—105	..	—105
Coorg	2	..	+2	..	..	..	+2	..
Madras	186	340	+154	..	147	—147	+186	+193
North-West Frontier	6,183	5,016	+1,167	444	11	+433	+5,739	+5,005
Punjab	37,345	36,309	+1,036	4,065	3,567	+498	+33,280	+32,742
Delhi	732	493	+259	189	34	+155	+563	+459
United Provinces	11,907	12,317	—410	455	365	+90	+11,452	+11,952
French and Portuguese Settlements	129	173	—44	..	..	..	+129	+173
India unspecified	107	52	+55	..	..	..	+107	+52
(B) INDIAN STATES	**3,646**	**4,874**	**—1,228**	**637**	**674**	**—37**	**+3,009**	**+4,200**
Baroda	22	12	+10	200	232	—32	—178	—220
Central India Agency	56	53	+3	162	158	+4	—106	—105
Cochin State	3	8	—5	8	..	+8	—5	+8
Gwalior	71	242	—171	7	25	—18	+64	+217
Hyderabad	150	249	—99	21	46	—25	+129	+203
Jammu and Kashmir	2,081	2,229	—148	93	94	—1	+1,988	+2,135
Mysore	107	127	—20	95	63	+32	+12	+64
Rajputana Agency	914	1,934	—1,020	51	55	—4	+863	+1,879
Sikkam	45	14	+31	..	..	..	+45	+14
Travancore	3	6	—3	..	1	—1	+3	+5
Western India Agency ..	194	..	+194	..	..	..	+194	..
(C) FOREIGN COUNTRIES ..	..	..	..	..	74	—74	..	—74
Africa	..	..	..	..	74	—74	..	—74
Kenya	..	..	..	..	62	—62	..	—63
Nyasaland	..	..	..	..	9	—9	..	—9
Tanganika	..	..	..	..	3	—3	..	—3

17. Nomadism among Selected Tribes.

Tribe.	Year of Census.	Tribal Census. Nomad. Males.	Tribal Census. Nomad. Females.	Tribal Census. Semi-Nomad. Males.	Tribal Census. Semi-Nomad. Females.	Tribal Census. Settled. Males.	Tribal Census. Settled. Females.	Regular Census. Males.	Regular Census. Females.
BALOCH (Indigenous) ..	1931	47,663	39,166	3,157	2,679	69,246	59,764	2,794	1,572
	1921	32,745	25,649	10,029	7,918	51,695	43,913	1,094	352
	1911	34,941	28,572	4,311	3,615	51,818	44,775	889	269
(i) *Eastern* ..	1931	34,580	27,857	1,406	1,155	45,116	38,572	1,044	442
	1921	25,835	19,556	3,560	2,483	30,773	25,801	798	199
	1911	24,192	19,050	2,336	1,863	34,392	29,499	431	156
Bugti ..	1931	16,193	13,302	34	28	533	478	37	8
	1921	12,373	9,300	2	2	536	504	17	3
	1911	10,541	8,160	25	23	313	292	14	2
Dombki ..	1931	119	104	..	..	3,727	3,149	97	45
	1921	53	32	..	..	3,201	2,670	58	35
	1911	416	324	38	36	2,737	2,325	29	8
Khetran ..	1931	688	582	473	477	7,755	7,090	80	16
	1921	988	870	333	212	7,670	7,018	27	5
	1911	639	604	443	401	6,278	5,774	12	2
Magasi ..	1931	235	193	..	..	6,974	5,877	3	4
	1921	1,917	1,484	18	14	2,638	2,194	16	1
	1911	631	467	..	..	9,119	7,525	22	13
Mari ..	1931	16,405	12,923	892	644	2,231	1,944	172	43
	1921	8,949	6,529	2,753	1,912	1,308	1,026	117	7
	1911	10,094	7,981	1,396	1,020	954	720	64	4
Rind ..	1931	906	724	7	6	22,281	18,626	386	194
	1921	1,111	942	453	342	15,248	12,245	332	63
	1911	1,864	1,514	428	378	14,454	12,378	192	59
Umrani ..	1931	..	..	..	..	1,406	1,194	27	14
	1921	444	399	..	..	138	111	12	..
	1911	..	..	6	5	500	460	14	4
Others ..	1931	34	29	..	..	208	214	242	118
	1921	..	..	1	1	34	33	222	85
	1911	7	..	..	..	37	25	84	64
(ii) *Western* ..	1931	13,083	11,309	1,751	1,524	24,020	21,190	1,750	1,130
	1921	6,910	6,093	6,469	5,435	20,922	18,112	296	153
	1911	10,749	9,522	1,975	1,752	17,426	15,276	458	113
BRAHUI ..	1931	35,951	30,661	4,415	3,595	39,378	33,034	3,784	1,770
	1921	33,219	26,865	16,727	13,463	36,745	29,977	2,270	468
	1911	55,588	44,335	12,228	9,968	24,133	20,062	1,146	327
(i) *Original Nucleus* ..	1931	3,203	2,757	5,295	275	3,193	2,697	370	165
	1921	5,153	4,354	1,170	1,028	3,249	2,790	173	38
	1911	5,514	4,448	437	370	2,279	1,914	72	13
Ahmadzai ..	1931	..	..	..	..	15	27	15	20
	1921	..	..	..	..	43	66	5	5
	1911	..	..	..	..	7	9	8	1
Iltazai ..	1931	46	32	..	..	66	58	..	..
	1921	135	86	20	15	104	91	..	..
	1911	63	40	..	..	22	31	..	..
Gurgnari ..	1931	504	431	32	36	255	201	7	..
	1921	525	442	41	37	165	175	6	..
	1911	958	785	13	13	147	117	6	2
Kalandrari ..	1931	333	245	..	..	410	333	7	2
	1921	1,755	1,601	41	53	558	516	7	1
	1911	759	567	97	91	279	216	3	..
Kambrari ..	1931	300	245	69	47	746	609	27	20
	1921	407	323	384	307	507	435	33	18
	1911	810	657	133	110	727	642	9	7
Mirwari ..	1931	374	349	18	17	585	532	3	..
	1921	539	416	46	48	824	717	..	..
	1911	990	798	16	11	444	395	..	..
Rodeni ..	1931	205	167	23	27	488	391	24	16
	1921	388	327	215	200	352	263	36	7
	1911	237	203	34	32	446	366	7	..
Sumalari ..	1931	1,441	1,288	153	148	628	546	287	107
	1921	1,405	1,159	423	368	696	527	86	7
	1911	1,697	1,398	144	113	207	138	39	3

17. Nomadism among Selected Tribes.—*contd.*

Tribe.	Year of Census.	Tribal Census.						Regular Census.	
		Nomad.		*Semi-Nomad.*		*Settled.*			
		Males.	Females.	Males.	Females.	Males.	Females.	Males.	Females.
(ii) *Sarawan* ..	1931	4,110	3,603	2,833	2,411	14,339	11,915	1,808	775
	1921	7,976	6,293	5,978	4,746	14,115	11,287	1,312	250
	1911	10,277	8,246	8,680	7,077	11,035	9,259	623	173
Bangulzai ..	1931	821	711	29	25	2,888	2,455	345	116
	1921	2,385	1,786	607	493	2,569	2,074	320	47
	1911	2,229	1,838	1,461	1,226	2,560	2,118	127	36
Kurd ..	1931	368	298	14	13	696	606	157	78
	1921	121	97	49	39	1,480	1,106	69	21
	1911	491	388	894	725	510	432	33	3
Lahri ..	1931	825	734	42	33	1,449	1,077	212	118
	1921	1,182	839	428	298	1,497	1,194	111	23
	1911	1,641	1,260	616	436	1,011	823	46	6
Langav ..	1931	323	281	1,109	914	2,020	1,686	179	136
	1921	674	567	2,972	2,435	1,363	1,059	184	47
	1911	1,077	852	3,675	3,087	1,175	997	80	36
Mamashahi ..	1931	138	129	21	14	1,226	981	150	68
	1921	239	181	165	124	1,069	907	89	16
	1911	869	742	197	134	1,013	829	64	18
Raisani ..	1931	193	171	4	2	1,175	992	128	51
	1921	313	289	363	292	696	579	66	20
	1911	104	77	71	58	894	743	24	6
Rustamzai ..	1931	..	..	..	..	101	76	40	26
	1921	12	8	..	..	333	275	7	1
	1911	..	..	1	..	332	290	8	16
Sarparra ..	1931	40	26	51	50	852	784	86	17
	1921	117	99	406	345	564	497	80	4
	1911	118	111	302	261	726	623	67	4
Satakzai ..	1931	315	235	427	324	124	83	57	21
	1921	283	209	91	72	532	385	16	..
	1911	654	514	5	5	43	37	13	7
Shahwani ..	1931	471	454	69	46	2,481	2,112	341	115
	1921	995	779	377	237	3,114	2,472	147	42
	1911	1,918	1,470	1,029	779	1,840	1,602	107	25
Zagr Mengal ..	1931	670	564	1,067	990	1,327	1,063	113	29
	1921	1,655	1,439	520	411	898	739	223	29
	1911	1,176	994	429	366	931	756	54	16
(iii) *Jhalawan* ..	1931	28,362	24,074	1,269	893	20,959	17,735	979	528
	1921	19,962	16,089	8,591	6,944	19,068	15,625	384	109
	1911	39,391	31,276	2,610	2,126	10,320	8,479	376	130
Bizanjav ..	1931	4,018	3,098	32	29	3,588	2,811	13	2
	1921	1,961	1,598	530	423	2,925	2,486	..	..
	1911	5,099	4,260	30	19	777	673	..	..
Haruni ..	1931	363	341	91	73	358	327	35	24
	1921	226	189	124	99	250	221	5	..
	1911	369	310	104	92	197	170	4	2
Mamasani ..	1931	2,780	2,494	581	372	2,177	1,866	62	22
	1921	3,639	2,980	2,608	2,087	1,873	1,586	59	13
	1911	5,864	5,753	181	152	1,375	1,088	54	21
Mengal ..	1931	9,093	7,673	246	192	4,346	3,782	655	384
	1921	6,270	5,226	1,493	1,240	5,207	4,202	235	58
	1911	12,096	9,242	790	637	2,125	1,664	188	63
Nichari ..	1931	134	118	..	..	766	611	51	25
	1921	39	28	333	250	680	495	35	25
	1911	1,327	1,075	50	30	617	461	66	15
Pandrani ..	1931	59	44	..	..	505	446	8	1
	1921	84	66	197	142	544	455	..	..
	1911	320	233	191	144	599	514	5	1
Sajdi ..	1931	1,307	1,054	30	22	504	358	2	2
	1921	1,130	874	172	140	1,016	804	1	..
	1911	1,769	1,421	16	14	453	336	1	..
Zahri ..	1931	10,608	9,252	289	205	8,715	7,534	153	68
	1921	6,613	5,128	3,134	2,563	6,483	5,376	49	13
	1911	12,547	9,981	1,248	1,038	4,177	3,573	58	27

17. Nomadism among Selected Tribes.—*contd.*

Tribe.	Year of Census.	Tribal Census. Nomad. Males.	Tribal Census. Nomad. Females.	Tribal Census. Semi-Nomad. Males.	Tribal Census. Semi-Nomad. Females.	Tribal Census. Settled. Males.	Tribal Census. Settled. Females.	Regular Census. Males.	Regular Census. Females.
(iv) *Miscellaneous* ..	1931	276	227	18	16	887	687	627	302
	1921	127	129	988	745	313	275	401	71
	1911	406	365	501	395	499	410	75	11
Nighari ..	1931	105	90	12	9	490	421	1	..
	1921	39	39	730	559	74	61	..	..
	1911	141	131	400	313	177	149	..	..
Rekizai ..	1931	39	39	6	7	244	196	2	1
	1921	5	4	252	186	112	94	..	..
	1911	2	2	89	75	245	198	..	..
Others ..	1931	132	98	..	..	153	70	624	301
	1921	83	86	6	..	127	120	401	71
	1911	263	232	12	7	77	63	75	11
PATHAN (INDIGENOUS) ..	1931	5,987	4,842	37,104	31,080	47,107	42,545	5,274	2,068
	1921	2,947	2,322	35,897	29,780	53,340	45,426	3,705	644
	1911	24,000	19,884	32,994	28,440	42,216	37,060	2,938	561
Babi ..	1931	..	..	1	3	102	88	..	..
	1921	..	..	..	..	..	..	..	..
	1911	2	1	1	3	159	140	11	6
Barech ..	1931	59	54	56	54	407	355	354	263
	1921	216	186	90	71	406	327	195	59
	1911	104	102	18	15	274	210	84	47
Jafar ..	1931	107	88	250	214	433	361	15	11
	1921	..	..	324	269	398	348	11	5
	1911	91	72	165	132	429	391	5	1
Kakar ..	1931	3,100	2,512	24,429	20,322	19,601	17,155	2,306	603
	1921	2,251	1,749	23,056	18,809	24,571	19,824	2,073	267
	1911	10,091	8,238	20,935	17,705	25,037	21,118	1,689	260
Dawi ..	1931	3	2	141	113	6	9	..	..
	1921	..	..	..	..	..	..	..	..
	1911	16	12	..	..	130	116	10	..
Dumar ..	1931	918	672	2,599	2,135	372	326	75	11
	1921	411	314	1,013	850	2,856	2,233	56	8
	1911	715	560	1,412	1,134	2,081	1,781	59	13
Sanzarkhel ..	1931	2,049	1,730	14,045	11,349	8,862	7,669	667	190
	1921	1,774	1,389	15,020	12,153	8,482	6,991	569	60
	1911	6,233	5,029	15,663	13,327	8,055	6,941	693	91
Sargara ..	1931	2	2	319	294	731	620	24	8
	1921	..	..	418	334	843	721	33	3
	1911	27	14	476	448	736	612	26	4
Snatia ..	1931	101	75	5,520	4,884	4,411	3,833	808	130
	1921	27	19	2,645	2,329	9,316	7,321	787	75
	1911	2,348	1,993	2,796	2,298	7,244	6,039	557	74
Targhara ..	1931	28	30	1,791	1,524	4,429	4,191	132	45
	1921	32	27	3,923	3,116	2,558	2,132	189	44
	1911	597	485	552	465	6,418	5,335	203	34
Others ..	1931	2	3	155	136	596	516	600	219
	1921	7	..	37	27	516	426	439	77
	1911	155	145	36	33	373	294	141	44
Kasi ..	1931	2	2	..	..	667	582	386	336
	1921	..	..	..	..	634	604	39	18
	1911	..	..	1	1	657	615	47	16
Luni ..	1931	326	283	57	53	1,491	1,304	7	..
	1921	24	28	136	114	1,520	1,362	3	..
	1911	296	266	7	4	1,185	1,049	8	1
Pani ..	1931	1,049	865	4,551	3,845	9,154	7,857	257	123
	1921	219	153	5,070	4,177	9,573	8,288	203	44
	1911	1,984	1,649	8,484	7,538	4,481	4,191	296	52
Main branch ..	1931	40	28	34	27	2,130	1,902	5	..
	1921	..	..	4	1	2,591	2,293	62	21
	1911	584	480	482	433	2,343	2,262	87	43
Isot ..	1931	12	13	928	793	409	397	3	..
	1921	39	19	117	115	1,254	1,057	..	..
	1911	394	315	942	879	124	103	55	..

17. Nomadism among Selected Tribes.—*concld.*

Tribe.	Year of Census.	Tribal Census. Nomad. Males.	Tribal Census. Nomad. Females.	Tribal Census. Semi-Nomad. Males.	Tribal Census. Semi-Nomad. Females.	Tribal Census. Settled. Males.	Tribal Census. Settled. Females.	Regular Census. Males.	Regular Census. Females.
Mandokhel ..	1931	..	..	2,169	1,765	267	231	126	77
	1921	2	2	1,857	1,462	247	205	73	22
	1911	154	137	2,278	2,031	142	123	79	..
Musakhel ..	1931	733	627	1,405	1,246	5,212	4,321	26	8
	1921	178	132	2,464	2,080	4,455	3,796	39	1
	1911	809	666	4,774	4,192	877	802	73	9
Zarkun ..	1931	24	23	15	14	1,074	842	28	3
	1921	..	..	57	41	1,000	921	..	..
	1911	43	51	8	3	995	901	2	..
Unspecified ..	1931	240	174	..	..	62	64	69	35
	1921	..	..	573	478	26	16	29	..
	1911	..	..	..	..	..	..	..	..
Shirani ..	1931	18	12	2,397	2,144	1,946	1,776	85	38
	1921	52	47	3,615	3,252	115	88	89	39
	1911	128	122	2,012	1,845	2,307	2,017	91	30
Tarin ..	1931	1,316	1,018	3,340	4,426	11,699	11,413	1,202	340
	1921	88	79	3,073	2,703	15,326	13,882	783	76
	1911	11,264	9,397	1,305	1,156	6,851	6,664	657	117
Abdal-Achakzai	1931	1,305	1,012	3,868	3,067	4,966	4,550	774	254
	1921	60	47	299	217	9,442	8,573	449	59
	1911	8,453	6,926	426	329	1,903	1,765	417	53
Spin Tarin ..	1931	11	6	1,467	1,353	3,371	3,230	241	30
	1921	27	30	2,757	2,468	2,218	1,868	231	14
	1911	718	624	821	777	1,149	1,015	25	5
Tor Tarin ..	1931	..	..	..	..	3,198	3,502	31	6
	1921	1	2	17	18	3,554	3,359	71	1
	1911	2,093	1,847	34	30	3,795	3,882	164	45
Others ..	1931	..	..	5	6	164	131	156	50
	1921	..	..	..	..	112	82	32	2
	1911	..	..	24	20	4	2	51	14
Zmarai ..	1931	..	..	..	..	1,526	1,363	..	..
	1921	60	51	530	385	340	333	1	..
	1911	14	13	63	39	610	482	7	..
Others ..	1931	10	8	24	22	383	319	662	351
	1921	37	20	3	..	457	370	308	136
	1911	26	24	3	2	226	183	43	31
Ghilzai ..	1931	4,160	3,625	1,199	754	1,349	1,067	1,394	561
	1921	2,656	2,242	152	122	1,704	1,292	1,380	111
	1911	7,560	6,139	450	371	1,341	982	1,538	205

CHAPTER IV.

AGE.

Reference to statistics.

83. The statistical data will be found in Imperial Table VII, parts A and B and Subsidiary Tables 18 to 22 at the end of this chapter.

Record of Age. Synchronous Areas.

84. Important and interesting as the record of specific age is, the Baluchistan age statistics have little charm for the statistician, for, age for each individual was recorded only in the synchronous areas and Kharan which represent only 15 per cent. of the total population consisting mainly of immigrants whose numbers vary at each successive census owing to changes in the constitution of the forces of the garrison stations, the nature of employment obtainable and the season of the year at which enumeration takes place. These areas are shown in black in map No. 6 printed opposite page 9 of this report.

85. The instructions to the enumerator were to enter in column 7 of the schedule the number of years to the nearest birth-day or the nearest age known for each individual, to enter 0 for infants less than six months old and one year for infants over 6 months of age. These instructions were different from those issued at previous censuses in so far as the enumerator was instructed at past censuses to record the number of completed years, ignoring fractions of a year, and to group all infants less than one year old under the age period 0.

A detailed examination of the age returns thus obtained is manifestly not likely to yield any useful results for scientific purposes. The only point of interest that is revealed by the Census of 1931 in respect of these statistics, is that the abnormalities to which reference was made in the 1911 report regarding the low proportion of the very young and the very old as well as an abnormal deficiency of females amongst the immigrants are, as will be seen from the marginal table, gradually disappearing, a clear indication that the immigration is assuming a semi-permanent and family character. Beyond this no illuminating conclusions are possible and I consider the collection and printing of this mass of information to be of doubtful utility, for, age statistics for Baluchistan in their present form will continue to be useless for any actuarial purposes so long as specific individual age is not recorded for the whole or a large majority of the indigenous population.

Year.	0—15		15—50		50 AND OVER.	
	Males.	Females.	Males.	Females.	Males.	Females.
1931 ..	15,014	12,590	61,846	16,709	3,337	1,353
1921 ..	8,677	6,618	64,522	9,885	3,950	1,184
1911 ..	6,326	5,032	40,428	7,914	2,517	790

Record of Age in Tribal Areas.

86. The record of specific age in these areas would have presented interesting and valuable results. Unfortunately it was not found expedient for reasons already discussed at great length in the 1911 report to record specific age for the indigenous tribesmen representing 85 per cent. of the total population. All that was considered possible was to divide up the population into non-adults and adults for each of the two sexes as at previous censuses. An attempt was, however, made to record specific age for each individual in Kharan where its enlightened Chief realising the object of the enquiry willingly volunteered to furnish a complete record on the standard schedule for the whole of its population numbering 23,358 persons. Before referring to these figures let us see what the figures for non-adults and adults for the rest of the tribal area stand for.

87. Crude figures are contained in Subsidiary table 20 at the end of this chapter. In the marginal table, the results obtained at the Census of 1931 are compared with those of 1911 and 1921.

Year.	Non-adults per 1,000 of each sex.		Adults per 1,000 of each sex.	
	Males.	Females.	Males.	Females.
1931 ..	406	383	594	617
1921 ..	412	387	588	613
1911 ..	391	366	609	634

It will be seen that the number of adults of both sexes fell during the decade ending with 1921 and rose again in 1931. This variation is due to the heavy toll that the great influenza epidemic took among the adult population of both sexes during the intercensal period 1911-1921.

88. On the whole, the surplus shown at previous censuses in the non-adult male population has been maintained except amongst the Hindus. The marginal table shows for each race the excess of male non-adults over female non-adults in 1,000 of each sex in 1911, 1921 and 1931. The largest increase, 72 per 1,000, occurs amongst Sayyids followed by Jatts (36). Both races take wives from alien tribes which, added to the natural precocity of Sayyid and Jatt females, accounts for the comparatively large increase. The Hindus alone are an exception. In their case the male adults exceed the females. The excess is the more remarkable because it has risen from 1 to 32 per 1,000 during the decennium under review. This is mainly due to the migration of the indigenous male element to the urban areas to which they have been driven by economic pressure. **Female Precocity.**

Race.	Non-adults in 1,000 of each sex. Male excess over females.		
	1911.	1921.	1931.
Indigenous ..	+25	+25	+23
Sayyid ..	+53	+69	+72
Miscellaneous ..	+34	+34	+9
Brahui ..	+26	+17	+24
Baluch ..	+25	+35	+18
Pathan ..	+22	+14	+25
Jatt ..	+19	+21	+36
Lasi ..	+11	+34	+37
Hindu ..	—1	+32	—32

89. The proportional figures for each administrative unit for 1931 and for each race for the three censuses 1911, 1921 and 1931 are given in Subsidiary tables 20 and 21. Comparison with other provinces and countries is not possible owing to the difficulty of assigning the exact age at which adolescence begins. In the instructions issued to the enumerators no definite age was fixed for the non-adult. The head of the family was simply asked to give the number of male and female members of his family who had attained the age of maturity and those who had not. In his report for 1901 Mr. Hughes-Buller remarked :—

"Several reasons appear to have influenced the committee of officers who devised the local forms in choosing these age limits. Boys were held to put away their childish things about their twelfth year. Twelve was also considered to be the age at which they don the *Toga Virilis*, in the shape of a pair of trousers, after which they are fit to carry arms and become a fair prey in tribal feuds. It was thought too, that girls became marriageable at the age of twelve. At the same time it is least arguable that the age-periods 'fifteen and under' and 'over fifteen' have been more appropriate for record. So far as my observation goes, maturity in Baluchistan is reached at a later age than in India. It is almost certain that boys have not reached the age of puberty at twelve years of age, and though they may have taken to trousers, I am doubtful if they would be counted by experts among the 'fighting men' of the tribe until two or three years later. Similarly although the Indian Legislature has adopted twelve, for the purposes of the Criminal Law as the age of consent, such enquiries as I have had an opportunity of making lead me to the belief that among the tribes living in the colder climate of the hills puberty is not generally reached by girls till fourteen or fifteen."

90. The same difficulty was experienced in 1911 in fixing upon the puberal age. After examining the subject in all its aspects, the age of fifteen was fixed upon as the most appropriate year at which to draw the line between the adults and the non-adults.

"Fifteen," says the 1911 report, "may err on the safe side, yet the margin is not so great as those accustomed to life in the warmth of India imagine. It seems to fit the males fairly well when we take them in the mass, though it probably over-steps the mark among the Jatt and other dwellers of the plains, where development seems to set in much more rapidly than in the uplands. But if it fits the males, it must necessarily fail to do justice to the superior precocity of the other sex; for a lass, as the Brahuis say, is like barley that shoots up apace, whereas a lad is like the more precious wheat that is slow of growth."

91. No solution of this difficult question could be found in the succeeding decennium when the joint investigations of the two able authors of the 1921 report had to be content with the following remarks :—

"At what age are we to put puberty ? Even in a single province like Baluchistan this varies with race, sex, environment and climate."

92. It must be admitted that it is not an easy matter to fix the right age for puberty. This is clearly brought out by the marginal statement in which the proportional statistics of non-adults in the tribal areas of Baluchistan are compared with those of persons of 0—15 years of age for certain Indian Provinces and States.

Province or State.	Year of Census.	PER 1,000 OF TOTAL POPULATION. *NON-ADULT. 0—15.	*ADULT. 15 and over.
Baluchistan (Tribal Areas only).	1931	394	606
	1921	391	609
Punjab ..	1931	401	599
	1921	403	597
N.-W. F. Province ..	1931	409	591
	1921	397	603
Bombay ..	1931	397	603
	1921	394	606
C. P. and Berar ..	1931	401	599
	1921	410	590
Madras ..	1931	389	611
	1921	377	623
Gwalior ..	1931	394	606
	1921	389	611
Kharan ..	1931	460	540

The comparison I am afraid is not in favour of taking the puberal age for Baluchistan at 15. It is an admitted fact that male as well as female precocity in this frontier province of sturdy highlanders and robust cultivators of the plains used to a hard life is comparatively lower than in most of the Indian Provinces and States. This fact is not proved by the marginal figures. The number of adults per 1,000 was 609 in 1921 and 606 in 1931 in Baluchistan whereas in the Bombay Presidency it was respectively 606 and 603 ; in the Central Provinces and Berar 590 and 599 ; and in Gwalior 611 and 606 for each of these two years. Precocity being comparatively lower in Baluchistan, the numbers of its adult population should be lower than in the provinces and states just named where owing to climatic and other reasons the young admittedly arrive at years of discretion at an earlier age. And considering the fact that the age period 0—15 oversteps the age of puberty in the provinces named above, the numbers of non-adults in Baluchistan should be much higher than those disclosed by these comparative figures. This is evidenced by the figures for Kharan where the number of males per 1,000 of the total population in the age-group 0—15 is 460 or 12 per cent. higher than the Corresponding proportion for the North-West Frontier Province. That the puberal age 15 for Baluchistan is a bit too high is quite clear. The right age would appear to be a little over 13 for females and slightly over 14 for males. But I must confess that I feel hardly less embarassed than my predecessor of 1911 who, while struggling to make use of these statistics expressed his embarrassment in the following terms :—

> " But whether or no there has been any speeding-up of the age of puberty, the fact unfortunately stares us in the face that we are unable to assign any particular age to puberty, varying as it does with the individual, with the race, with sex and with environment. Hence, much as I appreciate the accuracy of our statistics, it is a trifle embarrassing to know what to do with them now that I have got them. Comparison with other statistics seems scarcely feasible, for it would be hard to lay one's hands on any statistics that are really comparable."

93. The exact puberal age varies with race and locality. Even if we take 13 as the puberal age for females and 14 for males regardless of race and locality it is not possible to find corresponding data for any of the other Indian Provinces and States for purposes of comparison. The only use, in the circumstances, that I can possibly make of these figures is to use them in working out a rough estimate of the fighting strength of the local tribes. This has been done in Subsidiary Table 48 printed at the end of Chapter XII of this Report.

94. The statistics of adults and non-adults appear to me to be of doubtful utility and it is a matter for consideration by my successor whether they should be collected at future censuses in the form in which they have so far been collected and compiled. A great change is coming over the social life of the indigenous population under the impact of Western civilization and it should not be difficult to extend the standard schedule at future censuses to a much wider area in tribal territory.

* The division into Non-adult and adult applies only to Baluchistan.

Age Statistics for Kharan.

95. In spite of the difficulties which beset the record of age in tribal territory it was found possible to extend the standard schedule to Kharan, detailed crude statistics for which are given in Imperial Table VII part B.

Age Distribution in Kharan.

96. The instructions for recording age were the same as those issued for the synchronous areas. The crude ages recorded in the schedules were subjected in the Tabulation office to a process of smoothing which was briefly as follows. The ages actually returned were first grouped in alternate groups of 3 and 7, *i.e.*, 4—6 (which is a group of three), 7—13 (which is a group of seven), 14—16 (which is a group of three again), 17—23 (which again is a group of seven), and so on, and then redistributed into the quinary groups, namely, over 5 and under 10, over 10 and under 15 and so on, by halving the numbers in each of the adjoining alternate 3 and 7 years crude groups and then combining them into a quinary group by adding the halves. Thus, in order to find the population in the 5—10 group, the crude 4—6 and 7—13 groups were halved and added together. For the annual age periods up to 5 special adjustments, which I need not give in detail, were made.

97. The figures presented in Imperial Table VII, Part B, have been arrived at by this process. In the statement below, the age distribution of 1,000 of each sex in Kharan is compared with similar figures for certain other Indian Provinces.

Age group.	Bengal.		Bihar and Orissa.		Madras.		Bombay.		Kharan.	
	Males.	Females.	Males.	Females.	Males.	Females.	Males.	Females.	Males.	Females.
0—5 ..	148	163	149	154	145	144	142	159	154	212
0—1 ..	32	35	26	26	28	28	28	31	10	20
1—2 ..	24	28	27	28	28	28	27	31	26	47
2—3 ..	30	34	30	34	30	30	28	33	36	55
3—4 ..	31	34	33	34	30	30	29	32	41	49
4—5 ..	31	32	33	32	29	28	30	32	41	41
5—10 ..	137	131	141	129	131	126	132	131	180	131
10—15 ..	120	116	123	109	120	112	118	112	144	96
15—20 ..	88	106	83	86	87	92	88	91	70	84
20—25 ..	93	110	85	92	86	100	92	99	63	83
25—30 ..	90	88	86	89	81	90	89	88	66	86
30—35 ..	83	74	80	81	77	78	84	77	65	82
35—40 ..	65	54	64	64	67	62	68	61	64	66
40—45 ..	54	45	55	54	57	52	56	51	63	54
45—50 ..	39	34	43	41	43	40	42	39	40	34
50—55 ..	30	27	34	33	35	33	32	31	28	27
55—60 ..	20	19	22	25	26	25	22	23	21	17
60—65 ..	15	15	17	20	21	21	17	19	18	16
65—70 ..	7	7	7	9	10	10	8	8	9	5
70 and over ..	11	11	11	14	14	15	10	11	15	7

98. The variations in the earlier years are most remarkable. I hesitate to offer any explanation for various reasons beyond explaining the defect among males in the age periods 15—40 which is decidedly due to emigration. In spite of all the care that may be taken to procure accurate census returns, the record of age presents peculiar difficulties in a territory which is extremely primitive in its mode of life. In a large majority of cases, the age of persons well advanced in years had to be calculated from certain notable events which took place in their life-time. The record is necessarily only an approximate one and is intended to serve as a basis for further expansion of the inquiry in respect of the record of age at future censuses. One fact, however, so far as my enquiries go appears to be established and that is that the rate of female births

is undoubtedly higher in Kharan and that mortality among females between the ages of 3 and 10 is more appalling than among males. Poverty, ignorance, neglect, and, above all, the primitive mode of life which always keeps an abundant stock of victims ready to sacrifice to every visitation of small-pox, measles, whooping cough and all sorts of preventable diseases are among the principal causes of the high rate of mortality.

99. The graph on the opposite page illustrates the proportion of males and females in each age group. It will be seen that the number of children of both sexes increases steadily upto the third year after which the girls begin to decrease. The boys keep increasing but only for one year and after remaining stationary for another join the girls in their downward course. Taking the age group 0—5 as a unit, the number of girls exceeds that of the boys. After the age of 5, they lose their superiority of numbers, the boys maintaining their lead till the age group 15—20 is reached. Here emigration thins their ranks and the females once again recover their superiority which they maintain until they pass the age of 37 when, owing to mortality from natural causes, they fall behind never to rise again. The line of stability for males extends from the ages of about 25 to 45 and that of females from about 20 to 35. After 45, both lines run practically parallel.

Progressive Population.

100. The conclusion that has been drawn from the ever increasing population barring abnormal years in which famine and disease have played an important part, is that the population of this Province is essentially progressive. Let us see whether this view is supported by the statistics for Kharan on the basis of the Sundberg theory. Sundbärg divides the population into three age categories, 0—15, 15—50 and 50 and over, and three *types* namely progressive, Stationary and Retrogressive. His formula is that the middle category, *i.e.*, 15—50 always contains half the population of a country provided that it is not disturbed by migration or other abnormal causes. The type of population is determined by fluctuations in the other two age groups namely "0—15" and "50 and over." When the proportion in the "0—15" age group is more than twice that in group "50 and over", the population is called Progressive, when it is only twice as much it is Stationary, and when it is less than twice it is Retrogressive.

Province or State.	Distribution per 1,000 in the three age groups.		
	0—15	15—50	50 and over.
Kharan ..	460	458	82
Punjab ..	409	483	108
N.-W. F. Province ..	409	503	88
Bombay ..	397	512	91
Bihar and Orissa ..	402	502	96
C. P. and Berar ..	401	500	99
Madras ..	389	505	106
Mysore ..	401	499	100
Gwalior ..	394	520	86
Travancore ..	426	477	98
Ajmer-Merwara ..	388	520	92

The figures for Kharan for each of the three age categories "0—15, 15—50," and "50 and over" are compared in the marginal table with certain Indian Provinces and States.

The proportion in the youngest of the three categories is abnormally high. This is due possibly partially to defective age returns but largely to emigration. On the whole the figures indicate that the population is distinctly progressive.

Diagram No. 9.

KHARAN—DISTRIBUTION OF MALES AND FEMALES BY DIFFERENT AGE GROUPS.

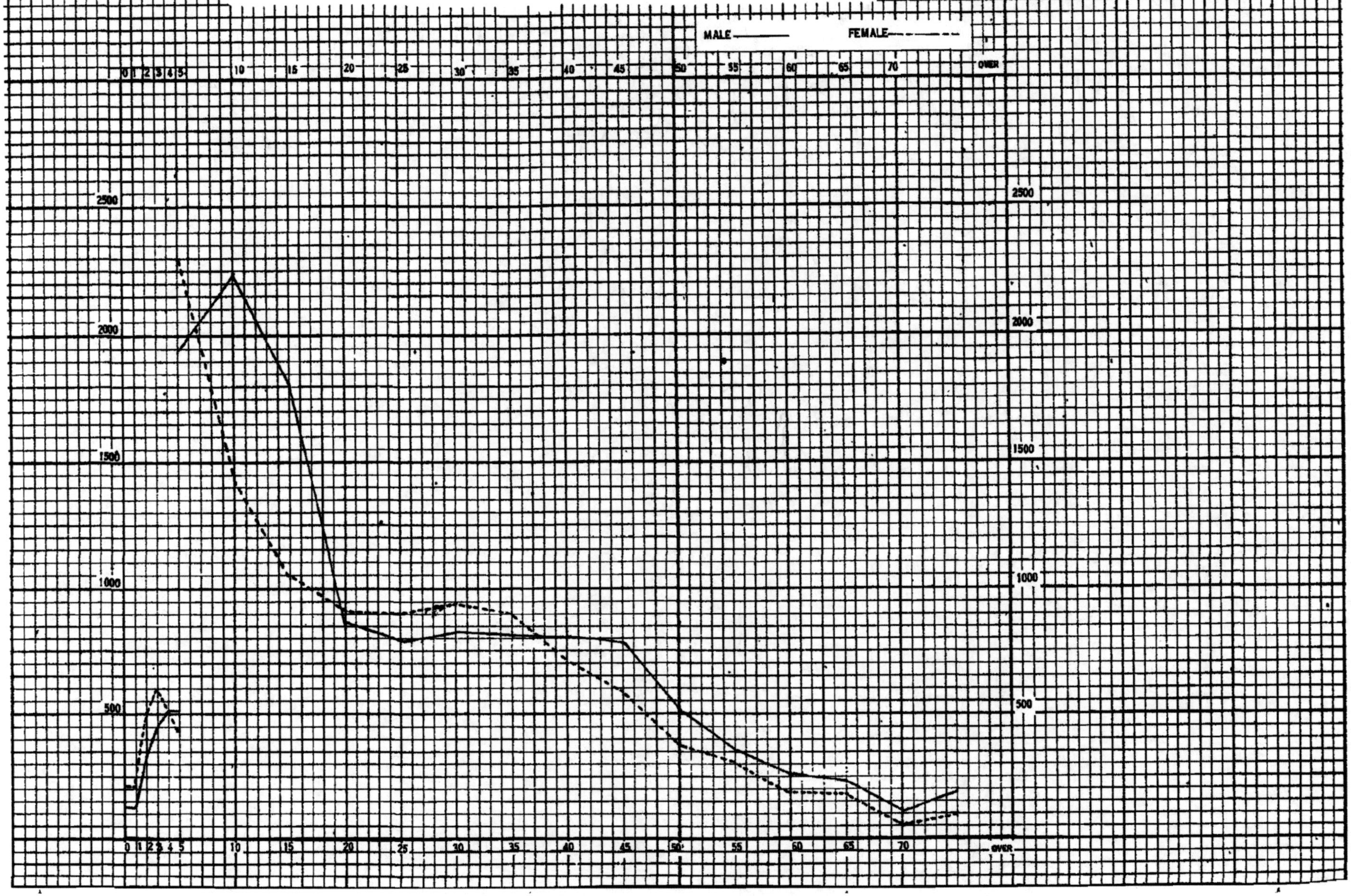

18.—Puberal Distribution by Race.

(Indigenous only).

Race or Tribe.	Non-adults *per mille*; persons.	Puberal Distribution of 1,000 of each sex.			
		Non-adults.		Adults.	
		Males.	Females.	Males.	Females.
1	2	3	4	5	6
INDIGENOUS ..	**395**	**406**	**383**	**594**	**617**
Baloch	**392**	**400**	**382**	**600**	**618**
Eastern	389	394	383	606	617
Western	399	414	382	586	618
Brahui	**405**	**416**	**392**	**584**	**608**
Original Nucleus	381	391	368	609	632
Sarawan	370	374	365	626	635
Jhalawan	422	436	406	564	594
Miscellaneous	411	442	374	558	626
Pathan	**410**	**422**	**397**	**578**	**603**
Kakar	409	422	396	578	604
Pani	386	384	389	616	611
Tarin	421	443	397	557	603
Others	428	441	414	559	586
Lasi	**384**	**402**	**365**	**598**	**635**
Jatt	**372**	**388**	**352**	**612**	**648**
Sayyid	**418**	**454**	**382**	**546**	**618**
Other Muslims	**383**	**387**	**378**	**613**	**622**
Hindu	**333**	**318**	**350**	**682**	**650**
Sikh	**159**	**125**	**250**	**875**	**750**

19.—Puberal Distribution by Locality.

(Indigenous only.)

District or State.	Non-adults *per mille*; persons.	PUBERAL DISTRIBUTION OF 1,000 OF EACH SEX.			
		Non-adults.		Adults.	
		Males.	Females.	Males.	Females.
1	2	3	4	5	6
BALUCHISTAN ..	**395**	**406**	**383**	**594**	**617**
Districts	**405**	**418**	**391**	**582**	**609**
Quetta-Pishin	422	452	389	548	611
Loralai	413	411	416	589	584
Zhob	399	407	391	593	609
Bolan	318	308	330	692	670
Chagai	411	427	393	573	607
Sibi	393	405	378	595	622
Administered Area	*383*	*396*	*368*	*604*	*632*
Mari-Bugti Country	*405*	*418*	*390*	*582*	*610*
States	**387**	**396**	**376**	**604**	**624**
Kalat	389	399	377	601	623
Sarawan	*357*	*353*	*361*	*647*	*639*
Jhalawan	*423*	*440*	*404*	*560*	*596*
Kachhi	*362*	*370*	*352*	*630*	*648*
Dombki-Kaheri Country	*365*	*359*	*372*	*641*	*628*
Makran	*409*	*426*	*389*	*574*	*611*
Kharan	*387*	*395*	*378*	*605*	*622*
Las Bela	378	385	370	615	630

20.—Puberal Distribution by Race for three Censuses.

(*Indigenous only*).

Race or Tribe.	Year of Census.	Non-adults *per mille*; persons.	Puberal Distribution of 1,000 of each sex. Non-adults. Males.	Non-adults. Females.	Adults. Males.	Adults. Females.
1	2	3	4	5	6	7
INDIGENOUS	1931	395	406	383	594	617
	1921	400	412	387	588	613
	1911	379	391	366	609	634
Baloch	1931	392	400	382	600	618
	1921	407	423	388	577	612
	1911	385	397	372	603	628
Eastern	1931	389	394	383	606	617
	1921	396	411	377	589	623
	1911	384	393	372	607	628
Western	1931	399	414	382	586	618
	1921	426	442	407	558	593
	1911	389	403	372	597	628
Brahui	1931	405	416	392	584	608
	1921	382	390	373	610	627
	1911	375	386	360	614	640
Original Nucleus	1931	381	391	368	609	632
	1921	374	377	370	623	630
	1911	371	384	356	616	644
Sarawan	1931	370	374	365	626	635
	1921	370	378	360	622	640
	1911	368	376	359	624	641
Jhalawan	1931	422	436	406	564	594
	1921	391	400	380	600	620
	1911	378	393	360	607	640
Miscellaneous	1931	411	442	374	558	626
	1921	398	399	397	601	603
	1911	398	400	396	600	604
Pathan	1931	410	422	397	578	603
	1921	433	440	426	560	574
	1911	402	412	390	588	610
Kakar	1931	409	422	396	578	604
	1921	435	440	429	560	571
	1911	397	405	388	595	612
Pani	1931	386	384	389	616	611
	1921	419	433	403	567	597
	1911	400	415	382	585	618
Tarin	1931	421	433	397	557	603
	1921	443	449	436	551	564
	1911	419	430	407	570	493
Others	1931	428	441	414	559	586
	1921	..	..	..	..	..
	1911	..	..	..	..	..
Lasi	1931	384	402	365	598	635
	1921	409	425	391	575	609
	1911	367	372	361	628	639
Jatt	1931	372	388	352	612	648
	1921	354	363	342	637	658
	1911	357	366	347	634	653
Sayyid	1931	418	454	382	546	618
	1921	424	457	388	543	612
	1911	395	420	367	580	633
Other Muslims	1931	383	387	378	613	622
	1921	393	410	376	590	624
	1911	360	376	342	624	658
Hindu	1931	333	318	350	682	650
	1921	320	335	303	665	697
	1911	315	315	316	685	684

21. Variation in Puberal Distribution by Locality Since 1911.

(Indigenous only).

District or State.	Year of Census.	Non-adults *per mille*; persons.	Puberal Distribution of 1,000 of each sex.			
			Non-adults.		Adults.	
			Males.	Females.	Males.	Females.
1	2	3	4	5	6	7
BALUCHISTAN	1931	395	406	383	594	617
	1921	400	412	387	588	613
	1911	379	391	366	609	634
Districts	1931	405	418	391	582	609
	1921	422	433	409	567	591
	1911	395	404	386	596	614
Quetta Pishin	1931	422	452	389	548	612
	1921	431	446	414	554	586
	1911	417	431	400	569	600
Loralai	1931	413	411	416	589	584
	1921	436	442	431	558	569
	1911	393	399	391	601	609
Zhob	1931	399	407	391	593	609
	1921	431	433	428	567	572
	1911	390	401	377	599	623
Bolan	1931	318	308	330	692	670
	1921	372	398	340	602	660
	1911	298	244	376	756	624
Chagai	1931	411	427	393	573	607
	1921	466	477	456	523	544
	1911	385	382	389	618	611
Sibi	1931	393	405	378	595	622
	1921	396	412	375	588	625
	1911	383	390	375	610	625
Administered Area	*1931*	*383*	*396*	*368*	*604*	*632*
	1921	*388*	*404*	*369*	*596*	*631*
	1911	*373*	*381*	*363*	*619*	*637*
Mari-Bugti Country	*1931*	*405*	*418*	*390*	*582*	*610*
	1921	*409*	*427*	*386*	*573*	*614*
	1911	*405*	*408*	*401*	*592*	*599*
States	1931	387	396	376	604	624
	1921	382	394	369	606	631
	1911	366	380	350	620	650
Kalat	1931	389	399	377	601	623
	1921	378	390	364	610	636
	1911	366	381	348	619	652
Sarawan	*1931*	*357*	*353*	*361*	*647*	*639*
	1921	*356*	*363*	*348*	*637*	*652*
	1911	*362*	*371*	*351*	*629*	*649*
Jhalawan	*1931*	*423*	*440*	*404*	*560*	*596*
	1921	*377*	*388*	*363*	*612*	*637*
	1911	*371*	*391*	*346*	*609*	*654*
Kachhi	*1931*	*362*	*370*	*352*	*630*	*648*
	1921	*339*	*354*	*321*	*646*	*679*
	1911	*348*	*364*	*330*	*636*	*670*
Dombki-Kaheri Country	*1931*	*365*	*359*	*372*	*641*	*628*
	1921	*365*	*374*	*356*	*626*	*644*
	1911	*359*	*364*	*354*	*636*	*646*
Makran	*1931*	*409*	*426*	*389*	*574*	*611*
	1921	*419*	*436*	*400*	*564*	*600*
	1911	*373*	*394*	*351*	*606*	*649*
Kharan	*1931*	*387*	*395*	*378*	*605*	*622*
	1921	*429*	*443*	*413*	*557*	*587*
	1911	*411*	*424*	*396*	*576*	*604*
Las Bela	1931	378	385	370	615	630
	1921	410	419	400	581	600
	1911	369	373	364	627	636

22.—Age Distribution of 1,000 of each sex in certain selected indigenous and semi-indigenous tribes.

(Kharan and Kasi-Nichari Villages).

Caste.	Males Number per mille, in each age group.						Females Number per mille, in each age group.					
	0—6	7—13	14—16	17—23	24—43	44 and over.	0—6	7—13	14—16	17—23	24—43	44 and over.
1	2	3	4	5	6	7	8	9	10	11	12	13
						KHARAN.						
Baloch (Indigenous)												
Rakhshani ..	211	239	51	89	257	153	275	138	52	119	300	116
Brahui (Indigenous)												
Gurgnari ..	271	187	83	125	167	167	194	278	..	139	222	167
Kambrari ..	184	211	53	158	289	105	306	111	83	83	250	167
Sumalari ..	160	277	76	88	218	181	265	135	85	95	275	145
Mamasani ..	208	230	50	76	268	168	284	132	59	102	322	101
Mengal ..	194	253	97	87	233	136	231	165	77	121	242	164
Sajdi ..	229	187	42	42	333	167	105	132	26	79	526	132
Other Muslims (Indigenous)												
Darzada ..	246	246	58	15	319	116	237	132	40	66	341	184
Lori ..	246	233	62	62	308	89	278	104	44	130	383	61
Nakib ..	252	229	70	44	259	146	273	150	26	100	296	155
Others ..	233	234	55	96	268	114	258	150	58	116	310	108
					KASI-NICHARI.							
Pathan (Indigenous)												
Kakar ..	151	160	63	145	378	103	193	187	42	145	349	84
Kasi ..	187	183	50	110	290	180	195	239	61	125	313	67
Pathan (Semi-Indigenous)												
Durrani	101	164	67	115	389	164	201	224	75	149	254	97
Ghilzai ..	156	150	54	145	382	113	157	187	52	134	366	104

CHAPTER V.

SEX.

Reference to Statistics.

101. Excepting Imperial Table III, the distribution of the population by sexes is given in all Imperial tables embodied in Part II of this report. In order to present the numbers more clearly for purposes of this chapter, the subsidiary tables noted in the margin have been prepared. These will be found at the end of this chapter.

23. General proportion of Sexes by Districts and States.
24. Sex variation by locality.
25. Sex variation by nomadism.

102. The instructions to enumerators were simple enough. In the synchronous areas including Kharan, the enumerator was asked to record the word male or female in column 5 of the schedule opposite the name of every individual. A few cases were discovered in the course of examination of enumeration books in which males had been shown erroneously as females and *vice vèrsa*. All such entries were corrected by reference to names in column 3 of the schedule before *slipcopying was begun*.

In the Tribal Areas which covered 85 per cent. of the population there was no possibility of error from this source as the entries in this case were made not by individuals but by families. On the whole the record both in synchronous and non-synchronous areas is as complete as can possibly be expected.

Proportion of Sexes.

103. At the Census of 1931 there were 488,414 males and 380,203 females in the whole Province which give a ratio of 778 females to 1,000 males. Taking the immigrants and the natural or indigenous population separately, the proportion of females to 1,000 males was 357 and 832 respectively.

In analysing the sex figures it is necessary to exclude the population of synchronous areas which is almost entirely composed of immigrants who generally leave their families behind at home or send them down to the plains to escape the winter. The statistics from which any satisfactory inferences can be drawn are those relating to the Tribal Areas inhabited by indigenous tribesmen and in order to present as complete a picture as possible, I have included in these figures the numbers of indigenous tribesmen who have taken their abode temporarily or permanently in the synchronous areas where they were enumerated. But in dealing with these sex statistics I have left out of account our tribal emigrants for the reasons explained in paragraph 138 of the report for 1911. The population which will thus be dealt with in this Chapter numbers only 760,125 out of a total of 868,617 persons.

Sex Ratio by Locality.

104. The sex ratio in the indigenous population of Baluchistan and each District and State at each of the three Censuses since 1911 is shown below :—

FEMALES PER 1,000 MALES.

	1911.	1921.	1931.
Baluchistan ..	**845**	**824**	**845**
Districts ..	**836**	**803**	**832**
Quetta-Pishin ..	853	836	881
Loralai ..	864	836	847
Zhob ..	824	795	811
Bolan ..	690	332	406
Chagai ..	820	805	823
Sibi Administered Area	823	778	819
Mari-Bugti Country ..	803	756	809
States ..	**852**	**842**	**857**
Kalat ..	848	836	852
Las Bela ..	880	881	883

Comparison with other Provinces.

105. A glance at the marginal table will show that the proportion of females to males in Baluchistan is much lower compared to other Indian Provinces excepting the adjoining Provinces of the Punjab and the North-West Frontier Province which in 1931 had a lower proportion of females than Baluchistan.

Province.	Proportion of Females to 100 Males.				
	1891.	1901.	1911.	1921.	1931.
Bombay including Sind ..	94	95	93	91	92
Bengal ..	99	96	95	--	92
Madras ..	102	103	103	102	102
Bihar and Orissa ..	102	105	104	103	100
Central Provinces and Berar ..	97	102	101	101	100
United Provinces ..	93	99	92	91	90
Punjab ..	84	85	82	83	83
North-West Frontier Province ..	82	85	86	85	84
Baluchistan	Not available	83	85	82	85

It will be observed that there is a preponderance of males in Baluchistan as a whole as well as in all its components. At the same time there are indications that while the proportion of women to men has been declining in India as a whole, it would appear to be on the increase in Baluchistan. This is illustrated in the marginal table which gives the proportion of females to 1,000 males for each of the principal indigenous races. The ratio fell between 1911 and 1921 and rose again between 1921 and 1931. The Baloch and Pathan women regained in 1931 the ratio of 1911. The Brahui women gained three, the Lasis and Sayyids each four per cent. The proportion in 1931 would have been appreciably higher than in 1911 but for the fact that the influenza epidemic of 1918 took a heavier toll among females. The Jatt and the indigenous Hindus alone do not appear to have completely recovered from the effects of the epidemic.

	Females to 1,000 Males.		
	1911.	1921.	1931.
Baloch ..	840	814	840
Brahui ..	802	796	827
Pathan ..	841	815	844
Lasi ..	870	877	912
Jatt ..	837	801	827
Sayyid ..	935	918	975
Indigenous Hindus ..	845	809	843

The sex proportions shown below for the principal tribes of Baluchistan speak for themselves :—

Tribe.	Females to 1,000 Males.			Tribe.	Females to 1,000 Males.		
	1911.	1921.	1931.		1911.	1921.	1931.
Indigenous ..	**845**	**824**	**845**	(3) *Jhalawan* ..	*797*	*808*	*838*
Baloch ..	**840**	**814**	**840**				
(a) *Eastern* ..	*824*	*788*	*828*	Bizanjav ..	838	832	776
Bugti ..	778	759	822	Mamasani ..	805	815	849
Khetran ..	920	899	908	Mengal ..	764	807	839
Mari ..	778	722	790	Zahri ..	811	803	863
Rind Jamali ..	..	836	851	**Pathan** ..	**841**	**815**	**844**
(b) *Western* ..	*871*	*861*	*864*	*Kakar* ..	*819*	*782*	*824*
Rais ..	896	908	911	Dumar ..	817	785	793
Rakhshani ..	861	844	840	Sanzarkhel ..	828	797	817
Rind ..	905	863	879	Sargara ..	852	818	859
Brahui ..	**802**	**796**	**827**	Snatia .	804	763	823
(1) *Original Nucleus* ..	*812*	*842*	*835*	Targhara ..	813	794	908
Kalandrari ..	768	920	773	*Pani* ..	*881*	*840*	*845*
Kambrari ..	843	790	808	Mandokhel ..	864	776	809
Sumalari ..	792	790	830	Musakhel ..	868	842	841
(2) *Sarawan* ..	*809*	*768*	*808*	*Shirani* ..	*886*	*886*	*893*
Bungalzai ..	818	748	810	*Tarin* ..	*863*	*869*	*879*
Langav ..	828	791	831	Abdal Achakzai ..	810	868	814
Shahwani ..	792	762	811	Spin Tarin ..	892	837	907
				Tor Tarin ..	954	928	1,086

Sex Proportion among Nomads.

106. Sex variations since 1911 among the nomads, semi-nomads and settled indigenous inhabitants shown in the margin indicate that the percentage of females is higher among the settled inhabitants than among the nomad or the semi-nomad. The statistics relating to Pathan and Baloch certainly support the view expressed in 1911 and endorsed in 1921 that one of the causes of paucity of females is nomadism which plays an important part in the life of the indigenous tribesmen. In the case of the Brahuis, however, the position is reversed for the ratio of females among the nomads is 858 against 832 and 831 for semi-nomad and settled inhabitants respectively. It is an admitted fact that the Brahuis, specially the Jhalawans, lead a nomadic life on a comparatively much larger scale and I must admit that I find it difficult to account for this phenomenon. All I can say is that to the Brahui, nomadism is a normal routine of life which tells less hardly on him than on the other two principal races.

Race.	Year.	Females to 1,000 Males.		
		Nomads.	Semi-Nomads.	Settled.
Baloch ..	1911 ..	818	839	864
	1921 ..	783	790	850
	1931 ..	826	832	864
Brahui ..	1911 ..	798	815	831
	1921 ..	809	805	816
	1931 ..	858	832	831
Pathan ..	1911 ..	828	862	878
	1921 ..	788	830	851
	1931 ..	801	840	903

Distribution by Age Groups.

107. The only age groups which it was found possible to record for the indigenous inhabitants, excepting Kharan where specific age was recorded for each individual, were adult and non-adult. The table in the margin shows the progress of female ratio to 100 males since 1911.

	Females per 100 Males.	
	Non-adult females per 100 male non-adults.	Adult females per 100 male adults.
1911 ..	79	88
1921 ..	79	87
1931 ..	81	89

Between 1911 and 1921, the proportion discloses a decrease among adult females caused by the influenza epidemic which claimed more victims among adults than among non-adults. Between 1921 and 1931, the ratio rose again in both age groups.

108. The subject of the causes of higher male births has been discussed at great length in previous reports. In 1911 Sir Denys Bray concluded his discussion with the following observation :—

"........The people themselves complacently attribute it in no small measure to their overwhelming desire for male issue, a desire which is as intense among the mothers of Baluchistan as it was among the mothers of the Jewish world, where, by the bye, it had roots much more ancient and much more deep down in human nature than that divine hope of bearing the promised Messiah in which we were taught to believe. And without in any way posing as being of the tribesmen's artless faith in the direct power of the wish to become father to the tact in this simple manner, I cannot but feel that the intensity of the desire for male issue and the universality of the belief in the inherent inferiority of the female sex are factors not to be overlooked in any discussion of sex-proportion in Baluchistan."

Although a Census Superintendent may be treading on dangerous ground when, leaving aside generally accepted theories, he expresses a personal opinion to solve one of nature's baffling puzzles, I cannot help endorsing the theory of intense desire which is so strongly backed by local public opinion. It is probably the stronger will-power that influences the sex. Unlike other seeds, they say, the human seed lies in the blood of the parents and it is the stronger will-power that has a direct influence on the sex of the seed every particle of which in the process of manufacture is under the command of the will-power of man. It is only when the father is indifferent to the sex of the issue that the desire or will-power of the mother prevails. The secrets of nature in this direction, however, still remain undiscovered. It will take many a long day before the scientist can dream of unravelling the mysteries of the process of manufacture of man and woman which lies hidden in the womb of darkness. All a Census Superintendent can perhaps safely suggest for the benefit of scientists, and countries anxious to effect a change in the ratio of sexes, is to invite them to study the voluminous Oriental medical literature and Oriental traditions which give information on artificial methods employed in the East to influence the sex of children. It will not perhaps be without interest to give here by way of illustration a couple of the more popular * prescriptions for sex and birth control.

*Kindly supplied by Hakim Islamulla Khan Ghauri of Quetta.

Prescriptions.

I.—For Sex Control (For mothers).

Take the rainbow crescent from the feather of a peacock and one pellet from the droppings of a hare. Powder them well and mix them up. In the second or third month of the child's life before seeing the light of day, administer the mixture to the mother. The sex of the hare will govern the sex of the child.

II.—For Birth Control (For fathers).

Take a little cotton and stuff both your nostrils, not so as to stop breathing altogether, but adjust it so as to allow of restricted breathing through the nose. This preliminary preparation will prevent conception.

Fertility and Mortality Returns.

Nature of Enquiry.

109. In 1911, statistics of children born to a father and the number of children that survived in his life-time from a single wife were collected for 6,641 fathers. In 1921 a slightly more elaborate form was used to collect this information. The enquiry extended to 3,582 families. In 1931, a much more detailed form adapted from a model prescribed by the Census Commissioner for India was used for this purpose. Particulars were asked for on the points noted in the margin in respect of each father instead of each mother as elsewhere in India. This change was considered advisable chiefly for political reasons. The following instructions were issued to those who were asked to fill up the form :—

1. Husband's age.
2. Age of wife.
3. Husband's occupation.
4. Husband's religion.
5. Duration of married life.
6. Sex of first child (whether quick or still born).
7. Husband's caste.
8. Total number of children born alive.
9. Number of children still alive.
10. Ages of children still living.
11. At what ages did children die ?
12. Permanent Residence of :—
    (a) Husband.
    (b) Wife.

1. State the requisite particulars for selected married persons alive.
2. In case of more than one wife, the above particulars should be given only for the wife who has been blessed with more children.
3. In the case of age, six months and over will be taken as one year.

The Statistics.

110. From the material thus collected the following five tables have been prepared :—

I. Sex of first born.
II. Size of family by occupation of husband.
III. Size of family by caste or religion.
IV. Size of family correlated with age of wife at marriage.
VI. Duration of marriage correlated with caste or religion of family.

These tables are printed at the end of this chapter as an appendix.

Table I.—Sex of first born confirms the observation so often made that there are more males first born than females. It is difficult, however, to prove that the sex of the first born influences the sex of the subsequent children, for, it will be seen that although the number of first born males in Kharan—the only tract inhabited by indigenous inhabitants for which specific age was recorded in detail—is 1,000 to 400 females first born, the number of surviving females in the age period 0—1 in the Census year was 1,756 per 1,000 males surviving in that year. This remarkable disparity is decidedly not due to appalling mortality among male infants. The numbers are very small and are hardly of any value for purposes of scientific investigation. The fact is that in a large number of cases male and female children have seen the light of day by rotation.

Table II—Size of Family by Occupation of Husband.—Speaking generally the average number of children born alive is highest in families connected with out-door occupations and lowest in those in which the father follows a sedentary occupation. The number of families examined for separate occupational groups is however very small and it is therefore not possible to draw any reliable inferences from them.

Table III—Size of Families by Caste or Religion.—The numbers of families examined and the rate of survivals per 1,000 births is shown in the margin. The improvement in the rate of survivals in the last decade compared to the previous intercensal period is remarkable. This improvement is undoubtedly due to greater amenities of life, and a greater measure of medical relief. Among the immigrant population the proportion of children surviving is 653 for all families examined. In the case of the indigenous population it is 669. Taking each indigenous race separately, " Unspecified Muslim " races for which 3,651 families were examined, top the list with 743 survivals per 1,000 children born. Brahuis come next with 732 followed by the indigenous Baloch 710, Jatt 708 and Hindus 645. The rate of survivals is comparatively low among the Lasis and the indigenous Pathans who have only 565 and 537 survivals per 1,000 children born.

Census year.	Number of families examined.	Survivals per thousand births.
1911 ..	6,641	613
1921 ..	3,582	622
1931 ..	39,744	669

SUBSIDIARY TABLES.

23. General Proportion of the Sexes by Districts and States.

District or State.	Number of Females to 1,000 Males. 1931. Tribal.	1931. Regular.	1921. Tribal.	1921. Regular.	1911. Tribal.	1911. Regular.	1901. Tribal and regular.
1	2	3	4	5	6	7	8
BALUCHISTAN	**856**	**382**	**836**	**229**	**850**	**279**	**820**
Districts	**855**	**382**	**830**	**229**	**848**	**280**	**741**
Quetta-Pishin	928	405	869	289	869	333	655
Loralai	849	318	841	124	859	166	794
Zhob	838	162	820	24	840	103	759
Bolan	736	317	754	181	926	253	305
Chagai	846	496	865	144	834	301	900
Sibi	828	473	795	257	829	266	780
Administered Area ..	*843*	*473*	*817*	*257*	*842*	*266*	*779*
Mari-Bugti Country ..	*808*	..	*755*	..	*802*	..	*782*
States	**857**	**406**	**841**	**217**	**851**	**208**	**897**
Kalat	853	406	835	321	847	210	898
Sarawan	*836*	*270*	*788*	*193*	*819*	*386*	*802*
Jhalawan	*855*	..	*825*	..	*800*	..	*947*
Kachhi	*832*	*13*	*818*	..	*848*	*500*	*850*
Dombki-Kaheri	*852*	..	*840*	..	*865*	..	*846*
Makran	*885*	*503*	*903*	*249*	*919*	*176*	..
Kharan	*868*	..	*838*	..	*869*	..	..
Las Bela	881	..	879	..	875	..	888

24.—Sex Variation by Locality (Indigenous only).

Locality.	Vital Statistics.		Census Statistics. Females to 1,000 Males.		
	Number of births recorded.	Proportion of survivals to 1,000 born.	Non-adults.	Adults.	All.
1	2	3	4	5	6
BALUCHISTAN	**1,58,494**	**669**	**810**	**893**	**845**
Districts	**48,098**	**565**	**805**	**899**	**832**
Quetta-Pishin	15,934	572	804	1,041	881
Loralai	15,266	544	864	845	847
Zhob	6,387	447	808	863	811
Bolan	151	430	802	725	406
Chagai	4,292	664	797	914	823
Sibi	6,068	634	774	869	818
(a) Administered Area ..	..	..	*789*	*887*	*819*
(b) Mari-Bugti Country ..	..	..	*756*	*846*	*809*
States	**1,10,396**	**715**	**814**	**887**	**857**
Kalat	1,00,332	732	808	884	852
Sarawan	*7,662*	*641*	*861*	*830*	*841*
Jhalawan	*10,739*	*820*	*787*	*912*	*855*
Kachhi	*54,178*	*729*	*792*	*855*	*833*
Dombki-Kaheri Country ..	*4,807*	*674*	*884*	*834*	*852*
Makran	*15,281*	*711*	*808*	*942*	*878*
Kharan	*7,656*	*794*	*830*	*892*	*868*
Las Bela	10,064	552	847	904	883

25.—Sex Variation by Nomadism (Tribal Census only).

Race and Tribe.	Year of Census.	Percentage of population that is			Females to 1,000 Males.		
		Nomad.	Semi-nomad.	Settled.	Nomad.	Semi-nomad.	Settled.
1	2	3	4	5	6	7	8
Baloch	**1931** **1921**	**40** **34**	**3** **10**	**57** **56**	**826** **783**	**832** **790**	**864** **850**
Eastern	1931 1921	43 42	2 6	55 52	807 757	780 697	856 838
Western	1931 1921	33 20	4 19	63 61	864 882	870 840	882 866
Brahui	**1931** **1921**	**47** **38**	**7** **19**	**46** **43**	**858** **809**	**832** **805**	**831** **816**
Original Nucleus ..	1931 1921	50 54	5 12	45 34	861 845	932 879	876 859
Sarawan	1931 1921	20 28	13 21	67 51	877 789	851 794	831 800
Jhalawan	1931 1921	59 42	4 18	37 40	856 806	799 808	831 819
Miscellaneous	1931 1921	24 10	2 67	74 23	822 1,016	889 754	775 846
Pathan	**1931** **1921**	**6** **3**	**42** **39**	**52** **58**	**801** **788**	**840** **830**	**903** **851**
Kakar	1931 1921	5 5	55 46	40 49	795 777	836 816	883 806
Pani	1931 1921	7 1	31 34	62 65	825 699	845 824	858 866
Others	1931 1921	9 4	7 52	84 44	800 877	907 871	833 888

Sex Table I.—Sex of first born. (Regular Area).

District or State.	Number of females first born.	Number of males first born.	Number of females first born per 1,000 males first born.	Number of slips examined.	REMARKS.
BALUCHISTAN	**423**	**833**	**508**	**1,376**	
Districts	**423**	**833**	**508**	**1,376**	
Quetta-Pishin	160	350	457	580	
Loralai	80	139	576	239	
Zhob	15	25	600	40	
Bolan	45	100	450	153	
Chagai	43	99	434	152	
Sibi	80	120	667	212	

Sex Table I.—Sex of first born. (Tribal Area).

District or State.	Number of females first born.	Number of males first born.	Number of females first born per 1,000 males first born.	Number of slips examined.	REMARKS.
BALUCHISTAN	**13,548**	**23,862**	**525**	**38,368**	
Districts	**3,367**	**5,263**	**643**	**8,684**	
Quetta-Pishin	1,341	1,891	709	3,248	
Loralai	956	1,572	608	2,553	
Zhob	368	606	607	975	
Bolan	10	23	435	33	
Chagai	345	471	732	819	
Sibi	347	700	495	1,056	
(*a*) *Administered Area* ..	*316*	*651*	*485*	*976*	
(*b*) *Mari-Bugti Country* ..	*31*	*49*	*633*	*80*	
States	**10,176**	**18,599**	**547**	**29,684**	
Kalat	9,536	17,485	545	27,866	
Sarawan	*719*	*1,281*	*561*	*2,080*	
Jhalawan	*1,499*	*1,901*	*789*	*3,457*	
Kachhi	*4,804*	*9,196*	*522*	*14,627*	
Dombki-Kaheri Country ..	*400*	*621*	*644*	*1,022*	
Makran	*1,400*	*2,699*	*519*	*4,179*	
Kharan	*714*	*1,787*	*400*	*2,501*	
Las Bela	640	1,114	575	1,818	

Sex Table II.—Size of families by occupation of husband.

Occupation of husband.	Number of families examined.	Total Number of children born.	Average per family.	Number of children surviving.	Proportion of surviving to total 1,000 born.
1	2	3	4	5	6
BALUCHISTAN	**39,744**	**163,001**	**4**	**108,949**	**669**
A. Production of Raw Materials	**33,385**	**139,575**	**4**	**93,407**	**669**
I.—EXPLOITATION OF ANIMALS AND VEGETATION.	*33,369*	*139,523*	*4*	*93,377*	*669*
1. *Pasture and Agriculture*	*33,368*	*139,522*	*4*	*93,356*	*669*
(a) *Cultivation*	*30,554*	*128,309*	*4*	*85,552*	*667*
1. Non-cultivating proprietors taking rent in money or kind.	11,193	43,445	4	30,866	810
5. Cultivating owners	16,663	74,683	4	47,841	641
6. Tenant Cultivators	1,559	6,124	4	4,058	663
7. Agricultural labourers	1,139	4,057	4	2,787	687
(b) *Cultivation of special crops, fruit, etc. (planters, managers, clerks and labourers.*	*13*	*35*	*3*	*28*	*800*
16. Market gardeners, flower and fruit growers	13	35	3	28	800
(c) *Forestry*	*13*	*51*	*4*	*32*	*627*
17. Forest Officers, rangers, guards, etc.	1	17	17	10	588
19. Collectors of forest produce	12	34	3	22	647
(d) *Stock raising*	*2,788*	*11,127*	*4*	*7,744*	*696*
21. Cattle and buffalo breeders and keepers	89	4,057	5	259	571
22. Breeders of transport animals	405	1,656	4	1,148	693
23. Sheep and goat breeders	2,056	8,028	4	5,721	713
23. (a) Herdsmen and shepherds	238	986	4	616	625
2. *Fishing and Hunting*	*1*	*1*	*1*	*1*	*1,000*
II.—EXPLOITATION OF MINERALS	*16*	*52*	*3*	*50*	*962*
4. *Non-Metallic Minerals*	*16*	*52*	*3*	*50*	*962*
40. Salt, saltpetre and other saline substances	16	52	3	50	962
B. Preparation and Supply of Material Substances	**3,680**	**14,192**	**4**	**8,976**	**631**
III.—INDUSTRY	*1,138*	*4,413*	*4*	*2,847*	*645*
5. *Textiles*	*43*	*174*	*4*	*129*	*741*
43. Cotton spinning, sizing and weaving	22	119	5	78	655
49. Dyeing, bleaching, printing, preparation and sponging of textiles.	21	55	3	51	927
7. *Wood*	*161*	*644*	*4*	*433*	*672*
55. Carpenters, turners and joiners, etc.	130	512	4	361	705
56. Basket makers and other industries of woody materials, including leaves and builders working with bamboo, reeds or similar materials.	31	132	4	72	545
8. *Metals*	*177*	*718*	*4*	*483*	*651*
59. Blacksmiths, other workers in iron, makers of implements.	165	688	4	432	658
60. Workers in brass, copper and bell-metal	4	25	6	9	360
61. Workers in other metals (except precious metals).	8	29	4	22	759
9. *Ceramics.*	*36*	*127*	*4*	*78*	*614*
64. Brick and tile makers	35	120	3	71	592
65. Other workers in ceramics	1	7	7	7	1,000
10. *Chemical products properly so-called and analogous*	*23*	*74*	*3*	*61*	*824*
67. Manufacture of aerated and mineral waters and ice.	4	10	3	6	600
68. Manufacture and refining of vegetable oils	5	16	3	11	688
70. Others	14	48	3	44	917

Sex Table II.—Size of families by occupation of husband—*continued.*

Occupation of husband.	Number of families examined.	Total Number of children born.	Average per family.	Number of children surviving.	Proportion of surviving to total 1,000 born.
1	2	3	4	5	6
11. *Food Industries*	*114*	*451*	*4*	*279*	*619*
71. Rice pounders and huskers and flour grinders	29	99	3	60	606
72. Grain parchers, etc.	16	57	4	39	684
73. Butchers	15	70	5	44	571
75. Sweetmeat and condiment makers ..	39	165	4	102	618
81. Others	15	60	4	34	567
12. *Industries of dress and the toilet*	*282*	*1,040*	*4*	*638*	*·613*
82. Boot, shoe, sandal and clog makers ..	135	592	4	345	583
83. Tailors, milliners, dressmakers and darners ..	46	158	4	106	655
84. Embroiderers, hat-makers and makers of other articles of wear.	10	55	3	31	564
85. Washing and cleaning	29	86	3	52	605
86. Barbers, hair-dressers and wig-makers ..	53	149	3	104	698
13. *Furniture Industries*	*27*	*100*	*4*	*75*	*750*
88. Cabinet-makers, carriage painters, etc. ..	27	100	4	75	750
14. *Building Industries*	*45*	*167*	*4*	*88*	*527*
90. Lime burners, cement workers; excavators and wellsinkers; stone cutters and dressers; brick layers and masons; builders (other than buildings made of bamboo or similar materials), painters, decorators of houses, tilers, plumbers, etc.	45	167	4	88	527
17. *Miscellaneous and undefined Industries*	*230*	*394*	*4*	*583*	*552*
97. Makers of clocks and surgical or scientific instruments, etc.	1	3	3	3	1,000
98. Makers of jewellery and ornaments ..	100	424	4	271	639
100. Scavenging	129	467	4	309	662
IV. TRANSPORT	*777*	*2,966*	*4*	*1,911*	*640*
19. *Transport by water*	*37*	*278*	*8*	*149*	*536*
102. Ship-owners, boat-owners and their employees, officers, mariners, etc. Ships brokers, boatmen and tow men.	37	278	8	149	536
20. *Transport by road*	*532*	*2,023*	*4*	*1,320*	*652*
106. Labourers employed on roads and bridges ..	15	71	5	43	606
107. Owners, managers and employees (excluding personal servants) connected with mechanically driven vehicles (including trams).	16	37	2	20	540
108 Owners, managers and employees (excluding personal servants) connected with other vehicles.	17	65	4	38	585
110. Pack elephant, camels, mule, ass and bullock-owners and drivers	446	1,761	4	1,170	665
111. Porters and messengers	38	89	2	49	651
21. *Transport by Rail*	*194*	*619*	*3*	*415*	*670*
113. Labourers employed on railway construction and maintenance and coolies and porters employed on railway premises	194	619	3	415	670
22. *Post Office Telegraph and Telephone service* ..	*14*	*46*	*3*	*27*	*587*
114. Post Office, Telegraph and Telephone service	14	46	3	27	587
V.—TRADE	*1,765*	*6,813*	*4*	*4,218*	*619*
23. *Banks, establishments of credit, exchange and insurance*	*35*	*196*	*6*	*90*	*459*
115. Bank managers, money-lenders, exchange and insurance agents, money changers and brokers and their employers.	35	196	6	90	459
24. *Brokerage, commission and export*	*70*	*59*	*3*	*41*	*695*
116. Brokers, commission agents, commercial travellors, warehouse owners and employees.	70	59	3	41	695

Sex Table II.—Size of families by occupation of husband—*continued.*

Occupation of husband.	Number of families examined.	Total Number of children born.	Average per family.	Number of children surviving.	Proportion of surviving to total 1,000 born.
1	2	3	4	5	6
25. *Trade in textiles*	*265*	*1,057*	*4*	*676*	*649*
117. Trade in piece-goods, wool, cotton, silk, hair and other textiles.	265	1,057	4	676	649
26. *Trade in skins, leather and furs*	*3*	*23*	*8*	*11*	*478*
118. Trade in skins, leather, furs, feather, horn, etc., and the articles made from those.	3	23	8	11	478
30. *Trade in chemical products*	*47*	*204*	*4*	*135*	*661*
123. Drugs, dyes, paints, petroleum, explosives, etc.	47	204	4	135	661
31. *Hotels, cafes, restaurants, etc.*	*21*	*100*	*5*	*53*	*530*
126. Vendors of wines, liquors, aerated waters and ice.	2	10	5	6	600
127. Owners and managers of hotels, cook shops, sarais, etc. (and employees).	18	88	5	45	511
128. Hawkers of drink and food-stuffs ..	1	2	2	2	1,000
32. *Other trade in food-stuffs*	*155*	*700*	*4*	*375*	*536*
129. Grain and pulse dealers	1	5	5	3	600
131. Dealers in dairy product, eggs and poultry ..	13	44	3	18	409
132. Dealers in animals for food	1	8	8	8	1,000
134. Dealers in other food-stuffs	137	635	5	340	542
135. Dealers in tobacco	2	2	1	1	500
137. Dealers in ganja	1	6	6	1	167
33. *Trade in clothing and toilet articles*	*18*	*60*	*3*	*43*	*717*
138. Trade in ready made clothing and other articles of dress and the toilet (hats, umbrellas, socks, ready made shoes, perfumes, etc.).	18	60	3	43	717
36. *Trade in means of transport*	*12*	*47*	*4*	*33*	*702*
144. Dealers and hirers of elephants, camels, horses, cattle, asses, mules, etc.	12	47	4	33	702
37. *Trade in fuel*	*20*	*79*	*4*	*40*	*557*
145. Dealers in firewood, charcoal, coal, cowdung, etc.	20	79	4	40	557
39. *Trade of other sorts*	*1,172*	*4,288*	*4*	*2,717*	*632*
150. General storekeepers and shopkeepers otherwise unspecified.	1,172	4,288	4	2,717	632
C.—Public Administration and Liberal Arts	**1,377**	**5,191**	**4**	**3,459**	**666**
VI.—PUBLIC FORCE	*221*	*916*	*4*	*542*	*592*
40. *Army*	*44*	*148*	*3*	*104*	*703*
153. Army (Imperial)	11	29	3	23	793
153 a. Levy service	1	1	1	1	1,000
154. Army (Indian States)	32	118	4	80	178
43. *Police*	*177*	*768*	*4*	*438*	*570*
157. Police	173	757	4	432	571
157 a. Levy service	4	11	3	6	545
VII.—PUBLIC ADMINISTRATION ..	*712*	*2,470*	*3*	*1,556*	*685*
44. *Public Administration*	*712*	*2,470*	*3*	*1,556*	*685*
159. Service of the State	427	1,330	3	920	692
160. Service of Indian and Foreign States ..	284	1,079	4	731	677
162. Village officials and servants other than watchmen.	1	8	8	5	625
VIII.—PROFESSIONS AND LIBERAL ARTS ..	*440*	*1,858*	*4*	*1,261*	*678*
45. *Religion*	*303*	*1,287*	*4*	*850*	*660*
165. Other religious workers	296	1,274	4	838	662
166. Servants in religious edifices, burial and burning grounds, pilgrim conductors, circumcisers, etc.	7	13	2	12	923

Sex Table II.—Size of families by occupation of husband—*concluded.*

Occupation of husband.	Number of families examined.	Total Number of children born.	Average per family.	Number of children surviving.	Proportion of surviving to total 1,000 born.
1	2	3	4	5	6
46. *Law*	*11*	*65*	*6*	*44*	*677*
168. Lawyers, clerks, petition-writers, etc. ..	11	65	6	44	677
47. *Medicines*	*18*	*67*	*4*	*56*	*836*
169. Registered medical practitioners including oculists.	11	29	3	23	793
170. Other persons practising the healing arts without being registered.	4	24	6	21	875
171. Dentists	1	7	7	6	857
172. Midwives, vaccinators, compounders, nurses, masseurs, etc.	1	5	5	4	800
173. Veterinary surgeons	1	2	2	2	1,000
48. *Instruction*	*18*	*61*	*3*	*46*	*754*
175. Clerks and servants connected with education	18	61	3	46	754
49. *Letters, arts and sciences (other than 44)*	*94*	*378*	*4*	*265*	*701*
178. Authors, editors, journalists and photographers	2	9	5	6	667
181. Horoscope casters, astrologers, fortune-tellers, wizards, witches and mediums.	1	5	5	4	800
182. Musicians (composers and performers other than military), actors, dancers, etc.	91	364	4	255	701
D.—Miscellaneous ..	**1,302**	**4,043**	**3**	**3,107**	**763**
IX.—PERSONS LIVING ON THEIR INCOME	*779*	*2,134*	*3*	*1,825*	*855*
50. *Persons living principally on their income* ..	*779*	*2,134*	*3*	*1,825*	*855*
185. Proprietors (other than of agricultural land) fund and scholarship-holders and pensioners.	779	2,134	3	1,825	855
X.—DOMESTIC SERVICE ..	*225*	*848*	*4*	*565*	*666*
51. *Domestic service*	*225*	*848*	*4*	*565*	*666*
186. Private motor drivers and cleaners ..	7	33	5	18	545
187. Other domestic service	218	815	4	547	671
XI.—INSUFFICIENTLY DESCRIBED OCCUPATIONS.	*35*	*162*	*5*	*107*	*660*
52. *General terms which do not indicate a definite occupation.*	*35*	*162*	*5*	*107*	*660*
188. Manufacturers, businessmen and contractors otherwise unspecified.	35	162	5	107	660
XII.—UNPRODUCTIVE ..	*263*	*899*	*3*	*610*	*679*
54. *Beggars, vagrants, prostitutes*	*263*	*899*	*3*	*610*	*679*
193. Beggars and vagrants	263	899	3	610	679

Sex Table III.—Size of family by caste or religion of family.

Caste or Religion.	Number of families examined.	Total Number of children born.	Average per family.	Number of children surviving.	Proportion of surviving to 1,000 born.	NUMBER OF FAMILIES WITH WIFE MARRIED AT 13—14	15—19	20—29	30 and over.
1	2	3	4	5	6	7	8	9	10
TOTAL ..	**39,744**	**163,001**	**4**	**108,949**	**668**	**8,130**	**17,587**	**12,369**	**1,708**
Indigenous	37,577	155,074	4	103,713	669	7,289	16,693	11,937	1,658
Semi-Indigenous ..	791	3,420	4	2,293	670	77	383	294	37
Aliens	1,376	4,507	3	2,943	653	764	461	138	13
Baloch	**9,325**	**38,367**	**4**	**27,315**	**712**	**1,725**	**4,227**	**2,962**	**411**
Indigenous	9,304	38,233	4	27,220	710	1,724	4,217	2,954	409
Semi-Indigenous ..	21	134	6	95	709	1	10	8	2
Brahui	**8,517**	**29,752**	**3**	**21,769**	**732**	**1,623**	**3,422**	**2,982**	**490**
Indigenous	8,517	29,752	3	21,769	732	1,623	3,422	2,982	490
Pathans	**6,502**	**35,445**	**5**	**19,304**	**545**	**1,169**	**3,214**	**1,874**	**245**
Indigenous	5,904	32,763	5	17,600	537	1,131	2,920	1,641	212
Semi-Indigenous ..	598	2,682	4	1,704	635	38	294	233	33
Lasi	**1,282**	**6,488**	**5**	**3,665**	**565**	**341**	**474**	**405**	**62**
Indigenous	1,282	6,488	5	3,665	565	341	474	405	62
Jatt	**7,083**	**27,000**	**4**	**19,106**	**708**	**1,050**	**3,591**	**2,255**	**187**
Indigenous	7,083	27,000	4	19,106	708	1,050	3,591	2,255	187
Sayyid	**786**	**3,908**	**5**	**2,169**	**555**	**121**	**313**	**240**	**62**
Other Muslim	**3,823**	**13,546**	**4**	**10,104**	**745**	**820**	**1,438**	**1,350**	**215**
Indigenous	3,651	12,942	3	9,610	743	782	1,359	1,297	213
Semi-Indigenous ..	172	604	4	494	538	38	79	53	2
Hindu Indigenous ..	**1,100**	**3,988**	**3**	**2,574**	**645**	**517**	**397**	**163**	**23**
Aliens	**1,376**	**4,507**	**3**	**2,943**	**653**	**764**	**461**	**138**	**13**
Muslim	626	2,047	3	1,320	645	314	227	75	10
Hindu	588	1,966	3	1,266	644	367	179	40	2
Sikh	116	320	3	238	744	60	43	13	..
Christian	40	174	4	119	684	23	12	10	1

Sex Table IV.—Average size of family correlated with age of wife at marriage. (Regular Area).

Age of wife at marriage.	Number of families.	Number of children born.	Average observed.	Number of children surviving.	Average observed.
1	2	3	4	5	6
ALL AGES	**1,376**	**4,507**	**3**	**2,943**	**2**
13—14	764	2,567	3	1,721	2
15—19	461	1,461	3	921	2
20—29	138	456	3	287	2
30 and over	13	23	2	14	1

Sex Table IV.—Average size of family correlated with age of wife at marriage. (Tribal Area).

Age of wife at marriage.	Number of families.	Number of children born.	Average observed.	Number of children surviving.	Average observed.
1	2	3	4	3	6
ALL AGES	**38,368**	**158,494**	**4**	**106,006**	**3**
13—14	7,366	28,520	4	18,582	3
15—19	17,076	70,304	4	46,066	3
20—29	12,231	51,578	4	36,163	3
30 and over	1,695	8,092	5	5,195	3

Sex Table VI.—Duration of marriage correlated with Caste, or Religion of Family.

Caste or Religion of family.	DURATION OF MARRIAGE WITH PRESENT WIFE.																	
	UNDER 10 YEARS.			10 YEARS.			11—19 YEARS.			20—31 YEARS.			32 YEARS.			33 YEARS AND OVER.		
	Number of families.	Number of children born.	Average Number of children.	Number of families.	Number of children born.	Average Number of children.	Number of families.	Number of children born.	Average Number of children.	Number of families.	Number of children born.	Average Number of children.	Number of families.	Number of children born.	Average Number of children.	Number of families.	Number of children born.	Average Number of children.
1	2	3	4	5	6	7	8	9	10	11	12	13	14	15	16	17	18	19
BALUCHISTAN ..	8,046	19,051	2	3,660	11,492	3	10,685	42,769	4	13,266	63,304	4	306	1,928	6	3,781	24,457	7
Indigenous	7,375	17,094	2	3,497	10,988	3	10,080	40,373	4	12,657	60,132	5	290	1,816	6	3,678	23,771	6
Semi-Indigenous	97	239	2	56	195	3	188	666	4	376	1,816	5	7	56	8	67	448	6
Aliens	574	818	1	107	309	3	417	1,730	4	233	1,356	6	9	56	6	36	238	7
Baloch	1,310	3,160	2	741	2,364	3	2,978	11,456	4	3,171	14,651	4	89	476	5	1,036	6,260	6
Indigenous	1,307	3,152	2	740	2,359	3	2,975	11,443	4	3,161	14,571	4	88	467	5	1,033	6,241	6
Semi-Indigenous	3	8	3	1	5	5	3	13	4	10	80	8	1	9	9	3	19	8
Brahui (Indigenous)	2,421	5,605	2	939	2,792	5	2,290	7,769	3	2,253	9,995	4	45	233	5	569	3,158	5
Pathan	1,632	4,348	3	506	2,190	4	1,630	8,745	5	1,896	12,846	7	88	754	8	750	6,562	9
Indigenous	1,561	4,160	3	464	2,036	4	1,482	8,220	6	1,608	11,408	7	84	710	8	705	6,229	9
Semi-Indigenous	71	188	3	42	154	3	148	525	4	288	1,438	5	4	44	11	45	333	8
Lasi (Indigenous)	158	433	3	97	388	4	258	1,330	4	619	3,366	5	7	42	6	153	1,139	7
Jatt (Indigenous)	923	2,271	2	671	1,654	2	1,550	5,895	4	3,134	12,512	4	27	176	6	778	4,494	6
Sayyid (Indigenous)	97	276	3	74	263	4	186	979	5	258	1,461	6	12	77	6	109	852	8
Other Muslim	716	1,694	2	398	1,148	3	1,109	3,936	4	1,341	5,494	4	19	85	4	240	1,189	5
Indigenous	693	1,651	2	385	1,112	3	1,072	3,808	4	1,263	5,196	4	17	82	5	221	1,093	5
Semi Indigenous	23	43	2	13	36	3	37	128	4	78	298	4	2	3	2	19	96	5
Hindu (Indigenous)	220	456	2	127	384	3	272	931	3	361	1,623	5	10	29	3	110	565	5
Aliens	574	818	1	107	309	3	417	1,730	4	233	1,356	6	9	56	6	36	238	7
Muslim	264	366	1	60	181	3	183	777	4	103	614	6	1	8	8	15	101	7
Hindu	236	331	1	36	99	3	185	755	4	108	627	6	7	45	6	16	109	7
Sikh	55	76	1	7	22	3	35	134	4	14	64	5	1	3	3	4	21	5
Christian	10	45	2	4	7	2	14	64	5	8	51	6	..	..	..	1	7	7

CHAPTER VI.

CIVIL CONDITION.

Reference to Statistics.

111. This chapter is intended to deal with statistics relating to the civil condition of the people which are contained in Imperial Tables VII and VIII.

Instructions to enumerators.

The instructions to enumerators were to record for each individual whether he or she was unmarried, married or widowed. A woman who had never married even though she were a prostitute or concubine was to be recorded as unmarried. Persons recognised by custom as married were to be entered as such even though they had not gone through the ceremony, and divorced persons were to be entered as widowed.

Scope of inquiry.

112. The inquiry embraced only the Regular Areas, and, in the Tribal Areas, only Kharan. In the rest of the Tribal Areas containing a population of 714,003 indigenous inhabitants, civil condition was not recorded. The total population thus dealt with numbers only 110,849 in the Regular Areas and 23,358 in Kharan.

The Regular Areas are mostly inhabited by immigrants consisting of troops, traders, artisans and others whose numbers are subject to fluctuations.

Civil condition.	Total.	Males.	Females.
Total ..	110,849	80,197	30,652
Unmarried ..	50,438	37,351	13,087
Married ..	55,020	39,362	15,658
Widowed ..	5,391	3,484	1,907

The absolute figures by civil condition for this part of the population are exhibited in the margin. The disparity between the numbers of males and females is very striking. The fact is that society here is living under conditions so artificial and abnormal that any detailed examination of figures for the Regular Areas would appear to be outside the scope of this chapter. We are thus left high and dry with only 23,358 residents of Kharan through whom we shall endeavour to have a peep at the matrimonial life prevailing in the greater part of the Province.

Main features.

113. The returns for Kharan were subjected to strict scrutiny personally by the Chief and may be taken to be fairly accurate. In every 1,000 of the total population there were 497 unmarried, 453 married and 50 widowed of both sexes. These consisted of 296 unmarried males, 201 unmarried females; 225 married males, 228 married females, 15 widowers and 35 widows. The marginal figures show how these proportional figures compare with those for Ajmere-Merwara. Calculated on the numerical strength of each sex, there were in every 1,000 males and 1,000 females, 553 unmarried males, 433 females; 419 married males, 491 married females; and 28 widowers and 76 widows. In the marginal table these ratios are compared with the figures for India, Burma, and Assam. Compared to India as a whole and Assam, the proportion of the unmarried is fairly high while the proportion for widowers and widows is remarkably low.

Civil condition.	Males.		Females.	
	Kharan.	Ajmere-Merwara.	Kharan.	Ajmere-Merwara.
Unmarried ..	296	238	201	150
Married ..	225	255	228	249
Widowed ..	15	35	35	73

Province.	Unmarried.		Married.		Widowed.	
	Males.	Females.	Males.	Females.	Males.	Females.
All India ..	479	346	467	499	54	155
Burma ..	561	521	392	374	47	11
Assam ..	536	415	420	444	44	141
Kharan ..	553	433	419	491	28	76

Universality of marriage.

114. Diagram No. 10 facing this page illustrates the three features of civil condition in Kharan. It brings out clearly the universality of marriage. Almost every one who is of marrigeable age gets married as soon as he or his parents are able to pay the bride-price. As age advances, the number of the unmarried goes on decreasing until it reaches the limit at 40 after which a few unmarried

Diagram No. 10.

SHOWING DISTRIBUTION BY CIVIL CONDITION OF 1,000 PERSONS OF EITHER SEX IN EACH AGE GROUP IN KHARAN.

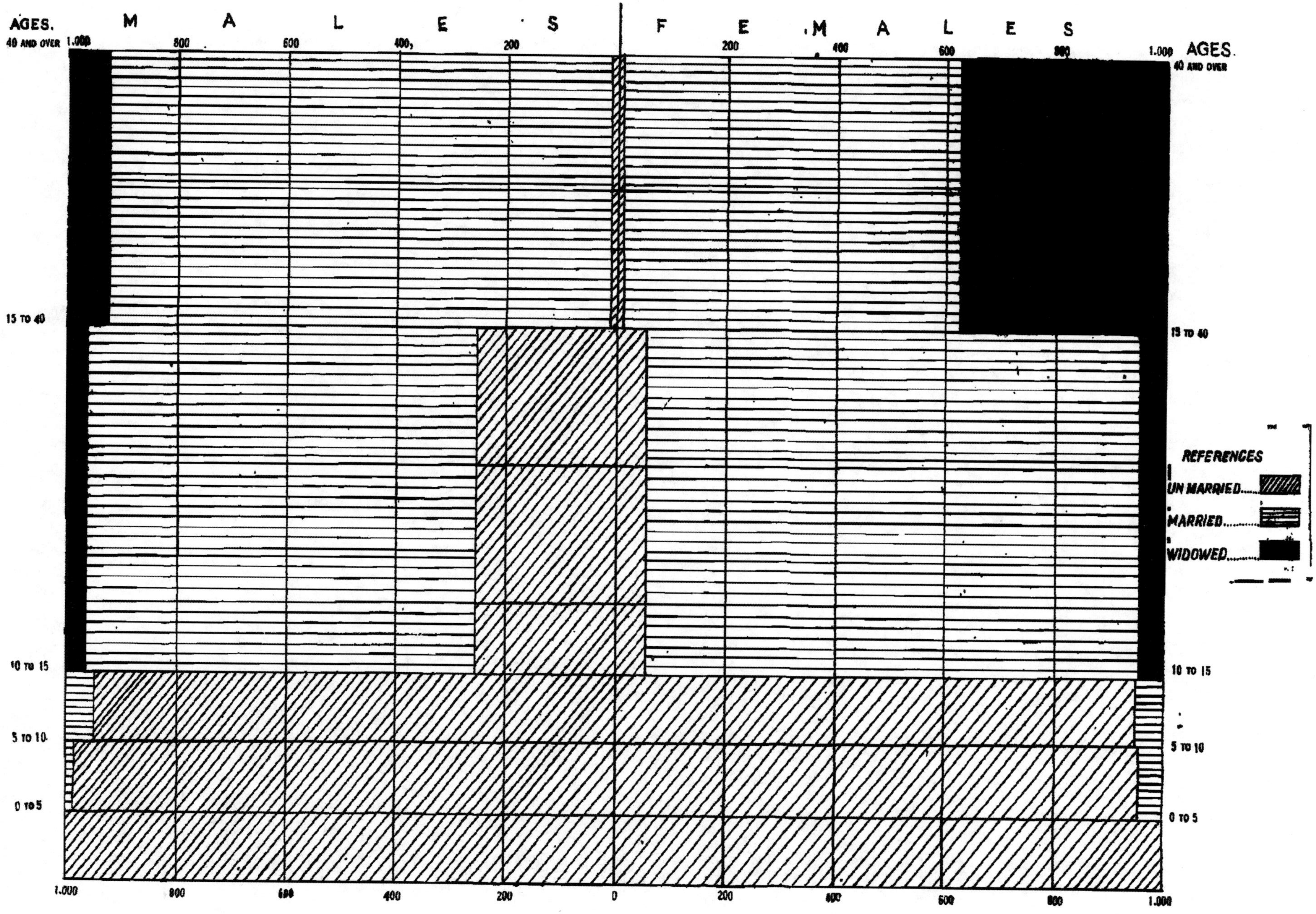

Diagram No. 11.

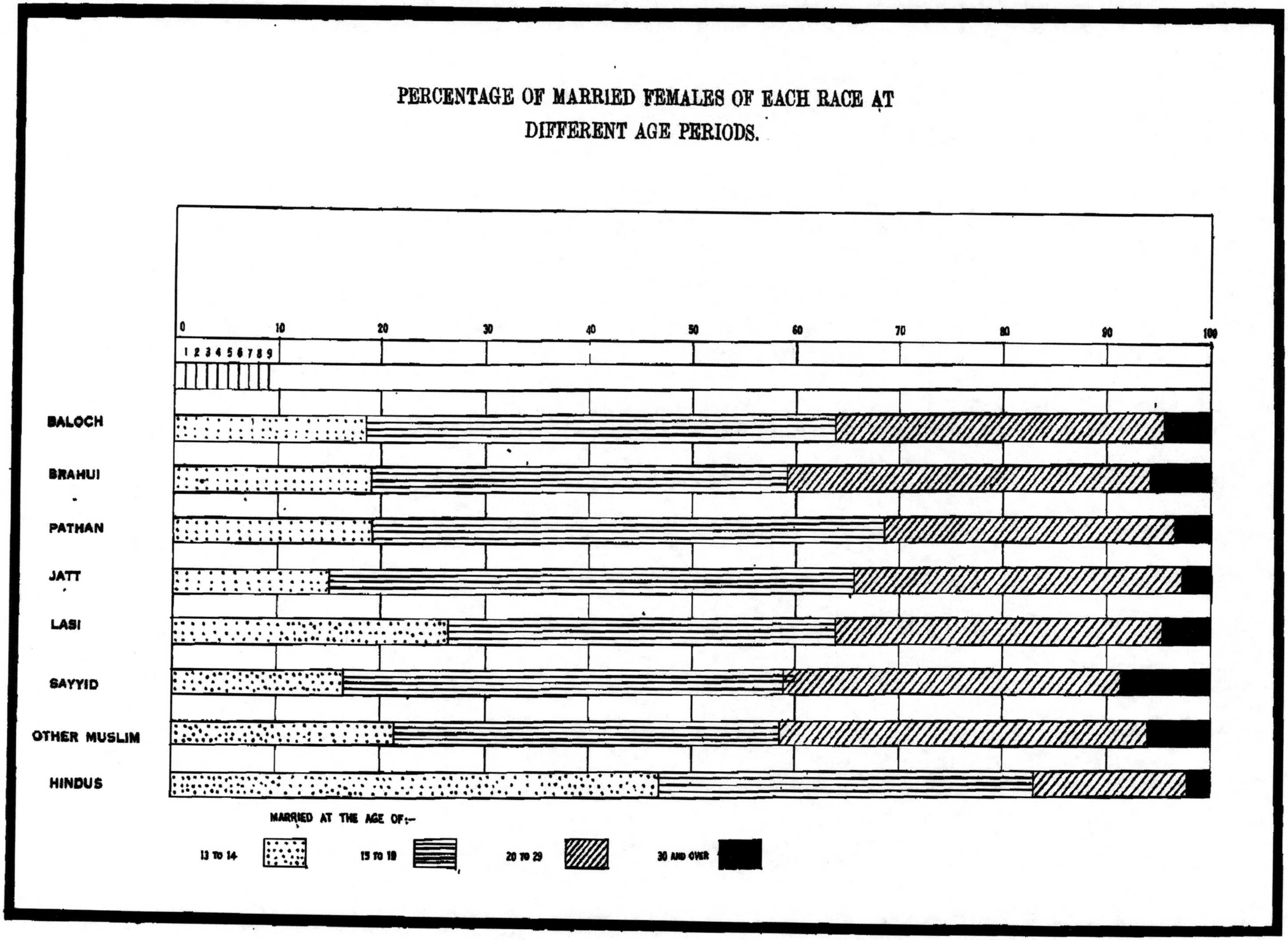

remain over till the end. These are obviously those who are unable to marry owing to lack of means or are unfit for married life owing to physical deformity, etc. The number of such persons of the ages of 15 and over was only 1,283 in 1931 in a population of 12,613 of those ages, or only 10 per cent.

The age of marriage.

115. The age at which marriage generally takes place was assumed at the Census of 1921 to be 16 for females and 22 for males. This was not based on statistical data which were not available. The statistics for Kharan indicate that there were one married male and one female per 1,000 of each sex in the age-group 0—5, 12 males and 45 females in the age-period 5—10 and 40 males and 229 females in the age-group 10—15. That is to say in a population of 10,745 persons of the ages of 0—15 years, only 4 per cent. were married, 1 male and 3 females. And if we calculate the ratios on the total population we find that in Kharan there were only 17 persons of both sexes per 1,000 of total population who had joined in wedlock below the age of 15. In the marginal table, figures of early marriages are compared with certain other Indian Provinces and States. The North West Frontier Province has the lowest proportion of all. Kharan comes next. Marriages below the age of 15 are practically unknown in Kharan. Those on paper are, excepting a very small percentage of marriages of girls, (for which female precocity is responsible) mostly marriages in name contracted in order to patch up blood-feuds or, in very rare instances, as mere tokens of affectionate regard between two friendly mothers or two friendly fathers. Such marriages strictly speaking are mere betrothals because actual marital relations are permitted as a rule some time after the couple attain puberty.

Province or State.	Married per 1,000 of each sex.					
	0—5		5—10		10—15	
	Males.	Females.	Males.	Females.	Males.	Females.
Kharan ..	1	1	12	45	40	229
Ajmere-Merwara	25	48	106	235	196	455
Assam ..	1	7	17	98	45	277
N. W. F. P. ..	..	..	5	18	23	121
Punjab ..	2	5	26	32	72	235
Jammu and Kashmir ..	..	..	18	42	51	217

Diagram No. 11 illustrates early and late marriages by each principal indigenous race. The marginal table will show that early marriages are more common among the Hindus than any other race. At the ages of 13-14 years, 47 per cent. Hindus, 27 Lasis, 19 Brahuis, 19 Pathans, 19 Baloch, 17 Sayyid and 15 per cent. Jatts enter into wedlock. There are 44 per cent. of all indigenous races who marry at the ages of 15—19 and 32 per cent. who marry between the ages of 20—29 years. Marriages at the advanced ages of 30 years and over are least common among the Hindus. 5 per cent. of the Lasis and 3 per cent. of Jatts marry at the ages of 30 years and over. Only 4 per cent. Pathans and Baloch and 6 per cent. 'other Muslims' marry late in life.

Indigenous inhabitants.	*Number of families out of a total of 39,744 families examined with wife married at*			
	13—14.	15—19.	20—29.	30 and over.
Baloch ..	1,724	4,217	2,954	409
Brahui ..	1,623	3,422	2,982	490
Pathan ..	1,131	2,920	1,641	212
Lasi ..	341	474	405	62
Jatt ..	1,050	3,591	2,255	187
Sayyid ..	121	313	240	62
Other Muslims ..	782	1,359	1,297	213
Hindu ..	517	397	163	23

Polygyny.

116. "Woe betide the man who marries more wives than one" is a standing joke! I have known many a case of plurality of wives but I have not seen one husband with more wives than one without an ironical smile on his face when you come to speak of plurality of wives in his presence. The lure to possess wives to the Islamic limit of four may be great but the condition of equal treatment to all imposed by Islam is almost impossible to fulfil, for rich and poor alike, and the complacent optimist who imagines a bed of roses and oversteps the limit seldom fails to find himself trapped in a bed of thorns.

Those in high families resort to Polygyny chiefly for political reasons and the rich as a luxury, while the poor as a rule cannot afford it except when one by custom inherits a brother's widow and marries her by her consent. I quote below an extract on this subject from Sir Denys Bray's Census Report for 1911. The views expressed in it are as true to-day as they were 20 years ago.

"Widow re-marriage (except may be in the proudest families) is the very general rule, continued widowhood the very rare exception. It would be unthrift indeed for tribesmen to suffer such easily convertible capital to lie idle. Nevertheless it is much more correct to keep a widow in the family than to dispose of her elsewhere. In most tribes she is the recognised perquisite of her deceased husband's brother; if he is unmarried or childless, the chances are that he'll avail himself of it briskly enough, especially as he usually gets her without paying a penny even though there are sons who inherit their father's estate. The freedom of choice that British rule has granted to widows has done little to shake his rights; indeed tribal opinion on the propriety of the match is sometimes so strong as to convert an apparent privilege into an irksome duty. And though no one has a prior claim to her hand in tribes (chiefly Baloch) where it is customary for a widow to revert to her parents' dominion, it is hardly too much to say that second marriage with the brother's widow is at the bottom of most of the polygamy from one end of the country to the other."

On the whole, the practice is not very popular, for, the husband of more wives than one seldom has peace at home. Both the favourite wife and the rest—one or more—make him thoroughly sick of life to rue the day on which by marrying a second wife he sowed the seed of dissension for his offspring and interminable worry for himself. With such secret under-currents in social life the numbers involved cannot be but insignificant so much so that the excess among married females for which polygamous marriages may be responsible is more than counter-balanced by the forced bachelorhood caused by the high rates of bride-price. This view is supported by the statistics for Kharan which show that while there are 517 men and 483 women among every 1,000 men and women of marriageable ages of 15 years and over, there are only 408 *married* men and 398 *married* women. There are thus 109 unmarried men and 85 unmarried women of marriageable age. Allowing only one wife to one man, we have a surplus of 24 men per 1,000 who have perforce to enjoy the mixed blessings of forced bachelorhood all through life.

Widowhood.

117. The numbers of widowers and widows in Kharan as disclosed by the Census of 1931 are exhibited in the marginal statement for India and certain selected Provinces. The number of both widowers and widows for Kharan is the lowest in India as a whole except that Muslim widowers in Assam and Bengal only have a slightly lower proportion. As regards the widows, Kharan goes at the bottom of the list with a remarkably low figure. It can safely be said that these figures of civil condition in Kharan represent approximately the conditions prevailing in the greater part of the Province.

Province.	*Widowers per 1,000 males.*		*Widowers per 1,000 females.*	
	Muslims.	Hindus.	Muslims.	Hindus.
All India ..	44	57	129	169
Kharan ..	28	..	76	..
Ajmere-Merwara ..	68	66	133	157
Assam ..	25	55	127	156
Bengal ..	22	45	140	226
Bombay ..	57	32	133	161
N.-W. F. Province ..	47	54	108	129
Punjab ..	68	85	105	142
United Provinces ..	73	80	123	156
Jammu and Kashmir ..	54	76	88	184

Civil condition for selected tribes.

118. The statistics of civil condition for selected tribes are contained in Subsidiary Table 27. The proportions per 1,000 of each sex for the principal tribes are given in the margin. The highest proportion of unmarried males is found among the Nakib, the lowest amongst the Mamasani. For unmarried females the Kasis top the list, the Rakhshanis coming last. The Kasis have more widowers than any other tribe. The Nakib have the lowest proportion of widowers and the highest proportion of widows. The disparity between the proportion of the widowed among the Nakib and other tribes is very striking and is due probably to the fact that the Nakib are a semi-depressed class whose widows are not in great demand.

Tribe.	Unmarried.	Married.	Widowed.
Rakhshani (Baloch)— ..			
Male ..	553	418	29
Female ..	*427*	*498*	*75*
Mamasani (Brahui)—			
Male ..	525	445	30
Female ..	*450*	*505*	*45*
Kasi (Pathan)—			
Male ..	573	393	34
Female ..	*498*	*435*	*67*
Nakib (Miscellaneous)—			
Male ..	581	403	16
Female ..	*436*	*437*	*127*

26. Distribution by Civil condition of 1,000 of each sex at certain ages among Muslims in Kharan.

Religion and Division.	Males. All Ages. Unmarried.	Married.	Widowed.	0—5. Unmarried.	Married.	Widowed.	5—10. Unmarried.	Married.	Widowed.	10—15. Unmarried.	Married.	Widowed.	15—40. Unmarried.	Married.	Widowed.	40 and over. Unmarried.	Married.	Widowed.
1	2	3	4	5	6	7	8	9	10	11	12	13	14	15	16	17	18	19
Kharan (Muslim)	553	420	27	999	1	..	987	12	1	956	40	4	249	715	36	7	917	76

Religion and Division.	Females. All Ages. Unmarried.	Married.	Widowed.	0—5. Unmarried.	Married.	Widowed.	5—10. Unmarried.	Married.	Widowed.	10—15. Unmarried.	Married.	Widowed.	15—40. Unmarried.	Married.	Widowed.	40 and over. Unmarried.	Married.	Widowed.
1	20	21	22	23	24	25	26	27	28	29	30	31	32	33	34	35	36	37
Kharan (Muslim)	433	491	76	999	1	..	954	45	1	767	229	4	53	905	42	8	621	371

27. Distribution by Civil condition of 1,000 of each sex at certain ages for selected indigenous tribes. (Kharan and Kasi-Nichari).

Distribution of 1,000 Males of each Age-group by Civil condition.

Tribe.	All Ages. Unmarried.	Married.	Widowed.	0—6. Unmarried.	Married.	Widowed.	7—13. Unmarried.	Married.	Widowed.	14—16. Unmarried.	Married.	Widowed.	17—23. Unmarried.	Married.	Widowed.	24—43. Unmarried.	Married.	Widowed.	44 and over. Unmarried.	Married.	Widowed.
1	2	3	4	5	6	7	8	9	10	11	12	13	14	15	16	17	18	19	20	21	22
BALOCH—																					
Rakhshani ..	553	418	29	999	1	..	989	9	2	848	134	18	515	455	30	62	895	43	6	902	92
BRAHUI—																					
Sumalari ..	525	437	38	1,000	..	..	939	61	..	667	222	111	429	476	95	77	865	58	..	953	47
Mamasani ..	525	445	30	997	3	..	995	5	..	793	195	12	452	516	32	46	913	41	14	891	95
PATHAN—																					
Kakar ..	601	348	51	1,000	..	..	1,000	..	..	905	95	..	833	167	..	264	664	72	118	647	235
Kasi ..	573	393	34	1,000	..	..	1,000	..	..	933	67	..	788	212	..	184	747	69	93	833	74
OTHER MUSLIMS—																					
Darzada ..	551	449	..	1,000	..	..	941	59	..	750	250	..	1,000	..	..	45	955	..	..	1,000	..
Lori ..	522	449	29	1,000	..	..	971	..	29	889	111	..	222	778	..	44	889	67	..	1,000	..
Nakib ..	581	403	16	1,000	..	..	1,000	..	..	850	150	..	680	280	40	41	939	20	..	940	60
Others ..	584	394	22	1,000	..	..	990	10	..	849	123	28	488	488	24	98	857	45	..	947	53

Distribution of 1,000 Females of each Age-group by Civil condition.

Tribe.	All Ages. Unmarried.	Married.	Widowed.	0—6. Unmarried.	Married.	Widowed.	7—13. Unmarried.	Married.	Widowed.	14—16. Unmarried.	Married.	Widowed.	17—23. Unmarried.	Married.	Widowed.	24—43. Unmarried.	Married.	Widowed.	44 and over. Unmarried.	Married.	Widowed.
1	23	24	25	26	27	28	29	30	31	32	33	34	35	36	37	38	39	40	41	42	43
BALOCH—																					
Rakhshani ..	427	498	75	997	3	..	910	88	2	354	640	6	48	939	13	8	924	68	7	546	447
BRAHUI—																					
Sumalari ..	435	520	45	1,000	..	..	852	148	..	294	647	59	263	737	..	..	982	18	35	724	241
Mamasani ..	450	505	45	1,000	..	..	957	43	..	289	711	..	175	818	7	7	962	31	21	631	348
PATHAN—																					
Kakar ..	392	530	78	1,000	..	..	968	32	..	286	714	..	..	1,000	..	17	948	35	..	214	786
Kasi ..	498	435	67	1,000	..	..	986	14	..	778	222	..	27	973	..	13	892	65	50	250	700
OTHER MUSLIMS—																					
Darzada ..	395	395	210	1,000	..	..	900	100	..	333	667	..	..	1,000	..	77	692	231	..	286	714
Lori ..	400	557	43	1,000	..	..	1,000	..	..	400	600	..	..	933	67	..	932	68	..	857	143
Nakib ..	436	437	127	1,000	..	..	938	62	..	357	643	..	93	870	37	12	907	81	..	357	643
Others ..	442	459	99	1,000	..	..	949	51	..	471	515	14	95	869	36	8	874	118	..	465	535

CHAPTER VII.

INFIRMITIES.

Reference to Statistics.

119. The statistics relating to infirmities are contained in Imperial Table IX printed at page 25 of part II of this volume and in the two Subsidiary Tables at the end of this chapter.

Scope of enquiry.

120. The infirmities for which statistics were collected through the machinery of the Census were:—

1. Insanity.
2. Deaf-muteness.
3. Blindness.
4. Leprosy.

Two different methods were employed for collecting the data. In the Regular Areas inhabited chiefly by the immigrant population which was subjected to a synchronous census, a separate column was provided in the schedule as elsewhere in India and the entry was made in this column against every individual suffering from any of these four physical disabilities. In the rest of the province classed as Tribal Areas inhabited by the indigenous tribesmen, the information was collected, as at the past two censuses, on a separate form in which the total number of males and females afflicted with each infirmity was recorded for each tribal section living in each hamlet. Other details as to civil condition, age and occupation recorded in the Regular Areas were omitted in the schedule for Tribal Areas.

Instructions to enumerators.

121. The instructions to enumerators ran as follows :—

Regular Areas (*Column* 18 *of the Schedule*).—Care is needed to prevent the entry of persons suffering from leucoderma, or white leprosy and other infirmities not falling within the scope of column 18. Persons blind of one eye should not be entered. Only those blind of both eyes should be included. A man must be both deaf and mute in order to be included in this column.

Tribal Areas.—When you have finished the enumeration of a Mauza put the following supplementary questions to the assembled headmen, and record the answers in the supplementary schedules in the manner indicated below :—

(Each family should be taken in the order in which it is entered in the House List).

(1) Are there in the family any persons who are—

(*a*) insane,
(*b*) totally blind of both eyes,
(*c*) deaf-mute from birth,
(*d*) leper ?

(2) Eye diseases in Baluchistan are common and often result in blindness. It will be interesting to ascertain the extent of blindness in the province and the age at which it generally occurs as well as its causes. In the case of the blind (blind of both eyes) give the present age of the person and also state the age at which he or she became blind. Causes of blindness, if known, should also be stated.

(3) If a person is simply weak-minded or weak-sighted, or hard of hearing or suffering from leucoderma (Pashto—*Praksho ;* Baluchi and Brahui—*Pisk* ; Jattki—Phulari; Persian —Bars) you should not enter him or her in the list. Persons suffering from leprosy (Brahui—*Noshadri ;* Persian—*Jazám* ; Punjabi—*Kohr*) should be entered in the list.

As the numbers of the infirm were very small, the figures were not tabulated by the slip system but were compiled direct from the schedules.

Accuracy of the results.

122. The difficulty of diagnosis, sentimental objections on the part of parents to disclose facts particularly in respect of females and the idiosyncrasies of the enumerator are well-known pitfalls in the path of accurate enumeration. This is exemplified by certain abnormal local variations at each successive Census both among males and females. Take, for instance, the figures for Quetta-Pishin, Zhob, Sarawan, Jhalawan, Kachhi, Makran and Las Bela. Quetta-Pishin returned 132 male infirm in 1911. The number dropped to 121 in 1921 and rose again to 192 in 1931. In Sarawan there were 191 male infirm in 1911; the number

fell to 137 in 1921 and 101 in 1931. The females similarly dropped from 96 in 1911 to 37 in 1931. In Jhalawan there were 104 male infirm in 1911 which more than doubled in 1921, and decreased by 47 in the following decade. Similarly the number of female infirm rose from 71 in 1911 to 137 in 1921 dropping again to 106 in 1931. The variations in Kachhi are still more puzzling. The number of male infirm was 326 in 1911 ; 284 in 1921 and only 185 in 1931, with 242 female infirm in 1911 and 161 in 1931. Makran and Las Bela figures show similar inexplicable variations. In Makran the number of females fell from 191 and 205 in 1911 and 1921 respectively to 91 in 1931. Las Bela had 197 male infirm in 1911 which fell to 108 and rose again to 159 in 1921 and 1931, the females being 108 in 1911 and 146 in 1921 increasing again to 103 in 1931.

The unreliability of the record is quite apparent. The variations in some cases are probably due both in 1921 and 1931 to better enumeration but in others they appear to be equally due to one or other of the causes mentioned above. The figures for leprosy as I shall show later on are certainly inaccurate for I believe, as did my predecessors of 1911 and 1921, that Baluchistan is free from leprosy as a local disease. Fortunately the numbers are very small. On the whole, however, they furnish sufficient indication of the general prevalence of the four important infirmities and their distribution in the Province.

General results.

123. In 1931, 2,744 persons (1,712 males ; 1,032 females) all told were returned as afflicted with the four infirmities in the whole Province. Of these, 421 were insane, 582 deaf-mute, 1,695 blind and 51 leper. Their distribution over Districts and States is shown below :—

Infirmities.	Districts.			States.		
	Total.	Males.	Females.	Total.	Males.	Females.
All-infirmities	1,269	820	449	1,480	895	585
Insane	186	138	48	235	157	78
Deaf-mute	278	204	74	304	192	112
Blind	781	458	323	914	525	389
Leper	24	20	4	27	21	6

Note.—Multiple infirmities were confined to five persons, *i.e.*, one insane male and one female and one blind female in Quetta-Pishin were also returned as deaf-mute, and two insane males in Kachhi were also returned as blind. These account for the difference of 5 in the totals.

124. In every 100 afflicted, 54 were contributed by States and 46 by Districts. The blind claim the highest percentage (62) followed by deaf-mutes (21), insane (15) and lepers (2).

The marginal statement shows the ratio of infirm per 100,000 of total population compared to other Indian Provinces and States as well as the Provincial increases since 1921 and the ratio of this increase to that of the total population. It will be seen that Baluchistan stands eleventh among the 26 Provinces and States taking all infirmities together. In insanity it stands fifth, in deaf-muteness tenth, in blindness ninth, in leprosy twenty-third. While it stands dangerously high in insanity, it is gratifying to see it so low in the list of leprosy. In fact, I should not be overstepping the mark if I were to say that among all Provinces and States in India, Baluchistan alone claims to be entirely free from leprosy as an indigenous malady—thanks to the one redeeming feature of its climate and of its inhospitable physical conformation which have kept the Province free from the devastating inroads of the demon of plague and the scourge of leprosy.

Province, State or Agency.	Infirm per 100,000 of population 1931.	Variation Increase+ Decrease— since 1921.	Ratio of Increase+ Decrease – infirm per 100,000 of increase of population.
Baluchistan ..	316	—556	—806
Ajmere-Merwara ..	501	+1,255	+1,930
Andamans and Nicobars	88	—39	—1,641
Assam ..	297	+5,918	+471
Bengal ..	226	+14,753	+423
Bihar and Orissa ..	263	+43,904	+1,004
Bombay (including Aden) ..	346	+27,152	+762
Burma ..	466	+10,940	+740
Central Provinces and Berar ..	434	+11,618	+578
Coorg ..	152	+112	+21,918
Delhi ..	141	+4	+3
Madras ..	285	+51,475	+1,170
N.-W. F. Province ..	206	—937	—539
Punjab ..	350	+2,873	+85
United Provinces ..	396	+46,015	+1,482
Baroda ..	456	+2,245	+709
Central India ..	272	+3,866	-613
Cochin ..	287	+873	+386
Gwalior ..	244	+170	+32
Hyderabad ..	154	—7,085	—361
Jammu and Kashmir ..	405	+2,850	+737
Mysore ..	198	+3,018	+522
Rajputana ..	337	+13,976	+1,003
Sikkim ..	184	+9	+32
Travancore ..	214	+3,732	+342
Western India States ..	535	(separate figures not available).	

Variation.

Year.	Total.			Insane.			Deaf-mute.			Blind.			Leper.		
	Total.	M.	F.	Total.	M.	F.	Total.	M.	F.	Total.	M.	F.	Total.	M.	F.
1911 ..	3,173	1,911	1,262	370	268	102	668	482	186	2,052	1,095	957	83	66	17
1921 ..	3,301	2,021	1,280	420	285	135	682	494	188	2,093	1,160	933	106	82	24
1931 ..	2,749	1,715	1,034	421	295	126	582	396	186	1,695	983	712	51	41	10

125. The marginal statement gives statistics of the total afflicted population as well as figures for each affliction recorded at the censuses of 1911, 1921 and 1931 for which complete figures are available. The Census of 1921 disclosed an increase of 128 afflicted since 1911 due probably to the excessive privations caused by drought and famine and a widespread outbreak of small-pox in the years preceding the Census. The results obtained at the 1931 Census show a decrease of 427 and 556 since 1911 and 1921 respectively.

126. The distribution of the infirm over Districts and States is given below :—

All Infirmities.

Year.	Districts.			States.		
	Total afflicted.	Males.	Females.	Total. afflicted.	Males.	Females.
1911	1,138	740	398	2,035	1,171	864
1921	1,278	831	447	2,023	1,190	833
1931	1,269	820	449	1,480	895	585

Each Infirmity.

Year.	Insane.			Deaf-mute.			Blind.			Leper.		
	Total.	M.	F.	Total.	M.	F.	Total.	M.	F.	Total.	M.	F.
1911—												
Districts	130	106	24	299	223	76	686	394	292	23	17	6
States	240	162	78	369	259	110	1,366	701	665	60	49	11
1921—												
Districts	177	127	50	249	185	64	819	492	327	33	27	6
States	243	158	85	433	309	124	1,274	668	606	73	55	18
1931—												
Districts	186	138	48	278	204	74	781	458	323	24	20	4
States	235	157	78	304	192	112	914	525	389	27	21	6

	Decrease.
Hyderabad ..	7,085
N.-W. F. Province ..	937
Baluchistan ..	556
Andamans and Nicobars ..	39

While Baluchistan does not occupy an enviable place in the general list of infirmities for India, it is satisfactory to note that it stands third among the four Provinces and States which alone have shown a decrease since 1921. The credit goes almost entirely to the States, for, the Districts contribute a net decrease of only 11 against the decrease of 545 in the States composed of 362 blind, 129 deaf-mute, 8 insane and 46 leper.

127. The improvement in the health bill of the States is ascribed by the Kalat State authorities to medical relief on a wider scale—thanks to the activities of the Medical Department and of Dr. Holland, C.I.E., M.B., of the Mission Hospital whose indefatigable activities both in Quetta and Shikarpur have done a great deal to reduce the number of the blind. For the improvement in the number of deaf-mutes and lepers and the insane, however, we must look for reasons in other directions.

Distribution by religions.

	1921.	1931.
Total afflicted ..	3,300	2,744
Muslim ..	3,184	2,629
Hindu ..	105	104
Sikh ..	7	8
Christian ..	4	3

128. The infirm in 1921 and 1931 were distributed among the various religions as shown in the margin. The Muslims have shown considerable improvement since 1921. The highest proportion is found among the indigenous Hindus who in 1931 had 43 afflicted in every 10,000 of their total population against 33 and 32 respectively of the indigenous and semi-indigenous Muslims.

Diagram No. 12. SHOWING PROPORTION OF PERSONS AFFLICTED WITH EACH INFIRMITY PER 10.000 OF TOTAL POPULATION OF DIFFERENT INDIGENOUS RACES.

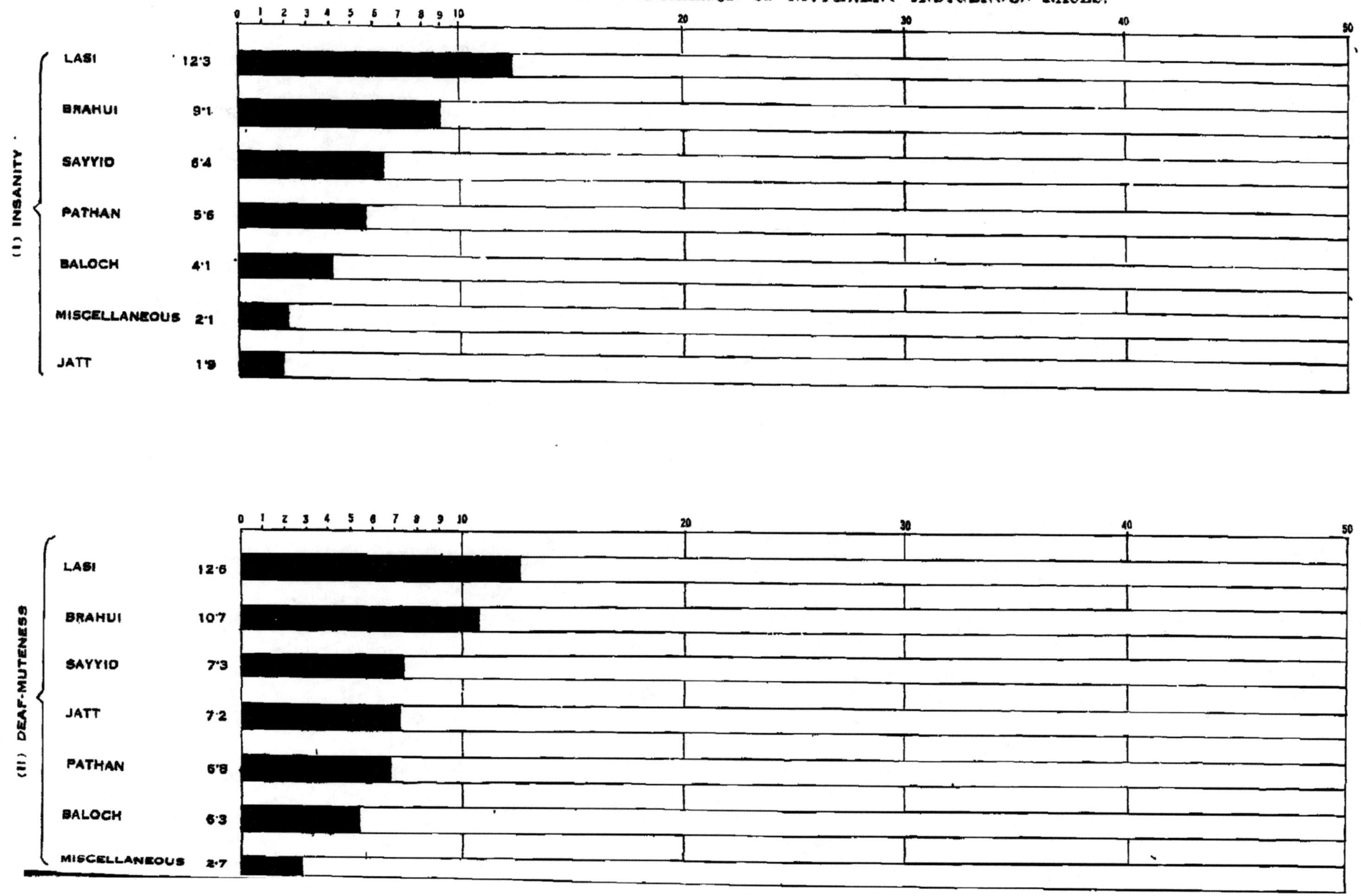

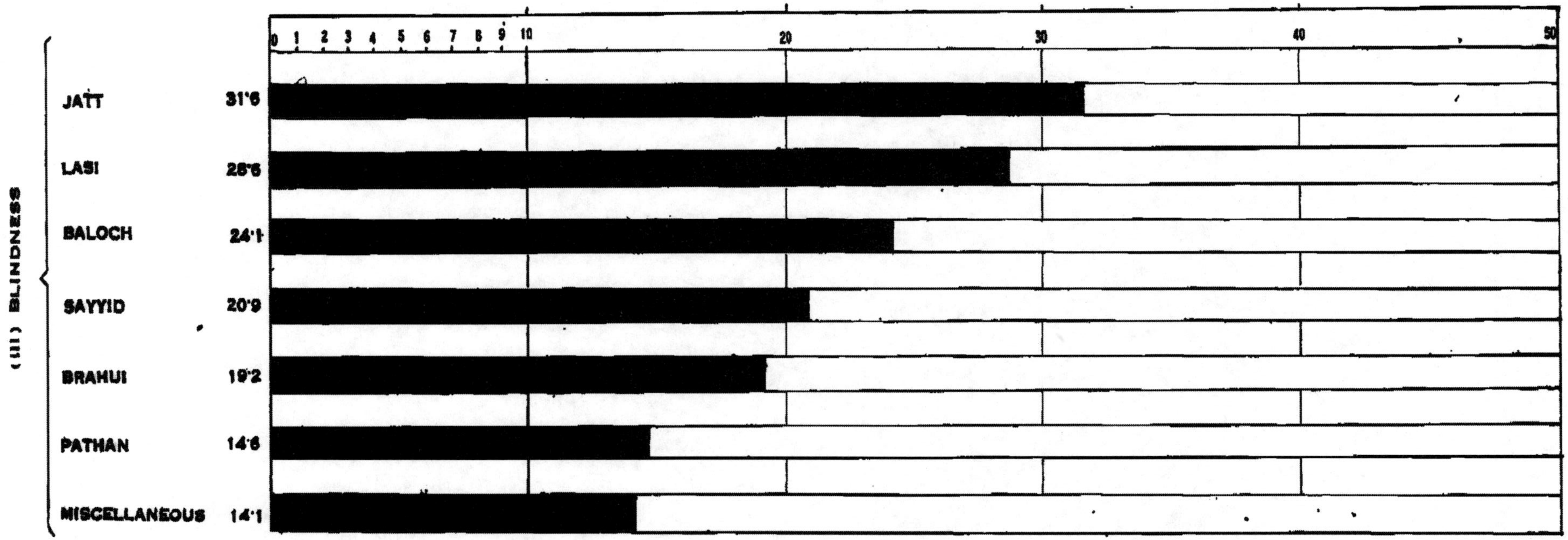
(III) BLINDNESS
JATT 31·6
LASI 28·6
BALOCH 24·1
SAYYID 20·9
BRAHUI 19·2
PATHAN 14·6
MISCELLANEOUS 14·1
0 1 2 3 4 5 6 7 8 9 10 20 30 40 50

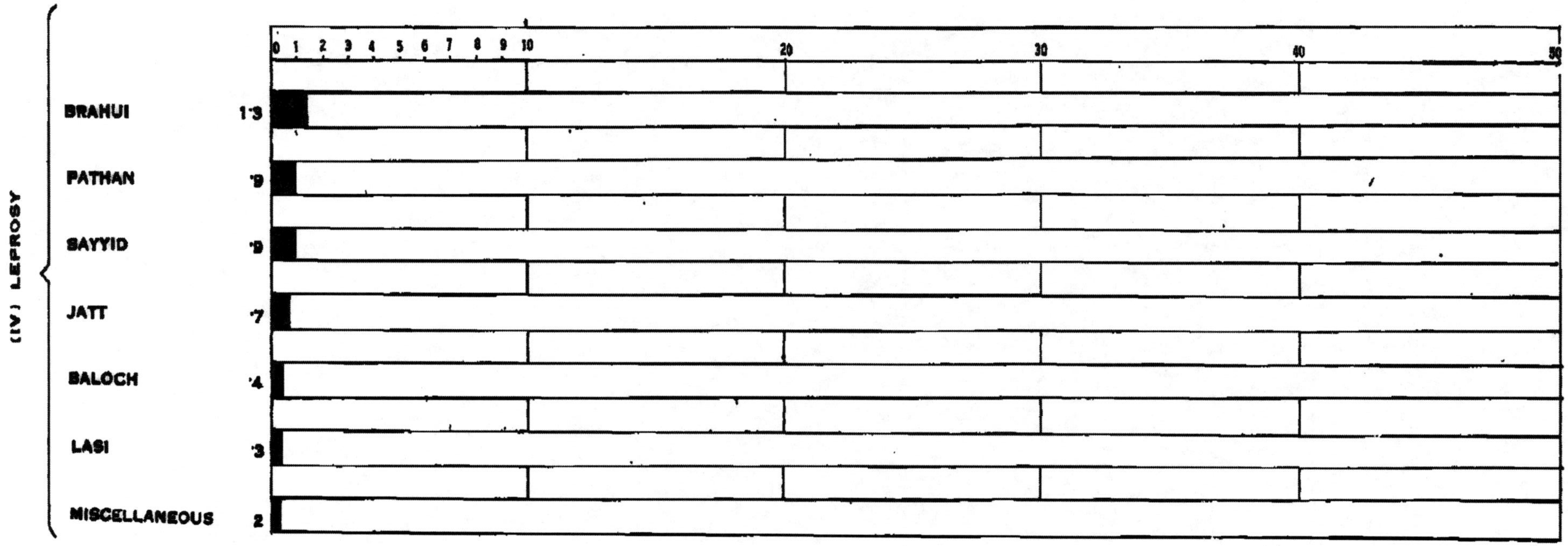
(IV) LEPROSY
BRAHUI 1·3
PATHAN ·9
SAYYID ·9
JATT ·7
BALOCH ·4
LASI ·3
MISCELLANEOUS 2
0 1 2 3 4 5 6 7 8 9 10 20 30 40 50

129. The racial distribution of the infirm as it stood in 1921 and 1931 is exhibited in the margin. Diagram No. 12 opposite this page illustrates their distribution for 1931. The figures for the Jatt, the Baloch, the Brahui and Others are decidedly suspect. The only explanation that I can offer for the large increase among Lasis is increased accuracy of enumeration. **Racial Distribution.**

Race.	Total afflicted. 1921.	Total afflicted. 1931.	Proportion of afflicted per 10,000 of total population of each race 1921.	Proportion of afflicted per 10,000 of total population of each race 1931.	Variation since 1921. Increase + Decrease —
Baloch ..	1,050	783	61	35	—26
Brahui ..	656	496	41	33	—8
Jatt ..	495	320	78	50	—28
Lasi ..	77	171	33	54	+21
Pathan ..	559	490	32	28	—4
Sayyid ..	56	77	28	35	+7
Others ..	240	110	35	19	—16

130. Taking in each indigenous race the more important tribes which have a sufficiently large number of infirm we get the following results :—

Tribe.	Proportion per 1,000 of its total population.	Tribe.	Proportion per 1,000 of its total population.
Baloch.		*Brahui.*	
Khetran	6	Mamashahi	7
Rakhshani	5	Shahwani	5
Dombki	5	Langav	5
Rind	5	Bizanjav	5
Bugti	3	Mengal	4
Mari	2	Zahri	2
Pathan.		*Others.*	
Kasi	10	Darzada	6
Zmarai	9	Lasi	5
Ghilzai	3	Jatt	4
Musakhel	3	Sayyid	4
Sherani	2	Hindus	4
Kakar	2		
Tarin	1		

The proportion of the infirm so far as the Pathans are concerned is highest amongst the Kasis and Zmarais. Among the Baloch, the Khetrans top the list; among "Others" the Darzadas head the list with 6 infirm per 1,000 of their total population.

131. The statement below gives the incidence of infirmities by Districts and States for the past three censuses :— **Distribution by Districts and States.**

District or State.	*Infirm per 10,000 of total population of each locality.* 1911.	1921.	1931.	Variation 1921 to 1931 Increase + Decrease —
DISTRICTS	*27*	*30*	*27*	—3
Quetta-Pishin	14	12	19	+7
Loralai	30	39	33	—6
Zhob	29	36	19	—17
Bolan	48	25	9	—16
Chagai	56	37	48	+11
Sibi	35	42	33	—9
STATES	*48*	*53*	*36*	*—17*
Sarawan	45	38	49	+11
Jhalawan	21	46	33	—13
Kachhi	61	66	33	—33
Dombki-Kaheri country ..	75	108	53	—55
Makran	56	62	32	—30
Kharan	38	44	34	—10
Las Bela	56	34	42	+8

INSANITY.

132. The total number of persons returned as insane at the Census of 1931 was 421 of whom 295 were males and 126 females.

Local Distribution.

The absolute figures by Districts and States will be found in Imperial Table IX printed at page 25 of Part II of this volume. In the margin are given proportional figures for 1921 and 1931. Taken as a whole, both Districts and States show practically no increase. This, however, is not the case, for these figures are exclusive of the 107 insane, 94 males and 13 females, who were sent to Mental hospitals in Sind and the Punjab between 1921 and 1931 and consisted of 49 indigenous males and 1 female of whom 35 were Pathans from Baluchistan, 5 Brahuis, 2 Baloch, 1 Sayyid, 3 other Muslim males and one female, and 3 Hindus. The rest included 8 male Pathan immigrants from Afghanistan; and 18 male and 7 female Muslim and 19 male and 5 female Hindu immigrants from India.

District or State.	*Proportion of insanes per 10,000 of total population.* 1921. Males.	1921. Females.	1931. Males.	1931. Females.
BALUCHISTAN ..	6	4	6	3
DISTRICTS ..	5	3	5	2
Quetta-Pishin ..	2	1	5	3
Loralai ..	8	4	5	3
Zhob ..	6	6	4	1
Bolan ..	..	..	..	..
Chagai ..	6	1	7	6
Sibi ..	6	4	5	2
STATES ..	8	5	7	4
Kalat ..	8	5	7	4
Sarawan ..	4	..	8	6
Jhalawan ..	10	5	13	8
Kachhi ..	8	5	4	1
Dombki-Kaheri country	9	3	1	2
Makran ..	9	9	5	3
Kharan ..	4	2	10	..
Las Bela ..	9	6	10	8

133. Taking the Census figures alone, we find that in every 100,000 inhabitants in the Province there are 48 who are insane. Including the 107 persons who were sent to mental hospitals, the proportion rises to 61 which places Baluchistan at the top, second only to Burma, among 26 Provinces and States in India shown in the margin. But if we include only the 50 indigenous insane the proportion falls to 54 reducing Baluchistan's place on the list from second to a bad enough fourth.

Province, State or Agency.	No. of insane per 100,000 of population 1931.	Variation per 100,000 of increase since 1921.
INDIA ..	34	+93
Ajmere-Merwara ..	39	+191
Andamans and Nicobars ..	24	—1,136
Assam	59	+106
Baluchistan	48	+1
Bengal	44	+81
Bihar and Orissa ..	21	+118
Bombay (including Aden) ..	48	+92
Burma	88	+90
Central Provinces and Berar	28	+72
Coorg	19	+3,136
Delhi	14	+8
Madras	33	+156
N. W. F. Province ..	31	+53
Punjab	29	+37
United Provinces ..	23	+136
Baroda	56	+120
Central India	23	+115
Cochin	53	+113
Gwalior	13	—1
Hyderabad	15	—16
Jammu and Kashmir ..	39	+36
Mysore	27	+158
Rajputana	23	+98
Sikkim	5	—21
Travancore	41	+73
Western India States ..	45	(separate figures not available).

Of the total number of insanes excluding inmates of asylums, the Districts have 40 and the States 58 per 100,000 of their respective populations. In the Districts, Chagai tops the list with 6 insane in every 10,000 of its inhabitants. Next comes Sibi Administered area with 5, followed by Quetta-Pishin and Loralai with 4 each. Zhob has 3 and the Mari-Bugti tribal area only 2.

In the States, the highest number of insanes is found in Jhalawan which has 10. Las Bela comes next with 9, with Sarawan a close third with 7. Kharan has 5, Makran 4, Kachhi 2 and Dombki-Kaheri 1. The distribution of the insane by locality is illustrated in map No. 9 on the opposite page.

Racial Distribution.

134. Of all the indigenous races in the Province, the Lasis contribute the largest proportion of insane per 10,000 of their total numerical strength. The Brahuis come next with 9 followed by Pathans and Sayyids who have 6 each. The Baloch have 4, Hindus 3, and Jatts and other Miscellaneous Muslim tribes 2 each. Of the principal tribes amongst the Baloch, the Rakhshanis have 8 insanes per 10,000 of their total numerical strength, the Magasis 7 and the Maris 4. Among Brahuis, the Bizanjav top the list with 15 followed by Mengals 10 and Zahris 7. The Kakars among the Pathans have only 5.

Variation.

135. Insanity on the whole has been on the increase in the Districts since 1911 while it shows an appreciable decrease in the States taken collectively. Among the Districts, Quetta-Pishin, the centre of charity, medical institutions

MAP No. 9.

PROPORTION OF INSANES PER 100,000 OF TOTAL POPULATION OF EACH DISTRICT AND DIVISION OF STATES.

I. CHAGAI
II. KHARAN
III. MAKRAN
IV. SARAWAN
V JHALAWAN
VI. LAS-BELA
VII. QUETTA-PISHIN
VIII. KACHHI
IX DOMBKI-KAHERI COUNTRY
X. BOLAN
XI. SIBI
XII. ZHOB
XIII. LORALAI

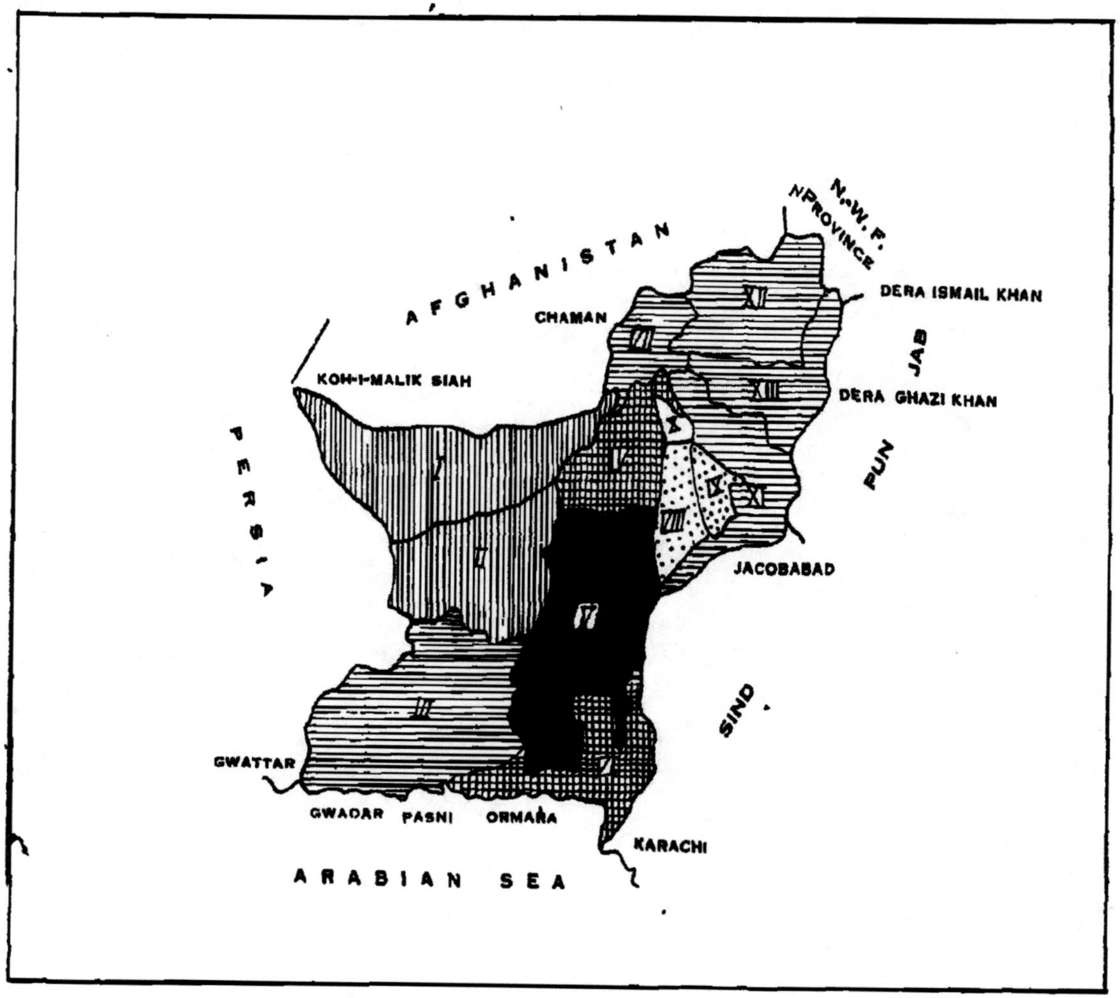

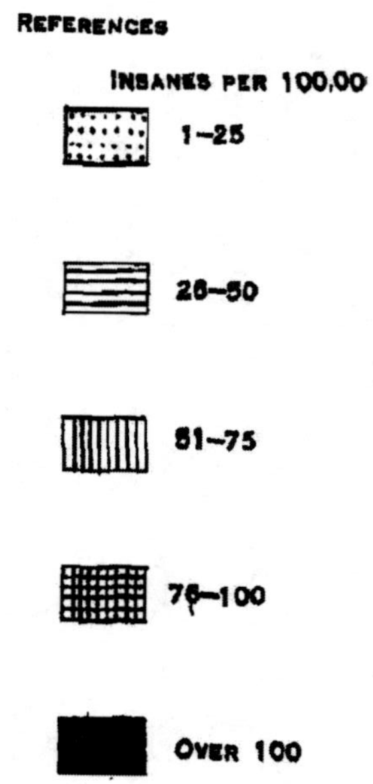

MAP No. 10.

PROPORTION OF DEAF-MUTES PER 100,000 OF TOTAL POPULATION OF EACH DISTRICT AND DIVISION OF STATES.

I. CHAGAI
II. KHARAN
III. MAKRAN
IV SARAWAN
V JHALAWAN
VI. LAS-BELA
VII. QUETTA-PISHIN
VIII. KACHHI
IX. DOMBKI-KAHERI COUNTRY
X. BOLAN
XI. SIBI
XII ZHOB
XIII. LORALAI

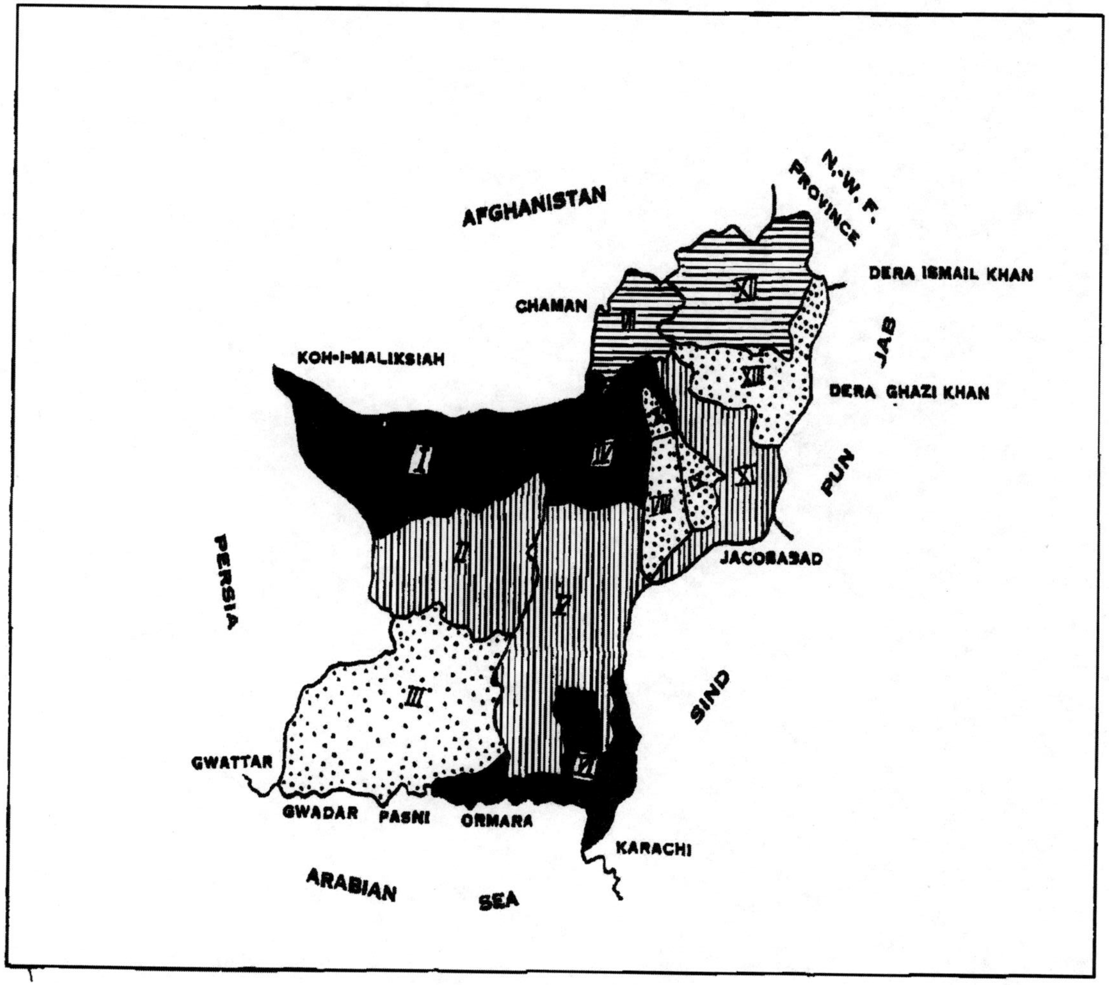

DEAF-MUTES PER 100,000

25–50

51–75

76–100

OVER 100

and drug smoking dens and other predisposing causes, contributes the largest increase. Of the remaining districts, Loralai and Sibi Administered area show increases while Zhob, Bolan, Chagai and Mari-Bugti tribal area show an appreciable decline. In the States, Sarawan, Kachhi, Dombki-Kaheri, Makran and Las Bela have shown an improvement since 1911. But there has been a large increase in Jhalawan where the number of insane has risen from 19 in 1911 to 93 in 1931. Jhalawan has 11 insane per 10,000 of its population against the maximum of 6 in the Districts areas and 9 in Las Bela. At the same time its three principal tribes namely, Bizanjav, Mengal and Zahri have also the largest proportion, *i.e.*, 15, 10 and 7 respectively against the maximum of 8 among the Baloch and 5 among the Pathan tribes. Unless this mushroom growth of the insane from 19 in 1911 to 60 in 1921 and 93 in 1931 is due to overzealous enumeration, Jhalawan's past and its present statistical history entitle it to the sorry distinction of being the centre of insanity in Baluchistan.

Causes of Insanity.

136. The causes of insanity have been described in the Census Report for 1911 as follows :—

> Insanity is variously regarded as the outcome of an excessive and heating diet, the result of a sudden shock, the punishment for perjury, or the malicious contrivance of the Jinns. But Kachhi folk put it down to the burning heat like most of their ills, and regard it as one of the ordinary endings of that racking headache they call *Loti*.

To these may be added the increasing use of Charas and Ganja as well as *Kohi Bhang* which is most destructive of the human brain. And lastly I suspect that hereditary syphilis which is believed to have assumed dangerous proportions in certain localities is not only responsible for some cases of insanity but also of deaf-muteness.

Province, State or Agency.	No. of deaf-mute per 100,000 of population 1931.	Variation per 100,000 of increase since 1921.
INDIA.	66	+120
Ajmere-Merwara	73	+418
Andamans and Nicobars	27	+252
Assam	75	+113
Baluchistan	67	+145
Bengal	70	+110
Bihar and Orissa	63	+147
Bombay (including Aden)	78	+230
Burma	116	+344
Central Provinces and Berar	78	—56
Coorg	62	+15,851
Delhi	23	—5
Madras	71	+274
N. W. F. Province	66	—173
Punjab	69	—95
United Provinces	52	+77
Baroda	52	+211
Central India	29	+23
Cochin	40	—7
Gwalior	37	—33
Hyderabad	26	+17
Jammu and Kashmir	159	+329
Mysore	60	+59
Rajputana	28	+39
Sikkim	149	+71
Travancore	57	+66
Western India States	91	(separate figures not available).

DEAF-MUTENESS.

Deaf-mutes in Baluchistan and other Parts of India.

137. The number of deaf-mutes disclosed by the Census of 1931 was 582 of whom 396 were males and 186 females. The marginal figures show how Baluchistan compares with other Indian Provinces and States. Baluchistan stands twelfth among 26 Provinces and States in respect of its deaf-mutes.

District or State.	*Deaf-mutes in 1931—Actual figures.* Total.	Male.	Female.	*Proportion per 10,000 of total population of each unit.* Total.	Male.	Female.
BALUCHISTAN	582	396	186	7	8	5
DISTRICTS	278	204	74	6	7	3
Quetta-Pishin	77	56	21	5	6	4
Loralai	26	21	5	3	4	1
Zhob	34	26	8	6	8	3
Bolan	2	1	1	..	3	8
Chagai	26	21	5	11	15	5
Sibi (Administered area)	84	55	29	10	11	8
„ Mari-Bugti country	29	24	5	5	8	2
STATES	304	192	112	8	9	6
Sarawan	36	26	10	13	17	8
Jhalawan	89	51	38	10	11	9
Kachhi	53	33	20	5	6	4
Dombki-Kaheri country	9	5	4	3	3	3
Makran	25	21	4	4	6	1
Kharan	23	17	6	10	14	6
Las Bela	69	39	30	11	12	10

138. In every 100,000 of its inhabitants there are 67 persons who are afflicted with deaf-muteness distributed over Districts and States as shown in the marginal table and illustrated in Map No. 10 facing this page. The disease claims more victims among males than females. In the Districts area, there are 7 males to every 3 female deaf-mutes; in the States there are 9 males to 6 females. In the Districts, the disease is comparatively more prevalent in Chagai where there are 15 male to 5 female afflicted. Next to Chagai comes Sibi Administered area which has 11 males to 8 females. In the Mari-Bugti tribal area there are 8 males to 2 females.

139. In the States, Sarawan heads the list with 17 males to 8 females. Kharan and Las Bela follow next with 14 and 12 males to 6 and 10 females respectively. Jhalawan stands third with 11 males to 9 females.

140. Grouping the various units according to geographical features, Quetta-Pishin, Loralai, Zhob, Sarawan and Jhalawan fall under the highlands group. Bolan may be ignored owing to its insignificant numbers. Chagai, Sibi, Makran, Kharan, Kachhi, Dombki-Kaheri and Las Bela belong to the lowlands-and-plains group.

A glance at the marginal table on page 75 gives the impression that deaf-muteness is more common in the lowlands-and-plains-group than in the highlands. In the latter group Sarawan and Jhalawan are the only exceptions and I suspect that the remarkably high ratio in their case is due to misinterpretation of the instructions. In the lowlands-and-plains group Makran, Kachhi and Dombki-Kaheri are the exceptions and the low numbers in their case are most probably due to emigration into Sind.

Racial Distribution.

141. The racial distribution is given in the margin for the principal indigenous races. The disease is more prevalent among the Lasis both among males and females. The Sayyids come next with 13 males. The Jatts stand third, the Brahuis fourth, Pathans fifth and Baloch sixth. Other miscellaneous tribes strange to say, come last. The highest proportion of female deaf-mutes is found among the Lasis and the lowest among the Sayyids and Miscellaneous tribes.

Race.	*Proportion per 10,000 of population.*	
	Males.	Females.
Baloch ..	8	3
Brahui ..	10	7
Pathan ..	9	5
Lasi ..	16	13
Jatt ..	11	7
Sayyid ..	13	2
Others ..	4	2

The principal tribes in the order of precedence among whom the disease is comparatively more prevalent are among Pathans, the Kasis 51 per 10,000 of their respective numerical strength, Sherani 10, Tarins 6, and Kakars 6. The proportion among the Kasis is the highest in the Province. But fortunately the actual number of deaf-mutes is only 10, the total strength of the tribe being 1,975. Among the Baloch the Khosas top the list with 26 followed by the Rakhshanis 15; among the Brahuis the Muhammadshahi and Bizanjav have 26 each, the Shahwani 16, Langav 8, Mengal 8 and Zahri 7.

Variation.

142. Deaf-muteness appears to be steadily decreasing. There was an increase of 12 males and 2 females between 1911 and 1921. This was probably due to change of definition in 1921. The Census of 1931 has revealed the fact that the numbers have fallen from 482 males and 186 females in 1911 and 494 males and 188 females in 1921 to 396 males and 186 females in 1931. The States account for a decrease of 117 males and 12 females since 1921 while the Districts show an increase of 19 males and 10 females.

Causes of deaf-muteness.

143. As to the causes of this malady, I would refer to paragraph 248 of the 1911 Report. To the general beliefs of the country folk on this subject, I can only add that it is commonly believed in some parts of the country that if a drop of rain fall accidentally into an infant's mouth before it learns to speak it results in deaf-muteness. Another belief is that if during the eclipse of the sun or the moon, one of the parents happens to be fast asleep at a certain point of time in the life of the child before it sees the light of day the child is born a deaf-mute. A belief of recent origin ascribes deaf-muteness to impaired health of one or both the parents caused by hereditary syphilis. I know at least of one case in which seven children were born in the family. The first, second, third, sixth and seventh were deaf-mutes. The fourth and fifth were not. All are dead except the sixth and seventh and yet the parents enjoy perfect health. The variations in the numbers and the causes, in short, are so eccentric that it appears wiser to leave analytical discussions to the better knowledge of my successors.

BLINDNESS.

Blindness in Baluchistan and other Parts of India.

144. The blind in the Province numbered 1,695 (983 males and 712 females). This gives a ratio of 195 per 100,000 of total population against 172 for the whole of India. There were 90 per 100,000 blind in the Districts

MAP No. 11.

PROPORTION OF BLIND PER 100,000 OF TOTAL POPULATION OF EACH DISTRICT AND DIVISION OF STATES.

I. CHAGAI
II. KHARAN
III. MAKRAN
IV. SARAWAN
V JHALAWAN
VI. LAS-BELA
VII. QUETTA-PISHIN
VIII. KACHHI
IX. DOMBKI-KAHERI COUNTRY
X. BOLAN
XI. SIBI
XII. ZHOB
XIII. LORALAI

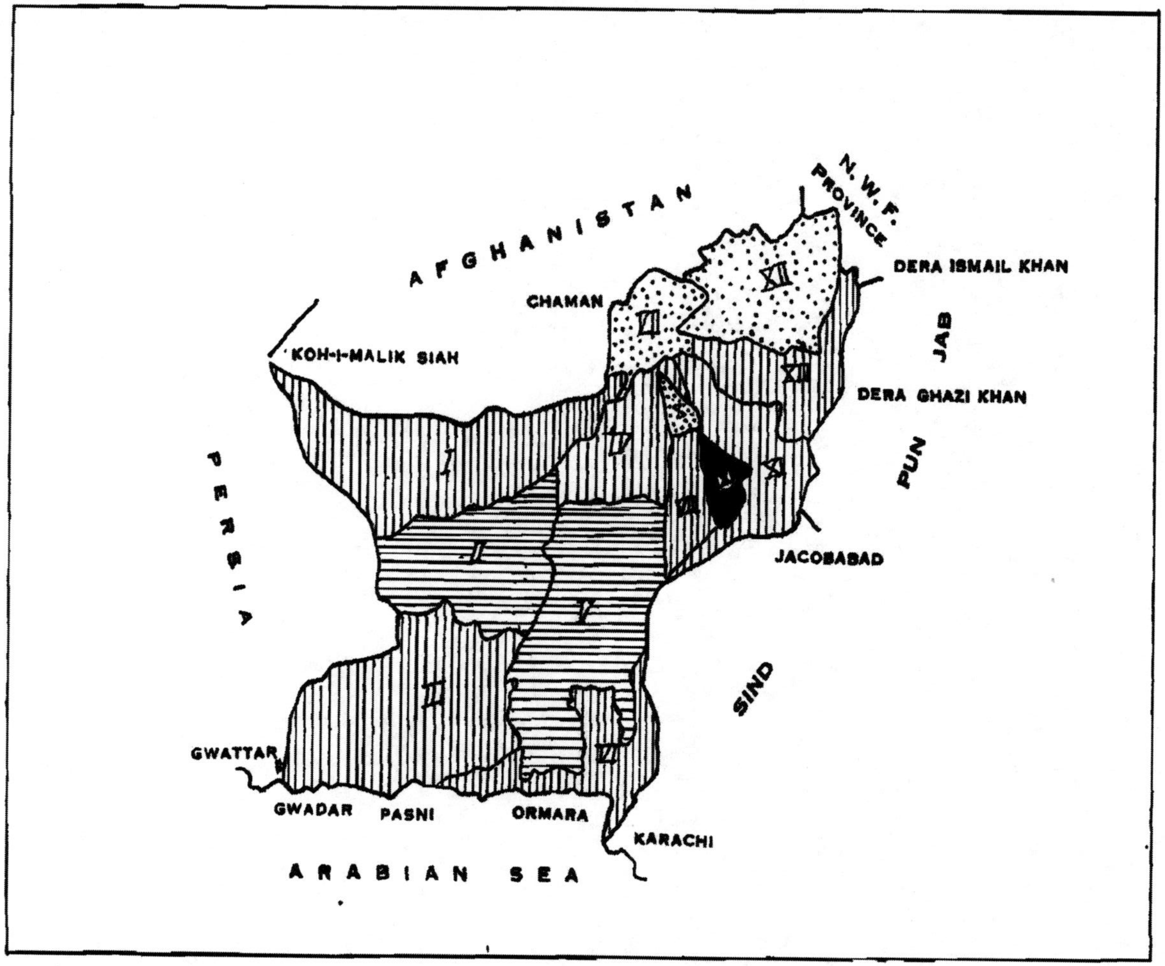

BLIND PER 100,000

UP TO 100

101–200

201–300

400–500

and 105 in the States in 1931. In every 100,000 of its inhabitants Baluchistan has 113 blind men and 82 blind women. The proportion of males and females in the Districts and States amounts to

	Males.	Females.
Districts	53	37
States	60	45

The proportion of both males and females is higher in the States than in the Districts. The chief causes are comparatively better climatic and economic conditions as well as greater medical facilities in the Districts. Baluchistan ranks ninth in the list of 26 Indian Provinces and States. Comparative figures are given in the margin.

Province, State or Agency.	Number of blind per 100,000 of population 1931.	Variation per 100,000 of increase since 1921.	Province, State or Agency.	Number of blind per 100,000 of population 1931.	Variation per 100,000 of increase since 1921.
INDIA ..	172	+353	N.-W. F. Province ..	102	−298
Ajmere-Merwara ..	386	+1,313	Punjab ..	245	+136
Andaman and Nicobars.	31	+168	United Provinces ..	291	+1,214
Assam ..	107	+175	Baroda ..	329	+391
Baluchistan ..	195	−577	Central India ..	206	+479
Bengal ..	73	+91	Cochin ..	132	+150
Bihar and Orissa ..	126	+508	Gwalior ..	182	+83
Bombay (including Aden).	178	+370	Hyderabad ..	87	−337
Burma ..	189	+217	Jammu and Kashmir	166	+272
Central Provinces and Berar.	262	+310	Mysore ..	100	+236
Coorg ..	61	+1,370	Rajputana ..	282	+855
Delhi ..	103	−2	Sikkim ..	24	−4
Madras ..	111	+344	Travancore ..	63	+139
			Western India States	395	(separate figures not available).

Local Distribution.

145. The proportion of the blind to 10,000 of total population of each local administrative unit is shown in the margin. The names are arranged in the order of numerical strength of the afflicted.

Districts.	Proportion per 10,000 of population.	States.	Proportion per 10,000 of population.
Chagai ..	29	Dombki-Kaheri country.	49
Loralai ..	24	Sarawan ..	28
Sibi-Administered area	24	Kachhi ..	25
Sibi-Mari-Bugti country ..	18	Makran ..	24
Zhob ..	10	Las Bela ..	21
Quetta-Pishin ..	9	Kharan ..	18
Bolan ..	4	Jhalawan ..	11

Blindness as pointed out in previous reports, flourishes in excessive heat and glare. The proportions for Loralai, Sibi and Sarawan would appear to weaken this inference, but the conclusions drawn in previous reports remain unchallenged, for, the high proportions have been traced to the Barkhan and Musakhel tahsils of the Loralai District and Sibi and Nasirabad tahsils of the Sibi Administered territory where heat and glare are as effective predisposing causes as in any other region notorious for its barrenness, scorching heat and glare. The high proportion for Sarawan is inexplicable. Perhaps in their winter migration, the "lame ducks" remained behind to escape enumeration in Kachhi.

146. The relative prevalence of blindness among males and females per 10,000 of total population of each locality is shown below :—

Districts.	*Proportion per 10,000 of total population.*		*States.*	*Proportion per 10,000 of total population.*	
	Males.	Females.		Males.	Females.
Chagai	17	12	Dombki-Kaheri country ..	27	22
Loralai	14	10	Sarawan	21	7
Sibi-Administered area ..	12	12	Makran	13	11
Sibi-Mari-Bugti country ..	12	6	Las Bela	13	8
Zhob	7	3	Kachhi	12	13
Quetta-Pishin	6	3	Kharan	11	7
Bolan	2	2	Jhalawan	7	4

It is difficult to offer an explanation for the remarkably low proportion of females in Sarawan.

147. The racial proportion per 10,000 of total population of each race, places the Jatts at the top with 38 males and 37 females. The Lasis rank second with 32 males and 22 females. The Baloch come next with 25 males and 24 females, followed by Sayyids who have 22 males and 19 females. The Brahuis and Pathans stand at the bottom with 17 males each and 13 and 12 females respectively.

148. The tribes which are most prominently prone to blindness are the Khetran and Rakhshani among the Baloch, the Muhammadshahi, Langav, Shahwani, Mengal and Zahri among the Brahuis; Zarkun, Musakhel and Zmarai among the Pathans.

Variation.

149. The largest decrease since 1911 and 1921 among the four infirmities is accounted for by blindness. The number of the blind has fallen from 2,052 in 1911 and 2,093 in 1921 to 1,695 in 1931. Compared to 1911, the Districts disclose an increase of 95 blind but since 1921 there has been a decrease of 38. The principal decrease is, however, accounted for by the States which had 452 and 360 fewer blind in 1931 than in 1911 and 1921 respectively. This satisfactory decline is attributed to medical institutions which between 1921 and 1931 performed 2,801 successful operations out of which credit is due to Doctor Holland of the Quetta Mission Hospital for 2,121.

LEPROSY.

Number of lepers.

150. The Census of 1931 puts the number of lepers at 51, against 83 in 1911 and 106 in 1921. The figures for all three censuses are most suspicious for they include patients afflicted with what is locally known as Noshádri. In leprous cases, the disease begins with a bronze patch on the arm, etc., without the accompaniment of pain. Slowly the bronze tint fades leaving the place a peculiarly dead white. In course of time the corrosive action begins and the patient's features become irrecognisable. He gradually loses his toes and fingers and in some cases his legs and arms as well. Noshádri on the other hand begins with a headache and giddiness followed by a swelling in the throat or the nose or the tonsils or in all simultaneously. After a few days the patient is unable to swallow even liquid food. The swelling in the nose is accompanied by a ticking sound. The swellings are extremely painful. There is a constant flow of watery matter from the nose. Eventually the swelling causes a hole in the palate when corrosive action begins resulting in course of time in the disappearance of the fleshy part of the nose and the upper lip.

Noshádri.

The Indian leper is shunned and feared. He is turned out of doors as a social outcast. On the other hand the Noshádri-stricken patient lives in the same house with other members of the family and is permitted to eat and drink from the ordinary household vessels. Separate vessels are provided only when the case assumes a hideous form. But the general belief is that contagion can only be passed through perspiration or by wearing the patient's shoes. The disease is confined to the region above the neck and never spreads to any other part of the body.

Cure for Noshádri.

The cure for Noshádri is simple enough. It consists of branding the affected parts, and the head with three equidistant brands from near the centre of the forehead in a straight line to the nape of the neck. After branding is over, the patient is given snuff locally prepared from indigenous herbs mixed with a little sacred earth from one of the shrines in Chagai. It is used twice daily, mornings and evenings. It causes sniffing which lasts for several minutes each time and causes a copious discharge of matter from the nose. The snuff course lasts for fourteen days during which the patient is made to live on simple wheaten bread. All other food, salt and sugar, etc., specially fat—even the smell of fat from the cooking pot—are strictly tabooed; only goat's milk is permitted. The patient begins to feel a change for the better on the 7th day and is discharged on the fourteenth day completely cured. I have seen a couple of successful cases. In both cases the cavity in the palate had filled up and the lost voice had been completely restored. Both patients looked perfectly healthy.

It is clear that Noshádri is not leprosy. And I believe that leprosy figures as collected by Census Agency minus those for Noshádri would leave the Province with an absolutely clean slate in respect of leprosy as a local disease. Between April 1921 and December 1930, altogether 16 lepers were sent from Baluchistan to the Leper Asylum in Tarn Taran. All these had been unloaded on us by our courteous neighbours of the North. They were all residents of Afghanistan, mostly Hazaras.

151. Of the other important infirmities figures for which have been collected through the local medical institution, only Syphilis and Tuberculosis deserve notice. No cases of Yaws have come to notice and only two cases of Filariasis were reported from the Zhob Militia Hospital beween 1921 and 1931. Thirty-seven cases of Ankylostomasis were recorded out of which 36 were reported from Mastung, and one from the Zhob Militia Hospital. The disease is probably due to drinking exposed Karez water and consumption of raw, unwashed vegetables—a habit common among the indigenous population of Mastung. **Other infirmities. Ankylostomasis.**

152. 4,039 cases of tuberculosis were treated in hospitals between 1921 and 1931 but the figures should not be taken to be accurate, for, some hospitals, specially hospitals for females, had kept no tabulated records while some were opened after 1921. At Quetta alone, 626 cases of tuberculosis were treated during this decade. This would give us an incorrect idea of the number of patients met with in Quetta during the summer months if we did not take into account the patients that take refuge in our Capital from other parts of India—especially Sind. Actual numbers are not available but they are not inconsiderable. **Tuberculosis.**

153. The total number of cases of Syphilis treated in all the dispensaries of Baluchistan between 1920 and 1930 was 10,919. This figure I believe is much below the mark. In the first place persons infected by this disease hesitate to disclose their secret. Then there are so many practitioners and *hakims* who specialise in this disease and attract a large number of patients. The patients too, in the first place mostly resort to them and to numerous indigenous and foreign patent medicines in order to escape exposure. It is feared that the actual number of sufferers from this disease has attained alarming proportions in certain local areas. **Syphilis.**

SUBSIDIARY TABLES.

28.—Incidence of Infirmities.

Particulars.	Year of Census.	Number afflicted per 100,000 of Total Population.										
		All infirmities.			*Insane.*		*Deaf-mute.*		*Blind.*		*Leper.*	
		Persons.	Males.	Females.	Males.	Females.	Males.	Females.	Males.	Females.	Males.	Females.
1	2	3	4	5	6	7	8	9	10	11	12	13
				By Locality.								
BALUCHISTAN ..	1911	380	409	343	57	28	103	50	235	260	14	5
	1921	413	438	378	62	40	107	56	252	276	18	7
	1931	316	351	271	60	33	81	49	201	187	8	3
DISTRICTS ..	1911	274	309	227	44	14	93	43	165	167	7	3
	1921	304	325	270	50	30	73	39	193	197	11	4
	1931	273	303	231	51	25	76	38	170	167	7	2
Quetta-Pishin ..	1911	139	172	90	33	2	52	23	86	63	1	2
	1921	115	139	72	21	10	31	8	85	54	2	..
	1931	185	213	145	53	28	62	37	93	82	6	2
Loralai ..	1911	297	342	240	51	19	80	31	191	184	20	6
	1921	390	453	307	83	39	70	28	272	234	30	6
	1931	329	361	288	54	31	44	13	246	241	16	3
Zhob ..	1911	293	322	253	64	23	92	57	161	170	5	3
	1921	364	353	381	63	56	88	74	196	241	6	9
	1931	193	231	137	43	13	75	34	110	87	3	4
Bolan ..	1911	477	201	1,159	67	..	67	..	67	1,159	..	..
	1921	249	172	365	..	..	34	282	137	282	..	..
	1931	85	58	163	..	..	29	82	29	82	..	..
Chagai ..	1911	563	571	553	88	55	220	83	274	401	..	14
	1921	370	395	330	61	12	99	37	236	281	..	..
	1931	479	547	390	66	57	153	48	306	276	22	10
Sibi ..	1911	350	399	284	34	9	133	60	226	213	7	2
	1921	422	452	380	57	36	114	58	267	282	13	4
	1931	333	371	284	50	17	99	54	219	213	4	..
Administered area	1911	404	431	367	38	9	141	54	248	301	6	8
	1921	320	331	305	31	3	86	50	208	246	6	6
	1931	384	394	370	63	26	111	76	214	269	6	..
Mari-Bugti country	1911	221	321	97	26	13	114	71	171	13	10	..
	1921	648	730	540	119	107	180	75	403	358	28	..
	1931	252	334	150	29	4	79	20	226	126	..	..
STATES ..	1911	484	515	447	71	40	114	57	308	344	22	6
	1921	534	578	482	76	49	150	72	325	350	27	10
	1931	365	409	313	72	42	88	60	240	208	10	3
Kalat ..	1911	471	501	437	66	32	95	49	318	349	22	7
	1921	564	604	514	75	48	157	73	345	381	27	12
	1931	355	397	307	67	35	83	52	238	216	10	4
Sarawan ..	1911	450	544	334	117	31	114	32	296	247	17	4
	1921	381	450	294	43	4	174	92	227	197	7	..
	1931	485	650	286	77	62	167	77	392	147	13	..
Jhalawan ..	1911	207	222	189	30	14	66	29	107	125	19	21
	1921	464	533	380	98	47	128	75	250	225	57	33
	1931	328	388	259	129	76	106	93	129	83	23	7
Kachhi ..	1911	612	650	568	62	21	118	66	466	479	4	2
	1921	659	687	624	77	50	239	77	363	497	7	..
	1931	327	320	335	35	8	57	41	226	279	5	6
Dombki-Kaheri country ..	1911	748	768	724	79	28	87	9	602	687	..	..
	1921	1,084	1,110	1,053	85	34	245	11	781	1,008	..	..
	1931	531	536	524	6	16	34	32	495	476	..	..
Makran ..	1911	556	554	557	55	61	93	58	337	435	69	3
	1921	619	634	602	85	94	98	73	404	423	48	12
	1931	317	345	285	47	31	58	13	241	241	..	..
Kharan ..	1911	379	388	370	91	47	74	48	223	275	..	..
	1921	436	464	403	40	16	66	63	351	308	7	16
	1931	342	464	203	96	..	136	55	216	147	16	..
Las Bela ..	1911	560	603	511	104	91	227	105	254	315	18	..
	1921	341	400	274	85	55	104	63	189	156	22	..
	1931	416	475	349	99	78	116	102	251	169	..	..

28.—Incidence of Infirmities—*concluded*.

Particulars.	Year of Census.	Number afflicted per 100,000 of total population.										
		All infirmities.			*Insane.*		*Deaf-mute.*		*Blind.*		*Leper.*	
		Persons.	Males.	Females.	Males.	Females.	Males.	Females.	Males.	Females.	Males.	Females.
1	2	3	4	5	6	7	8	9	10	11	12	13
				By Race.								
Indigenous Muslims ..	1911	399	445	344	60	29	117	53	253	257	15	5
	1921	457	511	392	70	42	124	38	296	284	22	8
	1931	339	391	278	68	35	91	50	223	191	10	3
Baloch ..	1911	468	519	407	55	35	126	60	322	308	16	4
	1921	606	623	585	73	71	120	71	408	438	21	5
	1931	352	394	301	55	27	81	34	252	239	6	..
Brahui ..	1911	322	341	297	62	35	85	64	174	189	20	9
	1921	411	473	332	70	31	135	73	240	208	28	20
	1931	325	385	252	96	54	101	70	172	126	17	3
Pathan ..	1911	280	339	209	57	16	108	34	166	157	8	2
	1921	321	393	233	65	29	86	36	226	164	18	4
	1931	277	345	196	76	30	89	47	167	117	13	2
Lasi ..	1911	572	707	418	148	77	310	70	236	271	13	..
	1921	332	372	286	73	63	105	55	178	166	16	..
	1931	538	619	448	120	99	162	125	325	224	12	..
Jatt ..	1911	625	653	590	37	22	150	81	464	487	2	..
	1921	809	858	690	94	42	259	68	493	580	11	..
	1931	499	526	467	38	9	109	74	377	375	7	9
Sayyid ..	1911	258	345	165	54	10	73	48	218	107	..	..
	1921	276	341	206	66	31	57	21	208	144	9	10
	1931	350	449	249	99	37	126	18	225	194	18	..
Miscellaneous ..	1911	450	490	406	71	30	97	33	287	333	35	10
	1921	334	385	279	53	20	102	49	198	203	32	6
	1931	191	204	176	16	26	39	15	149	131	..	4

29.—Incidence of Infirmities among females.

Particulars.	*Females afflicted per 1,000 afflicted males.*				
	All infirmities.	Insane.	Deaf-mute.	Blind.	Leper.
1	2	3	4	5	6
		By Locality.			
BALUCHISTAN	603	427	470	724	244
DISTRICTS	546	348	363	705	200
Quetta-Pishin	432	333	375	560	200
Loralai	636	462	238	780	125
Zhob	400	200	308	526	1,000
Bolan	1,000	..	1,000	1,000	..
Chagai	547	667	238	690	333
Sibi	603	275	430	766	..
Administered area ..	779	323	527	972	..
Mari-Bugti Country ..	363	111	208	525	..
STATES	656	497	583	741	286
Kalat	657	444	536	769	333
Sarawan	366	667	385	311	..
Jhalawan	570	500	745	548	273
Kachhi	870	200	606	1,023	1,000
Dombki-Kaheri Country ..	833	2,000	800	820	..
Makran	722	588	190	875	..
Kharan	379	..	353	594	..
Las Bela	648	697	769	595	..
		By Race.			
Indigenous Muslims ..	602	434	467	725	225
Baloch	643	412	350	797	143
Brahui	540	463	571	604	143
Pathan	480	329	447	597	167
Lasi	660	750	704	630	..
Jatt	734	188	565	824	1,000
Sayyid	540	400	143	457	..
Miscellaneous	746	1,400	333	761	1,000

CHAPTER VIII.

OCCUPATION.

SECTION I.—SCOPE OF ENQUIRY.

Statistical data. 154. The statistics dealt with in this Chapter are contained in the following Imperial and Subsidiary Tables :—

Imperial Tables X and XI.
Subsidiary Tables 30 to 37.

The Imperial Tables are printed in Part II of this Volume. The Subsidiary Tables will be found at the end of this Chapter.

Scheme of classification of occupations. 155. Before analysing the statistics it is necessary to explain the system on which the occupations have been recorded, and classified in the Imperial Tables. The whole range of occupations returned at the Census has been divided into four classes, subdivided into twelve sub-classes, as shown below :—

Class.	*Sub-class.*
A. Production of Raw Materials ..	I. Exploitation of Animals and Vegetation. II. Exploitation of Minerals.
B. Preparation and supply of material substances.	III. Industry. IV. Transport. V. Trade.
C. Public Administration and Liberal Arts ..	VI. Public Force. VII. Public Administration. VIII. Professions and Liberal Arts.
D. Miscellaneous	IX. Persons living on their income. X. Domestic Service. XI. Insufficiently described occupations. XII. Unproductive.

The sub-classes are divided into 55 Orders which are further sub-divided into 195 Groups. The complete scheme is based on the Bertillon Scheme approved by the International Statistical Institute and adapted to Indian conditions in 1911. The first change in the scheme was made in 1921 when the number of groups was increased from 69 to 191. The second modification took place at the Census of 1931 when the three Orders of Mines, Quarries of hard rocks and salt etc. were amalgamated with the two Orders of Metallic and Non-metallic Minerals and the number of Orders was reduced from 56 to 55. On the other hand the number of groups was raised from 191 to 195 with a reshuffling of groups as shown below :—

1921.	1931.
Group 3.—Agents, Managers of landed estates, clerks, rent collectors etc.	Sub-divided into Groups 2, 3 and 4.
Group 7.—Fruit, flower, vegetable, betelvine, pepper, spices, areca nut, etc., growers.	Groups 9-16.
Group 26.—Cotton spinning. Group 27.—Cotton sizing and weaving.	Combined in Group 43.
Group 31.—Wool carding and spinning. Group 32.—Weaving of woollen blankets. Group 33.—Weaving of woollen carpets.	Combined in Group 46.
Group 34.—Silk spinners. Group 35.—Silk weavers.	Combined in Group 47.
Group 52.—Makers of glass and crystal wares. Group 53.—Makers of glass bangles, glass beads, and necklaces and glass ear studs, etc. Group 54.—Makers of porcelain and crockery.	Combined in Group 65.

Group 75.—Manufacturers of tobacco, opium and ganja.	Group 78. Group 79. Group 80. Separate group assigned to each of these three.
Group 66.—Bakers and biscuit makers. Group 69.—Fish curers. Group 70.—Butter, cheese and ghee makers.	Combined in Group 81.
Group 79.—Other industries pertaining to dress gloves, socks, gaiters, belts, buttons, umbrellas, canes, etc. Group 82.—Other industries connected with the toilet, (tattooers, shampooers, bathhouses etc.)	Combined in Group 87.
Group 85.—Lime burners, cement workers. Group 86.—Excavators, earthworkers and well sinkers. Group 87.—Stone cutters and dressers. Group 88.—Brick layers and masons. Group 89.—Builders, painters, decorators of houses, tilers, plumbers etc. (other than buildings made of bamboo or similar materials).	Combined in Group 90.
Group 94.—Printers, lithographers, engravers, etc. Group 95.—Book-binders and stitchers, envelope-makers etc.	Combined in Group 95.
Group 99.—Makers of bangles or beads or necklaces of other materials than glass and makers of spangles, rosaries, lingams and sacred threads.	Combined in Group 99.
Group 102.—Contractors for the disposal of refuse, dust etc. Group 103.—Sweepers, scavengers.	Combined in Group 100.
Group 105.—Persons (other than labourers) employed in harbours and docks including pilots. Group 108.—Persons (other than labourers) employed on the maintenance of harbours and docks, streams, rivers and canals (including construction). Group 106.— Labourers in harbour works and dock yards. Group 109.—Labourers employed on the construction and maintenance of Harbours, docks, streams, rivers and canals (including construction).	Combined in Group 103.
Group 125.—Trade in Wood.	Divided into four separate Groups : Group 119.—Trade in wood (not firewood). Group 120.—Trade in barks. Group 121.—Trade in bamboos. Group 122.—Trade in thatches and other forest produce.
Group 132.—Grocers and sellers of vegetable oil, salt and other condiments. Group 134.—Sellers of sweetmeats, sugar, gur, and molasses.	Combined in Group 130.
Group 131.—Fish dealers. Group 135.—Cardamom, betel-leaf, vegetables, fruit and areca nut sellers.	Combined in Group 134.
Group 137.—Dealers in tobacco, opium, and ganja.	Divided into three Groups : Group 135.—Dealers in tobacco. Group 136.—Dealers in opium. Group 137.—Dealers in ganja.
Group 181.—Cooks, watercarriers, door-keepers, watchmen, and other in-door servants. Group 182.—Private grooms, coachmen, dog boys, etc.	Combined in Group 187.

Persons employed in theatres and other places of public entertainment, etc. in Group 101, are now classified in Group 183. Saddle-cloth makers in Group 40 of the last Census have been transferred to Embroideries in Group 50 of this Census and Saddle-cloth sellers to Group 117. Witches and Wizards have been transferred from Group 189 (*b*) to Group 181. Group 128 of this Census is a new group for hawkers of drink and food-stuffs.

156. For the purpose of filling up the return of occupation, two sets of instructions had to be issued to enumerators, one for the Regular or **Instructions to Enumerators.**

synchronous areas and Kharan which were censused on the Standard Indian Schedule, and the other for the Tribal Areas in which a modified form of the Standard Schedule was used. The forms of the two schedules with specimen entries are given below*:—

Standard Schedule.

Serial number of house or tenement.	Serial number of person.	Name.	Religion and Sect.	Male or Female.	Married, unmarried or widowed (enter Divorced persons as widowed).	Age (in years to nearest birthday).	Race, Tribe or Caste.	Earner or Dependent.	Principal occupation (this will be blank for dependents).	Subsidiary occupation (occupation of dependents may be given.)	Industry in which employed (for organized employees only).	Birth District (or Country).	Mother language.	Other language in common use.	Whether literate (i.e., able to write and read a letter).	Whether able to read and write English.	Insane, totally blind, Deaf-mute or Leper.
1	2	3	4	5	6	7	8	9	10	11	12	13	14	15	16	17	18
1	1	Anant Ram ..	Hindu (Sanatan)	Male	Married	37	Arora (Chawla)	Earner	Pleader	Landlord (Town property).	..	Rohtak (Punjab)	Urdu	Punjabi, English.	Urdu, English (S.L.C.,	English.)	..
	2	Female (wife of Anant Ram.)	Hindu (Sanatan)	Female	Married	35	Arora (Chawla)	Dependent	..	Embroidery	..	Rawalpindi (Punjab).	Punjabi	Urdu	Urdu (IV Primary)	..	..
	3	Son of Anant Ram.	Hindu (Sanatan)	Male	Unmarried.	12	Arora (Chawla)	Dependent	..	..	..	Rohtak (Punjab)	Punjabi	Urdu	Urdu (IV Primary)	..	..
	4	Daughter of Anant Ram.	Hindu (Sanatan)	Female	Unmarried.	6	Arora (Chawla)	Dependent	..	..	..	Rawalpindi (Punjab).	Punjabi	Urdu	Urdu	..	..

Local Schedule.

Serial No. of household or family.	Name of householder.	House or tent or both.	Race, tribe and caste.	Religion and Sect.	Mother-tongue.	Number of persons in the family. Males. Adults.	Males. Non-Adults.	Females. Adults.	Females. Non-Adults.	Occupation of earners in the family. Principal.	Subsidiary.	Number. Males.	Number. Females.	Dependents. Males.	Dependents. Females.	Industry in which employed.	Subsidiary occupation of dependents shown in columns 15 and 16. Subsidiary occupation.	Number. Males.	Number. Females.	Second language and number of persons in a family who can speak it. Second language.	Number. Males.	Number. Females.	Number of children born. Boys.	Girls.	Number of children who have died. Boys. Adults.	Boys. Non-Adults.	Girls. Adults.	Girls. Non-Adults.	Remarks.
1	2	3	4	5	6	7	8	9	10	11	12	13	14	15	16	17	18	19	20	21	22	23	24	25	26	27	28	29	30
1	Ali Muhammad	House	Belkhel Daulatzai.	Musalman Sunni.	Pashtu	3	2	2	4	Landlord (Non-cultivating).	..	1	..	3	6	..	Field Labour	2	1	Jafarki	3	2	3	5	1	..	1	2	*
										Shepherd.	..	1	..	..	..	..	Mat making	1	1		..	..	..	..	..	..	..	..	
2	Nur Ahmad ..	Tent	Barech Mirozai.	Musalman Sunni.	Pashtu	2	2	3	2	Tenant at will.	Shepherd	2	..	2	5	..	Embroidery	..	2	Brahui	2	1	1	2	..	..	..	1	
3	Turabaz ..	Both	Hasankhel Yusafzai.	Musalman Sunni.	Pashtu	1	3	2	3	Woodcutter and Seller.	Flock owner.	1	1	3	4	..	House-keeping.	..	1	Siraiki	1	1	2	3	..	..	..	..	
4	Yusaf Ali ..	Tent	Zarkhun Jamalzai.	Musalman Sunni.	Pashtu	4	2	1	1	Lorry driver	..	2	..	2	2	..	Field Labour	..	1	Eastern Balochi.	4	1	1	1	..	..	1	..	
										Levies Sowar	..	1	..	..	..														
										Shepherd	..	1	..	..	..														

The necessity for using two different forms arose from the fact that in the Regular Areas the unit of enumeration was the individual, while in the Tribal Areas the unit was the family. The form for the Tribal Areas proved to be extremely cumbersome for, although the unit of enumeration was the family, it was so devised as to facilitate the record of occupation for each individual. But as explained in the following paragraph, it had its advantages.

The following instructions were issued to enumerators for the Regular Areas :—

Columns 9 to 11.—The entry of occupation in Columns 9 to 11 is a matter requiring special care. The first thing is to distinguish between an earner and a dependent. Only those women and children will be entered as "earner" who help to augment the family income by permanent and regular work for which a return is obtained in cash or kind. As a rough and ready rule it may be assumed that boys and girls over the age of 10, who actually do field labour or tend cattle are adding to the family income and should, therefore, be entered in Column 10 as earner or 11 as working dependent according to whether they earn pay or not. Boys at school and college should be shown as dependents, though they may help to pay their own way by private tuition; in this case, "private tuition" will be entered in Column 11 against their names. Dependents who assist in the work of the family and contribute to its support without actually earning wages should be shown as dependents in Column 9 and under Subsidiary occupation in Column 11. Household work done by a woman in her house, will not count as subsidiary occupation. Women and children who are doing no manual work should be entered as "dependents" in Column 9, but not at all in either Column 10 or 11.

Domestic servants must be entered in Column 9 as earners, not dependent, and in Column 10 as cook, bhishti, etc. Persons temporarily out of employ should be shown in Column 9 as earners and in Column 10 as following their previous occupation.

When a man has two occupations, the principal one is that on which he relies mainly for his support and from which he gets the major part of his income. A subsidiary occupation should be entered if followed at any time of the year (whether followed through the year or during a part of it). If a man is a shop-keeper but makes mats in his spare time, the two occupations should be entered in Columns 10 and 11 respectively.

Where a person cultivates part of his land and sublets part, he should be shown in Column 10 as cultivator and in Column 11 as rent receiver, if he gets the greater part of his income from the self-cultivated land, and *vice versa* otherwise. If such a person has several profitable sources of income, as for instance, legal or medical work, etc., then that source from which he derives the greatest part of his income will be entered in Column 10, that source from which he derives the next greatest part of his income in Column 11.

Only one subsidiary occupation (the most important one) should be entered in Column 11. But if the most important one happens to be an agricultural occupation the next most important non-agricultural occupation should be entered.

Persons who have mortgaged their land with possession and derive no profit therefrom are not agriculturists in respect of that land. Agricultural labourers should be distinguished from tenants; the former receive their wages in cash or kind, the latter pay rent (*batai* or cash) to the landlord.

Prisoners should be classed as dependents and shown in Column 9; their occupations should be shown in column 11 as "Convict—rigorous imprisonment," "Convict—simple imprisonment," "Under trial," or "Civil Prisoner" as the case may be. Their previous occupation should not be shown. For patients in hospitals the occupation last followed should be entered in the appropriate Columns.

Stress must be laid on the importance of avoiding vague words like "labour" or "service" or "shop-keeping." The Enumerator must enter the exact kind of labour or service and the nature of goods sold. In the case of clerks, the occupation of their employer must also be shown, *e.g.*, lawyer's clerk, bank-clerk, *Shahukar ka Gumashta*.

Whenever large gangs of coolies are employed on earthwork of any kind, enter not only the word "earth-work," but also the nature of the undertaking (railway, road, canal, etc.), in connection with which it is being done. Pensioners should be shown Civil, Military or Political, as the case may be.

For shop-keepers and traders the nature of the articles sold should be stated. Mortgagees and persons who live mainly on money lent at interest or on stocks, bonds or other securities, such as shares in companies, should be entered as Capitalists (*Shahukars*). Persons who live by the receipt of alms should be recorded as religious mendicants, professional beggars, vagrants, etc., as the case may be.

The same set of instructions was applied to the Tribal Areas supplemented by the following additional instructions -

Columns 11—16. *Occupations of earners in the family and dependents.*—The main occupation by which each working member of the family earns his or her livelihood should be entered in Column 11 ; the occupation with which he or she mainly supplements it should be entered in Column 12. In case the main and supplementary occupation of all earning members is one and the same, the numbers of male and female earners if any should be entered in Columns 13 and 14 and the numbers of such members of the family as are dependent on them should be shown in Columns 15 and 16. (Totals of Columns 13-16 should tally with the totals of Columns 7-10). When, however, the main occupation of one or more earning members of the family is different a separate entry should be made for each such earning member but the dependents of all earning members should be shown together in Columns 15 and 16.

A glance at the specimen forms given above will show that the Census of 1931 went a step beyond its predecessors in so far as it enabled us to ascertain in the Tribal Areas the occupations of each and every worker whether male or female instead of assuming, as at earlier censuses, that the occupation of all adult male members was the same as that of the head of the family and that all non-adult male and female members and adult females were dependents excepting those female workers who represented separate family units by themselves. This change, by the way, strengthens the impression that there should be little difficulty in extending the Standard Schedule at future censuses in full detail to the Tribal Areas in Baluchistan, the Column of name being altered to " Name of male house-holder and sex of others ".

Value of the Statistics.

157. The occupation returns are admittedly the most complicated and troublesome at every stage of the operations. At the Enumeration stage the chief difficulties centered round the definition of Earners. Working and Non-working dependents and the Subsidiary occupations. At earlier censuses, the population was classified as " Actual Workers " and " Dependents ". No distinction was made between " Earners " and " Working dependents ". The subtle distinction between Workers and Dependents of earlier censuses was further complicated in 1931 by the division of Workers into Earners and Working dependents while multiple occupations presented conundrums which pretty well exercised the ingenuity as well as patience of both the part time, rushed enumerator and the reluctant victim of his searching, inconvenient enquiries. In the Tribal Areas, a tribesman at different times of the year is a

1. cultivating owner ;
2. tenant ;
3. field labourer :
4. Railway cooley ,
5. dwarf palm leaves seller ;
6. Levy sowar or footman etc. etc

Or if he has no agricultural land, he is a

1. flock owner :
2. porter :
3. mason's cooley on private construction work ;
4. mason's cooley in the Public Works Department ;
5. wood chopper ;
6. well sinker ;
7. field labourer ;
8. road cooley ;
9. brick-layer's cooley ;
10. Shop-keeper's chowkidar and so on.

His occupation changes almost from day to day.

Again take the case of the few shop-keepers who are scattered all over the Tribal Areas in small numbers. A shop-keeper sells

1. Atta, dal, ghee, spices, parched grains, country made sweats ;
2. cotton and silk and woollen cloth ;
3. petrol, drugs and dyes .
4. tobacco ;
5. ready-made clothes, boots and shoes ;
6. bangles ;
7. stationery ;
8. spirituous liquors.

And to add to the perplexities of the Enumerator. he is also a money-lender, a dealer in grains and wool.

It required considerable insight on the part of the Enumerator to pick out the principal, the dependent and the subsidiary occupations in each and every case. His difficulties were manifold but fortunately they were perhaps not so formidable as in other Provinces.

At the classification stage greater care had to be exercised in order to correct enumerators' mistakes and to classify the occupations correctly. All enumeration books on receipt in the Tabulation office were examined one by one personally by my able Assistant Superintendent for Tabulation and the entries were corrected or amplified where necessary by reference to the enumerators. No subordinate official was allowed to make any alterations in the schedules. The entries were classified on the following general principles :—

(1) Where a person both makes and sells, he is classified under the manufacturing or industrial head, the commercial one being reserved for trade pure and simple. On the same principle, where a person extracts some substance (such as salt-petre) from the ground and also refines it, he is shown under the mining and not under the industrial head.

(2) Industrial and trading occupations are divided into two main categories :—

(*a*) those where the occupation is classified according to the material worked in, and

(*b*) those where it is classified according to the use it serves.

Ordinarily, the first category is reserved for the manufacture or sale of articles the use of which is not finally determined, but it also includes that of specified articles for which there is no appropriate head in the second category. Thus, while shoe-making (Group 82) is classed with other industries of dress and toilet, the manufacture of certain leather articles such as water-bags, saddlery, etc., would fall within Group 51, " working in leather ".

(3) As a general rule, wherever a man's personal occupation is one which involves special training, *e.g.*, that of a doctor, engineer surveyor, etc., he is classed under the head reserved for that occupation. Thus a railway doctor is shown as a doctor and not as a railway employee. Only those Government servants are shown in Group 159 (Service of the State) who are engaged in general administration. Officers of the medical, irrigation. forest, post office and other similar services are classed under the special heads provided for these occupations.

Further doubtful points were cleared by occasional references to the Census Commissioner. When the working sheets were ready for Tahsils and divisions of States, the classification was marked on the sheets by the Tabulation Assistant Superintendent. A very reasonable degree of accuracy was thus achieved, and the occupation statistics here discussed may be accepted as representing such normal functional distribution of the population of Baluchistan as may be expected from an inquiry conducted through the Census agency.

Changes in the nature of the Occupational Census.

158. Before proceeding further it will be interesting to note the difference in the nature of the inquiry undertaken in 1931 in relation to earlier censuses. At the 1911 and 1921 censuses the occupation census was confined to the enumeration of—

(1) Actual workers (males and females, separately),
(2) Dependents on each occupation,
(3) Partially agriculturists in each occupation,

At the Census of 1931, the enquiry was intended to ascertain the numbers of—

(1) Earners (males and females separately),
(2) Working dependents (males and females separately),
(3) Non-working dependents,
(4) Subsidiary occupations of earners.

Thus the " actual workers " of 1911 and 1921 were split up in 1931 into Earners and Working dependents. All male and female workers who were in receipt of a definite wage in cash or kind were, as explained above, classed as earners while all other members of a family who actually helped to augment the family income but were not paid for the work they did were relegated to the category of working dependents. The remainder were all classed as non-working

Diagram No. 13.

DISTRIBUTION OF POPULATION BY MALE AND FEMALE WORKERS AND DEPENDENTS FOR 1911, 1921 & 1931.

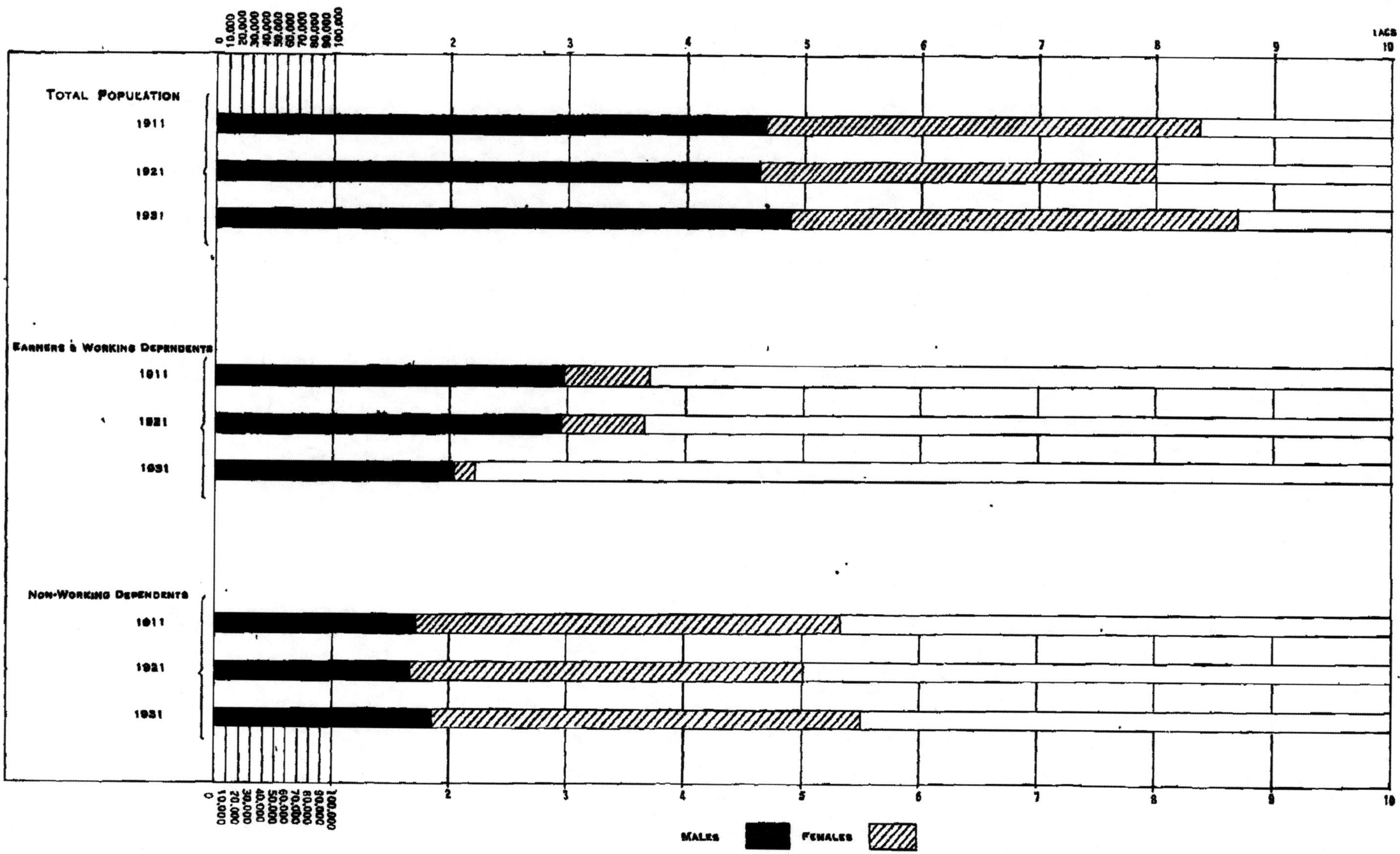

dependents. The occupation census of 1931 has thus lost by the change of definition a considerable number of persons of both sexes who were classed as "Actual Workers" in 1911 and 1921. This is an important point to remember when studying comparative statistics. In the following paragraphs, working dependents for 1931 have for facility of comparison been amalgamated with earners and compared with Actual Workers of earlier censuses. The other variations in the terms of the inquiry in 1931 are that in 1911 and 1921 the numbers of dependents were ascertained and recorded in the tables for each occupation on which they were dependent. But the numbers of males and females were not recorded separately. In 1931, the numbers of dependents (non-working) were not recorded for each occupation on which they were dependent but their numbers were tabulated for both males and females for the Province as a whole, by Districts and States, and by race and tribe. As regards the subsidiary occupations, agriculture was the only subsidiary occupation for which numbers were shown in the tables for 1911 and 1921. In 1931, however, all subsidiary occupations were ascertained and were shown in the tables separately under each occupational Group for both males and females.

SECTION II.—GENERAL REVIEW OF OCCUPATIONAL DISTRIBUTION.

(a) NUMBERS OF WORKERS AND DEPENDENTS.

159. With the above explanatory remarks, we can proceed to examine the occupational distribution of the population. In a total population of 868,617 in 1931, there were— **Working and non-working population.**

	Persons.	*Males.*	*Females.*
Earners	296,985	292,246	4,739
Working dependents	22,297	10,882	11,415
Non-working dependents ..	549,335	185,286	364,049

That is to say in every 1,000 of the population there were 342 earners, 26 working dependents and 632 non-working dependents composed of males and females in the following proportions :—

	Per 1,000 of total population.		
	Total.	Males.	Females.
Earners	342	336	6
Working dependents	26	13	13
Non-working dependents ..	632	213	419

As there is no record of working dependents for earlier censuses, the figures for 1931 are not comparable with those for 1921 and 1911. Taking the figures of earners plus working dependents of 1931 roughly to correspond with the Actual Workers of earlier censuses, the numbers of workers are compared in the margin for three Censuses and illustrated in Diagram No. 13.

	1931.	1921.	1911.
TOTAL POPULATION	868,617	799,625	834,703
Earners and working dependents ..	319,282	301,990	303,264
Non-working dependents ..	549,335	497,635	531,439

In every 1,000 of the total population there were 363 workers in 1911. The proportion rose to 378 in 1921 and fell to 368 in 1931, indicating a decrease of 10 in comparison to that of 1921. I can find no other satisfactory explanation than attributing it to the decrease of about 30,000 in 1921 and an increase of over 40,000 in 1931 in the total female population which resulted in lowering the proportion of dependents in 1921 and raising it in 1931, causing corresponding disturbances in the proportions of workers in the two inter-censal periods. Eliminating the abnormal Census year 1921, we find an increase of over five in the proportion of workers compared to 1911 which is not unsatisfactory for a Province whose industrial development is in its infancy and whose economic conditions do not permit of rapid advancement.

Numbers of workers and dependents by sex.

160. The total numbers of earners, working dependents and non-working dependents by sex are shown in the margin. We have just seen that in every 1,000 persons in Baluchistan in 1931, there were 342 earners, 26 working dependents and 632 non-working dependents. Among the 342 earners, there were 336 males and 6 females. The 26 working dependents were equally divided among males and females, while to the 632 non-working dependents, the males contributed one third of the drones and females two-thirds. Of the 342 earners 272 are accounted for by the indigenous, 11 by the semi-indigenous and 59 by the alien inhabitants, while 25 out of the 26 working dependents are claimed by the indigenous population alone.

	Total.	Males.	Females.
TOTAL POPULATION	868,617	488,414	380,203
Earners ..	296,985	292,246	4,739
Working dependents ..	22,297	10,882	11,415
Non-working dependents ..	549,335	185,286	364,049

Indigenous earners and dependents.

161. The marginal statement gives comparative figures of earners and dependents for each of the above three communities for 1921 and 1931. Indigenous earners have increased since 1921 by 9, semi-indigenous by 17 while the aliens have decreased by 9 per cent. The non-working dependents are distributed as under:—

	Workers (including working dependents).		*Dependents.*	
	1931.	1921.	1931.	1921.
TOTAL ..	319,282	301,990	549,335	497,635
Indigenous ..	257,594	237,007	502,530	466,937
Semi-indigenous ..	9,753	8,304	12,169	10,354
Alien ..	51,935	56,679	34,636	20,344

Total non-working dependents per 1,000 of total population ..	632
Indigenous	578
Semi-indigenous	14
Alien	40

Taking each class separately the highest proportion is found among the semi-indigenous who have 445 earners in every 1,000 of their total numerical strength. Next come the aliens with 400. The indigenous come last with only 339 earners but 661 dependents or 61 and 96 per 1,000 more than the other two communities. The effects of the increase of female population in 1931 are reflected in the high proportion of dependents among the indigenous inhabitants in 1931.

The following table gives comparative proportional figures for Baluchistan and other parts of India :—

WORKERS AND DEPENDENTS PER 1,000 OF TOTAL POPULATION.

Province or State.	*Earners.*		*Working-Dependents.*		*Non-working Dependents.*	
	Males.	Females.	Males.	Females.	Males.	Females.
Baluchistan	336	6	13	13	213	419
N.-W. F. Province	304	10	30	10	209	437
Punjab	280	19	36	33	230	402
Delhi	348	30	16	28	217	361
United Provinces	331	87	11	58	183	330
Travancore	219	71	32	115	252	275
Central Provinces and Berar	284	135	29	80	187	285
Rajputana	308	67	35	118	181	291
Ajmere-Merwara	314	56	29	125	185	291
Bihar and Orissa	282	118	7	9	209	375
Assam	274	61	46	71	203	345
Mysore	295	63	19	78	197	348
Central India Agency	315	151	18	27	180	309
Bombay	265	62	24	38	235	373
Burma	258	97	32	37	220	356
Bengal	244	31	6	7	270	442
Cochin	259	129	6	116	224	266
Hyderabad	225	108	68	69	217	313
Kashmir	206	15	61	245	265	208

Baluchistan enjoys the distinction of occupying the two extreme points in the field of functional distribution, the highest in India in respect of its male earners excepting the Delhi province ; and the lowest in respect of its females. The position of the male earners cannot be challenged but as regards the females, the figures should be taken with a pinch of salt. At first sight it is an enviable

Diagram No. 12.

EARNERS, WORKING DEPENDENTS AND NON-WORKING DEPENDENTS IN EVERY 1,000 OF TOTAL POPULATION OF EACH LOCALITY.

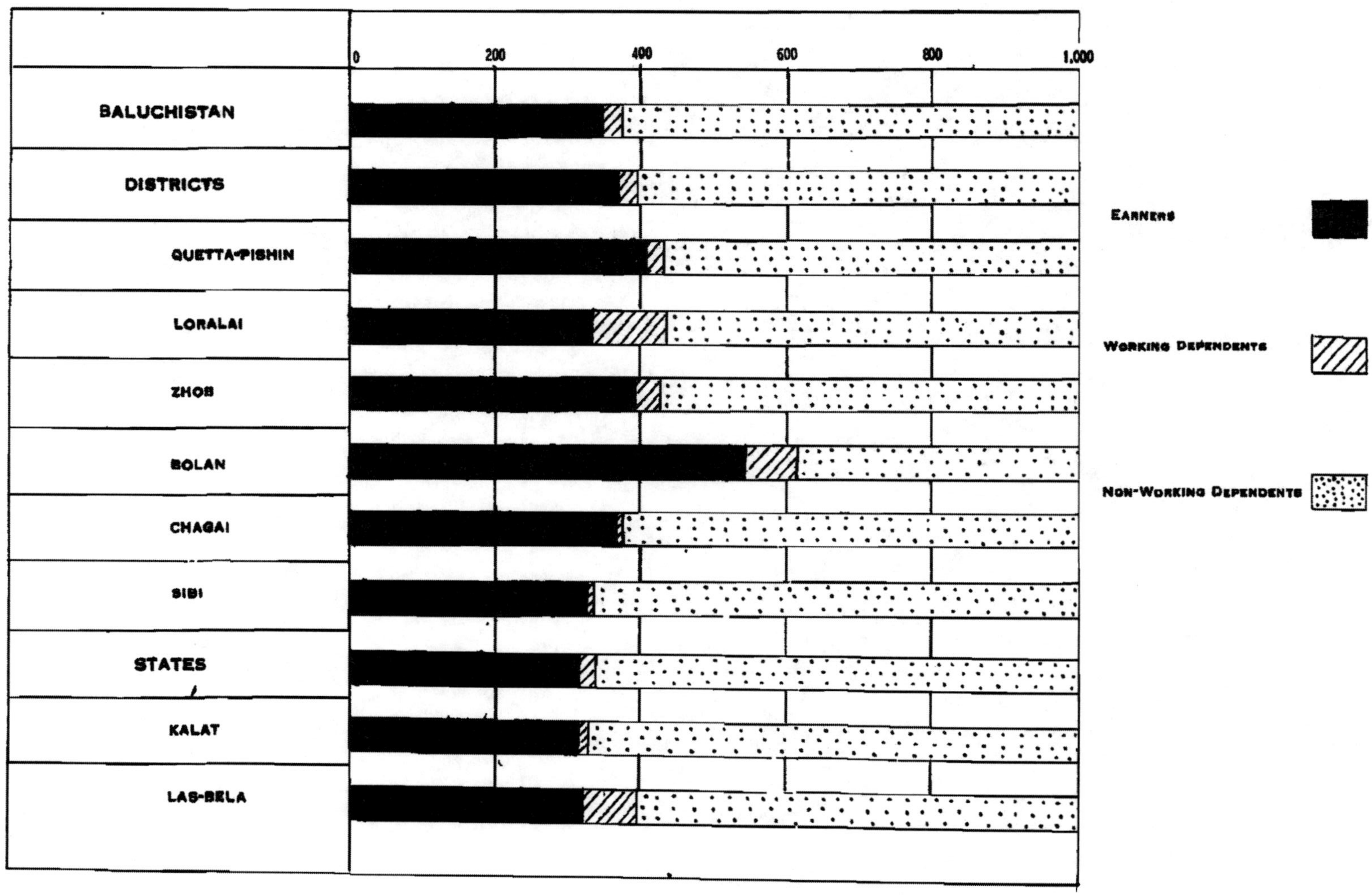

Diagram No. 13.

PERCENTAGE OF WORKERS IN EACH SUB-CLASS OF OCCUPATION FOLLOWED BY INDIGENOUS, SEMI-INDIGENOUS AND ALIEN INHABITANTS.

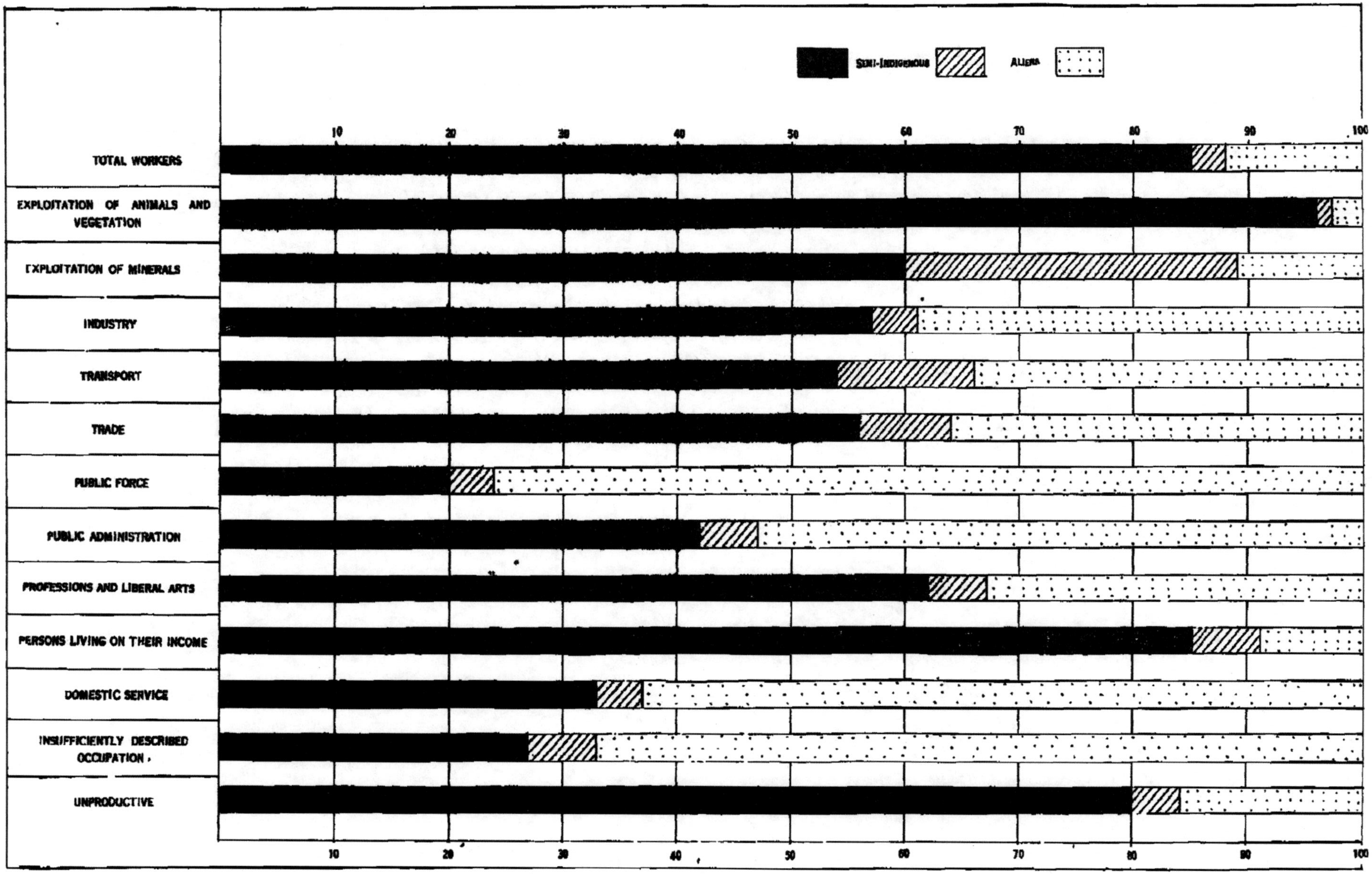

picture of most comfortable life for the females of Baluchistan compared to their Indian sisters. In fact, however, here the statistics have failed to do justice to the womenfolk of the province whose unenviable lot is depicted by Sir Denys Bray in the following extract from his Census Report for 1911.

In treating all children, whether girls or boys, as dependents on the main occupation of the head of the family, we can hardly have gone far wrong. In treating all women, in the self-same way, we have at any rate faithfully reflected economic conditions, not indeed as they actually are, but as they present themselves to the minds of the tribesmen at large. Speaking broadly—for in certain parts of the country where the tribal system is breaking up, conditions are a little different—a tribeswoman remains in a state of tutelage her whole life long: as a child she is subject to her father, as a married woman to her husband, as a widow to the heirs of one or the other. In theory she has no occupation at all: she is a mere dependent on the family into which she was born or into which she has married. In actual fact she is one of the hardest workers in the family, though most of her work is household drudgery and other lowly labour that a tribesman considers beneath his dignity. It is, for instance, the man himself who ploughs the land, sows the seed and waters the crops; the woman helps in the reaping and threshing, and grinds the daily corn. In a nomad family it is the man who sees to the breeding and shearing of his flocks; the woman pitches the tent, does the milking and the churning and the like, and often enough has to take flocks out to graze. And everywhere she is the hewer of wood and the drawer of water. But to treat her as a farmer in the one case or as a grazier in the other would be to do violence to the deep-rooted prejudices of the tribesmen regarding the position and functions of the sex.

The picture drawn in 1911 needs no retouching even after the lapse of 20 years. Were it possible to give the females their due share in the allocation of occupations, the proportion of our *dhobis*, cooks, flour-grinders, agricultural labourers, felt-makers, embroiders and midwives would have been staggeringly high. But presumably this applies to all areas where society is in a primitive state and living precarious.

Distribution of workers by locality.

162. The proportional distribution of workers (earners including working dependents of 1931 for facility of comparison) and dependents by Districts and States is shown in the margin for three censuses. It will be observed that workers have increased in the Districts by one but have decreased in the States by an equal number compared to 1911, Compared to 1921 however, both Districts and States show decreases of two and one respectively in every 1,000 of their respective populations.

PROPORTION PER 100 OF POPULATION OF EACH UNIT.

Districts and States.	1931.		1921.		1911.	
	Workers.	Dependents.	Workers.	Dependents.	Workers.	Dependents.
BALUCHISTAN	37	63	38	62	36	64
DISTRICTS ..	39	61	41	59	38	62
Quetta-Pishin ..	43	57	46	54	40	60
Loralai ..	42	58	35	65	35	65
Zhob ..	42	58	42	58	37	63
Bolan ..	62	38	73	27	61	39
Chagai ..	36	64	42	58	35	65
Sibi ..	33	67	37	63	37	63
STATES ..	34	66	35	65	35	65
Kalat ..	32	68	35	65	35	65
Las Bela ..	40	60	32	68	35	65

(b) MAIN OCCUPATIONS OF WORKERS AND THEIR NUMBERS IN EACH OCCUPATION.

Main occupations of workers.

163. A glance at the marginal table will give an idea of the functional distribution of earners and working dependents by the four main Classes of occupations for each of the three main groups. 68 per cent. of the earners are employed

PROPORTIONS OF EARNERS AND WORKING DEPENDENTS IN EACH CLASS PER 1,000 OF TOTAL POPULATION OF PROVINCE AMONG INDIGENOUS, SEMI-INDIGENOUS AND ALIEN INHABITANTS.

Classes.	Earners.	Working-Dependents.	Classes.	Earners.	Working Dependent.
Total all Classes ..	342	26	C. Public Administration and Liberal Arts	40	..
Indigenous ..	272	25	Indigenous ..	11	..
Semi-indigenous ..	11	1	Semi-indigenous ..	2	..
Alien ..	59		Alien ..	27	..
A. Production of raw-materials	231	118	D. Miscellaneous ..	13	1
Indigenous ..	225	17	Indigenous ..	6	..
Semi-indigenous ..	4	1	Alien ..	7	1
Alien ..	2				
B. Preparation and supply of material substances	58	7			
Indigenous ..	30	7			
Semi-indigenous ..	5	..			
Alien ..	23	..			

in the Production of raw materials, 17 in the Preparation and Supply of material substances, 12 in Public Administration and Liberal Arts and 3 in Miscellaneous professions. The indigenous inhabitants preponderate in Class A.—Agricultural and allied pursuits, their percentage being 97 with a small margin of only three per cent. for the semi-indigenous and aliens. In Class B.—Industry, Transport and Trade they contribute 52, the semi-indigenous 9 and the alien 39 per cent. of the total earners. The aliens preponderate in Class C.—Public Force, Public Administration and Professions and Liberal Arts, the percentages being Aliens 68 ; Indigenous 27 ; and Semi-indigenous 5. In Class D.—Domestic Service and Unproductive occupations, the indigenous inhabitants contribute 46 and aliens 54 per cent. These percentages have been calculated on the total number of earners in each Class.

Working Dependents.

164. The working dependents at the Census of 1931 numbered only 26 per 1,000 of total population. Of these 25 are contributed by the indigenous inhabitants and one is shared equally by the semi-indigenous and alien population. 18 are employed in Agricultural pursuits, seven in the Preparation and Supply of material substances and one only in Miscellaneous occupations. The percentage of working dependents to earners in each Sub-Class is indicated in the margin. For every 100 earners there are eight working dependents. The largest number of working dependents is found in Sub-Class I, but the highest proportion per cent. of total earners in each Class goes to Industry. The 439 working dependents under XII—Unproductive are all inmates of Jails.

Sub-Class.	Total carners.	Total working dependents.	Proportion of working dependents to 100 earners.
ALL OCCUPATIONS ..	296,985	22,297	8
I.—Exploitation of animals and vegetation ..	199,924	15,570	8
II.—Exploitation of Minerals ..	548	..	..
III.—Industry ..	19,461	5,934	30
IV.—Transport ..	17,801	163	1
V.—Trade ..	13,438	144	1
VI.—Public Force ..	25,858	..	..
VII.—Public Administration ..	3,694	..	..
VIII.—Professions and Liberal Arts ..	4,506	10	..
IX.—Persons living on their income ..	886	..	..
X.—Domestic Service ..	7,487	..	..
XI.—Insufficiently described occupations	887	3	1
XII.—Unproductive ..	2,495	473	19

Variation since 1921.

165. Variations since 1921 in the more important occupations selected for purposes of comparison with earlier censuses are exhibited in the margin. Agriculture and its allied occupations and Pasture have increased by three per cent. This is due to increase of population and partly to more favourable economic conditions during the last decade. Industry has increased by one per cent. while Transport, Trade, Arts and Professions and other miscellaneous occupations have remained practically stationary. Mechanical Transport has revolutionized the mode of transport and the numbers under this head ought to have shown an appreciable increase but for the fact that one motor lorry displaces at least half a dozen pack animal drivers within its beat. Administration and Domestic Service have gone down by two and three per cent. respectively. Retrenchment of establishments is responsible for the decrease in the former and abolition of slavery in the latter. Before 1927 when slavery was abolished, slaves were treated as servile dependents and classed as domestic servants. At the Census of 1931 they were free and were classed according to their actual means of livelihood.

Occupations.	Distribution of occupations. Workers (actual occupation).		Percentage of earners of each class to total earners.	
	1921.	1931.	1921.	1931.
TOTAL ..	301,990	319,282	100	100
Agriculture ..	172,746	183,700	57	57
Pasture ..	18,630	27,751	6	9
Industry ..	15,861	25,395	5	7
Transport ..	22,307	17,964	7	7
Trade ..	12,523	13,582	4	4
Administration ..	33,625	29,552	12	10
Arts and Professions ..	4,138	4,516	2	2
Domestic Service ..	16,055	7,487	5	2
Others ..	6,105	9,335	2	2

Subsidiary Occupations.

166. A subsidiary occupation means a secondary occupation followed continuously or intermittently by a person to augment the income derived from his principal means of livelihood. The instructions to enumerators were that where a man had more than one occupation, the one forming the primary means

Diagram No. 16.

RELATIVE PROPORTION OF OCCUPATIONS OF WORKING POPULATION IN 1921 AND 1931.

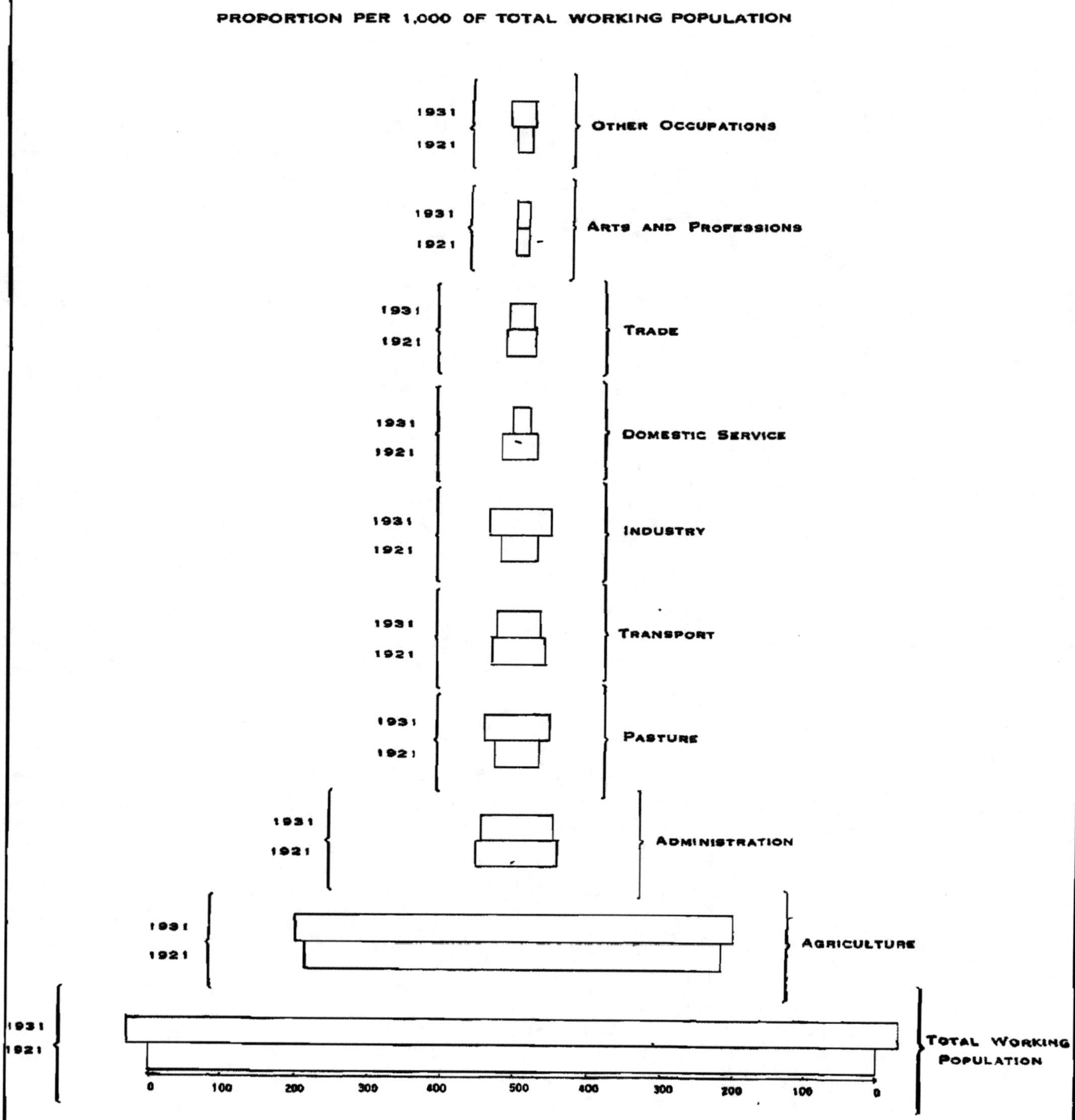

of subsistence should be recorded as the principal occupation and the other as subsidiary. Where there were more subsidiary occupations than one, the enumerator was asked to record the most lucrative, but if one of them was an agricultural one, the instructions were to enter the non-agricultural occupation. The accuracy of the return largely depends on the energy, ingenuity and personal knowledge of the enumerator. His difficulties are manifold. Firstly, rush of work or other causes may incline him to slackness resulting in the omission of entries in the column of subsidiary occupation which it is difficult for the supervising staff to detect. Secondly, if he is energetic and persistent, he may fail to elicit answers from persons inclined to intentional concealment. To my personal knowledge a fairly considerable number of gentlemen thought that their safety lay in following the time-honoured truth "Speech is silver, silence is gold." In spite of my repeated assurances that Census records are confidential and that the disclosure of such innocent and legitimate sources of auxiliary income as they possessed was absolutely harmless, they appear to have given preference to golden silence, for to my disappointment, I found at a later stage that all my efforts to convince them had fallen on deaf ears. The enumerator had to face another difficulty when he came to choose one subsidiary occupation from amongst many—a task which baffled even the person concerned with all his intimate personal knowledge to make the right selection. Take for instance the case of the indigenous agriculturist. As already explained, he is constantly flitting from agricultural to non-agricultural occupations almost from month to month in the course of the year. The following statement, however, shows that out of a total of 73,307 persons in the Province following subsidiary occupations, 50,241 were those following agriculture as their principal occupation :—

SUBSIDIARY OCCUPATIONS OF AGRICULTURISTS.

Occupation.	Total principal occupation.	Those returning subsidiary occupations.											
		I. Agriculture.	II. Minerals.	III. Industry.	IV. Transport.	V. Trade.	VI. Public Force.	VII. Public Administration.	VIII. Professions and Arts.	IX. Persons living on their income.	X. Domestic Service.	XI. Insufficiently described occupations.	XII. Unproductive.
1. Rent receivers (Non-cultivating owners) ..	11,513	1,196	..	251	152	171	5	92	166	107	29	21	48
2. Rent payers (cultivating owners). ..	104,559	29,661	7	845	1,872	6,364	127	307	476	367	70	160	155
3. Tenants-cultivators. ..	50,915	5,602	5	494	384	158	..	16	114	74	127	13	233
4. Agricultural labourers ..	6,002	329	..	16	26	..	..	7	3	7	..	1	13
5. Agents, managers of landed estates	9	..	..	..	..	..	..	..	..	..	..	..	..
Total ..	172,998	36,778	12	1,606	2,434	6,663	132	422	759	555	226	195	449

Of these 50,241, agricultural subsidiary occupations alone claim 36,788 while another 9,097 goes to camel transport and trade in camels leaving a balance of only about 5,000 for all other subsidiary occupations and this in spite of instructions to record a non-agricultural occupation in the case of multiple occupations one of which was agricultural. The results are manifestly disappointing. Nevertheless, I give in the following table such statistics as have been collected. They furnish at least some indication, though very meagre, of the directions in which the trend of economic advancement lies in these days.

NUMBER PER MILLE OF WORKING POPULATION.

	Earners (principal occupation only) and working dependents.	*Earners (principal and subsidiary occupations) and working dependents.*
ALL OCCUPATIONS	1,000	1,229
I.—Exploitation of animals and vegetation	675	849
II.—Exploitation of Minerals	1	2
III.—Industry	80	86
IV.—Transport	56	69
V.—Trade	42	68
VI.—Public Force	82	82
VII.—Public Administration	11	13
VIII.—Professions and Liberal Arts ..	15	18
IX.—Persons living on their income ..	3	5
X.—Domestic Service	24	24
XI.—Insufficiently described occupations ..	3	3
XII.—Unproductive	8	10

In every 1,000 earners (including working dependents) there are 229 persons who add to their income by devoting part of their time to auxiliary occupations in addition to their principal means of livelihood. These 229 persons are distributed among the various occupations as under :—

I.—Exploitation of animals and vegetation	174
II.—Exploitation of Minerals	1
III.—Industry	6
IV.—Transport	13
V.—Trade	26
VI.—Public Force	
VII.—Public Administration	2
VIII.—Professions and Liberal Arts	3
IX.—Persons living on their income	2
X.—Domestic Service	
XI.—Insufficiently described occupations	
XII.—Unproductive	2

The figures speak for themselves.

Occupations of females.

167. Among the 488,414 males and 380,203 females in the Province there were 292,246 male and 4,739 female earners; 10,882 male and 11,415 female working dependents; and 185,286 male and 364,049 female non-working dependents. Thus in every 1,000 of the population, there were 336 male and six female earners. Subsidiary Table 32 at the end of this chapter gives actual numbers and proportions of male and female earners in each Order and in some of the more important groups, the groups selected being those in which the number of female earners is comparatively large or their proportion is high.

It will be interesting to study the occupational distribution of female earners and working dependents by race in the following detailed table :—

Sub-Class.	BALOCH.		BRAHUI.		PATHAN.		LASI.		JATT.		SAYYID.		OTHER-MUSLIM.		HINDU.	
	Earners.	Working Dependents.	Earners.	Working Dependents.	Earners.	Working Dependents.	Earners.	Working Dependents.	Earners.	Working Dependents.	Earners.	Working Dependents.	Earners.	Working Dependents.	Earners.	Working Dependents.
TOTAL ..	1,234	4,830	474	1,395	417	2,017	163	717	331	922	57	550	683	281	141	123
I.—Exploitation of animals and vegetation ..	189	3,791	81	46	190	921	59	230	30	..	19	212	97	13	6	..
II.—Minerals ..	..	..	..	..	..	..	..	..	..	..	..	..	..	..	..	..
III.—Industry ..	849	1,030	270	1,348	33	1,087	72	482	196	922	6	338	390	268	64	123
IV.—Transport ..	18	6	59	1	29	1	..	..	17	..	16	..	30	..	50	..
V.—Trade ..	2	1	2	..	3	..	2	5	1	..	1	..	17	..	5	..
VI.—Public Force ..	..	..	..	..	..	..	..	..	..	..	..	..	..	..	..	..
VII.—Public Administration ..	..	..	..	..	..	..	..	..	..	..	..	..	..	..	..	..
VIII.—Professions and Liberal Arts ..	6	2	2	..	4	7	..	..	24	..	5	..	18	..	1	..
IX.—Persons living on their income ..	13	..	1	..	2	..	..	..	1	..	..	..	..	..	5	..
X.—Domestic Service ..	32	..	26	..	14	..	27	..	23	..	..	..	94	..	3	..
XI.—Insufficiently described occupations ..	..	..	..	..	..	..	..	..	..	..	..	..	..	..	..	..
XII.—Unproductive ..	125	..	33	..	142	1	3	..	39	..	10	..	37	..	7	..

Diagram No. 17.

OCCUPATIONS FOLLOWED BY WORKING POPULATION OF BALUCHISTAN

(PROPORTION PER CENT)

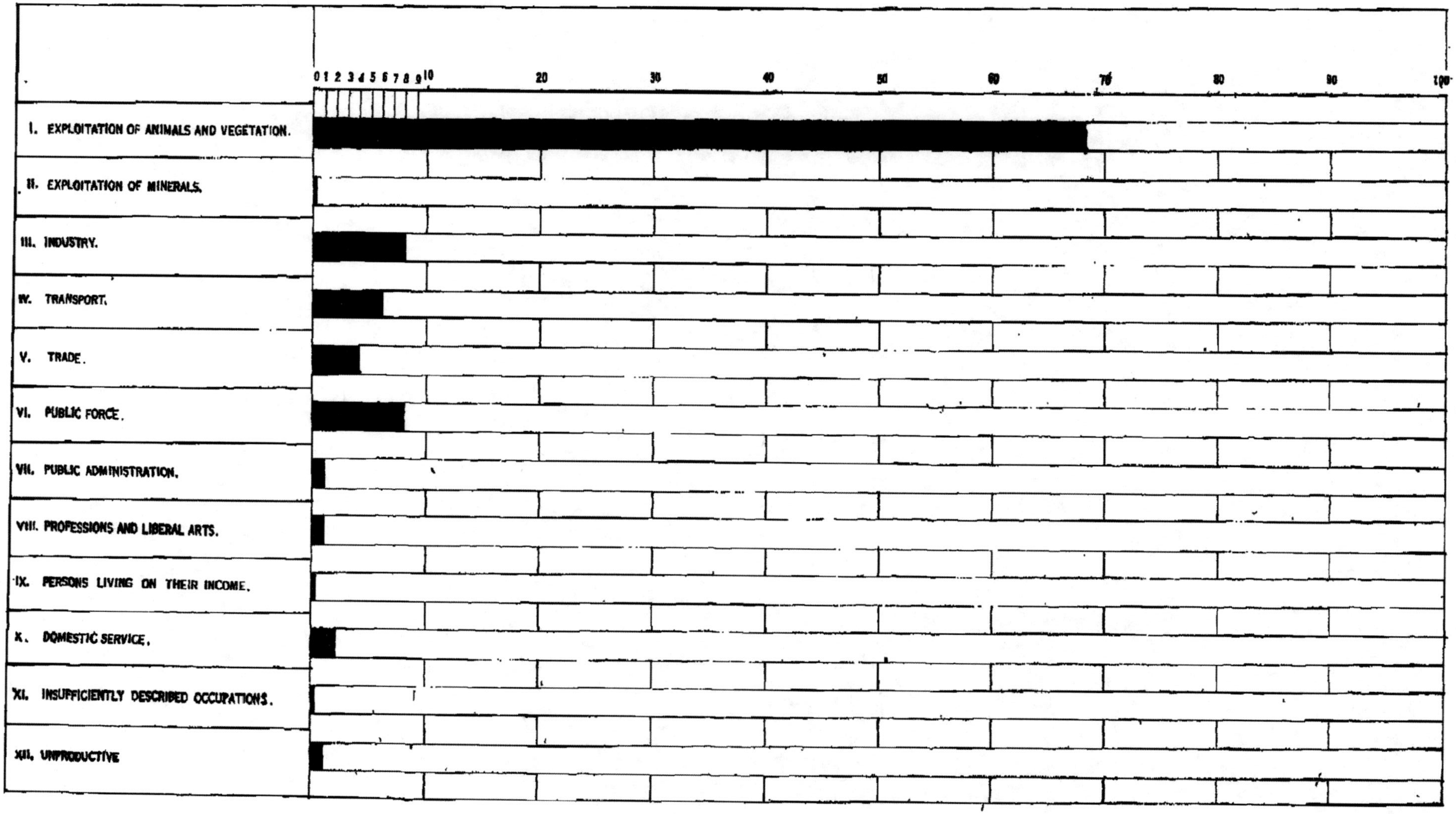

To the 4,739 female earners and 11,415 female working dependents, the indigenous and semi-indigenous inhabitants contribute 77 and 98 per cent. respectively. The distribution of these earners and working dependents in the indigenous races is compared in the margin with the "Actual workers" for 1921. The numbers of female earners have increased since 1921 in each race excepting "Other Muslims." This is accounted for largely by the abolition of slavery in 1927. At previous censuses slaves were classed as servile dependents and were lumped with domestic servants. In 1931 slaves were free and their actual means of livelihood were shown under the occupational groups concerned.

	FEMALE EARNERS.		
	1931.		1921.
	Earners.	Working Dependents.	Actual Workers.
INDIGENOUS ..	3,500	10,835	6,248
Baloch ..	1,234	4,830	117
Brahui ..	474	1,395	60
Pathan ..	417	2,017	69
Lasi ..	163	717	38
Jatt ..	331	922	10
Sayyid ..	57	350	20
Other Muslims ..	683	281	5,878
Hindu ..	141	123	50
SEMI-INDIGENOUS	150	308	33
Baloch ..	2	149	..
Pathan ..	142	159	21
Others ..	6	..	12

Twenty-eight per cent. of the earning females are employed as makers of baskets and mats of dwarf palm leaves, 10 per cent. as beggars and eight per cent. as scavengers. There are six per cent. earning females in each of the three groups—

Miscellaneous Domestic Service,
Non-cultivating proprietors, and
Porters and messengers,

and 4 per cent. in each of the following four groups:—

Midwives and nurses, etc.,
Agricultural labourers,
Rice pounders and flour grinders, etc., and
Wool-carding, spinning and weaving.

This distribution leaves 20 per cent. of female earners who are employed in other minor occupations. The chief occupations in which the 11,415 female working dependents help the male earners are—

		Percentage of female working dependents in each occupation followed.
1.	Agricultural labourers	43
2.	Makers of baskets and mats of dwarf palm leaves, etc.	22
3.	Tailors, milliners, etc.	13
4.	Wool carding, spinning and weaving	11
5.	Other occupations	11

SECTION III.—DETAILS OF CERTAIN IMPORTANT PRINCIPAL OCCUPATIONS.

Sub-Class I.—Exploitation of animals and vegetation. Agriculture.

168. This sub-class is divided into two Orders namely, Order 1—Pasture and Agriculture; Order 2—Fishing and hunting. Agriculture includes non-cultivating proprietors taking rent in money or kind; Estate agents, rent collectors; cultivating owners, tenants; agricultural labourers; market gardeners, flower and fruit growers; and forestry, the latter including forest employees, wood cutters and charcoal burners, and collectors of forest produce. Out of a total working population of 319,282 persons, no less than 185,468 or 58 per cent. are employed in one or other of the agricultural occupations enumerated above. The numbers represented by each of these groups in 1921 and 1931 are shown in the marginal table. It will be obserevd that there is an all round increase owing evidently to better economic conditions prevailing during the decade under review. The only exception is the group "Non-cultivating proprietors" which shows a decrease of 38 per cent. due mainly to economic pressure which has turned some

	1921.	1931.	
	Actual workers.	Earners and working-dependents.	Variations.
AGRICULTURE ..	172,746	185,468	+12,722
Non-cultivating proprietors ..	18,719	11,513	—7,206
Cultivating owners ..	152,593	104,559	+2,973
Tenants cultivators ..		51,007	
Estate agents and managers of owners and Government as well as rent collectors, etc. ..	8	26	+18
Agricultural labourers ..	617	16,595	+15,978
Market gardeners, etc. ..	766	873	+107
Forestry, etc. ..	43	895	+852

of the non-cultivating proprietors into cultivating owners, or has forced them into other channels to look for more lucrative means of livelihood throwing agricultural proprietorship into the background to be treated as a subsidiary occupation. This is evident from the large increase in the number of persons who have returned non-cultivating proprietorship as a subsidiary occupation.

The large increase of 15,978 among agricultural labourers is due to the distinction introduced in 1931 among working dependents and non-working dependents. Market gardening has reached its maximum limit and will show but little further progress unless marketing conditions in India are properly organized by the Agricultural Department. That agricultural pursuits are becoming more popular is clearly indicated by the increase of 22,539 since 1921 in the number of persons who have returned agriculture as a subsidiary occupation. And if further proof were needed it would be found in the number of ploughs in the province which have increased by over 15,000 since 1921.

Pasture.

169. Pasture includes the following occupational groups of the general scheme of occupations :—

21. Cattle and buffalo breeders and keepers.
22. Breeders of transport animals.
23. Herdsmen, shepherds and breeders of other animals.

The following statement gives the distribution of earners and working dependents in each of these three groups :—

	1921. *Actual workers.*	1931. *Earners and working dependents.*	*Variations.*
PASTURE	18,630	27,751	+9,121
Cattle and buffalo-breeders	1,713	1,449	—264
Breeders of transport animals	1,560	1,301	—259
Herdsmen, shepherds and breeders of other animals ..	15,357	25,001	+9,644
(*a*) Sheep and goat-breeders	12,551	23,816	+11,265
(*b*) Others	2,806	1,185	—1,621

The number of persons following pasture as a principal occupation shows a net increase of 9,121 between 1921 and 1931. In addition to the 27,751 workers in 1931, there were 30,838 persons who followed pasture as a subsidiary occupation. The increase falls chiefly under the Group "Sheep and goat-breeders" which accounts for 89 per cent. of the increase brought about by better grazing conditions which resulted in large increases in the number of animals as will be seen from the marginal statement which has been extracted from the records of the Cattle Census of 1931.

	1921.	1931.	Variation.
Sheep ..	1,143,610	1.347,591	+203,981
Goats ..	587,421	936,014	+348,593
Cows ..	89,141	106,873	+17,732
Young stock (calves)	40,705	54,513	+13,808
Buffaloes, Cow ..	3,788	4,218	+430
He-Camels ..	47,009	42,589	—4,420
She-Camels ..	46,823	62,222	+15,399
Horses ..	18,080	16,049	—2,031
Donkeys ..	49,869	68,037	+18,168

Fishing.

170. Fishing is a growing industry along the Las Bela and Makran coasts. The number of workers has risen from 1,600 in 1921 to 2,271 in 1931. Dried fish and fins are exported to Ceylon and China. If properly organised by the States concerned, fishing holds out promise of considerable expansion in future years.

Sub-Class II-Exploitation of Minerals.

171. This sub-class consists of (*a*) metallic minerals and (*b*) non-metallic minerals. The figures for 1921 and 1931 are compared in the margin. Chrome and coal are the principal minerals mined. Chrome mining received considerable impetus during the years of the Great War. The decrease under chrome is due to the general economic depression during the decade under review. The closing down of the Railway mines at Khost accounts for the decrease under coal.

	1921.	1931.	Variation.
	Actual workers.	Earners.	
MINERALS ..	1,839	548	—1,291
Other metallic minerals ..	863	176	—687
Non-metallic minerals ..	976	372	—604
(*a*) Coal ..	912	296	—616
(*b*) Saltpetre, etc. ..	64	76	+12

Sub-Class III-Industry.

172. This sub-class consists of 17 Orders. Figures for the more important ones for 1921 and 1931 are compared in the margin. Industry gives employment to 25,395 persons of whom 19,461 are earners and 5,934 working dependents. It partly supports another 2,137 persons who are employed or are interested in Industry as a subsidiary occupation. There is a general increase in numbers compared to 1921. In 1911, the Industrial Census only included establishments of 20 or more employees. In 1921, the scope of this part of the Census was widened so as to include all establishments containing 10 or more persons. At both censuses the Industrial Census was taken on special forms approved by the Government of India. At the Census of 1931, a column was provided in the Census schedule to obtain information regarding organised industries which were defined as under :—

	1921.	1931.	
	Actual workers.	Earners and working dependents.	Subsidiary earners.
INDUSTRY ..	15,832	25,395	2,137
Textiles ..	490	2,096	274
Hides and Skins, etc.	13	44	..
Wood ..	2,174	5,464	583
Metals ..	2,560	2,515	178
Ceramics ..	526	598	217
Chemical Products ..	146	293	81
Food Industries ..	1,717	1,823	180
Dress and Toilet ..	3,775	5,451	220
Furniture ..	4	585	11
Building ..	977	2,043	320
Means of Transport ..	32	109	3
Production and transmission of physical force ..	6	194	..
Miscellaneous ..	3,412	4,180	70

The minimum number of persons required to constitute a case of organized Industry is three—one paying the wage and two others working for wages simultaneously. But this minimum will only apply when the wage payer is also working himself. If he does not work then one wage-payer and three workmen is the minimum under the definition already given.

The information was collected but, later on owing to financial stringency, the tables were not printed.

Industrially, Baluchistan is very backward: The only industries of interest are those named in the margin with the numbers of persons employed in and supported by each in 1931. Woolcarding, spinning and weaving; embroideries, leather work; basket and mat-making from dwarf-palm leaves, are chief among the indigenous industries. The introduction of electric power in Quetta is likely to help industrial activities a great deal in future years.

Groups.	Total workers (earners and working dependents).	Total supported by Industry (inclusive of Subsidiary earners).
46. Woolcarding, spinning and weaving	1,670	1,804
50. Lace, crepe, embroideries, fringes, etc., and insufficiently described textile industries	..	4
51. Working in leather	41	41
52. Furriers and persons occupied with feathers and bristles ; brush makers	3	3
56. Basket makers, and other industries of woody materials, including leaves, and thatchers and builders working with bamboo, reeds or similar materials	4,448	4,803
60. Workers in brass, copper and bell metal	59	61
61. Workers in other metals (except precious metals)	118	125
64. Brick and tile makers	332	527
82. Boot, shoe, sandal and clog-makers..	1,121	1,229
88. Cabinet-makers, carriage painters, etc.	569	578
91. Persons engaged in making, assembling or repairing motor vehicles or cycles	109	112

Sub-Class IV-Transport.

173. The number of persons supported by the occupations falling under this sub-class, namely—

(*a*) Transport by air, (*c*) Transport by road,

(*b*) Transport by sea, (*d*) Transport by rail,

was 22,181 in 1931 consisting of 17,801 earners, 163 working dependents and 4,217 persons who follow these occupations as supplementary means of livelihood. The numbers under Transport by air are small owing to the fact that all enlisted employees have been shown under "Army (Imperial)" against Group 153. The Province possesses no navigable rivers or canals while the boatmen of the Las Bela and Makran coasts have been mostly classed as fishermen. 15,071 persons including 10,723 earners, 163 working dependents and 4,185 subsidiary earners are employed on Transport by road. Taking the workers alone (earners plus working dependents) the numbers have decreased by 2,418 since 1921. With the rapid substitution of mechanical transport for transport by camels and carts and tongas, the numbers of pack animal owners and drivers will continue to decrease. The progress of mechanical transport has also proved an inconvenient rival for the railway which has had to resort to retrenchment to effect economies.

Sub-Class V-Trade.

174. The total number of persons employed in this sub-class in 1931 was 13,582 against 12,523 of 1921. In addition to these, the Census of 1931 shows that there were 8,153 persons who were partly supported by Trade as a Subsidiary occupation.

Figures for the more important Groups are compared in the following statement :—

	Groups.	1921. *Actual workers.*	1931. *Earners (including working dependents.)*
	TOTAL ..	12,523	13,582
23.	Banks, etc.	313	100
24.	Brokerage, etc.	189	200
25.	Trade in textiles	3,195	2,363
26.	Trade in Skins, etc.	110	67
27.	Trade in Wood	35	18
28.	Trade in Metals	11	18
29.	Trade in Pottery, etc.	4	20
30.	Trade in Chemical-products	203	90
31.	Hotels, etc.	307	590
32.	Other trade in foodstuffs	3,767	2,854
33.	Trade in clothing, etc.	142	547
34.	Trade in furniture	99	78
35.	Trade in building material	6	4
36.	Trade in means of transport	230	332
37.	Trade in fuel	211	541
38.	Trade in articles of luxury	189	66
39.	Trade of other sorts	3,512	5,694

Trade in banking business, in textiles, chemical-products, foodstuffs other than hotels, and trade of all other sorts have appreciably decreased since 1921 owing to economic depression. On the other hand, insurance agents and brokers, etc., hotel managers and employees; persons employed in trade in means of transport and fuel have appreciably increased. It would appear that owing to paucity of capital and depression in trade, there is a growing tendency among the trading classes to devote their energies to more than one occupation in order to augment their income. This tendency is reflected in the fairly large numbers of subsidiary earners in several occupations.

Sub-Class VI-Public Force.

175. The numbers employed in this sub-class show a decrease of 1,402 persons since 1921. The numbers in the various groups of which this sub-class is composed including 136 subsidiary earners are given in the margin. A considerable proportion of the increase under Police is due to the inclusion under this Group of whole time local levymen recruited from the agricultural classes whose principal occupation was shown as agriculture in 1921.

	1931.	1921.
1. Army Imperial ..	19,603	24,659
2. Army Baluchistan States ..	526	658
3. Air Force ..	161	133
4. Police including local civil levies and village watchmen ..	5,704	1,946

The distribution of the workers among Indigenous and Alien categories is shown below :—

		ACTUAL FIGURES.	
		Indigenous.	*Alien.*
Imperial Army, including Air Force	..	921	18,682
Baluchistan States Army	..	503	23
Police and Levies	..	4,790	914

Sub-Class VII-Public-Administration.

176. This sub-class is composed of the following groups :—

Service of the State.
Service of Baluchistan States.
Municipal Service.
Village Officials, etc.

Retrenchment is responsible for the decrease under Service of Government and Service of the States. Village officials in 1931 included Patwaris and Lambardars. The distribution of workers in this sub-class among indigenous and alien inhabitants is shown below :—

	1921.	1931.		
	Actual workers.	Total (earners and working dependents).	Indigenous.	Aliens.
TOTAL	4,229	4,133	2,140	1,993
Service of the State	2,834	2,058	484	1,574
Service of Baluchistan States	944	1,163	1,089	74
Municipal Service	316	375	101	274
Village Officials, etc.	135	537	466	71

Sub-Class VIII-Professions and Liberal Arts.

177. In this sub-class, the Orders, Law, Medicine, and Instruction deserve notice. Lawyers and their clerks and petition-writers have increased from 41 in 1921 to 62 in 1931, 10 being indigenous and 52 aliens. Midwives have increased from 40 in 1921 to 197 of whom 116 are indigenous. Public instruction appears to be making satisfactory progress as will be seen from the numbers of teachers which has increased from 196 to 394 during the 10 years ending with 1931. The composition of the staff is 129 indigenous and 265 aliens. Advancement of education is seriously hampered by the paucity of qualified indigenous teachers.

While the world trade is believed to be groaning under the pressure of a widespread depression, places of public entertainment in Baluchistan appear to be enjoying unparalleled prosperity. The number of earners in this occupation has increased from 11 to 124 during the decennium under review. But Baluchistan is not an exception, for during the same period there has been an increase of 51 per cent. in the followers of this occupation in India as a whole. One feels puzzled as to which one to believe to be real—the wails of depression in business circles or the rapturous shouts of " encore " in places of public entertainment ! The money spent on increased entertainment is probably the reason for the businessmen's lament. The ultimate cause is surely to be sought in the psychology of mankind to-day.

Other Occupations.

178. The only other groups which show remarkable variations compared to 1921, are—

(*a*) Domestic Service ; decrease of 8,568.
(*b*) Labourers unspecified, decrease of 5,896.

The decrease under other Domestic Service is due to the emancipation of slaves who in 1931 were entered under the various occupations they actually followed. Similarly, unspecified labourers were classed in 1931 as porters and messengers.

Occupation by Race, Tribe or Caste.

179. The statement below shows the number of earners in each of the principal indigenous races as compared with the Census of 1921.

Race.	1931. Earners.	1931. Working Dependents.	1931. Non-working Dependents.	1921. Actual-workers.	1921. Dependents.	Percentage of earners of each race to total earners. 1931. Earners.	1931. Working-Dependents.	1931. Non-working Dependents.	1921. Actual-workers.	1921. Dependents.
Indigenous ..	236,602	21,177	502,346	237,007	466,937	100	100	100	100	100
Baloch ..	69,270	7,051	149,720	55,668	117,627	29	33	30	24	25
Brahui ..	48,789	1,896	101,903	55,066	104,668	21	9	20	23	23
Pathan ..	53,103	6,555	116,349	55,272	118,789	22	31	23	23	26
Lasi ..	8,863	2,575	20,374	7,197	16,015	4	12	4	3	3
Jatt ..	26,939	1,090	49,128	22,490	40,701	11	5	10	9	9
Sayyid ..	5,753	1,187	15,036	5,986	14,279	3	6	3	3	3
Other Muslim ..	17,527	694	39,370	28,192	43,574	7	3	8	12	9
Hindu ..	6,327	129	10,449	6,673	10,806	3	1	2	3	2

It will be observed that in every 100 earners, the Baloch claim 29, the Pathan 22, the Brahui 21 and the Jatt 11, while the remaining 17 are distributed over the other indigenous races. The statement below shows by indigenous races the number per 1,000 earners engaged in each of the following occupations :—

Occupation.	Number per 1,000 earners in each race engaged in each main occupation. Races (*Indigenous*). Baloch.	Brahui.	Pathan.	Lasi.	Jatt.	Sayyid.	Other Muslim.	Hindu.
TOTAL ..	1,000	1,000	1,000	1,000	1,000	1,000	1,000	1,000
Agriculture	829	653	761	642	823	663	580	9
Pasture	61	201	61	238	44	35	30	..
Other allied agricultural occupations ..	13	4	..	15	..	..	58	..
Minerals	1	..	2	5	2	..	4	..
Industry	24	20	22	21	64	28	157	34
Transport	29	51	54	35	23	46	44	47
Trade	5	6	20	10	4	48	18	813
Public Force	18	30	37	11	6	21	11	2
Public Administration	2	6	4	3	4	14	34	12
Professions and Liberal Arts ..	3	6	17	7	12	87	15	15
Persons living on their income ..	..	10	3	..	..	11	..	5
Domestic Service	7	9	8	9	7	12	28	45
Insufficiently described occupations ..	1	..	2	1	1	3	1	7
Unproductive	7	4	9	3	10	32	20	11

The order of precedence of each race in each of these occupations is shown in the following table :—

Occupations.	Baloch.	Brahui.	Pathan.	Lasi.	Jatt.	Sayyid.	Other Muslim.	Hindus.
Agriculture	1	5	3	6	2	4	7	8
Pasture	3	2	4	1	5	6	7	..
Other allied agricultural occupations ..	3	4	..	2	..	..	1	..
Minerals	..	..	4	1	3	..	2	..
Industry	5	8	6	7	2	4	1	3
Transport	7	2	1	6	8	4	5	3
Trade	7	6	3	5	8	2	4	1
Public Force	4	2	1	5	7	3	6	8
Public Administration	8	4	5	7	6	2	1	3
Professions and Liberal Arts ..	8	7	2	6	5	1	3	4
Persons living on their income ..	..	2	4	..	..	1	..	3
Domestic Service	8	5	6	4	7	3	2	1
Insifficiently described occupations ..	4	..	3	5	6	2	7	1
Unproductive	6	7	5	8	4	1	2	3

Diagram No. 18.

PROPORTION PER 1,000 WORKERS IN EACH SUB-CLASS OF OCCUPATION BY RACES.

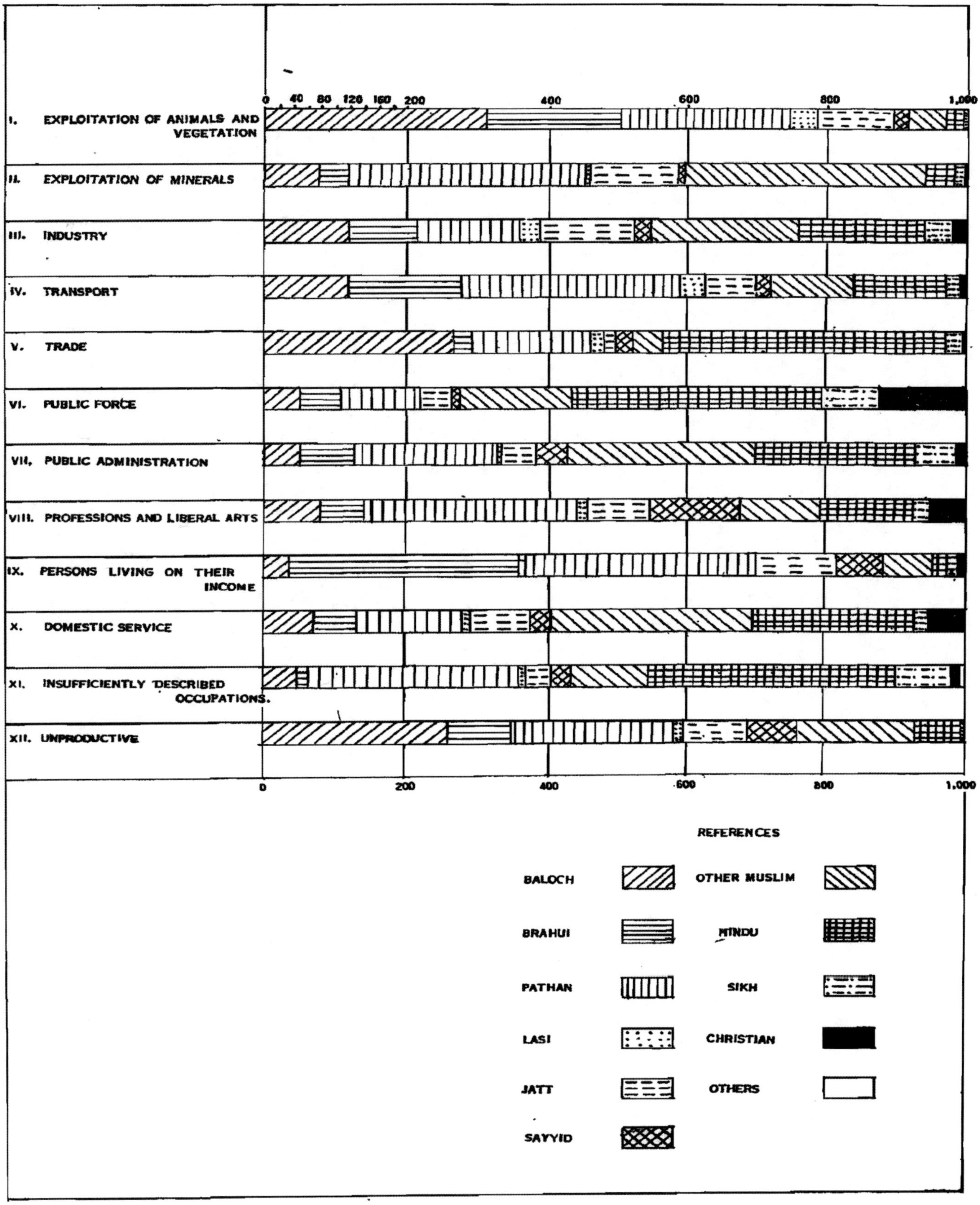

SUBSIDIARY TABLES.

30.—General Distribution of Occupations (*a*) Earners and Working Dependents.

Class, Sub-class and Order.	Number per 10,000 of total population.	Percentage of Earners.	Percentage of Working Dependents.
NON-WORKING DEPENDENTS	6,324	..	..
ALL OCCUPATIONS	4,520	..	..
Earners (Principal Occupation and Working Dependents)	3,676	93	7
A.—Production of Raw Materials	2,487	93	7
I.—Exploitation of Animals and Vegetation	2,481	93	7
1. Pasture and Agriculture	2,455	93	7
(*a*) Cultivation	2,115	94	6
(*b*) Cultivation of special crops, fruits, etc. (planters, managers, clerks and labourers)	10	99	1
(*c*) Forestry	10	56	44
(*d*) Stock raising	320	84	16
(*e*) Raising of small animals and insects	..	100	..
2. Fishing and hunting	26	98	2
II.—Exploitation of Minerals	6	100	..
3. Metallic minerals	2	100	..
4. Non-metallic minerals	4	100	..
B.—Preparation and Supply of Material Substances	656	89	11
III.—Industry	292	77	23
5. Textiles	24	41	59
6. Hides, skins and hard materials from the animal kingdom	..	80	20
7. Wood	63	51	49
8. Metals	29	99	1
9. Ceramics	7	98	2
10. Chemical Products properly so-called and analogous	3	100	..
11. Food Industries	21	98	2
12. Industries of dress and the toilet	63	65	35
13. Furniture Industries	7	99	1
14. Building Industries	24	100	..
15 Construction of means of transport	1	100	..
16. Production and transmission of physical force	2	100	..
17. Miscellaneous and undefined Industries	48	99	1
IV.—Transport	207	99	1
18. Transport by air	..	100	..
19. Transport by water	1	100	..
20. Transport by road	125	99	1
21. Transport by rail	74	100	..
22. Post Office, Telegraph and Telephone Services	6	100	..
V.—Trade	157	99	1
23. Banks, establishments of credit, exchange and insurance	1	100	..
24. Brokerage, commission and export	2	100	..
25. Trade in textiles	27	98	2
26. Trade in skins, leather and furs	1	100	..
27. Trade in wood	..	100	..
28. Trade in metals	..	100	..
29. Trade in pottery, bricks and tiles	..	100	..
30. Trade in chemical products	1	99	1
31. Hotels, cafes, restaurants, etc.	7	100	..
32. Other trade in food stuffs	33	99	1
33. Trade in clothing and toilet articles	7	100	..
34. Trade in furniture	1	100	..
35. Trade in building materials	..	100	..
36. Trade in means of transport	4	100	..
37. Trade in fuel	6	85	5
38. Trade in articles of luxury and those pertaining to Letters and the Arts and Sciences	1	100	..
39. Trade of the other sorts	66	100	..
C.—Public Administration and Liberal Arts	392	100	..
VI.—Public Force	298	100	..
40. Army	232	100	..
41. Navy	..	100	..
42. Air Force	2	100	..
43. Police	64	100	..
VII.—Public Administration	42	100	..
44. Public Administration	42	100	..
VIII.—Professions and Liberal Arts	52	100	..
45. Religion	29	100	..
46. Law	1	100	..
47. Medicine	10	100	..
48. Instruction	5	100	..
49. Letters, Arts and Sciences (other than 44)	7	99	1
D.—Miscellaneous	141	96	4
IX.—Persons living on their income	10	100	..
50. Persons principally living on their income	10	100	..
X.—Domestic Service	86	100	..
51. Domestic Service	86	100	..
XI.—Insufficiently Described Occupations	11	100	..
52. General terms which do not indicate a definite occupation	11	100	..
XII.—Unproductive	34	84	6
53. Inmates of jails, asylums, and alms houses	5	..	100
54. Beggars, vagrants, prostitutes	29	100	..
55. Other unclassified non-productive industries	..	..	..

30.—(*b*) Distribution of Subsidiary Earners.

Class, Sub-class and Order.	Number per 10,000 of total population.	Percentage recorded. Males.	Percentage recorded. Females.
ALL OCCUPATION	4,520	..	..
(EARNERS AS SUBSIDIARY TO OTHERS)	844	99	1
A.—Production of Raw Materials	640	76	..
I.—Exploitation of Animals and Vegetation	640	76	..
1. Pasture and Agriculture	636	75	..
(*a*) Cultivation	279	33	..
(*b*) Cultivation of special crops, fruit, etc., (planters, managers, clerks and labourers	..	..	..
(*c*) Forestry	2	..	..
(*d*) Stock raising	355	42	..
(*e*) Raising of small animals and insects	..	..	..
2. Fishing and hunting	4	1	..
II. Exploitation of Minerals	..	..	..
3. Metallic minerals	..	..	..
4. Non-metallic minerals	..	..	..
B.—Preparation and Supply of Material Substances	167	19	1
III.—Industry	25	2	1
5. Textiles	3	..	..
6. Hides, skins and hard materials from the animal kingdom	..	..	..
7. Wood	7	1	..
8. Metals	2	..	..
9. Ceramics	2	..	..
10. Chemical products properly so-called and analogous	1	..	..
11. Food Industries	2	..	..
12. Industries of dress and toilet	3	..	..
13. Furniture Industries	..	..	..
14. Building Industries	4	1	..
15. Construction of means of transport	..	..	..
16. Production and transmission of physical force	..	..	..
17. Miscellaneous and undefined Industries	1	..	..
IV.—Transport	48	6	..
18. Transport by air	..	..	..
19. Transport by water	..	..	..
20. Transport by road	48	6	..
21. Transport by rail	..	..	..
22. Post Office, Telegraph and Telephone Services	..	..	..
V.—Trade	94	11	..
23. Banks, establishments of credit, exchange and insurance	..	..	..
24. Brokerage, commission and export	..	..	..
25. Trade in textiles	8	1	..
26. Trade in skins, leather and furs	..	..	..
27. Trade in wood	..	..	..
28. Trade in metals	..	..	..
29. Trade in pottery, bricks and tiles	..	..	..
30. Trade in chemical products	1	..	..
31. Hotels, cafes, restaurant, etc.	..	..	..
32. Other trade in food stuffs	6	1	..
33. Trade in clothing and toilet articles	..	..	..
34. Trade in furniture	1	..	..
35. Trade in building materials	..	..	..
36. Trade in means of transport	67	8	..
37. Trade in fuel	..	..	..
38. Trade in articles of luxury and those pertaining to Letters and the Arts and Sciences	6	1	..
39. Trade of other sorts	5	..	..
C.—Public Administration and Liberal Arts	16	2	..
VI.—Public Force	1	..	..
40. Army	..	..	..
41. Navy	..	..	..
42. Air Force	..	..	..
43. Police	1	..	..
VII.—Public Administration	5	1	..
44. Public Administration	5	1	..
VIII—Professions and Liberal Arts	10	1	..
45. Religion	9	1	..
46. Law	..	..	..
47. Medicine	..	..	..
48. Instruction	..	..	..
49. Letters, Arts and Sciences (other than 44)	1	..	..
D.—Miscellaneous	21	2	..
IX.—Persons living on their Income	9	1	..
50. Persons principally living on their income	9	1	..
X.—Domestic Service	3	..	..
51. Domestic Service	3	..	..
XI.—Insufficiently described occupation	3	..	..
52. General terms which do not indicate a definite occupation	3	..	..
XII.—Unproductive	6	1	..
53. Inmates of jails, asylums and alms houses	..	..	..
54. Beggars, vagrants, prostitutes	6	1	..
55. Other unclassified non-productive industries	..	..	..

31.—Distribution by Sub-classes in Districts and States—(a) Earners (Principal Occupations) and Working Dependents.

Districts or States.	Total (1,000) Non-working Dependents.	Working Dependents.	Earners, Principal Occupation.	Number per mille of the total population occupied as Earners (Principal Occupation) and Working Dependents in I.—Exploitation of Animals and Vegetation.	II.—Exploitation of Minerals.	III.—Industry.	IV.—Transport.	V.—Trade.	VI.—Public Force.	VII.—Public Administration.	VIII.—Professions and Liberal Arts.	IX.—Persons living on their Income.	X.—Domestic Service.	XI.—Insufficiently Described Occupations.	XII.—Unproductive.
BALUCHISTAN ..	632	26	342	675	2	80	56	42	81	12	14	3	23	3	9
Districts ..	605	30	365	568	3	84	82	50	131	13	18	2	35	4	10
Quetta-Pishin ..	568	24	408	288	1	148	93	83	241	21	28	6	73	10	8
Loralai ..	579	90	331	790	..	48	33	31	60	7	12	..	10	1	8
Zhob ..	574	34	392	629	9	54	67	19	180	8	14	..	13	2	5
Bolan ..	382	79	539	93	17	117	417	52	87	50	12	..	20	3	132
Chagai ..	636	2	362	529	..	42	258	38	75	2	16	2	22	1	15
Sibi ..	673	3	324	782	2	49	57	37	26	8	11	..	17	2	9
States ..	664	20	316	819	..	73	22	33	13	10	9	4	8	..	9
Kalat ..	675	10	315	841	1	53	17	34	14	11	11	4	6	..	8
Las Bela ..	602	79	319	721	..	162	44	29	10	4	5	..	14	1	10

31.—(b) Earners (Subsidiary Occupations).

Districts or States.	Number per mille of total population of Earner having a Subsidiary Occupation. I.—Exploitation of Animals and Vegetation.	II.—Exploitation of Minerals.	III.—Industry.	IV.—Transport.	V.—Trade.	VI.—Public Force.	VII.—Public Administration.	VIII.—Professions and Liberal Arts.	IX.—Persons living on their Income.	X.—Domestic Service.	XI.—Insufficiently Described Occupations.	XII.—Unproductive.
BALUCHISTAN ..	758	..	29	57	111	2	6	12	11	4	3	7
Districts ..	727	..	26	42	151	3	9	13	15	3	4	7
Quetta-Pishin ..	707	..	13	46	63	..	4	11	49	3	11	3
Loralai ..	798	..	47	46	71	..	13	14	3	3	1	4
Zhob ..	823	..	11	88	16	18	2	23	6	3	5	5
Bolan ..	897	..	6	5	3	..	..	11	78	..	..	..
Chagai ..	841	..	25	41	45	1	4	13	14	5	7	4
Sibi ..	579	..	26	19	332	..	13	11	3	4	1	12
States ..	818	..	37	88	33	..	..	8	3	5	1	7
Kalat ..	867	..	31	42	24	..	..	10	14	3	1	8
Las Bela ..	655	1	33	224	61	..	..	3	2	16	1	4

32.—Occupations of Females by Sub-classes and Selected Orders and Groups.

Group No.	Occupation.	Number of Earners. Males.	Number of Earners. Females.	Number of females per 1,000 males.
	Total	2,92,246	4,739	16
	1. EXPLOITATION OF ANIMALS AND VEGETATION	1,99,231	693	3
	I.—PASTURE AND AGRICULTURE	1,97,003	687	4
	(a) Cultivation	1,72,469	526	3
1	Non-cultivating proprietors taking rent in money or kind	11,222	291	25
5	Cultivating owners	1,04,529	30	..
6	Tenant cultivators	50,905	10	..
7	Agricultural labourers	5,807	195	34
	(c) Forestry	464	36	78
17	Forest officers, rangers, guards, etc.	69	..	..
18	Wood cutters and charcoal burners	389	35	90
	(d) Stock Raising	33,187	125	4
21	Cattle and buffalo breeders and keepers	1,130	32	28
22	Breeders of transport animals	1,286	8	7
23	Herdsmen, shepherds and breeders of other animals	20,771	85	4
	2. Fishing and Hunting	2,228	6	3
27	Fishing and pearling	2,225	6	3
	III.—INDUSTRY	17,059	2,402	141
	5. Textiles	654	196	300
43	Cotton spinning, sizing and weaving	223	1	4
44	Jute pressing, spinning and weaving	..	16	16
45	Rope, twine, string and other fibres	77	10	130
46	Wool carding, spinning and weaving	273	167	612
49	Dyeing, bleaching, printing, preparation and sponging of textiles	66	2	20
	6. Hides, skins and Hard materials from the Animal Kingdom	27	8	296
51	Working in leather	24	8	333
	7. Wood	1,498	1,306	870
55	Carpenters, turners and joiners, etc.	959	..	..
56	Basket makers and other Industries of woody materials including leaves, and thatchers and builders working with bamboo, reeds or similar materials	492	1,306	2,654
	9. Ceramics	554	32	58
63	Potters and makers of earthenware	220	12	55
64	Brick and tile makers	310	20	65
	11. Food Industries	1,570	221	14
71	Rice pounders, huskers and flour grinding	151	186	1,199
72	Grain parchers, etc.	77	35	445
73	Butchers	430	..	..
75	Sweetmeat and condiment makers	263	..	..
81	Others	600	..	..
	12. Industries of Dress and the Toilet	3,324	209	63
82	Boot, shoe, sandal and clog-makers	1,117	1	1
83	Tailors, milliners, dress makers and darners	1,099	23	12
84	Embroiderers, hat makers and makers of other articles of wear	14	136	9,714
85	Washing and cleaning	496	48	97
	13. Furniture Industries	570	12	21
88	Cabinet makers, carriage painters, etc.	569	..	..
89	Upholsterers, tent-makers, etc.	1	12	12,000
	14. Building Industries	2,024	16	8
90	Lime burners, cement workers, excavators and well-sinkers, stone cutters and dressers, brick layers and masons, builders (other than building made of bamboo or similar materials) .. Painters, decorators of houses, tilers, plumbers, etc.	2,024	16	8
	17. Miscellaneous and Undefined Industries	3,754	402	107
98	Makers of jewellery and ornaments	742	..	..
100	Scavenging	2,893	402	139
	IV.—TRANSPORT	17,451	350	20
	20. Transport by Road	10,373	350	34
106	Labourers employed on roads and bridges	837	..	..
108	Owners, managers and employe, (excluding personal servants) connected with other vehicles	646	..	..
110	Pack elephant, camel, mule, ass and bullock owners and drivers	3,760	87	23
111	Porters and messengers	5,022	263	52
	V.—TRADE	13,381	57	4
	25. Trade in Textiles	2,320	2	1
117	Trade in piece-goods, wool, cotton, silk, hair and other textiles	2,320	2	1
	30. Trade in Chemical Products	86	3	35
125	Drugs, dyes, paints, petroleum, explosives, etc.	86	3	35
	31. Hotels, Cafes, Restaurants, etc.	584	6	10
126	Vendors of wine, liquors, aerated water and ice	76	..	..
127	Owners and managers of hotels, cook shops, sarais, etc., (and employees)	344	5	15
128	Hawkers of drink and food stuffs	164	1	6
	32. Other Trade in Food Stuffs	2,800	34	12
129	Grain and pulse dealers	451	5	11
130	Dealers in sweetmeats, sugar and spices	28	1	36
131	Dealers in dairy products, eggs and poultry	458	5	11
132	Dealers in animals for food	197	1	5
134	Dealers in other food stuffs	1,417	22	16
135	Dealers in tobacco	186	..	..
	33. Trade in Clothing and Toilet Articles	542	5	9
138	Trade in ready made clothing and other articles of dress and the toilet (hats, umbrellas, socks, ready made shoes, perfumes, etc.)	542	5	9
	36. Trade in means of Transport	329	2	6
144	Dealers and hirers of elephants, camels, horses, cattle, asses, mules, etc.	287	2	7
	37. Trade in Fuel	459	2	4
145	Dealers in firewood, charcoal, coal, cowdung, etc.	459	2	4
	39. Trade of other sorts	5,690	3	1
150	General storekeepers, shop-keepers otherwise unspecified	5,649	3	1
	VII.—PUBLIC ADMINISTRATION	3,698	1	..
	44 Public Administration	3,693	1	..
159	Service of the State	2,053	1	..
160	Service of Indian and Foreign States	1,161	..	..
161	Municipal and other local (not village) service	366	..	..
162	Village officials and sevants other than watchmen	111	..	..

32.—Occupations of Females by Sub-classes and Selected Orders and Groups—*concluded*.

Group No.	Occupation.	Number of Earners. Males.	Number of Earners. Females.	Number of females per 1,000 males.
	VIII.—Professions and Liberal Arts	**4,205**	**301**	**72**
	45 Religion	**2,481**	**17**	**7**
163	Priests, Ministers, etc. ..	2,052	11	5
164	Monks, nuns, religious mendicants	125	..	..
166	Servants in religious edifices, burial and burning grounds, pilgrim conductors, circumcisors, etc. ..	293	6	2
	47 Medicine	**655**	**217**	**331**
169	Registered medical practitioners including oculists ..	177	5	28
170	Other persons practising the healing arts without being registered ..	103	13	126
72	Midwives, vaccinators, compounders, nurses, masseurs, etc.	295	197	667
	48 Instruction	**397**	**54**	**136**
174	Professors and teachers of all kinds ..	339	48	142
175	Clerks and servants connected with education ..	58	6	103
	49 Letters, Arts and Sciences (other than 44)	**611**	**13**	**21**
182	Musicians (composers and performers other than military), actors, dancers, etc. ..	402	11	27
183	Managers and employees of places of public entertainments, race courses, societies, clubs	122	2	16
	IX.—Persons Living on their Income	**954**	**32**	**37**
	50 Persons living principally on their income	**854**	**32**	**37**
185	Proprietors (other than of agricultural land), fund and scholarship holders and pensioners ..	854	32	37
	X.—Domestic Service ..	**7,184**	**303**	**42**
	51. Domestic Service ..	**7,184**	**303**	**42**
186	Private motor drivers and cleaners	461	..	..
187	Other domestic service ..	6,723	303	45
	XI.—Insufficiently Described Occupations ..	**883**	**4**	**5**
	52. General terms which do not indicate a definite Occupation	**883**	**4**	**5**
188	Manufacturers, businessmen and contractors otherwise unspecified ..	396	..	..
189	Cashiers, accountants, bookkeepers, clerks and other employees in specified offices and warehouses and shops	472	4	8
	XII.—Unproductive ..	**1,899**	**596**	**314**
	54. Beggars, Vagrants, Prostitutes	**1,899**	**596**	**314**
193	Beggars and vagrants ..	1,882	461	245
194	Procurers and prostitutes ..	17	135	7,941

33.—Comparative Figures for Selected Occupations for 1911, 1921 and 1931.

Occupation.	Total Earners (1931) and Actual Workers (1911 and 1921) (Principal Occupation).									Variation Increase (+) Decrease (−).								
	1911 (*Actual Workers*).			1921 (*Actual Workers*).			1931 *Earners*.			1911—21.			1921—31.			1911—21.		
	Baluchistan.	Districts.	States.	Baluchistan.	Districts.	States.	Baluchistan.	Districts.	States.	Baluchistan.	Districts.	States.	Baluchistan.	Districts.	States.	Baluchistan.	Districts.	States.
TOTAL ..	303,284	156,718	146,566	301,990	171,219	180,771	296,985	169,050	127,935	−1,294	+14,501	−15,795	−5,005	−2,169	−2,830	−6,299	+12,332	−18,631
A.—Production of raw material	219,351	101,284	118,067	194,846	91,555	103,291	200,472	92,994	107,478	−24,505	−9,729	−14,776	+5,626	+1,439	+4,187	−18,879	−8,290	−10,589
I.—Exploitation of Animals and Vegetation.	218,115	100,125	117,990	193,007	89,796	103,211	199,924	92,530	107,394	−25,108	−10,329	−14,779	+6,917	+2,734	+4,183	−18,191	−7,595	−10,596
1. Pasture and agriculture ..	216,493	100,122	116,371	191,376	89,796	101,580	197,690	92,529	105,161	−25,117	−10,326	−14,791	+6,314	+2,733	+3,581	−18,803	−7,593	−11,210
(a) Cultivation ..	182,588	85,428	97,160	171,937	81,853	90,084	173,015	83,052	89,963	−10,651	−3,575	−7,076	+1,078	+1,199	−121	−9,573	−2,376	−7,197
(b) Cultivation of special crops fruit, etc. (planters, managers, clerks and labourers	1,021	547	474	766	670	96	362	822	40	−255	+123	−378	+96	+152	−56	−159	+275	−434
(c) Forestry ..	1,034	303	731	43	22	21	500	262	238	−991	−281	−710	+457	+240	+217	−534	−41	−493
(d) Stock raising ..	31,850	13,844	18,006	18,630	7,251	11,379	23,312	8,392	14,920	−13,220	−6,593	−6,627	+4,682	+1,141	+3,541	−8,538	−5,452	−3,086
(e) Raising of small animals and insects.	..	..	..	..	..	..	1	1	..	..	..	..	+1	+1	..	+1	+1	..
2. Fishing and hunting ..	1,622	3	1,619	1,631	..	1,631	2,234	1	2,233	+9	−3	+12	+603	+1	+602	+612	−2	+614
II.—Exploitation of Minerals ..	1,236	1,159	77	1,839	1,759	80	548	464	84	+603	+600	+3	−1,291	−1,295	+4	−688	−695	+7
3. Metallic minerals ..	3	3	..	863	863	..	176	175	1	+860	+860	..	−687	−688	+1	+173	+172	+1
4. Non-metallic minerals ..	1,233	1,156	77	976	896	80	372	289	83	−257	−260	+3	−604	−607	+3	−861	−867	+6
B.—Preparation and supply of material substances.	43,790	26,396	17,384	50,691	37,005	13,686	50,700	37,310	13,390	+6,911	+10,609	−3,698	+9	+305	−296	+6,920	+10,914	−3,994
III.—Industry ..	16,121	9,528	6,593	15,861	10,846	5,015	19,461	13,475	5,986	−260	+1,318	−1,578	+3,600	+2,629	+671	+3,340	+3,947	−607
5. Textiles ..	933	343	590	490	202	288	850	355	495	−443	−141	−302	+310	+153	+207	−83	+12	−95
6. Hides, skins and hard materials from the animal kingdom.	71	17	54	13	10	3	35	18	17	−58	−7	−51	+22	+8	+14	−36	+1	−37
7. Wood ..	1,866	689	1,177	1,874	1,090	784	2,804	735	2,069	+8	+401	−393	+930	−355	+1,285	+938	+46	+892
8. Metals ..	2,714	1,400	1,314	2,560	1,185	1,375	2,489	1,601	888	−154	−215	+61	−71	+516	−487	−225	+201	−426
9. Ceramics ..	271	93	178	526	387	139	586	432	154	+255	+294	−39	+60	+45	+15	+315	+339	−24
10. Chemical products properly so called and analogous.	122	39	83	146	44	102	292	242	50	+24	+5	+19	+146	+198	−52	+170	+203	−33
Food Industries ..	1,783	1,063	720	1,717	1,191	526	1,791	1,415	376	−66	+128	−194	+74	+224	−150	+8	+352	−344
Industries of dress and the toilet.	3,448	2,133	1,315	3,775	2,600	1,175	3,533	2,646	887	+327	+467	−140	−242	+46	−288	+85	+513	−428
3. Furniture Industries ..	42	37	5	304	304	..	582	567	15	+262	+267	−5	+278	+263	+15	+540	+530	+10
4. Building Industries ..	1,851	1,278	573	1,017	908	109	2,040	1,634	406	−834	−370	−464	+1,023	+726	+297	+189	+356	−167
15. Construction of means of transport.	25	25	..	32	32	..	109	109	..	+7	+7	..	+77	+77	..	+84	+84	..
16. Production and transmission of physical force.	..	..	..	6	6	..	194	191	3	+6	+6	..	+188	+185	+3	+194	+193	+3
17. Miscellaneous and undefined Industries.	2,995	2,411	584	3,401	2,987	414	4,156	3,530	626	+406	+576	−170	+755	+543	+215	+1,161	+1,119	+42
IV.—Transport ..	15,899	10,761	5,138	22,307	18,646	3,661	17,801	14,869	2,932	+6,408	+7,885	−1,477	−4,506	−3,777	−729	+1,902	+4,108	−2,206
18. Transport by air ..	..	..	..	..	..	..	40	40	..	..	..	..	+40	+40	..	+40	+40	..
19. Transport by water ..	220	..	220	12	..	12	81	..	81	−208	..	−208	+69	..	+69	−139	..	−139
20. Transport by road ..	11,884	7,125	4,759	13,304	9,732	3,572	10,723	8,033	2,690	+1,420	+2,607	−1,187	+2,581	+1,699	+882	−1,161	+908	−2,069
21. Transport by rail ..	3,307	3,287	20	8,564	8,543	21	6,385	6,345	40	+5,257	+5,256	+1	−2,179	−2,198	+19	+3,078	+3,058	+20
22. Post office, telegraph and telephone services.	488	349	139	427	371	56	572	451	121	−61	+22	−83	+145	+80	+65	+84	+102	−18

V.—Trade ..	11,760	6,107	5,653	12,523	7,513	5,010	13,438	8,966	4,472	+763	+1,406	−643	+915	+1,453	−538	+1,678	+2,859	−1,181
23. Banks, establishments of credit, exchange and insurance ..	254	109	145	313	224	89	100	100	..	+59	+115	−56	−213	−124	−89	+154	−9	−145
24. Brokerage, commission and export.	87	58	29	189	162	27	200	175	25	+102	+104	−2	+11	+13	−2	+113	+117	−4
25. Trade in textiles ..	1,971	1,027	944	3,195	1,968	1,227	2,322	1,605	717	+1,224	+941	+283	−873	−363	−510	+351	+378	−227
26. Trade in skins, leather and furs.	72	48	24	110	88	12	67	55	12	+38	+50	−12	−43	−43	..	−5	+7	−12
27. Trade in wood ..	223	5	218	35	35	..	18	18	..	−188	+30	−218	−17	−17	..	−205	+13	−218
28. Trade in metals ..	10	10	..	11	11	..	18	18	..	+1	+1	..	+7	+7	..	+8	+8	..
29. Trade in pottery, bricks, and tiles.	6	6	..	4	4	..	20	9	11	−2	−2	..	+16	+5	+11	+14	+3	+11
30. Trade in chemical products	342	218	124	203	123	80	89	87	2	−139	−95	−44	−114	−36	−78	−263	−131	−122
31. Hotels, cafes, restaurants, etc.	209	179	30	307	281	26	590	502	88	+98	+102	−4	+283	+221	+62	+381	+323	+58
32. Other trade in food stuffs	5,623	3,116	2,507	3,767	2,685	1,082	2,834	1,926	908	−1,856	−431	−1,425	−933	−759	+174	−2,789	−1,190	−1,599
33. Trade in clothing and toilet articles.	99	97	2	142	137	5	547	433	114	+43	+40	+3	+405	+296	+109	+448	+336	+112
34. Trade in furniture ..	390	146	244	99	99	..	78	75	3	−291	−47	−244	−21	−24	+3	−312	−71	−241
35. Trade in building materials	12	4	8	6	4	2	4	4	..	−6	..	−6	−2	..	−2	−8	..	−8
36. Trade in means of transport.	129	97	32	230	195	35	331	290	41	+101	+98	+3	+101	+95	+6	+202	+193	+9
37. Trade in fuel ..	167	127	40	211	150	61	401	432	29	+44	+23	+21	+250	+282	−32	+294	+305	−11
38. Trade in articles of luxury and those pertaining to letters and the arts and sciences.	312	250	62	189	169	20	66	66	..	−123	−81	−42	−123	−103	−20	−246	−184	−62
39. Trade of other sorts ..	1,853	610	1,243	3,512	1,168	2,344	5,693	3,171	2,522	+1,659	+558	+1,101	+2,181	+2,003	+178	+3,840	+2,561	+1,279
C.—PUBLIC ADMINISTRATION AND LIBERAL ARTS.	26,439	22,159	4,280	35,763	32,596	3,167	34,058	29,639	4,419	+9,324	+10,437	−1,118	−1,705	−2,957	+1,258	+7,619	+7,480	+139
VI.—Public Force ..	16,585	15,668	917	27,396	26,650	746	25,858	24,061	1,797	+10,811	+10,982	−171	−1,538	−2,589	+1,051	+9,273	+8,393	+880
40. Army ..	15,303	14,387	916	25,317	24,573	744	20,124	19,179	945	+10,014	+10,186	−172	−5,193	−5,394	+201	+4,821	+4,792	+29
41. Navy ..	..	..	..	..	..	..	..	..	..	..	..	..	..	..	..	..	..	..
42. Air Force ..	..	..	..	133	133	..	161	161	..	+133	+133	..	+28	+28	..	+161	+161	..
43. Police ..	1,282	1,281	1	1,946	1,944	2	5,573	4,721	852	+664	+663	+1	+3,627	+2,777	+850	+4,291	+3,440	+851
VII. Public Administration ..	5,228	3,655	1,573	4,229	3,137	1,092	3,694	2,359	1,335	−999	−518	−481	−535	−778	+243	−1,534	−1,296	−238
44. Public Administration ..	5,228	3,655	1,573	4,229	3,137	1,092	3,694	2,359	1,335	−999	−518	−481	−535	−778	+243	−1,534	−1,296	−238
VIII.—Professions and Liberal Arts	4,626	2,836	1,790	4,138	2,809	1,329	4,506	3,219	1,287	−488	−27	−461	+368	+410	−42	−120	+483	−503
45. Religion ..	2,578	1,365	1,213	2,102	1,162	940	2,498	1,645	853	+476	−203	−273	+396	+483	−87	−80	+280	−360
46. Law ..	72	43	29	41	37	4	61	52	9	−31	−6	−25	+20	+15	+5	−11	+9	−20
47. Medicine ..	492	456	36	696	664	32	872	776	96	+204	+208	−4	+176	+112	−64	+380	+320	+60
48. Instruction ..	396	351	45	224	204	20	451	409	42	−172	−147	−25	+227	+205	+22	+55	+58	−3
49. Letter, arts and sciences (other than 44)	1,088	621	467	1,075	742	333	624	337	287	−13	+121	−134	−451	−405	−46	+464	+284	+180
D.—MISCELLANEOUS ..																		
IX.—Persons living on their Income	13,714	6,879	6,835	20,690	10,063	10,627	11,755	9,107	2,648	+6,976	+3,184	+3,792	−8,935	−956	−7,979	−1,959	+2,228	−4,187
50. Persons principally living on their income.	155	139	16	245	207	38	886	404	482	+90	+68	+22	+641	+197	+444	+731	+265	+466
X.—Domestic Service ..	155	139	16	245	207	38	886	404	482	+90	+68	+22	+641	+197	+444	+731	+265	+466
51. Domestic service ..	10,389	5,099	5,790	16,055	6,511	9,544	7,487	6,439	1,048	+5,166	+1,412	+3,754	−8,568	−72	−8,496	−3,402	+1,340	−4,742
XI.—Insufficiently Described Occupations.	10,389	5,099	5,790	16,055	6,511	9,544	7,487	6,439	1,048	+5,166	+1,412	+3,754	−8,568	−72	−8,496	−3,402	+1,340	−4,742
	194	151	43	1,108	1,050	58	887	850	37	+914	+899	+15	−221	−200	−21	+693	+699	−6
52. General terms which do not indicate a definite occupation	194	151	43	1,108	1,050	58	887	850	37	+914	+899	+15	−221	−200	−21	+693	+699	−6
XII. Unproductive ..	2,476	1,490	986	3,282	2,295	987	2,495	1,414	1,081	+806	+805	+1	−787	−881	+94	+19	−76	+95
53. Inmates of jails, asylums and alms houses.	347	300	47	480	405	75	..	..	..	+133	+105	+28	−480	−405	−75	−347	−300	−47
54. Beggars, vagrants, prostitutes.	2,129	1,190	939	2,802	1,890	912	2,495	1,414	1,081	+673	+700	−27	−307	−476	+169	+366	+224	+142
55. Other unclassified non-productive industries.	..	..	..	..	..	..	..	..	..	..	..	..	..	..	..	..	..	..

34.—Occupational distribution for 1931 per 1,000 of

Caste.	Traditional Occupation.	SUB- I. Agriculture. Number per 1,000 workers engaged in each occupation.	Number of female workers per 1,000 male workers.	I. Pasture. Number per 1,000 workers engaged in each occupation.	Number of female workers per 1,000 male workers.	I. Others. Number per 1,000 workers engaged in each occupation.	Number of female workers per 1,000 male workers.	II. Number per 1,000 workers engaged in each occupation.	Number of female workers per 1,000 male workers.	III. Number per 1,000 workers engaged in each occupation.	Number of female workers per 1,000 male workers.	IV. Number per 1,000 workers engaged in each occupation.	Number of female workers per 1,000 male workers.
INDIGENOUS ..	.. .. ..	725	3	90	4	9	3	2	111	37	271	41	23
BALOCH. ..	.. .. ..	829	3	61	4	13	2	1	..	24	1,056	29	9
I. Eastern— ..	.. .. ..	910	2	37	..	·1	..	..	..	10	89	14	16
Bugti ..	Pillage and plunder, Flock owners and cultivating owners.	981	..	6	..	..	..	..	..	3	136	8	..
Dombki ..	Cultivating owners	923	..	24	..	..	..	..	..	7	..	15	..
Khetran ..	C. O., Horse breeders, and Flock owners ..	919	9	15	..	..	..	..	..	28	49	4	222
Magasi ..	C. O., and Horse breeders	944	·1	15	..	..	..	..	..	10	503	6	83
Mari ..	Pillage and plunder, Flock owners and C. O.	846	..	93	..	..	..	..	..	4	23	16	..
Rind Buledi ..	C. O. and Camel breeders	937	1	15	..	..	..	..	..	10	429	8	..
,, Jamali ..	Ditto	934	4	35	..	..	..	..	..	6	83	4	..
,, Khosa ..	Ditto	945	1	4	..	1	..	1	..	6	..	24	..
,, Lashari ..	Ditto	938	3	7	..	..	..	..	..	7	182	21	..
,, Unspecified	Ditto	927	..	12	..	..	..	..	..	13	30	28	..
Umrani ..	Ditto	898	..	13	..	..	..	..	..	29	..	ꞏꞏ	..
Others ..	Cultivating owners	325	..	17	..	87	..	..	..	136	..	261	23
II. Western ..	.. .. ..	673	6	107	7	37	2	2	..	49	2,145	58	6
Buledi ..	Cultivating owners	404	..	596	..	..	..	..	..	..	..	..	..
Dashti ..	C. O., Camel breeders and Flock owners ..	750	..	71	..	6	..	..	..	12	4,000	83	..
Gichki ..	N. C. O.	795	..	68	..	..	..	..	..	..	..	34	..
Kaudai ..	Cultivating owners	737	..	199	7	..	..	..	..	14	..	4	..
Rais ..	Ditto	610	..	24	..	221	..	13	..	25	2,100	40	..
Rakhshani ..	C. O. and N. C. O., Flock owners and Camel breeders.	606	24	165	13	2	..	1	..	23	500	80	11
Rind ..	C. O., Camel breeders and Flock owners ..	877	..	43	7	9	..	1	..	16	384	19	..
Sangur ..	C. O. and trade in fish	320	..	128	..	160	4	2	..	231	13,531	120	..
Sanjarani ..	C. O. and N. C. O., Flock owners and Camel breeders.	208	..	528	..	..	..	..	..	38	..	56	..
Others ..	Flock owners	456	..	200	..	6	..	2	..	67	303	111	10
BRAHUI ..	.. .. ..	653	2	201	2	4	11	..	..	20	376	51	24
I. Original Nucleus ..	.. .. ..	636	3	210	2	18	..	2	..	11	205	41	18
Ahmadzai ..	N. C. O.	313	..	..	..	..	..	..	..	62	..	250	..
Gurgnari ..	C. O and Flock owners	682	6	248	8	..	..	2	..	6	500	30	..
Iltazai ..	N. C. O.	852	..	130	..	..	..	..	..	..	..	18	..
Kalandrari ..	C. O. and Flock owners	802	..	150	..	..	..	..	..	23	..	11	..
Kambrari ..	Ditto	771	6	161	..	..	..	3	..	8	666	32	..
Mirwari ..	C. O. and N. C. O. and Flock owners ..	817	2	113	..	2	..	..	..	18	5,000	23	..
Rodeni ..	C. O. and Flock owners	563	..	67	..	169	..	..	..	11	..	71	32
Sumalari ..	Flock owners, C. O and tenants (All kinds)	459	1	324	2	..	..	3	..	7	100	51	26
II. Sarawan ..	.. .. ..	670	1	77	..	1	..	1	..	30	124	87	7
Bangulzai ..	C. O., Camel transport and Flock owners ..	741	3	28	..	..	..	1	..	20	..	91	..
Kurd ..	C. O.	587	..	97	..	16	..	6	..	84	1,792	64	..
Lahri ..	C. O., Camel transport and Flock owners ..	567	..	185	..	..	..	..	..	17	..	87	8
Langav ..	Camel transport, Flock owners, C. O. and tenants.	781	2	21	..	..	..	..	..	45	..	115	7
Mamashahi ..	C. O.	618	..	11	..	..	..	..	..	67	..	107	10
Raisani ..	C. O. and N. C. O.	461	2	66	..	..	..	..	..	33	..	82	31
Rustamzai ..	Ditto	573	..	..	..	..	..	11	..	101	..	135	..
Sarparra ..	C. O. and Flock owners	769	..	40	..	..	..	..	..	8	..	63	..
Satakzai ..	Flock owners	834	..	62	..	..	..	8	..	18	..	34	..
Shahwani ..	C. O., N. C. O., Flock owners and Camel transport.	716	1	47	..	..	..	..	..	18	..	96	10
Zagar Mengal ..	Ditto	559	..	194	..	..	..	..	..	18	152	66	..

NOTE.—C.O.=Cultivating Owner.
N.C.O.=Non-Cultivating Owner.

workers among selected tribes.

CLASSES.

V.		VI.		VII.		VIII. Religion.		VIII. Law.		VIII. Medicine.		VIII. Instruction.		VIII. Others.		IX.		X.		XI.		XII.	
Number per 1,000 workers engaged in each occupation.	Number of female workers per 1,000 male workers.	Number per 1,000 workers engaged in each occupation.	Number of female workers per 1,000 male workers.	Number per 1,000 workers engaged in each occupation.	Number of female workers per 1,000 male workers.	Number per 1,000 workers engaged in each occupation.	Number of female workers per 1,000 male workers.	Number per 1,000 workers engaged in each occupation.	Number of female workers per 1,000 male workers.	Number per 1,000 workers engaged in each occupation.	Number of female workers per 1,000 male workers.	Number per 1,000 workers engaged in each occupation.	Number of female workers per 1,000 male workers.	Number per 1,000 workers engaged in each occupation.	Number of female workers per 1,000 male workers.	Number per 1,000 workers engaged in each occupation.	Number of female workers per 1,000 male workers.	Number per 1,000 workers engaged in each occupation.	Number of female workers per 1,000 male workers.	Number per 1,000 workers engaged in each occupation.	Number of female workers per 1,000 male workers.	Number per 1,000 workers engaged in each occupation.	Number of female workers per 1,000 male workers.
32	4	22	..	7	..	8	8	..	..	1	490	1	23	2	..	3	30	10	97	1	..	9	240
5	6	18	..	2	..	2	..	..	..	..	160	..	99	1	..	..	929	7	70	1	..	7	383
4	7	9	..	1	..	2	..	..	..	..	67	..	111	2	..	..	..	6	17	..	..	4	177
1	..	1	..	..	..	..	..	..	..	..	..	..	..	..	..	..	..	..	..	..	..	..	1,000
2	..	14	..	2	..	1	..	..	..	..	..	..	..	..	..	8	..	..	..	1	..	3	143
1	143	7	..	1	..	5	..	..	..	..	..	..	500	6	..	..	..	2	125	2	..	10	351
1	..	..	..	..	..	2	..	..	..	..	..	..	..	3	..	..	..	9	..	..	..	10	47
6	..	19	..	..	..	1	..	..	..	1	..	..	..	3	..	..	..	8	..	..	..	3	..
12	..	9	..	2	..	2	..	..	..	..	..	..	..	..	..	..	..	5	100	..	..	..	..
1	..	7	..	..	..	2	..	..	..	..	..	..	..	..	..	..	..	6	..	..	..	5	1,000
6	..	6	..	2	..	4	..	..	..	..	..	..	..	..	..	1	..	..	..	..	..	..	..
..	..	10	..	4	..	3	..	..	..	..	1000	..	..	..	..	..	..	2	..	..	..	8	333
5	..	8	..	4	..	2	..	..	..	1	..	..	..	..	..	..	..	4	..	..	..	1	..
2	..	22	..	5	..	7	..	..	..	..	..	..	..	..	..	..	..	22	..	..	..	2	..
20	..	41	..	17	..	..	..	..	..	9	..	..	..	..	..	..	..	78	..	3	..	6	..
7	6	35	..	4	..	8	..	..	..	1	444	..	..	..	..	1	1,444	10	130	1	..	12	553
..	..	..	..	..	..	..	..	..	..	..	..	..	..	..	..	..	..	..	..	..	..	..	..
3	..	21	..	8	..	9	..	..	..	..	..	..	..	..	..	..	..	12	..	..	..	30	101
..	..	57	..	23	..	..	..	..	..	..	..	..	..	..	..	..	..	..	..	..	..	23	..
1	..	24	..	1	..	3	..	..	..	..	..	..	..	..	..	..	..	3	..	..	..	14	..
10	..	25	..	3	..	2	..	..	..	..	..	..	..	..	..	1	1,000	10	..	1	..	15	17,000
4	..	81	..	6	..	6	..	..	..	1	39	..	..	1	..	1	250	10	143	2	..	11	411
5	..	13	..	2	..	1	..	..	..	..	..	..	..	..	..	1	7,000	3	29	..	..	10	696
14	..	2	..	2	1	..	..	..	..	..	1,000	..	..	..	..	..	..	11	31	3	..	7	438
..	..	132	..	..	..	..	..	..	..	..	..	..	..	..	..	..	..	..	..	..	..	38	..
18	33	42	..	12	..	7	..	..	..	2	333	1	..	..	..	2	833	49	246	2	..	23	444
6	7	30	..	6	..	5	..	..	..	1	158	..	..	..	..	10	2	9	68	..	..	4	179
4	..	46	..	8	..	4	..	..	..	..	..	..	..	..	..	7	34	4	50	..	..	9	310
62	..	..	..	..	..	..	..	..	..	..	..	..	..	..	..	313	..	..	..	..	..	..	..
4	..	8	..	4	..	2	..	..	..	..	..	..	..	..	..	..	..	6	500	..	..	8	..
..	..	..	..	..	..	..	..	..	..	..	..	..	..	..	..	..	..	..	..	..	..	..	..
..	..	2	..	..	..	5	..	..	..	..	..	..	..	..	..	2	..	..	..	..	..	..	..
2	..	8	..	2	..	3	..	..	..	1	..	..	..	..	..	..	..	6	..	..	..	8	..
3	..	..	..	..	..	13	..	..	..	..	..	..	..	..	..	..	..	2	..	..	..	9	..
2	..	22	..	35	..	..	..	..	..	..	..	..	..	..	..	49	..	..	..	..	..	11	666
7	..	114	..	11	..	1	..	..	..	..	..	..	..	..	..	1	1,000	9	..	..	..	13	583
11	13	49	..	15	..	7	..	..	..	1	77	..	..	1	..	29	..	15	53	..	..	6	122
5	..	50	..	12	..	4	..	..	..	..	..	1	..	..	..	37	..	6	166	..	..	4	111
15	..	44	..	15	..	5	..	..	..	15	9	..	..	..	..	24	..	21	..	1	..	6	666
23	..	43	..	4	..	3	..	..	..	..	..	1	..	1	..	41	..	24	29	1	..	3	..
12	..	2	..	5	..	9	..	..	..	..	..	..	..	..	..	2	..	6	71	..	..	2	250
8	..	126	..	23	..	12	..	..	..	..	..	..	..	..	..	1	..	25	..	..	..	2	..
16	181	37	..	8	..	5	..	..	..	..	..	..	..	..	..	266	..	20	67	..	..	6	..
..	..	146	..	34	..	..	..	..	..	..	..	..	..	..	..	..	..	..	..	..	..	..	..
8	..	93	..	2	..	3	..	..	..	..	..	..	..	..	..	3	..	6	..	..	..	5	..
2	..	28	..	3	..	..	..	..	..	..	..	..	..	..	..	2	..	7	..	..	..	2	..
9	..	34	..	27	..	9	..	..	..	1	..	..	..	6	..	11	..	20	..	1	..	5	..
12	..	75	..	31	..	14	..	..	..	..	..	1	..	..	..	..	..	13	217	..	..	17	..

34.—Occupational distribution for 1931 per 1,000 of

Caste.	Traditional Occupation.	I. Agriculture. Number per 1,000 workers engaged in each occupation.	I. Agriculture. Number of female workers per 1,000 male workers.	I. Pasture. Number per 1,000 workers engaged in each occupation.	I. Pasture. Number of female workers per 1,000 male workers.	I. Others. Number per 1,000 workers engaged in each occupation.	I. Others. Number of female workers per 1,000 male workers.	II. Number per 1,000 workers engaged in each occupation.	II. Number of female workers per 1,000 male workers.	III. Number per 1,000 workers engaged in each occupation.	III. Number of female workers per 1,000 male workers.	IV. Number per 1,000 workers engaged in each occupation.	IV. Number of female workers per 1,000 male workers.
III. Jhalawan ..	.. .. ..	650	2	268	2	3	23	..	..	15	930	30	56
Bizanjav ..	C. O. and N. C. O. and Flock owners ..	633	7	257	..	16	..	..	..	59	199	16	..
Haruni ..	C. O. and Flock owners	668	..	218	..	..	..	..	..	8	..	67	..
Mamasni ..	Flock owners	614	7	300	14	..	..	..	..	8	1,000	44	7
Mengal ..	C. O. and N. C. O. and Flock owners ..	577	1	317	2	2	..	..	..	7	41	43	15
Nichari ..	C. O. and Camel transport	892	..	30	..	..	..	2	..	13	143	43	..
Pandrani ..	Cultivating owners	851	3	103	..	..	..	..	..	20	..	8	..
Sajidi ..	C. O., Flock owners and Camel breeders ..	816	..	86	..	2	1,000	..	..	18	4,000	23	..
Lahri ..	C. O. and N.C.O.. Flock owners and Camel breeders.	681	..	268	..	..	..	..	..	6	102	22	199
IV. Miscellaneous ..	.. .. ..	545	2	29	..	5	..	..	..	57	..	178	5
Nighari ..	Cultivating owners and occupancy tenants	954	..	3	..	..	..	..	..	3	..	..	..
Rekizai ..	Cultivating owners	901	..	20	..	..	..	..	..	13	..	13	..
Others ..	Ditto	218	8	32	..	10	..	..	..	100	..	323	5
PATHAN ..	.. .. ..	761	4	61	6	..	..	2	..	22	29	54	10
Babi ..	Cultivating owners	607	..	..	..	..	..	..	..	48	..	..	..
Barech ..	C. O., Flock owners and Camel breeders ..	338	..	27	..	..	..	..	..	75	..	296	..
Jafar ..	Cultivating owners	923	25	6	..	..	..	..	..	4	..	6	500
Kakar ..	.. .. ..	766	2	96	3	..	..	4	..	15	39	57	16
Dawi ..	Ditto	746	..	..	..	..	..	..	..	..	..	45	..
Dumar ..	C. O. and Flock owners	766	1	142	..	..	..	1	..	3	200	31	..
Hussain pasener	Cultivating owners	793	6	4	..	..	..	..	..	137	..	26	..
Sanzarkhel ..	C. O. and Flock owners	786	3	92	3	..	..	1	..	11	73	39	37
Sargara ..	Cultivating owners	733	5	46	..	..	..	..	..	16	..	119	14
Samatia ..	C. O. and Flock owners	737	3	26	18	..	..	3	..	11	16	96	2
Targhara ..	Ditto	868	2	17	..	..	..	1	..	8	87	29	..
Others ..	Cultivating owners	51	..	3	..	..	..	129	..	173	..	284	12
Kasi ..	C. O. and N. C. O.	384	..	2	..	..	..	5	..	33	..	313	..
Luni ..	C. O., N. C. O. and Flock owners. ..	876	5	19	..	..	..	..	..	21	211	8	125
Pani ..	.. .. ..	804	4	102	15	..	..	..	..	23	26	14	17
Main Branch ..	C. O. and N. C. O.	887	6	11	..	..	..	..	..	31	24	25	29
Isot ..	Ditto	887	..	15	..	..	..	..	..	32	..	24	..
Loun ..	Flock owners	234	..	717	15	..	..	..	..	..	..	33	..
Mandokhel ..	Cultivating and Flock owners	618	..	249	..	..	..	..	..	2	..	28	..
Musakhel ..	Ditto	841	5	83	32	..	..	..	..	28	35	2	167
Zarkun ..	Ditto	903	2	13	..	..	..	..	..	11	10	10	..
Unspecified ..	Cultivating owners	355	..	..	..	..	..	..	..	97	..	129	..
Shirani ..	C. O. and Flock owners	696	8	87	..	..	..	..	..	75	16	6	..
Tarin ..	.. .. ..	771	6	20	5	..	..	..	..	15	50	88	1
Abdal Achakzai	C. O. and Flock owners	730	6	30	6	..	..	1	..	12	..	74	2
Spin Tarin ..	Cultivating owners	865	10	11	..	..	..	..	..	10	160	58	..
Tortarin ..	Ditto	805	2	5	..	..	..	..	..	27	50	28	..
Unspecified ..	Ditto	317	..	5	..	..	..	..	..	67	..	337	..
Zamri ..	Cultivating owners	949	1	7	..	..	..	..	..	7	..	3	..
Other Pathan ..	Ditto	161	..	7	..	..	..	2	..	205	..	214	..
Lasi ..	.. .. ..	642	3	238	8	15	..	5	6,167	21	628	35	..
Angaria ..	C. O. and Cattle breeders	609	..	226	4	9	..	..	..	15	6,500	122	..
Burra ..	Ditto	625	..	316	..	2	..	..	..	1	..	8	..
Jamot ..	C. O. and N. C. O.	453	7	437	1	7	..	..	..	14	45	43	..
Runjha ..	C. O. and N. C. O. and Camel transport ..	870	2	7	..	..	..	..	..	35	..	17	..
Sheikh ..	C. O. and N.C.O. and Cattle breeders and sellers of grass and dwarf palm leaves.	672	..	201	4	22	..	..	..	38	1,556	19	..
Mongia ..	C. O., Flock owners and Cattle breeders	727	..	172	..	29	..	..	..	46	10,000	11	..
Shahok ..	Ditto	262	..	716	5	..	..	..	..	4	..	7	..
Mondra ..	Ditto	713	12	200	..	..	..	..	..	16	..	23	..
Gonga ..	Ditto	593	3	115	..	128	..	28	6,167	..	..	49	..
Unspecified ..	Ditto	..	..	..	..	260	..	..	..	..	..	..	..
JATT (INDIGENOUS)	Cultivating owners, tenants and Cattle breeders.	822	1	44	3	..	..	2	..	64	129	23	28

NOTE.—C.O.=Cultivating Owner.
N.C.O.=Non-Cultivating Owner.

-workers among selected tribes.

CLASSES.

V.		VI.		VII.		VIII.										IX.		X.		XI.		XII.	
						Religion.		*Law.*		*Medicine.*		*Instruction.*		*Others*									
Number per 1,000 workers engaged in each occupation.	Number of female workers per 1,000 male workers.	Number per 1,000 workers engaged in each occupation.	Number of female workers per 1,000 male workers.	Number per 1,000 workers engaged in each occupation.	Number of female workers per 1,000 male workers	Number per 1,000 workers engaged in each occupation.	Number of female workers per 1,000 male workers.	Number per 1,000 workers engaged in each occupation.	Number of female workers per 1,000 male workers.	Number per 1,000 workers engaged in each occupation.	Number of female workers per 1,000 male workers.	Number per 1,000 workers engaged in each occupation.	Number of female workers per 1,000 male workers.	Number per 1,000 workers engaged in each occupation.	Number of female workers per 1,000 male workers.	Number per 1,000 workers engaged in each occupation.	Number of female workers per 1,000 male workers.	Number per 1,000 workers engaged in each occupation.	Number of female workers per 1,000 male workers.	Number per 1,000 workers engaged in each occupation.	Number of female workers per 1,000 male workers.	Number per 1,000 workers engaged in each occupation.	Number of female workers per 1,000 male workers.
3	..	16	..	2	..	4	..	..	..	..	200	..	..	..	..	1	..	5	76	..	..	3	19
8	..	3	..	..	..	2	..	..	..	..	..	..	..	..	..	..	..	2	..	..	..	4	500
..	..	8	..	..	..	..	..	..	..	..	..	..	..	..	..	..	..	28	633	3	..	..	..
3	..	16	..	2	..	4	..	..	..	..	..	..	..	..	..	1	..	5	..	..	..	3	125
3	..	30	..	2	..	6	..	..	..	..	1,000	..	..	..	..	2	..	7	109	..	..	4	77
2	..	13	..	1	..	..	..	..	..	..	..	..	..	..	..	..	..	2	..	..	..	2	..
3	..	6	..	..	..	6	..	..	..	..	..	..	..	..	..	..	..	3	..	..	..	..	..
2	..	1	..	..	..	5	..	..	..	..	..	..	..	..	..	..	..	36	..	..	..	12	..
..	..	14	..	2	..	3	..	..	..	..	..	..	..	..	..	..	..	2	..	..	..	2	316
17	..	79	..	10	..	16	..	..	..	1	..	4	..	5	..	..	..	59	66	1	..	2	..
3	..	9	..	..	..	17	..	..	..	..	..	..	..	..	..	..	..	11	..	..	..	..	..
7	..	46	..	..	..	..	..	..	..	..	..	..	..	..	..	..	..	..	..	..	..	..	..
28	..	128	..	18	..	20	..	..	..	2	..	7	..	8	..	..	..	101	70	2	..	3	..
20	3	37	..	4	..	15	..	..	..	..	200	1	23	1	..	3	13	8	33	2	..	9	416
12	..	..	..	214	..	59	..	..	..	12	..	..	..	..	..	..	..	..	..	..	..	48	..
54	..	32	..	9	..	56	..	..	..	..	..	..	..	18	..	4	..	66	57	..	..	25	..
8	333	29	..	8	..	..	..	..	..	2	..	..	..	6	..	..	..	..	..	2	..	6	..
13	..	36	..	8	..	16	..	..	..	..	222	1	67	..	..	2	..	7	39	3	..	8	422
149	..	..	..	..	..	30	..	..	..	..	..	..	..	..	..	..	..	30	1,000	..	..	..	..
7	..	34	..	2	..	3	..	..	..	..	..	..	..	..	..	..	..	5	..	..	..	6	..
9	..	4	..	..	..	9	..	..	..	..	..	5	..	4	..	9	..	..	..	..	..	..	..
9	..	28	..	1	..	15	..	..	..	..	1,000	..	..	..	..	3	..	4	38	2	..	9	430
11	..	16	..	7	..	20	..	2	..	3	..	2	..	..	..	..	..	10	..	1	..	15	286
14	..	61	..	7	..	18	..	..	..	..	..	1	167	..	..	2	..	8	..	6	..	10	686
11	..	20	..	2	..	25	..	..	..	..	..	1	..	..	..	6	..	7	200	1	..	4	400
116	..	112	..	21	..	16	..	..	..	2	..	2	..	..	..	5	..	69	..	10	..	7	..
111	..	9	..	17	..	14	..	2	..	..	..	3	..	..	..	7	..	43	42	2	..	55	..
9	..	40	..	1	..	9	..	..	..	..	..	..	..	..	..	..	..	5	..	2	..	10	833
4	56	30	..	..	..	8	..	..	..	1	332	2	..	1	..	..	..	2	..	..	..	9	1,026
2	..	24	..	5	..	8	..	..	..	..	..	3	..	2	..	..	..	1	..	..	..	1	..
2	..	32	..	..	..	4	..	..	..	..	..	..	..	..	..	..	..	..	..	..	..	4	500
..	..	..	..	..	..	16	..	..	..	..	..	..	..	..	..	..	..	..	..	..	..	..	..
11	133	50	..	8	..	18	..	..	..	1	..	5	..	..	..	..	..	6	..	1	..	3	..
2	..	24	..	..	..	4	..	..	..	..	1,000	1	..	..	..	..	..	1	..	..	..	14	1,296
8	..	31	..	2	..	10	..	..	..	..	..	..	..	1	..	..	..	8	..	..	..	8	1,500
32	..	129	..	97	..	33	..	..	..	..	..	32	..	..	..	..	..	32	..	32	..	32	..
4	..	101	..	6	..	19	..	..	..	..	..	..	..	..	..	..	..	2	..	..	..	4	429
45	..	33	..	5	..	16	..	..	..	..	..	1	..	..	..	7	30	9	70	2	..	8	295
68	..	40	..	6	..	17	..	..	..	..	..	..	..	..	..	3	..	9	5	3	..	7	152
5	..	25	..	2	..	8	..	..	..	..	..	1	..	..	..	..	..	7	..	..	..	8	412
33	..	17	..	5	..	28	..	..	..	..	..	3	..	..	..	32	21	9	..	..	..	8	182
72	..	53	..	24	..	19	..	..	..	..	..	5	..	..	..	5	1,000	72	..	5	..	19	4,000
9	..	11	..	..	..	3	..	..	..	..	..	—	..	..	..	..	..	..	..	..	..	11	3,000
115	..	53	..	51	..	27	..	2	..	2	..	4	..	5	..	2	..	104	36	20	..	26	77
10	22	11	..	8	..	2	..	..	..	..	..	..	..	5	..	..	..	9	562	1	..	3	143
3	..	14	..	..	..	..	..	..	..	..	..	..	..	..	..	..	..	..	..	..	..	2	..
14	..	3	..	2	..	5	..	..	..	3	..	1	..	11	..	..	..	3	..	..	..	6	..
17	..	5	..	2	..	1	..	..	..	..	..	..	..	7	..	2	..	6	222	2	..	4	500
12	..	23	..	11	..	4	..	1	..	1	..	1	..	6	..	..	..	8	..	1	..	3	250
8	125	13	..	1	..	3	..	..	..	..	..	..	..	..	..	..	..	19	2,286	1	..	3	..
3	..	4	..	..	..	..	..	..	..	..	..	..	..	1	..	..	..	6	..	..	..	1	..
..	..	21	..	..	..	..	..	..	..	..	..	..	..	..	..	..	..	..	..	..	..	..	..
15	..	8	..	..	..	1	..	..	..	..	..	..	..	15	..	..	..	9	1,250	..	..	..	..
6	..	2	..	..	..	..	..	..	..	..	..	..	..	..	..	..	..	19	..	..	..	..	..
..	..	..	..	250	..	..	..	..	..	..	..	..	..	..	..	..	..	500	..	..	..	..	..
4	10	6	..	4	..	6	6	..	..	1	2,200	1	40	4	..	..	250	8	126	1	..	10	176

34.—Occupational distribution for 1931 per 1,000 of

Caste.	Traditional Occupation.	SUB- I. Agriculture. Number per 1,000 workers engaged in each occupation.	I. Agriculture. Number of female workers per 1,000 male workers.	I. Pasture. Number per 1,000 workers engaged in each occupation.	I. Pasture. Number of female workers per 1,000 male workers.	I. Others. Number per 1,000 workers engaged in each occupation.	I. Others. Number of female workers per 1,000 male workers.	II. Number per 1,000 workers engaged in each occupation.	II. Number of female workers per 1,000 male workers.	III. Number per 1,000 workers engaged in each occupation.	III. Number of female workers per 1,000 male workers.	IV. Number per 1,000 workers engaged in each occupation.	IV. Number of female workers per 1,000 male workers.
SAYYID ..	N. C. O. and spiritual leaders ..	**663**	**4**	**35**	**20**	..	..	..	..	**28**	**39**	**46**	**64**
Bukhari ..	Ditto	662	5	24	..	..	..	..	..	16	..	36	112
Chisti ..	Ditto	634	..	18	..	..	..	..	..	14	..	18	..
Gharshin ..	Ditto	676	..	23	..	..	..	..	..	144	..	10	..
Kaheri ..	Ditto	845	9	26	111	..	..	..	..	5	..	52	176
Mashwani ..	Ditto	558	10	3	..	..	..	..	..	54	56	122	..
Taran ..	Ditto	760	..	82	..	..	..	..	..	13	..	38	..
Ustarana ..	Ditto	832	5	5	..	..	..	..	..	54	91	45	..
Others ..	Ditto	·573	..	82	·39	2	..	..	..	31	154	72	44
OTHER MUSLIMS ..	.. .. ..	**580**	**8**	**30**	**17**	**58**	**2**	**4**	**18**	**157**	**165**	**44**	**41**
Darzada ..	C. O., occupancy tenants and tenants at-will	771	1	11	..	5	..	2	..	109	517	17	..
Dehwar ..	Cultivating owners	630	4	4	167	..	..	4	..	49	34	39	29
Gadra ..	Domestic servants and Field labourers ..	592	4	35	..	46	..	..	..	120	30	75	..
Gola ..	Ditto	918	..	..	..	..	..	..	..	18	..	..	..
Jat ..	Camel drivers and graziers	219	..	211	27	..	..	..	..	277	1,023	249	69
Khoja ..	General trades-men and trader in stores ..	28	..	..	..	..	..	..	..	47	667	..	..
Langah ..	Domestic service and musicians ..	545	..	18	500	6	..	..	..	30	667	6	..
Lori ..	Blacksmiths and domestic service ..	77	14	9	..	..	..	1	..	768	2	14	..
Med ..	Fishermen and transport by sea ..	5	..	..	..	872	2	..	..	53	1,348	19	..
Nakib ..	Tenants and C. O.	855	17	24	..	..	..	30	16	30	333	12	..
Sorozai ..	Domestic service and Field labour ..	778	10	22	..	8	..	..	..	46	299	83	74
Others ..	Domestic service and daily labour ..	631	19	15	..	..	..	..	..	103	115	18	..
Hindus ..	.. .. ..	**9**	**120**	..	..	..	..	..	..	**34**	**432**	**47**	**201**
Arora ..	General storekeepers and shopkeepers ..	9	*120*	..	..	..	..	..	..	33	453	45	224
Brahman ..	Ditto ..	..	..	..	..	..	..	..	..	27	2,000	213	..
Khatri ..	Ditto	..	..	..	..	..	..	..	..	39	..	8	..
Others ..	Ditto	..	..	..	..	..	..	15	..	90	..	134	..
SEMI-INDIGENOUS ..	.. .. ..	**134**	**1**	**177**	**7**	..	..	**18**	..	**105**	..	**245**	**51**
Baloch ..	.. .. ..	**862**	..	**44**	..	..	..	..	..	**20**	..	**8**	..
Buzdar ..	C. O. and Flock owners	881	..	46	..	..	..	..	..	9	..	2	..
Others ..	Flock owners and Field labourers ..	464	..	..	..	..	..	..	..	250	..	143	..
Pathan ..	.. .. ..	**103**	**1**	**236**	**7**	..	..	**7**	..	**117**	..	**283**	**58**
Durrani ..	Non-cultivating owners	171	..	7	..	..	..	6	..	202	..	161	12
Ghilzai ..	C. O. and Karez diggers	91	2	292	7	..	..	7	..	94	..	308	66
Others ..	Field labourers and daily labourers ..	49	..	17	..	..	..	8	..	250	..	267	..
Other Musalman ..	.. .. ..	**10**	..	**1**	..	..	..	**63**	..	**88**	..	**180**	**3**
Hazara ..	Cultivating owners	10	..	1	..	..	..	63	..	88	..	178	3
Others ..	C. O. and daily labourers	..	..	..	..	..	..	..	..	143	..	714	..

NOTE.—C.O.=Cultivating Owner.
N.C.O.=Non-Cultivating Owner.

workers among selected tribes.

CLASSES.																							
V.		VI.		VII.		VIII.										IX.		X.		XI.		XII.	
						Religion.		*Law.*		*Medicine.*		*Instruction.*		*Others.*									
Number per 1,000 workers engaged in each occupation.	Number of female workers per 1,000 male workers.	Number per 1,000 workers engaged in each occupation.	Number of female workers per 1,000 male workers.	Number per 1,000 workers engaged in each occupation.	Number of female workers per 1,000 male workers.	Number per 1,000 workers engaged in each occupation.	Number of female workers per 1,000 male workers.	Number per 1,000 workers engaged in each occupation.	Number of female workers per 1,000 male workers.	Number per 1,000 workers engaged in each occupation.	Number of female workers per 1,000 male workers.	Number per 1,000 workers engaged in each occupation.	Number of female workers per 1,000 male workers.	Number per 1,000 workers engaged in each occupation.	Number of female workers per 1,000 male workers.	Number per 1,000 workers engaged in each occupation.	Number of female workers per 1,000 male workers.	Number per 1,000 workers engaged in each occupation.	Number of female workers per 1,000 male workers.	Number per 1,000 workers engaged in each occupation.	Number of female workers per 1,000 male workers.	Number per 1,000 workers engaged in each occupation.	Number of female workers per 1,000 male workers.
48	4	21	..	14	..	79	11	..	..	2	..	6	..	..	..	11	..	12	..	3	..	32	57
78	5	9	..	14	..	79	5	..	..	1	..	7	..	..	..	20	..	12	..	3	..	39	39
6	..	20	..	14	..	169	..	2	..	..	..	8	..	..	..	2	..	12	..	..	..	83	79
13	..	27	..	10	..	43	..	..	..	..	..	17	..	..	..	10	..	10	..	17	..	..	..
32	..	11	..	..	..	11	..	..	..	..	..	..	..	..	..	..	..	2	..	..	..	16	..
45	..	79	..	31	..	85	..	..	..	..	..	..	..	..	..	3	..	9	..	..	..	11	..
6	..	16	..	3	..	44	..	..	..	3	..	..	..	..	..	..	..	..	..	3	..	32	250
9	..	9	..	5	..	18	..	..	..	..	..	..	..	..	..	9	..	..	..	..	..	14	..
30	..	38	..	20	..	94	22	2	..	6	..	6	..	2	..	1	..	24	..	3	..	14	77
18	58	11	..	34	..	7	..	..	..	1	3,600	..	..	7	..	..	..	28	239	1	..	20	116
14	..	3	..	11	..	14	..	..	..	3	3,500	..	..	1	..	..	..	15	162	1	..	23	32
7	..	8	..	208	..	16	..	..	..	1	1,000	1	..	2	..	..	..	18	31	4	..	9	63
19	138	27	..	10	..	4	..	..	..	2	..	..	..	2	..	1	..	59	1,429	2	..	5	600
..	..	..	..	..	..	..	..	..	..	..	..	..	..	..	..	..	..	9	..	..	..	55	..
2	..	11	..	5	..	1	..	..	..	..	..	..	..	4	..	..	..	11	..	..	..	10	..
823	..	..	..	28	..	..	..	..	..	..	..	..	..	..	..	..	..	65	..	..	..	9	..
6	..	..	..	6	..	..	..	..	..	..	..	..	..	6	..	..	..	..	..	..	..	377	432
1	..	1	..	15	..	4	..	1	..	1	2,000	..	..	43	..	..	..	18	..	..	..	47	62
15	1,500	2	..	2	..	1	..	..	..	..	..	..	..	..	..	..	..	31	684	..	..	..	..
17	..	4	..	5	..	4	..	2	..	..	..	..	..	..	..	..	..	6	..	1	..	10	105
17	73	7	..	25	..	4	..	..	..	..	..	..	..	..	..	..	..	59	73	..	..	1	..
20	..	71	..	15	..	6	..	1	..	8	8,000	..	..	32	..	1	..	4	..	..	..	75	69
813	1	2	..	12	..	12	14	..	..	2	..	..	..	1	..	5	28	45	11	7	..	11	109
828	1	1	..	6	..	6	30	..	..	2	..	..	..	1	..	5	28	46	11	7	..	11	97
160	..	40	..	14	..	494	..	..	..	13	..	..	..	13	..	..	..	13	..	13	..	..	..
835	..	..	..	..	..	16	..	..	..	..	..	..	..	..	..	..	..	71	..	31	..	..	..
119	..	15	..	582	..	..	..	..	..	..	..	..	..	..	..	..	..	..	..	..	..	45	500
117	4	110	..	17	..	19	..	..	..	3	80	1	182	2	..	6	..	31	87	5	..	10	182
3	..	24	..	10	..	15	..	..	..	..	..	..	..	..	..	..	..	7	333	..	..	7	333
4	..	19	..	11	..	16	..	..	..	..	..	..	..	..	..	..	..	5	500	..	..	7	333
..	..	107	..	..	..	..	..	..	..	..	..	..	..	..	..	..	..	36	..	..	..	..	..
138	4	31	..	16	..	23	..	..	..	3	8	1	286	2	..	3	..	21	51	4	..	12	125
143	7	64	..	59	..	65	..	..	..	11	500	5	667	6	..	11	..	53	74	17	..	19	..
138	4	20	..	8	..	14	..	..	..	1	..	1	..	1	..	1	..	14	28	1	..	9	173
115	..	127	..	12	..	33	..	..	..	4	..	4	..	..	..	4	..	53	83	..	..	57	167
76	..	431	..	22	..	3	..	..	..	7	..	2	..	5	..	21	..	76	7	11	..	4	167
77	..	432	..	22	..	3	..	..	..	7	..	2	..	5	..	21	..	76	7	11	..	4	167
..	..	..	..	143	..	..	..	..	..	..	..	..	..	..	..	..	..	..	..	..	..	..	..

35.—Number of Persons Employed in the Railway, Post and Telegraphs and Irrigation Departments.

(A) NUMBER OF PERSONS EMPLOYED ON THE 26TH FEBRUARY, 1931, IN THE IRRIGATION DEPARTMENT.

Class of persons employed.	European and Anglo-Indians.	Indians.	REMARKS.
TOTAL PERSONS EMPLOYED	..	213	
Persons directly employed	..	145	
Officers	..	2	
Upper Subordinates	..	5	
Lower ,,	..	11	
Clerks	..	12	
Peons and other servants	..	67	
Coolies	..	48	
Persons indirectly employed	..	68	
Contractors	..	4	
Contractors' regular employees	..	5	
Coolies	..	59	

(B) NUMBER OF PERSONS EMPLOYED ON THE 26TH FEBRUARY, 1931, IN THE POST OFFICE AND TELEGRAPH DEPARTMENT.

Class of persons employed.	POST OFFICE.		TELEGRAPH DEPARTMENT.		REMARKS.
	Europeans and Anglo-Indians.	Indians.	Europeans and Anglo-Indians.	Indians.	
TOTAL PERSONS EMPLOYED	4	341	30	228	
(1) Post and Telegraphs.					
Supervising Officers (including Probationary Superintendents and Inspectors of Post Offices and Assistant and Deputy Superintendents of Telegraphs and all officers of higher rank than these)	2	5	6	1	
Postmasters, including Deputy, Assistant, Sub and Branch Postmasters	1	49	..	..	
Signalling establishment including Warrant Officers, Non-commissoned Officers, Military Telegraphists and other employees	1	..	24	5	
Miscellaneous Agents, Schoolmasters, Station Masters, etc.	..	41	..	10	
Clerks of all kinds	..	84	..	3	
Postmen	..	80	..	..	
Skilled labour establishment including foremen, instrument makers, carpenters, blacksmiths, mechanics, sub-inspectors, linemen and lineriders and other employees	..	..	..	171	
Unskilled labour establishment including line coolies, cable guards, batterymen telegraph, messengers, peons, and other employees	..	60	..	38	
Road establishment consisting of overseers, runners, clerks and booking agents, boatmen, syces, coachmen, bearers, and others	..	..	..	..	
(2) Railway Mail Service	..	..	..	..	
Supervising Officers (including Superintendents and Inspectors of Sorting)	..	..	..	..	
Clerks of all kinds	..	..	..	..	
Sorters	..	..	..	..	
Mail Guards, mail agents, van peons	..	..	..	..	
(3) Combined Offices	..	..	..	..	
Signallers	..	7	..	..	
Messengers and other servants	..	15	..	..	

(C) NUMBER OF PERSONS EMPLOYED ON THE 20TH FEBRUARY, 1931, IN THE RAILWAY DEPARTMENT.

Class of persons employed.	Europeans and Anglo-Indians.	Indians.	REMARKS.
TOTAL PERSONS EMPLOYED	115	6,478	
Persons directly employed	115	6,293	
Officers	9	4	
Subordinates drawing more than Rs. 75/- per mensem	106	453	
Subordinates drawing from Rs. 20/- to 75/- per mensem	..	4,891	
Subordinates drawing under Rs. 20/- per mensem	..	945	
Persons indirectly employed	..	185	
Contractors	..	40	
Contractors' regular employees	..	125	
Coolies	..	20	

36.—Subsidiary Occupations of Agriculturists.

(Workers with Principal Occupation only).

	Occupation.	Baluchistan.	Districts.						States.	
			Quetta-Pishin.	Loralai.	Zhob.	Bolan.	Chaghai.	Sibi.	Kalat.	Las Bela.
	ALL RENT RECEIVERS (NON-CULTIVATING OWNERS)	11,513	982	1,078	504	19	358	1,257	7,070	245
	Rent receivers (Non-cultivating owners) who returned following subsidiary occupations	2,238	242	432	285	1	25	362	837	73
I	Ordinary cultivators	..	..	..	..	..	..	..	..	..
I	Tenants	81	5	20	..	..	..	24	32	..
I	Field labourers	123	34	19	20	..	..	46	4	..
I	Fruit, etc., growers	3	..	1	..	..	..	..	..	2
I	Cattle and buffalo breeders and keepers	225	..	23	..	..	..	16	182	4
I	Breeders of transport animals	6	1	..	..	..	..	..	..	5
I	Herdsmen, shepherds and breeders of other animals	742	10	176	78	..	12	47	407	12
I	Others	16	1	..	1	..	..	..	2	12
III	Industry	251	24	60	10	..	2	115	36	4
IV	Transport	152	45	12	44	1	2	3	37	8
V	Trade	171	52	26	36	..	..	14	35	8
VI	Public Force	5	..	..	4	..	1	..	..	..
VII	Public Administration	92	9	29	..	..	1	49	4	..
VIII	Religion	156	16	42	41	..	..	14	38	5
VIII	Medicine	5	..	..	3	..	..	1	1	..
VIII	Instruction	4	..	..	3	..	..	..	1	..
VIII	Letters and Arts and Sciences	1	..	..	..	..	..	..	..	1
IX	Persons living on their Income	107	38	6	1	..	7	18	30	7
X	Domestic Service	29	2	5	3	..	1	11	7	..
XI	Insufficiently described occupations	21	2	8	3	..	..	1	7	..
XII	Unproductive	48	3	5	18	..	..	3	14	5
	AGENTS, MANAGERS OF LANDED ESTATES	9	9	..	..	..	..	..	..	..
	Agents, etc., who returned following Subsidiary Occupations	..	..	..	..	..	..	..	..	..
	ALL RENT PAYERS (CULTIVATING OWNERS)	104,559	9,678	14,264	10,143	199	2,118	19,633	4,140	7,414
	Rent Payers who returned following Subsidiary Occupation	40,381	3,047	6,736	3,497	4	659	12,481	11,282	2,675
I	Non-cultivating owners	601	6	21	4	..	2	33	533	2
I	Tenants	4,992	169	479	79	..	41	507	3,494	223
I	Field labourers	643	72	170	11	..	..	40	311	39
I	Fruit, etc., growers	27	16	3	1	..	..	..	..	7
I	Cattle and buffalo breeders and keepers	1,626	..	413	1	..	4	73	1,015	120
I	Breeders of transport animals	966	11	3	..	..	87	..	5	860
I	Herdsmen, shepherds and breeders of other animals	20,538	1,229	4,798	2,502	..	444	5,918	4,973	674
I	Others	268	18	3	3	..	..	14	2	228
II	Exploitation of minerals	7	1	..	..	..	..	2	..	4
III	Industry	846	30	374	50	..	7	93	205	86
IV	Transport	1,872	385	117	500	1	19	23	483	344
V	Trade	6,334	528	97	46	..	30	5,524	55	54
VI	Public Force	127	..	5	121	..	..	1	..	..
VII	Public Administration	307	32	108	14	..	4	149	..	..
VIII	Religion	463	74	88	93	2	9	96	99	2
VIII	Medicine	8	6	2	..	..	..	..	..	..
VIII	Instruction	3	..	1	2	..	..	..	..	..
VIII	Letters and Arts and Sciences	2	..	1	..	..	..	..	1	..
IX	Persons living on their Income	367	326	8	16	1	7	4	5	..
X	Domestic Service	70	18	12	15	..	1	3	9	12
XI	Insufficiently described occupations	160	118	3	28	..	2	..	3	6
XII	Unproductive	155	8	30	11	..	2	1	89	14
	TENANTS OF ALL KINDS	50,915	3,003	3,364	546	29	606	13,079	28,878	1,378
	Tenants, etc., who returned following Subsidiary Occupations	7,220	349	786	110	2	129	2,260	3,460	174
I	Non-cultivating owners	142	1	..	1	..	5	10	125	..
I	Cultivating owners	477	10	8	23	..	18	..	412	..
I	Tenants	76	..	49	..	..	2	8	17	..
I	Field labourers	298	64	9	42	..	3	37	142	1
I	Fruit, etc., growers	3	..	..	..	..	..	2	1	..
I	Cattle and buffalo breeders and keepers	645	..	94	..	..	..	248	303	..
I	Breeders of transport animals	75	..	..	..	..	..	44	21	10
I	Herdsmen, shepherds and breeders of other animals	3,849	119	470	35	..	76	1,278	1,828	43
I	Others	37	..	..	..	..	..	20	..	17
II	Exploitation of minerals	5	..	..	..	..	..	..	5	..
III	Industry	494	14	50	3	..	1	72	350	4
IV	Transport	384	41	25	1	..	8	158	118	33

36.—Subsidiary Occupations of Agriculturists.

	Occupation.	Baluchistan.	Districts.						States.	
			Quetta-Pishin.	Loralai.	Zhob.	Bolan.	Chaghai.	Sibi.	Kalat.	Las Bela.
V	Trade	158	46	11	..	..	13	64	24	..
VI	Public Force	..	..	..	..	..	..	..	..	..
VII	Public Administration	16	..	4	..	..	1	10	1	..
VIII	Religion	85	5	3	1	..	1	46	24	5
	Medicine	5	..	..	..	..	..	3	2	..
	Instruction	..	..	..	..	..	..	..	..	..
	Letters and Arts and Sciences	24	..	4	..	..	..	11	9	..
IX	Persons living on their Income	74	37	..	..	2	..	11	24	..
X	Domestic Service	127	1	4	1	..	1	42	17	61
XI	Insufficiently described occupations	13	4	..	..	..	..	9	..	..
XII	Unproductive	233	1	5	3	..	..	187	37	..
	FIELD LABOURERS	**6,002**	**1,180**	**241**	**340**	**6**	**24**	**343**	**3,727**	**141**
	Field Labourers who returned following subsidiary Occupation	**402**	**72**	**27**	**31**	..	**1**	**18**	**247**	**6**
I	Non-cultivating owners	18	8	5	..	..	..	1	2	2
	Cultivating owners	114	18	..	..	..	..	..	96	..
	Tenants	64	10	..	..	..	..	2	52	..
	Cattle and buffalo breeders and keepers	4	..	..	..	..	1	..	1	2
	Herdsmen, shepherds and breeders of other animals	129	17	14	24	..	..	12	60	2
II	Industry	16	8	2	3	..	..	..	3	..
IV	Transport	26	4	..	..	..	..	..	22	..
VII	Public Administration	7	..	..	..	..	..	1	6	..
VIII	Religion	3	..	..	3	..	..	..	..	..
	Medicine	..	..	..	..	..	..	..	..	..
	Instruction	..	..	..	..	..	..	..	..	..
	Letters and Arts and Sciences	..	..	..	..	..	..	..	..	..
IX	Persons living on their Income	7	7	..	..	..	..	..	..	..
XI	Insufficiently described occupations	1	..	..	..	..	..	..	1	..
XII	Unproductive	13	..	6	1	..	..	2	4	..

37.—Certain Mixed Occupations.

(ACTUAL WORKERS ONLY.)

	Occupation.	Baluchistan.	Districts. Total.	Quetta Pishin.	Loralai	Zhob.	Bolan.	Chagai	Sibi.	States. Total.	Kalat.	Las-Bela.
	SHEEP AND GOAT BREEDING. ..	**47,332**	**35,448**	**2,077**	**7,772**	**4,796**	**8**	**1,970**	**8,926**	**21,883**	**17,249**	**4,634**
	(i) As Principal Occupation ..	**20,856**	**7,469**	**543**	**2,095**	**1,994**	**6**	**1,340**	**1,491**	**13,387**	**9,660**	**3,727**
	With following Subsidiary Occupations-											
I	Non-cultivating owners ..	302	115	4	31	32	..	35	13	187	168	19
I	Cultivating owners ..	604	144	17	76	32	..	19	..	460	458	2
I	Tenant cultivators ..	641	72	11	30	13	1	15	4	469	120	349
I	Agricultural labourers ..	236	100	15	48	34	..	..	3	136	100	36
I	Market gardeners, flower and fruit growers	..	..	..	..	..	..	..	..	..	..	..
I	Wood cutters	14	4	..	..	4	..	..	..	10	2	8
I	Cattle and buffalo breeders ..	14	..	..	..	..	..	..	..	14	..	14
I	Breeders of transport animals ..	628	12	..	12	..	..	..	..	616	5	611
I	Herdsmen, shepherds and breeders of other animals ..	350	213	3	80	61	..	23	46	137	91	46
I	Others	5	..	..	..	..	..	..	..	5	..	5
II	Exploitation of minerals ..	..	..	..	..	..	..	..	..	..	..	..
III	Industry	71	34	2	13	1	..	8	10	37	2	35
IV	Transport	1,456	208	11	106	65	..	18	8	748	44	704
V	Trade	706	430	16	373	13	..	7	21	276	224	52
VI	Public Force	2	2	..	..	2	..	..	..	..	..	..
VII	Public Administrations ..	4	4	..	..	..	..	..	4	..	..	..
VIII	Religion	33	32	7	6	12	..	7	..	1	1	..
VIII	Letters and Arts and Sciences ..	1	..	..	..	..	..	..	..	1	..	1
IX	Persons living on their income	4	4	..	..	4	..	..	..	..	..	..
X	Domestic Service	19	11	..	..	1	..	5	5	8	..	8
XI	Insufficiently described occupation	..	..	..	..	..	..	..	..	..	..	..
XII	Unproductive	12	10	4	1	..	..	3	2	2	2	..
	(ii) As Subsidiary Occupation ..	**26,476**	**17,980**	**1,534**	**5,577**	**2,802**	**2**	**630**	**7,435**	**8,496**	**7,589**	**907**
	With following Principal Occupations-											
I	Non-cultivating owners ..	742	323	10	176	78	..	12	47	419	407	12
I	Cultivating owners ..	20,538	14,891	1,229	4,798	2,602	..	444	5,918	5,647	4,973	674
I	Tenant cultivators ..	3,849	1,978	119	470	35	..	76	1,278	1,871	1,828	43
I	Agricultural labourers ..	129	67	17	14	24	..	..	12	62	60	2
I	Wood cutters, etc.	11	9	..	..	..	..	..	9	2	1	1
I	Cattle and buffalo breeders and keepers	4	..	..	..	..	..	..	..	4	..	4
I	Breeders of transport animals ..	16	4	..	4	..	..	..	..	12	..	12
I	Herdsmen, shepherds and breeders of other animals ..	350	213	3	80	61	..	23	46	137	91	46
I	Fishing and pearling ..	2	..	..	..	..	..	..	..	2	..	2
III	Industry	62	40	4	11	13	..	9	3	22	18	4
IV	Transport	280	184	36	8	7	..	27	106	96	24	72
V	Trade	228	115	99	9	..	2	1	4	113	96	17
VI	Public Force	129	102	6	4	65	..	25	2	27	15	12
VII	Public Administration ..	20	12	5	3	3	..	..	1	8	5	3
VIII	Religion	25	18	4	..	11	..	1	2	7	6	1
VIII	Medicine	5	5	..	..	..	..	..	5	..	..	..
VIII	Letters, Arts and Sciences .	5	..	..	..	..	..	..	..	5	4	1
IX	Persons living on their income	32	2	..	..	..	..	1	1	30	30	..
X	Domestic Service ..	28	13	1	..	1	..	10	1	15	14	1
XI	Insufficiently described occupations	1	1	..	..	1	..	..	..	..	..	..
XII	Unproductive	20	3	1	..	1	..	1	..	17	17	..
	PACK ANIMAL DRIVING	**6,782**	**2,533**	**867**	**337**	**214**	**15**	**288**	**622**	**4,249**	**2,268**	**1,981**
	(i) As Principal Occupation ..	**3,847**	**1,707**	**455**	**467**	**106**	**13**	**203**	**463**	**2,140**	**1,406**	**734**
	With following Subsidiary Occupations—											
I	Non-cultivating owners ..	55	45	4	..	25	..	2	14	10	7	3
I	Cultivating owners ..	15	15	14	..	1	..	..	..	..	..	..
I	Tenants cultivators	38	15	10	..	..	..	3	2	23	20	3
I	Agricultural labourers ..	60	8	2	6	..	..	..	..	52	48	4
I	Wood cutters	2	..	..	..	..	..	..	..	2	..	2
I	Cattle and buffalo breeders ..	5	..	..	..	..	..	..	..	5	3	2
I	Breeders of transport animals ..	29	..	..	..	..	..	..	..	29	23	6
I	Herdsmen, shepherds and breeders of other animals ..	222	127	5	10	5	..	7	100	95	24	71
II	Exploitation of minerals ..	..	..	..	..	..	..	..	..	..	..	..
III	Industry	169	140	..	7	..	..	2	131	29	24	5
IV	Transport	16	6	..	1	2	..	3	..	10	..	10
V	Trade	194	138	..	136	1	..	..	1	56	50	6
VI	Public Force ..	..	..	..	..	..	..	..	..	..	..	..
VII	Public Administration ..	..	..	..	..	..	..	..	..	..	..	..
VIII	Religion	4	1	..	..	..	..	1	..	3	..	3
IX	Persons living on their income ..	..	..	..	..	..	..	..	..	..	..	..
X	Domestic Service	4	..	..	..	..	..	..	..	4	1	3
XI	Insufficiently described occupation	..	..	..	..	..	..	..	..	..	..	..
XII	Unproductive	..	..	..	..	..	..	..	..	..	..	..

37.—Certain Mixed Occupations.

	Occupation.	Baluchistan.	Districts.							States.		
			Total.	Quetta Pishin.	Loralai.	Zhob.	Bolan.	Chagai	Sibi.	Total.	Kalat.	Las Bela.
	(ii) As Subsidiary Occupation ..	**2,935**	**826**	**152**	**370**	**108**	**2**	**35**	**159**	**2,109**	**862**	**1,247**
	With following Principal Occupations—											
I	Non-cultivating owners ..	75	32	17	12	1	1	1	..	43	35	8
I	Cultivating owners ..	964	163	96	3	43	1	8	12	801	479	322
I	Tenant cultivators ..	258	143	24	19	..	..	7	93	115	83	32
I	Agricultural labourers ..	24	2	2	..	..	..	..	..	22	22	..
I	Wood cutters	1	..	..	..	..	..	..	..	1	..	1
I	Cattle and buffalo breeders ..	71	..	..	..	..	..	..	..	71	..	71
I	Breeders of transport animals ..	204	77	..	63	..	..	4	10	127	63	64
I	Herdsmen, shepherds and breeders of other animals ..	924	181	6	105	64	..	6	..	743	41	702
I	Fishing and pearling ..	13	..	..	..	..	..	..	..	13	..	13
III	Industry	162	47	3	..	..	..	..	44	115	108	7
IV	Transport	9	..	..	..	..	..	..	..	9	2	7
V	Trade	188	176	3	168	..	..	5	..	12	2	10
VI	Public Force	..	..	..	..	..	..	..	..	..	..	..
VII	Public Administration ..	1	..	..	..	..	..	..	..	1	1	..
VIII	Religion	7	4	1	..	..	..	3	..	3	3	..
VIII	Medicine	..	..	..	..	..	..	..	..	11	11	..
IX	Persons living on their income	11	..	..	..	..	..	..	..	11	..	..
X	Domestic Service ..	8	..	..	..	..	..	..	..	8	..	8
XI	Insufficiently described occupations	..	..	..	..	..	..	..	..	..	..	..
XII	Unproductive	15	1	..	..	..	..	1	..	14	12	2

CHAPTER IX.

LITERACY.

180. This chapter deals with the statistics contained in the following tables :— **Reference to statistics.**

Particulars.	Table.	Part I of this Report page.	Part II of this Report page.
Literacy by Religion and Age ..	Imperial Table XIII ..	..	71
Literacy by selected Castes, Tribes or Races	Imperial Table XIV ..	..	79
Population of Political Agencies by Religion and Literacy.	Provincial Table II ..	..	128
Literacy among Muslims by Locality ..	Subsidiary Table 38 ..	126	.
Literacy among Indigenous Muslim tribes..	Subsidiary Table 39 ..	127	..
Number of Institutions and pupils according to the returns of the Education Department.	Subsidiary Table 40 ..	128	..

181. The criterion of Literacy for purposes of this chapter was whether a person could read a letter and write an answer to it. All children below five years of age were excluded from this inquiry. In the synchronous areas the information was collected in columns 16 and 17 of the Standard Schedule. In non-synchronous tracts a separate form was used. As the numbers in the latter were very small, the information was collected by families or hamlets and only numbers of literate persons were recorded with the names of the languages in which literate. **Definition of Literacy and instructions to Enumerators.**

The following instructions were issued to enumerators in the Regular Areas :—

" *Column* 16. A person should not be entered as literate unless he or she can write a " letter to a friend and read the answer to it. If a person can read and write in the Roman " Character, write 'Roman.' In the case of persons who are literate, one of the marginal " languages in which the individual is literate should be recorded in Column 16 adding the " class which the person concerned has passed or up to which he or she has studied. Otherwise " enter the word 'Literate' against all persons, who can both read and write a letter in any " other language. If illiterate make a cross thus ×. In the case of literates in English the " entry about Roman Character need not be made in this column.

a Arabic.
b Persian.
c Urdu.
d Lande-Sindhi.
e Lande-Punjabi.
f Sindhi.
g Gurmukhi.
h Hindi Nagri.
i Roman Urdu.

" *Column* 17. The question is whether the person enumerated is familiar with English " or not, *i.e.*, whether he or she can write and read a letter in English."

These instructions were applied *mutatis mutandis* to the Tribal Areas.

182. Education in Baluchistan is imparted by two different methods, namely, education by indigenous methods in mosques for Muslims and in temple Pathshalas for Hindus, and education in Government and aided schools. The former consists of two stages. In the first stage, the Muslim pupils are taught to read the holy Koran by rote in Arabic besides instruction in the principal religious formulæ which are essential for every Muslim to know as a true follower of the Holy Prophet of Islam. This education is imparted in the mosques by the village Mullas and is considered to be almost compulsory for every Muslim family. Instruction on these lines, though on the wane, is still carried on but the products of these mosque schools cannot fulfil even the simple requirements of our definition of literate. The Mulla is not a regular paid servant as in Government schools **Extent of Literacy.**

excepting the few who have been trained as teachers for elementary secular education and receive Rs. 20 per mensem when they open a school in which religious education is combined with elementary secular education. He is the Imām for prayers in the mosque. He performs all religious ceremonies for the whole village and receives remuneration from his congregation at harvest times, on ceremonial occasions and on festive days. This system of education has received a set back since the opening of Government schools in which religious education is not imparted.

The second stage in indigenous Muslim education consists of religious instruction to enable local youngmen to act as Mullas or priests and teachers in mosque schools. After completing his elementary spiritual instruction in his village, the candidate for the Mulla class leaves his home to receive education in Mohammadan Law under a Mulla of renown within the Province, in Kandahar, or in India. Students of this class are known as *Tālibs* and are able to read and write chiefly in Persian. Most of these *Tālibs* have no means of subsistence and while under instruction away from their homes they live on the charity of the villagers who provide them with cooked food and clothing, etc.

The second method of education is, as stated above, education in Government or aided schools.

Education among the indigenous and domiciled Hindus is imparted both in indigenous institutions known as Pathshalas attached to temples and in Government schools. The standard of literacy in their case is higher, for, a Hindu student educated in a Pathshala is able to carry on correspondence in his own vernacular, Lande-Sindhi or Lande-Punjabi. Moreover he is well trained in accounts and when he leaves the Pathshala, he is trained in business under the eye of his father until he is a full-fledged business man. The statistics discussed in this chapter deal with the products of all these institutions.

In a total population of 868,617 persons, Baluchistan can boast of only 40,775 literates. Of these, literate aliens from outside the Province numbered 31,578 or 774 *per mille*, while there were only 9,197 literates belonging to indigenous tribes. The latter consist of 5,101 Muslims in a total indigenous Muslim population of 743,172 and 4,084 Hindus in an indigenous Hindu population of 16,905, giving a proportion of 7 Muslim and 242 Hindu literates *per mille* of their respective total populations.

Literacy in Baluchistan is compared with that of some other Indian Provinces and States in Diagram No. 19.

Literacy by Districts and States.

183. Literacy by Political and Administrative divisions is exhibited in the marginal table. The Districts contribute 88 per cent. and the States 12 per cent. of the total literate population. Of the Districts, Quetta-Pishin accounts for 60 per cent. Zhob with 9 comes next followed by Sibi, Loralai and Chagai with 7, 7 and 3 per cent. respectively; Bolan with 2 per cent. comes last. In the States area, the Kalat State contributes 10 per cent. and Las Bela only 2. Taking the Kalat State Divisions separately, Kachhi stands foremost with 5 per cent. The remaining 5 per cent. is distributed among the remaining divisions of Kalat including Kharan. Literacy by Districts and States as also by indigenous, and alien population is illustrated in Diagram No. 20. In every 100 literates in the Province, the Quetta town and cantonment alone account for 50 per cent. Quetta is the capital of the province with a large military garrison and central Government Departmental offices. It is the biggest trade centre and possesses the largest number of schools.

Districts and States.	Total population.			Literates.		
	Persons.	Males.	Females.	Persons.	Males.	Females.
BALUCHISTAN ..	868,617	488,414	380,208	40,775	36,835	3,940
DISTRICTS ..	463,508	270,004	193,504	35,844	31,986	3,858
Quetta-Pishin ..	147,541	90,302	57,239	25,044	21,917	3,127
Loralai ..	86,087	47,936	38,151	2,746	2,587	159
Zhob ..	57,963	34,596	23,367	3,672	3,521	151
Bolan ..	4,688	3,466	1,222	717	649	68
Chagai ..	24,224	13,721	10,503	801	749	52
Sibi ..	143,005	79,983	63,022	2,864	2,563	301
STATES ..	405,109	218,410	186,699	4,931	4,849	82
Kalat ..	342,101	184,915	157,186	4,101	4,045	56
Las Bela ..	63,008	33,495	29,513	830	804	26

DIAGRAM NO. 19

TOTAL LITERATE AND ILLITERATE POPULATION OF BALUCHISTAN COMPARED WITH OTHER PROVINCES AND STATES OF INDIA.

Scale 1 Sq. Inch = 500,000 Persons

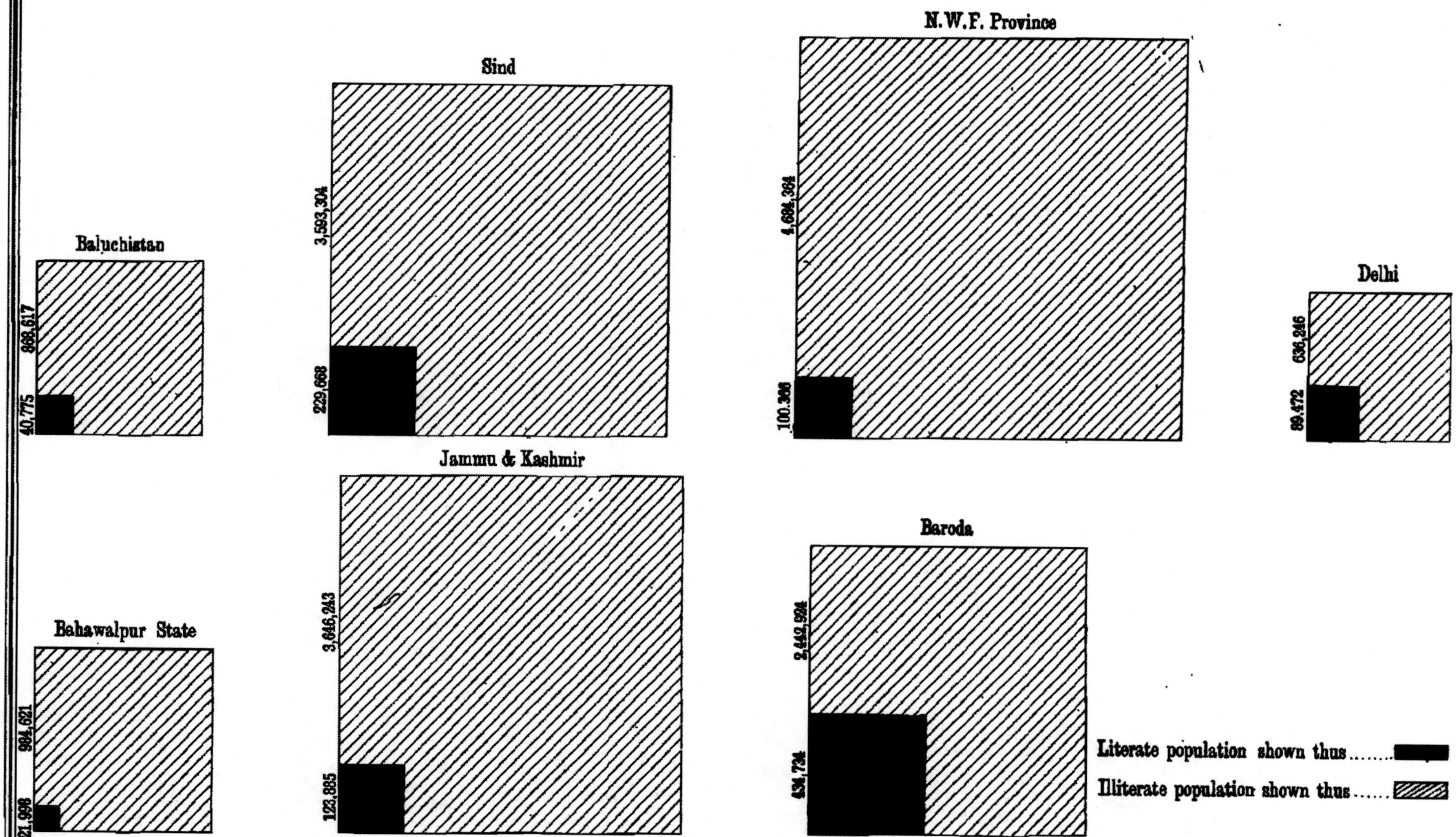

Reg No. 26. ED(E'Coy) 1833-550

DIAGRAM NO. 20

PROPORTION OF LITERACY TO TOTAL POPULATION IN BRITISH TERRITORY AND STATES IN BALUCHISTAN

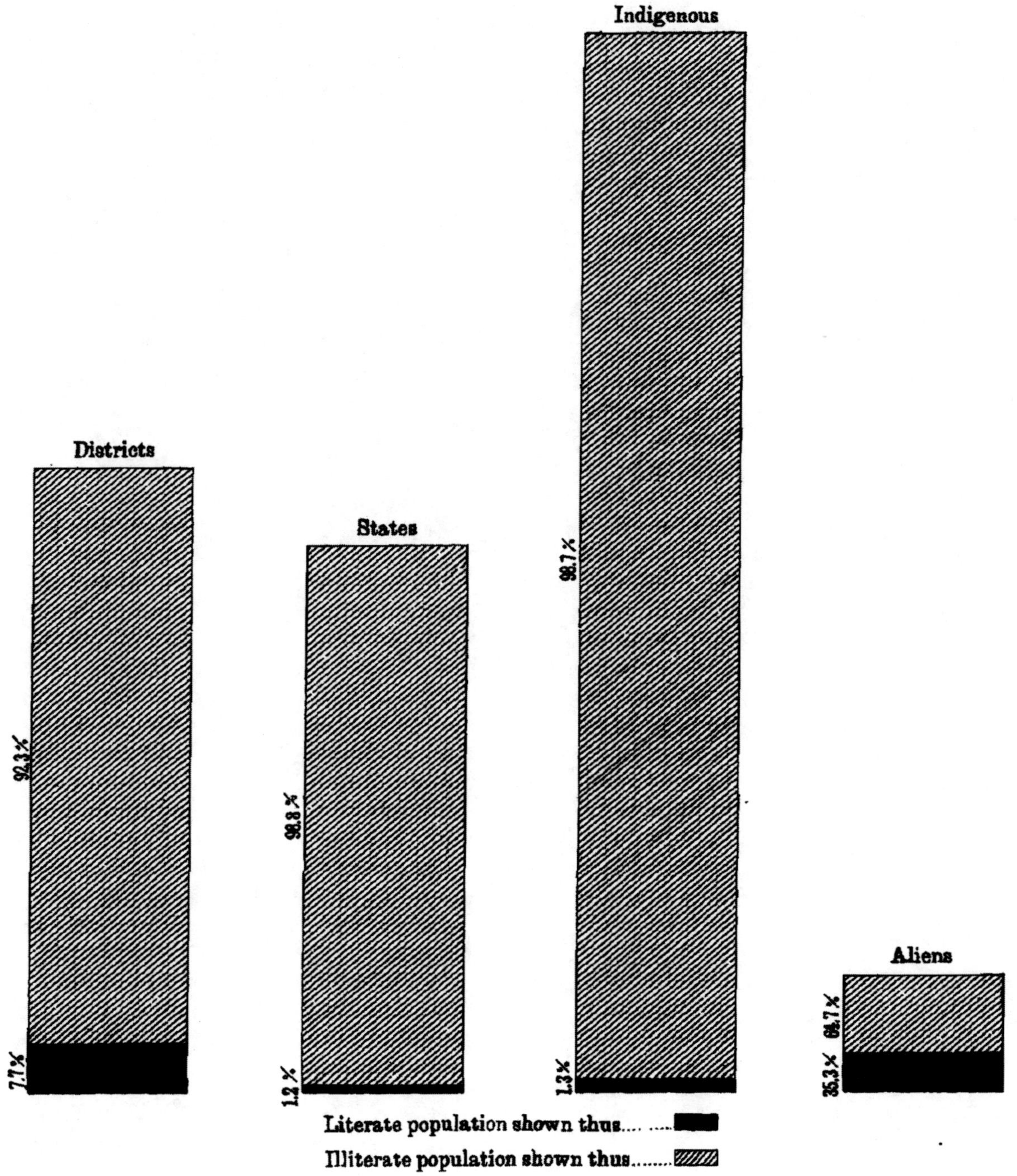

Reg No. 29. ED(E Coy) 1933.550

Literacy by religion.

184. Statistics of literacy by religion are given in the margin. It will be seen that in every 100 literates in the Province, there are 45 Hindus, 10 Sikhs, 31 Muslims (21 aliens and 10 indigenous inhabitants), 13 Christians and one belonging to other religions. The statistics of percentage on the total numerical strength of each religion are still more interesting. Literacy is highest among Zoroastrians. Out of every 100 of their population, the Zoroastrians have 71 literates; Christians 67; Sikhs 49; Hindus 34, and Muslims 2. Splitting the Muslims into aliens and indigenous, the percentage for the former rises to 20 while for the latter it falls to the negligible figure of one literate in every 100 indigenous inhabitants. Diagram No. 21 illustrates the ratio of literates to the population of each religion.

	Persons.	Males.	Females.
Muslims.			
(a) Indigenous and semi-indigenous ..	6,117	5,987	130
(b) Aliens ..	6,539	6,106	433
Hindus.			
(a) Indigenous ..	4,084	3,968	116
(b) Aliens ..	14,277	12,890	1,387
Sikhs.			
(a) Indigenous ..	12	11	1
(b) Aliens ..	4,181	3,658	523
Christians ..	5,369	4,075	1,294
Others ..	196	140	56

Racial Distribution of Indigenous Muslim literates.

185. Taking the literates by indigenous Muslim races we find that out of a total of 40,775 literates there were only 5,101 indigenous inhabitants who were returned as literate. The majority of these are literate only to this extent that they can decipher a letter and write a reply in Persian or Urdu and possibly include a small admixture of those who can only read the holy Korán in Arabic and can copy the words in that script without understanding the meaning. In the indigenous literate population, the Pathans have more literates than any other race. For every 100 indigenous literates there are 35 Pathans who can read and write; 20 Brahuis; 18 Baloch; 12 Sayyids; 7 others; 6 Jatts and 2 Lasis. Again, taking each tribe according to its numerical strength, we find that the Sayyids top the list as they did at the previous censuses. In every 1,000 Sayyids there are 27 who can read and write. The Pathans come next with 10 per 1,000 of indigenous Pathan population. They live almost entirely in tracts under direct British control where they enjoy comparatively greater facilities for education. The most watchful and adventurous of all indigenous races, the Pathans with their innate enthusiasm for religious instruction—they still supply most of the religious teachers—have taken full advantage of the facilities for secular education which Government has provided at their doors. The Brahuis stand third in the list with 7 literates per 1,000 of their total tribal strength. Here also greater educational facilities for Brahuis nearer Quetta and Mustung are responsible for this place of honour.

	Population.	Literates.		
		Persons.	Males.	Females.
Baloch ..	226,041	944	934	10
Brahui ..	152,588	1,012	1,004	8
Pathan ..	176,007	1,755	1,733	22
Lasi ..	31,812	115	115	..
Jatt ..	77,157	318	318	..
Sayyid ..	21,976	587	578	9
Other Indigenous Muslims ..	57,591	370	340	30

Sayyids,	27	Baloch,	4
Pathan,	10	Jatt,	4
Brahui,	7	Lasi	4
Other	6		

The ranks of "Others" have been swelled by the Khojas and Hazaras. The former belong to the trading class for whom reading and writing is essential. The Hazaras get their education in Military service and having lost a foothold in their own country have turned their attention to educating their children in the local schools of Quetta where they mostly reside.

The Baloch and the Jatt races have each 4 literates per 1,000 of their respective numerical strengths. The Baloch live chiefly in the Mari and Bugti country, the plains of Kachhi and in Chagai, Makran and Kharan. The nomadic habits of the Maris and the Bugtis, and the lack of educational institutions combined with their prejudices have been a stumbling block in the way of their educational advancement. Under the guidance of their enlightened chiefs, however, a considerable advance may be expected during the next decennium.

The Baloch of Kachhi, like the Jatt inhabiting that area, are mostly agriculturists. Owing to uncertainties of means of irrigation in this area, they have been rendered practically homeless. They are constantly on the move backwards and forwards between the Kalat State and Sind. They return to their deserted homes with the approach of normal floods in the Nari river. They return bag and baggage to Sind in search of livelihood when floods fail. In this impoverished state of life, educational advancement among the Baloch and Jatt of the plains of Kachhi is out of the question.

Literacy by Indigenous Muslim Tribes.

186. Let us now examine the statistics by tribes in order to ascertain which of the tribes are educationally more advanced. Here I must offer an apology before entering into the discussion, for, in many cases, the proportional figures exceed the actual numbers of our literates.

Taking the Baloch first of the three principal indigenous races inhabiting this province, namely, the Baloch, the Brahui, and the Pathan, the Rakhshani Baloch tribe is the most advanced with 106 literates per 10,000 of its total strength. Next come the Eastern Rind with 42 followed by the Khetran with 41 and the Magasis with 26.

Among the Brahuis, the Shahwanis who live largely in the vicinity of Quetta and Mustung top the list with 187 literates per 10,000. The Muhammadshahis come next with 183 followed by the Raisanis with 122, Lahris 105, Bangulzais, Langav and Mengal with 73, 45 and 39 respectively. The Zahris, as was expected, stand at the bottom with 8 literates in every 10,000.

Among the Pathans, the Snatia Kakars stand foremost with 146 literates per 10,000. The Tor Tarin with 120 stand second, Targharas third with 106, Abdal Achakzais fourth with 65. The Pani Mandokhel and Pani Musakhel go last with 45 and 41 respectively.

Literacy by Language for Indigenous Races and Tribes.

187. It will be seen from the marginal table that of the 40,775 literates in the whole province there are 11,588 literates in English, of whom only 484 are indigenous and semi-indigenous or 7 per 10,000 of their total population—a clear proof of the fact that literacy is largely confined at present to reading and writing a letter; for, English is taught only in the higher classes.

Tribe.	Total number of literates.	Literate in					
		Urdu.	Persian.	Arabic.	Sindhi.	Roman.	English.
A.—Baloch.							
Eastern-Rind ..	180	86	42	2	77	..	3
Khetran ..	70	59	11	..	..	..	9
Magasi ..	34	16	15	1	10	..	..
Rakhshani ..	256	39	232	5	..	..	4
B.—Brahui.							
Shahwani ..	114	78	65	3	..	..	4
Raisani ..	33	11	24	1	..	..	1
Muhammadshahi ..	50	24	39	..	..	..	..
Bangulzai ..	54	38	29	1	3	..	2
Langav ..	30	19	21	..	..	..	2
Mengal ..	104	55	58	3	1	4	12
Zahri ..	28	14	18	..	2	..	1
C.—Pathan.							
Snatia ..	288	197	122	12	..	..	6
Targhara ..	129	104	102	13	..	..	5
Tor Tarin ..	81	50	33	..	..	..	2
Abdal-Achakzai ..	128	84	61	..	..	..	3
Pani ..	131	75	70	13	..	..	13
,, Musakhel ..	56	16	40	4	..	..	4

Literacy in English.

188. In literacy in English, the lion's share goes to the Christians who contribute 45 per cent. Hindus follow with 28 per cent. Next come Muslims and Sikhs with 18 and 8 per cent. respectively. The proportion of literacy compared to total population is highest among Zoroastrians, 65 per cent. of whom are literate in English. The Christians are second with 64 per cent., the Sikhs third with 12, the Hindus fourth with 6 and the Muslims last with 0·3 per cent., or 3 literates per 1,000 of their total population.

Religion.	*Persons.*	*Males.*	*Females.*
TOTAL ..	11,588	10,063	1,525
Christians	5,198	3,934	1,264
Hindus	3,212	3,120	92
Muslims	2,055	1,997	58
Sikhs	987	930	57
Zoroastrians	109	61	48
Buddhists	12	9	3
Jains	2	2	..
Jews	6	6	..
Others	7	4	3

DIAGRAM NO. 21

THE RATIO OF LITERATES TO THE POPULATION OF EACH RELIGION IN BALUCHISTAN

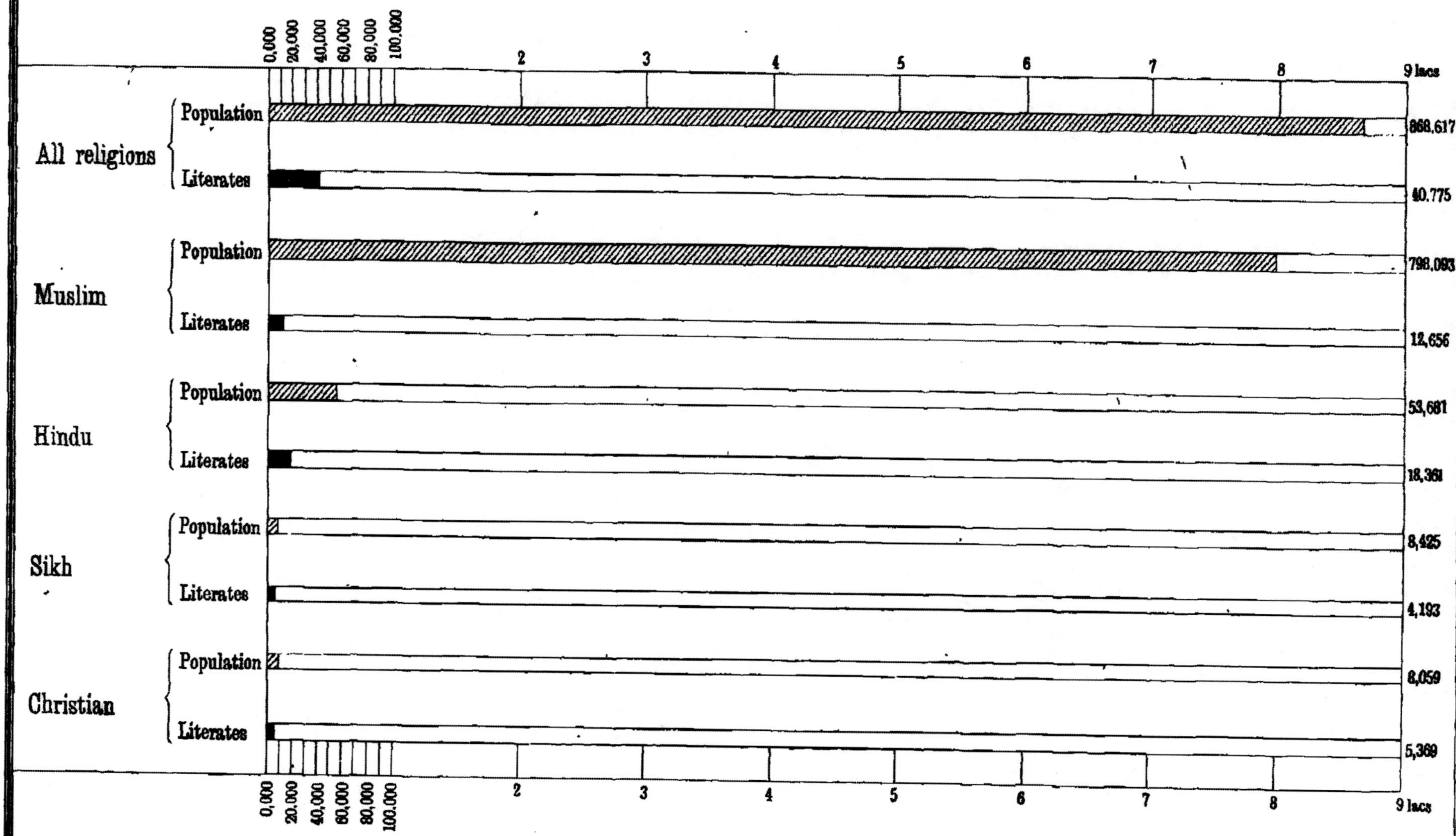

Literacy among females.

189. Of a total of 40,775 literates for all religions in the whole province, female literates in 1931 numbered only 3,940. Their distribution by religions is given in the margin. Excepting the indigenous Muslims, the population is of a fluid nature and the numbers vary from year to year. The statistics of the indigenous literates are therefore of real interest. In the marginal table figures are given of female literates for the more important tribes. Out of a total indigenous and semi-indigenous Muslim population of 765,096 there are all told 130 literate females, 98 in British territory and 32 in the States. Although female literacy shows a steady increase, the numbers having risen from 36 in 1911 and 85 in 1921 to 130 in 1931, the day is yet far off when progress of female education will begin to make a real start. One potent factor however which is indicative of better times for female education cannot be ignored, and this is the demand that has recently sprung up among educated local young men for educated wives. And it is a sign of the times that some of the more advanced parents of girls are taking a lively interest to co-operate in meeting the demand. The wish at least to educate girls is there; what is lacking are safeguards for female education which it is not easy to provide to the satisfaction of parents.

Religion.	*Female literates.*	*Female literates per 1,000 male literates.*
Hindus	1,503	89
Christians	1,294	318
Muslims	563	47
Sikhs	524	143
Zoroastrians	48	687
All other religions	8	114

Tribe.	*Female literates.*	*Tribe.*	*Female literates.*
A.—Baloch.		C.—Pathan.	
Indigenous.		*Indigenous.*	
Rind Eastern ..	1	Jafar ..	4
Rakhshani ..	2	Kakar Sanzarkhel	1
Rind Western ..	3	Kasi ..	1
Other Baloch ..	4	Pani Zarkun ..	1
Semi-Indigenous.		Tor Tarin ..	1
Buzdar ..	1	Other Pathans ..	14
B.—Brahui.		*Semi-Indigenous.*	
Ahmadzai ..	1	Durrani ..	32
Bangulzai ..	1	Ghilzai ..	6
Shahwani ..	1	Others ..	1
Muhammad Hasni	1	D.—Sayyids ..	9
Mengal ..	1	E.—Other Muslims	41
Others ..	3		

In the marginal statement are shown proportions of female literates per 1,000 male literates among indigenous Muslims. With the exception of the Baloch, Jatt and Lasi, there has been an all round increase over the figures of 1911 and 1921. The Baloch show an increase over the figures of 1921. The Jatt and Lasi still lag behind. Among the Sayyids the total number of literate females is 9 and among the Pathans 61 (Jaffars 4, Sanzarkhel, Kasi, Zarkun Pani and Tor Tarin one each), unspecified Pathans 14 and 32, 6, and 1 in the semi-indigenous Durrani, Ghilzai and the rest respectively. The Brahuis have 8 in all, one each in the Ahmadzai, Bangulzai, Shahwani, Muhammad Hasni and Mengal, and three among "Others" of the Miscellaneous group. The other Muslims claim 41 out of whom the Khojas alone return 24. The remaining 17 are divided among Sorozai 4, Dehwar 1, "Others" 1, and semi-indigenous Hazaras 11. The Baloch have 11 in all, Western Rind 3, Rakhshanis 2, the Eastern Rind 1, Others 4 and the semi-indigenous Buzdars 1.

Tribe.	Proportion of female literates per 1,000 male literates.		
	1911.	1921.	1931.
Indigenous Muslims ..	10	9	16
Sayyid ..	11	14	16
Pathan ..	2	4	13
Brahui ..	7	1	8
Others ..	14	53	88
Baloch ..	19	10	11
Jatt ..	9	3	..
Lasi ..	22	4	..

Variation in Literacy.

190. In the margin are given statistics of literates for 1911, 1921 and 1931. There is an all-round increase both under males and females as well as in the number of literates in English. There were 31 male and 2 female literates *per mille* in 1911. The numbers rose to 44 and 3 respectively in 1921, and to 5 for females in 1931, but the proportion

	Literates.			Literates in English.		
	Persons.	Males.	Females.	Persons.	Males.	Female.
1911 ..	27,925	26,202	1,723	6,321	5,541	780
1921 ..	37,380	34,905	2,475	9,291	8,454	837
1931 ..	40,775	36,835	3,940	11,588	10,063	1,525

for males fell to 43. Seventy-five per cent. of the total literate population are aliens whose numbers are subject to constant fluctuations which accounts for the decrease. Real educational progress in the country can only be gauged by an analysis of statistics of indigenous inhabitants who form 88 per cent. of the total population. The numbers of indigenous literate Muslims are given in the margin.

	Persons.	Males.	Females.
1911	3,481	3,446	35
1921	4,199	4,162	37
1931	5,101	5,022	79

Racial and Tribal Variation.

191. Variation by races and principal tribes among the indigenous Muslim literates is shown below—

Race and Tribe.	1911. Persons.	1911. Males.	1911. Females.	1921. Persons.	1921. Males.	1921. Females.	1931. Persons.	1931. Males.	1931. Females.
A. BALOCH	639	627	12	814	806	8	944	934	10
Rakhshani	104	104	..	149	147	2	256	254	2
Eastern Rind	82	81	1	178	178	..	180	179	1
Khetran	35	35	..	101	101	..	70	70	..
Magasi	35	31	4	21	20	1	34	34	..
B. BRAHUI	542	538	4	784	783	1	1,012	1,004	8
Shahwani	42	42	..	45	45	..	114	113	1
Mengal	56	56	..	52	52	..	104	103	1
Bangulzai	35	35	..	29	29	..	54	53	1
Muhammadshahi	11	10	1	43	43	..	50	50	..
Lahri	25	24	1	53	52	1	47	47	..
Raisani	16	16	..	32	32	..	33	33	..
Langav	74	74	..	65	65	..	30	30	..
C. PATHAN	940	938	2	1,256	1,251	5	1,755	1,733	22
Kakar-Snatia	181	181	..	168	168	..	288	288	..
Kasi	57	57	..	63	63	..	155	154	1
Kakar-Targhara	63	63	..	95	95	..	129	129	..
Abdal-Achakzai	61	61	..	79	79	..	128	128	..
Tor Tarin	89	89	..	128	128	..	81	80	1
Pani-Mandokhel	48	48	..	23	23	..	21	21	..
D. LASI	189	185	4	229	228	1	115	115	..
E. JATT	445	441	4	367	366	1	318	318	..
F. SAYYID	361	357	4	449	443	6	587	578	9
G. OTHERS	365	360	5	300	285	15	370	340	30

The Brahui and the Pathan show a high rate of advance of 87 per cent. each since 1911. Among the Baloch progress has been slower, the increase in the number of literates between 1911 and 1931 being only 48 per cent. The Lasi show a decline of 39 and the Jatt of 29 per cent. during these 20 years due evidently to migration into Sind where the educated have greater chances of employment. Looking at tribal figures, we find that education is most popular among the Muhammadshahi Brahuis who show an increase of 355 per cent. since 1911 (unfortunately however the actual number of literates was only 11 in 1911 and 50 in 1931). Second in order of merit are the Kasi Pathans with an increase of 172. Next come the Shahwani Brahuis with 171 followed by the Rakhshani Baloch with an increase of 146 per cent. since 1911. The high percentage of increase in these cases is due to comparatively greater educational facilities. The highest decrease occurs under Langav Brahuis and Mandokhel Pathans due to lack of educational facilities in remote localities. Percentage increases and decreases for the main tribes are given in the marginal table.

Race and Tribe.	*Increase* %+ *Decrease* %−	Race and Tribe.	*Increase* %+ *Decrease* %−
A. BALOCH ..	+47·7	C. PATHAN ..	+86·7
Rakhshani ..	+146·1	Kasi ..	+171·9
Eastern Rind ..	+119·5	Abdal Achakzai ..	+109·8
Khetran ..	+100·0	Kakar Targhara ..	+104·7
Magasi ..	−2·8	Kakar Snatia ..	+59·1
		Tor Tarin ..	−8·9
B. BRAHUI ..	+86·7	Pani Mandokhel ..	−56·2
Muhammadshahi ..	+354·5		
Shahwani ..	+171·4	D. LASI ..	−39·1
Raisani ..	+106·2		
Lahri ..	+88·0	E. JATT ..	−28·5
Mengal ..	+85·7		
Bangulzai ..	+64·2	F. SAYYID ..	+62·6
Langav ..	−59·4		
		G. OTHERS ..	+1·8

Variation by Districts and Divisions of States.

192. The numbers of literates *per mille* at the Censuses of 1911, 1921 and 1931 are shown in the margin. Quetta-Pishin, Bolan and Zhob show a steady increase since 1911. Loralai has stood fast since 1921 owing to changes in the population of the Military station. The decline occurs chiefly under Chagai and Sibi among the Districts, and in both the Kalat and Las Bela States. The decrease in Chagai is due to the withdrawal of troops and other literate establishments which had been posted all along the railway line during the Great War and subsequently the Afghan war. This is proved by the statistics of population. There has been an increase of 2,543 persons in the indigenous population between 1921 and 1931. On the other hand the number of aliens among whom the percentage of literacy is comparatively higher has fallen from 3,711 to 1,980. In spite of this decrease which affects the District as a whole, the number of literates among the indigenous tribesmen has actually risen from 95 in 1921 to 205 in 1931. The decline in Sibi has been brought about by the change in the date of Census. In 1921 the Census was taken on 18th March. In 1931 the date was changed to 26th February. During the winter months most of the Secretariat offices from Quetta as well as all Political Agents move down to Sibi for the annual Shahi Jirga, while owing to the annual Sibi Horse and Cattle Show which takes place during this period many visitors from Sind and elsewhere are present in Sibi. At the Census of 1921 all these persons were censused in Sibi and included in the population of that station. In 1931, however, all these functions took place before the date of Census and most of the visitors had dispersed before the Census took place. The Secretariat establishments from Quetta that remained in Sibi on the Census night were enumerated there but according to special instructions issued in 1931 these establishments were included in the population of the town of Quetta.

Districts and States.	1911	1921	1931.
DISTRICTS.			
Quetta-Pishin. ..	99	140	170
Bolan ..	143	132	153
Zhob ..	23	52	63
Chagai ..	24	53	33
Loralai ..	27	32	32
Sibi ..	33	32	20
STATES.			
Kalat ..	16	19	12
Las Bela ..	18	19	13

The decline in the number of literates in the States is due entirely to the annual migration into Sind. In order to prevent double enumeration in Sind, the Census was taken after the migratory population had filtered through the passes into Sind limits and we thus lost a large number of our permanent residents and with them the literate element.

Educated Un-employment.

193. Statistics of educated unemployment are contained in Imperial Table XII printed at page 69, Part II of this report. The census of this class of population was taken in the winter when most of the unemployed move down to the plains and the statistics are therefore of not much practical value.

Progress of Education.

194. In a province where the masses still lead a primitive life, the progress of education must necessarily be slow. The principal causes which have hitherto impeded the normal progress of education in the face of strenuous efforts on the part of District and Educational authorities are manifold. In the first place the nomadic habits of the people and their limited means do not permit of boys being sent to school to the detriment of domestic duties in which they take a prominent part. Again, inhabited villages are few and far between and most of them too small to call for separate schools. The schools are located at headquarters stations and in the larger villages which children from surrounding villages and hamlets cannot ordinarily attend owing to long distances from their homes. Again, as Urdu is the medium of instruction for want of an easier language, the lack of educated teachers with knowledge of local dialects has been a serious handicap. The most important obstacle, however, is the natural prejudice against foreign education which so far has caused serious harm to the interests of educational advancement. This prejudice was fostered by the Mullahs whose very existence depended on this profession. Twenty years ago Sir Denys Bray probed the native mind. The picture drawn by him is depicted in the following quotation:—

"Strong though the prejudice is against Urdu education, it is doubly strong against English. Even among the enterprising Pathans the prejudice is strong. The common idea is that the man that learns English will be sure to mumble English on his death-bed instead of reciting the *Kalima*; and to die with English on the lips is to take a passport to Hell. Small wonder that the death-bed scene of the wretch that knows English is a favourite theme of the sensational story-teller and an awful warning to others."

The remedy suggested by Sir Denys Bray twenty years ago was well received. The changed prescription then suggested was tried. But, although a change in the educational policy by which Mullas are now given stipends to undergo training in secular education to enable them to give instruction in Urdu and elementary arithmetic in their mosques has taken the edge off their antagonism, the prejudice has not yet completely died out.

Where society lives in such a frame of mind educational progress is faced with much uphill work. Yet it is satisfactory to note that school education has made slow but steady progress among indigenous inhabitants, for there were only 207 indigenous students in the schools in 1901 whereas in 1911 they numbered 1,475 and 2,447 in 1931. Details will be found in the Superintendent of Education's note which is printed as an appendix to this Chapter. And if further proof were needed that the cause of education is more hopeful to-day, it would be found in the change that has been brought about in the educational outlook of the province by the younger generation of educated local inhabitants who are demanding widespread education of all sorts not only for males but, to the annoyance and bitter surprise of the outgoing generation, for females also.

The motive power at the outset may be Government loaves and fishes and the demand for educated mothers as elsewhere in India, but here it appears necessary to utter a warning that, in the course of time, the increasing numbers of the educated will create a situation unwholesome both for themselves and their country. The remedy lies in changing the time-honoured curriculum which in the present stage of world civilization is only one of antiquarian interest. The educational department should take courage in both hands and devise a new curriculum which would make the future youngman a worthy citizen and befit him for loftier ideals, and finally open out a wider field of employment than the water tight compartments of Government services which, after all, can accommodate only a few. Education of the right type in which religious tuition takes its due share has never been resented even by the ignorant frontier Muslim, for, who can deny that the Muslim youth is often reminded from his very infancy of the immortal Persian poet Saadi's well known couplet :

پئے علم چوں شمع باید گداخت ۔ کہ بے علم نتواں خدا را شناخت

SUBSIDIARY TABLES.

38. Literacy among Muslims by Locality.

District or State.	Literates. Total. Persons.	Total. Males.	Total. Females.	Aliens. Males.	Aliens. Females.	Semi-Indigenous. Males.	Semi-Indigenous. Females.	Indigenous. Males.	Indigenous. Females.	Literates in 1,000 Indigenous Muslims. Males.	Literates in 1,000 Indigenous Muslims. Females.
BALUCHISTAN ..	**12,670**	**12,104**	**566**	**6,117**	**436**	**965**	**51**	**5,022**	**79**	**125**	**2**
DISTRICTS ..	**10,472**	**9,940**	**582**	**6,003**	**434**	**927**	**51**	**3,010**	**47**	**157**	**3**
Quetta-Pishin ..	6,701	6,303	398	3,956	325	748	44	1,599	29	368	8
Loralai ..	989	968	21	602	17	68	2	298	2	81	1
Zhob ..	1,094	1,062	32	767	29	45	2	250	1	91	1
Bolan ..	200	190	10	118	9	14	..	58	1	363	15
Chagai ..	363	355	8	119	3	6	..	230	5	203	5
Sibi ..	1,125	1,062	63	441	51	46	3	575	9	81	2
STATES ..	**2,198**	**2,164**	**34**	**114**	**2**	**38**	..	**2,012**	**32**	**95**	**2**
Kalat ..	1,778	1,770	8	73	2	37	..	1,660	6	93	1
Sarawan ..	516	516	..	5	..	24	..	487	..	327	..
Jhalawan ..	240	240	..	12	..	1	..	227	..	48	..
Kachhi ..	428	426	2	28	..	..	..	398	2	74	1
Dombki-Kaheri Country ..	101	101	..	14	..	..	..	87	..	66	..
Makran ..	323	319	4	12	2	11	..	296	2	82	1
Kharan ..	170	168	2	2	..	1	..	165	2	133	2
Las Bela ..	420	394	26	41	..	1	..	352	26	108	9

39.—Literacy among Indigenous Muslim tribes.

Race or Tribe.	Literates per 10,000 of total population.	Female literates to 1,000 male literates.	*Number per cent. of total literates who are literate in* Persian.	Urdu.	Arabic.	Sindhi.	Lande.	English.	Other languages.
INDIGENOUS MUSLIMS	69	16	52	55	3	4	2	6	..
BALOCH	42	11	54	51	1	13	..	5	..
(*i*) *Eastern*	29	2	30	73	1	23	..	8	..
Bugti	15	..	13	89	..	..	..	11	..
Khetran	41	..	16	84	..	..	..	13	..
Magasi	26	..	44	47	3	29	..	..	..
Mari	19	..	30	80	..	9	..	2	..
Rind	42	6	38	63	1	44	..	6	..
(*ii*) *Western*	66	18	75	32	1	4	..	2	..
Rakhshani	106	8	91	15	2	..	..	2	..
BRAHUI	66	8	64	47	1	1	..	4	1
(*i*) *Original Nucleus* ..	100	8	58	52	1	..	..	2	7
(*ii*) *Sarawan*	102	2	60	59	..	2	..	4	..
Bangulzai	73	19	54	70	2	6	..	4	..
Langav	45	..	70	63	..	..	..	7	..
(*iii*) *Jhalawan*	24	9	64	45	2	2	..	7	2
Bizanjav	29	..	82	16	3	5	..	..	..
Mamasani	34	29	54	66	..	..	..	3	..
Mongal	39	10	56	53	3	1	..	12	4
Zahri	8	..	64	50	..	7	..	4	..
(*iv*) *Miscellaneous* ..	770	13	77	22	1	..	..	2	..
PATHAN	100	13	45	65	5	..	..	8	..
(*i*) Kakar	96	1	50	61	7	..	..	5	..
Sanzarkhel	57	4	54	53	9	..	..	5	1
Snatia	146	..	42	68		..	..	2	..
Targhara	106	..	79	36	10	..	..	4	..
(*ii*) Pani	47	8	33	57	10	..	..	10	..
Musakhel	41	..	88	29	7	..	..	14	..
(*iii*) Tarin	73	4	43	67	1	..	..	6	..
Abdal Achakzai ..	65	..	48	66	..	..	..	2	..
Tor Tarin	120	12	62	62	..	..	..	2	..
LASI	36	..	14	86	..	28	..	..	..
JATT	41	..	67	52	6	12	..	2	..
SAYYID	267	16	65	51	3	2	..	7	1
OTHER MUSLIMS	64	88	31	41	..	1	33	7	..
(*i*) Darzada	64	..	60	50	2	2	..	..	..
(*ii*) Sorozai	10	235	33	67	..	..	..	..	..
(*iii*) Lori	14	..	63	50	..	..	..	13	..

40.—Number of institutions and pupils according to the returns of the Education Department.

Class of Institutions.	1931 (31st March, 1931).						1921 (31st March, 1921).					
	No. of Institutions.		No. of Scholars.				No. of Institutions.		No. of Scholars.			
			Males.		*Females.*				*Males.*		*Females.*	
	Tribal.	Regular.	Tribal.	Regular.	Tribal.	Regular.	Tribal.	Regular.	Tribal.	Regular.	Tribal.	Regular.
1	2	3	4	5	6	7	8	9	10	11	12	13
GRAND TOTAL ..	**267**	**27**	**4,565**	**3,981**	..	**1,424**	**314**	**14**	**4,423**	**1,681**	..	**989**
Secondary School Total for Boys ..	..	18	..	3,640	..	1,131	1	9	36	1,681	..	210
English ..	..	11	..	3,529	..	..	..	7	..	1,681	..	..
Vernacular for Girls ..	..	1	..	111	..	..	1	..	36	..	..	..
English ..	..	5	..	..	..	733	..	1	..	..	..	133
Vernacular ..	..	1	..	..	..	398	..	1	..	..	..	77
Primary School Total ..	82	9	2,014	341	..	293	66	5	1,622	..	..	380
For Boys ..	82	6	2,014	341	..	..	66	..	1,622	..	..	..
For Girls ..	..	3	..	..	..	293	..	5	..	..	..	380
Mullah School Total ..	185	..	2,551	..	..	..	247	..	2,765	..	..	399
Mixed ..	..	..	..	..	..	..	..	..	..	..	..	..
For Boys ..	185	..	2,551	..	..	..	247	..	2,765	..	..	399

APPENDIX.

NOTE ON THE PROGRESS OF EDUCATION IN BALUCHISTAN, 1921—1931.

By

KHAN BAHADUR MAULVI NAJAM-UD-DIN, B.A., I.E.S., SUPERINTENDENT OF EDUCATION IN BALUCHISTAN.

General.—In the note on the progress of education in 1911-1921 my predecessor described fully the history of education, the policy and the system in vogue in the Province. The policy and the system remain the same and there has been no change in these. However the story of the educational progress for the present decade is very satisfactory and encouraging as will be seen from a brief summary given below :—

During the last ten years all types of schools and scholars attending these have increased and the work has been greatly improved owing to the employment of better qualified and trained teachers. The five years expansion scheme sanctioned by the Government of India in 1927 gave the province a chance to increase its high schools and provide munificent building grants for the new Communal Secondary Schools which set up fine buildings with this opportune help. This also enabled us to open 12 more Primary Schools and put up three new school buildings and teachers' quarters besides building a new school and Boarding House at Pishin and extending the buildings of the Secondary School at Loralai.

Games and physical culture received special attention and our old boys called the "Sandemanians" had the proud distinction of being invited several times to join the Durand Football Tournament at Simla where they gave a very good account of themselves—once even beating the celebrated "Mohanbagans" of Bengal.

Primary Education.— Primary education which is the only kind of education in which the tribesmen take part, has been greatly extended—in fact in every village where the villagers have shown a desire, a primary school has been opened and thus education has been brought to the very doors of the native inhabitants. In 1921 there were 71 Primary Schools and 2,002 scholars, now there are 91 schools and 2,648 scholars.

The schools are now almost all manned with trained teachers and this has in its turn improved their work.

Four scholarships of Rs. 2/- each are given to local boys in each Primary School to encourage the poorer and brighter scholars to continue their studies during the full course in the village school.

Out of these 91 schools three schools are for girls, in which there are 293 scholars.

Middle Schools for boys.—The number of Middle Schools teaching English was four in 1921 and the number is still the same but the number of scholars in these has risen from 516 to 911. The increase is due to the raising of the three flourishing Primary Schools to the status of Middle Schools. Fees have been raised in these schools from Rs. 1/8/- per month to Rs. 3/- per month but the local boys still pay Re. 1/- per month.

The number of Vernacular Middle Schools is still the same, *viz.*, one but the school has been transferred from Gulistan to Pishin which is a more central place and surrounded by many village schools which act as feeders. An agricultural class has been added which is very popular with the local boys and tribesmen. The demand for English is so great that the educational authorities had to attach an English class to this institution for the benefit of those who wish to learn English as an optional subject. The number of scholars in this school has risen from 36 to 111.

Middle Schools for girls.—There are four Middle Schools for girls which are very well attended. There were 826 girls in these schools on 31st March 1931. The number of local girls is still very small, and every effort is made to encourage them to join these schools but they are usually taken away before they finish their education even in the Primary Department.

These girls schools send up candidates for the Middle School examination for females conducted by the Punjab Education Department and the results have usually been excellent.

Last year 23 girls were sent up from various schools and 21 of these came out successful.

These schools have quite good and comfortable buildings. The only drawback is the paucity of trained and well-qualified female teachers which is greatly retarding the progress of female education here.

APPENDIX.

High Schools.—The number of High Schools has gone up to six against two in the previous decade. The numbers of scholars has gone up to 2,500 against 1,129 in 1921.

All these schools have fine buildings which have been put up as already stated by public subscriptions and munificent aid from the Government. Fees have also been raised in this department and boys pay Rs. 5/- per mensem against Rs. 3/- Local boys pay only Rs. 2/- per mensem.

Last year 140 went up for Matriculation examination from these schools and 99 were declared successful.

During the last decade 56 local boys passed Matriculation and School Leaving Certificate examination from Baluchistan.

Some local boys now join the various Arts and Technical Colleges in the Punjab and as the Government of India has sanctioned some scholarships of varying values from Rs. 20/- to Rs. 50/- per mensem the local Government tries to encourage these students by granting them such scholarships as are available.

European Schools.—There are two European schools in Quetta. Grammar School which is an undenominational school and is wholly maintained by fees and Government grants. It has a good building and good attendance.

The Presentation Convent School which is maintained by the Roman Catholic Community and grants from the Government and other public bodies, is also in a very flourishing state.

Both the schools send up candidates for the various Cambridge Examinations and the results are usually very satisfactory.

Both schools admit Indians freely. In March 1931 there were 254 pupils in these two institutions, *viz.*, 145 boys and 109 girls.

Normal School.—This school has been working satisfactorily throughout the decade and turning out trained teachers for Primary Schools and thus it has been found possible to weed out inefficient and untrained teachers from these schools. It is intended to raise the status of this school so that it may train vernacular teachers for Secondary Schools but the present financial stringency has stood in the way of a definite scheme being put up to the Government.

Mosque Schools.—More interest has been taken in the mosque school. The grant given by the Government of India for the five year expansion scheme enabled the Education Department to train some 29 Mullahs. After passing through the training each Mullah gets Rs. 20/- per mensem if he opens a school in any village in British Baluchistan. Every such school has to keep an attendance and an admission and withdrawal register and the Mullah has to supply information to the education department about the number of pupils on rolls.

These Mullahs usually teach Qurán-i-Sharif and books on theology but now some of them teach Urdu reading and writing and a little elementary arithmetic. The experiment is being watched by the Education Department with much interest. Thus it will be seen that the progress has been satisfactory and encouraging in every branch of education and that there is every hope of further development in the future.

CHAPTER X.

LANGUAGE.

---

195. The statistics on which this chapter is based are contained in Imperial Table XV. Part I of this table gives the distribution of the population by mother-tongues, while Part II shows the extent of bilingualism. Comparative figures for past three censuses, proportional figures by Districts and States for the principal local languages and comparative figures of tribal numerical strengths and tribal languages will be found in the three subsidiary tables at the end of this chapter. **Statistical data.**

196. The instructions to enumerators were to record a person's genuine mother-tongue as first spoken from the cradle and to enter in a separate column any other language or languages habitually spoken by a person in addition to the mother-tongue, in daily or domestic life. Infants and deaf-mutes were credited with their mothers' mother-tongues. The information was collected on the Standard Schedule in the Regular or Synchronous areas and a modified form was used in the Tribal Areas. Here the mother-tongue of the head of the family was assumed to be the mother-tongue of all other members of the family. For the record of the secondary languages, however, a separate column was provided in the modified schedule and the enumerator was asked to enter the names of subsidiary language or languages spoken together with the number of speakers. **Nature of the inquiry.**

197. In Imperial Table XV, the languages censused in Baluchistan have been grouped under the following heads:— **Classification of languages.**

A. Vernaculars of India;
B. Vernaculars of other Asiatic countries and Africa;
C. European languages.

According to linguistic affinities, however, the languages are classified by the Linguistic Survey of India into ten main families, namely,

1. Austric,
2. Tibeto-Chinese,
3. Karen,
4. Mán,
5. Dravidian,
6. Indo-European,
7. Semitic,
8. Hemetic,
9. Mongolian,
10. Malayo-Polynesian.

The families represented in Baluchistan together with the numbers of speakers are shown below:—

Family of languages.	*Numbers of persons speaking the languages.*		
	1911.	1921.	1931.
1. Indo-European	688,967	659,015	740,152
2. Dravidian	145,378	140,180	127,693
3. Tibeto-Chinese	5	183	637
4. Semitic	87	6	10
5. Mongolian	13	..	7
6. Malayo-Polynesian	..	..	1
7. Unclassed languages	253	241	117

The Indo-European and the Dravidian are the only two families which are vernaculars of Baluchistan. The rest, excepting 21 males and 19 females whose mother-tongue is Chinese and who have settled down permanently in Baluchistan, are all immigrants whose numerical strength varies chiefly with fluctuations in the composition of the garrison troops.

Numbers of languages spoken and of speakers according to Census classification.

198. Altogether 51 languages were spoken in Baluchistan in 1931. Of these, 7 were vernaculars of Baluchistan, 27 vernaculars of other parts of India, 7 vernaculars of other Asiatic countries and Africa, and 10 European languages. The marginal summary gives the numbers of speakers of each of these 51 languages. In every 1,000 of the total population. 852 persons speak Indo-European languages, 147 Dravidian languages, and all the rest one. Or taking the Census classification, 897 per 1,000 of total population speak vernaculars of Baluchistan, 91 speak vernaculars of other parts of India, and 6 each speak vernaculars of other Asiatic countries and Africa, and European languages.

Families of Languages.	*Languages with numbers of speakers.*				
	I.—Vernaculars of Baluchistan.				
Indo-European Family.	(1) Balochi	266,957	(5) Jattki Sindhi and Lasi, Unspecified Jagdali and Jatki		145,010
	(2) Dehwari	5,233			
	(3) Pashto	207,181			
	(4) Lahnda or Western-Punjabi	27,283			651,664
Dravidian Family	(6) Brahui	127,479			
		127,479			
Unclassed	(7) Lori Chini	117			
		117			
	II.—Vernaculars of other parts of India.				
Indo-European Family.	(1) Kashmiri	201	(10) Gujrati		618
	(2) Lahnda or Western Punjabi	23,071	(11) Punjabi		19,515
			(12) Central Pahari		3,169
	(3) Sindhi	8,022	(13) Eastern Pahari		4,653
	(4) Marathi	789			
	(5) Konkani	93	(14) Western Pahari		25
	(6) Bengali	93			
	(7) Eastern Hindi	39	(15) Pahari unspecified		54
	(8) Western ,,	17,092			
	(9) Rajasthani	530			77,964
Dravidian Family	(16) Tamil	150	(18) Kanarese		10
	(17) Malayalam	12	(19) Telugu		42
					214
Tibeto-Chinese Family.	(20) Tibetan	21	(25) Sanwar		38
	(21) Sharpa Bhotia	6	(26) Magari		24
	(22) Sikkim ,,	2	(27) Rong or Lepcha		2
	(23) Kiranti	488			
	(24) Gurang	16			597
	III.—Vernaculars of other Asiatic Countries and Africa.				
Indo-European Family.	(1) Persian	5,020	(2) Armenian		1
Tibeto-Chinese Family.	(3) Chinese	40			5,021
		40			
Semitic Family	(4) Arabic	9	(5) Hebrew		1
					10
Mongolian Family	(6) Turkish	7			
		7			
Malayo-Polynesian Family	(7) Javanese	1			
		1			
	IV.—European Languages.				
Indo-European Family.	(1) Italian	1	(7) Irish		16
	(2) French	9	(8) English		5,369
	(3) Portuguese	3	(9) Danish		2
	(4) Spanish	55	(10) German		4
	(5) Welsh	9			
	(6) Scotch	35			5,503

Variation.

The numbers of persons speaking the various languages in 1911, 1921 and 1931 are compared in the marginal table. The increases on the whole are due to increases of population. Taking the indigenous languages separately, however, we notice interesting variations. Since 1921, the indigenous and semi-indigenous population has increased by 59,445. On the other hand, the numbers of persons speaking vernaculars of Baluchistan show an increase of 57,501 only. This means that Baluchistan vernaculars have lost 1,944 of their adherents since 1921, for there is a corresponding increase in the numbers of speakers of languages other than the vernaculars of Baluchistan. This variation indicates that the indigenous inhabitants of the Province are showing a preference for foreign languages. In point of fact this is not the case. The decrease is partly due to inter-marriages in families speaking non-racial or foreign languages. Where such unions take place, the wife assumes the racial title of her husband but retains her mother tongue together with her children. The major portion of the decrease however, is accounted for by an erroneous return in the case of about 1,000 indigenous Hindus, who really speak Sindhi-Jatki but returned their mother-tongue as only Sindhi and have therefore been shown under Vernaculars of other parts of India.

	1911.	1921.	1931.
Baluchistan Vernaculrs	769,022	721,759	779,260
Languages of other parts of India	57,388	69,211	78,775
Languages of other Asiatic countries and Africa	3,936	3,598	5,079
European languages	4,358	5,057	5,503

Vernaculars of Baluchistan.

199. The Vernaculars of Baluchistan consist of 7 main languages with five dialects under Western Punjabi and two under Sindhi. Statistics for each of these for three Censuses are given in the following table. :—

NUMBERS SPEAKING VERNACULARS OF BALUCHISTAN.

Language.	1911.	1921.	1931.	Variation. 1911-31.	Variation. 1921-31.
1. Balochi	232,987	225,127	266,957	+33,970	+41,830
2. Pashto	227,553	201,873	207,181	−20,372	+5,308
3. Sindhi	55,545	94,876	143,210	+87,665	+48,334
(a) Jatki-Sindhi	14,940	58,474	97,412	+82,472	+38,938
(b) Lasi	40,605	36,402	45,798	+ 5,193	+9,396
4. Brahui	145,299	139,727	127,479	− 17,820	− 12,248
5. Lahnda or Western Punjabi ..	99,806	53,647	29,083	−70,723	− 24,564
(a) Khetrani	16,071	17,495	18,232	+2,161	+737
(b) Siraiki	31,254	21,916	7,381	−23,873	−14,535
(c) Jafarki	606	1,361	1,670	+1,064	+309
(d) Jatki	1,519	436	1,025	−494	+589
(e) Jagdali	50,356	12,439	775	−49,581	−11,664
6. Persian (Dehwari)	7,579	6,268	5,233	−2,346	−1,035
7. Lori-Chini	253	241	117	−136	−124

In every 100 speakers of vernaculars of Baluchistan, 34 speak Balochi, 27 Pashto, 6 Sindhi-Lasi, 12 Sindhi-Jatki, 16 Brahui and 4 Lahnda. Dehwari and Lori-Chini both represent less than one per cent. These percentages are compared in the margin with those for 1911. Between 1911 and 1931, Balochi has increased by 4 and Sindhi by 11, while Pashto has decreased by 3, Lahnda by 9, Brahui by 3 and Dehwari and Lori-Chini have both together fallen from one to less than one.

PERCENTAGE OF VERNACULARS OF BALUCHISTAN IN 1911 AND 1931.

	1911.	1931.
1. Balochi ..	30	34
2. Pashto ..	30	27
3. Sindhi ..	7	18
4. Lahnda ..	13	4
5. Brahui ..	19	16
6. Dehwari and Lori-Chini ..	1	1
	100	100

Linguistic Map.

200. The distribution of the various vernaculars of the Province, by Districts and States is shown in the map at the beginning of this chapter. The key to this map will be found in the appendix to this chapter. A more detailed examination of each Provincial vernacular is contained in the following paragraphs.

Balochi.

201. "The home of Balóchi" as the Linguistic Survey describes it, "is as its name implies, Baluchistan, but it extends beyond the usually recognised limits of the Province. On the East it reaches to the Indus, as far North as Dera Ghazi Khan, although the country along the banks of that river is mainly inhabited by Indians whose language is Lahnda. Northward in Baluchistan it extends to near Quetta, and as we go westwards, it is found even further than this, up to the valley of the Helmand, where Pashto becomes the main language of the country. Still further west, where the lower course of the Helmand runs south to north we come to the Persian province of Seistan. Here Balochis are found mixed with Persians and the language of the tract is partly Balochi and partly Persian. Indeed, nomadic Balochis are found still further north, in Karman and as far as Central Khurasan. South of Quetta Balochi is the language of the greater part of Baluchistan. It extends westwards as the principal language of the country over Persian Baluchistan as far as Bampur and is spoken by at least a part of the population as far as Jask."

Eastern Balochi	376,822
Western "	324,899
Unspecified	2,865
Total ..	704,586

Brahui wedges in in the central parts of Baluchistan dividing Balochi into Eastern and Western dialects. The Linguistic Survey puts the numbers of all Balochi speakers at 704,586 of which Balochi speakers in Persian territory were estimated at 200,000. According to the Census of 1931, the Balochi speakers in the tracts in the Indian Empire above described numbered 628,086 as shown in the margin against a total Baloch population of 1,333,215 in the above tracts excluding Persia.

	Balochi speakers.	*Baloch population.*
Baluchistan	263,777	229,473
Bombay	297,768	435,439
Punjab	60,985	624,695
Elsewhere in India	5,556	43,608
	628,086	1,333,215

The numbers of Balochi speakers in Baluchistan for past three censuses are given in the margin. There has been an increase of 20 per cent. in the number of Balochi speakers since 1921 which is entirely due to increase of population.

	Balochi speakers.	*Baloch. population*
1911	232,987	172,473
1921	225,127	176,336
1931	266,957	229,473

In Baluchistan, Balochi is not the exclusive language of the Baloch. Out of 266,957 Balochi speakers in 1931, there were only 195,646 Baloch Balochi speakers in a total Baloch population of 229,473, 33,002 Brahuis, 1,681 Lasi, 1,303 Jatt, 1,120 Sayyid, 219 Pathan and 30,806 other Muslims besides 11 Indigenous Hindus and 3,169 aliens of all classes. Balochi is spoken by 31 per cent. of the total population of the Province and 35 of the indigenous population. It is the most popular language because it is the easiest to learn and also because it carries with it an atmosphere of superiority over the Brahui and Lahnda-Jattki. Until quite recently Balochi no doubt held the mastery. But economic development of Sind has lent renewed energy to its old rival Sindhi-Jatki or Sindhi-Siraiki, and Balochi has thereby received a set-back which will result in the gradual absorption by Sindhi of both Balochi and Lahnda-Jattki or Lahnda-Jagdali. An indication of this tendency is afforded by the fact that 10,754 Baloch returned Sindhi dialects as their mother-tongues in 1931.

202. "Roughly speaking we may say," writes Sir George Grierson in his Linguistic Survey, "that the country in which the majority of the population use Pashto as their language, is Southern and Eastern Afghanistan, the country to the west of Indus from its southward bend down to Dera Ismail Khan, and a strip of Northern Baluchistan."

Pashto is divided into two sections,—the North-Eastern, called Pakhto and the South-Western known as Pashto. Pashto spoken in Baluchistan belongs to the second category.

The marginal statement shows the number of indigenous Muslims who use the language as their mother tongue. It has not been able to reach the figure of 1911 though it has recorded an increase over that of 1921. The decrease compared to 1911 is due to decrease in population.

	1911.	1921.	1931.	Variation% 1921-31.
Pashto ..	201,775	185,965	186,263	+·02

Pashto is spoken by 24 per cent. of the total population of the Province. The 207,181 Pashto speakers of 1931 consisted of 169,769 indigenous Pathan Pashto speakers, 15,332 Sayyids, 902 Baloch, 504 Hindus, 125 Jat and 20,549 semi-indigenous and alien Pathans and others. There were, all told, 188,093 indigenous Pathans in 1911, 174,061 in 1921 and 176,007 in 1931. Out of these there were 183,132 Pashto speakers in 1911 ; in 1921 and 1931 they numbered, 168,681 and 169,769 respectively. This shows that there were—

4,961 indigenous Pathans in 1911,

5,380 in 1921, and

6,238 in 1931,

whose mother tongue was not Pashto. It appears that the Pathans are adopting Sindhi-Jatki as their mother-tongue in increasing numbers, the numbers of indigenous Pathans who returned Sindhi-Jatki as their mother-tongue in 1931, being 3,550. Comparison with earlier censuses is not possible owing to separate figures for Sindhi-Jatki not being available.

203. Dehwari is slowly but steadily losing ground as will be seen from the marginal table. Between 1911 and 1931 it has lost 2,346 or 31 per cent. of its adherents. The Dehwars are giving up their own language in favour of others. In 1931, there were 731 Dehwars who returned languages other than Dehwari as their mother-tongue as shown in the margin. **Dehwari.**

	1911.	1921.	1931.
Dehwari-speakers ..	7,579	6,268	5,233
Dehwar tribe ..	7,326	5,455	5,317
TOTAL NUMERICAL STRENGTH OF DEHWAR TRIBE ..			5,317
Languages spoken :—			
1. Dehwari ..	..	..	.. 4,586
2. Brahui ..	..	..	.. 481
3. Jatki Sindhi	..	..	.. 107
4. Balochi ..	..	..	.. 109
5. Pashto ..	..	..	.. 33
6. Other languages	..	..	.. 1

204. Lahnda is a member of the "Outer sub-branch" of the "Indo-Aryan Branch" of the "Aryan Sub-family" of the Indo-European family of languages. The "Outer sub-branch" is divided into three groups, namely,— **Lahnda or Western Punjabi.**

(1) North-Western group, consisting of (*a*) Lahnda, and (*b*) Sindhi,
(2) Southern group consisting of Marathi and Konkani, and
(3) Eastern group, consisting of Oriya, Bihari, Bengali and Assamese languages.

Lahnda and Sindhi are the two languages with which we are here concerned.

Both Lahnda and Sindhi are derived from old Sanskrit. The area in which Lahnda is spoken comprises Western Punjab, part of the North-Western Frontier Province and parts of Baluchistan. Its Eastern boundary runs from north to south-west starting from near Jammu, passing near Gujranwala, Lyallpur, Montgomery, including Bahawalpur State, till it meets the Sindh boundary where it crosses into Sind as well as the plains of Baluchistan. In its westward march it changes its name frequently. It is known as Pothawari in the neighbourhood of Rawalpindi. Further north-westward it is known as Hindko. The other names by which it is known are Multani of Multan, Jatki of other surrounding districts, Thalochari of Mianwali etc., and Jangli of Shahpur, Gujrat and Gujranwala etc. As it crosses the Indus westwards, it is known as Derawali. It has numerous other names which change, as they say, after every 12 *kos.* (30 to 40 miles) until on the Eastern frontiers of Baluchistan it takes the tribal names of Jafiri or Jafarki and Khetrani, while in the interior up in the Kachhi and the Sibi plains of Baluchistan it falls back to its original name Jatki and its Sindhi title Siraiki which are the dialects of the Jatt husbandmen of these areas.

The above description does not necessarily mean that the home of Lahnda was in Western Punjab or elsewhere in India whence it spread out westwards. This is a point which is for the historian of the future to decide.

The dialects of Lahnda which are spoken in Baluchistan are, beginning from the East, Jafarki, Khetrani, Siraiki, Jattki or Jagdali and Jatki. Jafarki has acquired this name from the Jafar Pathan tribe of Musakhel in the Loralai district, who are the only speakers of this dialect. Khetrani derives its name from the Khetran tribe in the Barkhan Tahsil of the Loralai district. Jatki is so called because it is the mother-tongue of the Jat (جت) camelmen found chiefly in the Mari and Bugti tribal areas. Jattki (جتکی) or Jagdali derives its name from the original nucleus of the Jatt cultivating class which settled down in the plains of Kachhi and its neighbourhood. Siraiki is applicable both to Lahnda-Jatki and Sindhi-Jattki. Lahnda dialects are spoken by 6 per cent. of the total population.

The marginal statement gives statistics for Lahnda and its dialects for 1911, 1921 and 1931. The variations in Jafarki and Khetrani are due mainly to increase of population. The variations in Siraiki and Jagdali or Jattki are important and stand in need of explanation. Between 1911 and 1931, the two together have lost 73,454 of their adherents. This figure is based on the Census returns. But suspecting that the enumerator had fallen into the pitfall of erroneous

	1911.	1921.	1931.
Lahnda or Western Punjabi ..	99,806	53,647	29,083
(*a*) Khetrani ..	16,071	17,495	18,232
(*b*) Siraiki ..	31,254	21,916	7,381
(c) Jafarki ..	606	1,361	1,670
(*d*) Jatki ..	1,519	436	1,025
(*e*) Jagdali or Jattki	50,356	12,439	775

classification, my predecessor of 1911 made a rough division of Jattki between Sindhi and Lahnda. According to that estimate he put the numbers of Lahnda-Siraiki and Lahnda-Jatki speakers at 48,040 as shown in the margin. These figures are much lower than those. disclosed by the Census returns of 1911. Yet they show a sufficiently large decline amounting to no less than 39,884 speakers. The fact is that the Lahnda-Siraiki and Lahnda-Jattki or Jagdali have both fallen a prey to the irresistible attacks of Sindhi which has many advantages over its rival the Lahnda, the more important ones being closer association owing to the proximity of habitats, and much wider, more lucrative and easier field of employment opened out by the Sukkur Barrage scheme—causes which have added large numbers of converts to Sindhi as will be seen from the following paragraph.

Jatki ..	16,786
Siraiki ..	31,254
	48,040

Sindhi.

205. Sindhi dialects are spoken by 16 per cent. of the total populaion of the Province. The statistics for Sindhi and its components are given in the margin. The increase under Lasi is attributable in the main to increase of population. The increase under Sindhi-Jattki is, however, due entirely to its conquests over Lahnda-Jattki and Lahnda-Siraiki. The above figures are based on census returns. The rough estimates framed in 1911 as explained above put the figures for Sindhi-Jattki and Sindhi-Jattki unspecified at 48,510 against 14,940 as disclosed by the Census returns for that year. According to actual Census returns, the gain to Sindhi between 1911 and 1931 amounts to 82,472. According to the estimated figure, however, it falls to 48,902 which in itself is very remarkable. The fact is that both Lahnda and Sindhi are sister languages and the dividing line between the two is very thin. Years of prolonged association in circumstances most favourable to Sindhi, have depleted the ranks of Lahnda and this process is sure to continue apace in the absence of reinforcements for Lahnda for which there is no inducement at all to beat the lure of prosperity and comfort offered by Sind.

	1911.	1921.	1931.
Jattki Sindhi ..	14,940	58,474	97,412
Lasi ..	40,605	36,402	45,798

Brahui.

206. It has been decided beyond a shadow of doubt that Brahui belongs to the Dravidian family of languages. How the Brahui nucleus came to occupy an isolated tract in Central Baluchistan still remains a mystery. The latest information on the subject is contained in the following quotation from the Census of India Report for 1931 :—

> " It seems therefore necessary to regard the Dravidian speakers as having been the latest pre-Indo-European occupants of Upper India, as having reached India from the north-west where their language remains among the Brahui, who actually regard the Mohanjo-daro ruins (in Sind) as the work of their ancestors, and as having brought with them the ancient civilization of Mesopotamia, Asia Minor and the Eastern Mediterranean."

Efforts were made to elucidate the Brahui claim in respect of the archælogical discovery in Sind but without success. The claim is one which deserves systematic investigation both in Sind and Baluchistan in view of the fact that in 1931 there were 79,561 Brahui speakers in Sind against 127,479 of Baluchistan. It is not improbable that the home of the Brahuis might have been in Sind from where they spread out to the headquarters of the Sewa dynasty in Kalat and gradually further northwards into Western Afghanistan where they are found leading a nomadic life in numbers which local estimates put at a figure far in excess of the Brahui population of both Baluchistan and Sind taken together.

Brahui speakers in Baluchistan in 1931 represented 15 per cent. of the population of the Province. That Brahui is not a progressive language is proved by the figures in the margin. Between 1911 and 1931 the number of Brahui speakers has fallen from 145,299 to 127,479—a decrease of 17,820 or 12 per cent. in a period of 20 years. Out of 152,588 Brahuis in the Province, only 116,688 have returned Brahui as their mother-tongue. The remaining 35,900 speak Baluchi (33,002), Sindhi dialects (2,377), Pashtu (309) and other languages (212). Besides the Brahuis the non-Brahui tribes which have returned Brahui as their mother-tongue are the Sorozai freed slaves (3,688), Loris

	Brahui speakers.
1911 ..	145,299
1921 ..	130,727
1931 ..	127,479

(1,984), Baloch (1,547), Nakib (849), Dehwars (624) and others (2,094). These accretions are not indicative of any expansive popularity of the language, for, the Sorozais freed slaves were domestic servants while the others are tribal artisans, cultivators or traders who have settled down within Brahui tribal limits and had perforce in the course of years to adopt Brahui as their mother-tongue.

Vernaculars of other parts of India.

207. The speakers of languages of other parts of India have increased from 57,388 in 1911 and 69,211 in 1921 to 78,775 in 1931. The increases are largely due to the increasing influx of immigrants as well as increases in the population of the garrison stations. The decrease in Punjabi and the corresponding increase in Western Punjabi are due to change of classification in 1931. The numbers of speakers of the more important languages are shown in the margin for the past three Censuses.

	1911.	1921.	1931.	Variation 1921-31.	Variation 1911-31.
TOTAL ..	57,388	69,211	78,775	+9,564	+21,387
Punjabi ..	27,542	35,378	19,515	−15,863	−8,027
Hindustani ..	10,983	16,267	16,628	+361	+5,645
Lahnda ..	168	4,556	23,071	+18,515	+22,903
Sindhi ..	14,429	3,661	8,022	+4,361	−6,407
Eastern Pahari ..	1,956	2,949	4,653	+1,704	+2,697
Central „ ..	302	2,452	3,169	+717	+2,867
Marathi ..	846	1,124	789	−335	−57
Other languages ..	1,162	2,824	2,928	+104	+1,766

(1) Vernaculars of other Asiatic Countries and Africa, and (2) European languages.

208. The speakers of languages of Asiatic countries other than India and of Africa as well as speakers of European languages have increased since 1911 and 1921 as shown below :—

	1921-31.	1911-31.
Other Asiatic languages	1,481	1,144
European languages	446	1,145

The principal increases fall under the languages named below and are due to increase in the number of immigrants :—

	1921-31.	1911-31.
Other Asiatic languages.		
Persian	+1,429	+1,187
Other Asiatic and African languages	+52	—43
European languages.		
English	+313	+1,020
Other European languages	+133	+125

Racial Distribution.

209. The linguistic distribution *per mille* of each indigenous race for three Censuses is shown in the following table :—

Language.	Year.	Linguistic Distribution per mille of each race.							
		Indigenous Muslim.	Baloch.	Pathan.	Brahui.	Jatt.	Lasi.	Sayyid.	Others.
Balochi ..	1911 1921 1931	313 325 347	870 852 866	1 3 1	210 201 216	48 20 17	52 25 53	43 72 51	302 546 535
Pashto ..	1911 1921 1931	275 271 246	4 4 4	974 968 965	8 3 2	2 3 2	.. .. ..	707 731 698	16 19 5
Brahui ..	1911 1921 1931	198 204 168	17 14 7	2 4 3	773 789 765	3 2 5	30 7 1	52 51 38	123 127 127
Jātki ..	1911 1921 1931	192 184 224	108 127 120	21 23 29	8 6 14	878 925 969	918 968 944	151 111 181	248 222 244
Others ..	1911 1921 1931	22 16 15	1 3 3	2 2 2	1 1 3	69 50 7	 2	47 35 32	111 86 89

Separate figures for Jattki-Sindhi and Jattki-Lahnda are not available for 1911 and 1921. For purposes of comparison, the figures for the two languages for 1931 have therefore been amalgamated.

In the total indigenous population of the Province numbering 760,125, 347 in every 1,000 speak Balochi, 246 Pashtu, 224 Jattki (Jatki-Lahnda plus Jatki-Sindhi), 168 Brahui and 15 other minor languages. Taking each race separately, we find that of all indigenous races, the Jatt top the list with 969 per 1,000 of their total numerical strength as speakers of their racial language. Next come the Pathans with 965 followed by the Lasis, 944. The Baloch have only 866 while the Brahuis come last with only 765. The Sayyids and 'Others' hardly need any explanation in view of the fact that their avocations are of a cosmopolitan nature which necessitate a knowledge of the various languages in varying degrees.

Jattki is the most popular non-racial language among the Baloch, the Pathan and the Sayyids; Balochi among the Brahui, the Lasi, the Sayyids, the Jatts and 'Others.'

The year 1921 was an abnormal year and comparison with that year will not yield satisfactory results. Taking therefore the figures for 1911 and 1931, in which normal conditions prevailed, we find that the Baloch, the Pathan and the Sayyids have been giving up their racial languages in favour mostly of Jattki as is indicated by the following figures :—

	Jattki speakers per mille.		
	Baloch.	*Pathan.*	*Sayyid.*
1911	108	21	151
1931	120	29	181

On the other hand, Balochi is losing ground among the Jatt, the number of Jatt Balochi speakers having declined since 1911 from 48 to 17 *per mille*. Balochi however seems to be still popular among the Lasi and the Sayyid. To sum up, Jattki (Jattki-Sindhi) appears to be the most promising language of the future among the masses, though Urdu which is the court language and the medium of education may in time claim the major portion of the educated class.

Bilingualism. 210. The following table shows the extent of bilingualism prevalent in the Province in 1911, 1921 and 1931 :—

Language.	Year.	Indigenous Muslim.	Secondary language per mille of each race.						
			Baloch.	Pathan.	Brahui.	Jatt.	Lasi.	Sayyid.	Others.
ALL ..	1911	202	342	30	268	132	143	167	272
	1921	126	191	16	202	47	82	96	155
	1931	109	126	48	139	54	17	114	94
Balochi ..	1911	37	18	6	94	32	32	27	42
	1921	31	23	8	75	22	44	15	25
	1931	19	13	9	40	26	14	27	6
Pashto ..	1911	6	7	4	10	1	..	23	4
	1921	6	8	1	13	..	..	11	6
	1931	7	8	2	16	3	..	9	6
Brahui ..	1911	68	89	7	81	21	79	97	175
	1921	37	31	10	56	5	29	51	99
	1931	30	43	9	36	19	3	43	50
Jattki ..	1911	62	104	11	41	14	17	8	23
	1921	43	112	..	48	14	8	17	15
	1931	43	109	6	25	17	..	4	18
Others ..	1911	20	34	2	42	64	15	12	28
	1921	9	17	2	10	6	1	2	10
	1931	22	7	33	41	5	..	49	24

Bilingualism would appear to be on the decline. In Baluchi, bilingualism has fallen between 1911 and 1931 from 37 to 19, in Brahui from 68 to 30, in Jattki from 62 to 43, in other miscellaneous languages from 29 to 22. Pashto alone has shown a negligible increase of one *per mille*. Taking each race separately we find that bilingualism among the Baloch has decreased between 1911 and 1931 from 342 per 1,000 to 126; among the Brahuis from 268 to 139; among Jatts and Lasis from 132 and 143 to 54 and 17 respectively and so also amongst the Sayyids and others from 167 and 272 to 114 and 94 respectively.

The all round decrease, I may note, is apparent not real. At the Censuses of 1911 and 1921, when a second language was returned by a family, all members of that family were assumed to be speakers of that second language. In 1931, a different method was adopted by which the actual numbers of persons in a family using a second language were recorded in separate columns provided for the purpose. The enumeration of 1931 has thus recorded the actual numbers of speakers which should be naturally lower than those of earlier Censuses.

SUBSIDIARY TABLE.

41—Distribution of total population by languages classified according to Linguistic Survey.

Family, Sub-Family, Branch and Sub-Branch.	Group.	Language.	Total Number of Speakers. 1931.	1921.	1911.	Number per 10,000 of Population of Province. 1931.	1921.	1911.
1	2	3	4	5	6	7	8	9
TOTAL ..	..	..	**868,617**	**799,625**	**834,703**	**10,000**	**10,000**	**10,000**
I.—LANGUAGES OF INDIA.	..	..	**58,035**	**790,970**	**826,410**	**9,378**	**9,892**	**9,901**
Tibeto-Chinese Family ..	..	..	**597**	**182**	**3**	**7**	**2**	..
Tibeto-Burman Sub-Family.	..	..	**597**	**182**	**3**	**7**	**2**	..
Tibeto-Himalyan Branch	..	..	**597**	**182**	**3**	**7**	**2**	..
	Tibetan ..	..	29	20	2	..	..	..
		Bhotia of Tibet ..	21	20	2	..	..	..
		Bhotia of Sharpa ..	6	..	..	..	..	..
		Bhotia of Sikkim ..	2	..	..	..	..	..
	Pronominalized Himalayan.	..	488	..	..	6	..	..
		Kiranti ..	488	..	..	6	..	..
		(a) Limbu ..	262	..	..	3	..	..
		(b) Rai or Jimdar ..	226	..	..	3	..	..
	Non-Pronominalized Himalayan.	..	80	..	1	1	..	..
		Gurang ..	16	..	1	..	..	..
		Sunwar ..	38	..	..	1	..	..
		Magari ..	24	..	..	..	..	..
		Rong or Lepcha ..	2	..	..	..	..	..
	Burma ..	..	..	162	..	..	2	..
		Burmese ..	..	162	..	..	2	..
Dravidian Family ..	..	..	**127,810**	**140,421**	**145,631**	**1,471**	**1,756**	**1,745**
	Dravida ..	..	172	389	59	2	5	1
		Tamil ..	150	349	55	2	5	1
		Malayalam ..	12	11	2	..	..	..
		Kanarese ..	10	29	2	..	..	..
	Andhra Language ..	Telegu ..	42	64	20	..	..	..
	North-Western Language	Brahui ..	127,479	139,727	145,299	1,468	1,748	1,741
	Un-classed language	Lori Chini ..	117	241	253	1	3	3
Indo-European Family ..	..	..	**729,628**	**650,367**	**680,776**	**8,400**	**8,134**	**8,156**
Aryan Sub-Family ..	..	..	**729,628**	**650,367**	**680,776**	**8,400**	**8,134**	**8,156**
Eranian Branch ..	..	..	**479,371**	**433,268**	**468,119**	**5,519**	**5,419**	**5,608**
	Eastern ..	..	**479,371**	**433,268**	**468,119**	**5,519**	**5,419**	**5,608**
		Pashto ..	207,181	201,873	227,553	2,385	2,525	2,726
		Balochi ..	266,957	225,127	232,987	3,074	2,816	2,791
		Persian ..	5,233	6,268	7,579	60	78	91
Dardic Branch ..	..	..	**201**	**165**	**16**	**2**	**2**	..
	Dard ..	..	201	165	16	2	2	..
		Kashmiri ..	201	165	16	2	2	..
Outer Sub-Branch ..	..	..	**204,361**	**157,942**	**170,954**	**2,853**	**1,975**	**2,048**
	North-Western ..	..	**203,386**	**156,740**	**169,948**	**2,342**	**1,960**	**2,036**
		Lahanda or Western Punjabi	50,354	45,328	48,099	580	567	576
		Sindhi ..	151,232	98,537	69,974	1,741	1,232	838
		Unspecified ..	1,800	12,875	51,875	21	161	621
	Southern ..	..	**862**	**1,124**	**846**	**10**	**14**	**10**
		Marathi ..	789	1,124	846	9	14	10
		Konkani ..	93	..	..	1	..	..
	Eastern ..	..	**93**	**78**	**160**	**1**	**1**	**2**
		Oriya ..	..	8	3	..	..	..
		Bihari ..	..	..	144	..	..	2
		Bengali ..	93	70	13	1	1	..
Mediate Sub-Branch ..	..	..	**39**	..	..	..	..	..
	Mediate ..	..	**39**	..	..	..	..	..
		Eastern Hindi ..	39	..	..	..	..	..
Inner Sub-Branch ..	..	..	**45,656**	**58,992**	**41,687**	**526**	**738**	**500**
	Central ..	..	**37,755**	**53,591**	**39,429**	**435**	**670**	**478**
		Western Hindi ..	17,092	16,757	10,983	197	210	132
		Rajasthani ..	530	962	324	6	12	4
		Gujrati ..	618	494	580	7	6	7
		Panjabi ..	19,515	35,378	27,542	225	442	330
	Pahari ..	..	**7,901**	**5,401**	**2,258**	**91**	**68**	**27**
		Central Pahari ..	3,169	2,452	302	36	31	4
		Eastern Pahari, Khaskura or Naipali	4,653	2,949	1,956	54	37	23
		Western Pahari ..	25	..	..	..	..	..
		Pahari unspecified ..	54	..	..	1	..	..

SUBSIDIARY TABLES.

41—Distribution of total population by languages classified according to Linguistic Survey—*concluded.*

Family, Sub-Family, Branch and Sub-Branch.	Group.	Language.	Total number of Speakers.			Number per 10,000 of Population of Province.		
			1931.	1921.	1911.	1931.	1921.	1911.
1	2	3	4	5	6	7	8	9
II.—LANGUAGES FOREIGN TO INDIA.	..	..	10,582	8,655	8,293	122	108	99
Indo-European Family:—	..	..	10,524	8,648	8,191	121	108	98
Aryan Sub-Family ..	..	..	5,021	3,591	3,833	58	45	46
Eranian Branch ..	..	..	5,021	3,591	3,833	58	45	46
	Persian ..	..	5,020	3,591	3,833	58	45	46
		Persian ..	5,020	3,591	3,833	58	45	46
	Armenian ..	..	1	..	..	..	..	..
		Armenian ..	1	..	..	..	..	..
	Romanic ..	..	68	2	1	1	..	..
		Italian ..	1	..	..	..	..	..
		French ..	9	2	1	..	..	..
		Spanish ..	3	..	..	..	..	..
		Portuguese ..	55	..	..	1	..	..
	Celtic ..	..	60	..	..	..	..	..
		Welsh ..	9	..	..	..	..	..
		Scotch ..	35	..	..	..	..	..
		Irish ..	16	..	..	..	..	..
	Bolto-slavonic ..	..	..	2	..	..	..	..
		Russian ..	..	2	..	..	..	..
	Teutonic ..	..	5,375	5,053	4,357	62	63	52
		English ..	5,369	5,053	4,349	62	63	52
		Danish ..	2	..	..	..	..	..
		German ..	4	..	8	..	..	..
Tibeto-Chinese Family ..	..	..	40	1	2	1	..	..
Tai-Chinese Sub-Family	..	..	40	1	2	1	..	..
Chinese Branch ..	..	..	40	1	3	..	..	..
	Chinese ..	..	40	1	2	..	..	..
		Chinese ..	40	1	2	..	..	..
Semitic Family ..	..	..	10	6	87	..	..	1
		Arabic ..	9	6	78	..	..	1
		Hebrew ..	1	..	9	..	..	..
Mongolian Family ..	..	..	7	..	13	..	..	..
	Ural Altaic ..	..	7	..	7	..	..	..
		Turkish ..	7	..	7	..	..	..
	Japanese ..	..	..	..	6	..	..	..
		Japanese ..	..	..	6	..	..	..
Malayo-Polynesian Family	..	..	1	..	..	..	..	..
	Malayan ..	..	1	..	..	..	..	..
		Javanese ..	1	..	..	..	..	..

42.—Distribution by Language of Population of each District (for Indigenous only).

District or State.	Number per 10,000 of the Population Speaking.															
	Balochi.				*Pashto.*				*Brahui.*				*Local Sindhi (Jatki Sindhi and Lasi).*			
	As mother tongue.	As subsidiary to Pashto.	As subsidiary to Brahui.	As subsidiary to Local Sindhi.	As mother tongue.	As subsidiary to Balochi.	As subsidiary to Brahui.	As subsidiary to Local Sindhi.	As mother tongue.	As subsidiary to Balochi.	As subsidiary to Pashto.	As subsidiary to Local Sindhi.	As mother tongue.	As subsidiary to Balochi.	As subsidiary to Brahui.	As subsidiary to Pashto.
1	2	3	4	5	6	7	8	9	10	11	12	13	14	15	16	17
BALUCHISTAN	3,470	14	84	47	2,464	16	34	4	1,676	212	27	30	1,877	807	1	46
DISTRICTS	2,636	30	107	25	5,230	35	68	5	695	113	53	5	680	258	2	37
Quetta Pishin	226	11	9	..	8,593	34	179	..	967	16	86	..	1	..	..	..
Loralai	282	53	12	..	6,833	47	18	..	68	..	56	..	..	..	..	..
Zhob	11	2	..	..	9,954	2	21	..	28	..	1	..	..	..	..	..
Bolan	2,722	21	837	..	541	87	79	..	4,265	1,653	2	..	..	29	..	225
Chagai	5,192	62	1,329	..	636	35	246	..	3,917	1,593	354	..	2	17	..	1
Sibi	5,961	36	50	69	1,326	39	10	14	522	12	4	15	1,839	694	4	96
Administered Area ..	3,132	62	85	118	2,266	67	18	24	893	20	6	25	3,144	1,189	8	164
Mari-Bugti Country ..	9,950	..	..	..	1	..	..	..	..	..	..	..	..	..	..	..
STATES	4,209	..	64	79	15	..	5	3	2,543	300	4	51	2,937	349	..	54
Kalat	4,601	..	76	66	18	1	5	3	2,889	351	5	59	2,144	386	..	37
Sarawan	1,527	2	293	..	178	..	58	..	6,252	312	60	..	..	..	..	..
Jhalawan	2,111	..	103	..	2	..	..	..	7,721	185	..	6	157	..	..	..
Kachhi	3,450	1	48	73	4	1	..	1	981	210	..	128	5,015	1,081	..	80
Dombki-Kaheri Country ..	2,322	..	127	487	3	..	6	40	648	13	..	232	6,965	653	..	160
Makran	9,937	..	..	22	4	..	..	..	44	5	..	..	..	..	..	..
Kharan	9,995	3	..	..	5	6	..	..	..	3,079	..	..	..	..	..	..
Las-Bela	2,080	..	..	70	2	..	..	..	670	20	..	8	7,237	149	..	144

43.—Comparison of Tribe and Language Tables.

Tribe, Race or Caste.	Mother-tongue.	Strength of Tribe.		No. speaking tribal language only.		No. speaking tribal language and some other language.		REMARKS.
		Males.	Females.	Males.	Females.	Males.	Females.	
BALOCH.								
INDIGENOUS.								
(i) Eastern.								
Bugti	Balochi	16,797	13,816	16,506	13,554	212	159	Local Sindhi and Brahui.
Dombki	,,	3,943	3,298	3,786	3,158	1,945	922	Local Sindhi.
Khetran	Lahnda (Khetran)	8,997	8,165	8,617	7,907	2,539	398	Balochi & Pashto.
Magasi	Blochi	7,212	6,074	6,151	5,183	5,038	4,081	Local Sindhi.
Mari	,,	19,700	15,554	17,577	14,707	750	91	Pashto & Lahnda.
Rind Buledi	,,	3,093	2,616	2,479	2,124	1,153	966	Local Sindhi.
,, Jamali	,,	3,557	3,028	3,410	2,912	2,360	1,407	Local Sindhi & Lahnda.
,, Khosa	,,	2,535	2,084	2,466	2,028	1,424	1,005	.. ,, Brahui.
,, Lashari	,,	3,808	3,391	2,462	2,165	1,593	209	,, ,, ,,
,, Unspecified	,,	10,695	8,515	9,691	7,945	1,094	854	,, ,, ,,
Umrani	,,	1,433	1,208	1,288	1,076	296	264	Local Sindhi.
Baloch Unspecified	,,	484	361	367	332	204	35	,, ,, & Western Hindi.
(ii) Western.								
Buledi	,,	84	74	84	74	..	..	
Dashti	,,	543	453	542	453	6	..	Brahui.
Gichki	,,	142	151	142	150	2	..	Western Hindi & Persian
Kaudai	,,	1,231	1,077	1,214	1,068	9	7	Brahui.
Rais	,,	2,068	1,883	2,067	1,882	49	17	,,
Rakhshani	,,	13,104	11,002	12,835	10,795	4,077	3,027	,,
Rind	,,	16,531	14,524	16,215	14,282	238	160	Local Sindhi.
Sangur	,,	3,924	3,410	3,924	3,410	94	15	,,
Sanjrani	,,	208	193	194	182	15	7	Brahui.
Others	,,	2,771	2,304	2,558	2,158	207	66	Western Hindi & Brahui.
SEMI-INDIGENOUS								
Buzdar	Balochi	953	785	866	713	314	75	Lahnda & Pashto.
Others	,,	39	28	30	25	9	1	Sindhi.
BRAHUI.								
(i) Original Nucleus.								
Ahmadzai	Balochi	30	47	..	..	..	..	
Gurgnari	Brahui	798	668	723	611	117	12	Local Sindhi & Balochi.
Iltazai	,,	112	90	112	90	7	..	,, ,, ,,
Kalandrari	Brahui	750	580	642	497	58	5	Pashto.
Kambrari	Balochi	1,142	923	350	275	45	23	Brahui.
Mirwari	,,	980	898	734	681	11	7	,,
Rodeni	Brahui	734	601	534	464	128	31	Local Sindhi & Balochi.
Sumalari	,,	2,516	2,079	2,179	1,821	819	491	Balochi and Pashto.
(ii) Sarawan.								
Bangulzai	Brahui	4,083	3,306	3,170	2,578	736	220	Balochi, Western Hindi & Local Sindhi.
Kurd	,,	1,235	995	961	756	330	110	Western Hindi & Dehwari.
Lahri	,,	2,528	1,962	2,444	1,893	561	259	Local Sindhi and Dehwari.
Langav	Balochi	3,631	3,017	2,156	1,939	919	567	Dehwari, Western Hindi & Brahui.
Mamashahi	Brahui	1,535	1,193	1,440	1,117	316	175	Balochi & Western Hindi.
Raisani	,,	1,500	1,216	1,452	1,183	461	182	Dehwari & Pashto.
Rustumzai	,,	141	102	131	97	41	16	Balochi.
Sarparra	,,	1,029	877	971	820	162	62	Western Hindi, Pashto & Balochi.
Satakzai	Pashto	923	663	882	637	336	134	Pashto & Balochi.
Shahwani	Brahui	3,362	2,727	2,051	2,434	721	114	Western Hindi, Pashto & Balochi.
Zagr Mengal	,,	3,177	2,646	2,946	2,456	1,090	499	Balochi & Pashto.
(iii) Jhalawan.								
Bizanjav	Balochi	7,651	5,940	6,797	5,202	868	740	Brahui.
Haruni	Brahui	847	765	594	549	31	..	Western Hindi & Pashto.
Mamasani	Balochi & Brahui	5,602	4,754	5,595	4,751	2,356	1,948	Brahui or Balochi.
Mengal	Brahui	14,344	12,033	13,545	11,293	1,139	303	Local Sindhi, Balochi & Western Hindi.
Nichari	,,	951	754	939	744	43	26	Pashto.
Pandrani	,,	572	491	561	481	214	83	Local Sindhi.
Sajdi	Balochi	1,843	1,436	1,283	987	15	11	Brahui.
Zahri	Brahui	19,765	17,059	18,565	16,204	410	103	Local Sindhi & Balochi.
(iv) Miscellaneous.								
Nighari	Brahui	608	520	595	515	1	..	Lori Chini.
Rekizai	,,	291	243	291	243	..	..	
Others	,,	848	465	627	298	383	58	Western Hindi & Pashto.
PATHAN.								
INDIGENOUS.								
Babi	Pashto	103	91	7	6	..	..	
Barech	,,	886	724	800	640	356	153	Brahui & Western Hindi.
Jafar	Lahnda (Jafarki)	805	674	698	603	364	66	Pashto & Balochi.
Kakar.								
Dawi	Pashto	150	124	150	124	9	1	
Dumar	,,	3,964	3,144	3,958	3,141	99	11	Western Hindi & Brahui.
Hussain Pasenr	,,	414	391	414	391	20	..	,, ,,
Sanzar Khel	,,	25,623	20,938	25,561	20,912	472	55	,, ,, & Persian.
Sargara	,,	1,076	924	1,076	924	20	..	,, ,,
Shatia	,,	10,840	8,922	10,824	8,914	1,537	41	,, ,, & Brahui.
Targara	,,	6,380	5,790	6,380	5,790	297	4	,, ,,
Others	,,	790	361	653	262	232	30	,, ,,
Kasi	,,	1,055	920	854	767	309	27	,, ,, & Brahui.
Luni	,,	1,881	1,700	1,817	1,637	12	..	,, ,,

43.—Comparison of Tribe and Language Tables.—*concluded.*

Tribe, Race or caste.	Mother tongue.	Strength of Tribe.		No. speaking tribal language only.		No. speaking tribal language and some other language.		Remarks.
		Males.	Females.	Males.	Females.	Males.	Females.	
PATHAN—*concld.*								
Pani.								
Main Branch ..	Pashto ..	2,209	1,957	1,267	1,097	186	94	Unspecified Jagdali or, Jatki & Brahui.
Isot ..	„ ..	1,352	1,203	1,352	1,203	149	116	„ „ „ „
Laun ..	„ ..	305	238	304	238	1	..	Landah.
Mando Khel ..	„ ..	2,562	2,073	2,562	2,073	69	2	Western Hindi.
Musa Khel ..	„ ..	7,376	6,202	7,362	6,195	310	209	Unspecified Jagdali & Brahui.
Zarkun ..	„ ..	1,141	982	1,017	879	391	284	Balochi.
Unspecified ..	„ ..	66	35	13	6	12	6	Western Hindi.
Shirani ..	„ ..	4,446	3,970	4,444	3,968	76	11	„ „ & Persian.
Tarin.								
Abdal Achakzai	„ ..	10,913	8,883	10,912	8,881	391	10	„ „ „
Spin Tarin ..	„ ..	5,090	4,619	4,621	4,177	148	2	„ „
Tor Tarin ..	„ ..	3,229	3,508	3,191	3,478	159	2	„ „
Unspecified ..	„ ..	325	187	321	186	76	4	„ „
Zmarai ..	„ ..	1,526	1,363	1,526	1,363	309	7	Persian.
Other Pathans ..	„ ..	965	612	603	364	351	116	Western Hindi & Persian.
SEMI-INDIGENOUS								
Durrani ..	Pashto & Persian	1,541	869	1,450	807	729	209	(1) Persian & (2) Pashto.
				(1) 1,218	682	551	124	
				(2) 232	125	178	85	
Ghilzai ..	Pashto ..	8,102	6,007	7,969	5,926	554	117	Western Hindi & Persian.
Others ..	„ ..	329	170	225	73	123	17	„ „ „
LASI.								
Angaria ..	Local Sindhi (Lasi)	2,116	1,850	2,113	1,849	..	..	
Burra ..	„ ..	1,895	1,516	1,884	1,507	..	..	
Jamot ..	„ ..	3,050	2,765	2,774	2,536	190	166	Balochi & Brahui.
Runjha ..	„ ..	2,387	2,269	2,387	2,269	138	44	Balochi.
Sheikh ..	„ ..	2,270	2,036	1,756	1,546	..	..	
Mongia ..	„ ..	1,393	1,268	1,334	1,221	..	..	
Shahoke ..	„ ..	727	588	720	585	1	1	Balochi.
Mondra ..	„ ..	1,724	1,507	1,724	1,507	..	..	
Gonga ..	„ ..	1,065	1,378	1,006	1,321	..	..	
Unspecified ..	„ ..	8	..	5	..	..	..	
JATT.								
INDIGENOUS ..	Local Sindhi, (Jatki Sindi.)	42,227	34,930	38,094	31,516	1,892	780	Balochi & Brahui.
SAYYID.								
INDIGENOUS.								
Bukhari ..	Pashto ..	5,585	6,199	4,298	5,079	341	7	Western Hindi & Persian.
Chishti ..	„ ..	928	909	455	426	9	1	„ „
Gharshin ..	„ ..	542	473	365	294	24	4	Persian & Western Hindi.
Kaheri ..	Local Sindhi (Jatki Sindi).	652	563	462	385	7	..	Balochi.
Mashwani ..	Pashto ..	593	447	516	398	342	248	Brahui.
Taran ..	„ ..	672	548	671	548	35	7	Western Hindi.
Ustrana ..	„ ..	356	282	348	272	16	6	Balochi.
Others ..	„ ..	1,799	1,428	849	678	117	14	Western Hindi & Persian.
OTHER MUSLIM.								
INDIGENOUS.								
Darzada ..	Balochi ..	4,831	4,508	4,752	4,440	10	2	Western Hindi.
Dehwar ..	Dehwari ..	2,934	2,383	2,406	1,976	835	718	Brahui.
Gadra ..	Local Sindi (Jatki Sindi.) ..	4,530	3,396	4,535	3,390	..	..	
Gola ..	„ ..	264	213	264	213	..	..	
Jat ..	„ ..	1,798	1,438	1,143	908	..	..	
Khoja ..	„ ..	177	175	142	148	—	..	
Langah ..	Balochi ..	255	251	163	161	20	17	Local Sindhi
Lori ..	„ ..	3,044	2,609	1,617	1,389	314	190	Brahui, Western Hindi & Pashto.
Med ..	„ ..	1,566	1,475	1,218	1,149	..	..	
Nakib ..	„ ..	3,814	3,340	3,237	2,927	32	..	Local Sindhi & Brahui.
OTHERS.								
(*a*) Sorozai ..	„ ..	5,829	5,335	3,351	3,237	348	333	Brahui.
(*b*) Others ..	„ ..	1,831	1,586	1,589	1,398	48	58	Pashto & Brahui.
SEMI-INDIGENOUS								
Hazara ..	Persian ..	2,226	849	2,176	825	1,269	214	Western Hindi & Pashto.
Others ..	„ ..	16	8	5	..	1	..	Western Hindi.
HINDUS.								
INDIGENOUS.								
Arora ..	Local Sindi (Jatki Sindi)	8,825	7,534	6,527	5,786	966	26	Brahui & Balochi.
Brahman ..	„ ..	97	60	37	24	..	..	
Khatri ..	Sindhi ..	166	93	102	50	70	9	Western Hindi.
Others ..	Local Sindhi ..	87	43	59	28	2	..	Balochi & Brahui.
SIKH.								
INDIGENOUS.								
Sikh Unspecified ..	Local Sindhi ..	35	13	30	12	24	..	Balochi.

APPENDIX.

KEY TO LINGUISTIC MAP.

(1) *Quetta-Pishin District*—

POPULATION 147,541

Pashto (77,177), 52·3 %.
Baluchi (1,895), 1·3 % not shown.
Brahui (8,063), 5·5 % (of whom 18·6 % speak Pashto).
Foreign languages (60,406), 40·9 %.

(2) *Loralai District*—

POPULATION 86,087

Pashto (56,384), 65·5 %.
Balochi (4,562), 5·3 %, (Pashto 11·6 %, Western Punjabi 16 %).
Western Punjabi (19,435), 22·6 %, Balochi 15·4 %, Pashto 5·9 %.
Foreign languages (5,706), 6·6 %.

(3) *Zhob District*—

POPULATION 57,930

Pashto (50,854), 87·9 %.
Foreign languages (6,999), 12·1 %.

(4) *Bolan*—

POPULATION 4,688

Pashto (215), 4·6 % not shown.
Balochi (713), 15·2 %, (Brahui 57·8 %).
Western Punjabi (33), 0·7 % not shown.
Brahui (1,044), 23·3 %, (Balochi 19·5 %, Sindhi 5·4%).
Foreign languages (2,683), 57·2 %.

(5) *Chagai District*—

POPULATION .. .. 24,224.

Pashto (2,371), 9·8 %, (Balochi 7 %, Brahui 35·9 %).
Balochi (11,224), 46·3 %, (Brahui 31·96 %).
Brahui (8,277), 34·2 %, (Balochi 34·1%, Pashto 6·9 %).
Foreign languages (2,362), 9·7 %.

(6) *Sibi District*—

POPULATION 143,005

Balochi (78,646), 55 %, (Sindhi 11·7 %).
Pashto (19,279), 13·5 %.
Western Punjabi (3,499), 2·4 % not shown.
Sindhi (14,487), 10·1 %, (Balochi 7·6 %).
Brahui (6,887), 4·8 %, (Balochi 9·5 %, Sindhi 25·9 %).
Foreign languages (20,207), 14·2 %.

(7) *Sarawan*—

POPULATION 28,464

Pashto (705), 2·5 % not shown.
Balochi (4,271), 15 %, (Dehwari 22 %, Brahui 20·4 %).
Dehwari (5,101), 17·9 %, (Brahui 45 %).
Brahui (17,486), 61·4 %, (Dehwari 10·2 %).
Foreign languages (901), 3·2 % not shown.

(8) *Jhalawan*—

POPULATION 88,978

Balochi (18,741), 21·1 %, (Brahui 8·8 %).
Sindhi (1,446), 1·6 % not shown.
Brahui (68,498), 77 %.
Foreign languages 0·3 % not shown.

(9) *Kachhi*—

Population 105,886

Balochi (36,413), 34·4 % (Sindhi 31·8 %, Brahui 6·5 %).
Western Punjabi (5,780), 5·5 % (Sindhi 28·5 %).
Sindhi (53,040), 50·1 %.
Brahui (10,341), 9·8 % (Sindhi 10·4 %).
Foreign languages (112), 0·2 % not shown.

(10) *Dombki-Kaheri Country*—

Population 26,953

Balochi (6,250), 23·3 % (Sindhi 28·1 %).
Sindhi (18,747), 69·3 %.
Brahui (1,744), 6·6 % (Balochi 19·6 %, Sindhi 24·7 %).
Foreign langages (212), 0·8 % not shown.

(11) *Makran*—

Population 68,462

Balochi (67,829), 99·1 %.
Brahui (303), 0·4 % not shown.
Foreign languages (33), 0·5 % not shown.

(12) *Kharan*—

Population 23,358

Balochi (23,304), 99·8 % (Brahui 31·4 %).
Foreign languages (54), 0·2 % not shown.

(13) *Las Bela*—

Population 63,008

Balochi (13,058), 20·7 % (Sindhi 7·2 %, Brahui 18·8 %.)
Sindhi (45,453), 72·1 %.
Brahui (4,208), 6·7 % (Sindhi 21·5 %).
Foreign languages (292), 0·5 % not shown.

CHAPTER XI.

RELIGION.

---

211. The absolute figures dealt with in this chapter are contained in Imperial Table XVI. The figures of religions of the urban population are given in Imperial Table V. Statistics of literates in each religion and the summary figures for the principal religions for each District and State are contained in Imperial Tables XIII and XX respectively. The numbers of followers of each of the main religions in each Tahsil and Division of the States will be found in Provincial Table II. All these tables are printed in Part II of this volume. The proportional figures for each religion in each District and State and in the urban areas with variation since 1911 are given in the Subsidiary Tables at the end of this chapter. **Reference to Statistics.**

212. The enumerators were asked to record the religion of each individual in column 4 of the Standard Schedule and column 5 of the Tribal Schedule. The following instructions were issued for the guidance of enumerators and supervising officers :— **Instructions to Enumerators.**

Regular Areas—*Column* 4 (*Religion and Sect*).—Enter here the religion which each person returns, as Hindu, Muslim, Sikh, Jain, Christian, Parsi, and the sect of religion followed by each person as he returns it. In the case of aboriginal tribes who are not Hindus, Buddhist. Christian, etc., the name of the tribe should be entered in this column. Sect is in all cases required for Christians.

The answer which each person gives about his religion must be accepted and entered in column 4. If a man says that he is a Jain or Sikh he should be entered as such. Brahmos, Aryas and Dev Samajists should be recorded as such but the enumerators should not refuse to add within brackets the word 'Hindu' after the name of the sects of those Brahmos, Aryas and Dev Samajists who desire that they should be definitely entered as 'Hindu.' Similar procedure may be followed in the case of Buddhists, Jains or Sikhs who express a definite desire to be returned as Hindu also. The religion of Aryas should be entered as Vedic Dharma.

If a Jain desires his sect to be recorded it should be recorded in brackets after his religion, *e.g.*, Swetambar, Degambar, Swetambar-Sthakbashi and Swetambar-Tarapanthi.

In the case of famine orphans made over to the charge of a Mission, but not baptised, the religion of the parents if known, should be entered. If the religion of the parents cannot be ascertained, the predominant religion of the district or locality should be recorded.

In the case of Chuhras who return themselves as Hindu, Musalman or Sikh enter the sect to which they profess to belong. Those who return no religion should be entered simply as Chuhras.

Persons returning themselves as Adharmis should be recorded as such. In the case of Sansis and others, whose religion is tribal, the tribe should be entered in this column.

In the case of Christians belonging to definite tribes or races, the term Indian Christian should not be entered in column 8, but the tribe to which the individual really belongs.

The main sects of the Hindus will be noted, *e.g.*, Sanatan Dharam, Radha Swami, River Worship, Zind Kaliana, Vaishnava, etc. Sub-divisions of these sects are not needed.

For Mussalmans such sects as Sunni, Shia, Ahl-i-Hadis, Ahmadi, Zikri, Taib should be recorded.

For Sikhs the main sects will be Kesdhari and Sahjdhari or Mona. Special sub-divisions such as Hazuri, Nihang, and Sultani should be entered in addition to the sect. Similarly such minor divisions as Udasi, Nanakpanthi, Nirmala should, if stated, be noted.

In the case of Parsis, (Zoroastrians) enter whether Kadmi or Shahnshahi. All women and children should be shown as belonging to the religion and sect of persons on whom they are dependent, unless they clearly belong to another.

Tribal Areas—*Column 5, Religion and Sect.*—Here enter the various religions and sects such as Sunni, Shia, Zikri, Taib, etc., in the case of Muslims, and Sanatan, Brahmo, Dev Samaji, Arya, etc., for Hindus. In the case of Sikhs enter Kesdhari or Sahjdhari. If there are any other sects such as Dev Margi among the Hindus and Namdharis among the Sikhs record what the people tell you. In the case of Christians enter their denominations. But you must be very careful not to put impertinent questions to any one or to offer any comment or criticism regarding any religion whatsoever.

Accuracy of the Results.

213. The instructions were so clear and the questions and answers so simple that hardly any doubt can be entertained as to the normal accuracy of the results of the Census of this Province which outside the synchronous areas is inhabited mainly by Muslims of the Sunni sect. Religions other than Islam, excepting a small percentage of Hindus and Sikhs, are represented only in the synchronous areas. Here the tail end of the Indian agitation in respect of religious clssification made itself slightly felt in the early stages of the operations but the excitement was nipped in the bud by taking precautionary measures in consultation with representatives of the various communities. The numbers of the followers of each religion as disclosed by the Census may, therefore, be taken to be as accurate as the figures of population by sexes.

Numerical Strength of each Religion.

214. The marginal summary gives the numerical strength of each religion represented in Baluchistan at the Census of 1931. The figures are illustrated in the map at the beginning of this Chapter. The Muslims predominate enormously, claiming 919 in every 1,000 of the total population including temporary immigrants. The Hindus contribute 62, Sikhs 10, Christians 9 and all other religions less than one. These numbers include 5,249 Chuhras who are not ordinarily recognised as members of the communities with which they have been lumped up and although they have lost in this Province much of the unpleasantness of the curse of untouchability in social circles, they would only be claimed as Hindus, Muslims or Sikhs for purposes other than social or religious.

Religion.	Total.	Males.	Females.
Muslim	798,093	440,089	358,004
Hindu	53,681	36,180	17,501
Sikh	8,425	6,270	2,155
Christian	8,059	5,637	2,422
Jain	32	20	12
Buddhist	68	53	15
Zoroastrian	167	90	77
Jew	17	14	3
Tribal	32	25	7
Others	43	36	7

Muslim Chuhras ..	546
Hindu Chuhras ..	4,533
Sikh Chuhras ..	134
Others	36
	5,249

Proportion amongst Indigenous Inhabitants.

215. Taking the indigenous population and immigrants separately, the proportion of Muslims rises to 978 in every 1,000 indigenous inhabitants of all creeds while that of the Hindus falls from 62 to 22. No other religion, excepting 48 Sikhs, is represented in the Tribal Areas.

	Indigenous.	Aliens.
Muslim ..	765,094	32,999
Hindu ..	16,905	36,776
Sikh ..	48	8,377

VARIATION OF PROPORTIONAL DISTRIBUTION BY RELIGION.

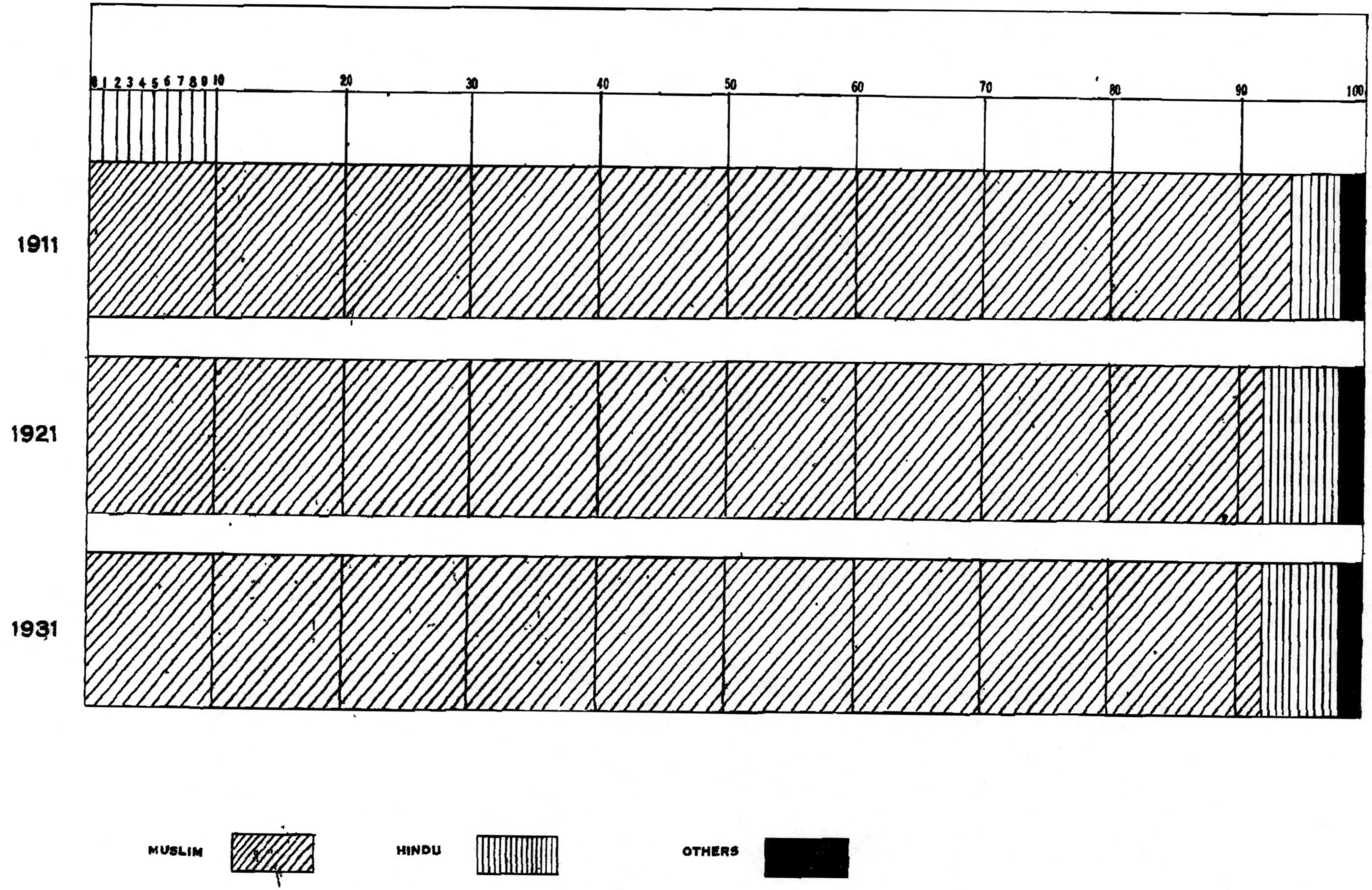

Distribution by Districts and States.

216. The distribution of the various religions by locality for each of the past three censuses is given in Subsidiary Table 44. The distribution for 1931 is shown in the following table :—

District or State.	Total population.	Muslim.	Hindu.	Sikh.	Christian.	Zoroastrian	Jew.	Jain.	Buddhist.	No religion	Tribal.	Chuhras.
BALUCHISTAN ..	**868,617**	**798,093**	**53,681**	**8,425**	**8,059**	**167**	**17**	**32**	**68**	**7**	**32**	**36**
Districts ..	**463,508**	**405,309**	**41,432**	**8,368**	**8,044**	**167**	**15**	**32**	**68**	**7**	**32**	**34**
Quetta-Pishin ..	147,541	107,945	26,718	5,255	7,370	161	15	32	40	5	..	..
Loralai ..	86,087	81,812	3,504	562	209	..	..	..	..	..	..	..
Zhob ..	57,963	53,844	2,839	1,134	115	..	..	..	27	..	..	4
Bolan ..	4,688	3,229	1,165	173	91	..	..	..	..	..	..	30
Chagai ..	24,224	22,769	1,313	117	25	..	..	..	..	..	..	..
Sibi ..	143,005	135,710	5,893	1,127	234	6	..	..	1	2	32	..
States ..	**405,109**	**392,784**	**12,249**	**57**	**15**	..	**2**	..	..	..	..	**2**
Kalat ..	342,101	331,234	10,806	42	15	..	2	..	..	..	..	2
Sarawan ..	*28,464*	*27,722*	*729*	*10*	*3*	..	..	..	..	..	..	..
Jhalawan ..	*88,978*	*88,780*	*197*	*1*	..	..	..	..	..	..	..	..
Kachhi ..	*105,886*	*98,852*	*7,019*	*12*	*1*	..	..	..	..	..	..	*2*
Dombki-Kaheri country ..	*26,953*	*24,349*	*2,588*	*16*	..	..	..		..	..	..	..
Makran ..	*68,462*	*68,213*	*233*	*3*	*11*	..	*2*	..	..	..	..	..
Kharan ..	*23,358*	*23,318*	*40*	..	..	..	..	..	..	..	..	..
Las Bela ..	63,008	61,550	1,443	15	..	..	..	..	..	..	..	..

Variation.

217. The percentage of increase or decrease since 1911 in each class of population under each of the three religions indigenous to the Province, namely, Muslim, Hindu and Sikh is shown below. The variation of proportional distribution by religion for three censuses is illustrated in Diagram No. 22 on the opposite page.

Religion.	Percentage of Increase+ Decrease—		
	1911-21.	1911-31.	1921-31.
Muslim —	—7	+1	+9
Indigenous	—8	—0·2	+8
Semi-indigenous	—27	—14	+13
Alien	+33	+46	+9
Hindu—	+37	+43	+5
Indigenous	+17	+13	—3
Alien	+50	+63	+9
Sikh—	—8	+0·4	+9
Indigenous	—67	—98	—94
Alien	+23	+50	+21

MUSLIMS.

Muslim Population.

218. According to the Census of 1931, the Muslims in the Province numbered 798,093 (males 440,089, females 358,004) out of a total population of 868,617 (males 488,414, females 380,203). There were 405,309 Muslims in British and Administered territory and 392,784 in the States. The Muslims represent 92 per cent. of the total population in the Province as a whole, 87 per cent. in British and Administered territory, and 97 per cent. in the States. In the total Muslim population of the Province, there are 743,172 indigenous, 21,922 semi-indigenous and 32,999 alien immigrants. The indigenous Muslims represent 85, the semi-indigenous 4 and alien immigrants 3 per cent. of the total population of the Province.

Variations.

219. The natural growth of population since 1911 received a set-back between 1911 and 1921 due to the combined influence of influenza and other epidemics as well as drought and famine which took a heavy toll and caused emigration resulting in a decrease in the Muslim population of no less than 6 per cent. between 1911 and 1921. In spite of the adverse opening balance and the fact that the last decennium was not entirely free from natural

calamities, the Census of 1931 has revealed an increase of 1 per cent. in the total Muslim population since 1911 and 9 per cent. since 1921. Excluding alien immigrants whose numbers fluctuate from year to year according to varying conditions of business and employment and the composition of troops, the indigenous Muslims show a gain of 8 per cent. between 1921 and 1931 and a loss of 0·2 between 1911 and 1931. These variations among the indigenous population are distributed over Districts and States as shown below :—

Districts and States.	Percentage of Increase+ Decrease— 1911-21.	1911-31.	1921-31.
Districts	—6	+6	+9
Quetta-Pishin	—7	—6	+2
Loralai	+5	+7	+2
Zhob	—21	—17	+2
Bholan	+67	+166	+59
Chagai	+11	+38	+24
Sibi	—7	+26	+34
States	+8	+10	+7
Kalat	+6	+14	+4
Sarawan	*—15*	*—58*	*—48*
Jhalawan	*—9*	*+2*	*+12*
Kachhi	*—19*	*+17*	*+45*
Dombki-Kaheri country	*—17*	*+19*	*+44*
Makran	*+1*	*—4*	*—5*
Kharan	*+22*	*+1*	*—16*
Las Bela	—17	+3	+25

In the Districts the increase in the last decennium is distributed uniformly between Quetta-Pishin, Loralai and Zhob it being only 2 per cent. The high percentage for Chagai is due to the transfer of the Shorarud Tahsil from the Quetta-Pishin to the Chagai District. In the case of Bolan the actual numbers are very small and the small accession of numbers is responsible for the violent disturbance in percentage increase. The high percentage for Sibi is largely due to natural increases as well as to the return to their homes of considerable numbers of Maris and Bugtis who had emigrated into Sind and the Punjab at the Census of 1921 owing to famine conditions.

In the States, Sarawan shows a decrease of 48 per cent. since 1921 while Jhalawan, Kachhi and Dombki-Kaheri country contribute increases of 12, 45 and 44 respectively. Makran and Kharan show decreases of 5 and 16 per cent. respectively while the population of Las Bela has increased since 1921 by 25 per cent. The abnormal variations in Sarawan, Jhalawan, Kachhi and Dombki-Kaheri divisions are due largely to the winter migration of the population of Sarawan and Jhalawan into Kachhi and Dombki-Kaheri. In order to ascertain the true proportion of variation in these areas it is necessary to deal with them as a single unit. The indigenous Muslim population in these four divisions was 253,147 in 1911. In 1921 it declined to 217,031 and rose in 1931 to 238,732. The net loss thus amounted to 14 per cent. between 1911 and 1921 which added to the normal natural increase, say, at 10 per cent. means a decrease of 24 per cent. caused by the world wide outbreak of influenza followed by drought and famine which latter scattered thousands away in all directions particularly Sind and the Punjab frontier. The recovery in the following decennium was only 9 per cent., amply proving that a considerable proportion of the emigrants of the preceding decade did not find it possible to return home during the last decennium. The increase since 1921 is attributable largely to the influence of natural growth. The rate would have been appreciably higher but for the fact that a considerable number of tribesmen who had migrated to Sind did not return to be included in the Census returns for Baluchistan.

The Semi-indigenous inhabitants lost ground between 1911 and 1921 to the extent of 26 per cent. but since 1921 have shown signs of recovery, the increase between 1921 and 1931 being 13 per cent. The Alien Muslims increased from 22,627 in 1911 to 30,195 in 1921 and 32,999 in 1931, the percentage of increase being 33 between 1911 and 1921, 9 between 1921 and 1931 and 46 since 1911.

Muslim Sects.

220. In the marginal statement are given figures for the Muslim sects at the past three censuses. The only sects which are indigenous to the Province are Sunni and Zikri and about 1,000 Shiahs among the Dombkis. The classification of some of the Dombkis as Shiahs is a doubtful item and needs further searching inquiry. The rest of the sects noted above are to be found exclusively among the immigrants chiefly from the Punjab. The whole of the indigenous population is of the Sunni Hanafi sect, excepting the 24,231 Zikris whose disappearance from future returns is only a matter of time. With the extension of education, the sect which has been the victim of ridicule for all time, will follow in the footsteps of the Taib sect whose followers under pressure of ridicule had to retire peacefully into the folds of its parent sect, the Sunni Hanafis.

	1911.	1921.	1931.
Sunni ..	749,909	705,716	767,114
Zikri ..	27,588	23,301	24,231
Shiah ..	4,823	3,739	5,961
Ahmadi ..	47	64	122
Ahl-i-Hadis ..	17	18	108
Sufi ..	1	..	..
Unspecified ..	263	639	537

HINDUS.

Hindu Population.

221. The Hindus numbered 53,681 in 1931 out of a total population of 868,617. Hinduism is the second largest religion in the Province but represents only 6 per cent. of the total population. The community is composed of 16,905 persons who are indigenous to the Province and 36,776 immigrants from Sind, Punjab and other Indian Provinces. Of the 16,905 indigenous Hindus, 5,136 are found in the Districts and 11,769 in the States. The majority of the alien Hindus, however, are met with in the Districts their actual numbers being 36,296 in the various Districts and only 480 in the States. Thus the percentage of the indigenous Hindus works out to only 2 in the total population against 6 for all Hindus and 4 for alien Hindus, or against 92 for all Muslims (Indigenous, Semi-indigenous and Aliens), and 98 for the indigenous Muslims in the whole of the indigenous population.

The alien Hindus include 4,533 Chuhras who have been classed as Hindus merely by courtesy on the part of the enumerators as in the case of Muslim and Sikh Chuhras who have nothing in common whatsoever with any of the three religions. Their beliefs are indefinite and they are untouchables pure and simple though the degree of untouchability has been slightly modified to suit local conditions on the frontier. If these Chuhras were excluded the proportion of all Hindus in the Province would drop from 6 to 5 per cent.

Local Distribution of Hindus.

222. Indigenous Hindus muster most strongly in the plains, their proportion per cent. of the total population of each locality being 41 in Kachhi, 15 in Dombki-Kaheri and 14 in Sibi. Las Bela has 8 per cent., Loralai 7, Quetta-Pishin 6, and Sarawan 4. The rest 5 per cent. are scattered over other Districts and Divisions of Kalat State. The alien Hindus are found mostly in Quetta and other garrison and headquarters stations as will be seen from the marginal figures. The alien Hindu element in the rural areas is conspicuous by its absence.

	Per cent.
Quetta-Pishin	70
Sibi	10
Zhob	8
Loralai	6
Other stations	6

Hindu Sects.

223. Of the 53,681 Hindus, 30,282 males and 14,663 females returned themselves as followers of the orthodox Brahmanic faith, 2,642 males and 1,414 females as Aryas, 7 males as Brahmos and 3,249 males and 1,424 females as belonging to other Hindu sects. The Brahmanic faith represents about 84 per cent. of the total Hindu population. Of these, 61 per cent. live in the Districts and 23 in the States. The Aryas contribute only 7 per cent; nearly three-fourths are found in Quetta-Pishin and the rest are scattered over other Districts, their numbers being only nominal in the States.

Variation.

224. The actual numerical strength of Hindus at each of the past three censuses is shown in the margin. Taking both indigenous and aliens together, the Hindus increased by 37 per cent. between 1911 and 1921. Between 1921 and 1931, the rate of increase fell to 5 per cent. During the twenty years ending with 1931, the Hindus have increased by 43 per cent. This rate would appear to

	Hindus.	
	Indigenous.	Alien.
1911 ..	14,985	22,617
1921 ..	17,479	33,869
1931 ..	16,905	36,776

be astonishingly high. Splitting the immigrants from the indigenous Hindus, we discover the real cause of this high rate of increase. The increase among the indigenous element was only 17 per cent. and even this rate was not due to natural causes for the indigenous Hindus gained at the expense of the Sikhs who lost 1,958 of their indigenous adherents by absorption by the Hindus and thus helped to raise the percentage of natural increase from 4 to 17.

In the following decade, 1921-31, though the Hindus increased in the aggregate by 5 per cent., the indigenous Hindus actually decreased by 3 per cent. in spite of a further accession of 793 persons who had returned themselves as Sikh at previous censuses. To arrive at the rate of natural growth, these 793 persons should be excluded. The rate of decrease thus rises to 8 per cent. between 1921 and 1931. The fact is that the high rate of increase shown by the Hindus is due mainly to a larger influx of temporary immigrants engaged in trade and the professions as well as in Civil and Military employ. The rate of natural increase can only be ascertained by separating the immigrants from the indigenous inhabitants and by doing so we arrive at disappointing conclusions which show that while the alien Hindus have increased by 63 per cent., the indigenous inhabitants have actually decreased by 6 per cent. during the past twenty years, excluding of course the adventitious gain by the conversion of 2,751 Sikhs. This decrease is not due to a high death-rate. It is true that, as pointed out in the Census Report for 1921, migration specially in hard times leaves the Hindu as a rule untouched. But continued world depression and unfavourable seasons extending over a series of years have taxed the patience of even the local accommodating Hindus who were obliged to seek refuge in comparatively more prosperous parts of Sind.

SIKHS.

Sikhs.

225. The Sikhs in Baluchistan represent slightly less than 1 per cent. of the total population. Their actual numbers for the past three censuses are shown in the margin. During the past twenty years they have lost 2,751 of their adherents among the indigenous inhabitants in consequence of change of faith. The only link between these persons and the Sikh religion were the Sikh scriptures. They knew little of their own. They read the Sikh scriptures but performed other rites in the manner of their brethren in Sind. A hint from their religious teachers whose visits have become more frequent of late had the desired effect and they almost bodily went back to the religion which they in reality professed.

	Sikhs.	
	Indigenous.	Aliens.
1911 ..	2,799	5,591
1921 ..	841	6,900
1931 ..	48	8,377

The principal Sikh sects returned at the Census of 1931 were Kesdhari and Sahjdhari. Their numbers for the past three censuses are shown in the margin. Among the principal local religious bodies the Sikhs are perhaps the only community in the Province who have made sustained and systematic efforts to bring the members of their community under strict religious control. The appreciable increase in the numbers of the Kesdharis, though only at the cost of the Sahjdharis, shows plainly enough that their efforts have not been fruitless.

	Kesdhari.	Sahjdhari.	Others.
1911 ..	4,613	3,777	..
1921 ..	6,603	1,138	..
1931 ..	7,489	735	201

OTHER RELIGIONS.

Christians.

226. Fourth among the religions in order of numerical strength comes Christianity. In 1931 the Christians numbered 8,059, composed of 5,637 males and 2,422 females. Their numbers for the past three censuses by nationality are given in the margin. The Christians have increased in the aggregate by 31 per cent. between 1911 and 1921, by 20 per cent. between 1921 and 1931 and by 58 per cent. during the

		1911.	1921.	1931.
All Christians ..	Total ..	5,085	6,693	8,059
	Males ..	3,941	5,214	5,637
	Females ..	1,144	1,479	2,422
European and allied races	Total ..	4,210	4,751	5,024
	Males ..	3,382	3,966	3,802
	Females ..	828	785	1,222
Anglo-Indian ..	Total ..	123	234	379
	Males ..	64	129	200
	Females ..	59	105	179
Indian ..	Total ..	752	1,708	2,656
	Males ..	495	1,119	1,635
	Females ..	257	589	1,021

20 years beginning with 1911. The increase among the males was 32 per cent. between 1911 and 1921 and 8 per cent. between 1921 and 1931. The females increased between 1911 and 1921 by 29 and between 1921 and 1931 by 64 per cent. Of the total increase of 2,974 since 1911, the Indian Christians have contributed 64, European and allied races 27 and Anglo-Indians 9 per cent. The increase is due mainly to fluctuations in the strength of the European regiments, partly to conversion among aliens and to a small extent to fluctuations in the composition of the Railway staff as well as to industrial expansion.

Other Religions.

227. Statistics for other minor religions are given in the margin. These are all aliens and are constantly shifting with changes among the troops, excepting the Zoroastrians who appear to have come to stay. They are mostly businessmenand Government employees. The community though numerically insignificant is influential and has the proud distinction of claiming perhaps the only two merchant princes of the Province. The community does not appear to be of the progressive type owing evidently to lower fertility caused by too much inbreeding.

	1911.	1921.	1931.
Zoroastrian ..	170	165	167
Buddhist ..	16	160	68
Jain ..	10	17	32
Tribal ..	..	..	32
Jew ..	57	19	17
Others ..	1	5	43

Religious Movements and Changes in Religious beliefs.

228. The Muslims have no Tabligh movement in the Province. They have no religious organisation on modern lines excepting a few Anjumans which are showing a tendency to be run on sectarian lines and whose efforts are directed chiefly towards secular affairs. Religious beliefs are undergoing slow but steady modifications some in the right directions, others otherwise. There is a general tendency among the younger generation towards modernisation particularly in respect of dress and personal appearance. The Purda system which among the large majority of the rural population exists only within religious limits has begun its funeral march in the urban areas and my successor in office of 1961 should be able to write its epitaph. The more enlightened class is looking askance at the Pirs and Mullas whose influence is sure to wane as modern education advances. The same remarks apply to veneration for shrines. The movement is a part of the general Islamic revival. Its main object is to reform all customs which have overstepped religious limits, and bride price is going to be the target for its first attacks. The abolition of slavery has opened a new chapter in the social history of Baluchistan.

229. The Shudhi movement has little scope in the Province but considering that there has been a remarkable increase in the number of Hindu Chuhras during the past decennium, the movement does not appear to be entirely unknown. It is however confined to the alien Chuhras who have returned themselves as Hindu Chuhras. The headman of this community is now a member of the Hindu Panchayat of Quetta and is allowed to take part in its discussions relating to cases of his community. On the whole there is a general religious awakening among all communities. Christianity is silently carrying on its work of uplift among the alien depressed classes. This is the only religion which has a systematic proselytising organisation.

SUBSIDIARY TABLES.

44.—General Distribution of the Population by Religion.

District or State.	Number per 1,000 of the population who are														
	Muslim.			Hindu.			Sikh.			Christian.			Others.		
	1931.	1921.	1911.	1931.	1921.	1911.	1931.	1921.	1911.	1931.	1921.	1911.	1931.	1921.	1911.
1	2	3	4	5	6	7	8	9	10	11	12	13	14	15	16
BALUCHISTAN ..	919	917	938	62	64	45	10	10	10	9	8	6	..	1	1
Districts ..	875	873	911	89	92	62	18	18	13	17	16	12	1	1	2
Quetta-Pishin ..	732	755	836	181	163	104	35	35	19	50	45	36	2	2	5
Loralai ..	950	951	950	41	44	37	7	4	11	2	1	1	..	..	1
Zhob ..	929	923	968	49	60	19	20	15	10	2	2	2	..	..	1
Bolan ..	689	680	678	249	268	250	37	32	51	19	19	12	6	1	9
Chagai ..	940	895	974	54	87	23	5	12	2	1	2	1	..	4	..
Sibi ..	949	934	926	41	54	62	8	11	9	2	1	2	..	..	1
Administered Area	*921*	*907*	*899*	*63*	*75*	*84*	*13*	*16*	*13*	*3*	*2*	*2*	..	..	*2*
Mari-Bugti Country	*994*	*992*	*989*	*6*	*8*	*11*	..	..	..	..	..	..	..	..	..
States ..	970	966	965	30	34	28	..	..	7	..	..	..	..	..	..
Kalat ..	968	966	963	32	34	28	..	..	9	..	..	..	..	..	..
Sarawan ..	*974*	*982*	*982*	*26*	*17*	*16*	..	*1*	*2*	..	..	..	..	..	..
Jhalawan ..	*998*	*995*	*994*	*2*	*5*	*6*	..	..	..	..	..	..	..	..	..
Kachhi ..	*934*	*907*	*910*	*66*	*93*	*77*	..	..	*13*	..	..	..	..	..	..
Dombki-Kaheri Country.	*903*	*866*	*874*	*97*	*134*	*54*	..	..	*72*	..	..	..	..	..	..
Makran ..	*996*	*997*	*997*	*4*	*3*	*2*	..	..	..	..	..	*1*	..	..	..
Kharan ..	*998*	*998*	*998*	*2*	*2*	*2*	..	..	..	..	..	..	..	..	..
Las-Bela ..	977	971	970	23	29	29	..	..	1	..	..	..	..	..	..

45.—Christians—Numbers and Variation.

District or State.	Actual number of Christians in			Variation per cent.		
	1931.	1921.	1911.	1921-31.	1911-21.	1911-31.
1	2	3	4	5	6	7
BALUCHISTAN ..	8,059	6,693	5,085	+20	+31	+58
Districts ..	8,044	6,678	5,030	+20	+33	+60
Quetta-Pishin	7,370	6,139	4,564	+20	+35	+61
Loralai	209	101	71	+107	+42	+194
Zhob	115	141	168	—18	—16	—32
Bolan	91	69	26	+32	+165	+250
Chagai	25	45	9	—44	+400	+178
Sibi	234	183	192	+28	—5	+22
Administered Area ..	*234*	*183*	*192*	*+28*	*—5*	*+22*
Mari-Bugti Country ..	..	..	..	..	..	..
States	15	15	55	..	—73	—73
Kalat	15	13	51	+15	—75	—71
Sarawan	*3*	*2*	*5*	*+50*	*—60*	*—40*
Jhalawan	..	..	..	..	..	..
Kachhi	*1*	..	*6*	*+100*	..	*—83*
Dombki-Kaheri Country ..	..	..	..	..	..	..
Makran	*11*	*11*	*40*	..	*—73*	*—73*
Kharan	..	..	..	..	..	..
Las-Bela ..	..	2	4	—100	—50	—100

46.—Religions of Urban and Rural Population.

District or State.	Year.	Number per thousand of urban population who are					Number per thousand of rural population who are				
		Muslim.	Hindu.	Sikh.	Christian.	Others.	Muslims.	Hindus.	Sikh.	Christian.	Others.
1	2	3	4	5	6	7	8	9	10	11	12
BALUCHISTAN ..	1931 ..	515	336	69	77	3	972	26	2	..	..
	1921 ..	493	347	74	81	5	964	33	3	..	..
	1911 ..	538	315	62	81	4	969	25	6	..	..
Districts	1931 ..	472	363	76	86	3	974	21	4	1	..
	1921 ..	442	379	82	92	5	959	35	5	1	..
	1911 ..	466	359	73	97	5	971	24	5	..	..
Quetta-Pishin	1931 ..	439	377	75	109	..	988	11	1	..	..
	1921 ..	410	387	86	111	6	986	12	2	..	..
	1911 ..	452	356	62	124	6	976	17	6	1	..
Loralai	1931 ..	490	382	95	33	..	981	18	1	..	..
	1921 ..	486	457	36	21	..	977	21	2	..	..
	1911 ..	426	324	231	19	..	970	27	3	..	..
Zhob	1931 ..	511	353	119	13	4	982	10	7	1	..
	1921 ..	616	217	151	16	..	948	47	4	1	..
	1911 ..	604	312	66	17	1	986	5	7	2	..
Bolan	1931 ..	627	248	74	36	15	729	248	13	9	1
	1921 ..	..	..	..	..	..	680	268	32	19	1
	1911 ..	..	..	..	..	..	678	258	51	12	1
Chagai	1931 ..	..	..	..	..	..	940	55	4	1	..
	1921 ..	..	..	..	..	..	895	91	12	2	..
	1911 ..	..	..	..	..	..	974	24	2	..	..
Sibi	1931 ..	647	286	44	22	1	971	24	5	..	..
	1921 ..	581	357	42	18	2	953	37	9	1	..
	1911 ..	492	414	66	23	5	951	42	6	1	..
Administered Area ..	*1931* ..	*646*	*287*	*44*	*22*	*1*	*954*	*37*	*9*	..	..
	1921 ..	*581*	*357*	*42*	*18*	*2*	*935*	*51*	*13*	*1*	..
	1911 ..	*492*	*414*	*66*	*23*	*5*	*934*	*57*	*8*	*1*	..
Mari-Bugti Country ..	*1931* ..	..	..	..	..	..	*995*	*5*	..	..	..
	1921 ..	..	..	..	..	..	*992*	*8*	..	..	..
	1911 ..	..	..	..	..	..	*989*	*11*	..	..	..
States	1931 ..	898	104	2	1	..	972	28	..	..	..
	1921 ..	885	106	9	..	..	968	32	..	..	..
	1911 ..	895	94	10	1	..	966	27	7	..	..
Kalat	1931 ..	894	103	2	1	..	970	30	..	..	..
	1921 ..	879	111	10	..	..	966	34	..	..	..
	1911 ..	899	93	7	1	..	964	27	9	..	..
Sarawan	*1931* ..	*872*	*126*	*2*	..	..	*995*	*5*	..	..	..
	1921 ..	*879*	*111*	*10*	..	..	*996*	*4*	..	..	..
	1911 ..	*899*	*93*	*7*	*1*	..	*993*	*6*	*1*	..	..
Jhalawan	*1931* ..	..	..	..	..	..	*998*	*2*	..	..	..
	1921 ..	..	..	..	..	..	*995*	*5*	..	..	..
	1911 ..	..	..	..	..	..	*994*	*6*	..	..	..
Kachhi	*1931* ..	..	..	..	..	..	*934*	*66*	..	..	..
	1921 ..	..	..	..	..	..	*907*	*93*	..	..	..
	1911 ..	..	..	..	..	..	*910*	*77*	*13*	..	..
Dombki-Kaheri Country ..	*1931* ..	..	..	..	..	..	*904*	*96*	..	..	..
	1921 ..	..	..	..	..	..	*866*	*134*	..	..	..
	1911 ..	..	..	..	..	..	*874*	*54*	72	..	..
Makran	*1931* ..	*939*	*59*	*1*	*1*	..	*999*	*1*	..	..	..
	1921 ..	..	..	..	..	..	*997*	*3*	..	..	..
	1911 ..	..	..	..	..	..	*997*	*2*	*1*	..	..
Kharan	*1931* ..	..	..	..	..	..	*999*	*1*	..	..	..
	1921 ..	..	..	..	..	..	*998*	*2*	..	..	..
	1911 ..	..	..	..	..	..	*998*	*2*	..	..	..
Las-Bela	1931 ..	890	107	3	..	..	982	18	..	..	..
	1921 ..	898	95	7	..	..	975	25	..	..	..
	1911 ..	882	95	22	1	..	970	29	1	..	..

CHAPTER XII.

RACE, TRIBE OR CASTE.

SECTION I.—SCOPE OF ENQUIRY.

Statistical data.

230. The absolute statistics with which this Chapter is principally concerned are those contained in Imperial Tables IVII, XVIII and XIX. Table XVII shows the various races and principal tribes and castes in each race in the Province and their distribution by Districts and States. Table XVIII shows the numerical strengths of the various tribes and races for three Censuses, 1911, 1921 and 1931 and variations for inter-censal periods. Table XIX gives the distribution of European and allied races and Anglo-Indians by race and age, for each District and State.

Statistics for certain selected races and tribes have also been tabulated by civil condition, occupations and literacy. These are contained in Imperial Tables VIII, XI and XIII and are discussed in Chapters VI, VIII and IX. Statistics of incidence of infirmities in each race are given in Subsidiary Table 28 at the end of chapter VII in which variations have been explained. Proportional figures relating to the numerical strength of each race and tribe, etc., will be found in the Subsidiary Tables at the end of this chapter.

How the statistics were collected.

231. The Province is inhabited by indigenous and semi-indigenous races and immigrants from India and foreign countries. The instructions to enumerators were to record tribal names in the Census schedules for the indigenous and semi-indigenous inhabitants, castes and sub-castes for Indians, and nationality for foreigners. At past censuses the practice was to record the name of the tribe, its clan, section and sub-section and even the group to which each family claimed to belong. This information was collected in great detail in 1911 and a Statistical Analysis of the various tribes was prepared for local administrative purposes. The task of compiling a similar analysis at each successive Census is extremely troublesome and expensive and it was decided that at the Census of 1931 only the name of the tribe should be recorded. To ensure accuracy, however, a detailed tribal index was compiled in vernacular from Sir Denys Bray's Statistical Analysis and supplied to all enumerators who were instructed to record only the name of the tribe and in order to facilitate classification, its lowest sub-division also. In practice, however, these instructions proved to be totally unworkable owing to the inability of the tribesmen to give answers to the point and the enumerators had to be permitted to record as at earlier censuses the name of tribe, clan, section and sub-section, etc., actually returned by the house-holder, comparing and correcting the entries in the schedules where necessary in accordance with the entries in the Index. On receipt of the enumeration books in the Tabulation Office, each and every entry was examined and the name of the tribe to which each family belonged was marked in the schedules opposite each house-holder in red ink and the red ink entries only were copied on the slips. Doubtful entries were corrected where necessary by reference to enumerators. The work of classification was extremely laborious but it ensured accuracy and resulted in a saving of considerable time at later stages of tabulation.

For the record of castes of Indian immigrants a detailed set of instructions was issued requiring the enumerators to record castes and sub-castes for Hindus and Muslims and nationality for foreigners.

Necessity or advisability of retaining returns of race, tribe or caste.

232. The retention of the return of race and tribe is as necessary and advisable for this Province as the retention of the return of caste is unnecessary and useless. The whole Provincial administrative superstructure rests on the Tribal system and it is essential to compile the tribal returns not only for their administrative value but also for their utility for measuring the gradual progress of the indigenous population in various walks of life which fall within the purview of a census of population. On the other hand the return of caste serves no useful purpose at all so far as this Province is concerned and its compilation entails an amount of labour and expense out of all proportion to its utility. This

Diagram No. 23.

INDIGENOUS, SEMI-INDIGENOUS AND ALIEN POPULATION OF BALUCHISTAN IN 1911, 1921 & 1931.

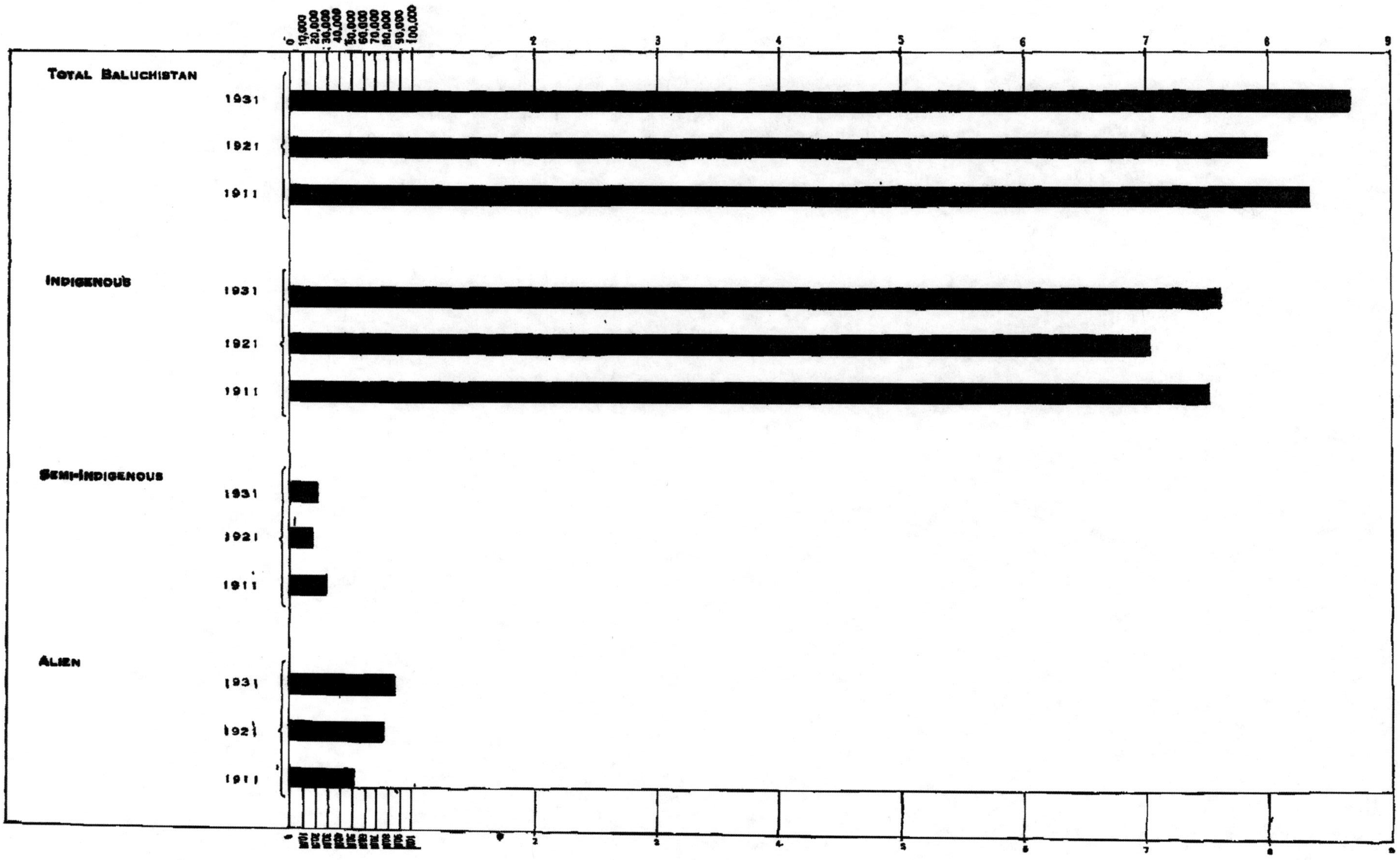

question was raised by me at the Conference of Census Officers which was held in Delhi in January 1931 and it was decided that castes which have a population of less than 2 *per mille* should not be tabulated. This curtailment afforded only nominal relief because the castes with a population of 2 *per mille* could only be sorted out after all the processes of enumeration, slip-copying, sorting and compilation had been gone through. I can see absolutely no use for the caste return for this Province, and I believe it hardly serves any useful purpose for other Provinces in the compressed form in which it is published. I am inclined to suggest a twofold solution. Firstly, that a complete return of all castes returned should be prepared in all Provinces in full detail and a consolidated statement published as an appendix to the Census Commissioner's report, only such castes appearing in Provincial Reports as may be selected on local considerations by each Province. This will be a useful record for ethnological purposes but the question is whether in view of the present tendency to discard caste, it will be possible to collect reliable data. The second alternative is to select the castes for which statistics are required from each Province and to supply each Superintendent with a list of their names in time to enable him to issue the requisite instructions before commencement of enumeration.

SECTION II—DISTRIBUTION OF POPULATION BY RACE, TRIBE AND CASTE.

Indigenous, semi-indigenous and alien population.

233. The population of Baluchistan falls into three main groups, Indigenous, Semi-indigenous and Alien. The indigenous group consists of the permanent resident population. The semi-indigenous are all trans-Indus tribesmen from the Derajat or Afghanistan but as they are not connected with the resident tribesmen by ties of kinship or common weal and woe they have been treated as a separate group for convenience of statistical analysis. The alien group consists mainly of temporary immigrants from India and foreign countries. The population for 1931 which falls under each of these three groups is shown in the margin. It will be seen that 88 per cent. of the population are Indigenous, 3 Semi-Indigenous and 9 Aliens. Detailed accounts as to the origin, etc., and distribution of each race and the more important tribes have already been published in previous reports and the Gazetteers and it is not necessary to go over the ground again. In the following paragraphs the remarks regarding the various races and tribes, etc., have therefore been confined mainly to numbers for 1931 and variations compared to earlier Censuses.

	Population.		
	Total.	Males.	Females.
TOTAL ..	868,617	488,414	380,203
Indigenous ..	760,125	411,941	348,184
Semi-indigenous ..	21,922	13,206	8,716
Alien ..	86,570	63,267	23,303

Indigenous Population.

Indigenous.

234. The principal indigenous Muslim races living in the Province are Pathan, Baloch, Brahui, Lasi, Jatt, Sayyid and other minor tribes. The numerical strength of each and its proportion per 1,000 of total indigenous population are shown in the margin. The fighting strength of each race and tribe has been worked out roughly and shown in Subsidiary Table 48 which will be found at the end of this chapter.

Race.	Actual strength.	Proportion to 1,000 of total indigenous population.	Race.	Actual strength.	Proportion to 1,000 of total indigenous population.
Pathan ..	176,007	232	Jatt ..	77,157	101
Baloch ..	226,041	297	Sayyid ..	21,976	29
Brahui ..	152,588	207	Others ..	57,691	71
Lasi ..	31,812	41	Hindus ..	16,905	22

Pathans.

Indigenous Tribes.

235. The Pathans represent 21 per cent. of the total population and 23 per cent. of the total indigenous population of the Province. They are divided for Census purposes into six main divisions namely Tarin, Kakar, Pani, Miani, Shirani and Kasi. The proportions of these divisions and their sub-divisions to the total population and to all indigenous Pathans are shown in the margin. A brief account of each of these tribal units is given below.

	Proportion per cent. to total population.	Proportion per cent. to total indigenous Pathans.		Proportion per cent. to total population.	Proportion per cent. to total indigenous Pathans.
Tarin ..	4·3	21·0	Isot ..	0·3	1·4
Abdal Achakzai..	2·3	11·1	Laun ..	0·1	0·5
Spin Tarin ..	1·1	5·5	Mandokhel ..	0·5	2·4
Tor Tarin ..	0·8	3·9	Musakhel ..	1·6	7·9
Unspecified ..	0·1	0·5	Zarkun ..	0·2	0·9
Kakar ..	10·3	51·0	Unspecified ..	..	0·2
Sanzarkhel ..	5·4	26·8	Miani ..	0·9	4·4
Snatia ..	2·3	11·5	Luni ..	0·4	2·0
Targara ..	1·4	6·9	Jafar ..	0·2	1·0
Sargara ..	0·2	0·9	Zmarai ..	0·3	1·4
Dumar ..	0·9	4·4	Shirani ..	1·0	5·0
Dawi ..	0·1	0·5	Kasi ..	0·2	1·0
Pani ..	3·2	15·7	Others (including Barech).	0·4	1·9
Main Branch ..	0·5	2·4			

Tarin.

236. The Tarins numbered 36,754 (19,557 males, 17,197 females) in 1931. They represent a little over 4 per cent. of the total population of Baluchistan and 21 per cent. of all indigenous Pathans. The figures for three censuses and variations are given in the marginal table. The Tarins have increased by 2 per cent. since 1921, but compared to 1911, they are fewer by about 2 per cent. indicating that they have not yet been able to make up the losses from the influenza epidemic of the previous decade. The Achakzais and Spin Tarins have recorded modest increases during the decennium under review but the Tor Tarins have decaeased by 4 per cent. which is due partly to over 600 members of the tribe being in India for purposes of trade at the time of Census.

	Population.			Variation per cent.		
	1931.	1921.	1911.	1921-31.	1911-21.	1911-31.
TARIN ..	36,754	36,010	37,411	+2·1	—3·7	—1·8
Abdal Achakzai ..	19,796	19,146	20,272	+3·4	—5·5	—2·3
Spin Tarin ..	9,703	9,613	5,134	+1·0	+87·2	+89·1
Tor Tarin ..	6,737	7,023	11,890	—4·1	—40·9	—43·3
Unspecified ..	512	228	115	+124·6	+98·3	+345·2

Kakar.

237. The total numerical strength of the Kakars in 1931 was 89,831 (49,237 males, 40,594 females) or a little over 10 per cent. of the total population of the Province. Amongst all individual tribes in all races, the Kakars are the most numerous. The strength of its components for three censuses with percentage variations is shown in the margin. The Sanzarkhel clan alone more than equals all other clans taken together. The Kakars have recorded a decrease of about 3 per cent. since 1921. Their losses in the preceding decennium amounted to 12 per cent. which were attributed largely to the influenza epidemic and famine and partly to emigration to Afghanistan. The percentage of loss was so high that the tribe does not appear to have been able even to make up the deficiency between 1921 and 1931. The decrease in 1931 is also partly due to the temporary emigration to India of about 2,000 Kakars of various clans for purposes of trade.

	Population.			Variation per cent.		
	1931.	1921.	1911.	1921-31.	1911-21.	1911-31.
KAKAR ..	89,831	92,600	105,073	—2·9	—11·9	—14·6
Sanzarkhel ..	46,561	46,438	56,032	+0·3	—17·1	—16·9
Snatia ..	19,762	22,519	23,349	—12·2	—3·4	—15·4
Targara ..	12,170	12,021	14,089	+1·2	—14·7	—13·6
Sargara ..	2,000	2,352	2,343	—15·0	+0·4	—14·6
Dumar ..	7,108	7,741	7,755	—8·2	—0·2	—8·3
Dawi ..	274	..	284	..	..	—3·5
Others ..	1,956	1,529	1,221	+24·4	+25·2	+60·1

Diagram No. 24.

POPULATION OF INDIGENOUS RACES OF BALUCHISTAN FOR 1911, 1921 AND 1931.

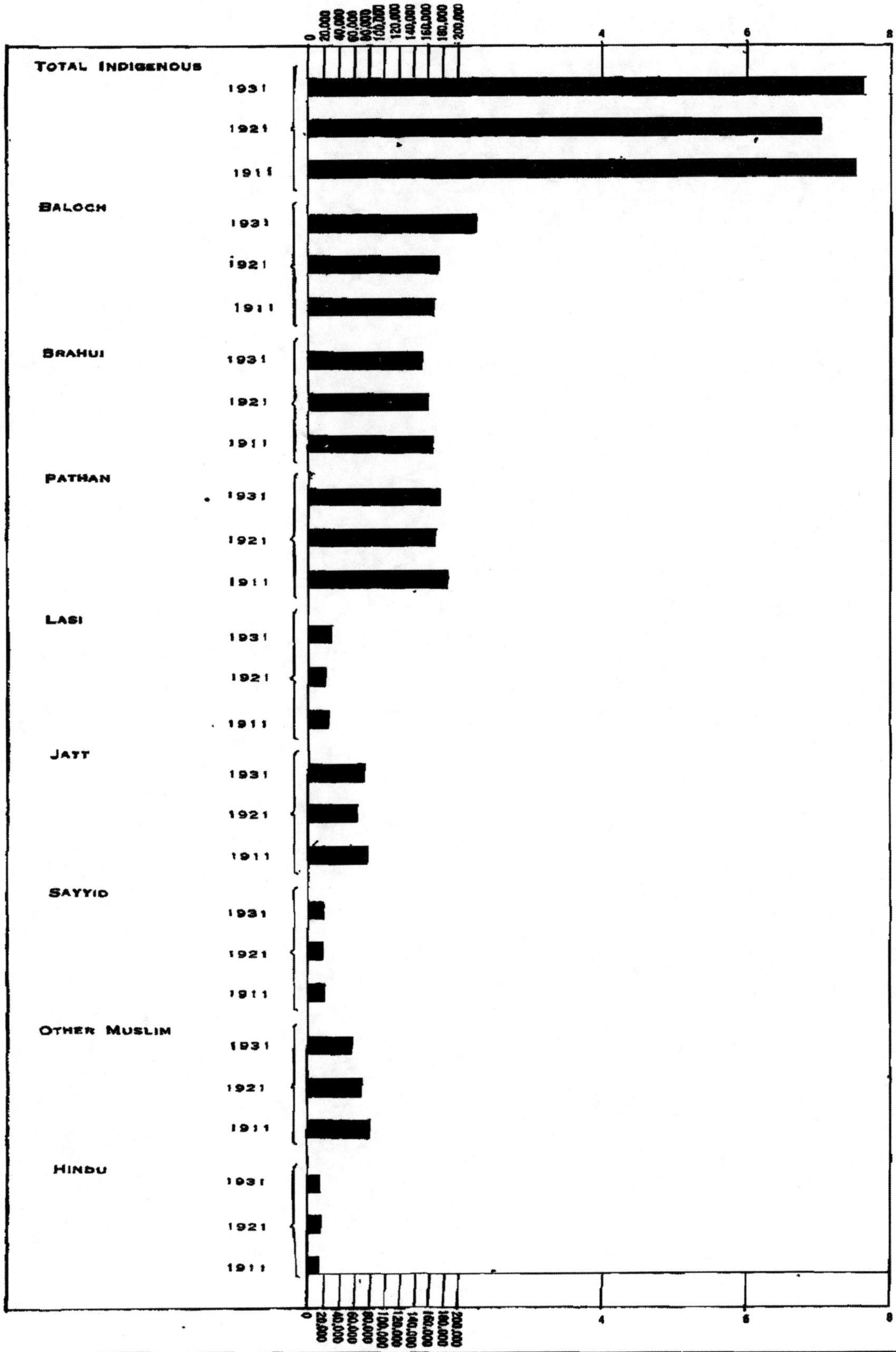

Pani.

238. The Panis represent slightly more than 3 per cent. of the total population of the Province and 16 per cent. of the indigenous Pathans. They numbered 27,701 in 1921 and 28,675 in 1911. They are divided into the 6 marginally named main branches which in their respective local areas are treated as separate tribes. Taken as a whole the Panis show a decrease of 26 persons over the figures of 1921. This is accounted for mostly by the migratory habits of the various tribes.

	Population.			Variation per cent.		
	1931.	1921.	1911.	1921-31.	1911-21.	1911-31.
PANI ..	27,701	27,727	28,675	−0·1	−3·3	−3·3
Main Branch ..	4,166	4,972	6,714	−16·2	−25·9	−37·9
Isot ..	2,555	2,601	2,812	−1·8	−7·5	−9·1
Laun ..	543	1,081	..	−49·8	..	..
Mandokhel ..	4,635	3,870	4,944	+19·8	−21·8	−6·2
Musakhel ..	13,578	13,145	12,202	+3·3	+7·7	+11·3
Zarkun ..	2,123	2,017	2,003	+5·2	+0·7	+6·0
Unspecified ..	101	41	..	+146·3	..	..

Miani.

239. The Miani tribes—Luni, Jafar and Zmarai all told numbered 7,949 in 1931 against 6,242 and 5,330 in 1921 and 1911. The numerical strength of each tribe for four censuses is shown in the margin. In spite of the heavy toll taken by the influenza epidemic in the 1911-21 decennium, all three tribes have shown a continuous increase since 1901 as will be seen by the following percentage increases.

	1931.	1921.	1911.	1901.
Luni ..	3,581	3,187	2,816	2,582
Jafar ..	1,479	1,355	1,286	1,033
Zmarai ..	2,889	1,700	1,228	531

	1901-11.	1911-21.	1921-31.	1901-31.
Luni	9	13	12	38
Jafar	19	5	9	43
Zmarai	131	39	70	477

The highest rate of increase is disclosed by the Zmarais who have increased by 477 per cent. during the 30 years ending with 1931. The following table reveals interesting variations in the proportions of males and females at each of the four censuses :—

Proportion per cent. of Males and Females.

	Males.				Females.			
	1931.	1921.	1911.	1901.	1931.	1921.	1911.	19[illegible]
Luni ..	53	53	53	51	47	47	47	4[illegible]
Jafar ..	54	54	53	53	46	46	47	47
Zmarai ..	53	55	57	60	47	45	43	40

It will be observed that there were 49 females in every 100 Lunis in 1901 ; they declined to 47 in 1911 and stood at the latter figure in 1921 and 1931. Similarly there were 47 females in every 100 Jafars in 1901 and 1911, but fell to 46 in 1921 and remained steady during the following decade. On the other hand there were 40 females in every 100 Zmarais. Their proportion rose to 43 in 1911, 45 in 1921 and 47 in 1931. These variations indicate that while the population of the three tribes has been increasing from census to census, the proportion of Luni and Jafar females has been continuously decreasing while that of Zmarai females has been steadily increasing, the variations in the number of females per 1,000 of total population of both sexes being

	Increase	Decrease.
Luni	..	20
Jafar	..	10
Zmarai	30	..

I have not been able to trace the cause of these remarkable variations. Unless they are due to faulty enumeration of which the above figures give no indication, it would appear that of all the Pathans fertility is highest among the three Miani tribes particularly the Zmarais.

Shirani.

240. The Shiranis decreased by 15 per cent. between 1911 and 1921. The chief causes of the decrease were influenza and emigration to Afghanistan during

the 1919 disturbances. Between 1921 and 1931, the tribe has made a remarkable recovery, the increase over 1921 being 15 per cent. They have, however, not yet quite reached their strength of 1911 as will be seen from the marginal figures.

	1931.	1921.	1911.
Shirani ..	8,416	7,297	8,552

Kasi.

241. As was expected the Kasis have shown an increase of 53 per cent. since 1921. Their total strength was 1,975 in 1931 and 1,295 in 1921. They live mostly in the vicinity of Quetta where they enjoy greater amenities of civilized life.

Barech.

242. The Barech numbered 1,610 in 1931, 1,550 in 1921 and 854 in 1911. They are all permanent inhabitants of Shorawak in Afghan territory and should strictly speaking be treated as Semi-indigenous or Alien. In any case they are not indigenous to Baluchistan at all. In Afghan territory they depend entirely on flood irrigation from the Pishin Lora in British territory. When floods fail a wholesale emigration sets in in search of employment in Baluchistan and Sind. A very small number have settled down semi-permanently in Quetta and elsewhere.

Baloch.

Baloch.

243. The Baloch are divided into two main branches, the Eastern and Western. The tribes included in each are shown in the margin with their respective numbers for three censuses.

	1931.	1921.	1911.		1931	1921	1911
Eastern Baloch	*150,364*	*109,005*	*111,919*	*Western Baloch*	*75,677*	*64,390*	*57,271*
1. Bugti ..	30,613	22,737	19,370	1. Buledi ..	158	1,289	1,340
2. Dombki ..	7,241	6,046	5,913	2. Dashti ..	996	4,474	1,149
3. Khetran ..	17,162	17,123	14,153	3. Gichki ..	293	575	554
4. Magasi ..	13,286	8,282	17,777	4 Kaudai ..	2,308	1,694	1,132
5. Mari ..	35,254	22,601	22,233	5. Rais ..	3,951	5,696	4,147
6. Rind ..	43,322	30,736	31,267	6. Rakhshani ..	24,106	21,677	20,068
7. Umrani ..	2,641	1,104	989	7. Rind ..	31,055	17,136	14,561
8. Others ..	845	376	217	8. Sangur ..	7,334	4,336	5,798
				9. Sanjrani ..	401	481	121
				10. Others ..	5,075	7,032	8,401

Eastern Baloch-Bugti.

244. The Bugtis represent a little less than 4 per cent. of the total population of the Province and 18 per cent. of the total strength of the indigenous Baloch. They numbered 30,613 (16,797 males and 13,816 females) in 1931. Out of these, 29,435 (16,158 males and 13,277 females) were censused within their own tribal limits. The remaining 1,178 were scattered over different parts of the Province the majority (440 males and 409 females) being enumerated in Kachhi. The Census of 1931 has disclosed an increase of 35 per cent. in the number of Bugtis since 1921 and 58 per cent. since 1911. The increase which has been explained in Chapter III is attributed partly to natural growth but mainly to the return of temporary emigrants from Sind and Dera Ghazi Khan. The tribe is divided into seven clans (Durrag Nothani, Khalpar, Masori, Mondrani, Pirozani Nothani, Raheja and Shambani) which are sub-divided into a large number of sections and sub-sections, etc. The tribal Chief whose headquarters are at Dera Bugti belongs to the Bibrakzai section of the Raheja clan.

Dombki.

245. The Dombkis numbered 7,241 (3,943 males, 3,298 females) in 1931, or a little less than one per cent. of the total population, and 3 per cent. of the indigenous Baloch race. They have recorded an increase of 20 per cent. since 1921, and 22 per cent. compared to 1911. The Dombki-Kaheri division of the Kalat State is the home of the tribe with the Sardar's headquarters at Lahri. The tribe is divided into several clans. The Sardar belongs to the Jalalkhanzai section of the Mirozai clan. 5,254 Dombkis were censused in the Dombki-Kaheri country and 1,945 in the Administered Area of the Sibi District.

Khetran.

246. The Khetrans numbered 17,162 (8,997 males, 8,165 females) in 1931. They have increased by 21 per cent. since 1911 but only 2 *per mille* compared to 1921. They represent 2 per cent. of the total population of the Province and 7 per cent. of the indigenous Baloch.

The Khetrans live mostly in the Barkhan Tahsil of the Loralai District. They are a very mixed tribe containing an appreciable admixture of Afghan, Baloch and Jatt elements. They are divided into three main clans, Dhara, Ispani and Phalliat. The division is not based on ethnic grounds, but was made in pre-British days for the sake of convenience in military expeditions, etc. The Sardar of the tribe belongs to the Mazarani section of the Ispani clan and lives at Haji Kot.

247. The total strength of the Magasis in 1931 was 13,286 (7,212 males, 6,074 females) against 8,282 in 1921 and 17,777 in 1911. They recorded a decrease of 53 per cent. between 1911 and 1921 and a decrease of 25 per cent. between 1911 and 1931 in spite of an increase of 60 per cent. between 1921 and 1931. The heavy fall in 1921 was due mainly to migration into Sind owing to adverse economic conditions. The Magasis like most other tribes are a very mixed tribe which has affiliated several clans and sections from other rival and neighbouring tribes. They live in the Jhal tribal area with the Sardar's headquarters at Jhal and belong to the Jhalawan wing of the Brahui confederacy. A good many clans of the Magasis have separated from the parent tribe and have settled down in various parts of the Punjab, in Sind and the Bahawalpur State. **Magasi.**

248. Next to the Rind Baloch tribe the Maris are the most numerous Baloch tribe in Baluchistan. They numbered 35,254 (19,700 males, 15,554 females) in 1931 against 22,601 in 1921, and 22,233 in 1911. The tribe represents a little over four per cent. of the total population of the Province and 15 per cent. of the indigenous Baloch. It has recorded a surprising increase of 56 per cent. between 1921 and 1931 and of 59 per cent. since 1911. The alleged causes of the variation have been explained in Chapter III. The tribe is divided into three main clans, Bahawalanzai, Bijarani and Loharani composed of more heterogeneous elements than any other Baloch tribe. The home of the tribe is what is known as the Mari country. But they are flock-owning nomads almost to a man and are constantly moving from place to place within their own country and abroad as indicated by the marginal figures showing the various localities in which they were censused in 1931. The only tracts which were free from the unwelcome visitations of their flocks of sheep and goats were Chagai, Kharan and Makran. The Mari chief comes of the Bahawalanzai section of the Ghazani clan with headquarters at Kahan generally known as Mari-Kahan. **Mari.**

Locality where censused.	*Numbers.*
Mari country	24,615
Sibi Administered Area	7,822
Loralai District	1,731
Jhalawan	411
Kachhi	355
Las Bela	148
Quetta-Pishin	88
Zhob	26
Bolan	22
Sarawan	18
Dombki-Kaheri country	18

249. The Rinds are the most numerous of all Baloch tribes, their proportion to the total population of the Province being 9 per cent. and to the total indigenous Baloch 33 per cent. They are divided into Eastern and Western Rinds. The Eastern branch numbering 43,322 in 1931 is largely found in Kachhi and the Sibi District, while the Western numbering 31,055 live mostly in Makran, Kharan and Chagai. The Eastern Rind have increased between 1921 and 1931 by 41 and between 1911 and 1931 by 39 per cent., the increase being due largely to the return of emigrants. They include Buledis (5,709), Jamali (6,585), Khosas (4,619), Lasharis (7,199) and other unspecified Rind (19,210). **Rind.**

250. The Umranis show an increase from 989 in 1911 and 1,104 in 1921 to 2,641 in 1931, which is due to the return of temporary emigrants from Sind. **Umranis.**

251. Very striking variations are noticeable among all Western Baloch tribes. In the aggregate, the Western Baloch contribute an increase of 18 per cent. between 1921 and 1931 and of 12 per cent. between the preceding decennium. The internal variations except in the case of the Rakhshanis are apparently due to change in classification of certain tribal units which at previous censuses were not classed as Rind. The increases of 11 and 8 per cent. between 1921 and 1931 and 1911 and 1931 respectively among the Rakhshanis are due largely to natural growth of population and partly to the effects of migration. **Western Baloch.**

BRAHUIS.

252. The origin of the Brahuis still lies shrouded in mystery. All that historical research has been able to add to our knowledge on the subject since the question of origin of the Brahui language was solved by Sir Denys Bray in 1911 is that the Dravidian races of India to which the real Brahuis belong came from the North-West and brought with them the ancient civilization of Mesopotamia, Asia Minor and the Eastern Mediterranean. **Origin of Brahuis.**

It is stated that the Brahuis in Sind regard the Mohenjo-daro ruins recently discovered by the Archæological Department to be the work of their ancestors. This statement is not believed in some quarters to be well-founded and enquiries made in Baluchistan have so far failed to elicit any corroborative evidence beyond the simple fact that Brahui traditions claim Aleppo as the original home of the Brahuis. The inquiries made by Sir Denys Bray in 1911 were extremely searching and it is hopeless to expect that further local inquiries will result in any really useful additions to our existing knowledge.

253. To revert to the 1911 report again, the Brahui race is composed of extremely heterogeneous elements. It is called Brahui and is treated as such because of its philological affinities and its confederate unity for military and political ends. The true Brahui tribes who are generally believed to be Brahui by race as well as language are only eight out of 30 Brahui tribes into which the Brahui race is divided and represents a population of only 85 in every 1,000 of the total Brahui population of Baluchistan as revealed by the Census of 1931.

Brahui population.

254. The Brahuis are divided into four main branches, Original Nucleus or the true Brahuis, Sarawans, Jhalawans and Miscellaneous. The population of each of these branches for three Censuses together with the numbers of Brahui speakers is given in the following table :—

	1931.	1921.	1911.	VARIATION PER CENT.	
				1921-31.	1911-31.
1. Original Nucleus	12,958	17,956	15,047	—28	—14
2. Sarawans	41,848	51,957	55,370	—19	—24
3. Jhalawans	94,807	86,772	94,708	+9	+0·1
4. Miscellaneous	2,975	3,049	2,662	—2	+12
Total Brahuis	*152,588*	*159,734*	*167,787*	*—5*	*—9*
Speakers of Brahui language	*127,479*	*139,727*	*145,299*	*—9*	*—12*

The Brahui population shows a decline of five per cent. between 1921 and 1931 and of nine per cent. between 1911 and 1931. The decline is most remarkable in the case of the Original Nucleus and the Sarawans. But for the fact that over 20,000 Jhalawan Brahuis returned to their homes from Kachhi and Sind just on the date of Census, the decrease in the case of the Jhalawans would have been much larger. Detailed statistics for three censuses with percentage variations, etc., for each of the tribes falling under the four main sections named above are given in Subsidiary Table 47 at the end of this chapter.

Brahui disintegration.

255. The variations shown above furnish unmistakable indication of increasing disintegration which was prophesied in 1911. The view did not find much support from the statistical evidence of 1921 which was to the following effect:—

"The marginal figures however, indicate that during the decade the process of disintegration has certainly not been actively at work. It is true that the Brahuis as a whole have declined but this decrease is distinctly less than that of the Pathans, and can be attributed to influenza, famine and migration, while the real Brahui stock—the Brahui nucleus—shows an actual increase."

If evidence was lacking in 1921, there is plenty of it to be found in the figures for 1931. The Brahui race has decreased by nine per cent. between 1911 and 1931, and by five per cent. between 1921 and 1931. On the other hand the Brahui language shows a decline of 12 per cent. between 1911 and 1931, and of nine per cent. between 1921 and 1931. The figures need no comment. Not only emigration into Sind but also disintegration within provincial limits is thinning the ranks of the Brahui race which in fact means the Brahui Confederacy. The causes that are insidiously at work to bring about this sorry state of affairs have been discussed in the report for 1911 (Paragraphs 36, 37 and 270—278). To follow up later developments, is, I consider, beyond the scope of this report. All that I can add is that the Brahui race or Brahui confederacy, call it by whatever name we chose, has never been placed in such a predicament before as it is to-day. Its fate was foretold in 1911 and it appears that the prophesy is well on the way to its fulfilment. The question is so important and interesting that I feel no hesitation in quoting once more the relative extract from the 1911 Census Report in order to refresh the memories of both friends and foes of the time-honoured institution established by Nasir Khan the Great and reformed and fostered by that great sympathetic statesman-friend of the gentry and hero of the ignorant masses of the Province—the late Sir Robert Sandeman—who sacrificed his life in the wilds of Baluchistan with the comprehensive word "Baloch" on his lips even in the last moments of life. This is what Sir Denys Bray said in 1911 :—

"And added to the absence of natural checks to Brahui disintegration, there are a multitude of positive disintegrating forces such as the growth of a selfish individualism among the tribesmen at large and most significant of all among the chiefs, the inevitably disintegrating influence of peace under a foreign administration, the increasing tendency to migrate beyond the limits of the country, and the consequent tendency to settle outside it. Taking one thing with another, I am forced to the regretful conclusion that unless the many disintegrating influences are arrested and some counterinfluence, such as the purging and strengthening of the Jirga system, speedily arises to put new life into tribal and racial unity, the Brahui tribes have seen their best days, and that the Brahui race is doomed in the future, let us hope in the very distant future, to absorption into some more virile community."

Other indigenous Muslim races.

256. The other important indigenous Muslim races inhabiting the Province are Lasi, Jatt and Sayyid. Their numbers for three censuses are shown in the margin.

	1931.	1921.	1911.
Lasi	31,812	23,212	27,779
Jatt	77,157	63,191	78,397
Sayyid	21,976	20,265	21,296

Lasi.

257. The Lasi represent about four per cent. of the total population of the Province, and about five per cent. of the indigenous Muslims. They are found exclusively in the Las Bela State and are all settled inhabitants but when rainfall is deficient, they migrate to Sind in large numbers. At the Censuses of 1911 and 1921 the race was divided into five Rajes. After the close of the Census of 1921 local inquiries, however, disclosed that the Lasis were divided into nine Rajes (five major and four minor). At the present Census the figures have been tabulated for nine. The strength of each Raj for three censuses is shown in the margin. Comparison with previous censuses is impracticable owing to change of classification but a glance at the marginal statement will show that on the whole there has been a considerable increase during the decennium under review, which is attributable partly to natural growth but mainly to better agricultural prospects which resulted in the return of the families who had migrated to Sind and other provinces at the time of the Census of 1921.

	Population.			Variation per cent.		
	1931.	1921.	1911.	1921-31.	1911-21.	1911-31.
LASI ..	31,812	23,212	27,779	+37·0	−16·4	+14·5
Main-rajes.						
Angaria ..	3,966	3,363	3,146	+17·9	+6·9	+26·1
Burra ..	3,411	4,279	5,374	−20·3	−20·4	−36·5
Jamot ..	5,815	6,663	9,724	−12·7	−31·4	−40·2
Runjha ..	4,656	5,027	5,103	−7·4	−1·5	−8·7
Sheikh ..	4,306	3,725	4,432	+15·6	−15·9	−2·8
Sub-rajes.						
Mongia ..	2,661	..	..	..	..	..
Shahok ..	1,315	..	..	..	..	..
Mondra ..	3,231	..	..	..	..	..
Gonga ..	2,443	..	..	..	..	..
Unspecified ..	8	155	..	−94·8	..	..

Jatt.

258. The Jatt represent one-eleventh of the total population of the Province and over 10 per cent. of the indigenous Muslims. They are found chiefly in Kachhi, the Dombki-Kaheri country, the Sibi District and the Las Bela State. They form the bulk of the cultivating class of these tracts. The increase in their numbers during the decade is due partly to natural increase but largely to the return of emigrants from Sind in consequence of more favourable agricultural prospects at home.

Sayyid.

259. A detailed account of the origin, etc. of the Sayyids in Baluchistan is given in Mr. Hughes-Buller's interesting report for 1901. Their numbers for past three censuses are shown in the margin. It will be observed that the Sayyids have increased by eight per cent. between 1921 and 1931 and by three per cent. between 1911 and 1931, in spite of the fact that about 1,000 members of this community living in the Pishin Tahsil were absent from their homes in 1931, carrying on trade in other provinces.

	1931.	1921.	1911.
SAYYID ..	21,976	20,265	21,296

Other Muslims.

260. The other indigenous Muslims represent about seven per cent. of the total population of the Province. Their respective strength, for three censuses are given in the marginal table. An interesting feature of this group of indigenous tribes is that they have been blessed with an additional member namely the Sorozais. These are freed slaves who have been shown under different names of "Ghulam," "Servile dependents" and "Tribal followers" respectively at the censuses of 1901, 1911 and 1921. Taken as a whole these tribes show a decrease of 20 per cent. during the decennium 1921—31 and of 30 per cent. during the 20 years ending with 1931. With the exception of the Dehwars, all these tribes are regarded as social inferiors of the principal races and there is therefore a tendency on their part to disguise their identity under borrowed tribal names. This is particularly noticeable in the case of the Sorozais freed slaves, whose numbers have diminished by 55 per cent. between 1921 and 1931 and by 60 per cent. between 1911 and 1931.

	Population.			Variation per cent.		
	1931.	1921.	1911.	1921-31.	1911-21.	1911-31.
OTHER MUSLIMS ..	57,591	71,766	82,068	−19·8	−12·5	−29·8
Darzada ..	9,339	10,685	10,257	−12·5	+4·2	−8·9
Dehwar ..	5,317	5,455	7,326	−2·5	−25·5	−27·4
Gadra ..	7,935	6,958	7,201	+14·0	−3·4	+10·2
Gola ..	477	172	834	+177·3	−79·4	−42·8
Jat ..	3,236	3,726	5,630	−13·1	−34·4	−43·0
Khoja ..	352	311	367	+13·2	−15·3	−4·1
Langah ..	506	1,371	570	−63·1	+140·5	−11·2
Lori ..	5,653	6,890	10,936	−17·9	−37·0	−48·3
Med. ..	3,041	1,628	2,494	+86·2	−34·7	+21·9
Nakib ..	7,154	5,577	6,536	+28·3	−14·7	+9·4
Sorozai ..	11,164	24,888	27,982	−55·1	−11·1	−60·1
Others ..	3,417	4,105	1,885	−16·8	+117·9	+81·3

Indigenous Hindus and Sikhs.

261. There were 16,905 indigenous Hindus and 48 indigenous Sikhs, all told in the whole Province in 1931. Their numbers for three censuses are shown in the margin. Reconversion of Sikhs to Hinduism accounts for increase in the one and decrease in the other. On the whole the indigenous Hindus show a continuous decline the causes for which have been explained in the Chapter on Religion. The distribution of indigenous Hindus by caste is exhibited in the marginal table. The majority belong to the great Hindu trading caste, the Aroras.

	Population.			Variation per cent.		
	1931.	1921.	1911.	1921-31.	1911-21.	1911-31.
Hindu ..	16,905	17,479	14,985	−3·3	+16·6	+12·0
Sikh ..	48	841	2,799	−94·3	−69·9	−98·3

	Baluchistan.	Districts.	States.
TOTAL	16,905	5,136	11,769
Arora	16,359	4,770	11,589
Brahman	157	95	62
Khatri	259	220	39
Others	130	51	79

SEMI-INDIGENOUS.

262. The semi-indigenous population composed of the marginal races represents about three per cent. of the total population of the Province. They numbered 21,922 in 1931, 18,653 in 1921 and 29,515 in 1911. During the past 20 years they have decreased by 7,593 persons or 24 per cent. The numbers of this part of the population fluctuate from year to year according to grazing prospects.

Pathan ..	17,018
Baloch ..	1,805
Other Muslim (Hazaras)	3,099

ALIENS.

263. The alien immigrants numbered 86,570 in 1931, consisting of 32,999 Muslims, 36,776 Hindus, 8,377 Sikhs, 5,403 Europeans and Anglo-Indians, and 3,015 others. To the total alien population of 1931, Muslims contributed 38 per cent., Hindus 42, Sikhs 10, Europeans and Anglo-Indians and others 10 per cent. Variations in their numbers are indicated in the margin. The alien immigrants have increased by 33,776 or 64 per cent. in the 20 years ending with 1931, the communal per centages of the increases being Muslims 78, Hindus 63, Sikhs 50, Europeans and Anglo-Indians 25 and others 74. The chief attractions are Government service, trade and industrial pursuits and skilled and unskilled labour.

	Population.			Variation per cent.		
	1931.	1921.	1911.	1921-31.	1911-21.	1911-31.
ALL ALIENS ..	86,570	77,023	52,794	+12·4	+45·9	+63·9
Muslim ..	32,999	29,195	18,523	+13·4	+57·6	+78·3
Hindu ..	36,776	33,869	22,617	+8·6	+49·8	+62·6
Sikh ..	8,377	6,900	5,591	+21·4	+23·4	+49·8
Europeans and Anglo-Indians..	5,403	4,985	4,333	+7·1	+15·0	+24·7
Others ..	3,015	2,074	1,730	+45·5	+19·8	+74·3

264. The principal castes represented in Baluchistan in the three principal Indian communities are shown below with the numerical strength of each as revealed by the Census of 1931 :—

Muslim.		*Hindu.*		*Sikh.*	
Baloch ..	1,627	Arora ..	7,157	Jatt ..	2,612
Pathan ..	5,581	Gurkha ..	5,029	Chuhra ..	134
Jatt ..	5,532	Khatri ..	4,263	Sikh ..	2,070
Sayyid ..	1,679	Rajput ..	3,937	Other castes ..	3,561
Rajput ..	6,305	Brahman ..	3,546		
Sheikh ..	5,077	Arya ..	1,725		
Awan ..	1,959	Depressed castes ..	7,346		
Chuhras ..	546	Others ..	3,773		
Others ..	5,693				

SUBSIDIARY TABLES.

47.—Variation by Caste, Tribe, Race or Nationality.

Caste, Tribe or Race.	Total Population.			Percentage of Variation.			Percentage of the population of each caste to the total population of the Province.		
	1931.	1921.	1911.	1921 to 1931.	1911 to 1921.	1911 to 1931.	1931.	1921.	1911.
1	2	3	4	5	6	7	8	9	10
TOTAL	868,617	799,625	834,703	+8·6	—4·2	+4·1	100	100	100
BALOCH	229,473	176,386	172,478	+30·1	+2·2	+33·0	26·4	22·0	20·6
Indigenous	226,041	173,395	169,190	+30·4	+2·5	+33·6	26·0	21·7	20·3
Eastern	150,364	109,005	111,919	+37·9	—2·6	+34·3	17·3	13·6	13·4
Bugti	30,613	22,737	19,370	+34·1	+17·4	+58·0	3·5	2·8	2·3
Dombki	7,241	6,046	5,913	+19·8	+2·2	+22·4	0·8	0·8	0·7
Khetran	17,162	17,123	14,153	+0·2	+21·0	+21·3	2·0	2·1	1·7
Magasi	13,286	8,282	17,777	+60·4	—53·4	—25·3	1·5	1·0	2·1
Mari	35,254	22,601	22,233	+56·0	+1·7	+58·6	4·1	2·8	2·7
Rind Eastern	43,322	30,736	31,267	+40·9	—1·7	+38·5	5·0	3·9	3·8
Umrani	2,641	1,104	989	+139·2	+11·6	+167·0	0·3	0·1	0·1
Baloch unspecified	845	376	217	+124·7	+73·3	+289·4	0·1	0·1	..
Western	75,677	64,390	57,271	+17·5	+12·4	+32·1	8·7	8·1	6·9
Buledi	158	1,289	1,340	—87·7	—3·8	—88·2	..	0·2	0·2
Dashti	996	4,474	1,149	—77·7	+289·4	—13·3	0·1	0·6	0·1
Gichki	293	575	554	—49·0	+3·8	—47·1	..	0·1	0·1
Kaudai	2,308	1,694	1,132	+36·2	+49·7	+103·9	0·3	0·2	0·1
Reis	3,951	5,696	4,147	—30·6	+37·4	—4·7	0·5	0·7	0·5
Rakhshani	24,106	21,677	20,068	+11·2	+8·0	+20·1	2·8	2·7	2·4
Rind Western	31,055	17,136	14,561	+81·2	+17·7	+113·3	3·6	2·1	1·8
Sangur	7,334	4,336	5,798	+69·1	—25·2	+26·5	0·8	0·5	0·7
Sanjrani	401	481	121	—16·6	+297·5	+231·4	..	0·1	..
Others	5,075	7,032	8,401	—27·8	—16·2	—39·6	0·6	0·9	1·0
Semi-Indigenous	1,805	2,578	3,094	—30·0	—16·7	—41·7	0·2	0·3	0·3
Buzdar	1,738	1,196	1,224	+45·3	—2·3	+42·0	0·2	0·1	0·1
Others	67	1,382	1,870	—95·1	—26·1	—96·4	..	0·2	0·2
Aliens	1,627	363	189	+348·2	+92·1	+760·8	0·2	..	..
Brahui	152,588	159,734	167,787	—4·5	—4·8	—9·1	17·6	20·0	20·1
Original Nucleus	12,958	17,956	15,047	—27·8	+19·3	—13·9	1·5	2·2	1·8
Ahmadzai	77	119	25	—35·3	+376·0	+208·0	..	..	..
Gurgnari	1,466	1,391	2,041	+5·4	—31·9	—28·2	0·2	0·2	0·2
Iltazai	202	451	156	—55·2	+189·1	+29·5	..	..	..
Kalandrari	1,330	4,532	2,012	—70·6	+125·3	—33·9	0·2	0·6	0·2
Kambrari	2,065	2,414	3,095	—14·4	—22·0	—33·3	0·2	0·3	0·4
Mirwari	1,878	2,590	2,654	—27·5	—2·4	—29·2	0·2	0·3	0·3
Rodeni	1,335	1,788	1,325	—25·3	+34·9	+0·7	0·2	0·2	0·2
Sumalari	4,605	4,671	3,739	—1·4	+24·9	+23·2	0·5	0·6	0·5
Sarawan	41,848	51,957	55,370	—19·4	—6·2	—24·4	4·8	6·6	6·7
Bangulzai	7,389	10,281	11,595	—28·1	—11·3	—36·3	0·8	1·3	1·4
Kurd	2,230	2,982	3,476	—25·2	—14·2	—35·8	0·3	0·4	0·4
Lahri	4,490	5,572	5,839	—19·4	—4·6	—23·1	0·5	0·7	0·7
Langav	6,648	9,301	10,979	—28·5	—15·3	—39·4	0·8	1·2	1·3
Mamashahi	2,728	2,790	3,866	—2·2	—27·8	—29·4	0·3	0·4	0·4
Raisani	2,716	2,618	1,977	+3·7	+32·4	+37·4	0·3	0·3	0·2
Rustumzai	243	636	656	—61·8	—3·1	—62·9	..	0·1	0·1
Sarparra	1,906	2,112	2,212	—9·7	—4·5	—13·8	0·2	0·3	0·3
Satakzai	1,586	1,588	1,278	—0·1	+24·3	+24·1	0·2	0·2	0·2
Shahwani	6,089	8,163	8,770	—25·4	—6·9	—30·6	0·7	1·0	1·1
Zagr Mengal	5,823	5,914	4,722	—1·5	+25·2	+23·3	0·7	0·7	0·6
Jhalawan	94,807	86,772	94,708	+9·3	—8·4	+0·1	10·9	10·8	11·3
Bizanjav	13,591	9,923	10,858	+37·0	—8·6	+25·2	1·6	1·2	1·3
Haruni	1,612	1,114	1,248	+44·7	—10·7	+29·2	0·2	0·1	0·2
Mamasani	10,356	14,845	13,489	—30·2	+10·1	—23·2	1·2	1·9	1·6
Mengal	26,377	24,021	26,805	+9·8	—10·4	—1·6	3·0	3·0	3·2
Nichari	1,705	1,885	3,641	—9·5	—48·2	—53·2	0·2	0·2	0·4
Pandrani	1,063	1,488	2,007	—28·6	—25·9	—47·0	0·1	0·2	0·2
Sajdi	3,279	4,137	4,011	—20·7	+3·1	—18·2	0·4	0·5	0·5
Zahri	36,824	29,359	32,649	+25·4	—10·1	+12·8	4·2	3·7	3·9
Miscellaneous	2,975	3,049	2,662	—2·4	+14·6	+11·8	0·4	0·4	0·3
Nighari	1,128	1,502	1,311	—24·9	+14·6	—13·9	0·1	0·2	0·1
Reikizai	534	653	611	—18·2	+6·9	—12·6	0·1	0·1	0·1
Others	1,313	894	740	+46·9	+20·8	+77·4	0·2	0·1	0·1
Pathan	198,606	192,164	214,517	+3·4	—10·4	—7·4	22·9	24·1	25·7
Indigenous	176,007	174,061	188,093	+1·1	—7·5	—6·4	20·3	21·8	22·5
Babi	194	..	323	..	..	—39·9	..	..	..
Barech	1,610	1,550	854	+3·8	+81·5	+88·5	0·2	0·2	0·1
Jafar	1,479	1,355	1,286	+9·1	+5·4	+15·0	0·2	0·2	0·2
Kakar	89,831	92,600	105,073	—2·9	—11·9	—14·5	10·3	11·5	12·6
Dawi	274	..	284	..	..	—3·5	..	..	..
Dumar	7,108	7,741	7,755	—8·2	—0·2	—8·3	0·8	0·9	0·9
Hussain Pasenr	805	..	492	..	..	+63·6	0·1	..	0·1
Sanzarkhel	46,561	46,438	56,032	+0·3	—17·1	—16·9	5·4	5·8	6·7
Sargara	2,000	2,352	2,343	—15·0	+0·4	—14·6	0·2	0·3	0·3
Snatia	19,762	22,519	23,349	—12·2	—3·4	—15·4	2·3	2·8	2·8
Targhara	12,170	12,021	14,089	+1·2	—14·7	—13·6	1·4	1·5	1·7
Others	1,151	1,629	729	—24·7	+109·7	+57·9	0·1	0·2	0·1
Kasi	1,975	1,295	1,337	+52·5	—3·1	+47·7	0·2	0·2	0·2
Luni	3,581	3,187	2,816	+12·4	+13·2	+2·2	0·4	0·4	0·3

47.—Variation by Caste, Tribe, Race or Nationality—(*Concld.*).

Caste, Tribe or Race.	Total Population.			Percentage of Variation.			Percentage of the population of each caste to the total population of the Province.		
	1931.	1921.	1911.	1921 to 1931.	1911 to 1921.	1911 to 1931.	1931.	1921.	1911.
1	2	3	4	5	6	7	8	9	10
Pani	27,701	27,727	28,675	−0·1	−3·3	−3·4	3·2	3·5	3·4
Main Branch	4,166	4,972	6,714	−16·2	−25·9	−37·9	0·5	0·6	0·8
Isot	2,555	2,601	2,812	−1·8	−7·5	−9·1	0·3	0·3	0·3
Laun	543	1,081	..	−49·8	..	..	0·1	0·1	..
Mandokhel	4,635	3,870	4,944	+19·8	−21·8	−6·2	0·5	0·5	0·6
Musakhel	13,578	13,145	12,202	+3·3	+7·7	+11·3	1·6	1·7	1·5
Zarkun	2,123	2,017	2,003	+5·2	+0·7	+6·0	0·2	0·3	0·2
Unspecified	101	41	..	+146·3	..	..	..	..	..
Shirani	8,416	7,297	8,552	+15·3	−14·7	−1·6	1·0	0·9	1·0
Tarin	36,754	36,010	37,411	+2·0	−3·7	−1·8	4·3	4·5	4·5
Abdal Achakzai	19,756	19,146	20,272	+3·4	−5·5	−2·3	2·3	2·4	2·4
Spin Tarin	9,709	9,613	5,134	+1·0	+87·2	+89·1	0·1	1·2	0·6
Tor Tarin	6,737	7,023	11,890	−4·1	−40·9	−43·3	0·8	0·9	1·4
Unspecified	512	228	115	+124·6	+98·3	+345·2	0·1	..	..
Zmarai	2,889	1,700	1,228	+69·9	+38·4	+135·3	0·3	0·2	0·2
Other Pathan	1,577	1,340	538	+17·7	+149·1	+193·1	0·2	0·2	0·1
Semi-Indigenous	17,018	13,467	22,317	+26·4	−39·7	−23·7	2·0	1·7	2·7
Durrani	2,410	2,344	2,927	+2·8	−19·9	−17·7	0·3	0·3	0·4
Ghilzai	14,109	9,659	18,586	+46·1	−48·0	−24·1	1·6	1·2	2·2
Pathan unspecified	499	1,464	804	−65·9	+82·0	−37·9	0·1	0·2	0·1
ALIENS	5,581	4,636	4,107	+20·4	+12·9	+35·9	0·6	0·6	0·5
Lasi Panj Raj	31,812	23,212	27,779	+37·0	−16·4	+14·5	3·7	2·9	3·3
Angaria	3,966	3,363	3,146	+17·9	+6·9	+26·1	0·5	0·4	0·4
Burra	3,411	4,279	5,374	−20·3	−20·4	−36·5	0·4	0·5	0·6
Jamot	5,815	6,663	9,724	−12·7	−31·4	−40·2	0·7	0·9	1·2
Runjha	4,656	5,027	5,103	−7·4	−1·5	−8·7	0·5	0·6	0·6
Sheikh	4,306	3,725	4,432	+15·6	−15·9	−2·8	0·5	0·5	0·5
Unspecified	9,658	155	..	+6,131·0	..	..	1·1	..	..
JATT	82,689	66,982	78,400	+23·4	−14·6	+5·4	9·5	8·4	9·4
Indigenous	77,157	63,191	78,397	+22·1	−19·4	−1·6	8·9	7·9	9·4
Aliens	5,532	3,791	3	+45·9	..	..	0·6	0·5	..
SAYYID	23,655	21,542	22,183	+9·8	−2·9	+6·6	2·7	2·7	2·7
Indigenous	21,976	20,265	21,296	+8·4	−4·8	+3·2	2·5	2·5	2·6
Bukhari	11,784	9,501	9,750	+24·0	−2·5	+20·9	1·4	1·2	1·2
Chishti	1,837	1,229	1,500	+49·5	−18·1	+22·4	0·2	0·1	0·2
Gharshin	1,015	786	796	+29·1	−1·3	+27·5	0·1	0·1	0·1
Kaheri	1,215	796	938	+52·6	−15·1	+29·5	0·1	0·1	0·1
Mashwani	1,040	924	1,008	+12·5	−8·3	+3·2	0·1	0·1	0·1
Taran	1,220	955	1,237	+27·7	−22·8	−1·4	0·1	0·1	0·1
Ustrana	638	623	764	+2·4	−18·5	+16·5	0·1	0·1	0·1
Others	3,227	5,451	5,303	−40·8	+2·8	−37·3	0·4	0·7	0·7
Aliens	1,679	1,277	887	+31·5	+44·0	+89·3	0·2	0·2	0·1
OTHER MUSLIMS	79,270	93,507	99,509	−15·2	−6·0	−20·3	9·1	11·7	11·9
Indigenous	57,591	71,766	82,068	−19·8	−12·5	−29·8	6·6	9·0	9·8
Darzada	9,339	10,685	10,257	−12·5	+4·2	−8·9	1·1	1·3	1·2
Dehwar	5,317	5,455	7,326	−2·5	−25·5	−27·4	0·6	0·7	0·9
Gadra	7,935	6,958	7,201	+14·0	−3·4	+10·2	0·9	0·9	0·9
Gola	477	172	834	+177·3	−79·4	−42·8	0·1	..	0·1
Jat	3,236	3,726	5,680	−13·1	−34·4	−43·0	0·4	0·5	0·7
Khoja	352	311	367	+13·2	−15·3	−4·1	..	..	..
Langah	506	1,371	570	−63·1	+140·5	−11·2	0·1	0·2	0·1
Lori	5,653	6,890	10,936	−17·9	−37·0	−48·3	0·6	0·9	1·3
Med	3,041	1,628	2,494	+86·2	−34·7	+21·9	0·3	0·2	0·3
Nakib	7,154	5,577	6,536	+28·3	−14·7	+9·4	0·8	0·7	0·8
Sorozai	11,164	24,888	27,982	−55·1	−11·1	−60·1	1·3	3·1	3·3
Others	3,417	4,105	1,885	−16·8	+117·9	+81·3	0·4	0·5	0·2
Semi-Indigenous	3,099	2,613	4,104	+18·6	−36·3	−24·5	0·3	0·3	0·5
Hazara	3,075	1,997	2,454	+54·0	+18·6	+25·3	0·3	0·2	0·3
Other Muslim	24	616	1,650	−96·1	−62·7	−98·5	..	0·1	0·2
Alien Muslim	18,580	19,128	13,337	−2·9	+43·4	+39·3	2·2	2·4	1·6
HINDU	53,681	51,348	37,602	+4·5	+36·5	+42·8	6·1	6·4	4·5
Indigenous	16,905	17,479	14,985	−3·3	+16·6	+12·0	1·9	2·2	1·8
Aliens	36,776	33,869	22,617	+8·6	+49·8	+62·6	4·2	4·2	2·7
SIKH	8,425	7,741	8,390	+8·8	−7·7	+0·4	1·0	0·9	1·1
Indigenous	48	841	2,799	−94·3	−69·9	−98·3	..	0·1	0·4
Aliens	8,377	6,900	5,591	+21·4	+23·4	+49·8	1·0	0·8	0·7
MISCELLANEOUS	8,418	7,059	6,063	+19·3	+16·4	+38·8	1·0	0·9	0·7
European	5,024	4,751	4,210	+5·7	+12·8	+19·3	0·6	0·6	0·5
Anglo-Indian	379	234	123	+64·5	+90·2	+208·1	..	..	..
Indian-Christian	2,656	1,706	752	+55·5	+127·1	+253·2	0·3	0·2	0·1
Others	359	366	978	−1·9	−62·6	−63·3	0·1	0·1	0·1

48.—Rough Estimate of the fighting strength of each race and tribe in 1931.

Race and Tribe.	Males. Total.	Males. Non-adult.	Males. Adult.	Fighting strength of each tribe.
1	2	3	4	5
INDIGENOUS	**396,626**	**161,039**	**235,587**	**195,924**
BALOCH	**120,066**	**48,093**	**71,973**	**59,966**
Eastern	**81,210**	**32,005**	**49,205**	**41,084**
Bugti	16,760	6,907	9,853	8,177
Dombki	3,846	1,486	2,360	1,975
Khetran	8,917	3,772	5,145	4,253
Magasi	7,209	2,716	4,493	3,772
Mari	19,528	8,281	11,247	9,294
Rind Buledi	3,009	1,201	1,808	1,507
Rind Jamali	3,535	1,367	2,168	1,815
Rind Khosa	2,477	951	1,526	1,278
Rind Lashari	3,735	1,373	2,362	1,990
Rind Unspecified	10,546	3,337	7,209	6,154
Umrani	1,406	539	867	726
Unspecified	242	75	167	143
Western	**38,856**	**16,088**	**22,768**	**18,882**
Buledi	84	35	49	41
Dashti	525	206	319	267
Gichki	136	55	81	67
Kaudai	1,220	501	719	597
Rais	2,035	881	1,154	950
Rakhshani	12,319	4,963	7,356	6,124
Rind Western	16,349	6,858	9,491	7,856
Sangur	3,910	1,620	2,290	1,899
Sanjrani	191	102	89	70
Others	2,087	867	1,220	1,011
BRAHUI	**79,744**	**33,137**	**46,607**	**38,633**
Original nucleus	**6,692**	**2,619**	**4,073**	**3,404**
Ahmadzai	15	5	10	9
Gurgnari	791	281	510	431
Iltazai	112	53	59	48
Kalandrari	743	297	446	372
Kambrari	1,115	490	625	513
Mirwari	977	352	625	527
Rodeni	710	272	438	367
Sumalari	2,229	869	1,360	1,137
Sarawan	**21,336**	**7,973**	**13,363**	**11,230**
Bangulzai	3,738	1,362	2,376	2,002
Kurd	1,078	403	675	567
Lahri	2,316	913	1,403	1,171
Langav	3,452	1,297	2,155	1,810
Mamasani	1,385	471	914	776
Raisani	1,372	513	859	722
Rustamzai	101	37	64	54
Sarparra	943	362	581	487
Satakzai	866	296	570	483
Shahwani	3,021	1,085	1,936	1,634
Zagr Mengal	3,064	1,234	1,830	1,524
Jhalawan	**50,596**	**22,050**	**28,546**	**23,486**
Bizanjav	7,638	3,309	4,329	3,564
Haruni	812	364	448	367
Mamasani	5,540	2,333	3,207	2,653
Mengal	13,689	6,279	7,410	6,041
Nichari	900	331	569	479
Pandrani	564	216	348	293
Sajdi	1,841	768	1,073	889
Zahri	19,612	8,450	11,162	9,201
Miscellaneous	**1,120**	**495**	**625**	**513**
Nighari	607	259	348	287
Rekizai	289	139	150	121
Others	224	97	127	105
PATHAN	**90,198**	**38,064**	**52,134**	**43,114**
Babi	103	44	59	49
Barech	532	199	333	280
Jafar	790	321	469	390
Kakar	46,931	19,786	27,145	22,452
Dawi	150	82	68	53
Dumar	3,889	1,628	2,261	1,872
Husain Paseni	414	182	232	191
Sanzarkhel	24,956	10,151	14,805	12,309
Sargara	1,052	429	623	518
Snatia	10,032	4,348	5,684	4,681
Targara	6,248	2,901	3,347	2,722
Others	190	65	125	106
Kasi	669	271	398	331
Luni	1,874	845	1,029	842
Pani	14,754	5,664	9,090	7,615
Main Branch	2,204	811	1,393	1,173
Isot	1,349	529	820	685
Laun	302	128	174	144
Mandokhel	2,436	986	1,450	1,206
Musakhel	7,350	2,712	4,638	3,903
Zarkun	1,113	498	615	504
Shirani	4,361	1,893	2,468	2,032
Tarin	18,355	8,138	10,217	8,380
Abdal Achakzai	10,139	4,499	5,640	4,626
Spin Tarin	4,849	1,995	2,854	2,368
Tor Tarin	3,198	1,573	1,625	1,305
Unspecified	169	71	98	81
Zmarai	1,526	810	716	563
Other Pathans	303	93	210	180
Lasi	*16,622*	*6,677*	*9,945*	*8,283*
Jatt	*41,542*	*16,134*	*25,408*	*21,254*
Sayyid	*10,576*	*4,804*	*5,772*	*4,714*
Other Muslims	*30,079*	*11,653*	*18,426*	*15,418*
Hindu	*7,767*	*2,473*	*5,294*	*4,517*
Sikh	*32*	*4*	*28*	*25*

APPENDIX.

BILINGUALISM AND NOMADISM BY RACES AND BY TAHSILS.

——:-o-:——

This table has been prepared under the orders of the Census Commissioner for India in connection with the enquiry relating to cultural border zones.

STATISTICS RELATING TO
Bilingualism and Nomadism
Tribal

Race.	TOTAL POPULATION.			MOTHER TONGUE.			OTHER					
	Total.	Males.	Females.	Language.	*Number of Speakers.* Males.	Females.	*Balochi.* Males.	Females.	*Pashto.* Males.	Females.	*Brahui.* Males.	Females.
1	2	3	4	5	6	7	8	9	10	11	12	13
I.—BALUCHISTAN ..	757,768	408,217	349,551	..	408,217	349,551	11,961	4,952	4,042	1,202	14,927	9,612
A.—Indigenous inhabitants.	737,301	396,626	340,675	..	396,626	340,675	11,882	4,877	3,506	1,088	14,470	9,381
1. BALOCH ..	221,675	120,066	101,609	Balochi ..	105,796	88,963	..	..	620	129	5,508	3,606
				Dehwari ..	110	100	..	..	..	..	97	87
				Pashto ..	425	327	2	..	..	..	1	..
				Khetrani ..	8,610	7,912	2,017	318	678	192	..	..
				Saraiki ..	687	632	87	20	..	..	20	2
				Jatki Sindhi ..	3,709	3,076	269	68	27	17	162	8
				Lasi ..	63	67	20	17	..	..	8	9
				Brahui ..	632	519	8	59	19	..	..	..
				Sindhi ..	5	1	2	..	1	..	3	1
				Punjabi ..	1	..	1	..	1	..	..	..
				Persian ..	28	22	..	..	..	..	..	..
2. BRAHUI ..	147,034	79,744	67,290	Balochi ..	10,276	15,812	..	..	76	20	2,909	2,357
				Dehwari ..	11	6	..	..	..	..	6	2
				Pashto ..	123	96	21	10	..	..	3	..
				Khetrani ..	6	3	5	3	..	..	..	..
				Saraiki ..	15	11	..	..	..	..	1	1
				Jatki Sindhi ..	882	700	123	70	5	..	42	2
				Lasi ..	82	93	2	6	..	..	1	1
				Brahui ..	59,341	50,563	3,654	2,088	1,142	372	..	..
				Sindhi ..	1	..	1	..	..	..	1	..
				Persian ..	7	6	..	..	..	..	..	..
3. PATHAN ..	168,665	90,198	78,467	Balochi ..	178	169	..	..	..	..	52	39
				Pashto ..	87,084	75,719	587	358	..	..	856	383
				Jafirki ..	701	605	217	39	221	58	..	..
				Khetrani ..	118	105	3	..	51	32	..	..
				Saraiki ..	7	5	..	..	1	..	1	..
				Jatki Sindhi ..	1,839	1,655	359	7	11	8	34	20
				Brahui ..	246	188	1	..	3	1	..	..
				Persian ..	25	21	4	5	4	..	1	..
4. LASI ..	31,799	16,622	15,177	Balochi ..	826	737	..	..	..	..	..	..
				Lasi ..	15,766	14,417	1,112	676	..	..	326	267
				Brahui ..	14	8	..	..	2	..	..	..
				Sindhi ..	16	15	..	..	..	..	..	..
5. JATT ..	76,180	41,542	34,638	Balochi ..	586	501	..	..	1	..	87	30
				Dehwari ..	3	1	..	..	..	..	..	..
				Pashto ..	38	34	..	..	..	..	3	..
				Jafirki ..	4	10	..	..	6	3	..	..
				Saraiki ..	2,404	2,265	41	21	..	..	47	21
				Jatki Sindhi ..	36,041	29,429	1,397	477	149	72	891	411
				Lasi ..	2,072	2,146	178	121	..	..	166	130
				Jatki ..	8	7	..	..	1	..	..	..
				Brahui ..	184	148	10	6	10	7	..	..
				Sindhi ..	2	..	..	..	..	..	..	..
				Punjabi ..	110	97	25	14	..	..	..	..
6. SAYYID ..	21,145	10,576	10,569	Balochi ..	585	462	..	..	20	5	132	89
				Dehwari ..	139	138	..	..	4	4	5	4
				Pashto ..	7,252	7,607	14	6	..	..	326	247
				Jafirki ..	158	160	73	63	19	6	..	..
				Khetrani ..	424	350	205	31	2	1	..	..
				Saraiki ..	88	85	..	..	..	..	..	..
				Jatki Sindhi ..	1,279	1,156	83	15	6	1	96	12
				Lasi ..	142	139	29	21	..	..	6	4
				Brahui ..	409	378	25	11	48	37	..	..
				Sindhi ..	28	28	4	7	13	7	6	2
				Urdu ..	7	2	..	..	..	..	..	..
				Punjabi ..	15	19	..	..	..	..	..	..
				Persian ..	50	43	6	..	3	..	7	..
7. OTHER MUSLIM ..	56,229	30,079	26,150	Balochi ..	15,555	14,425	..	..	49	24	548	46
				Dehwari ..	2,142	1,747	..	..	..	..	902	761
				Pashto ..	160	120	..	..	..	..	3	..
				Khetrani ..	12	15	4	5	2	2	..	..
				Saraiki ..	99	75	1	1	..	..	..	..
				Jatki Sindhi ..	2,654	2,136	145	60	..	..	68	26
				Lasi ..	5,065	3,892	221	138	..	..	48	31
				Brahui ..	3,931	3,313	117	60	71	26	..	..
				Lori Chini ..	64	47	3	3	15	11	43	31
				Persian ..	407	380	7	5	..	..	211	165

CULTURAL BORDER ZONES.

by Races, and by Tahsils.

Areas.)

LANGUAGES.										PERSONS LIVING IN OCCUPIED.							
Urdu.		*Punjabi.*		*Persian.*		*Arabic.*		*English.*		*Houses.*		*Chhappar.*		*Kizhdi. (Blanket tent).*		*Both (Houses and Kizhdis).*	
Males.	Females.	Males.	Females.	Males.	Females.	Males.	Females.	Males.	Females.	Males.	Females.	Males.	Females.	Males.	Females.	Males.	Females.
14	15	16	17	18	19	20	21	22	23	24	25	26	27	28	29	30	31
5,128	301	261	16	1,308	177	72	4	92	3	183,269	160,042	71,313	61,063	104,277	87,370	49,358	41,076
4,744	266	246	3	1,001	145	60	4	71	3	178,831	156,980	70,903	60,769	99,464	83,243	47,428	39,683
208	30	4	..	89	9	..	..	1	..	38,002	32,651	31,244	27,113	47,663	39,166	3,157	2,679
..	..	..	..	..	..	..	..	..	..	..	..	..	..	..	..	..	..
3	..	..	..	..	..	..	..	..	..	..	..	..	..	..	..	..	..
14	1	11	1	..	..	..	..	..	..	..	..	..	..	..	..	..	..
4	..	..	..	..	..	..	..	..	..	..	..	..	..	..	..	..	..
9	..	..	..	3	..	..	..	..	..	..	..	..	..	..	..	..	..
..	..	..	..	..	..	..	..	..	..	..	..	..	..	..	..	..	..
19	..	1	..	1	..	..	..	1	..	..	..	..	..	..	..	..	..
1	..	..	..	1	..	..	..	..	..	..	..	..	..	..	..	..	..
..	..	..	..	..	..	..	..	..	..	..	..	..	..	..	..	..	..
..	..	..	..	..	..	..	..	5	..	..	..	..	..	..	..	..	..
203	5	5	..	16	3	..	..	3	..	31,455	26,589	7,923	6,445	35,951	30,861	4,415	3,595
..	..	..	..	48	22	..	..	..	..	..	..	..	..	..	..	..	..
1	1	..	..	..	..	..	..	..	..	..	..	..	..	..	..	..	..
..	..	..	..	..	..	..	..	..	..	..	..	..	..	..	..	..	..
..	..	..	..	..	..	..	..	..	..	..	..	..	..	..	..	..	..
7	..	..	..	7	8	..	..	2	..	..	..	..	..	..	..	..	..
..	..	..	..	..	..	..	..	..	..	..	..	..	..	..	..	..	..
1,049	53	2	..	186	29	7	1	9	3	..	..	..	..	..	..	..	..
1	..	..	..	..	..	..	..	..	..	..	..	..	..	..	..	..	..
5	..	..	..	..	..	..	..	..	..	..	..	..	..	..	..	..	..
45	4	..	..	..	..	..	..	..	..	..	..	..	..	..	..	..	..
2,073	38	148	2	396	16	35	2	39	..	46,316	41,863	791	742	5,987	4,842	37,101	31,080
..	..	..	..	..	..	..	..	..	..	..	..	..	..	..	..	..	..
..	..	..	..	..	..	..	..	..	..	..	..	..	..	..	..	..	..
1	..	..	..	1	..	..	..	1	..	..	..	..	..	..	..	..	..
1	..	..	..	1	..	..	..	..	..	..	..	..	..	..	..	..	..
88	12	..	..	..	..	..	..	..	..	..	..	..	..	..	..	..	..
7	2	..	..	..	..	..	..	..	..	..	..	..	..	..	..	..	..
..	..	..	..	..	..	..	..	..	..	5,517	5,239	9,827	8,853	1,276	1,685	..	..
..	..	..	..	..	..	..	..	..	..	..	..	..	..	..	..	..	..
2	..	..	..	..	..	..	..	..	..	..	..	..	..	..	..	..	..
..	..	..	..	..	..	..	..	..	..	..	..	..	..	..	..	..	..
..	..	..	..	..	..	..	..	1	..	30,780	25,622	8,452	7,012	2,084	1,824	226	180
..	..	..	..	..	..	..	..	..	..	..	..	..	..	..	..	..	..
8	..	3	..	1	..	..	..	..	..	..	..	..	..	..	..	..	..
..	..	..	..	..	..	..	..	..	..	..	..	..	..	..	..	..	..
..	..	..	..	..	..	..	..	..	..	..	..	..	..	..	..	..	..
57	..	..	..	58	18	..	..	2	..	..	..	..	..	..	..	..	..
..	..	..	..	..	..	..	..	1	..	..	..	..	..	..	..	..	..
5	..	..	..	..	..	..	..	..	..	..	..	..	..	..	..	..	..
4	2	..	..	..	..	..	..	..	..	..	..	..	..	..	..	..	..
2	..	..	..	..	..	..	..	..	..	..	..	..	..	..	..	..	..
..	..	..	..	..	..	..	..	..	..	..	..	..	..	..	..	..	..
19	5	..	..	17	3	3	1	..	..	7,620	8,079	282	244	620	485	2,054	1,761
30	14	..	..	2	2	..	..	..	..	..	..	..	..	..	..	..	..
333	5	2	..	63	2	15	..	5	..	..	..	..	..	..	..	..	..
..	..	..	..	..	..	..	..	..	..	..	..	..	..	..	..	..	..
..	..	..	..	..	..	..	..	..	..	..	..	..	..	..	..	..	..
49	3	..	..	52	17	1	..	..	..	..	..	..	..	..	..	..	..
..	..	..	..	..	..	..	..	..	..	..	..	..	..	..	..	..	..
29	24	..	..	..	..	..	..	..	..	..	..	..	..	..	..	..	..
..	..	..	..	..	..	..	..	..	..	..	..	..	..	..	..	..	..
..	..	..	..	..	..	..	..	..	..	..	..	..	..	..	..	..	..
..	..	..	..	..	..	..	..	..	..	..	..	..	..	..	..	..	..
8	2	..	..	..	..	..	..	..	..	..	..	..	..	..	..	..	..
72	18	..	..	4	..	..	..	..	..	11,533	10,354	12,311	10,326	5,868	5,168	367	302
26	2	..	..	..	..	..	..	..	..	..	..	..	..	..	..	..	..
7	..	1	..	2	..	..	..	..	..	..	..	..	..	..	..	..	..
..	..	..	..	..	..	..	..	..	..	..	..	..	..	..	..	..	..
..	..	..	..	..	..	..	..	..	..	..	..	..	..	..	..	..	..
4	4	..	..	1	..	..	..	..	..	..	..	..	..	..	..	..	..
..	..	..	..	..	..	..	..	..	..	..	..	..	..	..	..	..	..
208	25	..	..	17	6	..	..	..	..	..	..	..	..	..	..	..	..
..	..	..	..	..	..	..	..	..	..	..	..	..	..	..	..	..	..
26	6	..	..	..	..	..	..	..	..	..	..	..	..	..	..	..	..

Race.	Total Population.			Mother Tongue.			Other					
				Language.	Number of Speakers.		Balochi.		Pashto.		Brahui.	
	Total.	Males.	Females.		Males.	Females.	Males.	Females.	Males.	Females.	Males.	Females.
1	2	3	4	5	6	7	8	9	10	11	12	13
8. Hindus ..	14,330	7,767	6,763	Pashto ..	241	191	..	..	..	..	..	..
				Khetrani ..	337	284	135	..	22	1	..	..
				Saraiki ..	7	1	..	..	..	..	..	..
				Jatki Sindhi ..	5,800	5,225	180	13	91	..	5 4	8
				Lasi ..	750	600	57	..	..	..	20	..
				Sindhi ..	599	411	281	55	15	2	129	68
				Urdu ..	29	18	..	..	1	..	..	..
				Punjabi ..	4	3	..	..	..	..	..	..
9. Sikhs ..	44	32	12	Jatki Sindhi ..	6	8	3	..	1	..	..	..
				Sindhi ..	26	4	20	..	..	..	..	..
B.—Semi-Indigenous inhabitants.	15,117	8,367	6,750	..	8,367	6,750	34	18	170	35	185	65
1. Other Muslims	90	51	39	Pashto ..	12	10	..	..	..	..	..	..
				Persian ..	39	29	..	..	2	3	..	..
2. Pathan ..	13,322	7,401	5,921	Balochi ..	49	53	..	..	6	..	9	6
				Pashto ..	7,289	5,817	33	18	..	..	125	57
				Khetrani ..	3	..	..	..	..	..	..	..
				Jatki Sindhi ..	15	12	..	..	..	1	..	1
				Brahui ..	11	15	..	..	2	1	..	..
				Urdu ..	3	2	..	..	1	—	..	..
				Punjabi ..	2	2	..	..	1	..	..	..
				Persian ..	29	20	..	..	6	2	1	..
3. Baloch ..	1,705	915	790	Balochi ..	862	736	..	..	141	28	..	1
				Pashto ..	33	33	..	..	..	..	..	..
				Khetrani ..	2	1	..	..	..	..	..	..
				Jatki Sindhi ..	14	18	..	..	..	..	..	..
				Jatki ..	1	..	1	..	1	..	..	..
				Punjabi ..	1	..	..	..	..	..	..	..
				Persian ..	2	2	..	..	..	..	..	..
C.—Aliens ..	5,350	3,224	2,126	..	3,224	2,126	150	39	194	44	186	101
1. Muslims ..	3,818	2,173	1,645	Balochi ..	707	544	..	..	7	5	50	44
				Dehwari ..	24	20	..	..	..	..	16	12
				Pashto ..	107	68	3	..	..	..	11	10
				Jafirki ..	11	7	1	..	1	1	..	..
				Saraiki ..	135	113	17	..	..	..	1	2
				Jatki Sindhi ..	514	429	9	8	40	25	..	..
				Lasi ..	38	31	4	1	..	..	..	..
				Jatki ..	33	19	7	5	6	5	..	..
				Brahui ..	4	6	..	..	3	2	..	..
				Sindhi ..	3	2	..	..	—	..	1	1
				Urdu ..	27	12	1	..	3	..	..	..
				Gujrati ..	1	..	..	..	..	..	..	..
				Punjabi ..	307	181	19	11	33	1	11	4
				Persian ..	10	9	2	3	..	..	1	..
				Jagdali ..	252	204	..	..	..	..	..	..
2. Hindus ..	1,088	754	334	Balochi ..	3	2	..	..	..	..	..	..
				Pashto ..	6	..	..	..	..	..	..	..
				Saraiki ..	269	149	..	..	..	..	..	..
				Jatki Sindhi ..	18	10	4	1	..	..	3	1
				Lasi ..	12	..	..	..	..	..	..	..
				Jatki or Jagdali ..	9	8	..	..	..	..	..	..
				Sindhi ..	174	57	26	8	2	3	74	26
				Urdu ..	40	8	..	..	..	..	..	..
				Gujrati ..	3	..	..	..	..	..	..	..
				Punjabi ..	219	100	24	2	45	1	14	1
				Central Pahari ..	1	..	..	..	..	..	..	..
3. Sikh ..	441	294	147	Saraiki ..	1	..	..	..	..	..	..	..
				Sindhi ..	249	136	..	..	..	..	..	..
				Punjabi ..	44	11	32	..	51	..	4	..
4. Christians ..	3	3	..	Punjabi ..	3	..	..	..	..	..	..	..
II.—DETAILS BY DISTRICTS AND TAHSILS	354,158	190,873	163,285	..	190,873	163,285	6,529	2,404	3,618	1,060	3,540	2,404
I.—Quetta Pishin District.	76,242	39,554	36,688	..	39,554	36,688	..	..	..	..	..	..
Quetta Tahsil ..	15,990	8,779	7,211	..	8,779	7,211	55	19	1,065	234	612	93
A.—Indigenous ..	15,098	8,277	6,821	..	8,277	6,821	53	19	1,024	227	530	81
1. Baloch ..	481	281	200	Balochi ..	165	110	..	..	20	8	4	2
	..	..	..	Pashto ..	14	13	..	..	..	..	1	..
	..	..	..	Brahui ..	73	55	..	..	18	..	..	..
	..	..	..	Sindhi ..	1	..	1	..	..	..	1	..
	..	..	..	Persian ..	28	22	..	..	..	..	..	..

Nomadism.

LANGUAGES.										OCCUPIED.							
Urdu.		*Punjabi.*		*Persian.*		*Arabic.*		*English.*		*Houses.*		*Chhappar.*		*Kizhdi.*		*Both (Houses and Kizhdis).*	
Males.	Females.	Males.	Females.	Males.	Females.	Males.	Females.	Males.	Females.	Males.	Females.	Males.	Females.	Males.	Females.	Males.	Females.
14	15	16	17	18	19	20	21	22	23	24	25	26	27	28	29	30	31
1	..	69	..	..	..	..	..	..	..	7,576	6,631	73	34	13	12	105	86
..	..	..	..	..	..	..	..	..	..	..	..	..	..	..	..	..	..
17	..	..	..	..	..	..	..	..	..	..	..	..	..	..	..	..	..
..	..	..	..	..	..	..	..	..	..	..	..	..	..	..	..	..	..
96	10	..	..	40	10	..	..	..	..	..	..	..	..	..	..	..	..
..	..	..	..	..	..	..	..	1	..	..	..	..	..	..	..	..	..
..	..	..	..	..	..	..	..	..	..	..	..	..	..	..	..	..	..
1	..	..	..	..	..	..	..	..	..	32	12	..	..	..	..	..	..
1	..	..	..	..	..	..	..	..	..	..	..	..	..	..	..	..	..
155	5	6	4	144	10	5	..	8	..	2,289	1,750	15	8	4,321	3,757	1,742	1,235
..	..	..	..	..	..	..	..	..	..	..	..	..	..	..	..	..	..
7	2	3	..	..	..	..	..	..	..	47	39	..	..	2	..	2	..
6	..	..	..	7	..	..	..	..	..	..	..	..	..	..	..	..	..
128	2	2	4	136	10	5	..	3	..	1,982	1,487	12	7	4,184	3,646	1,223	781
..	..	..	..	..	..	..	..	..	..	..	..	..	..	..	..	..	..
..	..	..	..	..	..	..	..	..	..	..	..	..	..	..	..	..	..
2	1	..	..	..	..	..	..	..	..	..	..	..	..	..	..	..	..
..	..	..	..	..	..	..	..	..	..	..	..	..	..	..	..	..	..
..	..	..	..	..	..	..	..	..	..	..	..	..	..	..	..	..	..
12	..	..	..	..	..	..	..	..	..	..	..	..	..	..	..	..	..
..	..	..	..	1	..	..	..	..	..	260	224	3	1	135	111	517	454
..	..	..	..	..	..	..	..	..	..	..	..	..	..	..	..	..	..
..	..	..	..	..	..	..	..	..	..	..	..	..	..	..	..	..	..
..	..	..	..	..	..	..	..	..	..	..	..	..	..	..	..	..	..
..	..	1	..	..	..	..	..	..	..	..	..	..	..	..	..	..	..
..	..	..	..	..	..	..	..	..	..	..	..	..	..	..	..	..	..
..	..	..	..	..	..	..	..	..	..	..	..	..	..	..	..	..	..
129	25	7	5	19	2	2	..	15	..	2,149	1,812	395	286	492	370	188	158
17	12	..	..	..	..	..	..	..	..	1,299	957	198	160	488	370	188	158
16	6	1	..	4	..	..	..	..	..	..	..	..	..	..	..	..	..
..	..	..	..	..	..	..	..	..	..	..	..	..	..	..	..	..	..
..	..	..	..	..	..	..	..	..	..	..	..	..	..	..	..	..	..
..	..	..	..	..	..	..	..	..	..	..	..	..	..	..	..	..	..
..	..	..	..	..	..	..	..	..	..	..	..	..	..	..	..	..	..
1	..	6	5	..	..	..	..	..	..	..	..	..	..	..	..	..	..
3	2	..	..	1	2	..	..	..	..	..	..	..	..	..	..	..	..
3	1	..	..	..	..	..	..	..	..	..	..	..	..	..	..	..	..
5	..	..	..	4	..	..	..	1	..	..	..	..	..	..	..	..	..
..	..	..	..	..	..	..	..	..	..	..	..	..	..	..	..	..	..
32	2	..	..	5	..	..	..	7	..	..	..	..	..	..	..	..	..
3	..	..	..	..	..	..	..	1	..	..	..	..	..	..	..	..	..
..	..	..	..	..	..	..	..	..	..	701	208	49	36	4	..	..	..
..	..	..	..	..	..	..	..	..	..	..	..	..	..	..	..	..	..
..	..	..	..	..	..	..	..	..	..	..	..	..	..	..	..	..	..
..	..	..	..	..	..	..	..	..	..	..	..	..	..	..	..	..	..
..	..	..	..	..	..	..	..	..	..	..	..	..	..	..	..	..	..
..	..	..	..	..	..	..	..	..	..	..	..	..	..	..	..	..	..
19	2	..	..	..	..	2	..	1	..	..	..	..	..	..	..	..	..
..	..	..	..	..	..	..	..	..	..	..	..	..	..	..	..	..	..
1	..	..	..	1	..	..	..	..	..	..	..	..	..	..	..	..	..
22	..	..	..	2	..	..	..	3	..	..	..	..	..	..	..	..	..
1	..	..	..	..	..	..	..	..	..	..	..	..	..	..	..	..	..
..	..	..	..	..	..	..	..	..	..	146	57	148	90	..	..	..	..
..	..	..	..	..	..	..	..	..	..	..	..	..	..	..	..	..	..
6	..	..	..	2	..	..	..	1	..	..	..	..	..	..	..	..	..
..	..	..	..	..	..	..	..	..	..	3	..	..	..	..	..	..	..
3,995	130	253	12	763	56	64	3	68	..	79,264	71,254	15,331	12,706	49,451	40,306	46,327	39,019
..	..	..	..	..	..	..	..	..	..	29,641	28,539	323	265	1,598	1,279	7,992	6,605
2,448	61	..	..	387	37	37	2	48	..	7,730	6,347	11	10	182	159	856	695
2,302	56	..	..	352	31	35	2	44	..	7,236	5,960	9	10	176	156	856	695
66	..	..	..	2	..	..	..	1	..	228	153	..	..	25	23	28	24
2	..	..	..	..	..	..	..	..	..	..	..	..	..	..	..	..	..
18	..	..	..	..	..	..	..	..	..	..	..	..	..	..	..	..	..
1	..	..	..	..	..	..	..	..	..	..	..	..	..	..	..	..	..
15	..	..	..	..	..	..	..	5	..	..	..	..	..	..	..	..	..

Race	Total Population: Total	Males	Females	Mother-Tongue: Language	Number of Speakers: Males	Females	Other — Balochi: Males	Females	Pashto: Males	Females	Brahui: Males	Females
1	2	3	4	5	6	7	8	9	10	11	12	13
2. Brahui ..	6,045	3,276	2,769	Balochi ..	365	327	..	..	59	12	1	..
				Pashto ..	39	28	1	..	..	..	5	2
				Brahui ..	2,864	2,408	14	12	767	146	..	..
				Sindhi ..	1	..	1	..	..	..	1	..
				Persian ..	7	6	..	..	..	..	..	..
3. Pathan ..	7,504	4,103	3,401	Balochi ..	65	66	..	..	..	..	..	--
				Pashto ..	3,887	3,228	32	7	..	..	436	70
				Brahui ..	135	95	..	..	3	1	..	..
				Persian ..	16	12	..	..	4	..	1	..
4. Lasi ..	12	8	4	Brahui ..	8	4	..	..	2	..	..	..
5. Jatt ..	45	25	20	Pashto ..	6	8	..	..	..	..	3	..
				Jatki ..	8	7	..	..	1	..	..	..
				Brahui ..	9	5	..	..	..	..	..	..
				Sindhi ..	2	..	..	..		..	..	..
Sayyid ..	569	325	244	Balochi ..	29	12	..	..	16	2	6	3
				Pashto ..	203	157	..	..	..	..	37	1
				Brahui ..	91	74	..	..	48	37	6	2
				Persian ..	2	1	..	..	..	..	..	..
7. Other Muslim ..	403	230	173	Balochi ..	9	6	..	..	9	2	..	..
				Pashto ..	28	19	..	..	..	..	3	..
				Brahui ..	151	107	4	..	62	17	..	..
				Persian ..	42	41	..	..	..	..	3	..
8. Hindu ..	39	29	10	Sindhi ..	29	10	..	..	15	2	22	1
B.—Semi-Indigenous ..	**714**	**379**	**335**	..	**379**	**335**	**1**	..	**6**	**3**	**59**	**8**
1. Pathan ..	678	362	316	Pashto ..	337	292	1	..	..	..	58	8
				Brahui ..	2	5	..	..	2	1	..	..
				Persian ..	23	19	..	..	4	2	..	..
2.—Other Muslim ..	36	17	19	Pashto ..	10	8	..	..	..	..	..	..
				Persian ..	7	11	..	..	..	..	..	..
C.—Alien ..	**178**	**123**	**55**	..	**123**	**55**	**1**	..	**35**	**4**	**23**	**4**
1. Muslim ..	108	67	41	Pashto ..	32	23	..	..	..	..	5	4
				Brahui ..	4	6	..	..	3	2	..	..
				Urdu ..	1	..	..	..	1	..	..	..
				Punjabi ..	23	6	1	..	5	..	1	..
				Persian ..	7	6	..	..	..	..	..	..
2.—Hindu ..	61	48	13	Urdu ..	13	1	..	..	2	..	..	..
				Gujrati ..	1	..	..	..	..	..	..	..
				Punjabi ..	33	12	..	..	18	1	13	..
				Central Pahari ..	1	..	..	..	..	..	..	..
3. Sikh ..	9	8	1	Western Punjabi ..	8	1	..	..	6	1	4	..
Pishin Tahsil ..	**49,131**	**24,614**	**24,517**	..	**24,614**	**24,517**	**2**	**3**	**67**	**31**	..	..
A.—Indigenous ..	**47,642**	**23,754**	**23,888**	..	**23,754**	**23,888**	**2**	**3**	**51**	**29**	—	..
1. Baloch ..	118	68	50	Balochi ..	41	29	..	..	39	26	..	..
				Pashto ..	25	20	..	..	..	..	..	..
				Brahui ..	2	1	..	..	1	..	..	..
2. Brahui ..	64	37	27	Pashto ..	14	8	..	..	..	..	..	..
				Brahui ..	23	19	..	..	10	3	..	..
3. Pathan ..	38,959	19,856	19,103	Pashto ..	19,856	19,103	2	3	..	..	..	..
				Pashto ..	28	30	..	..	..	—	..	..
4. Sayyid ..	8,384	3,729	4,655	Pashto ..	3,729	4,655	..	..	..	..	..	..
5. Other Muslim	116	63	53	Pashto ..	35	23	..	..	..	..	..	..
6. Hindu ..	1	1	..	Urdu ..	1	..	..	..	1	..	..	..
B.—Semi-Indigenous .	**1,448**	**838**	**615**	..	**838**	**615**	..	..	**9**	**2**	..	..
1. Pathan ..	1,441	828	613	Pashto ..	823	610	..	..	..	..	..	..
				Urdu ..	1	1	..	..	1	..	..	..
				Punjabi ..	2	2	..	.	1	..	..	..
				Persian ..	2	..	..	..	2	..	..	..
2. Other Muslim	7	5	2	Persian ..	5	2	..	..	5	2	..	..
C.—Alien ..	**41**	**27**	**14**	..	**27**	**14**	..	..	**7**	..	..	..
1.—Muslim ..	28	20	8	Pashto ..	5	3	..	..	..	..	..	..
				Urdu ..	1	--	-	..	1	..	..	..
				Punjabi ..	9	3	..	..	4	..	..	..
				Western Punjabi ..	5	2	..	..	2	..	..	..
2.—Hindu ..	13	7	6	Sindhi ..	1	1	..	..	..	..	..	..
				Punjabi ..	6	5	..	..	..	..	..	..

Nomadism.

Languages.										Occupied.							
Urdu.		*Punjabi.*		*Persian.*		*Arabic.*		*English.*		*Houses.*		*Chhappar.*		*Kizhdi.*		*Both (Houses and Kizhdis).*	
Males.	Females.	Males.	Females.	Males.	Females.	Males.	Females.	Males.	Females.	Males.	Females.	Males.	Females.	Males.	Females.	Males.	Females.
14	15	16	17	18	19	20	21	22	23	24	25	26	27	28	29	30	31
177	5	..	..	1	..	..	..	2	..	3,036	2,582	8	10	116	92	115	85
12	..	..	..	..	..	..	..	..	..	..	..	..	..	..	..	..	..
733	18	..	..	118	17	7	1	4	..	..	..	..	..	..	..	..	..
1	..	..	..	..	..	..	..	..	..	..	..	..	..	..	..	..	..
5	..	..	..	..	..	..	..	..	..	..	..	..	..	..	..	..	..
42	..	..	..	..	..	..	..	..	..	3,388	2,315	..	..	11	6	704	580
969	20	..	..	192	12	13	1	30	..	..	..	..	..	..	..	..	..
63	..	..	..	..	..	..	..	..	..	..	..	..	..	..	..	..	..
5	..	..	..	..	..	..	..	..	..	..	..	..	..	..	..	..	..
2	..	..	..	..	..	..	..	..	..	7	2	..	..	1	2	..	..
5	..	..	..	1	..	..	..	..	..	22	18	..	..	..	..	3	2
5	..	..	..	..	..	..	..	..	..	..	..	..	..	..	..	..	..
..	..	..	..	..	..	..	..	..	..	..	..	..	..	..	..	..	..
2	..	..	..	..	..	..	..	..	..	..	..	..	..	..	..	..	..
11	..	..	..	5	2	..	..	..	..	294	207	1	..	24	33	6	4
49	..	..	..	21	..	15	..	2	..	..	..	..	..	..	..	..	..
11	6	..	..	..	..	..	..	..	..	..	..	..	..	..	..	..	..
1	..	..	..	..	..	..	..	..	..	..	..	..	..	..	..	..	..
..	..	..	..	..	..	..	..	..	..	280	173	..	..	..	..	..	..
7	..	..	..	1	..	..	..	..	..	..	..	..	..	..	..	..	..
59	7	..	..	11	..	..	..	..	..	..	..	..	..	..	..	..	..
14	..	..	..	..	..	..	..	..	..	..	..	..	..	..	..	..	..
18	..	..	..	..	..	..	..	..	..	29	10	..	..	..	..	..	..
101	3	..	..	26	4	2	..	3	..	378	333	2	..	4	2	..	..
87	2	..	..	20	4	2	..	3	..	356	314	2	..	4	2	..	..
2	1	..	..	..	..	..	..	..	..	..	..	..	..	..	..	..	..
12	..	..	..	..	..	..	..	..	..	..	..	..	..	..	..	..	..
..	..	..	..	..	..	..	..	..	..	17	19	..	..	..	..	..	..
..	..	..	..	..	..	..	..	..	..	..	..	..	..	..	..	..	..
45	2	..	..	9	2	..	..	1	..	121	54	..	..	2	1	..	..
8	..	..	..	3	..	..	..	..	..	65	40	..	..	2	1	..	..
3	2	..	..	1	2	..	..	..	..	..	..	..	..	..	..	..	..
..	..	..	..	1	..	..	..	..	..	..	..	..	..	..	..	..	..
9	..	..	..	..	..	..	..	1	..	..	..	..	..	..	..	..	..
3	..	..	..	..	..	..	..	..	..	..	..	..	..	..	..	..	..
..	..	..	..	..	..	..	..	..	..	48	13	..	..	..	..	..	..
1	..	..	..	1	..	..	..	..	..	..	..	..	..	..	..	..	..
16	..	..	..	2	..	..	..	..	..	..	..	..	..	..	..	..	..
1	..	..	..	..	..	..	..	..	..	..	..	..	..	..	..	..	..
4	..	..	..	1	..	..	..	..	..	8	1	..	..	..	..	..	..
1,259	13	6	..	136	..	4	..	10	..	20,838	21,240	311	255	242	225	3,223	2,797
1,222	12	4	..	122	..	4	..	8	..	20,191	20,791	311	255	212	203	3,040	2,639
..	..	..	..	1	..	..	..	..	..	68	50	..	..	..	..	..	..
..	..	..	..	..	..	..	..	..	..	..	..	..	..	..	..	..	..
..	..	..	..	..	..	..	..	..	..	..	..	..	..	..	..	..	..
1	..	..	..	..	..	..	..	..	..	37	27	..	..	..	..	..	..
..	..	..	..	..	..	..	..	..	..	..	..	..	..	..	..	..	..
960	18	3	..	91	..	4	..	5	..	16,622	16,289	311	255	212	203	2,711	2,356
..	..	4	..	..	..	..	..	..	..	28	30	..	..	..	..	..	..
257	..	1	..	30	..	..	..	2	..	3,400	4,372	..	..	..	..	329	283
..	..	..	..	..	..	..	..	..	..	36	23	..	..	..	..	..	..
..	..	..	..	..	..	..	..	1	..	1	..	..	..	..	..	..	..
33	..	2	..	12	..	..	..	..	..	620	485	..	..	30	22	188	153
31	..	..	..	12	..	..	..	..	..	615	433	..	..	30	22	183	158
..	..	..	..	..	..	..	..	..	..	..	..	..	..	..	..	..	..
..	..	..	..	..	..	..	..	..	..	..	..	..	..	..	..	..	..
..	..	..	..	..	..	..	..	..	..	..	..	..	..	..	..	..	..
2	..	2	..	..	..	..	..	..	..	5	2	..	..	..	..	..	..
4	..	..	..	2	..	..	..	2	..	27	14	..	..	..	..	..	..
..	..	..	..	1	..	..	..	..	..	20	8	..	..	..	..	..	..
..	..	..	..	1	..	..	..	..	..	..	..	..	..	..	..	..	..
..	..	..	..	..	..	..	..	..	..	..	..	..	..	..	..	..	..
2	..	..	..	..	..	..	..	..	..	..	..	..	..	..	..	..	..
..	..	..	..	..	..	..	..	1	..	7	6	..	..	..	..	..	..
2	..	..	..	..	..	..	..	1	..	..	..	..	..	..	..	..	..

Bilingualism and

Race.	TOTAL POPULATION.			MOTHER TONGUE.			OTHER					
				Language.	*Number of Speakers.*		*Balochi.*		*Pashto.*		*Brahui.*	
	Total.	Males.	Females.		Males.	Females.	Males.	Females.	Males.	Females.	Males.	Females.
1	2	3	4	5	6	7	8	9	10	11	12	13
Chaman Tahsil ..	**11,121**	**6,161**	**4,960**	..	**6,161**	**4,960**	..	—	..	..	..	..
A.—Indigenous ..	**11,079**	**6,140**	**4,939**	..	**6,140**	**4,939**	..	..	..	..	..	..
1. PATHAN ..	11,068	6,134	4,934	Pashto ..	6,134	4,934	..	..	..	..	..	..
2. SAYYID ..	11	6	5	Pashto ..	6	5	..	..	..	..	..	..
B.—Semi-Indigenous ..	**38**	**19**	**19**	..	**19**	**19**	..	..	..	..	..	..
1. PATHAN ..	38	19	19	Pashto ..	19	19	..	..	..	..	..	..
C.—Alien ..	**4**	**2**	**2**	..	**2**	**2**	..	..	—	..	..	..
1. MUSLIM ..	4	2	2	..	2	2	..	..	..	..	..	..
II.—Loralai District ..	**79,784**	**43,153**	**36,631**	..	**43,153**	**36,631**	**2,906**	**551**	**1,601**	**365**	**220**	**169**
Duki Tahsil ..	**17,621**	**9,489**	**8,132**	..	**9,489**	**8,132**	**224**	**138**	**607**	**350**	**1**	..
A.—Indigenous ..	**12,102**	**6,515**	**5,587**	..	**6,515**	**5,587**	**221**	**138**	**373**	**235**	**1**	..
1. BALOCH ..	1,037	591	446	Balochi ..	173	129	..	..	121	74	..	..
				Pashto ..	167	128	..	..	..	..	..	..
				Khetrani ..	251	199	7	4	200	133	..	..
2. BRAHUI ..	253	143	110	Balochi ..	1	..	..	..	..	..	..	..
				Pashto ..	12	10	..	..	..	..	1	..
				Brahui ..	130	100	11	6	9	..	..	..
3. PATHAN ..	9,114	4,865	4,249	Pashto ..	4,865	4,249	198	128	..	..	..	..
4. JATT ..	9	5	4	Pashto ..	5	4	..	..	..	..	..	..
5. SAYYID .	1,336	716	620	Pashto ..	698	599	3	—	..	..	..	..
				Sindhi ..	18	21	..	..	13	7	..	..
6. OTHER MUSLIM ..	78	38	40	Balochi ..	34	35	..	..	26	21	..	..
				Pashto ..	4	5	—	..	..	..	..	..
7. HINDU ..	275	157	118	Pashto ..	152	118	..	..	..	..	..	..
				Jatki Sindhi ..	5	..	2	..	4	..	..	..
B.—Semi-Indigenous ..	**5,438**	**2,917**	**2,521**	..	**2,917**	**2,521**	**2**	..	**209**	**10**	..	..
1. PATHAN ..	5,358	2,873	2,485	Pashto ..	2,873	2,485	1	..	109	..	..	..
2. BALOCH ..	80	44	36	Balochi ..	23	19	..	..	18	10	..	.
				Pashto ..	20	17	..	..	..	..	..	..
				Jatki ..	1	..	1	..	1	..	..	..
C.—Alien ..	**81**	**57**	**24**	..	**57**	**24**	**1**	..	**25**	**5**	..	..
1. MUSLIM ..	52	33	19	Balochi ..	10	7	..	..	7	5	..	.
				Pashto ..	22	12	1		..	..	..	..
				Punjabi ..	1	..	..	..	1	..	..	..
2. HINDU ..	29	24	5	Pashto ..	4	..	..	..	..	..	..	..
				Punjabi ..	20	5	..	..	17	..	..	..
Bori Tahsil ..	**13,203**	**7,387**	**5,816**	..	**7,387**	**5,816**	**4**	..	**50**	**9**	..	..
A.—Indigenous ..	**10,971**	**6,187**	**4,784**	..	**6,187**	**4,784**	**4**	—	**44**	**8**	..	..
1. BALOCH ..	28	20	8	Balochi ..	8	3	..	..	5	..	..	..
				Pashto ..	10	5	1	..	..	..	..	..
				Khetrani ..	1	..	..	..	..	..	..	..
				Sindhi ..	1	..	..	..	1	..	..	..
2. BRAHUI ..	138	73	65	Balochi ..	20	15	..	..	8	4	..	..
				Pashto ..	3	2	1	..	..	..	..	..
				Brahui ..	50	48	..	..	27	3	..	..
3. PATHAN ..	10,285	5,800	4,485	Pashto ..	5,795	4,482	2	..	..	..	..	..
				Brahui ..	5	3	..	..	..	..	..	..
4. JATT ..	12	8	4	Pashto ..	8	4	..	..	..	..	..	..
5. SAYYID ..	307	175	132	Pashto ..	175	132	..	..	..	..	..	..
7. OTHER MUSLIM	28	15	13	Pashto ..	15	13	..	..	..	..	..	..
8. HINDU ..	173	96	77	Pashto ..	89	73	..	..	..	..	..	..
				Khetrani ..	3	1	..	..	3	1	..	..
				Punjabi ..	4	3	..	..	—	..	..	..
B.—Semi-Indigenous ..	**2,191**	**1,168**	**1,023**	..	**1,168**	**1,023**	..	..	..	..	..	..
1. PATHAN ..	2,184	1,165	1,019	Pashto ..	1,165	1,019	..	..	..	..	..	..
2. BALOCH ..	7	3	4	Pashto ..	3	4	..	..	..	..	..	—

Nomadism.

Languages.										Occupied.							
Urdu.		*Punjabi.*		*Persian.*		*Arabic.*		*English.*		*Houses.*		*Chhappar.*		*Kizhdi.*		*Both (Houses and Kizhdis).*	
Males.	Females.	Males.	Females.	Males.	Females.	Males.	Females.	Males.	Females.	Males.	Females.	Males.	Females.	Males.	Females.	Males.	Females.
14	15	16	17	18	19	20	21	22	23	24	25	26	27	28	29	30	31
25	..	..	..	22	..	..	..	..	..	1,078	952	1	..	1,174	895	3,913	3,113
25	..	..	..	22	..	..	..	..	..	1,069	949	1	..	1,174	895	3,896	3,095
25	..	..	..	22	..	..	..	..	..	1,069	949	1	..	1,169	890	3,895	3,095
..	..	..	..	..	..	..	..	..	..	..	..	..	..	5	5	1	..
..	..	..	..	..	..	..	..	..	..	2	1	..	..	..	..	17	18
..	..	..	..	..	..	..	..	..	..	2	1	..	..	..	..	17	18
..	..	..	..	..	..	..	..	..	..	2	2	..	..	..	..	..	..
..	..	..	..	..	..	..	..	..	..	2	2	..	..	..	..	..	..
90	2	100	10	108	2	12	..	1	..	26,529	22,534	405	357	7,930	6,614	8,289	7,126
26	..	4	..	2	..	..	..	..	..	5,406	4,566	167	174	3,481	3,021	435	371
23	..	3	..	2	..	..	..	..	..	5,199	4.447	158	170	784	645	374	325
2	..	..	..	..	..	..	..	..	..	467	337	..	..	121	89	..	..
..	..	..	..	..	..	..	..	..	..	..	..	..	..	..	..	..	..
..	..	..	..	..	..	..	..	..	..	..	..	..	..	..	..	..	..
..	..	..	..	..	..	..	..	..	..	59	52	..	..	65	45	19	13
..	..	..	..	..	..	..	..	..	..	..	..	..	..	..	..	..	..
1	..	1	..	..	..	..	..	..	..	..	..	..	..	..	..	..	..
19	6	..	..	1	..	..	..	..	..	3,939	3,492	153	162	523	441	170	164
..	..	..	..	..	..	..	..	..	..	1	..	..	..	4	4	..	..
1	..	..	..	..	..	..	..	..	..	309	420	..	..	61	58	146	142
..	..	..	..	..	..	..	..	..	..	7	8	5	8	7	8	19	16
..	..	2	..	..	..	..	..	..	..	157	118	..	..	..	..	..	..
..	..	1	..	..	..	..	..	..	..	160	100	4	1	2,692	2,374	61	46
..	..	..	..	..	..	..	..	..	..	124	71	1	..	2,687	2,368	61	46
..	..	..	..	..	..	..	..	..	..	36	29	3	1	5	6	..	..
..	..	1	..	..	..	..	..	..	..	..	..	..	..	..	..	..	..
3	..	..	..	..	..	..	..	..	..	47	19	5	3	5	2	..	..
2	..	..	..	..	..	..	..	..	..	25	14	5	3	3	2	..	..
1	..	..	..	..	..	..	..	..	..	..	..	..	..	..	..	..	..
..	..	..	..	..	..	..	..	..	..	22	5	..	..	2	..	..	..
80	..	76	4	89	..	4	..	..	..	5,016	3,827	140	94	1,009	844	1,222	1,051
23	..	73	..	5	..	4	..	..	..	4,633	3,520	140	94	300	225	1,114	945
1	..	..	..	..	..	..	..	..	..	20	8	..	..	..	..	..	..
..	..	..	..	..	..	..	..	..	..	..	..	..	..	..	..	..	..
..	..	..	..	..	..	..	..	..	..	73	63	..	..	..	..	..	..
2	..	..	..	..	..	..	..	..	..	..	..	..	..	..	..	..	..
20	..	3	..	5	..	4	..	..	..	4,261	3,233	127	84	300	223	1,012	943
..	..	3	..	..	..	..	..	..	..	8	4	..	..	..	..	..	..
..	..	..	..	..	..	..	..	..	..	173	130	..	..	..	..	2	2
..	..	67	..	..	..	..	..	..	..	2	3	13	10	..	..	..	..
..	..	..	..	..	..	..	..	..	..	96	77	..	..	..	..	..	..
5	..	2	4	84	..	..	..	..	..	351	293	..	..	709	619	108	106
5	..	2	4	84	..	..	..	..	..	348	204	..	..	709	619	108	106
..	..	..	..	..	..	..	..	..	..	3	4	..	..	..	..	..	..

Race.	Total Population.			Mother Tongue.			Other					
				Language.	Number of Speakers.		Balochi.		Pashto.		Brahui.	
	Total.	Males.	Females.		Males.	Females.	Males.	Females.	Males.	Females.	Males.	Females.
1	2	3	4	5	6	7	8	9	10	11	12	13
C.—Alien ..	**41**	**32**	**9**	..	**32**	**9**	..	..	**6**	**1**	..	..
1. Muslim ..	31	22	9	Pashto ..	8	5	..	..	..	..	..	..
				Punjabi ..	14	4	..	..	5	1	..	..
2. Hindu ..	9	9	..	Urdu ..	2	..	..	..	..	..	..	..
				Punjabi ..	7	..	..	..	1	..	..	..
3. Sikh ..	1	1	..	Punjabi ..	1	..	..	..	..	..	.	.
Sanjawi Tahsil ..	**6,147**	**3,381**	**2,766**	..	**3,381**	**2,766**	..	..	**11**	**7**	..	..
A.—Indigenous ..	**6,009**	**3,296**	**2,713**	..	**3,296**	**2,713**	..	..	**9**	**7**	..	..
1. Baloch ..	30	17	13	Balochi ..	5	3	..	..	..	..	..	..
				Pashto ..	2	3	..	..	..	..	..	..
				Khetrani ..	10	7	..	..	6	3	..	..
2. Brahui ..	13	7	6	Balochi ..	7	6	..	..	3	4	..	..
3. Pathan ..	5,322	2,908	2,414	Pashto ..	2,908	2,414	..	..	..	..	..	..
4. Sayyid ..	644	364	280	Pashto ..	364	280	..		..	..	..	..
B.—Semi-Indigenous ..	**114**	**70**	**44**	..	**70**	**44**	..	..	..	..	..	..
1. Pathan ..	76	50	26	Pashto ..	50	26	..	..	..	..	.	..
2. Other Muslim ..	37	20	17	Pashto ..	2	2		..	..	..	..	..
				Persian ..	18	15	..	.	..	..	..	..
3. Baloch ..	1	..	1	Persian ..	..	1	..	..	..	..	..	..
C.—Alien ..	**24**	**15**	**9**	..	**15**	**9**	..	..	**2**	..	..	..
1. Muslim ..	23	14	9	Pashto ..	11	6	..	..	..	..	..	..
				Urdu ..	1	..	..	..	1	..	..	..
				Punjabi ..	2	3	..	..	..	..	..	..
2. Hindu ..	1	1	..	Urdu ..	1	..	..	..	1	..	..	..
Barkhan Tahsil ..	**20,124**	**10,692**	**9,482**	..	**10,692**	**9,482**	**2,335**	**292**	**551**	**12**	..	..
A.—Indigenous ..	**18,587**	**9,777**	**8,810**	..	**9,777**	**8,810**	**2,295**	**285**	**486**	**6**	..	..
1. Baloch ..	17,100	8,970	8,130	Balochi ..	784	586	..	..	50	..	..	..
				Khetrani ..	8,185	7,544	1,950	255	413	6	..	..
				Punjabi ..	1	..	1		1	..	..	..
2. Brahui ..	5	3	2	Balochi ..	3	2	..	..	..	..	..	..
3. Pathan ..	85	43	42	Pashto ..	19	19	..	..	..	..		..
				Jafirki ..	7	4	2	..	..	..	..	..
				Khetrani ..	17	19	3	..	2	..	..	..
4. Sayyid ..	770	422	348	Khetrani ..	422	348	204	30	1	..	..	..
5. Other Muslim ..	11	6	5	Khetrani ..	6	5	..	..	..	..	..	..
6. Hindu ..	616	333	283	Khetrani ..	333	282	135	..	19	..	..	..
B.—Semi-Indigenous ..	**658**	**385**	**273**	..	**385**	**273**	**3**	..	**44**	**1**	..	..
1. Pathan ..	97	68	29	Pashto ..	65	29	3	..	..	..	..	..
				Khetrani ..	3	..	..	..	..	..	..	..
2. Baloch ..	561	317	244	Balochi ..	315	243	..	..	43	1	..	..
				Persian ..	2	1	..	..	1	..	.	..
C.—Alien ..	**879**	**530**	**349**	..	**530**	**349**	**37**	**7**	**21**	**5**	..	..
1. Muslim ..	825	477	348	Balochi ..	418	320	..	..	..	..	..	..
				Pashto ..	13	4	2	..	..	..	..	..
				Jatki ..	31	18	6	5	6	5	..	..
				Punjabi ..	15	6	5	2	7	..	..	..
2. Hindu ..	50	50	..	Punjabi ..	50	..	22	..	8	..	..	..
3. Sikh ..	3	2	1	Punjabi ..	2	1	2	..	..	..	..	..
4. Christian ..	1	1	..	Punjabi ..	1	..	..	..	..	..	..	.
Musakhel Tahsil ..	**22,689**	**12,204**	**10,485**	..	**12,204**	**10,485**	**343**	**121**	**382**	**87**	**219**	**169**
A.—Indigenous ..	**20,824**	**11,189**	**9,635**	..	**11,189**	**9,635**	**309**	**121**	**250**	**69**	**219**	**169**
1. Baloch ..	283	163	120	Balochi ..	6	3	..	..	..	..	..	..
				Pashto ..	150	112	..	..	..	..	..	..
				Khetrani ..	8	5	4	2	4	2	..	..
2. Pathan ..	19,954	10,731	9,223	Pashto ..	10,037	8,622	10	7	..	..	219	169
				Jafirki ..	694	601	215	39	221	58	..	..
3. Jatt ..	16	5	11	Balochi ..	1	1	..	..	..	..	..	..
				Jafirki ..	4	10	.	..	6	3	..	..
4. Sayyid ..	562	285	277	Balochi ..	3	2	..	..	..	..	..	..
				Pashto ..	114	108	3	3	..	..	..	..
				Jafirki ..	158	160	73	63	19	6	..	..
				Sindhi ..	10	7	4	7	..	..	..	..
5. Other Muslim ..	8	4	4	Balochi ..	4	4	..	..	..	..	..	..
6. Hindu ..	1	1	..	Khetrani ..	1	..	..	..	..	..	..	..

Nom dism.

Languages.										Occupied.							
Urdu.		*Punjabi.*		*Persian.*		*Arabic.*		*English.*		*Houses.*		*Chhappar.*		*Kizhdi.*		*Both (Houses and Kizhdis).*	
Males.	Females.	Males.	Females.	Males.	Females.	Males.	Females.	Males.	Females.	Males.	Females.	Males.	Females.	Males.	Females.	Males.	Females.
14	15	16	17	18	19	20	21	22	23	24	25	26	27	28	29	30	31
2	..	1	..	..	..	..	..	..	..	32	9	..	..	..	..	..	..
2	..	1	..	..	..	..	..	..	..	22	9	..	..	..	..	..	..
..	..	..	..	..	..	..	..	..	..	..	..	..	..	..	..	..	..
..	..	..	..	..	..	..	..	..	..	9	..	..	..	..	..	..	..
..	..	..	..	..	..	..	..	..	..	..	..	..	..	..	..	..	..
..	..	..	..	..	..	..	..	..	..	1	..	..	..	..	..	..	..
9	..	..	..	6	2	6	..	..	..	182	147	..	..	584	417	2,665	2,202
9	..	..	..	6	2	3	..	..	..	140	122	..	..	534	417	2,622	2,174
..	..	..	..	..	..	..	..	..	..	3	1	..	..	..	..	14	12
..	..	..	..	..	..	..	..	..	..	..	..	..	..	..	..	..	..
..	..	..	..	..	..	..	..	..	..	..	..	..	..	..	..	..	..
..	..	..	..	2	2	..	..	..	..	3	4	..	..	..	..	4	2
9	..	..	..	3	..	3	..	..	..	116	100	..	..	491	389	2,301	1,925
..	..	..	..	1	..	..	..	..	..	18	17	..	..	43	28	303	235
..	..	..	..	..	..	3	..	..	..	36	22	..	..	..	..	34	22
..	..	..	..	..	..	3	..	..	..	18	4	..	..	..	..	32	22
..	..	..	..	..	..	..	..	..	..	18	17	..	..	..	..	2	..
..	..	..	..	..	..	..	..	..	..	..	..	..	..	..	..	..	..
..	..	..	..	..	..	..	..	..	..	..	1	..	..	..	..	..	..
..	..	..	..	..	..	..	..	..	..	6	3	..	..	..	..	9	6
..	..	..	..	..	..	..	..	..	..	5	3	..	..	..	..	9	6
..	..	..	..	..	..	..	..	..	..	..	..	..	..	..	..	..	..
..	..	..	..	..	..	..	..	..	..	..	..	..	..	..	..	..	..
..	..	..	..	..	..	..	..	..	..	1	..	..	..	..	..	..	..
13	1	13	6	..	..	..	..	1	..	8,020	7,236	98	89	1,777	1,402	797	705
13	1	11	1	..	..	..	..	..	..	7,636	6,986	90	80	1,536	1,232	515	512
13	1	11	1	..	..	..	..	..	..	6,998	6,448	84	74	1,424	1,140	464	468
..	..	..	..	..	..	..	..	..	..	..	..	..	..	..	..	..	..
..	..	..	..	..	..	..	..	..	..	..	..	..	..	..	..	..	..
..	..	..	..	..	..	..	..	..	..	..	..	..	..	3	2	..	..
..	..	..	..	..	..	..	..	..	..	29	27	..	..	9	10	5	5
..	..	..	..	..	..	..	..	..	..	..	..	..	..	..	..	..	..
..	..	..	..	..	..	..	..	..	..	..	..	..	..	..	..	..	..
..	..	..	..	..	..	..	..	..	..	270	223	6	6	100	80	46	39
..	..	..	..	..	..	..	..	..	..	6	5	..	..	..	..	..	..
..	..	..	..	..	..	..	..	..	..	333	283	..	..	..	..	..	..
2	..	1	..	..	..	..	..	..	..	133	110	..	..	94	73	158	90
..	..	..	..	..	..	..	..	..	..	14	5	..	..	..	..	54	24
..	..	..	..	..	..	..	..	..	..	..	..	..	..	..	..	..	..
2	..	1	..	..	..	..	..	..	..	119	105	..	..	94	73	104	66
..	..	..	..	..	..	..	..	..	..	..	..	..	..	..	..	..	..
3	..	6	5	..	..	..	..	1	..	251	140	8	9	147	97	124	103
..	..	..	..	..	..	..	..	..	..	198	139	8	9	147	97	124	103
1	..	6	5	..	..	..	..	..	..	..	..	..	..	..	..	..	..
2	..	..	..	..	..	..	..	..	..	..	..	..	..	..	..	..	..
..	..	..	..	..	..	..	..	..	..	..	..	..	..	..	..	..	..
..	..	..	..	..	..	..	..	..	..	50	..	..	..	..	..	..	..
..	..	..	..	..	..	..	..	1	..	2	1	..	..	..	..	..	..
..	..	..	..	..	..	..	..	..	..	1	..	..	..	..	..	..	..
8	..	2	..	11	..	2	..	..	..	7,905	6,758	..	..	1,129	930	3,170	2,797
7	..	2	..	10	..	2	..	..	..	7,651	6,563	..	..	784	666	2,754	2,406
..	..	..	..	..	..	..	..	..	..	53	36	..	..	12	5	98	79
1	..	..	..	..	..	..	..	..	..	..	..	..	..	..	..	..	..
4	..	2	..	7	..	2	..	..	..	7,393	6,321	..	..	772	661	2,566	2,241
..	..	..	..	..	..	..	..	..	..	..	..	..	..	..	..	..	..
..	..	..	..	..	..	..	..	..	..	5	11	..	..	..	..	..	..
..	..	..	..	..	..	..	..	..	..	..	..	..	..	..	..	..	..
1	..	..	..	3	..	..	..	..	..	195	191	..	..	..	..	90	86
..	..	..	..	..	..	..	..	..	..	..	..	..	..	..	..	..	..
..	..	..	..	..	..	..	..	..	..	..	..	..	..	..	..	..	..
..	..	..	..	..	..	..	..	..	..	..	..	..	..	..	..	..	..
1	..	..	..	..	..	..	..	..	..	4	4	..	..	..	..	..	..
..	..	..	..	..	..	..	..	..	..	1	..	..	..	..	..	..	..

Race.	Total Population. Total.	Males.	Females.	Mother Tongue. Language.	Number of Speakers. Males.	Females.	Other — Balochi. Males.	Females.	Pashto. Males.	Females.	Brahui. Males.	Females.
1	2	3	4	5	6	7	8	9	10	11	12	13
B.—Semi-Indigenous ..	**1,464**	**784**	**680**	..	**784**	**680**	..	..	**80**	**17**	..	..
1. Baloch ..	43	19	24	Balochi ..	19	24	..	..	..	..	..	..
2. Pathan ..	478	270	208	Pashto ..	270	208	..	..	..	..	..	..
3. Baloch ..	943	495	448	Balochi ..	485	436	..	..	80	17	..	..
				Pashto ..	10	12	..	..	..	..	..	..
C.—Alien ..	**401**	**231**	**170**	..	**281**	**170**	**34**	..	**52**	**1**	..	..
1. Muslim ..	321	188	133	Balochi ..	154	109	..	..	..	..	..	..
				Pashto ..	3	5	..	..	..	..	..	..
				Jafirki ..	11	7	1	..	1	1	..	..
				Jatki ..	1	1	1	..	..	..	..	..
				Punjabi ..	19	11	2	..	6	..	..	..
2. Hindu ..	80	43	37	Punjabi ..	43	37	30	..	45	..	..	..
III.—Zhob District ..	**48,345**	**26,309**	**22,036**	..	**26,309**	**22,036**	..	3	8	1	..	..
Fort Sandeman Tahsil ..	**25,754**	**13,896**	**11,858**	..	**13,896**	**11,858**	..	..	2	..	..	..
A.—Indigenous ..	**25,549**	**13,779**	**11,770**	..	**13,779**	**11,770**	..	..	..	..	..	..
1. Baloch ..	26	15	11	Balochi ..	5	7	..	..	..	..	..	..
				Pashto ..	10	4	..	..	..	..	..	..
2. Pathan ..	24,580	13,260	11,320	Pashto ..	13,260	11,320	..	..	..	..	..	..
3. Sayyid ..	881	470	411	Pashto ..	470	411	..	..	..	..	..	..
4. Other Muslim	61	33	28	Pashto ..	33	28	..	..	..	..	..	..
5. Jatt ..	1	1	..	Pashto .	1	..	..	..	..	..	..	..
B.—Semi-Indigenous ..	**193**	**111**	**82**	..	**111**	**82**	..	..	2	..	..	..
1. Pathan ..	169	95	74	Pashto ..	94	74	..	..	..	..	..	..
				Persian ..	1	..	..	..	..	..	..	..
2. Other Muslim ..	2	2	..	Persian ..	2	..	..	..	2	..	..	..
3. Baloch ..	22	14	8	Balochi ..	14	8	..	..	..	..	..	..
C.—Alien ..	**12**	**6**	**6**	..	**6**	**6**	..	..	..	..	..	..
1. Muslim ..	9	3	6	Punjabi .	3	6	..	..	..	..	..	..
2. Hindu ..	2	2	..	Punjabi ..	2	..	..	..	..	..	..	..
3. Christian ..	1	1	..	Punjabi ..	1	..	..	..	..	..	..	..
Hindubagh Tahsil ..	**10,112**	**5,433**	**4,679**	..	**5,433**	**4,679**	..	3	1	..	..	..
A.—Indigenous ..	**10,068**	**5,398**	**4,670**	..	**5,398**	**4,670**	..	3	..	..	..	..
1. Pathan ..	9,980	5,347	4,633	Pashto ..	5,347	4,633	..	3	..	..	..	..
2. Sayyid ..	88	51	37	Pashto ..	51	37	..	..	..	..	..	..
B.—Semi-Indigenous ..	**41**	**32**	**9**	Pashto ..	**32**	**9**	..	..	..	..	..	..
1. Pathan ..	41	32	9	Pashto ..	32	9	..	..	..	..	..	..
C.—Alien ..	**3**	**3**	..	..	**3**	..	..	..	..	..	..	..
2. Muslim ..	3	3	..	Urdu ..	1	..	..	..	..	..	..	..
				Punjabi ..	2	..	..	..	..	..	..	..
Killa Saifulla Tahsil ..	**12,479**	**6,980**	**5,499**	..	**6,980**	**5,499**	..	..	6	1	..	..
A.—Indigenous ..	**12,315**	**6,863**	**5,452**	..	**6,863**	**5,452**	..	..	1	..	..	..
1. Baloch ..	2	1	1	Balochi ..	1	1	..	..	1	..	..	..
2. Pathan ..	12,241	6,824	5,417	Pashto ..	6,824	5,417	..	..	..	..	..	..
3. Sayyid ..	70	36	34	Pashto ..	36	34	..	..	..	..	..	..
4. Other Muslim ..	2	2	..	Pashto ..	2	..	..	..	..	..	..	..
B.—Semi-Indigenous ..	**151**	**107**	**44**	..	**107**	**44**	..	..	1	1	..	..
1. Pathan ..	147	104	43	Pashto ..	104	43	..	..	..	..	..	..
2. Other Muslim ..	4	3	1	Persian ..	3	1	..	..	1	1	..	..
C.—Alien ..	**13**	**10**	**3**	..	**10**	**3**	..	..	4	..	..	..
1. Muslim ..	5	5	..	Punjabi ..	5	..	..	..	3	..	..	..
2. Hindu ..	8	5	3	Pashto ..	2	..	..	..	..	..	..	..
				Urdu ..	2	3	..	..	..	..	..	..
				Punjabi ..	1	..	..	..	1	..	..	..

Nomadism.

Languages.										Occupied.							
Urdu.		*Punjabi.*		*Persian.*		*Arabic.*		*English.*		*Houses.*		*Chhappar.*		*Kizhdi.*		*Both (Houses and Kizhdis).*	
Males.	Females.	Males.	Females.	Males.	Females.	Males.	Females.	Males.	Females.	Males.	Females.	Males.	Females.	Males.	Females.	Males.	Females.
14	15	16	17	18	19	20	21	22	23	24	25	26	27	28	29	30	31
..	..	..	..	1	..	..	..	..	..	82	62	..	..	302	238	400	380
..		..	..	..	..	..	..	..	..	..	..	..	..	..	..	19	24
..	..	..	..	..	..	..	..	..	..	3	2	..	..	266	206	1	..
..	..	..	..	1	..	..	..	..	..	79	60	..	..	36	32	380	356
..	..	..	..	..	..	..	..	..	..	..	..	..	..	..	..	..	..
1	..	..	..	..	..	..	..	..	..	172	133	..	..	43	26	16	11
..	..	..	..	..	..	..	..	..	..	129	96	..	..	43	26	16	11
..	..	..	..	..	..	..	..	..	..	..	..	..	..	..	..	..	..
..	..	..	..	..	..	..	..	..	..	..	..	..	..	..	..	..	..
..	..	..	..	..	..	..	..	..	..	..	..	..	..	..	..	..	..
1	..	..	..	..	..	..	..	..	..	..	..	..	..	..	..	..	..
..	..	..	..	..	..	..	..	..	..	43	37	..	..	..	..	..	..
40	4	141	2	71	1	9	1	3	..	2,806	2,466	2	..	1,674	1,340	21,827	18,280
15	..	12	..	45	1	8	1	3	..	2,206	1,999	2	..	548	436	11,140	9,428
13	..	12	..	45	1	8	1	2	..	2,194	1,992	..	..	548	436	11,087	9,342
..	..	..	..	..	..	..	..	..	..	4	4	..	..	..	..	11	7
..	..	..	..	..	..	..	..	..	..	..	..	..	..	..	..	..	..
11	..	12	..	42	1	8	1	2	..	2,169	1,971	..	..	522	421	10,569	8,928
2	..	..	..	3	..	..	..	..	..	12	10	..	..	26	15	432	386
..	..	..	..	..	..	..	..	..	..	8	7	..	..	..	..	25	21
..	..	..	..	..	..	..	..	..	..	1	..	..	..	..	..	..	..
..	..	..	..	..	..	..	..	..	..	6	1	2	..	..	..	103	81
..	..	..	..	..	..	..	..	..	..	4	1	2	..	..	..	89	73
..	..	..	..	..	..	..	..	..	..	..	..	..	..	..	..	..	..
..	..	..	..	..	..	..	..	..	..	2	..	..	..	..	..	..	..
..	..	..	..	..	..	..	..	..	..	..	..	..	..	..	..	14	8
2	..	..	..	..	..	..	..	1	..	6	6	..	..	..	..	..	..
..	..	..	..	..	..	..	..	1	..	3	6	..	..	..	..	..	..
2	..	..	..	..	..	..	..	..	..	2	..	..	..	..	..	..	..
..	..	..	..	..	..	..	..	..	..	1	..	..	..	..	..	..	..
13	3	127	2	21	..	..	..	..	..	516	392	..	..	408	323	4,509	3,964
13	3	..	..	21	..	1	..	..	..	502	385	..	..	395	322	4,501	3,963
13	3	127	2	21	..	1	..	..	..	500	385	..	..	395	322	4,452	3,926
..	..	..	..	..	..	..	..	..	..	2	..	..	..	..	..	49	37
..	..	..	..	..	..	..	..	..	..	13	7	..	..	13	1	6	1
..	..	..	..	..	..	..	..	..	..	13	7	..	..	13	1	6	1
..	..	..	..	..	..	..	..	..	..	1	..	..	..	..	..	2	..
..	..	..	..	..	..	..	..	..	..	1	..	..	..	..	..	2	..
..	..	..	..	..	..	..	..	..	..	..	..	..	..	..	..	..	..
13	1	2	..	5	..	..	..	..	..	84	75	..	..	718	581	6,178	4,843
11	..	2	..	5	..	..	..	..	..	69	70	..	..	712	578	6,082	4,804
1	..	..	..	..	..	..	..	..	..	1	1	..	..	..	..	..	..
10	..	..	..	4	..	..	..	..	..	68	69	..	..	712	578	6,044	4,770
..	..	1	..	..	..	..	..	..	..	..	..	..	..	..	..	36	34
..	..	1	..	1	..	..	..	..	..	..	..	..	..	..	..	2	..
2	1	..	..	..	..	..	..	..	..	5	2	..	..	6	3	96	39
1	..	..	..	..	..	..	..	..	..	2	1	..	..	6	3	96	39
1	1	..	..	..	..	..	..	..	..	3	1	..	..	..	..	..	..
..	..	..	..	..	..	..	..	..	..	10	8	..	..	..	..	..	..
..	..	..	..	..	..	..	..	..	..	5	..	..	..	..	..	..	..
..	..	..	..	..	..	..	..	..	..	5	3	..	..	..	..	..	..
..	..	..	..	..	..	..	..	..	..	..	..	..	..	..	..	..	..
..	..	..	..	..	..	..	..	..	..	..	..	..	..	..	..	..	..

Race.	Total Population.			Mother Tongue.			Other					
				Language.	Number of Speakers.		Balochi.		Pashto.		Brahui.	
	Total.	Males.	Females.		Males.	Females.	Males.	Females.	Males.	Females.	Males.	Females.
1	2	3	4	5	6	7	8	9	10	11	12	13
IV.—Bolan District ..	**514**	**296**	**218**	..	**296**	**218**	**77**	**50**	..	..	**212**	**162**
A.—Indigenous ..	**488**	**279**	**209**	..	**279**	**209**	**70**	**47**	..	..	**200**	**153**
1. Baloch ..	224	124	100	Balochi ..	122	100	..	..	..	..	122	99
				Brahui ..	2	..	2	..	..	..	..	..
2. Brahui ..	223	127	96	Balochi ..	62	44	..	..	..	..	61	43
				Brahui ..	65	52	65	47	..	..	..	..
3. Pathan ..	1	1	..	Pashto ..	1	..	1	..	..	..	..	..
4. Other Muslim ..	40	27	13	Balochi ..	25	13	..	..	..	..	17	11
				Brahui ..	2	..	2	..	..	..	..	..
B.—Semi-Indigenous ..	**1**	**1**	..	..	**1**	..	..	..	..	—	..	..
1. Pathan ..	1	1	..	Pashto ..	1	..	1	..	..	..	..	..
C.—Alien ..	**25**	**16**	**9**	..	**16**	**9**	..	..	..	..	**12**	**9**
1. Muslim ..	15	8	7	Balochi ..	7	6	..	..	..	..	7	6
				Punjabi ..	1	1	1	1	..	..	1	1
2. Hindu ..	10	8	2	Jatki Sindhi ..	4	1	4	1	..	..	3	1
				Urdu ..	2	..	1	..	..	..	..	..
				Punjabi ..	2	1	..	..	..	..	1	1
V.—Chagai District ..	**19,516**	**10,573**	**8,943**	..	**10,573**	**8,943**	**1,690**	**1,124**	**328**	**228**	**2,340**	**1,897**
Nushki Tahsil ..	**9,154**	**4,908**	**4,246**	..	**4,908**	**4,246**	**1,162**	**717**	**79**	**18**	**1,529**	**1,307**
A.—Indigenous ..	**9,021**	**4,840**	**4,181**	..	**4,840**	**4,181**	**1,142**	**702**	**79**	**18**	**1,510**	**1,290**
1. Baloch ..	3,347	1,811	1,536	Balochi ..	1,801	1,521	..	..	5	..	1,158	998
				Brahui ..	10	15	8	10	..	..	..	..
2. Brahui ..	4,883	2,635	2,248	Balochi ..	145	121	..	..	..	..	134	115
				Brahui ..	2,490	2,127	1,042	651	74	13	..	..
3. Pathan ..	198	97	101	Pashto ..	85	94	47	19	..	..	71	65
				Brahui ..	12	7	1	..	..	..	..	..
4. Sayyid ..	248	129	119	Balochi ..	97	70	..	..	..	..	60	45
				Pashto ..	8	4	2	..	..	..	1	..
				Brahui ..	24	45	24	11	..	..	..	..
5. Other Muslim ..	345	168	177	Balochi ..	140	157	..	..	..	..	86	67
				Brahui ..	20	13	12	6	..	..	..	..
				Persian ..	8	7	6	5	..	..	..	..
B.—Semi-Indigenous ..	**30**	**18**	**17**	..	**13**	**17**	**16**	**11**	..	..	**19**	**17**
1. Pathan ..	30	13	17	Pashto ..	10	16	16	11	..	..	19	17
				Persian ..	3	1	..	..	..	..	..	..
C.—Alien ..	**103**	**55**	**48**	..	**55**	**48**	**4**	**4**	..	..	..	..
1. Muslim ..	101	54	47	Jatki Sindhi ..	52	44	1	1	..	..	..	..
				Persian ..	2	3	2	3	..	..	..	..
2. Hindu ..	2	1	1	Sindhi ..	1	1	1	..	..	..	..	..
Dalbandin Tahsil (Including Western Sanjrani).	**8,251**	**4,423**	**3,828**	..	**4,428**	**3,828**	**528**	**407**	**42**	**18**	**513**	**336**
A.—Indigenous ..	**8,112**	**4,354**	**3,758**	..	**4,354**	**3,758**	**523**	**398**	**38**	**18**	**488**	**318**
1. Baloch ..	3,525	1,905	1,620	Balochi ..	1,803	1,539	..	..	21	10	197	131
				Pashto ..	2	1	..	—	..	..	..	..
				Brahui ..	100	80	37	23	..	..	..	..
2. Brahui ..	3,432	1,853	1,579	Balochi ..	869	758	—	—	6	..	119	68
				Pashto ..	5	4	4	2	..	—	..	..
				Brahui ..	979	817	454	351	3	7	..	..
3. Pathan ..	290	146	144	Balochi ..	96	85	..	..	..	..	48	34
				Pashto ..	50	57	13	11	..	..	22	25
				Persian ..	...	2	..	2	..	..	..	..
4. Sayyid ..	463	254	209	Balochi ..	248	202	..	..	..	..	50	32
				Pashto ..	4	6	3	1	..	..	2	1
				Brahui ..	2	1	1	..	..	..	..	..
5. Other Muslim ..	402	196	206	Balochi ..	183	191	..	..	2	—	50	27
				Brahui ..	13	15	11	8	6	6	..	..
B.—Semi-Indigenous ..	**74**	**38**	**36**	..	**38**	**36**	**2**	**1**	**4**	..	**13**	**8**
1. Pathan ..	72	36	36	Balochi ..	22	22	..	..	2	..	6	..
				Pashto ..	14	14	2	1	—	..	7	6
2. Other Muslim ..	2	2	..	Persian ..	2	..	..	..	2	..	..	..
C.—Alien ..	**65**	**31**	**34**	..	**31**	**34**	**3**	**8**	..	..	**12**	**11**
1. Muslim ..	65	31	34	Balochi ..	25	25	..	..	..	..	12	11
				Punjabi ..	3	8	3	8	..	..	..	..
				Jatki Sindhi ..	3	1	..	..	..	..	..	..

Nomadism.

Languages.										Occupied.							
Urdu.		*Punjabi.*		*Persian.*		*Arabic.*		*English.*		*Houses.*		*Chhappar.*		*Kizhdi.*		*Both (Houses and Kizhdis).*	
Males.	Females.	Males.	Females.	Males.	Females.	Males.	Females.	Males.	Females.	Males.	Females.	Males.	Females.	Males.	Females.	Males.	Females.
14	15	16	17	18	19	20	21	22	23	24	25	26	27	28	29	30	31
..	..	..	..	..	..	..	..	..	..	253	175	..	..	40	39	3	4
..	..	..	..	..	..	..	..	..	..	236	166	..	..	40	39	3	4
..	..	..	..	..	..	..	..	..	..	124	100	..	..	..	..	..	..
..	..	..	..	..	..	..	..	..	..	..	..	..	..	..	..	..	..
..	..	..	..	..	..	..	..	..	..	84	53	..	..	40	39	3	4
..	..	..	..	..	..	..	..	..	..	..	..	..	..	..	..	..	..
..	..	..	..	..	..	..	..	..	..	1	..	..	..	..	..	..	..
..	..	..	..	..	..	..	..	..	..	27	13	..	..	..	..	..	..
..	..	..	..	..	..	..	..	..	..	..	..	..	..	..	..	..	..
..	..	..	..	..	..	..	..	..	..	1	..	..	..	..	..	..	..
..	..	..	..	..	..	..	..	..	..	1	..	..	..	..	..	..	..
2	1	..	..	..	..	..	..	..	..	16	9	..	..	..	..	..	..
..	..	..	..	..	..	..	..	..	..	8	7	..	..	..	..	..	..
..	..	..	..	..	..	..	..	..	..	..	..	..	..	..	..	..	..
..	..	..	..	..	..	..	..	..	..	8	2	..	..	..	..	..	..
..	..	..	..	..	..	..	..	..	..	..	..	..	..	..	..	..	..
2	1	..	..	..	..	..	..	..	..	..	..	..	..	..	..	..	..
187	50	9	..	38	16	..	..	..	..	1,252	1,102	1,706	1,481	3,249	2,883	4,366	3,527
48	5	..	..	17	1	..	..	..	..	431	359	1,363	1,119	195	163	2,919	2,605
48	5	..	..	17	1	..	..	..	..	414	343	1,350	1,112	195	163	2,881	2,563
10	5	..	..	6	1	..	..	..	..	176	152	692	559	6	4	937	821
..	..	..	..	..	..	..	..	..	..	190	138	502	396	189	159	1,754	1,555
..	..	..	..	..	..	..	..	..	..	..	..	..	..	..	..	..	..
37	..	..	..	9	..	..	..	..	..	23	29	32	32	..	..	42	40
1	..	..	..	..	..	..	..	..	..	..	..	..	..	..	..	..	..
..	..	..	..	2	..	..	..	..	..	15	14	51	49	..	..	63	56
..	..	..	..	..	..	..	..	..	..	..	..	..	..	..	..	..	..
..	..	..	..	..	..	..	..	..	..	..	..	..	..	..	..	..	..
..	..	..	..	..	..	..	..	..	..	10	10	73	76	..	..	85	91
..	..	..	..	..	..	..	..	..	..	..	..	..	..	..	..	..	..
..	..	..	..	..	..	..	..	..	..	..	..	..	..	..	..	..	..
..	..	..	..	..	..	..	..	..	..	12	13	..	..	..	..	1	4
..	..	..	..	..	..	..	..	..	..	12	13	..	..	..	..	1	4
..	..	..	..	..	..	..	..	..	..	..	..	..	..	..	..	..	..
..	..	..	..	..	..	..	..	..	..	5	3	13	7	..	..	37	38
..	..	..	..	..	..	..	..	..	..	4	2	13	7	..	..	37	38
..	..	..	..	..	..	..	..	..	..	..	..	..	..	..	..	..	..
..	..	..	..	..	..	..	..	..	..	1	1	..	..	..	..	..	..
137	45	9	..	21	15	..	..	..	..	175	183	343	312	3,054	2,720	851	613
131	45	9	..	21	15	..	..	..	..	166	174	343	312	3,002	2,670	843	602
53	15	3	..	9	6	..	..	..	..	124	132	106	119	1,519	1,252	156	117
..	..	..	..	..	..	..	..	..	..	..	..	..	..	..	..	..	..
17	..	5	..	1	..	..	..	..	..	7	5	233	190	977	946	636	438
1	1	..	..	..	..	..	..	..	..	..	..	..	..	..	..	..	..
13	7	1	..	..	..	..	..	..	..	..	..	..	..	..	..	..	..
3	4	..	..	..	..	..	..	..	..	12	15	..	..	123	114	11	15
1	..	..	..	3	3	..	..	..	..	..	..	..	..	..	..	..	..
..	..	..	..	..	..	..	..	..	..	..	..	..	..	..	..	..	..
5	2	..	..	..	..	..	..	..	..	15	12	4	3	201	168	34	26
2	1	..	..	..	..	..	..	..	..	..	..	..	..	..	..	..	..
..	..	..	..	..	..	..	..	..	..	..	..	..	..	..	..	..	..
29	9	..	..	2	..	..	..	..	..	8	10	..	..	182	190	6	6
7	6	..	..	6	6	..	..	..	..	..	..	..	..	..	..	..	..
6	..	..	..	..	..	..	..	..	..	4	5	..	..	26	20	8	11
4	..	..	..	..	..	..	..	..	..	4	5	..	..	24	20	8	11
..	..	..	..	..	..	..	..	..	..	..	..	..	..	..	..	..	..
2	..	..	..	..	..	..	..	..	..	..	..	..	..	2	..	..	..
..	..	..	..	..	..	..	..	..	..	5	4	..	..	26	30	..	..
..	..	..	..	..	..	..	..	..	..	5	4	..	..	26	30	..	..
..	..	..	..	..	..	..	..	..	..	..	..	..	..	..	..	..	..
..	..	..	..	..	..	..	..	..	..	..	..	..	..	..	..	..	..

Race.	Total Population.			Mother Tongue.			Other					
				Language.	Number of Speakers.		Balochi.		Pashto.		Brahui.	
	Total.	Males.	Females.		Males.	Females.	Males.	Females.	Males.	Females.	Males.	Females.
1	2	3	4	5	6	7	8	9	10	11	12	13
Shorarud Sub-Tahsil ..	**2,111**	**1,242**	**869**	..	**1,242**	**869**	..	..	**205**	**197**	**298**	**255**
A.—Indigenous ..	**1,252**	**669**	**583**	..	**669**	**583**	..	..	**205**	**197**	**282**	**241**
1. BALOCH ..	1	1	..	Balochi ..	1	..	..	..	1	..	..	..
2. BRAHUI ..	468	237	231	Brahui ..	237	231	..	..	201	194	..	..
3. PATHAN ..	15	9	6	Pashto ..	9	6	..	..	..	..	..	..
4. SAYYID ..	749	412	337	Pashto ..	412	337	..	..	..	..	282	241
5. OTHER MUSLIM ..	19	10	9	Balochi ..	7	6	..	..	..	..	..	..
				Brahui ..	3	3	..	..	3	3	..	..
B.—Semi-Indigenous ..	**859**	**573**	**286**	..	**573**	**286**	..	..	**16**	**14**	..	..
1. PATHAN ..	859	573	286	Pashto ..	573	286	..	..	16	14	..	..
VI.—Sibi District ..	**129,757**	**70,988**	**58,769**	..	**70,988**	**58,769**	**1,762**	**621**	**739**	**201**	**161**	**85**
Sibi Tahsil ..	**17,742**	**9,535**	**8,207**	..	**9,535**	**8,207**	**579**	**161**	**275**	**120**	**140**	**70**
A.—Indigenous ..	**16,221**	**8,724**	**7,497**	..	**8,724**	**7,497**	**575**	**156**	**234**	**95**	**140**	**70**
1. BALOCH ..	4,199	2,266	1,933	Balochi ..	1,522	1,431	..	..	2	2	1	..
				Pashto ..	4	5	..	..	..	..	..	..
				Khetrani ..	48	44	..	..	36	31	..	..
				Saraiki ..	17	15	11	10	..	..	2	2
				Jatki Sindhi ..	646	415	83	22	27	17	4	3
				Brahui ..	29	23	1	1	..	..	..	..
2. BRAHUI ..	1,602	889	713	Balochi ..	31	30	..	..	..	..	..	..
				Pashto ..	35	27	11	4	..	..	2	..
				Jatki Sindhi ..	160	121	116	70	..	..	..	..
				Brahui ..	663	535	40	16	9	3	..	..
3. PATHAN ..	5,257	2,765	2,492	Balochi ..	2	1	..	..	..	..	..	..
				Pashto ..	1,271	1,112	50	33	..	..	12	6
				Jatki Sindhi ..	1,492	1,379	263	..	11	8	2	1
4. JATT ..	4,059	2,255	1,804	Balochi ..	126	121	..	..	..	..	..	..
				Saraiki ..	298	200	..	..	..	..	..	..
				Jatki Sindhi ..	1,773	1,439	..	..	62	34	117	58
				Brahui ..	58	44	..	..	..	..	..	..
5. SAYYID ..	325	171	154	Pashto ..	60	55	..	..	..	..	..	..
				Jatki Sindhi ..	111	99	..	..	..	..	..	..
6. OTHER MUSLIM ..	63	43	20	Balochi ..	10	5	..	..	..	..	..	..
				Pashto ..	5	2	..	..	..	..	..	..
				Jatki Sindhi ..	28	18	..	..	..	..	..	..
7. HINDU ..	716	335	381	Jatki Sindhi ..	335	381	..	..	87	..	..	..
B.—Semi-Indigenous ..	**855**	**449**	**406**	..	**449**	**406**	..	..	**1**	..	..	..
1. PATHAN ..	854	448	406	Pashto ..	443	403	..	..	..	..	..	..
				Jatki Sindhi ..	5	3	..	..	1	..	..	..
2. OTHER MUSLIM .	1	1	..	Persian ..	1	..	..	..	..	..	..	..
C.—Alien ..	**665**	**362**	**304**	..	**362**	**304**	**4**	**5**	**40**	**25**	..	..
1. MUSLIM ..	642	344	298	Jatki Sindhi ..	338	238	4	4	40	25	..	..
				Punjabi ..	6	10	..	..	..	..	..	..
2. HINDU ..	14	11	3	Urdu ..	2	..	..	..	..	..	..	..
				Punjabi ..	9	3	..	1	..	..	..	..
3. SIKH ..	10	7	3	Punjabi ..	7	3	..	..	..	..	..	..
Shahrig Tahsil ..	**16,137**	**8,629**	**7,508**	..	**8,629**	**7,508**	**1**	..	**275**	**11**	**15**	**11**
A.—Indigenous ..	**15,677**	**8,366**	**7,311**	..	**8,366**	**7,311**	**1**	..	**271**	**11**	**15**	**11**
1. BALOCH ..	2,195	1,243	952	Balochi ..	1,211	926	..	..	243	..	..	..
				Pashto ..	32	26	1	..	..	..	..	..
2. BRAHUI ..	38	20	18	Pashto ..	10	13	..	..	..	..	..	..
				Brahui ..	10	5	..	..	3	..	..	..
3. PATHAN ..	11,754	6,186	5,568	Pashto ..	6,186	5,568	..	..	..	..	..	..
4. JATT ..	35	18	18	Pashto ..	18	18	..	..	..	..	..	..
5. SAYYID ..	1,580	851	729	Pashto ..	851	729	..	..	..	..	..	..
6. OTHER MUSLIM ..	74	48	26	Balochi ..	17	5	..	..	10	..	..	..
				Lori Chini ..	31	21	..	..	15	11	15	11
B.—Semi-Indigenous ..	**453**	**257**	**196**	..	**257**	**196**	..	..	..	..	..	..
1. PATHAN ..	453	257	196	Pashto ..	257	196	..	..	..	..	..	..
C.—Alien ..	**7**	**6**	**1**	..	**6**	**1**	..	..	**4**	..	..	..
1. MUSLIM ..	2	1	1	Punjabi ..	1	1	..	..	..	..	..	..
2. HINDU ..	5	5	..	Jatki Sindhi ..	5	..	..	..	4	..	..	..

Nomadism.

Languages.										Occupied.							
Urdu.		*Punjabi.*		*Persian.*		*Arabic.*		*English.*		*Houses.*		*Chhappar.*		*Kizhdi.*		*Both (Houses and Kizhdis).*	
Males.	Females.	Males.	Females.	Males.	Females.	Males.	Females.	Males.	Females.	Males.	Females.	Males.	Females.	Males.	Females.	Males.	Females.
14	15	16	17	18	19	20	21	22	23	24	25	26	27	28	29	30	31
..	..	..	..	..	..	..	..	..	..	646	560	..	..	..	..	596	309
..	..	..	..	..	..	..	..	..	..	618	540	..	..	..	..	51	43
..	..	..	..	..	..	..	..	..	..	1	..	..	..	..	..	..	..
..	..	..	..	..	..	..	..	..	..	186	188	..	..	..	..	51	43
..	..	..	..	..	..	..	..	..	..	9	6	..	..	..	..	..	..
..	..	..	..	..	..	..	..	..	..	412	337	..	..	..	..	..	..
..	..	..	..	..	..	..	..	..	..	10	9	..	..	..	..	..	..
..	..	..	..	..	..	..	..	..	..	..	..	..	..	..	..	..	..
..	..	..	..	..	..	..	..	..	..	23	20	..	..	..	..	545	266
..	..	..	..	..	..	..	..	..	..	28	20	..	..	..	..	545	266
22	..	1	..	1	..	2	..	6	3	18,783	16,488	12,595	10,653	34,960	28,151	4,350	3,527
26	..	..	..	..	..	..	..	6	..	8,086	7,073	..	..	1,274	986	175	148
19	..	..	..	..	..	..	..	5	..	7,713	6,766	..	..	881	588	175	148
2	..	..	..	..	..	..	..	..	..	1,850	1,674	..	..	388	239	28	20
..	..	..	..	..	..	..	..	..	..	..	..	..	..	..	..	..	..
..	..	..	..	..	..	..	..	..	..	..	..	..	..	..	..	..	..
..	..	..	..	..	..	..	..	..	..	..	..	..	..	..	..	..	..
..	..	..	..	..	..	..	..	..	..	..	..	..	..	..	..	..	..
..	..	..	..	..	..	..	..	..	..	..	..	..	..	..	..	..	..
..	..	..	..	..	..	..	..	..	..	467	376	..	..	432	337	..	..
..	..	..	..	..	..	..	..	..	..	..	..	..	..	..	..	..	..
..	..	..	..	..	..	..	..	..	..	..	..	..	..	..	..	..	..
17	..	..	..	..	..	..	..	5	..	..	..	..	..	..	..	..	..
..	..	..	..	..	..	..	..	..	..	2,607	2,357	..	..	11	7	147	128
..	..	..	..	..	..	..	..	..	..	..	..	..	..	..	..	..	..
..	..	..	..	..	..	..	..	..	..	..	..	..	..	..	..	..	..
..	..	..	..	..	..	..	..	..	..	2,255	1,804	..	..	..	..	..	..
..	..	..	..	..	..	..	..	..	..	..	..	..	..	..	..	..	..
..	..	..	..	..	..	..	..	..	..	..	..	..	..	..	..	..	..
..	..	..	..	..	..	..	..	..	..	..	..	..	..	..	..	..	..
..	..	..	..	..	..	..	..	..	..	171	154	..	..	..	..	..	..
..	..	..	..	..	..	..	..	..	..	..	..	..	..	..	..	..	..
..	..	..	..	..	..	..	..	..	..	43	20	..	..	..	..	..	..
..	..	..	..	..	..	..	..	..	..	..	..	..	..	..	..	..	..
..	..	..	..	..	..	..	..	..	..	..	..	..	..	..	..	..	..
..	..	..	..	..	..	..	..	..	..	335	381	..	..	..	..	..	..
..	..	..	..	..	..	..	..	..	..	6	3	..	..	443	408	..	..
..	..	..	..	..	..	..	..	..	..	5	3	..	..	443	403	..	..
..	..	..	..	..	..	..	..	..	..	..	..	..	..	..	..	..	..
..	..	..	..	..	..	..	..	..	..	1	..	..	..	..	..	..	..
1	..	..	..	..	..	..	..	1	..	362	304	..	..	..	..	..	..
..	..	..	..	..	..	..	..	..	..	344	298	..	..	..	..	..	..
..	..	..	..	..	..	..	..	..	..	..	..	..	..	..	..	..	..
..	..	..	..	..	..	..	..	..	..	11	3	..	..	..	..	..	..
1	..	..	..	..	..	..	..	1	..	..	..	..	..	..	..	..	..
..	..	..	..	..	..	..	..	..	..	7	3	..	..	..	..	..	..
..	..	..	..	..	..	..	..	..	..	3,577	3,387	88	143	806	612	4,158	3,366
..	..	..	..	..	..	..	..	..	..	3,336	3,203	88	143	806	612	4,136	3,358
..	..	..	..	..	..	..	..	..	..	13	13	..	..	6	3	1,224	936
..	..	..	..	..	..	..	..	..	..	..	..	..	..	..	..	..	..
..	..	..	..	..	..	..	..	..	..	..	..	..	..	..	..	20	18
..	..	..	..	..	..	..	..	..	..	..	..	..	..	..	..	..	..
..	..	..	..	..	..	..	..	..	..	3,024	2,886	88	143	720	565	2,354	1,974
..	..	..	..	..	..	..	..	..	..	17	16	..	..	..	..	1	2
..	..	..	..	..	..	..	..	..	..	282	288	..	..	80	44	489	397
..	..	..	..	..	..	..	..	..	..	..	..	..	..	..	..	48	26
..	..	..	..	..	..	..	..	..	..	..	..	..	..	..	..	..	..
..	..	..	..	..	..	..	..	..	..	235	183	..	..	..	..	22	13
..	..	..	..	..	..	..	..	..	..	235	183	..	..	..	..	22	13
..	..	..	..	..	..	..	..	..	..	6	1	..	..	..	..	..	..
..	..	..	..	..	..	..	..	..	..	1	1	..	..	..	..	..	..
..	..	..	..	..	..	..	..	..	..	5	..	..	..	..	..	..	..

Race.	Total Population. Total.	Males.	Females.	Mother Tongue. Language.	Number of Speakers. Males.	Females.	Balochi. Males.	Females.	Pashto. Males.	Females.	Other… Brahui. Males.	Females.
1	2	3	4	5	6	7	8	9	10	11	12	13
Nasirabad Tahsil ..	**35,260**	**19,322**	**15,938**	..	**19,322**	**15,938**	**866**	**238**	**13**	**8**	..	.
A.—Indigenous ..	**34,081**	**18,588**	**15,493**	..	**18,588**	**15,493**	**843**	**230**	**13**	**8**	..	..
1. Baloch ..	17,390	9,385	8,005	Balochi ..	8,048	6,845	.	..	..	..	..	.
				Pashto ..	9	10	..	..	..	..	..	..
				Saraiki ..	616	575	75	10	..	..	..	..
				Jatki Sindhi ..	682	553	39	27	..	..	..	..
				Brahui ..	30	22	..	..	..	..	..	..
2. Brahui ..	4,271	2,349	1,922	Balochi ..	8	6	..	..	..	..	..	..
				Brahui ..	2,341	1,916	321	98	13	8	..	..
3. Pathan ..	188	103	85	Pashto ..	9	5	7	5	..	..	..	..
				Saraiki ..	6	4	..	..	..	..	..	..
				Jatki Sindhi ..	88	76	14	7	..	..	..	..
4. Lasi ..	31	16	15	Sindhi ..	16	15	..	..	..	..	..	..
5. Jatt ..	9,598	5,281	4,317	Jatki Sindhi ..	5,281	4,317	363	80	..	..	..	..
6. Sayyid ..	163	84	79	Balochi ..	2	2	..	..	..	..	..	..
				Saraiki ..	21	15	..	..	..	..	..	..
				Jatki Sindhi ..	61	62	2	2	..	..	..	..
7. Other Muslim ..	1,685	928	757	Balochi ..	8	4	..	..	..	..	..	..
				Saraiki ..	29	26	1	1	..	..	..	..
				Jatki Sindhi ..	891	727	1	..	..	..	..	..
8. Hindu ..	725	416	309	Jatki Sindhi ..	416	309	..	..	..	..	..	..
9. Sikhs ..	30	26	4	Jatki Sindhi ..	26	4	20	..	..	..	..	..
C.—Alien ..	**1,179**	**734**	**445**	..	**734**	**445**	**23**	**3**	..	..	..	..
1. Muslim ..	360	206	154	Saraiki ..	47	37	17	..	..	..	..	..
				Jatki Sindhi ..	98	81	4	3	..	..	..	..
				Punjabi .	61	36	2	..	..	..	..	..
2. Hindu ..	434	279	155	Saraiki ..	269	149	..	..	..	..	..	..
				Sindhi ..	10	6	..	..	..	..	..	..
3. Sikhs ..	385	249	136	Sindhi ..	249	136	..	..	..	..	..	..
Kohlu Sub-Tahsil ..	**5,394**	**2,966**	**2,428**	..	**2,966**	**2,428**	**315**	**226**	**180**	**62**	.	
A.—Indigenous ..	**5,350**	**2,939**	**2,411**	..	**2,939**	**2,411**	**312**	**222**	**178**	**59**	..	
1. Baloch ..	4,547	2,490	2,057	Balochi ..	2,379	1,940	..	..	105	7	..	
				Khetrani ..	107	113	56	57	19	7	..	..
				Brahui ..	3	4	..	..	..	..	..	..
				Sindhi ..	1	..	1	..	..	..	..	..
2. Brahui ..	62	41	21	Balochi ..	2	..	..	..	..	..	..	..
				Pashto ..	5	4	5	4	..	..	..	..
				Khetrani ..	6	3	5	3	..	..	..	..
				Brahui .	28	14	25	14	2	..	..	..
3. Pathan ..	706	392	314	Pashto ..	291	228	209	133	..	..	..	..
				Khetrani ..	101	86	..	..	49	32	..	..
4. Sayyid ..	19	10	9	Pashto ..	8	7	6	5	..	..	..	..
				Khetrani ..	2	2	1	1	1	1	..	..
5. Other Muslim ..	16	6	10	Khetrani ..	6	10	4	5	2	2	..	..
B.—Semi-Indigenous ..	**27**	**14**	**13**	..	**14**	**13**	**3**	**4**	..	..	..	..
1. Pathan ..	18	9	9	Pashto ..	9	9	2	4	..	..	..	..
2. Baloch ..	9	5	4	Balochi ..	2	3	..	..	..	..	..	..
				Khetrani ..	2	1	..	..	..	..	..	..
				Punjabi ..	1	..	1	..	..	..	..	..
C. Alien ..	**17**	**13**	**4**	..	**13**	**4**	..	..	**2**	**3**	..	..
1. Muslim ..	2	2	..	Pashto ..	1	..	..	..	..	..	..	..
				Western Punjabi ..	1	..	..	..	..	..	..	..
2. Hindu ..	15	11	4	Sindhi ..	4	4	..	..	2	3	..	..
				Punjabi ..	7	..	..	..	..	..	..	..
Mari Country ..	**24,860**	**13,880**	**10,980**	..	**13,880**	**10,980**	**40**	**34**	..	..	..	..
A.—Indigenous ..	**24,836**	**13,866**	**10,970**	..	**13,866**	**10,970**	**40**	**34**	..	..	..	..
1. Baloch ..	24,615	13,745	10,870	Balochi ..	13,745	10,870	..	..	..	..	..	..
2. Sayyid ..	80	43	37	..	43	37	..	..	..	..	..	..
3. Other Muslim ..	33	17	16	..	17	16	..	..	..	..	..	..
4. Hindu ..	108	61	47	..	61	47	38	33	..	..	..	..
B.—Semi-Indigenous ..	**3**	**2**	**1**	..	**2**	**1**	..	..	..	..	..	..
1. Pathan ..	3	2	1	Urdu ..	2	1	..	..	..	..	..	..
C.—Alien ..	**21**	**12**	**9**	..	**12**	**9**	**2**	**1**	..	..	..	..
1. Hindu ..	21	12	9	Jagdali ..	6	8	..	..	..	..	..	..
				Sindhi ..	4	1	2	1	..	..	..	..
				Urdu ..	2	..	..	..	..	..	..	..

Nomadism.

LANGUAGES.										OCCUPIED.							
Urdu.		*Punjabi*		*Persian.*		*Arabic.*		*English.*		*Houses.*		*Chhappar.*		*Kizhdi.*		*Both (Houses and Kizhdis).*	
Males.	Females.	Males.	Females.	Males.	Females.	Males.	Females.	Males.	Females.	Males.	Females.	Males.	Females.	Males.	Females.	Males.	Females.
14	15	16	17	18	19	20	21	22	23	24	25	26	27	28	29	30	31
..	..	..	..	..	..	..	..	..	..	6,140	5,143	12,801	10,502	364	280	17	13
..	..	..	..	..	..	..	..	..	..	5,721	4,916	10,486	10,284	364	280	17	13
..	..	..	..	..	..	..	..	..	..	3,300	2,030	6,066	5,057	12	12	7	6
..	..	..	..	..	..	..	..	..	..	..	..	..	..	..	..	..	..
..	..	..	..	..	..	..	..	..	..	..	..	..	..	..	..	..	..
..	..	..	..	..	..	..	..	..	..	..	..	..	..	..	..	..	..
..	..	..	..	..	..	..	..	..	..	..	..	..	..	..	..	..	..
..	..	..	..	..	..	..	..	..	..	297	247	1,838	1,487	204	181	10	7
..	..	..	..	..	..	..	..	..	..	..	..	..	..	..	..	..	..
..	..	..	..	..	..	..	..	..	..	29	23	74	62	..	..	..	..
..	..	..	..	..	..	..	..	..	..	..	..	..	..	..	..	..	..
..	..	..	..	..	..	..	..	..	..	..	..	..	..	..	..	..	..
..	..	..	..	..	..	..	..	..	..	..	..	16	15	..	..	..	..
..	..	..	..	..	..	..	..	..	..	1,451	1,223	3,682	3,007	148	87	..	..
..	..	..	..	..	..	..	..	..	..	65	63	19	16	..	..	..	..
..	..	..	..	..	..	..	..	..	..	..	..	..	..	..	..	..	..
..	..	..	..	..	..	..	..	..	..	..	..	..	..	..	..	..	..
..	..	..	..	..	..	..	..	..	..	181	151	747	606	..	..	..	..
..	..	..	..	..	..	..	..	..	..	..	..	..	..	..	..	..	..
..	..	..	..	..	..	..	..	..	..	..	..	..	..	..	..	..	..
..	..	..	..	..	..	..	..	..	..	372	275	44	34	..	..	..	..
..	..	..	..	..	..	..	..	..	..	26	4	..	..	..	..	..	..
..	..	..	..	..	..	..	..	..	..	419	227	315	218	..	..	..	..
..	..	..	..	..	..	..	..	..	..	82	54	124	100	..	..	..	..
..	..	..	..	..	..	..	..	..	..	..	..	..	..	..	..	..	..
..	..	..	..	..	..	..	..	..	..	..	..	..	..	..	..	..	..
..	..	..	..	..	..	..	..	..	..	236	127	43	28	..	..	..	..
..	..	..	..	..	..	..	..	..	..	..	..	..	..	..	..	..	..
..	..	..	..	..	..	..	..	..	..	101	46	148	90	..	..	..	..
4	2	..	3	..	1	..	..	..	..	562	473	..	..	2,404	1,955	..	..
4	..	..	1	..	1	..	..	..	..	535	456	..	..	2,404	1,955	..	..
4	..	..	1	..	..	..	..	..	..	116	120	..	..	2,374	1,937	..	..
..	..	..	..	..	..	..	..	..	..	..	..	..	..	..	..	..	..
..	..	..	..	..	..	..	..	..	..	..	..	..	..	..	..	..	..
..	..	..	..	..	1	..	..	..	..	..	..	..	..	..	..	..	..
..	..	..	..	..	..	..	..	..	..	11	3	..	..	30	18	..	..
..	..	..	..	..	..	..	..	..	..	..	..	..	..	..	..	..	..
..	..	..	..	..	..	..	..	..	..	..	..	..	..	..	..	..	..
..	..	..	..	..	..	..	..	..	..	..	..	..	..	..	..	..	..
..	..	..	..	..	..	..	..	..	..	392	314	..	..	..	..	..	..
..	..	..	..	..	..	..	..	..	..	..	..	..	..	..	..	..	..
..	..	..	..	..	..	..	..	..	..	10	9	..	..	..	..	..	..
..	..	..	..	..	..	..	..	..	..	..	..	..	..	..	..	..	..
..	..	..	..	..	..	..	..	..	..	6	10	..	..	..	..	..	..
..	2	..	..	..	..	..	..	..	..	14	13	..	..	..	..	..	..
..	2	..	..	..	..	..	..	..	..	9	9	..	..	..	..	..	..
..	..	..	..	..	..	..	..	..	..	5	4	..	..	..	..	..	..
..	..	..	..	..	..	..	..	..	..	..	..	..	..	..	..	..	..
..	..	..	..	..	..	..	..	..	..	..	..	..	..	..	..	..	..
..	2	..	..	..	..	..	..	..	..	13	4	..	..	..	..	..	..
..	..	..	..	..	..	..	..	..	..	2	..	..	..	..	..	..	..
..	..	..	..	..	..	..	..	..	..	..	..	..	..	..	..	..	..
..	..	..	..	..	..	..	..	..	..	11	4	..	..	..	..	..	..
..	2	..	..	..	..	..	..	..	..	..	..	..	..	..	..	..	..
..	..	..	..	..	..	..	..	..	..	308	258	6	8	13,566	10,714	..	..
..	..	..	..	..	..	..	..	..	..	302	256	..	..	13,564	10,714	..	..
..	..	..	..	..	..	..	..	..	..	237	203	..	..	13,508	10,667	..	..
..	..	..	..	..	..	..	..	..	..	14	14	..	..	29	23	..	..
..	..	..	..	..	..	..	..	..	..	..	..	..	..	17	16	..	..
..	..	..	..	..	..	..	..	..	..	51	39	..	..	10	8	..	..
..	..	..	..	..	..	..	..	..	..	2	1	..	..	..	..	..	..
..	..	..	..	..	..	..	..	..	..	2	1	..	..	..	..	..	..
..	..	..	..	..	..	..	..	..	..	4	1	6	8	2	..	..	..
..	..	..	..	..	..	..	..	..	..	4	1	6	8	2	..	..	..
..	..	..	..	..	..	..	..	..	..	..	..	..	..	..	..	..	..
..	..	..	..	..	..	..	..	..	..	..	..	..	..	..	..	..	..

Race.	Total Population. Total.	Males.	Females.	Mother Tongue. Language.	Number of Speakers. Males.	Females.	Other: Balochi. Males.	Females.	Pashto. Males.	Females.	Brahui. Males.	Females.
1	2	3	4	5	6	7	8	9	10	11	12	13
Bugti Country ..	**30,364**	**16,656**	**13,708**	..	**16,656**	**13,708**	..	..	..	..	..	..
A.—Indigenous ..	**29,878**	**16,387**	**13,491**	..	**16,387**	**13,491**	..	..	..	..	..	..
1. BALOCH ..	29,452	16,168	13,284	Balochi ..	16,168	13,284		..	..	..	..	..
2. PATHAN ..	1	1	..	Pashto ..	1	..	..	..	..	..	..	..
3. OTHER MUSLIM ..	261	138	123	Balochi ..	138	123	..	..	..	..	..	..
4. HINDU ..	164	80	84	Sindhi ..	80	84	..	..	..	..	..	..
B.—Semi-Indigenous ..	**2**	**2**	..	..	**2**	..	..	..	..	..	..	..
1. PATHAN ..	2	2	..	Pashto ..	2	..	..	..	..	..	..	..
C.—Alien ..	**284**	**267**	**217**	..	**267**	**217**	..	..	..	..	..	..
1. MUSLIM ..	456	252	204	Jagdali ..	252	204	..	..	..	..	..	..
2. HINDUS ..	28	15	13	Jagdali ..	12	9	..	..	..	..	..	..
				Sindhi ..	3	4	..	..	..	..	..	..
III.—DETAILS BY STATES AND THEIR DIVISIONS.	403,610	217,344	186,266	..	217,344	186,266	5,485	2,581	255	106	11,252	7,142
Kalat State ..	**340,602**	**183,849**	**156,753**	..	**183,849**	**156,753**	**3,740**	**1,441**	**258**	**106**	**10,624**	**6,676**
A.—Indigenous ..	**339,330**	**183,100**	**156,280**	..	**183,100**	**156,280**	**3,718**	**1,431**	**249**	**106**	**10,457**	**6,581**
1. BALOCH ..	106,579	57,361	49,218	Balochi ..	54,603	46,785	..	..	7	2	4,009	2,367
				Dehwari ..	110	100	..	..	..	..	87	87
				Saraiki ..	54	42	1	..	..	..	18	..
				Jatki Sindhi ..	2,381	2,108	117	19	..	..	158	5
				Brahui ..	211	182	6	5	..	..	..	..
				Sindhi ..	2	1	..	..	..	..	1	1
2. BRAHUI ..	117,230	63,468	53,792	Balochi ..	13,774	11,303	..	..	..	..	2,616	2,090
				Dehwari ..	11	6	..	..	98	50	6	2
				Saraiki ..	15	11	..	..	..	..	1	1
				Jatki Sindhi ..	722	579	7	..	5	..	42	2
				Lasi ..	16	25	..	..	..	..	..	..
				Brahui ..	48,980	41,868	1,598	813	24	..	..	..
3. PATHAN ..	1,151	618	533	Balochi ..	15	17	..	.	..	..	4	5
				Pashto ..	240	225	15	6	..	..	95	58
				Saraiki ..	1	1	..	..	1	..	1	..
				Jatki Sindhi ..	259	200	82	..	..	..	32	19
				Brahui ..	94	83	..	..	..	..	..	..
				Persian ..	9	7	4	3	..	..	..	..
4. LASI ..	881	510	371	Balochi ..	336	266	..	..	..	..	..	..
				Lasi ..	171	104	1	..	..	..	24	20
				Brahui ..	3	1	..	..	..	..	..	..
5. JATT ..	58,081	31,815	26,266	Balochi ..	446	378	..	..	..	..	67	30
				Dehwari ..	3	1	..	..	..	..	..	..
				Saraiki ..	2,196	2,065	41	21	..	..	47	21
				Jatki Sindhi ..	28,987	23,673	1,044	396	87	38	774	353
				Brahui ..	83	64	3	..	10	7	..	..
				Punjabi ..	100	85	25	14	..	..	..	..
6. SAYYID ..	3,567	1,876	1,691	Balochi ..	163	137	..	..	4	3	16	9
				Dehwari ..	139	138	..	..	4	4	5	4
				Pashto ..	63	51	..	..	..	..	4	4
				Saraiki ..	67	70	..	..	..	..	..	..
				Jatki Sindhi ..	1,107	995	81	13	6	1	96	12
				Lasi ..	1	1	..	..	..	..	1	1
				Brahui ..	289	257	..	..	..	..	..	..
				Punjabi ..	1	1	..	..	..	..	..	..
				Persian ..	46	41	6	..	3	..	7	..
7. OTHER MUSLIM ..	41,531	21,966	19,565	Balochi ..	13,910	12,867	..	..	2	1	394	441
				Dehwari ..	2,142	1,747	..	..	..	..	902	761
				Saraiki ..	70	49	..	..	..	..	..	..
				Jatki Sindhi ..	1,735	1,396	144	60	..	..	68	26
				Lori ..	12	5	..	..	..	..	5	2
				Brahui ..	3,707	3,143	88	46	..	..	..	..
				Lori Chini ..	33	26	..	..	..	..	28	20
				Persian ..	357	332	1	..	..	..	208	165
8. HINDU ..	10,316	5,480	4,836	Saraiki ..	7	1	..	..	..	..	..	..
				Jatki Sindhi ..	5,044	4,535	178	18	..	..	514	8
				Sindhi ..	429	300	243	22	..	..	107	67
9. SIKH ..	14	6	8	Jatki Sindhi ..	6	8	3	..	..	..	..	..
B.—Semi-Indigenous ..	**362**	**212**	**150**	..	**212**	**150**	**7**	**2**	**4**	..	**29**	**18**
1. PATHAN ..	323	194	129	Balochi ..	27	31	..	..	4	..	3	6
				Pashto ..	148	79	7	2	..	..	25	12
				Jatki Sindhi ..	10	9	..	..	..	..	1	..
				Brahui ..	9	10	..	..	..	..	..	..
2. BALOCH ..	39	18	21	Balochi ..	4	3	..	..	..	..	..	1
				Jatki Sindhi ..	14	18	..	..	..	..	..	..

Nomadism.

LANGUAGES.										OCCUPIED.							
Urdu.		*Punjabi.*		*Persian.*		*Arabic.*		*English.*		*Houses.*		*Chhappar.*		*Kizhdi.*		*Both (Houses and Kizhdis).*	
Males.	Females.	Males.	Females.	Males.	Females.	Males.	Females.	Males.	Females.	Males.	Females.	Males.	Females.	Males.	Females.	Males.	Females.
14	15	16	17	18	19	20	21	22	23	24	25	26	27	28	29	30	31
..	..	..	..	..	..	..	..	..	..	110	104	..	..	16,546	18,604	..	..
..	..	..	..	..	..	..	..	..	..	93	91	..	..	16,294	18,400	..	..
..	..	..	..	..	..	..	..	..	..	10	7	..	..	16,158	13,277	..	..
..	..	..	..	..	..	..	..	..	..	1	..	..	..	..	..	..	..
..	..	..	..	..	..	..	..	..	..	2	..	..	..	136	123	..	..
..	..	..	..	..	..	..	..	..	..	80	84	..	..	..	..	..	..
..	..	..	..	..	..	..	..	..	..	2	..	..	..	..	..	..	..
..	..	..	..	..	..	..	..	..	..	2	..	..	..	..	..	..	..
..	..	..	..	..	..	..	..	..	..	15	13	..	..	252	204	..	..
..	..	..	..	..	..	..	..	..	..	..	..	..	..	252	201	..	..
..	..	..	..	..	..	..	..	..	..	15	13	..	..	..	..	..	..
..	..	..	..	..	..	..	..	..	..	..	..	..	..	..	..	..	..
999	166	2	..	401	101	3	1	21	..	104,095	88,788	55,982	48,857	54,826	47,064	2,581	2,057
989	156	1	..	401	101	3	1	13	..	94,593	79,758	39,137	34,018	47,629	40,983	2,490	2,004
916	143	1	..	372	95	3	1	8	..	93,907	79,335	39,087	33,968	47,616	40,978	2,490	2,004
74	10	..	..	71	2	..	..	..	..	24,003	20,085	22,545	19,656	10,664	9,341	149	136
..	..	..	..	..	..	..	..	..	..	..	..	..	..	..	..	..	..
4	..	..	..	..	..	..	..	..	..	..	..	..	..	..	..	..	..
9	..	..	..	3	..	..	..	..	..	..	..	..	..	..	..	..	..
1	..	1	..	1	..	..	..	1	..	..	..	..	..	..	..	..	..
11	..	..	..	12	1	..	..	1	..	26,638	22,506	3,517	2,771	31,510	27,085	1,803	1,430
..	..	..	..	48	22	..	..	..	..	..	..	..	..	..	..	..	..
7	..	..	..	7	8	..	..	2	..	..	..	..	..	..	..	..	..
216	28	..	..	59	12	..	..	..	..	..	..	..	..	..	..	..	..
31	2	..	..	5	..	..	..	..	..	595	519	5	4	17	10	1	..
1	..	..	..	1	..	..	..	1	..	..	..	..	..	..	..	..	..
1	..	..	..	1	..	..	..	..	..	..	..	..	..	..	..	..	..
20	12	..	..	..	..	..	..	..	..	..	..	..	..	..	..	..	..
2	2	..	..	..	..	..	..	..	..	..	..	..	..	..	..	..	..
..	..	..	..	..	..	..	..	..	..	110	86	204	169	196	116	..	..
..	..	..	..	..	..	..	..	..	..	..	..	..	..	..	..	..	..
..	..	..	..	..	..	..	..	..	..	26,861	22,201	3,803	3,094	926	792	222	176
57	10	..	..	53	28	..	..	2	..	..	..	..	..	..	..	..	..
4	2	..	..	..	..	..	..	..	..	..	..	..	..	..	..	..	..
3	3	..	..	10	1	3	1	..	..	1,648	1,494	149	132	51	31	28	34
30	14	..	..	2	2	..	..	..	..	..	..	..	..	..	..	..	..
18	4	..	..	4	2	..	..	1	..	..	..	..	..	..	..	..	..
49	3	..	..	52	17	..	..	..	..	..	..	..	..	..	..	..	..
18	8	..	..	..	..	..	..	..	..	..	..	..	..	..	..	..	..
7	2	..	..	..	..	..	..	..	..	..	..	..	..	..	..	..	..
43	9	..	..	2	..	..	..	..	..	8,703	7,687	8,832	8,142	4,249	3,594	182	142
26	2	..	..	..	..	..	..	..	..	..	..	..	..	..	..	..	..
4	4	..	..	1	..	..	..	..	..	..	..	..	..	..	..	..	..
142	12	..	..	..	..	..	..	..	..	..	..	..	..	..	..	..	..
12	6	..	..	..	..	..	..	..	..	..	..	..	..	..	..	..	..
17	..	..	..	..	..	..	..	..	..	5,343	4,746	29	..	3	4	105	86
78	10	..	..	40	10	..	..	..	..	..	..	..	..	..	..	..	..
1	..	..	..	..	..	..	..	..	..	6	8	..	..	..	..	..	..
5	..	..	..	21	6	..	..	..	..	203	141	7	7	2	2	..	..
2	..	..	..	7	..	..	..	..	..	185	120	7	7	2	2	..	..
3	..	..	..	14	6	..	..	..	..	..	..	..	..	..	..	..	..
..	..	..	..	..	..	..	..	..	..	..	..	..	..	..	..	..	..
..	..	..	..	..	..	..	..	..	..	18	21	..	..	..	..	..	..
..	..	..	..	..	..	..	..	..	..	..	..	..	..	..	..	..	..

Race.	Total Population. Total.	Males.	Females.	Mother Tongue. Language.	Number of Speakers. Males.	Females.	Other: Balochi. Males.	Females.	Pashto. Males.	Females.	Brahui. Males.	Females.
1	2	3	4	5	6	7	8	9	10	11	12	13
C.—Alien ..	860	587	323	..	537	323	25	7	..	..	138	77
1. MUSLIM ..	561	318	243	Balochi ..	93	77	..	..	..	..	31	27
				Dehwari ..	24	20	..	..	..	..	16	12
				Pashto ..	10	8	..	..	..	..	6	6
				Saraiki ..	88	76	..	..	..	..	1	2
				Jatki Sindhi ..	23	15	..	..	..	..	..	..
				Sindhi ..	3	2	..	..	..	..	1	1
				Urdu ..	11	3	..	..	..	..	..	..
				Punjabi ..	66	42	2	..	..	..	9	3
2. HINDU ..	280	203	77	Balochi ..	3	2	..	..	..	..	..	..
				Sindhi ..	151	40	23	7	..	..	74	26
				Urdu ..	12	3	..	..	..	..	..	..
				Gujrati ..	2	..	..	..	..	..	..	..
				Punjabi ..	35	32	..	..	..	..	..	..
3. SIKH ..	18	15	3	Saraiki ..	1	..	..	..	..	..	..	..
				Punjabi ..	14	3	..	..	..	..	..	..
4. CHRISTIAN ..	1	1	..	Panjabi ..	1	..	..	..	..	..	..	..
Sarawan ..	28,285	15,404	12,881	..	15,404	12,881	546	300	110	61	1,921	1,627
A.—Indigenous ..	27,952	15,190	12,762	..	15,190	12,762	546	300	110	61	1,858	1,586
1. BALOCH ..	857	483	374	Balochi ..	291	210	..	..	..	..	256	174
				Dehwari ..	110	100	..	..	..	..	97	87
				Brahui ..	82	64	4	1	..	..	..	..
2. BRAHUI ..	18,944	10,406	8,538	Balochi ..	1,599	1,455	..	--	..	..	2	5
				Dehwari ..	11	6	..	--	96	50	6	2
				Brahui ..	8,796	7,077	466	253	..	..	..	..
3. PATHAN ..	546	293	253	Pashto ..	216	189	3	2	..	..	90	58
				Brahui ..	73	60	..	..	..	..	..	..
				Persian ..	4	4	..	..	..	..	..	..
4. JATT ..	103	61	42	Brahui ..	61	42	..	..	10	7	..	..
5. SAYYID ..	759	403	556	Dehwari ..	139	138	..	..	4	4	5	4
				Pashto ..	59	48	..	..	..	..	4	4
				Brahui ..	168	138	..	..	..	..	..	..
				Punjabi ..	1	1	..	..	..	..	..	..
				Persian ..	36	31	..	..	..	..	1	..
6. OTHER MUSLIM ..	6,177	3,260	2,917	Balochi ..	262	453	..	..	..	..	200	266
				Dehwari ..	2,142	1,747	..	..	..	..	902	761
				Brahui ..	508	398	58	36	..	..	..	..
				Persian ..	348	319	..	..	..	..	205	165
7. HINDU ..	566	284	282	Sindhi ..	281	282	15	8		..	90	60
B.—Semi-Indigenous ..	178	116	62	..	116	62	..	..	..	..	20	12
1. PATHAN ..	178	116	62	Pashto ..	116	62	..	..	..	..	20	12
C.—Alien ..	155	98	57	..	98	57	..	..	..	..	43	29
1. MUSLIM ..	96	58	38	Dehwari ..	24	20	..	..	..	..	16	12
				Pashto ..	6	8	..	..	..	..	6	6
				Sindhi ..	3	2	..	..	..	..	1	1
				Urdu ..	7	..	..	..	..	..	2	..
				Punjabi ..	18	8	..	..	..	..	6	3
2. HINDU ..	52	35	17	Sindhi ..	19	8	..	..	..	..	12	7
				Urdu ..	7	3	..	..	..	..	..	..
				Punjabi ..	9	6	..	..	..	..	..	..
3. SIKH ..	7	5	2	Punjabi ..	5	2	..	..	..	..	..	..
Jhalawan ..	88,916	47,925	40,991	..	47,925	40,991	547	421	9	..	990	796
A.—Indigenous ..	88,692	47,758	40,934	..	47,758	40,934	518	412	9	..	921	775
1. BALOCH ..	1,777	938	839	Balochi ..	787	704	..	..	..	..	33	12
				Jatki Sindhi ..	25	22	..	..	..	..	..	..
				Brahui ..	124	112	2	4	..	..	..	..
				Sindhi ..	2	1	..	..	..	..	1	1
2. BRAHUI ..	75,395	40,614	34,781	Balochi ..	6,397	4,921	..	..	..	..	732	627
				Lasi ..	16	25	--	..	..	..	..	..
				Jatki Sindhi ..	568	462	..	..	5	..	39	2
				Brahui ..	33,633	29,373	504	405	4	..	..	..
3. PATHAN ..	57	25	32	Balochi ..	1	..	..	..	..	..	..	..
				Pashto ..	6	10	..	..	..	..	1	..
				Brahui ..	18	22	..	..	..	..	..	..
4. LASI ..	508	306	202	Balochi ..	132	97	..	..	..	..	..	..
				Lasi ..	171	104	1	..	..	..	24	20
				Brahui ..	3	1	..	..	..	..	..	..
5. JATT ..	7	3	4	Brahui ..	3	4	..	..	..	..	..	..
6. SAYYID ..	276	142	134	Balochi ..	24	21	..	..	..	..	1	..
				Pashto ..	1	..	..	..	..	..	..	..
				Lasi ..	1	1	..	..	..	..	1	1
				Brahui ..	116	112	..	..	..	..	..	..
7. OTHER MUSLIM ..	10,645	5,707	4,938	Balochi ..	2,547	2,234	..	..	..	..	82	108
				Lasi ..	12	5	..	..	..	..	5	2
				Brahui ..	3,148	2,699	8	3	..	..	..	..
8. HINDU (ARORA) ..	27	23	4	Jatki Sindhi ..	23	4	3	..	..	..	3	..

Nomadism.

Languages.										Occupied.							
Urdu.		*Punjabi.*		*Persian.*		*Arabic.*		*English.*		*Houses.*		*Chhappar.*		*Kizhdi.*		*Both (Houses and Kizhdis).*	
Males.	Females.	Males.	Females.	Males.	Females.	Males.	Females.	Males.	Females.	Males.	Females.	Males.	Females.	Males.	Females.	Males.	Females.
14	15	16	17	18	19	20	21	22	23	24	25	26	27	28	29	30	31
68	23	..	..	8	..	..	..	5	..	483	277	43	38	11	8	..	..
..	..	..	..	..	..	..	..	..	..	264	197	43	38	11	8	..	..
16	12	..	..	..	..	..	..	..	..	..	..	..	..	..	..	..	..
6	6	..	..	..	..	..	..	..	..	..	..	..	..	..	..	..	..
..	..	..	..	..	..	..	..	..	..	..	..	..	..	..	..	..	..
..	..	..	..	..	..	..	..	..	..	..	..	..	..	..	..	..	..
4	1	..	..	..	..	..	..	1	..	..	..	..	..	..	..	..	..
..	..	..	..	2	..	..	..	..	..	..	..	..	..	..	..	..	..
20	2	..	..	5	..	..	..	3	..	..	..	..	..	..	..	..	..
..	..	..	..	..	..	..	..	..	..	..	..	..	..	..	..	..	..
19	2	..	..	..	..	..	..	..	..	203	77	..	..	..	..	..	..
..	..	..	..	..	..	..	..	..	..	..	..	..	..	..	..	..	..
..	..	..	..	..	..	..	..	..	..	..	..	..	..	..	..	..	..
1	..	..	..	..	..	..	..	1	..	..	..	..	..	..	..	..	..
..	..	..	..	..	..	..	..	..	..	..	..	..	..	..	..	..	..
2	..	..	..	1	..	..	..	..	..	15	3	..	..	..	..	..	..
..	..	..	..	..	..	..	..	..	..	1	..	..	..	..	..	..	..
585	193	1	..	123	51	..	..	3	..	14,706	12,384	2	17	287	228	409	252
541	170	1	..	112	45	..	..	1	..	14,492	12,265	2	17	287	228	409	252
1	..	..	..	..	..	..	..	..	..	481	372	..	..	..	..	2	2
..	..	..	..	..	..	..	..	..	..	..	..	..	..	..	..	..	..
1	..	1	..	1	..	..	..	1	..	..	..	..	..	..	..	..	..
..	..	..	..	..	..	..	..	..	..	9,777	8,086	2	17	287	228	340	207
..	..	..	..	48	22	..	..	..	..	..	..	..	..	..	..	..	..
178	89	..	..	18	9	..	..	..	..	..	..	..	..	..	..	..	..
30	2	..	..	1	..	..	..	..	..	292	253	..	..	..	..	..	..
20	12	..	..	..	..	..	..	..	..	..	..	..	..	..	..	1	..
2	2	..	..	..	..	..	..	..	..	..	..	..	..	..	..	..	..
4	2	..	..	..	..	..	..	..	..	61	42	..	..	..	..	..	..
30	14	..	..	2	2	..	..	..	..	403	356	..	..	..	..	..	..
16	4	..	..	2	2	..	..	..	..	..	..	..	..	..	..	..	..
18	8	..	..	..	..	..	..	..	..	..	..	..	..	..	..	..	..
..	..	..	..	..	..	..	..	..	..	..	..	..	..	..	..	..	..
4	2	..	..	..	..	..	..	..	..	..	..	..	..	..	..	..	..
41	9	..	..	..	..	..	..	..	..	3,194	2,874	..	..	..	..	66	43
26	2	..	..	..	..	..	..	..	..	..	..	..	..	..	..	..	..
140	12	..	..	..	..	..	..	..	..	..	..	..	..	..	..	..	..
10	6	..	..	..	..	..	..	..	..	..	..	..	..	..	..	..	..
20	6	..	..	40	10	..	..	..	..	284	282	..	..	..	..	..	..
..	..	..	..	10	6	..	..	..	..	116	62	..	..	..	..	..	..
..	..	..	..	10	6	..	..	..	..	116	62	..	..	..	..	..	..
44	23	..	..	1	..	..	..	2	..	98	57	..	..	..	..	..	..
16	12	..	..	..	..	..	..	..	..	58	38	..	..	..	..	..	..
6	6	..	..	..	..	..	..	..	..	..	..	..	..	..	..	..	..
4	1	..	..	..	..	..	..	1	..	..	..	..	..	..	..	..	..
..	..	..	..	1	..	..	..	..	..	..	..	..	..	..	..	..	..
8	2	..	..	..	..	..	..	..	..	..	..	..	..	..	..	..	..
8	2	..	..	..	..	..	..	..	..	35	17	..	..	..	..	..	..
..	..	..	..	..	..	..	..	..	..	..	..	..	..	..	..	..	..
1	..	..	..	..	..	..	..	1	..	..	..	..	..	..	..	..	..
1	..	..	..	..	..	..	..	..	..	5	2	..	..	..	..	..	..
50	..	..	..	17	8	..	..	4	..	15,856	13,615	2,232	1,721	28,844	24,829	993	826
36	..	..	..	15	8	..	..	3	..	15,695	13,562	2,232	1,721	28,838	24,825	993	826
..	..	..	..	..	..	..	..	..	..	252	201	..	..	681	636	5	2
..	..	..	..	..	..	..	..	..	..	..	..	..	..	..	..	..	..
..	..	..	..	..	..	..	..	..	..	..	..	..	..	..	..	..	..
1	..	..	..	..	..	..	..	..	..	12,206	10,490	2,011	1,539	25,494	21,994	903	758
7	..	..	..	7	8	..	..	2	..	..	..	..	..	..	..	..	..
25	..	..	..	7	..	..	..	..	..	..	..	..	..	..	..	..	..
..	..	..	..	..	..	..	..	..	..	22	32	..	..	3	..	..	..
1	..	..	..	..	..	..	..	..	..	..	..	..	..	..	..	..	..
..	..	..	..	..	..	..	..	..	..	..	..	..	..	..	..	..	..
..	..	..	..	..	..	..	..	..	..	110	86	..	..	196	116	..	..
..	..	..	..	..	..	..	..	..	..	..	..	..	..	..	..	..	..
..	..	..	..	..	..	..	..	..	..	3	4	..	..	..	..	..	..
..	..	..	..	..	..	..	..	..	..	121	125	..	..	21	9	..	..
1	..	..	..	..	1	..	..	..	1	..	..	..	..	..	..	..	..
..	..	..	..	..	..	..	..	..	..	..	..	..	..	..	..	..	..
..	..	..	..	..	..	..	..	..	..	2,959	2,621	221	182	2,442	2,069	85	66
2	..	..	..	..	..	..	..	..	..	..	..	..	..	..	..	..	..
..	..	..	..	..	..	..	..	..	..	22	3	..	..	1	1	..	..

Race.	Total Population.			Mother Tongue.			Other					
				Language.	Number of Speakers.		Balochi.		Pashto.		Brahui.	
	Total.	Males.	Females.		Males.	Females.	Males.	Females.	Males.	Females.	Males.	Females.
1	2	3	4	5	6	7	8	9	10	11	12	13
B.—Semi-Indigenous ..	29	14	15	..	14	15	5	2	..	..	3	2
1. Pathan. ..	29	14	15	Pashto ..	5	5	5	2	..	..	3	2
				Brahui ..	9	10	..	..	..	..	..	..
C.—Alien ..	195	153	42	..	153	42	24	7	..	..	66	21
1. Muslim ..	31	21	10	Pashto ..	4	..	..	..	..	..	..	..
				Saraiki ..	2	2	..	..	..	..	1	2
				Urdu ..	1	..	..	..	..	..	1	..
				Punjabi ..	14	8	1	..	..	..	2	..
2. Hindu ..	164	132	32	Sindhi ..	132	32	23	7	..	..	62	19
Kachhi ..	105,805	57,764	48,041	..	57,764	48,041	1,239	324	16	4	3,233	749
A.—Indigenous ..	*105,316*	*57,492*	*47,824*	..	*57,492*	*47,824*	*1,238*	*324*	*16*	*4*	*3,198*	*721*
1. Baloch ..	38,239	20,865	17,374	Balochi ..	18,550	15,332	..	..	1	..	1,397	371
				Saraiki ..	54	42	1	..	..	..	18	..
				Jatki Sindhi ..	2,256	1,994	95	2	..	..	158	5
				Brahui ..	5	6	..	..	..	..	..	..
2. Brahui ..	11,826	6,450	5,376	Balochi ..	711	643	..	..	..	..	234	107
				Saraiki ..	15	11	..	..	..	..	1	1
				Jatki Sindhi ..	154	117	7	..	..	..	3	..
				Brahui ..	5,570	4,605	325	117	4	..	..	..
3. Pathan ..	258	131	127	Pashto ..	13	18	4	..	..	..	4	..
				Saraiki ..	1	1	..	..	1	..	1	..
				Jatki Sindhi ..	109	104	7	..	..	..	32	19
				Brahui ..	3	1	..	..	..	..	..	..
				Persian ..	5	3	4	3	..	..	..	..
4. Jatt ..	44,237	24,266	19,971	Balochi ..	444	377	..	..	..	..	87	30
				Dehwari ..	3	1	..	..	..	..	..	..
				Saraiki ..	2,196	2,065	41	21	..	..	47	21
				Jatki Sindhi ..	21,604	17,510	446	120	1	..	430	82
				Brahui ..	19	18	3	..	..	..	..	..
5. Sayyid ..	1,201	621	580	Balochi ..	8	7	..	..	2	3	2	3
				Saraiki ..	67	70	..	..	..	..	..	..
				Jatki Sindhi ..	531	486	37	6	4	1	92	12
				Brahui ..	5	7	..	..	..	..	..	..
				Persian ..	10	10	6	..	3	..	6	..
6. Other Muslim ..	2,583	1,440	1,143	Balochi ..	136	98	..	..	..	..	76	16
				Saraiki ..	70	49	..	..	..	..	..	..
				Jatki Sindhi ..	1,141	911	64	35	..	..	68	26
				Brahui ..	51	46	22	7	..	..	..	..
				Lori-Chini ..	33	26	..	..	..	..	28	20
				Persian ..	9	13	1	..	..	..	3	..
7. Hindu ..	6,972	3,719	3,253	Saraiki ..	7	1	..	..	..	..	..	..
				Jatki Sindhi ..	3,712	3,252	175	13	..	..	511	8
B.—Semi-Indigenous ..	56	28	28	..	28	28	..	..	..	..	1	1
1. Pathan ..	23	14	9	Jatki Sindhi ..	14	9	..	..	..	..	1	..
2. Baloch ..	33	14	19	Balochi ..	..	1	..	..	..	..	..	1
				Jatki Sindhi ..	14	18	..	..	..	..	..	..
C.—Alien ..	433	244	189	..	244	189	1	..	..	..	34	27
1. Muslim ..	368	206	102	Balochi ..	71	59	..	..	..	..	31	27
				Saraiki ..	84	66	..	..	..	..	..	..
				Jatki Sindhi ..	14	8	..	..	..	..	..	..
				Urdu ..	3	3	..	..	..	..	2	..
				Punjabi ..	34	26	1	..	..	..	1	..
2. Hindu ..	58	32	26	Urdu ..	5	..	..	..	..	..	..	..
				Gujrati ..	1	..	..	..	..	..	..	..
				Punjabi ..	26	26	..	..	..	..	..	..
3. Sikh ..	7	6	1	Punjabi ..	6	1	..	..	..	..	..	..
Dombki-Kaheri Country	26,953	14,553	12,400	..	14,553	12,400	1,322	383	95	38	388	272
A.—Indigenous ..	26,915	14,535	12,380	..	14,535	12,380	1,320	383	95	38	386	272
1. Baloch ..	6,442	3,501	2,941	Eastern Balochi ..	3,401	2,849	..	..	..	..	33	1
				Jatki Sindhi ..	100	92	52	17	..	..	..	..
2. Brahui ..	1,744	931	813	Brahui ..	931	813	303	38	16	..	..	..
3. Pathan ..	226	132	94	Jatki Sindhi ..	132	94	75	..	..	..	..	..
4. Jatt ..	*13,731*	7,483	*6,248*	*Jatki Sindhi* ..	*7,383*	*6,163*	588	277	77	38	*344*	*271*
				Punjabi ..	100	85	25	14	..	..	..	..
5. Sayyid ..	1,091	579	512	Pashto ..	3	3	..	..	..	..	..	..
				Jatki Sindhi ..	576	509	44	7	2	..	4	..
6. Other Muslim	1,079	594	485	Jatki Sindhi ..	594	485	80	25	..	..	..	..
7. Hindu ..	2,588	1,309	1,279	Jatki Sindhi ..	1,309	1,279	150	5	..	..	5	..
8. Sikh ..	14	6	8	Jatki Sindhi ..	6	8	3	..	..	..	..	..

Nomadism.

Languages.										Occupied.							
Urdu.		*Punjabi.*		*Persian.*		*Arabic.*		*English.*		*Houses.*		*Chhappar.*		*Kishdi.*		*Both (Houses and Kishdis).*	
Males.	Females.	Males.	Females.	Males.	Females.	Males.	Females.	Males.	Females.	Males.	Females.	Males.	Females.	Males.	Females.	Males.	Females.
14	15	16	17	18	19	20	21	22	23	24	25	26	27	28	29	30	31
1	..	..	..	..	..	..	..	..	..	12	18	..	..	2	2	..	..
1	..	..	..	..	..	..	..	..	..	..	..	..	..	..	..	..	..
..	..	..	..	..	..	..	..	..	..	12	13	..	..	2	2	..	..
18	..	..	..	2	..	..	..	1	..	149	40	..	..	4	2	..	..
..	..	..	..	..	..	..	..	..	..	17	8	..	..	4	2	..	..
..	..	..	..	..	..	..	..	..	..	..	..	..	..	..	..	..	..
..	..	..	..	1	..	..	..	..	..	..	..	..	..	..	..	..	..
2	..	..	..	1	..	..	..	1	..	..	..	..	..	..	..	..	..
11	..	..	..	..	..	..	..	..	..	132	32	..	..	..	..	..	..
165	17	..	..	122	17	..	..	5	..	50,459	42,059	3,471	2,833	3,274	2,684	560	465
159	17	..	..	117	17	..	..	3	..	50,230	41,879	3,432	2,798	3,270	2,682	560	465
25	7	..	..	8	..	..	..	..	..	18,299	15,217	2,200	1,856	366	301	..	..
4	..	..	..	..	..	..	..	..	..	..	..	..	..	..	..	..	..
9	..	..	..	3	..	..	..	..	..	..	..	..	..	..	..	..	..
..	..	..	..	..	..	..	..	..	..	..	..	..	..	..	..	..	..
4	..	..	..	2	1	..	..	..	..	3,730	3,143	119	67	2,041	1,701	560	465
..	..	..	..	..	..	..	..	..	..	..	..	..	..	..	..	..	..
23	..	..	..	32	3	..	..	..	..	..	..	..	..	..	..	..	..
..	..	..	..	4	..	..	..	..	..	127	123	..	..	4	4	..	..
1	..	..	..	1	..	..	..	1	..	..	..	..	..	..	..	..	..
1	..	..	..	1	..	..	..	..	..	..	..	..	..	..	..	..	..
..	..	..	..	..	..	..	..	..	..	..	..	..	..	..	..	..	..
..	..	..	..	..	..	..	..	..	..	..	..	..	..	..	..	..	..
..	..	..	..	..	..	..	..	..	..	22,970	18,950	1,018	803	278	218	..	..
..	..	..	..	..	..	..	..	..	..	..	..	..	..	..	..	..	..
33	..	..	..	28	..	..	..	2	..	..	..	..	..	..	..	..	..
2	3	..	..	..	..	..	..	..	..	619	568	..	..	2	3	..	..
34	3	..	..	37	13	..	..	..	..	..	..	..	..	..	..	..	..
3	..	..	..	..	..	..	..	..	..	..	..	..	..	..	..	..	..
..	..	..	..	..	..	..	..	..	..	766	616	95	72	579	455	..	..
4	4	..	..	1	..	..	..	..	..	..	..	..	..	..	..	..	..
..	..	..	..	..	..	..	..	..	..	..	..	..	..	..	..	..	..
2	..	..	..	..	..	..	..	..	..	..	..	..	..	..	..	..	..
14	..	..	..	..	..	..	..	..	..	3,719	3,253	..	..	..	..	..	..
..	..	..	..	..	..	..	..	..	..	28	28	..	..	..	..	..	..
..	..	..	..	..	..	..	..	..	..	14	9	..	..	..	..	..	..
..	..	..	..	..	..	..	..	..	..	14	19	..	..	..	..	..	..
..	..	..	..	..	..	..	..	..	..	..	..	..	..	..	..	..	..
6	..	..	..	5	..	..	..	2	..	201	152	39	35	4	2	..	..
..	..	..	..	..	..	..	..	..	..	163	125	39	35	4	2	..	..
..	..	..	..	..	..	..	..	..	..	..	..	..	..	..	..	..	..
..	..	..	..	..	..	..	..	..	..	..	..	..	..	..	..	..	..
5	..	..	..	4	..	..	..	2	..	..	..	..	..	..	..	..	..
..	..	..	..	..	..	..	..	..	..	32	26	..	..	..	..	..	..
..	..	..	..	..	..	..	..	..	..	..	..	..	..	..	..	..	..
1	..	..	..	1	..	..	..	..	..	6	1	..	..	..	..	..	..
71	1	..	..	47	22	..	..	..	..	8,238	7,107	4,108	3,382	1,848	1,611	359	300
69	1	..	..	43	22	..	..	..	..	8,225	7,092	4,103	3,377	1,848	1,611	359	300
5	1	..	..	..	..	..	..	..	..	2,130	1,801	1,144	942	227	198	..	..
20	..	..	..	2	..	..	..	..	..	175	150	5	3	751	660	..	..
..	..	..	..	..	..	..	..	..	..	127	90	5	4	..	..	..	..
24	..	..	..	25	18	..	..	..	..	3,827	3,208	2,786	2,290	648	574	222	176
1	..	..	..	1	..	..	..	..	..	..	..	..	..	..	..	..	..
15	..	..	..	15	4	..	..	..	..	436	377	115	101	..	..	28	34
3	..	..	..	..	..	..	..	..	..	320	265	48	37	222	179	4	4
1	..	..	..	..	..	..	..	..	..	1,204	1,193	..	..	..	..	105	86
										6	8	..	..	..	..	..	..

Race.	Total Population. Total.	Males.	Females.	Mother Tongue. Language.	Number of Speakers. Males.	Females.	Other — Balochi. Males.	Females.	Pashto. Males.	Females.	Brahui. Males.	Females.
1	2	3	4	5	6	7	8	9	10	11	12	13
B.—Semi-Indigenous ..	10	5	5	..	5	5	2	..	..	..	2	..
1. Pathan ..	10	5	5	Pashto ..	5	5	2	..	..	..	2	..
C.—Alien ..	28	13	15	..	13	15	..	..	..	..	..	..
1. Muslim ..	26	11	15	Saraiki ..	2	8	..	..	..	..	..	..
				Jatki Sindhi ..	9	7	..	..	..	..	..	..
2. Sikhs ..	2	2	..	Saraiki and Jatki Sindhi.	2	..	..	..	..	..	..	..
Makran ..	67,285	35,700	31,585	..	35,700	31,585	53	..	..	..	..	..
A.—Indigenous ..	67,207	35,651	31,556	..	35,651	31,556	53	..	..	..	..	..
1. Baloch ..	44,561	23,671	20,890	Balochi ..	23,671	20,890	..	..	..	..	..	..
2. Brahui ..	5,074	2,767	2,307	Balochi ..	2,767	2,307	..	..	..	..	..	..
3. Pathan ..	21	15	6	Pashto ..	15	6	..	..	..	..	..	..
4. Lasi ..	373	204	169	Balochi ..	204	169	..	..	..	..	..	..
5. Jatt ..	3	2	1	Balochi ..	2	1	..	..	..	..	..	..
6. Sayyid ..	95	51	44	Balochi ..	51	44	..	..	..	..	..	..
7. Other Muslim ..	16,957	8,821	8,136	Balochi ..	8,821	8,136	..	..	..	..	..	..
8. Hindus ..	123	120	3	Sindhi ..	120	3	53	..	..	..	..	..
B.—Semi-Idigenous ..	29	20	9	..	20	9	..	..	..	..	..	..
1. Pathan ..	23	16	7	Pashto ..	16	7	..	..	..	..	..	..
2. Other Muslim ..	6	4	2	Balochi ..	4	2	..	..	..	..	..	..
C.—Alien ..	49	29	20	..	29	20	..	..	..	..	..	..
1. Muslim ..	40	22	18	Western Balochi ..	22	18	..	..	..	..	..	..
2. Hindu ..	6	4	2	Balochi ..	3	2	..	..	..	..	..	..
				Gujrati ..	1	..	..	..	..	..	..	..
3. Sikhs ..	2	2	..	Punjabi ..	2	..	..	..	..	..	..	..
4. Christian ..	1	1	..	Punjabi ..	1	..	..	..	..	..	..	..
Kharan ..	23,358	12,508	10,855	..	12,508	10,855	33	13	14	3	4,096	3,235
A.—Indigenous ..	23,298	12,474	10,824	..	12,474	10,824	33	13	10	3	4,093	3,229
1. Baloch ..	14,703	7,903	6,800	Western Balochi ..	7,903	6,800	..	..	6	2	2,380	1,809
2. Brahui ..	4,277	2,300	1,977	Western Balochi ..	2,300	1,977	..	..	..	..	1,648	1,351
3. Pathan ..	43	22	21	Balochi ..	14	17	..	..	..	..	4	5
				Pashto ..	8	4	8	4	..	..	..	..
4. Sayyid ..	145	80	65	Western Balochi ..	80	65	..	..	2	..	13	6
5. Other Muslim ..	4,090	2,144	1,946	Western Balochi ..	2,144	1,946	..	..	2	1	36	51
6. Hindu ..	40	25	15	Sindhi ..	25	15	25	19	..	..	12	7
B.—Semi-Indigenous ..	60	29	31	..	29	31	..	..	4	..	3	6
1. Pathan ..	60	29	31	Pashto ..	2	..	..	..	..	..	..	..
				Balochi ..	27	31	..	..	4	..	3	6
Las Bela State ..	63,008	33,495	29,513	..	33,495	29,513	1,745	1,090	2	..	628	465
A.—Indigenous ..	62,761	33,339	29,422	..	33,339	29,422	1,737	1,089	1	..	627	465
1. Baloch ..	6,496	3,441	3,055	Balochi ..	3,206	2,851	..	..	..	..	11	5
				Lasi ..	63	67	20	17	..	..	8	9
				Brahui ..	172	137	27	20	..	..	..	..
2. Brahui ..	8,277	4,586	3,691	Balochi ..	3,089	3,201	..	..	..	..	68	41
				Lasi ..	66	68	2	6	..	..	1	1
				Brahui ..	531	422	84	80	..	..	..	..
3. Pathan ..	12	9	3	Pashto ..	9	3	1	3	..	..	1	..
Lasi ..	30,875	16,088	14,787	Balochi ..	490	471	..	..	..	..	..	..
				Lasi ..	15,595	14,313	1,111	677	..	..	302	247
				Brahui ..	3	3	..	..	..	..	..	..
4. Jatt ..	4,323	2,129	2,194	Balochi ..	13	1	..	..	1	..	..	..
				Lasi ..	2,072	2,146	178	121	..	..	166	130
				Brahui ..	34	35	7	6	..	..	..	..
				Punjabi ..	10	12	..	..	..	..	..	..
5. Sayyid ..	329	167	162	Lasi ..	141	148	29	21	..	..	5	3
				Brahui ..	3	1	..	..	..	..	..	..
				Urdu ..	7	2	..	..	..	..	..	..
				Punjabi ..	14	18	..	..	..	..	..	..
				Persian ..	2	3	..	..	..	..	..	..
6. Other Muslim ..	11,053	6,141	4,912	Balochi ..	1,053	993	..	..	..	..	1	..
				Lasi ..	5,053	3,887	221	138	..	..	43	2
				Brahui ..	35	32	..	..	..	..	..	..
7. Hindu ..	1,396	778	618	Lasi ..	750	600	57	..	..	..	21	..
				Urdu ..	28	18	..	..	..	..	..	..
B.—Semi-Indigenous ..	1	1	..	..	1	..	..	..	1	..	..	..
1. Other Muslims ..	1	1	..	Persian ..	1	..	..	..	1	..	..	..
C.—Alien ..	248	155	91	..	155	91	8	1	..	..	1	..
1. Muslim ..	184	111	73	Lasi ..	38	31	4	1	..	..	..	..
				Urdu ..	11	9	1	..	..	..	..	..
				Gujrati ..	1	..	..	..	..	..	..	..
				Punjabi ..	60	33	3	..	..	..	..	..
				Persian ..	1	..	..	..	..	..	1	..
2. Hindu ..	47	32	15	Lasi ..	12	..	..	..	..	..	..	..
				Urdu ..	5	1	..	..	..	..	..	..
				Punjabi ..	15	14	..	..	..	..	..	..
3. Sikhs ..	15	12	3	Punjabi ..	12	3	..	..	..	..	..	..

Nomadism.

LANGUAGES.										OCCUPIED.							
Urdu.		*Punjabi.*		*Persian.*		*Arabic.*		*English.*		*Houses.*		*Chhappar.*		*Kizhdi.*		*Both (Houses and Kizhdis).*	
Males.	Females.	Males.	Females.	Males.	Females.	Males.	Females.	Males.	Females.	Males.	Females.	Males.	Females.	Males.	Females.	Males.	Females.
14	15	16	17	18	19	20	21	22	23	24	25	26	27	28	29	30	31
2	..	..	..	4	..	..	..	..	..	..	..	5	5	..	..	..	..
2	..	..	..	4	..	..	..	..	..	..	..	5	5	..	..	..	..
..	..	..	..	..	..	..	..	..	..	13	15	..	..	..	..	..	..
..	..	..	..	..	..	..	..	..	..	11	15	..	..	..	..	..	..
..	..	..	..	..	..	..	..	..	..	..	..	..	..	..	..	..	..
..	..	..	..	..	..	..	..	..	..	2	..	..	..	..	..	..	..
91	..	..	..	35	..	..	..	1	..	1,086	958	28,704	25,471	5,741	4,995	169	161
91	..	..	..	35	..	..	..	1	..	1,046	988	28,698	25,466	5,738	4,991	169	161
36	..	..	..	33	..	..	..	..	..	375	443	19,099	16,774	4,055	3,541	142	132
2	..	..	..	2	..	..	..	1	..	234	182	1,361	1,138	1,172	987	..	..
..	..	..	..	..	..	..	..	..	..	14	6	..	..	1	..	..	..
..	..	..	..	..	..	..	..	..	..	..	..	204	169	..	..	..	..
..	..	..	..	..	..	..	..	..	..	..	..	2	1	..	..	..	..
..	..	..	..	..	..	..	..	..	..	16	12	34	31	1	1	..	..
..	..	..	..	..	..	..	..	..	..	318	295	7,969	7,353	507	459	27	29
53	..	..	..	..	..	..	..	..	..	89	..	29	..	2	3	..	..
..	..	..	..	..	..	..	..	..	..	18	7	2	2	..	..	..	..
..	..	..	..	..	..	..	..	..	..	14	5	2	2	..	..	..	..
..	..	..	..	..	..	..	..	..	..	4	2	..	..	..	..	..	..
..	..	..	..	..	..	..	..	..	..	22	13	4	3	3	4	..	..
..	..	..	..	..	..	..	..	..	..	15	11	4	3	3	4	..	..
..	..	..	..	..	..	..	..	..	..	3	2	..	..	..	..	..	..
..	..	..	..	..	..	..	..	..	..	1	..	..	..	..	..	..	..
..	..	..	..	..	..	..	..	..	..	2	..	..	..	..	..	..	..
..	..	..	..	..	..	..	..	..	..	1	..	..	..	..	..	..	..
21	6	..	..	57	3	3	1	..	..	4,248	3,630	620	589	7,635	6,636	..	..
19	6	..	..	50	3	3	1	..	..	4,219	3,599	620	589	7,635	6,636	..	..
7	2		..	30	2	..	..	..	..	2,466	2,051	102	84	5,335	4,665	..	..
4	..	..	..	8	..	..	..	..	..	516	455	19	7	1,765	1,515	..	..
..	..	..	..	..	..	..	..	..	..	..	..	..	..	..	..	..	..
..	..	..	..	..	..	..	..	..	..	13	15	..	..	9	6	..	..
1	..	..	..	10	1	3	1	..	..	53	47	..	..	27	18	..	..
2	..	..	..	2	..	..	..	..	..	1,146	1,016	499	498	499	432	..	..
5	4	..	..	..	..	..	..	..	..	25	15	..	..	..	..	..	..
2	..	..	..	7	..	..	..	..	..	29	31	..	..	..	..	..	..
..	..	..	..	..	..	..	..	..	..	29	31	..	..	..	..	..	..
2	..	..	..	7	..	..	..	..	..	..	..	..	..	..	..	..	..
..	..	1	..	..	..	..	..	8	..	9,412	9,035	16,845	14,344	7,197	6,081	41	53
..	..	1	..	..	..	..	..	4	..	9,265	8,949	16,840	14,341	7,193	6,079	41	53
..	..	..	..	..	..	..	..	..	..	206	177	1,751	1,648	1,443	1,177	41	53
..	..	..	..	..	..	..	..	..	..	..	..	..	..	..	..	..	..
..	..	..	..	..	..	..	..	..	..	..	..	..	..	..	..	..	..
..	..	..	..	..	..	..	..	..	..	375	343	1,825	1,591	2,386	1,757	..	..
..	..	..	..	..	..	..	..	..	..	..	..	..	..	..	..	..	..
..	..	..	..	..	..	..	..	..	..	..	..	..	..	..	..	..	..
..	..	1	..	..	..	..	..	2	..	9	3	..	..	..	..	..	..
..	..	..	..	..	..	..	..	..	..	5,400	5,151	9,607	8,669	1,081	967	..	..
..	..	..	..	..	..	..	..	..	..	..	..	..	..	..	..	..	..
..	..	..	..	..	..	..	..	..	..	..	..	..	..	..	..	..	..
..	..	..	..	..	..	..	..	1	..	159	342	964	911	1,006	941	..	..
..	..	..	..	..	..	..	..	1	..	..	..	..	..	..	..	..	..
..	..	..	..	..	..	..	..	..	..	..	..	..	..	..	..	..	..
..	..	..	..	..	..	..	..	..	..	..	..	..	..	..	..	..	..
..	..	..	..	..	..	..	..	..	..	115	124	52	38	..	..	..	..
..	..	..	..	..	..	..	..	..	..	..	..	..	..	..	..	..	..
..	..	..	..	..	..	..	..	..	..	..	..	..	..	..	..	..	..
..	..	..	..	..	..	..	..	..	..	..	..	..	..	..	..	..	..
..	..	..	..	..	..	..	..	..	..	..	..	..	..	..	..	..	..
..	..	..	..	..	..	..	..	..	..	2,223	2,191	2,641	1,484	1,277	1,237	..	..
..	..	..	..	..	..	..	..	..	..	..	..	..	..	..	..	..	..
..	..	..	..	..	..	..	..	..	..	..	..	..	..	..	..	..	..
..	..	..	..	..	..	..	..	..	..	778	618	..	..	..	..	..	..
..	..	..	..	..	..	..	..	..	..	..	..	..	..	..	..	..	..
..	..	..	..	..	..	..	..	..	..	1	..	..	..	..	..	..	..
..	..	..	..	..	..	..	..	..	..	1	..	..	..	..	..	..	..
..	..	..	..	..	..	..	..	4	1	146	86	5	3	4	2	..	..
..	..	..	..	..	..	..	..	..	..	102	68	5	3	4	2	..	..
..	..	..	..	..	..	..	..	..	..	..	..	..	..	..	..	..	..
..	..	..	..	..	..	..	..	..	..	..	..	..	..	..	..	..	..
..	..	..	..	..	..	..	..	2	..	..	..	..	..	..	..	..	..
..	..	..	..	..	..	..	..	1	..	..	..	..	..	..	..	..	..
..	..	..	..	..	..	..	..	..	..	32	15	..	..	..	..	..	..
..	..	..	..	..	..	..	..	1	..	..	..	..	..	..	..	..	..
..	..	..	..	..	..	..	..	..	..	..	..	..	..	..	..	..	..
..	..	..	..	..	..	..	..	..	..	12	3	..	..	..	..	..	..

CENSUS OF INDIA, 1931.

VOLUME IV.

BALUCHISTAN.

PART II.—TABLES.

PART II.

CONTENTS.

IMPERIAL TABLES.

PROVINCIAL TABLES.

TABLE I.

AREA, HOUSES AND POPULATION.

1. The Census of 1931 embraced the whole Province which for purposes of Census was divided into (*a*) Regular Areas and (*b*) Tribal Areas. The Regular Areas were censused synchronously on the 26th of February 1931 as in other Indian Provinces on the Standard Form. Enumeration in the Tribal Areas occupied by indigenous inhabitants was non-synchronous commencing between July and October 1930 and ending between December 1930 and the first fortnight of February 1931. A simplified form to suit primitive conditions of life was used in these tracts except in Kharan where, with the willing co-operation of the Chief, the Standard Indian form was used. The figures of population represented by each of these methods are summarised below :—

	Persons.	*Males.*	*Females.*
(1) Synchronously Censused ..	110,849	80,197	30,652
(2) Non-synchronously censused			
(*a*) On a simplified form ..	734,410	395,714	338,696
(*b*) On the standard form..	23,358	12,503	10,855
Total (2) ..	757,768	408,217	349,551
Total for the Province	868,617	488,414	380,203

2. The area of the Province, 134,638 square miles, has undergone no change since 1911. The following changes in the areas of Districts have, however, taken place since 1921 owing to territorial transfers :—

Districts.	*Area in 1921.*	*Area in 1931.*	*Remarks.*
Quetta-Pishin	5,220	(1) 4,806	(1) Due to transfer of Shorârud Sub-tahsil with an area of 414 square miles from Quetta-Pishin to Chagai.
Chagai	19,622	20,036	
Sibi	11,193	(2) 11,187	(2) Due to transfer of Railway line between Jhatpat and Pirak Railway stations covering an area of 6 miles, from Sibi to Bolan and of retransfer of Quat Mandai with an area of 12 square miles from the Sibi Tahsil to the Mari Country.
Bolan	353	359	
Sibi Administered Area	3,925	(2) 3,907	
Mari Country	3,392	3,404	

3. " House " means only occupied houses and includes not only permanent houses but also blanket tents and other movable or temporary dwellings. The figures for 1931 are exclusive of houses in strictly Military areas.

4. Statistics of area and population by Tahsils will be found in Provincial Table I.

5. The definition of " village " is given on the flyleaf of Table III ; that of " town " on that of Table IV.

TABLE I.—AREA, HOUSES AND POPULATION.

TABLE I.—AREA, HOUSES AND POPULATION.

District or State.	Area in Square Miles.	Towns.	Villages.	Occupied Houses.			Population.								
							Persons.			Males.			Females.		
				Total.	In Towns.	In Villages.	Total.	Urban.	Rural.	Total.	Urban.	Rural.	Total.	Urban.	Rural.
1	2	3	4	5	6	7	8	9	10	11	12	13	14	15	16
BALUCHISTAN ..	134,638	17	3,501	166,644	17,945	148,699	868,617	102,602	766,015	488,414	71,561	416,858	380,208	31,041	349,162
DISTRICTS ..	54,228	12	1,425	90,116	15,559	74,557	463,508	92,025	371,483	270,004	65,913	204,091	193,504	26,112	167,392
Quetta-Pishin ..	4,806	6	376	28,172	10,806	17,366	147,541	68,757	78,784	90,302	48,727	41,575	57,239	20,030	37,209
Loralai ..	7,525	2	429	16,402	780	15,622	86,087	5,321	80,766	47,936	4,070	43,866	38,151	1,251	36,900
Zhob ..	10,315	2	251	12,675	1,070	11,605	57,963	6,581	51,382	34,596	5,573	29,023	23,367	1,008	22,359
Bolan ..	359	1	28	1,635	434	1,201	4,688	1,834	2,854	3,466	1,455	2,011	1,222	379	843
Chagai ..	20,036	..	72	6,187	..	6,187	24,224	..	24,224	13,721	..	13,721	10,503	..	10,503
Sibi ..	11,187	1	269	25,045	2,469	22,576	143,005	9,532	133,473	79,983	6,088	73,895	63,022	3,444	59,578
Administered Area ..	*3,907*	*1*	*242*	*17,550*	*2,469*	*15,081*	*87,781*	*9,532*	*78,249*	*49,447*	*6,088*	*43,359*	*38,334*	*3,444*	*34,890*
Mari-Bugti Country ..	*7,280*	..	*27*	*7,495*	..	*7,495*	*55,224*	..	*55,224*	*30,536*	..	*30,536*	*24,688*	..	*24,688*
STATES ..	80,410	5	2,076	76,528	2,386	74,142	405,109	10,577	394,532	218,410	5,648	212,762	186,699	4,929	181,770
Kalat ..	73,278	4	1,797	65,007	1,693	63,314	342,101	7,237	334,864	184,915	3,912	181,003	157,186	3,325	153,861
Sarawan ..	*5,230*	*2*	*186*	*6,281*	*1,074*	*5,207*	*28,464*	*4,816*	*23,648*	*15,545*	*2,534*	*13,011*	*12,919*	*2,282*	*10,637*
Jhalawan ..	*20,795*	..	*475*	*14,139*	..	*14,139*	*88,978*	..	*88,978*	*47,987*	..	*47,987*	*40,991*	..	*40,991*
Kachhi ..	*4,060*	..	*589*	*18,255*	..	*18,255*	*105,886*	..	*105,886*	*57,844*	..	*57,844*	*48,042*	..	*48,042*
Dombki-Kaheri Country	*1,369*	..	*123*	*4,592*	..	*4,592*	*26,953*	..	*26,953*	*14,553*	..	*14,553*	*12,400*	..	*12,400*
Makran ..	*23,269*	*2*	*305*	*16,464*	*619*	*14,845*	*68,462*	*2,421*	*66,041*	*36,483*	*1,378*	*35,105*	*31,979*	*1,043*	*30,936*
Kharan ..	*18,565*	..	*119*	*6,276*	..	*6,276*	*23,358*	..	*23,358*	*12,503*	..	*12,503*	*10,855*	..	*10,856*
Las-Bela ..	7,132	1	279	11,521	693	10,828	63,008	3,340	59,668	33,495	1,736	31,759	29,513	1,604	27,909

TABLE II.

VARIATION IN POPULATION SINCE 1901.

Census results for 1891, 1901, 1911, 1921 and 1931 may be summarised thus :—

Year.	Area in square miles dealt with	Population.		
		Total.	Estimated.	Enumerated.
1891 ..	20,568	171,752	142,473	29,279
1901 ..	82,950	810,746	459,728	351,018
1911 ..	134,638	834,703	..	834,703
1921 ..	134,638	799,625	2,231	797,394
1931 ..	134,638	868,617	..	868,617

The first census of 1891 was too rough and fragmentary to lend itself for comparison in this table. Similarly comparison with the figures for 1901 is misleading because western Sinjrani in Chagai as well as Makran and Kharan were excluded from the census and the figures for the Jhalawan Division of the Kalat State based on estimates were found to be very considerably exaggerated.

The figures of population for previous censuses differ in some cases from those given in this table in previous reports owing to subsequent inter-district territorial transfers specified on the flyleaf of Imperial Table I. The adjustments thus made are shown below :—

Name of unit or area.	District, etc. from which transferred.	District, etc. to which transferred.	Persons.
Shorarud Sub-tahsil..	Quetta-Pishin District.	Chagai District ..	1,273
Nasirabad Railway Tahsil.	Sibi District ..	Bolan-Kachhi-Nushki Railway District.	1,256
Quat Mandai Valley..	Sibi District—Administered Area.	Sibi District (Mari Tribal Country.)	935

Variations due to other causes are discussed in Part I of this volume.

TABLE II.—VARIATION IN POPULATION SINCE 1901.

TABLE II.—VARIATION IN POPULATION SINCE 1901.

District or State.	Persons.				Variation: Increase + Decrease −			Net Variation in period 1901 to 1931. Increase (+) Decrease (−)	Males.				Females.			
	1931	1921	1911	1901	1921 to 1931	1911 to 1921	1901 to 1911		1931	1921	1911	1901	1931	1921	1911	1901
1	2	3	4	5	6	7	8	9	10	11	12	13	14	15	16	17
BALUCHISTAN ..	868,617	799,625	834,703	810,746	+68,992	−35,078	+23,957	+57,871	488,414	461,000	466,419	445,520	380,203	338,625	368,284	365,226
DISTRICTS ..	463,508	420,648	414,412	382,106	+42,860	+6,236	+32,306	+81,402	270,004	255,014	239,181	219,523	193,504	165,634	175,231	162,583
Quetta-Pishin ..	147,541	135,809	125,569	113,025	+11,732	+10,240	+12,544	+34,516	90,302	86,422	75,390	68,372	57,239	49,387	50,179	44,653
Loralai ..	86,087	82,473	80,769	68,332	+3,614	+1,704	+12,437	+17,755	47,936	46,973	44,923	38,088	38,151	35,500	35,846	30,244
Zhob ..	57,963	56,668	70,366	69,718	+1,295	−13,698	+ 648	− 11,755	34,596	35,136	40,346	39,637	23,367	21,533	30,020	30,081
Bolan ..	4,688	4,874	2,880	2,762	−186	+1,994	+118	+1,926	3,466	3,942	2,080	2,105	1,222	932	800	657
Chagai ..	24,224	22,616	18,423	16,751	+1,608	+4,193	+1,672	+7,473	13,721	13,835	10,184	8,832	10,503	8,781	8,239	7,919
Sibi ..	143,005	118,208	116,405	111,518	+24,797	+1,803	+4,887	+31,487	79,983	68,707	66,258	62,489	63,022	49,501	50,147	49,029
Administered Area ..	*87,781*	*80,249*	*80,687*	*76,271*	*+7,532*	*−438*	*+4,416*	*+11,510*	*49,447*	*47,047*	*46,439*	*42,739*	*38,334*	*33,202*	*34,248*	*33,532*
Mari-Bugti Country ..	*55,224*	*37,959*	*35,718*	*35,247*	*+17,265*	*+2,241*	*+471*	*+19,977*	*30,536*	*21,660*	*19,819*	*19,750*	*24,688*	*16,299*	*15,899*	*15,497*
STATES ..	405,109	378,977	420,291	428,840	+26,132	−41,314	−8,349	−23,531	218,410	205,986	227,238	225,997	186,699	172,991	193,053	202,843
Kalat ..	342,101	328,281	359,086	372,531	+13,820	−30,805	−13,445	−30,430	184,915	179,003	194,598	196,279	157,186	149,278	164,488	176,252
Sarawan ..	*28,464*	*54,262*	*63,781*	*65,549*	*−25,798*	*−9,519*	*−1,768*	*−37,085*	*15,545*	*30,422*	*35,082*	*36,366*	*12,919*	*23,840*	*28,699*	*29,183*
Jhalawan ..	*88,978*	*79,710*	*84,398*	*224,073*	*+9,268*	*−4,688*	*−139,675*	*−135,095*	*47,987*	*43,687*	*46,880*	*115,077*	*40,991*	*36,023*	*37,518*	*108,996*
Kachhi ..	*105,886*	*75,153*	*92,759*	*63,367*	*+30,733*	*−17,606*	*+29,392*	*+42,519*	*57,844*	*41,349*	*50,191*	*34,251*	*48,042*	*33,804*	*42,568*	*29,116*
Dombki-Kaheri Country ..	*26,953*	*19,558*	*23,543*	*19,542*	*+7,395*	*−3,985*	*+4,001*	*+7,411*	*14,553*	*10,628*	*12,624*	*10,585*	*12,400*	*8,930*	*10,919*	*8,957*
Makran ..	*68,462*	*71,860*	*71,942*	..	*−3,398*	*−82*	*+71,942*	*+68,462*	*36,483*	*37,826*	*37,698*	..	*31,979*	*34,034*	*34,244*	..
Kharan ..	*23,358*	*27,738*	*22,663*	..	*−4,380*	*+5,075*	*+22,663*	*+23,358*	*12,503*	*15,091*	*12,123*	..	*10,855*	*12,647*	*10,540*	..
Las-Bela ..	63,008	50,696	61,205	56,109	+12,312	−10,509	+5,096	+6,899	33,495	26,983	32,640	29,718	29,513	23,713	28,565	26,391

TABLE III.

TOWNS AND VILLAGES CLASSIFIED BY POPULATION.

1. For definition of "Town" see fly-leaf of table IV.

2. The term "Village" is the revenue village including attached hamlets. In the states areas it includes not only revenue mauzas with attached hamlets, but also residential villages with out-lying hamlets as well as localities which often containing practically no permanent dwellings are regularly occupied at certain seasons of the year by semi-nomadic population.

3. The following unclassed population is included in the figures given in column 18 of the table owing to there being no village within reasonable distance in which the figures could be included :—

District.	Road-side gangs.	Railway gang huts.	Total.
Quetta-Pishin ..	36	346	382
Loralai ..	102	..	102
Zhob ..	220	368	588
Bolan ..	..	436	436
Chagai ..	68	719	787
Sibi ..	18	257	275

4. Altogether 530 persons were enumerated in trains, 265 on platforms, 29 in boats and 601 in encampments. These have been included in the population of adjoining villages.

TABLE III.—TOWNS AND VILLAGES CLASSIFIED BY POPULATION.

District or State.	Total No. of inhabited Towns and Villages.	Population.	Under 500.		500 to 1,000.		1,000 to 2,000.		2,000 to 5,000.		5,000 to 10,000.		10,000 to 20,000.		20,000 to 50,000.		Encampments, Boats, Road and Railway Population, Unclassed.
			Number.	Population.	Number.	Population.	Number.	Population.	Number.	Population.	Number.	Population.	Number.	Population.	Number.	Population.	
1	2	3	4	5	6	7	8	9	10	11	12	13	14	15	16	17	18
BALUCHISTAN ..	3,518	868,617	3,145	408,109	254	169,526	86	116,106	27	81,612	4	30,422	..	..	2	60,272	2,570
DISTRICTS ..	1,437	463,508	1,229	161,483	137	93,844	49	65,142	16	49,775	4	30,422	..	..	2	60,272	2,570
Quetta-Pishin ..	382	147,541	333	38,003	32	22,305	11	15,406	4	11,173	..	..	..	..	2	60,272	382
Loralai ..	431	86,087	386	47,445	35	22,976	8	10,243	2	5,321	..	..	..	..	..	..	102
Zhob ..	253	57,963	228	31,122	17	10,833	6	8,839	2	6,581	..	..	..	..	..	..	588
Bolan ..	29	4,688	28	2,418	..	..	1	1,834	..	..	..	..	..	..	..	..	436
Chagai ..	72	24,224	56	8,415	9	6,583	7	8,439	..	..	..	..	..	..	..	..	787
Sibi ..	270	143,005	198	34,080	44	31,147	16	20,381	8	26,700	4	30,422	..	..	..	..	275
Administered Area	*243*	*87,781*	*188*	*32,063*	*41*	*28,961*	*12*	*14,776*	*1*	*2,174*	*1*	*9,532*	..	..	..	..	*275*
Mari-Bugti Country	*27*	*55,224*	*10*	*2,017*	*3*	*2,186*	*4*	*5,605*	*7*	*24,526*	*3*	*20,890*	..	..	..	..	..
STATES ..	2,081	405,109	1,916	246,626	117	75,682	37	50,964	11	31,837	..	..	..	..	..	..	..
Kalat ..	1,801	342,101	1,667	211,734	93	59,372	32	44,975	9	26,020	..	..	..	..	..	..	..
Sarawan ..	*188*	*28,464*	*180*	*18,677*	*3*	*1,912*	*4*	*4,503*	*1*	*3,372*	..	..	..	..	..	..	..
Jhalawan ..	*475*	*88,978*	*436*	*47,643*	*29*	*18,892*	*5*	*7,505*	*5*	*14,938*	..	..	..	..	..	..	..
Kachhi ..	*589*	*105,886*	*550*	*69,357*	*25*	*13,904*	*13*	*19,434*	*1*	*3,191*	..	..	..	..	..	..	..
Dombki-Kaheri Country.	*123*	*26,953*	*111*	*12,891*	*6*	*4,201*	*4*	*5,342*	*2*	*4,519*	..	..	..	..	..	..	..
Makran ..	*307*	*68,462*	*277*	*44,100*	*25*	*17,408*	*5*	*6,954*	..	..	..	..	..	..	..	..	..
Kharan ..	*119*	*23,358*	*113*	*19,066*	*5*	*3,055*	*1*	*1,237*	..	..	..	..	..	..	..	..	..
Las Bela ..	280	63,008	249	34,892	24	16,310	5	5,989	2	5,817	..	..	..	..	..	..	..

TABLE IV.

TOWNS CLASSIFIED BY POPULATION WITH VARIATION FOR FORTY YEARS.

1. *Town.*—A town has been defined for Census purposes as including :—

(1) Every Municipality.

(2) All Civil Lines not included in municipal limits.

(3) Every Cantonment.

(4) Every other continuous collection of houses inhabited by not less than 5,000 persons, which may be selected for treatment as a town with regard to the character of its population, the relative density of its dwellings, its importance as a trade centre and its historic associations.

2. In the case of towns named in column 1 of this Table the numerical test has not been strictly applied in order to prevent the exclusion of certain headquarters and other stations which have a population of less than 5,000 but possess other urban characteristics.

3. Quetta and Loralai are the only places which have regular cantonments. For convenience of comparison, however, the Military stations of Fort Sandeman, Pishin and Chaman, though not cantonments in the strict sense of the word, have been shown separately from their adjoining civil stations.

4. The population of the town of Quetta consists of the following :—

	Total.	Males.	Females.
1. Quetta Municipality proper ..	27,071	17,965	9,106
2. Railway premises ..	2,112	1,451	661
3. Kasi and Nichari villages ..	4,963	2,895	2,068
4. Suburbs ..	735	527	208

Owing to rapid expansion of the Town area the adjoining villages of Kasi and Nichari with a population of 2,895 males and 2,068 females in 1931 and 755 males and 615 females in 1921, respectively, have been absorbed in the Quetta Municipality.

5. Figures are not available for Chaman, Fort Sandeman, Kalat and Bela for 1891 and for Mastung for 1891 and 1901.

6. The Kalat Town includes Kalat, Pase Shahr, Khel and Gom ; Mastung Town includes Dadezai, Mutriba, Ghulaman, Ashkanu, Khawasam, Gilkand, Sheikhan, Fatima, Muhammad Taki, Behram Shahi, Kot Saidan, Kot Sardar Muhammad Shahi, Tindlan and Pir Kanu. Bela Town includes, Balochi, Moriani, Got Sipahian, Akbani, Radhan Chatani and Notani.

7. The following places have been treated as towns for the first time with the approval of the local Government :—

1. Panjgur.
2. Pasni.
3. Machh.

Where figures for past Censuses are available, they have been shown within brackets, but not included in the totals.

8. The names of places treated as towns at each of the Censuses of 1891 to 1931, are shown below :—

1891.	1901.	1911.	1921.	1931.
1. Quetta ..	1. Quetta ..	1. Quetta ..	1. Quetta ..	1. Quetta.
2. Sibi ..	2. Sibi ..	2. Sibi ..	2. Sibi ..	2. Sibi.
3. Loralai ..	3. Fort Sandeman.	3. Fort Sandeman.	3. Fort Sandeman.	3. Fort Sandeman.
4. Pishin ..	4. Chaman ..	4. Chaman ..	4. Chaman ..	4. Chaman.
	5. Loralai ..	5. Mastung ..	5. Mastung ..	5. Mastung.
	6. Pishin ..	6. Bela ..	6. Bela ..	6. Bela.
		7. Loralai ..	7. Loralai ..	7. Loralai.
		8. Pishin ..	8. Pishin ..	8. Pasni.
		9. Kalat ..	9. Kalat ..	9. Machh.
				10. Pishin.
				11. Kalat.
				12. Panjgur.

9. The net variation during 1891 to 1931 in the population of the places treated as towns is shown below :—

Particulars.	No. of towns.	Population.
Total population of places treated as towns in 1891 ..	4	25,952
Total population of places treated as towns in 1901 ..	6	40,033
(*a*) Places treated as towns in 1891, but omitted in 1901 ..	..	..
(*b*) Places treated as towns in 1901 which were not so treated in 1891	2	5,785
Total population of places treated as towns in 1911 ..	9	59,593
(*a*) Places treated as towns in 1901, but omitted in 1911 ..	..	..
(*b*) Places treated as towns in 1911 which were not so treated in 1901	3	9,984
Total population of places treated as towns in 1921 ..	9	79,063
(*a*) Places treated as towns in 1911, but omitted in 1921 ..	..	..
(*b*) Places treated as towns in 1921 which were not so treated in 1911	..	..
Total population of places treated as towns in 1931.. ..	12	102,602
(*a*) Places treated as towns in 1921, but omitted in 1931 ..	..	..
(*b*) Places treated as towns in 1931 which were not so treated in 1921	3	4,255
Net variation in aggregate population of places treated as towns during the decades 1891 to 1931 :—		
(*a*) 1921 to 1931	..	23,539
(*b*) 1911 to 1921	..	19,470
(*c*) 1901 to 1911	..	19,560
(*d*) 1891 to 1901	..	14,081
(*e*) 1891 to 1931	..	76,650

10. As the cantonments have been treated as separate towns in 1931, the number of towns as shown above does not tally with that shown in Imperial Table V.

TABLE IV.—TOWNS CLASSIFIED BY POPULATION WITH VARIATION FOR FORTY YEARS.

Name of Town.	District or State.	Description of Towns, (Municipality, Suburbs, Cantonments, etc.)	Population.					Variation Increase (+) Decrease (—)				Variation in period 1891 to 1931. Increase (+) Decrease (—)	Males.			Females.		
			1931	1921	1911	1901	1891	1921 to 1931	1911 to 1921	1901 to 1911	1891 to 1901		1931	1921	1911	1931	1921	1911
1	2	3	4	5	6	7	8	9	10	11	12	13	14	15	16	17	18	19
	BALUCHISTAN ..		**102,602**	**79,063**	**59,598**	**40,033**	**25,952**	**+ 23,539**	**+ 19,470**	**+ 19,560**	**+ 14,061**	**+ 76,650**	**71,561**	**60,099**	**43,049**	**31,041**	**18,964**	**16,544**
CLASS III	**(20,000 – 50,000).**																	
1. Quetta ..	Quetta-Pishin ..	*Municipality and suburbs.*	*34,881*	*27,220*	*17,021*	*13,517*	*11,302*	*+ 7,661*	*+ 10,199*	*+ 3,504*	*+ 2,215*	*+ 23,579*	*22,838*	*19,024*	*11,456*	*12,043*	*8,196*	*5,565*
2. Do. ..	Do. ..	*Cantonment* ..	*25,391*	*21,781*	*16,901*	*11,067*	*7,500*	*+ 3,610*	*+ 4,880*	*+ 5,834*	*+ 3,567*	*+ 17,891*	*19,589*	*18,385*	*13,813*	*5,802*	*3,396*	*3,088*
CLASS V	**(5,000 – 10,000).**																	
3. Sibi ..	Sibi ..	Town ..	9,532	6,386	6,597	4,551	2,944	+ 3,146	– 211	+ 2,046	+ 1,607	+ 6,588	6,088	4,548	4,900	3,444	1,838	1,697
CLASS VI	**(Under 5,000).**																	
4. Fort Sandeman	Zhob ..	Town ..	3,944	4,228	3,391	3,552	..	– 284	+ 837	– 161	+ 3,552	+ 3,944	2,976	4,101	2,941	968	127	450
Do. ..	Do. ..	Cantonment ..	2,637	..	Included in Fort Sandeman Town.			+ 2,637	..	..	..	+ 2,637	2,597	..	..	40	..	..
5. Chaman ..	Quetta-Pishin ..	Town .	3,696	4,226	2,009	2,233	..	– 530	+ 2,217	– 224	+ 2,233	+ 3,696	2,547	3,618	1,605	1,149	608	404
Do. ..	Do. ..	Cantonment ..	2,354	..	Included in Chaman Town			+ 2,354	..	..	..	+ 2,354	1,923	..	..	431	..	..
6. Mastung ..	Kalat State ..	Town ..	3,372	4,569	5,007	..	..	– 1,197	– 438	+ 5,007	..	+ 3,372	1,888	2,609	2,775	1,484	1,960	2,232
7. Bela ..	Las-Bela State ..	Do. ..	3,340	2,712	3,006	(4,183)	..	+ 628	– 294	+ 3,006	..	+ 3,340	1,736	1,431	1,559	1,604	1,281	1,447
8. Loralai ..	Loralai .	Do. ..	2,695	4,303	2,936	3,561	3,674	– 1,608	+ 1,367	– 625	– 113	– 979	1,913	3,728	2,428	782	575	508
Do. ..	Do. ..	Cantonment ..	2,626	..	Included in Loralai Town.			+ 2,626	..	..	..	+ 2,626	2,157	..	..	469	..	..
9. Pasni ..	Kalat State ..	Port ..	1,989	(1,446)	(1,253)	..	..	+ 1,989	..	..	..	+ 1,989	1,090	(788)	(657)	899	(658)	(596)
10. Machh ..	Bolan ..	Town ..	1,834	(794)	(519)	..	..	+ 1,834	..	..	..	+ 1,834	1,455	(626)	(386)	379	(168)	(133)
11. Pishin ..	Quetta-Pishin ..	Do. ..	1,625	1,804	754	1,552	532	– 179	+ 1,050	– 798	+ 1,020	+ 1,093	1,064	1,461	517	561	343	237
Do. ..	Do. ..	Cantonment ..	810	..	Included in Pishin Town.			+ 810	..	..	..	+ 810	766	..	..	44	..	..
12. Kalat ..	Kalat State ..	Town ..	1,444	1,834	1,971	(2,000)	..	– 390	– 137	+ 1,971	..	+ 1,444	646	1,194	1,055	798	640	916
13. Panjgur ..	Do. ..	Do. ..	432	(530)	(452)	..	..	+ 432	..	..	..	+ 432	288	(389)	(345)	144	(141)	(107

TABLE V.

TOWNS ARRANGED TERRITORIALLY WITH POPULATION BY RELIGION.

Columns 30—32 under "Others" consist of 28 Chuhras (24 males, 4 females) in Machh, 1 male of indefinite belief in Sibi and 2 males and 3 females in Quetta Cantonment.

Details of the Civil and Military population in the various Cantonments are given below :—

Cantonment.	Population.								
	Total.			*Military.*			*Civil.*		
	Total.	Males.	Females.	Total.	Males.	Females.	Total.	Males.	Females.
Quetta ..	25,391	19,589	5,802	11,740	11,730	10	13,651	7,859	5,792
Pishin ..	810	766	44	672	672	..	138	94	44
Chaman ..	2,354	1,923	431	1,923	1,9?3	.	431	..	431
Loralai ..	2,626	2,157	469	1,359	1,359	..	1,267	798	469
Fort Sandeman	2,637	2,597	40	2,336	2,336	..	301	261	40
Total ..	33,818	27,082	6,786	18,030	18,020	10	15,788	9,012	6,776

The Military figures represent persons subject to Military Law living at the time of Census within strictly Military area.

TABLE V.—TOWNS ARRANGED TERRITORIALLY WITH POPULATION BY RELIGION.

District or State.	Town, Municipality, Suburb, Cantts., etc.	Population.			Hindu.			Sikh.			Jain.			Buddhist.			Muslim.			Christian.			Zoroastrian.			Jew.			Others.		
		P.	M.	F.	P.	M.	F.	P.	M.	F.	P.	M.	F.	P.	M.	F.	P.	M.	F.	P.	M.	F.	P.	M.	F.	P.	M.	F.	P.	M.	F.
1	2	3	4	5	6	7	8	9	10	11	12	13	14	15	16	17	18	19	20	21	22	23	24	25	26	27	28	29	30	31	32
BALUCHISTAN ..		102,802	71,561	31,041	34,484	24,850	9,634	7,029	5,194	1,835	32	20	12	68	53	15	52,853	35,776	17,077	7,918	5,537	2,381	167	90	77	17	14	3	34	27	7
DISTRICTS ..		92,025	65,913	26,112	33,387	24,193	9,194	7,002	5,172	1,830	32	20	12	68	53	15	43,416	30,820	12,596	7,904	5,526	2,378	167	90	77	15	12	3	34	27	7
Quetta-Pishin ..	Quetta :—	34,881	22,838	12,043	11,956	8,038	3,918	3,310	2,180	1,130	25	13	12	29	16	13	18,101	11,799	6,3[illegible]2	1,319	716	603	137	72	65	4	4	..	..	..	..
	Municipality	*34,146*	*22,311*	*11,835*	*11,767*	*7,896*	*3,871*	*3,263*	*2,145*	*1,118*	*25*	*13*	*12*	*29*	*16*	*13*	*17,660*	*11,482*	*6,178*	*1,266*	*685*	*581*	*132*	*70*	*62*	*4*	*4*	..	..	..	..
	Suburbs	*735*	*527*	*208*	*189*	*142*	*47*	*47*	*35*	*12*	..	..	..	..	..	..	*441*	*317*	*124*	*53*	*31*	*22*	*5*	*2*	*3*	..	..	..	..	..	..
	Quetta-Cantonment.	25,391	19,589	5,802	10,188	7,719	2,469	1,476	1,219	257	7	7	..	11	9	2	7,980	6,385	1,595	5,693	4,232	1,461	23	11	12	8	5	3	5	2	3
	Pishin Town ..	1,625	1,064	561	371	231	140	105	69	36	..	..	..	..	..	..	1,081	718	363	68	46	22	..	..	..	..	..	..	..	..	..
	Pishin Cantonment.	810	766	44	475	456	19	2	2	..	..	..	..	..	..	..	289	271	18	44	37	7	..	..	..	..	..	..	..	..	..
	Chaman Town	3,696	2,547	1,149	1,230	842	388	148	103	45	..	..	..	..	..	..	2,154	1,508	646	161	91	70	..	..	..	3	3	..	..	..	..
	Chaman Cantonment.	2,354	1,923	431	1,631	1,260	371	112	107	5	..	..	..	..	..	..	530	506	24	80	49	31	1	1	..	..	..	..	..	..	..
Loralai ..	Loralai Town ..	2,695	1,913	782	767	548	219	292	205	87	..	..	..	..	..	..	1,571	1,119	452	65	41	24	..	..	..	..	..	..	..	..	..
	Loralai Cantonment.	2,626	2,157	469	1,263	970	293	214	202	12	..	..	..	..	..	..	1,037	903	134	112	82	30	..	..	..	..	..	..	..	..	..
Zhob ..	Fort Sandeman Town.	3,944	2,976	968	1,046	724	322	228	164	64	..	..	..	27	27	..	2,610	2,042	568	33	19	14	..	..	..	..	..	..	..	..	..
	Fort Sandeman Cantonment.	2,637	2,597	40	1,278	1,257	21	559	559	..	..	..	..	..	..	..	750	731	19	50	50	..	..	..	..	..	..	..	..	..	..
Bolan ..	Machh Town ..	1,834	1,455	379	455	362	93	136	114	22	..	..	..	..	..	..	1,149	916	233	66	39	27	..	..	..	..	..	..	28	24	4
Sibi ..	Sibi Town ..	9,532	6,088	3,444	2,727	1,786	941	420	248	172	..	..	..	1	1	..	6,164	3,922	2,242	213	124	89	6	6	..	..	..	..	1	1	..
STATES ..		10,577	5,648	4,929	1,097	657	440	27	22	5	..	..	..	..	..	..	9,437	4,956	4,481	14	11	3	..	..	..	2	2	..	..	..	..
Kalat ..	Kalat Town ..	1,444	646	798	344	169	175	..	..	..	..	..	..	..	..	..	1,100	477	623	..	..	..	..	..	..	..	..	..	..	..	..
	Mastung Town..	3,372	1,888	1,484	260	156	104	10	8	2	..	..	..	..	..	..	3,099	1,723	1,376	3	1	2	..	..	..	..	..	..	..	..	..
	Pasni Port ..	1,989	1,090	899	62	62	..	2	2	..	..	..	..	..	..	..	1,924	1,025	899	1	1	..	..	..	..	..	..	..	..	..	..
	Panjgur Town	432	288	144	77	54	23	..	..	..	..	..	..	..	..	..	343	223	120	10	9	1	..	..	..	2	2	..	..	..	..
Las-Bela ..	Bela Town ..	3,340	1,736	1,604	354	216	138	15	12	3	..	..	..	..	..	..	2,971	1,508	1,463	..	..	..	..	..	..	..	..	..	..	..	..

P = Persons; M = Males; F = Females.

TABLE V.—TOWNS ARRANGED TERRITORIALLY WITH POPULATION BY RELIGION.

TABLE VI

BIRTHPLACE.

1. The arrangement of countries and districts of birth is based on the principle laid down by the Census Commissioner for India.

2. Birthplace was recorded for the non-indigenous population only. The birthplace of the indigenous inhabitants was assumed to be the same as the District or State in which they were enumerated, excepting temporary immigrants whose birthplace was taken to be the District or State in which they permanently reside.

3. Of a total population of 868,617 persons (488,414 males and 380,203 females), 778,564 persons were born in Baluchistan. The rest were born in the countries named below :—

	Total.	Males.	Females.
A.—Born in Indian Provinces and States ..	66,542	50,061	16,481
B.—Born in Other Asiatic Countries ..	19,344	12,959	6,385
(a) Afghanistan ..	14,953	9,572	5,381
(b) Nepal ..	3,868	3,120	748
(c) Persia ..	417	189	228
(d) China ..	34	24	10
(e) Other Asiatic Countries ..	72	54	18
C.—Born in Europe ..	4,082	3,298	784
(a) United Kingdom ..	3,917	3,195	722
(b) Other European Countries	165	103	62
D.—Born in Africa ..	29	18	11
(a) Egypt ..	18	9	9
(b) Other African Countries ..	11	9	2
E.—Born in America ..	41	26	15
(a) Canada ..	21	14	7
(b) Other American Countries	20	12	8
F.—Born in Australasia ..	15	12	3

TABLE VI.—

District, State, Province or Country where born.	DISTRICT OR STATE											
	Baluchistan.			District or Administered								
				Quetta-Pishin.			Loralai.			Zhob.		
	Persons.	Males.	Females.	Persons.	Males.	Females.	Persons.	Males.	Females.	Persons.	Males.	Females.
1	2	3	4	5	6	7	8	9	10	11	12	13
TOTAL	**868,617**	**488,414**	**380,203**	**147,541**	**90,302**	**57,239**	**86,087**	**47,936**	**38,151**	**57,963**	**34,596**	**23,367**
A. Born in India	*845,106*	*472,101*	*373,005*	*135,271*	*81,024*	*54,247*	*79,172*	*44,041*	*35,131*	*56,576*	*33,292*	*23,284*
I. WITHIN BALUCHISTAN	*778,564*	*422,040*	*356,524*	*93,564*	*49,881*	*43,683*	*73,681*	*39,894*	*33,787*	*49,904*	*27,559*	*22,345*
(i) Districts and Administered Territories.	*369,599*	*201,032*	*168,567*	*91,685*	*48,664*	*43,021*	*73,222*	*39,613*	*33,609*	*49,757*	*27,416*	*22,341*
Quetta-Pishin	94,029	50,000	44,029	90,808	48,044	42,764	203	124	79	335	279	56
Loralai	72,920	39,437	33,483	90	56	34	72,155	38,972	33,183	109	70	39
Zhob	49,837	27,424	22,413	228	158	70	300	190	110	49,234	27,009	22,225
Bolan	619	370	249	19	9	10	..	..	..	..	..	..
Chagai	21,353	11,770	9,583	297	204	93	89	64	25	12	7	5
Sibi	130,841	72,031	58,810	243	193	50	475	263	212	67	51	16
(ii) States	*408,965*	*221,008*	*187,957*	*1,879*	*1,217*	*662*	*459*	*281*	*178*	*147*	*143*	*4*
Kalat	346,838	188,046	158,792	1,875	1,216	659	459	281	178	147	143	4
Las-Bela	62,127	32,962	29,165	4	1	3	..	...	..	..	..	..
II. PROVINCES AND STATES IN INDIA BEYOND BALUCHISTAN.	*66,542*	*50,061*	*16,481*	*41,707*	*31,143*	*10,564*	*5,491*	*4,147*	*1,344*	*6,672*	*5,733*	*939*
(a) Provinces and States Adjacent to Baluchistan.	*48,792*	*35,982*	*12,810*	*29,558*	*21,653*	*7,905*	*4,034*	*2,980*	*1,054*	*5,366*	*4,506*	*860*
(i) *British Territory*	*47,282*	*34,734*	*12,548*	*28,717*	*20,970*	*7,747*	*3,960*	*2,912*	*1,048*	*5,138*	*4,289*	*849*
Bombay including Aden	4,805	3,502	1,303	3,198	2,319	879	167	108	59	80	64	16
Aden	1	..	1	1	..	1	..	..		..	..	..
North-West Frontier Province—Districts and Administered Territories.	6,148	4,742	1,406	3,611	2,674	937	583	478	105	1,328	1,130	198
Punjab	36,329	26,490	9,839	21,908	15,977	5,931	3,210	2,326	884	3,730	3,095	635
(ii) *Feudatory States*	*1,510*	*1,248*	*262*	*841*	*683*	*158*	*74*	*68*	*6*	*228*	*217*	*11*
Bombay States	459	396	63	314	277	37	6	4	2	3	1	2
North-West Frontier Province—Agencies and Tribal Areas.	35	20	15	20	10	10	10	7	3	..	..	..
Punjab States	1,016	832	184	507	396	111	58	57	1	225	216	9
(b) Other Provinces and States in India.	*17,514*	*13,915*	*3,599*	*11,930*	*9,339*	*2,591*	*1,457*	*1,167*	*290*	*1,302*	*1,223*	*79*
(i) *British Territory*	*13,830*	*10,922*	*2,908*	*9,782*	*7,649*	*2,133*	*1,181*	*932*	*249*	*879*	*822*	*57*
Ajmer-Merwara	117	73	44	99	62	37	..	..	..	1	1	..
Andamans and Nicobars	2	2	..	1	1	..	..	..	..	..	..	..
Assam	10	4	6	7	2	5	1	1	..	1	1	..
Bengal	578	352	226	467	260	207	13	7	6	72	69	3
Bihar and Orissa	44	35	9	28	23	5	12	8	4	3	3	..
Burma	60	36	24	56	33	23	..	..	..	4	3	1
Central Provinces and Berar.	203	120	83	109	63	46	72	42	30	1	..	1
Coorg	2	1	1	2	1	1	..	..	..	..	..	..
Delhi	752	536	216	611	429	182	39	29	10	12	12	..
Madras	186	119	67	164	101	63	9	7	2	2	2	..
United Provinces of Agra and Oudh.	11,876	9,644	2,232	8,238	6,674	1,564	1,035	838	197	783	731	52
(ii) *Feudatory States*	*3,684*	*2,993*	*691*	*2,148*	*1,690*	*458*	*276*	*235*	*41*	*423*	*401*	*22*
Assam States (*i.e.*, Manipur and Tribal Areas).	7	2	5	7	2	5	..	..	..	..	..	..
Baroda State	22	11	11	10	6	4	..	..	..	..	..	..
Central India Agency	56	35	21	45	26	19	8	6	2	2	2	..
Gwalior State	71	53	18	43	34	9	18	13	5	9	5	4
Hyderabad State	150	105	45	139	99	40	2	1	1	..	..	..
Kashmir State	2,081	1,793	288	1,205	1,010	195	165	145	20	263	252	11
Madras States	6	5	1	5	4	1	..	..	..	..	..	..
(a) Cochin	3	2	1	2	1	1	..	..	..	..	..	..
(b) Travancore	3	3	..	3	3	..	..	..	..	..	..	..
Mysore State	107	64	43	87	53	34	3	3	..	10	5	5
Rajputana Agency	914	713	201	375	279	96	79	66	13	115	114	1
Sikkim State	45	36	9	25	16	9	..	..	..	20	20	..
United Provinces States	31	24	7	22	16	6	1	1	..	4	3	1
Western India Agency	194	152	42	185	145	40	..	..	..	..	..	

BIRTHPLACE.

WHERE ENUMERATED.

TERRITORY.									STATES.					
Bolan.			*Chagai.*			*Sibi.*			*Kalat.*			*Las-Bela.*		
Persons.	Males.	Females.	Persons.	Males.	Females.	Persons.	Males.	Females.	Persons.	Males.	Females.	Persons.	Males.	Females.
14	15	16	17	18	19	20	21	22	23	24	25	26	27	28
4,688	**3,466**	**1,222**	**24,224**	**13,721**	**10,503**	**143,005**	**79,983**	**63,022**	**342,101**	**184,915**	**157,186**	**63,008**	**33,495**	**29,513**
4,581	*3,373*	*1,208*	*23,047*	*12,966*	*10,081*	*141,497*	*79,080*	*62,417*	*341,964*	*184,835*	*157,129*	*62,998*	*33,490*	*29,508*
2,483	*1,770*	*713*	*21,256*	*11,627*	*9,629*	*135,122*	*74,495*	*60,627*	*340,011*	*183,644*	*156,367*	*62,543*	*33,170*	*29,373*
1,265	*886*	*379*	*20,392*	*11,121*	*9,271*	*132,253*	*72,696*	*59,557*	*1,024*	*635*	*389*	*1*	*1*	..
234	165	69	53	33	20	1,995	1,125	870	400	229	171	1	1	..
44	44	..	2	1	1	520	294	226	..	..	..	..	..	..
50	47	3	2	2	..	21	18	3	2	..	2	..	..	..
594	358	236	..	..	..	6	3	3	..	..	..	..	..	..
23	15	8	20,302	11,066	9,236	46	31	15	584	383	201	..	..	..
320	257	63	33	19	14	129,665	71,225	58,440	38	23	15	..	..	..
1,218	*884*	*334*	*864*	*506*	*358*	*2,869*	*1,799*	*1,070*	*338,987*	*183,009*	*155,978*	*62,542*	*33,169*	*29,373*
1,218	884	334	864	506	358	2,865	1,796	1,069	338,978	183,002	155,976	442	228	214
..	..	..	..	..	..	4	3	1	9	7	2	62,100	32,941	29,159
2,098	*1,603*	*495*	*1,791*	*1,339*	*452*	*6,375*	*4,585*	*1,790*	*1,953*	*1,191*	*762*	*455*	*320*	*135*
1,488	*1,119*	*369*	*1,132*	*817*	*315*	*4,998*	*3,555*	*1,443*	*1,813*	*1,068*	*745*	*403*	*284*	*119*
1,438	*1,081*	*357*	*1,102*	*795*	*307*	*4,771*	*3,330*	*1,391*	*1,788*	*1,050*	*738*	*368*	*257*	*111*
152	116	36	120	76	44	733	535	198	173	147	26	182	137	45
..	..	..	..	..	..	..	..	..	..	..	..	..	..	..
121	94	27	93	70	23	330	241	89	42	27	15	40	28	12
1,165	871	294	889	649	240	3,708	2,604	1,104	1,573	876	697	146	92	54
50	*38*	*12*	*30*	*22*	*8*	*227*	*175*	*52*	*25*	*18*	*7*	*35*	*27*	*8*
4	4	..	2	2	..	100	85	15	4	4	..	26	19	7
..	..	..	1	1	..	3	1	2	..	..	..	1	1	..
46	34	12	27	19	8	124	89	35	21	14	7	8	7	1
608	*482*	*126*	*658*	*521*	*137*	*1,368*	*1,025*	*343*	*139*	*122*	*17*	*52*	*36*	*16*
524	*409*	*115*	*313*	*242*	*71*	*1,018*	*754*	*264*	*102*	*90*	*12*	*31*	*24*	*7*
..	..	..	..	..	..	..	..	..	17	10	7	..	..	..
..	..	..	1	1	..	..	..	..	..	..	..	..	..	..
..	..	..	..	..	..	1	..	1	..	..	..	..	..	..
11	6	5	2	2	..	13	8	5	..	..	..	..	..	..
..	..	..	..	..	..	1	1	..	..	..	..	..	..	..
..	..	..	..	..	..	..	..	..	..	..	..	..	..	..
7	4	3	..	..	..	15	12	3	..	..	..	..	..	..
8	7	1	18	14	4	54	38	16	10	7	3	..	..	..
..	..	..	3	3	..	6	4	2	1	1	..	..	..	..
498	392	106	289	222	67	928	691	237	74	72	2	31	24	7
84	*73*	*11*	*345*	*279*	*66*	*350*	*271*	*79*	*37*	*32*	*5*	*21*	*12*	*9*
..	..	..	..	..	..	..	..	..	..	..	..	..	..	..
..	..	..	..	..	..	..	..	..	..	..	..	12	5	7
..	..	..	..	..	..	1	1	..	..	..	..	..	..	..
..	..	..	..	..	..	1	1	..	..	..	..	..	..	..
..	..	..	2	1	1	5	3	2	2	1	1	..	..	..
75	66	9	184	161	23	162	132	30	27	27	..	..	..	..
..	..	..	..	..	..	..	..	..	1	1	..	..	..	..
..	..	..	..	..	..	..	..	..	1	1	..	..	..	..
..	..	..	..	..	..	..	..	..	..	..	..	..	..	..
..	..	..	..	..	..	7	3	4	..	..	..	..	..	..
9	7	2	158	116	42	171	128	43	7	3	4	..	..	..
..	..	..	..	..	..	..	..	..	..	..	..	..	..	..
..	..	..	1	1	..	3	3	..	..	..	..	..	..	..
..	..	..	..	..	..	..	..	..	..	..	..	9	7	2

TABLE VI.—

District, State, Province or Country where born.	DISTRICT OR STATE											
	BALUCHISTAN.			DISTRICT OR ADMINISTERED								
				Quetta-Pishin.			*Loralai.*			*Zhob.*		
	Persons.	Males.	Females.	Persons.	Males.	Females.	Persons.	Males.	Females.	Persons.	Males.	Females.
1	2	3	4	5	6	7	8	9	10	11	12	13
(c) FRENCH AND PORTUGUESE SETTLEMENTS.	129	104	25	112	91	21	..	..	..	4	4	..
(d) INDIA UNSPECIFIED ..	107	60	47	107	60	47	..	..	..	..	..	..
B. *Born in other Asiatic Countries.*	*19,344*	*12,959*	*6,385*	*8,275*	*6,046*	*2,229*	*6,848*	*3,847*	*3,001*	*1,338*	*1,260*	*78*
* (i) WITHIN BRITISH DOMINIONS.	*20*	*10*	*10*	*19*	*9*	*10*	..	..	..	*1*	*1*	..
Ceylon ..	12	3	9	12	3	9	..	..	..	..	..	..
Straits Settlements and Malaya.	5	4	1	5	4	1	..	..	..	..	..	..
Elsewhere ..	3	3	..	2	2	..	..	..	..	1	1	..
(ii) OUTSIDE BRITISH DOMINIONS.	*19,324*	*12,949*	*6,375*	*8,256*	*6,037*	*2,219*	*6,848*	*3,847*	*3,001*	*1,337*	*1,259*	*78*
Afghanistan ..	14,953	9,572	5,381	4,808	3,438	1,370	6,817	3,818	2,999	800	723	77
China ..	34	24	10	34	24	10	..	—	..	..	..	..
Nepal ..	3 868	3,120	748	3,236	2,489	747	19	19	..	532	531	1
Elsewhere ..	469	233	236	178	86	92	12	10	2	5	5	..
C. *Born in Europe* ..	*4,082*	*3,298*	*784*	*3,918*	*3,181*	*737*	*65*	*47*	*18*	*46*	*42*	*4*
* WITHIN BRITISH DOMINIONS ..	*4,060*	*3,286*	*774*	*3,897*	*3,170*	*727*	*65*	*47*	*18*	*45*	*41*	*4*
(i) United Kingdom and Irish Free State.	4,041	3,277	764	3,878	3,161	717	65	47	18	45	41	4
(ii) British Possessions in Europe.	19	9	10	19	9	10	..	..	..	..	..	..
CONTINENTAL EUROPE ..	*22*	*12*	*10*	*21*	*11*	*10*	..	..	..	*1*	*1*	..
D. *Born in Africa* ..	*29*	*18*	*11*	*26*	*16*	*10*	..	..	..	*3*	*2*	*1*
* (i) WITHIN BRITISH DOMINIONS	*5*	*3*	*2*	*2*	*1*	*1*	..	..	..	*3*	*2*	*1*
Mauritius ..	1	..	1	1	..	1	..	..	..	..	..	..
Transvaal ..	3	2	1	..	..	..	..	..	..	3	2	1
Elsewhere ..	1	1	..	1	1	..	..	..	..	..	..	..
(ii) OUTSIDE BRITISH DOMINIONS.	*18*	*9*	*9*	*18*	*9*	*9*	..	..	..	..	..	..
Elsewhere ..	18	9	9	18	9	9	..	..	..	..	..	..
(iii) AFRICA UNSPECIFIED ..	*6*	*6*	..	*6*	*6*	..	..	..	..	..	..	..
E. *Born in America* ..	*41*	*26*	*15*	*38*	*25*	*13*	*1*	..	*1*	..	..	..
* (i) WITHIN BRITISH DOMINIONS	*27*	*18*	*9*	*26*	*18*	*8*	*1*	..	*1*	..	..	..
British Guiana ..	1	..	1	1	..	1	..	..	..	..	..	..
Canada ..	21	14	7	20	14	6	1	..	1	..	..	..
Elsewhere ..	5	4	1	5	4	1	..	..	..	..	..	..
(ii) OUTSIDE BRITISH DOMINIONS.	*7*	*4*	*3*	*7*	*4*	*3*	..	..	..	..	..	..
United States ..	4	2	2	4	2	2	..	..	..	..	..	..
Elsewhere ..	3	2	1	3	2	1	..	..	..	..	..	..
(iii) AMERICA UNSPECIFIED ..	*7*	*4*	*3*	*5*	*3*	*2*	..	..	..	..	..	..
F. *Born in Australasia.* ..	*15*	*12*	*3*	*13*	*10*	*3*	*1*	*1*	..	..	..	..
* (i) WITHIN BRITISH DOMINIONS	*4*	*4*	..	*2*	*2*	..	*1*	*1*	..	..	..	..
Australia ..	2	2	..	..	..	..	1	1	..	..	..	..
New Zealand ..	2	2	..	2	2	..	..	..	..	..	..	..
(ii) OUTSIDE BRITISH DOMINIONS.	..	..	..	..	..	..	..	..	..	..	..	..
(iii) AUSTRALASIA UNSPECIFIED.	11	8	3	11	8	3	..	..	..	..	..	..

*Means "Within the British Empire and Mandated Territories."

BIRTH-PLACE.

WHERE ENUMERATED.

TERRITORY.									STATES.					
Bolan.			*Chagai.*			*Sibi.*			*Kalat.*			*Las-Bela.*		
Persons.	Males.	Females.	Persons.	Males.	Females.	Persons.	Males.	Females.	Persons.	Males.	Females	Persons.	Males.	Females.
14	15	16	17	18	19	20	21	22	23	24	25	26	27	28
2	2	..	1	1	..	9	5	4	1	1	..	..	..	..
..	..	..	..	..	..	..	..	..	..	..	..	..	..	..
94	*85*	*9*	*1,176*	*754*	*422*	*1,468*	*883*	*585*	*135*	*79*	*56*	*10*	*5*	
..	..	..	..	..	..	..	..	..	..	..	..	..	..	..
..	..	..	..	..	..	..	..	..	..	..	..	..	..	..
..	..	..	..	..	..	..	..	..	..	..	..	..	..	..
..	..	..	..	..	..	..	..	..	..	..	..	..	..	..
94	*85*	*9*	*1,176*	*754*	*422*	*1,468*	*883*	*585*	*135*	*79*	*56*	*10*	*5*	
69	60	9	1,020	679	341	1,402	820	582	35	32	3	2	2	..
..	..	..	..	..	..	..	..	..	..	..	..	..	..	..
25	25	..	..	..	..	56	56	..	..	..	..	..	..	..
..	..	..	156	75	81	10	7	3	100	47	53	8	3	
13	*8*	*5*	..	..	..	*38*	*19*	*19*	*2*	*1*	*1*	..	..	..
13	*8*	*5*	..	..	..	*38*	*19*	*19*	*2*	*1*	*1*	..	..	..
13	8	5	..	..	..	38	19	19	2	1	1	..	..	..
..	..	..	..	..	..	..	..	..	..	..	..	..	..	..
..	..	..	..	..	..	..	..	..	..	..	..	..	..	..
..	..	..	..	..	..	..	..	..	..	..	..	..	..	..
..	..	..	..	..	..	..	..	..	..	..	..	..	..	..
..	..	..	..	..	..	..	..	..	..	..	..	..	..	..
..	..	..	..	..	..	..	..	..	..	..	..	..	..	..
..	..	..	..	..	..	..	..	..	..	..	..	..	..	..
..	..	..	..	..	..	..	..	..	..	..	..	..	..	..
..	..	..	..	..	..	..	..	..	..	..	..	..	..	..
..	..	..	..	..	..	..	..	..	..	..	..	..	..	..
..	..	..	..	..	..	*2*	*1*	*1*	..	..	..	..	..	..
..	..	..	..	..	..	..	..	..	..	..	..	..	..	..
..	..	..	..	..	..	..	..	..	..	..	..	..	..	..
..	..	..	..	..	..	..	..	..	..	..	..	..	..	..
..	..	..	..	..	..	..	..	..	..	..	..	..	..	..
..	..	..	..	..	..	..	..	..	..	..	..	..	..	..
..	..	..	..	..	..	..	..	..	..	..	..	..	..	..
..	..	..	..	..	..	..	..	..	..	..	..	..	..	..
..	..	..	..	..	..	*2*	*1*	*1*	..	..	..	..	..	..
..	..	..	*1*	*1*	..	..	..	..	..	..	..	..	..	..
..	..	..	*1*	*1*	..	..	..	..	..	..	..	..	..	..
..	..	..	1	1	..	..	..	..	..	..	..	..	..	..
..	..	..	..	..	..	..	..	..	..	..	..	..	..	..
..	..	..	..	..	..	..	..	..	..	..	..	..	..	..
..	..	..	..	..	..	..	..	..	..	..	..	..	..	..

TABLE VII.

AGE, SEX AND CIVIL CONDITION.

PART "A"—BALUCHISTAN.

PART "B"—KHARAN.

For purposes of Census, Baluchistan was divided into (*i*) Regular Areas (Population 110,849) and (*ii*) Tribal Areas (Population 757,768). The Regular Areas covered all Towns, Cantonments, Railway premises, District and Tahsil headquarters stations inhabited almost entirely by aliens from India and elsewhere. The Tribal Areas comprised the rest of the Province representing 757,768 persons practically exclusively indigenous. Specific Age and Civil condition were recorded for each individual throughout the Regular Areas but in the Tribal Areas the return could be extended only to Kharan. In view of the diversity of conditions prevailing in the two areas owing to the temporary nature of the sojourn of aliens, the table has been split up into two parts. Part "A" contains a summary for the non-indigenous population or, to be more accurate, for the Regular Areas in which aliens predominate. Part "B" gives statistics for Kharan representing exclusively indigenous population, in order to give an indication of conditions prevailing amongst indigenous tribesmen.

2. The age groups in this table are shown as 5-10, 10-15, etc. etc. This is in accordance with the usual statistical practice. The entry 5-10 for instance, refers to all persons who have reached the age of 5 but have not reached the age of 10, *i.e.* those whose completed ages are either 5, 6, 7, 8 or 9, but not 10.

TABLE VII.—AGE, SEX AND CIVIL CONDITION.

PART "A"—BALUCHISTAN.

Age and Civil Condition.	Population.			Hindu.			Sikh.			Muslim.			Christian.			Others.		
	P.	M.	F.	P.	M.	F.	P.	M.	F.	P.	M.	F.	P.	M.	F.	P.	M.	F.
1	2	3	4	5	6	7	8	9	10	11	12	13	14	15	16	17	18	19
Grand Total ..	**868,617**	**488,414**	**380,203**	**53,681**	**36,180**	**17,501**	**8,425**	**6,270**	**2,155**	**798,093**	**440,089**	**358,004**	**8,059**	**5,637**	**2,422**	**359**	**238**	**121**
Total Civil Condition Unspecified.	**757,768**	**408,217**	**349,551**	**15,615**	**8,521**	**7,094**	**485**	**326**	**159**	**741,665**	**399,367**	**342,298**	**3**	**3**	..	..	..	..
Total Civil Condition Specified.	**110,849**	**80,197**	**30,652**	**38,066**	**27,659**	**10,407**	**7,940**	**5,944**	**1,996**	**56,428**	**40,722**	**15,706**	**8,056**	**5,634**	**2,422**	**359**	**238**	**121**
Unmarried ..	50,438	37,351	13,087	15,584	11,264	4,320	3,527	2,693	834	26,052	19,336	6,716	5,091	3,948	1,143	184	110	74
Married ..	55,020	39,362	15,658	20,608	15,204	5,404	4,156	3,054	1,102	27,438	19,520	7,918	2,661	1,467	1,194	157	117	40
Widowed ..	5,391	3,484	1,907	1,874	1,191	683	257	197	60	2,938	1,866	1,072	304	219	85	18	11	7
0—1 ..	**2,566**	**1,285**	**1,281**	**960**	**488**	**472**	**177**	**79**	**98**	**1,238**	**623**	**615**	**187**	**93**	**94**	**4**	**2**	**2**
Unmarried ..	2,566	1,285	1,281	960	488	472	177	79	98	1,238	623	615	187	93	94	4	2	2
Married ..	..	..	..	..	..	..	..	..	..	..	..	..	..	..	..	..	..	..
Widowed ..	..	..	..	..	..	..	..	..	..	..	..	..	..	..	..	..	..	..
1—2 ..	**2,160**	**1,115**	**1,045**	**784**	**401**	**383**	**152**	**78**	**74**	**1,043**	**540**	**503**	**174**	**93**	**81**	**7**	**3**	**4**
Unmarried ..	2,160	1,115	1,045	784	401	383	152	78	74	1,043	540	503	174	93	81	7	3	4
Married ..	..	..	..	..	..	..	..	..	..	..	..	..	..	..	..	..	..	..
Widowed ..	..	..	..	..	..	..	..	..	..	..	..	..	..	..	..	..	..	..
2—3 ..	**2,380**	**1,212**	**1,168**	**830**	**427**	**403**	**161**	**83**	**78**	**1,208**	**608**	**600**	**173**	**90**	**83**	**8**	**4**	**4**
Unmarried	2,380	1,212	1,168	830	427	403	161	83	78	1,208	608	600	173	90	83	8	4	4
Married ..	..	..	..	..	..	..	..	..	..	..	..	..	..	..	..	..	..	..
Widowed ..	..	..	..	..	..	..	..	..	..	..	..	..	..	..	..	..	..	..
3—4 ..	**2,235**	**1,125**	**1,110**	**766**	**385**	**381**	**154**	**81**	**73**	**1,144**	**571**	**573**	**166**	**86**	**80**	**5**	**2**	**3**
Unmarried ..	2,235	1,125	1,110	766	385	381	154	81	73	1,144	571	573	166	86	80	5	2	3
Married ..	..	..	..	..	..	..	..	..	..	..	..	..	..	..	..	..	..	..
Widowed ..	..	..	..	..	..	..	..	..	..	..	..	..	..	..	..	..	..	..
4—5 ..	**2,015**	**1,056**	**959**	**665**	**338**	**327**	**134**	**79**	**55**	**1,043**	**544**	**499**	**166**	**92**	**74**	**7**	**3**	**4**
Unmarried ..	2,015	1,056	959	665	338	327	134	79	55	1,043	544	499	166	92	74	7	3	4
Married ..	..	..	..	..	..	..	..	..	..	..	..	..	..	..	..	..	..	..
Widowed ..	..	..	..	..	..	..	..	..	..	..	..	..	..	..	..	..	..	..
Total 0—5 ..	*11,356*	*5,793*	*5,563*	*4,005*	*2,039*	*1,966*	*778*	*400*	*378*	*5,676*	*2,886*	*2,790*	*866*	*454*	*412*	*31*	*14*	*17*
Unmarried	11,356	5,793	5,563	4,005	2,039	1,966	778	400	378	5,676	2,886	2,790	866	454	412	31	14	17
Married ..	..	..	..	..	..	..	..	..	..	..	..	..	..	..	..	..	..	..
Widowed ..	..	..	..	..	..	..	..	..	..	..	..	..	..	..	..	..	..	..
5—10 ..	**8,484**	**4,682**	**3,802**	**2,793**	**1,489**	**1,304**	**572**	**335**	**237**	**4,455**	**2,502**	**1,953**	**632**	**343**	**289**	**32**	**13**	**19**
Unmarried ..	8,287	4,620	3,667	2,715	1,458	1,257	558	331	227	4,356	2,476	1,880	627	343	284	31	12	19
Married ..	197	62	135	78	31	47	14	4	10	99	26	73	5	..	5	1	1	..
Widowed ..	..	..	..	..	..	..	..	..	..	..	..	..	..	..	..	..	..	..
10—15 ..	**7,764**	**4,539**	**3,225**	**2,598**	**1,502**	**1,096**	**520**	**309**	**211**	**4,129**	**2,453**	**1,676**	**484**	**260**	**224**	**33**	**15**	**18**
Unmarried ..	6,963	4,328	2,635	2,274	1,402	872	468	296	172	3,725	2,360	1,365	464	255	209	32	15	17
Married ..	791	206	585	321	99	222	51	12	39	398	90	308	20	5	15	1	..	1
Widowed ..	10	5	5	3	1	2	1	1	..	6	3	3	..	..	..	..	..	..
15—20 ..	**14,260**	**10,686**	**3,574**	**5,355**	**4,081**	**1,274**	**1,225**	**935**	**290**	**6,806**	**4,992**	**1,814**	**827**	**644**	**183**	**47**	**34**	**13**
Unmarried ..	7,797	7,180	617	2,531	2,390	141	606	568	38	3,955	3,612	343	671	587	84	34	23	11
Married ..	6,303	3,383	2,920	2,759	1,640	1,119	613	362	251	2,771	1,321	1,450	147	49	98	13	11	2
Widowed ..	160	123	37	65	51	14	6	5	1	80	59	21	9	8	1	..	..	..
20—25	**19,215**	**15,008**	**4,207**	**6,940**	**5,415**	**1,525**	**1,569**	**1,248**	**321**	**9,188**	**7,068**	**2,120**	**1,465**	**1,237**	**228**	**53**	**40**	**13**
Unmarried ..	8,516	8,246	270	2,475	2,430	45	629	619	10	4,233	4,083	150	1,151	1,094	57	28	20	8
Married ..	10,339	6,464	3,875	4,326	2,869	1,457	924	617	307	4,769	2,833	1,936	296	126	170	24	19	5
Widowed ..	360	298	62	139	116	23	16	12	4	186	152	34	18	17	1	1	1	..
25—30 ..	**16,649**	**13,388**	**3,261**	**5,682**	**4,584**	**1,098**	**1,111**	**926**	**185**	**8,874**	**6,697**	**1,677**	**1,439**	**1,149**	**290**	**43**	**32**	**11**
Unmarried ..	4,092	3,981	111	861	845	16	264	261	3	2,123	2,054	69	833	811	22	11	10	1
Married ..	11,931	8,888	3,043	4,590	3,551	1,039	818	638	180	5,921	4,370	1,551	570	307	263	32	22	10
Widowed ..	626	519	107	231	188	43	29	27	2	330	273	57	36	31	5	..	..	..
30—35 ..	**13,027**	**10,612**	**2,415**	**4,450**	**3,693**	**757**	**863**	**729**	**134**	**6,748**	**5,509**	**1,284**	**935**	**653**	**282**	**36**	**28**	**8**
Unmarried ..	2,034	1,958	76	436	427	9	153	150	3	1,129	1,086	43	310	289	21	6	6	..
Married ..	10,304	8,093	2,211	3,773	3,077	696	675	546	129	5,245	4,122	1,123	582	327	255	29	21	8
Widowed ..	689	561	128	241	189	52	35	33	2	369	301	68	43	37	6	1	1	..
35—40 ..	**7,300**	**5,837**	**1,463**	**2,323**	**1,897**	**426**	**477**	**394**	**83**	**3,929**	**3,174**	**755**	**544**	**352**	**192**	**27**	**20**	**7**
Unmarried ..	629	584	45	123	118	5	37	35	2	384	362	22	80	65	15	5	4	1
Married ..	5,960	4,764	1,196	1,980	1,635	345	403	329	74	3,141	2,537	604	416	249	167	20	14	6
Widowed ..	711	489	222	220	144	76	37	30	7	404	275	129	48	38	10	2	2	..

P= Persons ; M= Males ; F= Females.

TABLE VII.—AGE, SEX AND CIVIL CONDITION.

PART "A" BALUCHISTAN.—(*concld.*)

Age and Civil Condition.	Population.			Hindu.			Sikh.			Muslim.			Christian.			Others.		
	P.	M.	F.	P.	M.	F.	P.	M.	F.	P.	M.	F.	P.	M.	F.	P.	M.	F.
1	2	3	4	5	6	7	8	9	10	11	12	13	14	15	16	17	18	19
40-45 ..	**5,079**	**3,985**	**1,094**	**1,604**	**1,280**	**324**	**334**	**277**	**57**	**2,714**	**2,152**	**562**	**404**	**258**	**146**	**23**	**18**	**5**
Unmarried ..	353	322	31	70	66	4	14	14	..	218	204	14	49	36	13	2	2	..
Married ..	4,047	3,242	805	1,318	1,087	231	286	236	50	2,116	1,715	401	310	190	120	17	14	3
Widowed ..	679	421	258	216	127	89	34	27	7	380	233	147	45	32	13	4	2	2
45—50 ..	**3,025**	**2,330**	**695**	**875**	**674**	**201**	**206**	**172**	**34**	**1,736**	**1,352**	**384**	**198**	**125**	**73**	**10**	**7**	**3**
Unmarried ..	163	138	25	36	34	2	5	5	..	105	90	15	15	7	8	2	2	..
Married ..	2,234	1,847	387	634	524	110	171	145	26	1,272	1,074	198	150	99	51	7	5	2
Widowed ..	628	345	283	205	116	89	30	22	8	359	188	171	33	19	14	1	..	1
50-55 ..	**1,984**	**1,480**	**504**	**562**	**414**	**148**	**131**	**105**	**26**	**1,163**	**879**	**284**	**120**	**76**	**44**	**8**	**6**	**2**
Unmarried ..	104	82	22	22	21	1	4	3	1	66	54	12	10	2	8	2	2	..
Married ..	1,402	1,156	246	381	312	69	106	87	19	820	692	128	90	62	28	5	3	2
Widowed ..	478	242	236	159	81	78	21	15	6	277	133	144	20	12	8	1	1	..
55—60 ..	**1,020**	**733**	**287**	**334**	**233**	**101**	**64**	**52**	**12**	**566**	**413**	**153**	**50**	**30**	**20**	**6**	**5**	**1**
Unmarried ..	58	48	10	17	16	1	3	3	..	30	26	4	8	3	5	..	..	..
Married ..	633	534	99	188	160	28	47	40	7	368	310	58	27	21	6	3	3	..
Widowed ..	329	151	178	129	57	72	14	9	5	168	77	91	15	6	9	3	2	1
60—65 ..	**779**	**535**	**244**	**253**	**174**	**79**	**44**	**33**	**11**	**437**	**300**	**137**	**40**	**25**	**15**	**5**	**3**	**2**
Unmarried ..	40	35	5	10	10	..	2	2	..	24	21	3	4	2	2	..	..	..
Married ..	445	370	75	127	111	16	28	24	4	266	217	49	21	16	5	3	2	1
Widowed ..	294	130	164	116	53	63	14	7	7	147	62	85	15	7	8	2	1	1
65-70 ..	**333**	**218**	**115**	**107**	**69**	**38**	**19**	**12**	**7**	**183**	**124**	**59**	**23**	**12**	**11**	**1**	**1**	..
Unmarried ..	15	12	3	4	4	..	2	2	..	7	6	1	2	..	2	..	..	..
Married ..	173	140	33	53	44	9	9	5	4	98	84	14	13	7	6	..	..	..
Widowed ..	145	66	79	50	21	29	8	5	3	78	34	44	8	5	3	1	1	..
70 and over	**574**	**371**	**203**	**185**	**115**	**70**	**27**	**17**	**10**	**329**	**221**	**108**	**29**	**16**	**13**	**4**	**2**	**2**
Unmarried ..	31	24	7	5	4	1	4	4	..	21	16	5	1	..	1	..	..	..
Married ..	261	213	48	80	64	16	11	9	2	154	129	25	14	9	5	2	2	..
Widowed ..	282	134	148	100	47	53	12	4	8	154	76	78	14	7	7	2		2

P= Persons; M= Males; F= Females.

TABLE VII.—AGE, SEX AND CIVIL CONDITION.
PART "B"—KHARAN.

Age and Civil Condition.	Population.			Muslim.			Hindu.		
	P.	M.	F.	P.	M.	F.	P.	M.	F.
1	2	3	4	5	6	7	8	9	10
ALL RELIGIONS ..	23,358	12,503	10,855	23,318	12,478	10,840	40	25	15
Unmarried ..	11,608	6,910	4,698	11,592	6,900	4,692	16	10	6
Married ..	10,571	5,244	5,327	10,553	5,235	5,318	18	9	9
Widowed ..	1,179	349	830	1,173	343	830	6	6	..
0—1 ..	339	123	216	339	123	216	..	..	..
Unmarried ..	339	123	216	339	123	216	..	..	..
Married ..	..	..	..	..	..	..	..	..	..
Widowed ..	..	..	..	..	..	..	..	..	..
1—2 ..	833	320	513	832	320	512	1	..	1
Unmarried ..	832	320	512	831	320	511	1	..	1
Married ..	1	..	1	1	..	1	..	..	..
Widowed ..	..	..	..	..	..	..	..	..	..
2—3 ..	1,056	456	600	1,054	455	599	2		1
Unmarried ..	1,055	455	600	1,053	454	599	2	1	1
Married ..	1	1	..	1	1	..	..	..	..
Widowed ..	..	..	..	..	..	..	..	..	..
3—4 ..	1,041	514	527	1,039	514	525	2	..	2
Unmarried ..	1,040	514	526	1,038	514	524	2	..	2
Married ..	1	..	1	1	..	1	..	..	..
Widowed ..	..	..	..	..	..	..	..	..	..
4—5 ..	958	514	444	958	514	444	..	..	..
Unmarried ..	956	513	443	956	513	443	..	..	..
Married ..	2	1	1	2	1	1	..	..	..
Widowed ..	..	..	..	..	..	..	..	..	..
Total 0—5 ..	*4,227*	*1,927*	*2,300*	*4,222*	*1,926*	*2,296*	*5*	*1*	*4*
Unmarried ..	4,222	1,925	2,297	4,217	1,924	2,293	5	1	4
Married ..	5	2	3	5	2	3	..	..	..
Widowed ..	..	..	..	..	..	..	..	..	..
5—10 ..	3,671	2,247	1,424	3,669	2,246	1,423	2	1	1
Unmarried ..	3,578	2,219	1,359	3,576	2,218	1,358	2	1	1
Married ..	90	26	64	90	26	64	..	..	..
Widowed ..	3	2	1	3	2	1	..	..	..
10—15 ..	2,847	1,806	1,041	2,845	1,805	1,040	2	1	1
Unmarried ..	2,525	1,726	799	2,523	1,725	798	2	1	1
Married ..	310	72	238	310	72	238	..	..	..
Widowed ..	12	8	4	12	8	4	..	..	..
15—20 ..	1,773	863	910	1,768	860	908	5	3	2
Unmarried ..	702	550	152	700	548	152	2	2	..
Married ..	1,035	290	745	1,033	290	743	2	..	2
Widowed ..	36	23	13	35	22	13	1	1	..
20—25 ..	1,693	788	905	1,685	784	901	8	4	4
Unmarried ..	377	322	55	374	319	55	3	3	..
Married ..	1,275	441	834	1,270	440	830	5	1	4
Widowed ..	41	25	16	41	25	16	..	..	..
25—30 ..	1,758	821	937	1,750	816	934	8	5	3
Unmarried ..	99	87	12	98	86	12	1	1	..
Married ..	1,595	701	894	1,589	698	891	6	3	3
Widowed ..	64	33	31	63	32	31	1	1	..
30—35 ..	1,702	811	891	1,697	806	891	5	5	..
Unmarried ..	53	48	5	52	47	5	1	1	..
Married ..	1,574	728	846	1,572	726	846	2	2	..
Widowed ..	75	35	40	73	33	40	2	2	..
35—40 ..	1,520	807	713	1,519	806	713	1	1	..
Unmarried ..	20	15	5	20	15	5	..	..	..
Married ..	1,383	756	627	1,382	755	627	1	1	..
Widowed ..	117	36	81	117	36	81	..	..	..
40—45 ..	1,371	782	589	1,369	780	589	2	2	..
Unmarried ..	12	7	5	12	7	5	..	..	..
Married ..	1,240	741	499	1,238	739	499	2	2	..
Widowed ..	119	34	85	119	34	85	..	..	..
45—50 ..	871	504	367	870	503	367	1	1	..
Unmarried ..	3	1	2	3	1	2	..	..	..
Married ..	720	477	243	720	477	243	..	..	..
Widowed ..	148	26	122	147	25	122	1	1	..
50—55 ..	642	351	291	641	350	291	1	1	..
Unmarried ..	6	3	3	6	3	3	..	..	..
Married ..	500	327	173	500	327	173	..	..	..
Widowed ..	136	21	115	135	20	115	1	1	..
55—60 ..	450	265	185	450	265	185	..	..	..
Unmarried ..	4	3	1	4	3	1	..	..	..
Married ..	305	235	70	305	235	70	..	..	..
Widowed ..	141	27	114	141	27	114	..	..	..
60—65 ..	397	229	168	397	229	168	..	..	..
Unmarried ..	3	1	2	3	1	2	..	..	..
Married ..	258	201	57	258	201	57	..	..	..
Widowed ..	136	27	109	136	27	109	..	..	..
65—70 ..	175	117	58	175	117	58	..	..	..
Unmarried ..	2	2	..	2	2	..	..	..	..
Married ..	117	99	18	117	99	18	..	..	..
Widowed ..	56	16	40	56	16	40	..	..	..
70 and over ..	261	185	76	261	185	76	..	..	..
Unmarried ..	2	1	1	2	1	1	..	..	..
Married ..	164	148	16	164	148	16	..	..	..
Widowed ..	95	36	59	95	36	59	..	..	..

P= Persons; M= Males; F= Females.

TABLE VIII.

CIVIL CONDITION BY AGE FOR SELECTED TRIBES.

This table gives statistics for the whole of Kharan, and the Kasi and Nichari villages of the Quetta-Pishin District. These are the only areas inhabited by indigenous tribesmen which have been brought under the Standard Schedule for the first time in the history of the Census of this Province. The numbers are no doubt small but they are not without interest as a rough index of conditions prevailing among local tribesmen.

TABLE VIII.—CIVIL CONDITION BY AGE FOR SELECTED TRIBES.

Caste, Tribe or Race.	Locality.	Sex.	Population dealt with.	Unmarried. Total.	Unmarried. 0 to 6	Unmarried. 7 to 13	Unmarried. 14 to 16	Unmarried. 17 to 23	Unmarried. 24 to 43	Unmarried. 44 and over.	Married. Total.	Married. 0 to 6	Married. 7 to 13	Married. 14 to 16	Married. 17 to 23	Married. 24 to 43	Married. 44 and over.	Widowed. Total.	Widowed. 0 to 6	Widowed. 7 to 13	Widowed. 14 to 16	Widowed. 17 to 23	Widowed. 24 to 43	Widowed. 44 and over
Baloch Indigenous-Rakhshani	KHARAN.	Males	7,785	4,306	1,644	1,839	335	358	123	7	3,251	2	17	53	316	1,787	1,076	228	..	3	7	21	87	110
		Females	6,688	2,858	1,836	838	124	38	17	5	3,332	5	81	224	745	1,852	425	498	..	2	[illegible]	10	136	348
Brahui Indigenous ..		Males	2,112	1,122	428	487	95	80	28	4	928	1	8	20	81	501	317	62	..	..	3	7	21	31
		Females	1,806	798	495	231	34	30	4	4	911	..	15	75	153	542	126	97	..	1	2	1	21	72
Gurgnari ..		Males	48	29	13	9	4	3	..	..	19	..	..	..	3	8	8	..	..	..	..	..	..	..
		Females	36	15	7	8	..	..	..	..	19	..	2	..	5	8	4	2	..	..	..	..	..	2
Kambrari ..		Males	38	22	7	8	2	3	2	..	14	..	..	..	2	9	3	2	..	..	..	1	..	1
		Females	36	17	11	4	2	..	..	..	14	..	..	1	3	8	2	5	..	..	..	..	1	4
Sumalari ..		Males	238	125	38	62	12	9	4	..	104	..	4	4	10	45	41	9	..	..	2	2	3	2
		Females	200	87	53	23	5	5	..	1	104	..	4	11	14	54	21	9	..	..	1	..	1	7
Mamasani ..		Males	1,637	859	339	375	65	56	20	4	729	1	2	16	64	401	245	49	..	..	1	4	18	26
		Females	1,405	632	399	178	24	25	3	3	709	..	8	59	117	436	89	64	..	..	..	1	14	4[illegible]
Mengal ..		Males	103	63	20	24	10	8	1	..	38	..	2	..	1	23	12	2	..	..	..	..	..	[illegible]
		Females	91	38	21	13	3	..	1	..	40	..	1	3	11	18	7	13	..	1	1	..	3	[illegible]
Sajdi ..		Males	48	24	11	9	2	1	1	..	24	..	..	..	1	15	8	..	..	..	..	..	..	..
		Females	38	9	4	5	..	..	..	..	25	..	..	1	3	18	8	4	..	..	..	..	2	2
Other Muslims Indigenous.		Males	2,113	1,226	506	487	107	82	44	..	845	..	4	17	76	505	243	42	..	1	2	4	22	13
		Females	1,914	834	503	266	40	18	7	..	873	..	15	49	185	525	99	207	..	..	1	8	65	133
Darzada ..		Males	69	38	17	16	3	1	1	..	31	..	1	1	..	21	8	..	..	..	..	..	..	..
		Females	76	30	18	9	1	..	2	..	30	..	1	2	5	18	4	16	..	..	..	..	6	10
Lori ..		Males	146	81	36	33	8	2	2	..	61	..	..	1	7	40	13	4	..	1	..	..	3	..
		Females	115	46	32	12	2	..	..	..	64	..	..	3	14	41	6	5	..	..	..	1	3	1
Nakib ..		Males	568	330	143	130	34	17	6	..	229	..	..	6	7	138	78	9	..	..	..	1	3	5
		Females	542	236	148	76	5	5	2	..	237	..	5	9	47	146	30	69	..	..	..	2	13	54
Others ..		Males	1,330	777	310	308	62	62	35	..	524	..	3	9	62	306	144	29	..	..	2	3	16	8
		Females	1,181	522	305	169	32	13	3	..	542	..	9	35	119	320	59	117	..	..	1	5	43	68
Pathan Indigenous ..	KASI-NICHARI.	Males	631	371	106	108	33	66	49	9	233	..	..	3	15	148	67	27	..	..	..	..	15	12
		Females	463	213	90	100	16	1	5	1	217	..	2	9	60	138	8	33	..	..	..	..	8	25
Kakar ..		Males	331	199	50	53	19	40	33	4	115	..	..	2	8	83	22	17	..	..	..	..	9	8
		Females	166	65	32	30	2	..	1	..	88	..	1	5	24	55	3	13	..	..	..	..	2	11
Kasi .		Males	300	172	56	55	14	26	16	5	118	..	..	1	7	65	45	10	..	..	..	..	6	4
		Females	297	148	58	70	14	1	4	1	129	..	1	4	36	83	5	20	..	..	..	..	6	14
Pathan (Semi-indigenous.)		Males	394	221	50	61	23	36	45	6	148	..	1	..	14	95	38	25	..	..	1	1	12	11
		Females	268	124	48	55	11	8	1	1	120	..	..	6	29	74	11	24	..	..	..	1	8	15
Durrani ..		Males	208	115	21	34	14	17	25	4	78	..	..	..	6	51	21	15	..	..	..	1	5	9
		Females	134	70	27	30	7	5	1	..	52	..	..	3	15	27	7	12	..	..	..	..	6	6
Ghilzai ..		Males	186	106	29	27	9	19	20	2	70	..	1	..	8	44	17	10	..	..	1	..	7	2
		Females	134	54	21	25	4	3	..	1	68	..	..	3	14	47	4	12	..	..	..	1	2	9
Other Muslims (Semi-indigenous). Hazara ..		Males	339	172	53	56	13	20	26	4	143	..	..	..	2	93	48	24	..	..	..	1	16	7
		Females	268	129	66	47	9	5	1	1	130	..	..	2	27	86	15	9	..	..	..	..	4	5

TABLE IX.

INFIRMITIES.

1. The record of infirmities was confined to insanity, deaf-mutism, blindness of both eyes and leprosy.

2. This table consists of two parts. Part I gives infirmities by ages Part II gives their distribution by districts and divisions of States.

3. In a total population of 868,617, the total number of afflicted was 2,744. Of the latter, 120 were censused in the Regular Areas with a total population of 110,849 persons representing the alien population for which infirmities were recorded by ages. The remaining 2,624 afflicted were censused in Tribal Areas with a total population (practically all indigenous) of 757,768 persons censused on a simplified form omitting age.

4. Dual infirmities were recorded in the case of 5 persons, *i.e.*, one insane female, one insane male and one blind female in Quetta-Pishin were also returned as deaf-mute, and two insane males in Kachhi sub-division of the Kalat State were also returned as blind.

5. These tables are exclusive of 107 insane (males 94, females 13) and 16 male lepers who were sent out of the Province to asylums in other Provinces during the past decade.

PART I—DISTRIBUTION BY AGE.

Age.	Population afflicted.			Insane.			Deaf-mute.			Blind.			Leper.		
	P.	M.	F.	P.	M.	F.	P.	M.	F.	P.	M.	F.	P.	M.	F.
1	2	3	4	5	6	7	8	9	10	11	12	13	14	15	16
0—1 ..	..	..	..	..	..	..	..	..	..	..	..	..	..	..	..
1—2 ..	..	..	..	..	..	..	..	..	..	..	..	..	..	..	..
2—3 ..	1	1	..	..	..	..	1	1	..	..	..	..	..	..	..
3—4 ..	..	..	..	..	..	..	..	..	..	..	..	..	..	..	..
4—5 ..	1	1	..	1	1	..	..	..	..	..	..	..	..	..	..
Total 0—5 ..	2	2	..	1	1	..	1	1	..	..	..	..	..	..	..
5—10 ..	4	3	1	1	1	..	1	1	..	3	2	1	..	..	..
10—15 ..	7	6	1	1	1	..	3	2	1	3	3	..	..	..	..
15—20 ..	7	6	1	2	2	..	4	3	1	..	..	..	1	1	..
20—25 ..	9	7	2	4	3	1	2	2	..	3	2	1	..	..	..
25—30 ..	14	10	4	5	3	2	3	3	..	6	4	2	..	..	..
30—35 ..	15	9	6	4	2	2	3	2	1	8	5	3	..	..	..
35—40 ..	12	9	3	6	3	3	1	1	..	5	5	..	..	..	..
40—45 ..	10	9	1	6	5	1	2	2	..	2	2	..	..	..	..
45—50 ..	8	8	..	3	3	..	1	1	..	4	4	..	..	..	..
50—55 ..	6	4	2	..	..	..	2	2	..	3	2	1	1	..	1
55—60 ..	7	6	1	..	..	..	1	1	..	6	5	1	..	..	..
60—65 ..	7	5	2	..	..	..	..	..	..	7	5	2	..	..	..
65—70 ..	3	..	3	..	..	..	..	..	..	3	..	3	..	..	..
70 and over ..	9	4	5	..	..	..	1	..	1	9	4	5	..	..	..
Unspecified ..	2,624	1,624	1,000	388	271	117	557	375	182	1,633	940	693	49	40	9
Total ..	2,744	1,712	1,032	421	295	126	582	396	186	1,695	983	712	51	41	10

PART II—DISTRIBUTION BY DISTRICTS.

	P.	M.	F.	P.	M.	F.	P.	M.	F.	P.	M.	F.	P.	M.	F.
BALUCHISTAN	2,744	1,712	1,032	421	295	126	582	396	186	1,695	983	712	51	41	10
DISTRICTS ..	1,266	819	447	186	138	48	278	204	74	781	458	323	24	20	4
Quetta-Pishin ..	275	192	83	64	48	16	77	56	21	131	84	47	6	5	1
Loralai ..	283	173	110	38	26	12	26	21	5	210	118	92	9	8	1
Zhob ..	112	80	32	18	15	3	34	26	8	58	38	20	2	1	1
Bolan ..	4	2	2	..	..	..	2	1	1	2	1	1	..	..	..
Chagai ..	116	75	41	15	9	6	26	21	5	71	42	29	4	3	1
Sibi ..	476	297	179	51	40	11	113	79	34	309	175	134	3	3	..
Administered Area	*337*	*195*	*142*	*41*	*31*	*10*	*84*	*55*	*29*	*209*	*106*	*103*	*3*	*3*	..
Mari-Bugti Country	*139*	*102*	*37*	*10*	*9*	*1*	*29*	*24*	*5*	*100*	*69*	*31*	..	..	..
STATES ..	1,478	893	585	235	157	78	304	192	112	914	525	389	27	21	6
Kalat ..	1,216	734	482	179	124	55	235	153	82	780	441	339	24	18	6
Sarawan ..	*138*	*101*	*37*	*20*	*12*	*8*	*36*	*26*	*10*	*80*	*61*	*19*	*2*	*2*	..
Jhalawan ..	*292*	*186*	*106*	*93*	*62*	*31*	*89*	*51*	*38*	*96*	*62*	*34*	*14*	*11*	*3*
Kachhi ..	*346*	*185*	*161*	*24*	*20*	*4*	*53*	*33*	*20*	*265*	*131*	*134*	*6*	*3*	*3*
Dombki-Kaheri Country.	*143*	*78*	*65*	*3*	*1*	*2*	*9*	*5*	*4*	*131*	*72*	*59*	..	..	..
Makran ..	*217*	*126*	*91*	*27*	*17*	*10*	*25*	*21*	*4*	*165*	*88*	*77*	..	..	..
Kharan ..	*80*	*58*	*22*	*12*	*12*	..	*23*	*17*	*6*	*43*	*27*	*16*	*2*	*2*	..
Las-Bela ..	262	159	103	56	33	23	69	39	30	134	84	50	3	3	..

P=Persons; M=Males; F=Females.

TABLE X.

PART I.—OCCUPATION OR MEANS OF LIVELIHOOD—TOTALS FOR PROVINCE, DISTRICTS AND STATES.

1. Groups which are blank for the whole province have been omitted from both parts of the Table. Their numbers and names are given below :—

No.	Name.
8	Cultivators of Jhum, Taungya and shifting areas.
9	Cinchona.
10	Coccanut.
11	Coffee.
12	Ganja.
13	Pan-vine.
14	Rubber.
15	Tea.
20	Collectors of lac.
25	Silkworms.
26	Lac cultivation.
29	Gold.
30	Iron.
31	Lead, Silver and Zinc.
32	Manganese.
33	Tin and Wolfram.
36	Petroleum.
37	Building Materials (including stone, material for cement manufacture and clays).
38	Mica.
39	Precious and semi-precious stones.
41	Other non-metallic minerals.
48	Hair (horse-hair), etc.
53	Bone, ivory, horn, shell, etc., workers (except buttons).
57	Smelting, forging and rolling of iron and other metals.
62	Workers in mints, die-sinkers, etc.
66	Manufacture of matches, fireworks and other explosives.
69	Manufacture and refining of mineral oils.
74	Makers of sugar, molasses and gur.
76	Toddy drawers.
78	Manufacturers of Tobacco.
79	Manufacturers of Opium.
80	Manufacturers of Ganja.
92	Carriage, Cart, Palki, etc., makers and wheel wrights.
96	Makers of musical instruments.
103	Persons (other than labourers) employed in harbours, docks, rivers and canals, including pilots.
104	Labourers employed on harbours, docks, rivers and canals.
120	Trade in barks.
121	Trade in bamboos and canes.
122	Trade in thatches and other forest produce.
143	Dealers and hirers in other carriages, carts, boats, etc.
149	Dealers in rags, stable refuse, etc.
155	Navy.
191	Labourers and workmen otherwise unspecified.
195	Other unclassified non-productive industries.

2. In Part I, the prisoners undergoing rigorous imprisonment have been shown as working dependents under Group No. 192 and included in the total of working dependents in the heading. All other classes of prisoners numbering 280 (279 males ; 1 female) have also been shown under Group No. 192 as earners but they are excluded from the total earners and included among non-working dependents in the heading. Consequently the totals of columns 4 and 5, 11 and 12, and 18 and 19 of this part differ from the total of earners in the heading by the number shown in them against Group No. 192. Similarly in Part II, 279 males and 1 female have been shown against Group No. 192 under the heading "Principal Occupation" (Columns 4 and 5) with the necessary distribution under Districts, etc. The figures have been included, as in Part I, in the totals of the Order, Sub-Class and Class. The Grand totals in the top line of the Table thus fall short of the sum of the details below them by 280 persons (279 males ; 1 female).

TABLE X, PART I.—OCCUPATION OR MEANS
TOTALS FOR PROVINCE,

BALUCHISTAN.

Total Earners	..	..	.. 296,985
Total Working dependents		..	.. 22,297
Total Non-working dependents { Males .. 185,286; Females .. 364,049 }			.. 549,335
Total Population	..	..	.. 868,617

Group Number.	Occupation.	Total following occupation.	As Principal Occupation.		As Working Dependents.		As Subsidiary to other Occupation.	
			M.	F.	M.	F.	M.	F.
1	2	3	4	5	6	7	8	9
	TOTAL FOR PROVINCE	392,869	292,525	4,740	10,882	11,415	72,901	406
	CLASS A.—PRODUCTION OF RAW MATERIALS ..	271,617	199,779	693	9,915	5,655	55,429	146
	SUB-CLASS I. EXPLOITATION OF ANIMALS AND VEGETATION	271,057	199,231	693	9,915	5,655	55,417	146
	ORDER I. PASTURE AND AGRICULTURE	*268,492*	*197,003*	*687*	*9,894*	*5,636*	*55,127*	*145*
	(a) *Cultivation*	*207,964*	*172,489*	*526*	*5,725*	*4,960*	*24,200*	*64*
1	Non-cultivating proprietors taking rent in money or kind ..	26,020	11,222	291	..	..	14,459	48
2	Estate Agents and Managers of owners	10	9	..	..	..	1	..
3	Estate Agents and Managers of Government	2	2	..	..	..	..	..
4	Rent Collectors, clerks, etc.	15	15	..	..	..	..	..
5	Cultivating owners	106,197	104,529	30	..	..	1,635	3
6	Tenant cultivators	57,690	50,905	10	90	2	6,679	4
7	Agricultural labourers	18,030	5,807	195	5,635	4,958	1,426	9
	(b) *Cultivation of special crops, fruit, etc., (Planters, Managers, Clerks and Labourers)*	*909*	*862*	..	*6*	*5*	*36*	..
16	Market gardeners, flower and fruit growers	909	862	..	6	5	36	..
	(c) *Forestry*	*1,029*	*464*	*36*	*340*	*55*	*134*	..
17	Forest Officers, rangers, guards, etc.	74	69	..	..	..	5	..
18	Wood-cutters and Charcoal burners	938	389	35	339	55	120	..
19	Collectors of forest produce	17	6	1	1	..	9	..
	(d) *Stock Raising-*	*58,589*	*23,187*	*125*	*3,823*	*616*	*30,757*	*81*
21	Cattle and buffalo breeders and keepers	3,992	1,130	32	203	84	2,542	1
22	Breeders of transport animals	3,120	1,286	8	7	..	1,781	38
23	Herdsmen, shepherds and breeders of other animals ..	51,477	20,771	85	3,613	532	26,434	42
	(e) *Raising of small animals and insects*	*1*	*1*	..	..	..	..	..
24	Birds, bees, etc.	1	1	..	..	..	..	..
	ORDER 2. FISHING AND HUNTING	*2,565*	*2,228*	*6*	*21*	*19*	*290*	*1*
27	Fishing and Pearling	2,561	2,225	6	21	19	289	1
28	Hunting	4	3	..	..	..	1	..
	SUB-CLASS II. EXPLOITATION OF MINERALS ..	560	548	..	..	..	12	..
	ORDER 3. METALLIC MINERALS	*181*	*176*	..	..	..	*5*	..
34	Other metallic minerals (chrome)	181	176	..	..	..	5	..
	ORDER 4. NON-METALLIC MINERALS	*379*	*372*	..	..	..	*7*	..
35	Coal	297	296	..	..	..	1	..
40	Salt, salt-petre and other saline substances	82	76	..	..	..	6	..
	CLASS B.—PREPARATION AND SUPPLY OF MATERIAL SUBSTANCES	71,446	47,891	2,809	493	5,748	14,287	220
	SUB-CLASS III. INDUSTRY	27,582	17,059	2,402	255	5,679	1,974	163
	ORDER 5. TEXTILES	*2,370*	*654*	*196*	*33*	*1,213*	*233*	*41*
42	Cotton ginning, cleaning and pressing	10	8	..	..	..	2	..
43	Cotton spinning, sizing and weaving	263	223	1	..	..	38	1
44	Jute pressing, spinning and weaving	32	..	16	1	15	..	..
45	Rope, twine, string and other fibres ..	178	77	10	..	..	87	4
46	Wool carding, spinning and weaving	1,804	273	167	32	1,198	102	32
47	Silk spinning and weaving	8	7	..	..	..	1	..
49	Dyeing, bleaching, printing, preparation and sponging of textiles	71	66	2	..	..	3	..
50	Lace, crepe, embroideries, fringes, etc., and insufficiently described textile industries	4	..	..	..	..	..	4
	ORDER 6. HIDES, SKINS, AND HARD MATERIALS FROM THE ANIMAL KINGDOM	*44*	*27*	*8*	*4*	*5*	..	..
51	Working in leather	41	24	8	4	5	..	..
52	Furriers and persons occupied with feathers and bristles ; brush makers	3	3	..	..	..	..	..

OF LIVELIHOOD.
DISTRICTS AND STATES.

DISTRICTS.			STATES.		
Total Earners	..	169,050	Total Earners	..	127,935
Total Working dependents	..	14,078	Total Working dependents	..	8,219
Total Non-working dependents — Males .. 96,368; Females .. 184,012	..	280,380	Total Non-working dependents — Males .. 88,918; Females .. 180,037	..	268,955
Total Population	..	463,508	Total Population	..	405,109

Total following occupation.	As Principal Occupation.		As Working Dependents.		As Subsidiary to other Occupation.		Total following occupation.	As Principal Occupation.		As Working Dependents		As Subsidiary to other Occupation.	
	M.	F.	M.	F.	M.	F.		M.	F.	M.	F.	M.	F.
10	11	12	13	14	15	16	17	18	19	20	21	22	23
281,745	166,913	2,297	6,882	7,196	48,168	289	161,124	125,612	2,448	4,000	4,219	24,783	117
139,701	92,632	862	6,153	5,321	35,123	110	131,916	107,147	331	3,762	334	20,306	36
139,234	92,168	362	6,153	5,321	35,120	110	131,823	107,063	331	3,762	334	20,297	36
139,232	*92,167*	*362*	*6,153*	*5,321*	*35,119*	*110*	*129,260*	*104,836*	*325*	*3,741*	*315*	*20,008*	*35*
107,280	*82,766*	*286*	*3,393*	*4,825*	*15,959*	*51*	*100,684*	*89,723*	*240*	*2,332*	*135*	*8,241*	*13*
16,976	4,003	195	..	..	12,739	39	9,044	7,219	96	..	..	1,720	9
10	9	..	..	..	1	..	..	..	..	..	..	..	
2	2	..	..	..	..	..	..	..	..	..	..	..	..
15	15	..	..	..	..	..	..	..	..	..	..	..	..
56,625	56,033	2	..	..	588	2	49,572	48,496	28	..	..	1,047	1
22,628	20,650	9	55	..	1,912	2	35,062	30,255	1	35	2	4,767	2
11,024	2,054	80	3,338	4,825	719	8	7,006	3,753	115	2,297	133	707	1
852	*822*	..	*6*	..	*24*	..	*57*	*40*	..	..	*5*	*12*	..
852	822	..	6	..	24	..	57	40	..	..	5	12	..
749	*261*	*1*	*337*	*55*	*95*	..	*280*	*203*	*35*	*3*	..	*39*	..
72	67	..	..	..	5	..	2	2	..	..	..	..	..
677	194	1	337	55	90	..	261	195	34	2	..	30	..
..	..	..	..	..	..	..	17	6	1	1	..	9	..
30,350	*8,317*	*75*	*2,417*	*441*	*19,041*	*59*	*28,239*	*14,870*	*50*	*1,406*	*175*	*11,716*	*22*
1,185	277	27	..	..	880	1	2,807	853	5	203	84	1,662	..
858	619	..	..	..	204	35	2,262	667	8	7	..	1,577	3
28,307	7,421	48	2,417	441	17,957	23	23,170	13,350	37	1,196	91	8,477	19
1	*1*	..	..	..	..	..	..	..	..	..	..	..	..
1	1	..	..	..	..	..	..	..	..	..	..	..	..
2	*1*	..	..	..	*1*	..	*2,563*	*2,227*	*6*	*21*	*19*	*289*	*1*
1	1	..	..	..	..	..	2,560	2,224	6	21	19	289	1
1	..	..	..	..	1	..	3	3	..	..	..	..	..
467	464	..	..	..	3	..	93	84	..	..	..	9	..
175	*175*	..	..	..	..	..	*6*	*1*	..	..	..	*5*	..
175	175	..	..	..	..	..	6	1	..	..	..	5	..
292	*289*	..	..	..	*3*	..	*87*	*83*	..	..	..	*4*	..
290	289	..	..	..	1	..	7	7	..	..	..	..	..
2	..	..	..	..	2	..	80	76	..	..	..	4	..
50,088	36,278	1,037	302	1,865	10,468	143	21,380	11,618	1,772	191	3,883	3,819	77
16,679	12,762	713	154	1,807	1,144	99	10,853	4,297	1,689	101	3,872	830	64
455	*319*	*36*	*2*	*4*	*86*	*8*	*1,915*	*335*	*160*	*31*	*1,209*	*147*	*33*
10	8	..	..	..	2	..	..	..	..	..	..	..	..
107	96	..	..	..	10	1	156	127	1	..	..	28	..
..	..	..	..	..	..	..	32	..	16	1	15	..	..
4	4	..	..	..	..	..	174	73	10	..	..	87	4
264	149	34	2	4	72	3	1,540	124	133	30	1,194	30	29
8	7	..	..	..	1	..	..	..	..	..	..	..	..
58	55	2	..	..	1	..	13	11	..	..	..	2	..
4	..	..	..	..	..	4	..	..	..	..	..	..	..
24	*18*	..	*4*	*2*	..	..	*20*	*9*	*8*	..	*3*	..	..
21	15	..	4	2	..	..	20	9	8	..	3	..	..
3	3	..	..	..	..	..	..	..	..	..	..	..	..

M. = Males; F. = Females.

TABLE X, PART I.—OCCUPATION OR MEANS
TOTAL FOR PROVINCE.

Group Number.	Occupation.	BALUCHISTAN. Total following occupation.	As Principal Occupation. M.	F.	As Working Dependents. M.	F.	As Subsidiary to other Occupation. M.	F.
1	2	3	4	5	6	7	8	9
	ORDER 7. WOOD	*6,047*	*1,498*	*1,306*	*144*	*2,516*	*483*	*100*
54	Sawyers	47	47	..	..	..	..	..
55	Carpenters, turners, and joiners, etc.	1,197	959	..	10	..	228	..
56	Basket makers, and other industries of woody materials, including leaves and thatchers and builders working with bamboo, reeds or similar materials.	4,803	492	1,306	134	2,516	255	100
	ORDER 8. METALS	*2,693*	*2,489*	..	*21*	*5*	*178*	..
58	Makers of arms, guns, etc.	487	487	..	..	..	..	..
59	Blacksmiths, other workers in iron, makers of implements	2,020	1,826	..	20	5	169	..
60	Workers in brass, copper and bell-metal	61	59	..	..	..	2	..
61	Workers in other metals (except precious metals)	125	117	..	1	..	7	..
	ORDER 9. CERAMICS	*815*	*554*	*32*	..	*12*	*217*	..
63	Potters and makers of earthenware	264	220	12	..	10	22	..
64	Brick and tile makers	527	310	20	..	2	195	..
65	Other workers in ceramics	24	24	..	..	..	..	..
	ORDER 10. CHEMICAL PRODUCTS PROPERLY SO CALLED AND ANALOGOUS	*374*	*292*	..	*1*	..	*81*	..
67	Manufacture of aerated and mineral waters, and ice	28	28	..	..	..	..	..
68	Manufacture and refining of vegetable oils	136	63	..	..	..	73	..
70	Others	210	201	..	1	..	8	..
	ORDER 11. FOOD INDUSTRIES	*2,003*	*1,570*	*221*	*12*	*20*	*170*	*10*
71	Rice pounders and huskers and flour grinders	412	151	186	..	14	56	5
72	Grain parchers, etc.	152	77	35	..	..	35	5
73	Butchers	501	430	..	..	..	71	..
75	Sweetmeat and condiment makers	265	263	..	..	..	2	..
77	Brewers and distillers	49	49	..	..	..	..	..
81	Others	624	600	..	12	6	6	..
	ORDER 12. INDUSTRIES OF DRESS, AND THE TOILET	*5,671*	*3,324*	*209*	*26*	*1,892*	*211*	*9*
82	Boot, shoe, sandal and clog makers	1,229	1,117	1	3	..	108	..
83	Tailors, milliners, dress makers and darners	2,642	1,099	23	16	1,480	22	2
84	Embroiderers, hat makers and makers of other articles of wear	564	14	136	5	404	1	4
85	Washing and cleaning	584	496	48	2	8	27	3
86	Barbers, hair-dressers and wig-makers	648	594	1	..	..	53	..
87	Other industries connected with the toilet	4	4	..	..	..	..	..
	ORDER 13. FURNITURE INDUSTRIES	*596*	*570*	*12*	..	*3*	*9*	*2*
88	Cabinet-makers, carriage painters, etc.	578	569	..	..	..	9	..
89	Upholsterers, tent-makers, etc.	18	1	12	..	3	..	2
	ORDER 14. BUILDING INDUSTRIES	*2,363*	*2,024*	*16*	*3*	..	*319*	*1*
90	Lime burners, cement workers; Excavators and well sinkers; Stone cutters, and dressers; Brick layers, and masons; Builders (other than buildings made of bamboo or similar materials), painters, decorators of houses, tilers, plumbers, etc.	2,363	2,024	16	3	..	319	1
	ORDER 15. CONSTRUCTION OF MEANS OF TRANSPORT	*112*	*109*	..	..	..	*3*	..
91	Persons engaged in making, assembling or repairing motor vehicles or cycles	111	109	..	..	..	2	..
93	Ship, boat, aeroplane builders	1	..	..	..	..	1	..
	ORDER 16. PRODUCTION AND TRANSMISSION OF PHYSICAL FORCE.	*194*	*194*	..	..	..	..	..
94	Heat, light, electricity, motive power, etc., gas works and electric light and power	194	194	..	..	..	..	..
	ORDER 17. MISCELLANEOUS AND UNDEFINED INDUSTRIES	*4,250*	*3,754*	*402*	*11*	*13*	*70*	..
95	Printers, engravers, book binders, etc.	65	65	..	..	..	..	..
97	Makers of clocks and surgical or scientific instruments, etc.	39	39	..	..	..	..	..
98	Makers of jewellery and ornaments	783	742	..	3	..	38	..
99	Other miscellaneous and undefined industries (toy-making, taxidermy, etc.)	42	15	..	..	..	27	..
100	Scavenging	3,321	2,893	402	8	13	5	..
	SUB-CLASS IV. TRANSPORT	22,181	17,451	350	155	8	4,172	45
	ORDER 18. TRANSPORT BY AIR	*40*	*40*	..	..	..	..	..
101	Persons concerned with aerodromes and aeroplanes	40	40	..	..	..	..	..
	ORDER 19. TRANSPORT BY WATER	*85*	*81*	..	..	..	*4*	..
102	Ship-owners, boat-owners and their employees, officers, mariners, etc.; Ship brokers, boatmen and tow men	85	81	..	..	..	4	..

OF LIVELIHOOD.
DISTRICTS AND STATES.

DISTRICTS.							STATES.						
Total following occupation.	As Principal Occupation.		As Working Dependents.		As Subsidiary to other Occupation.		Total following occupation.	As Principal Occupation.		As Working Dependents.		As Subsidiary to other Occupation.	
	M.	F.	M.	F.	M.	F.		M.	F.	M.	F.	M.	F.
10	11	12	13	14	15	16	17	18	19	20	21	22	23
1,602	589	146	111	372	302	82	4,445	909	1,160	33	2,144	181	18
47	47	..	..	..	..	..	..	..	..	..	..	..	..
300	207	..	3	..	96	..	891	752	..	7	..	132	..
1,249	335	146	108	372	206	82	3,554	157	1,160	26	2,144	49	18
1,761	1,601	..	12	3	145	..	932	888	..	9	2	33	..
483	483	..	..	..	..	..	4	4	..	..	..	..	..
1,147	990	..	12	3	142	..	873	836	..	8	2	27	..
61	59	..	..	..	2	..	..	..	..	..	..	..	..
70	69	..	..	..	1	..	55	48	..	1	..	6	..
627	400	32	..	..	195	..	188	154	..	..	12	22	..
86	69	12	..	..	4	..	179	151	..	..	10	18	..
518	307	20	..	..	191	..	9	3	..	..	2	4	..
24	24	..	..	..	..	..	..	..	..	..	..	..	..
265	242	..	1	..	22	..	109	50	..	..	..	59	..
28	28	..	..	..	..	..	..	..	..	..	..	..	..
27	13	..	..	..	14	..	109	50	..	..	..	59	..
210	201	..	1	..	8	..	..	..	..	..	..	..	..
1,516	1,397	18	..	..	99	2	487	173	203	12	20	71	8
203	130	18	..	..	53	2	209	21	168	..	14	3	3
21	21	..	..	..	..	..	131	56	35	..	..	35	5
405	367	..	..	..	38	..	96	63	..	..	..	33	..
249	247	..	..	..	2	..	16	16	..	..	..	..	..
49	49	..	..	..	..	..	..	..	..	..	..	..	..
589	583	..	..	..	6	..	35	17	..	12	6	..	..
4,150	2,568	78	16	1,413	69	7	1,521	756	131	11	479	142	2
664	633	1	..	..	30	..	565	484	..	3	..	78	..
2,449	1,004	15	15	1,404	10	1	193	95	8	1	76	12	1
40	8	21	..	8	..	3	524	6	115	5	396	1	1
506	441	40	..	1	20	3	79	55	8	2	7	7	..
489	479	1	..	..	9	..	159	115	..	..	..	44	..
3	3	..	..	..	..	..	1	1	..	..	..	..	..
576	567	..	..	..	9	..	20	3	12	..	3	..	2
575	566	..	..	..	9	..	3	3	..	..	..	..	..
1	1	..	..	..	..	..	17	..	12	..	3	..	2
1,803	1,619	15	..	..	169	..	560	405	1	3	..	150	1
1,803	1,619	15	..	..	169	..	560	405	1	3	..	150	1
111	109	..	..	..	2	..	1	..	..	..	..	1	..
111	109	..	..	..	2	..	..	..	..	..	..	..	..
..	..	..	..	..	..	..	1	..	..	..	..	1	..
191	191	..	..	..	..	..	3	3	..	..	..	..	..
191	191	..	..	..	..	..	3	3	..	..	..	..	..
3,598	3,142	388	9	13	46	..	652	612	14	2	..	24	..
65	65	..	..	..	..	..	..	..	..	..	..	..	..
39	39	..	..	..	..	..	..	..	..	..	..	..	..
366	345	..	1	..	20	..	417	397	..	2	..	18	..
39	14	..	..	..	25	..	3	1	..	..	..	2	..
3,089	2,679	388	8	13	1	..	232	214	14	..	..	4	..
16,982	14,575	294	78	4	2,002	34	5,199	2,876	56	82	4	2,170	11
40	40	..	..	..	..	..	..	..	..	..	..	..	..
40	40	..	..	..	..	..	..	..	..	..	..	..	..
..	..	..	..	..	..	..	85	81	..	..	..	4	..
	..	..	..	..	..	..	85	81	..	..	..	4	..

M. = Males ; F. = Females.

TABLE X, PART I.—OCCUPATION OR MEANS
TOTAL FOR PROVINCE,

Group Number.	Occupation.	BALUCHISTAN. Total following occupation.	As Principal Occupation. M.	As Principal Occupation. F.	As Working Dependents. M.	As Working Dependents. F.	As Subsidiary to other Occupation. M.	As Subsidiary to other Occupation. F.
1	2	3	4	5	6	7	8	9
	ORDER 20. TRANSPORT BY ROAD	*15,071*	*10,373*	*350*	*155*	*8*	*4,140*	*45*
105	Persons (other than labourers) employed on the construction and maintenance of roads and bridges	63	63	..	..	..	..	..
106	Labourers employed on roads and bridges	979	837	..	2	..	140	..
107	Owners, managers and employees (excluding personal servants) connected with mechanically driven vehicles (including trams)	47	44	..	..	..	3	..
108	Owners, managers and employees (excluding personal servants) connected with other vehicles	678	646	..	..	..	32	..
109	Palki, etc., bearers and owners	1	1	..	..	..	..	..
110	Pack elephant, camel, mule, ass and bullock owners and drivers	6,928	3,760	87	141	5	2,906	27
111	Porters and messengers	5,375	5,022	263	12	3	1,057	18
	ORDER 21. TRANSPORT BY RAIL	*6,408*	*6,385*	..	..	..	*23*	..
112	Railway employees of all kinds other than coolies	3,121	3,117	..	..	..	4	..
113	Labourers employed on Railway construction and maintenance, and coolies and porters employed on Railway premises	3,287	3,268	..	..	..	19	..
	ORDER 22. POST OFFICE, TELEGRAPH AND TELEPHONE SERVICES	*577*	*572*	..	..	..	*5*	..
114	Post-office, Telegraph and Telephone services	577	572	..	..	..	5	..
	SUB-CLASS V. TRADE	21,735	18,381	57	83	61	3,141	13
	ORDER 23. BANKS, ESTABLISHMENTS OF CREDIT, EXCHANGE AND INSURANCE	*112*	*100*	..	..	..	*12*	..
115	Bank managers, money lenders, exchange and insurance agents, money changers and brokers, and their employees	112	100	..	..	..	12	..
	ORDER 24. BROKERAGE, COMMISSION AND EXPORT	*216*	*200*	..	..	..	*16*	..
116	Brokers, commission agents, commercial travellers, ware-house owners and employees	216	200	..	..	..	16	..
	ORDER 25. TRADE IN TEXTILES	*3,051*	*2,320*	*2*	*41*	..	*682*	*6*
117	Trade in piece-goods, wool, cotton, silk, hair and other textiles	3,051	2,320	2	41	..	682	6
	ORDER 26. TRADE IN SKINS, LEATHER AND FURS	*101*	*67*	..	..	..	*34*	..
118	Trade in skins, leather, furs, feathers, horn, etc., and the articles made from these	101	67	..	..	..	34	..
	ORDER 27. TRADE IN WOOD	*19*	*18*	..	..	..	*1*	..
119	Trade in wood (not firewood)	19	18	..	..	..	1	..
	ORDER 28. TRADE IN METALS	*18*	*18*	..	..	..	..	..
123	Trade in metals, machinery, knives, tools, etc.	18	18	..	..	..	..	..
	ORDER 29. TRADE IN POTTERY, BRICKS AND TILES	*20*	*20*	..	..	..	..	..
124	Trade in pottery, bricks and tiles	20	20	..	..	..	..	..
	ORDER 30. TRADE IN CHEMICAL PRODUCTS	*133*	*86*	*3*	*1*	..	*43*	..
125	Drugs, dyes, paints, petroleum, explosives, etc.	133	86	3	1	..	43	..
	ORDER 31. HOTELS, CAFES, RESTAURANTS, ETC.	*601*	*584*	*6*	..	..	*11*	..
126	Vendors of wine, liquors, aerated waters and ice	78	76	..	..	..	2	..
127	Owners and managers of hotels, cook shops, sarais, etc. (and employees)	353	344	5	..	..	4	..
128	Hawkers of drink and food stuffs	170	164	1	..	..	5	..
	ORDER 32. OTHER TRADE IN FOOD STUFFS	*3,402*	*2,800*	*34*	*13*	*7*	*545*	*3*
129	Grain and pulse dealers	487	451	5	..	..	31	..
130	Dealers in sweetmeat, sugar and spices	29	28	1	..	..	..	..
131	Dealers in Dairy product, eggs and poultry	552	458	6	5	6	75	3
132	Dealers in animals for food	454	197	1	..	..	256	..
133	Dealers in fodder for animals	60	54	..	..	..	6	..
134	Dealers in other food stuffs	1,621	1,417	22	8	1	173	..
135	Dealers in tobacco	189	186	..	..	..	3	..
136	Dealers in opium	3	2	..	..	..	1	..
137	Dealers in Gania	7	7	..	..	..	..	..
	ORDER 33. TRADE IN CLOTHING AND TOILET ARTICLES	*561*	*542*	*5*	..	..	*14*	..
138	Trade in ready-made clothing and other articles of dress and the toilet (hats, umbrellas, socks, ready-made shoes, perfumes, etc.)	561	542	5	..	..	14	..
	ORDER 34. TRADE IN FURNITURE	*132*	*78*	..	..	..	*54*	..
139	Trade in furniture, carpets, curtains and bedding	85	31	..	..	..	54	..
140	Hard-ware, cooking utensils, porcelain, crockery, glass-ware, bottles, articles for gardening, etc.	47	47	..	..	..	..	..

OF LIVELIHOOD.
DISTRICTS AND STATES.

DISTRICTS.							STATES.						
Total following occupation.	As Principal Occupation.		As Working Dependents.		As Subsidiary to other Occupation.		Total following occupation.	As Principal Occupation.		As Working Dependents.		As Subsidiary to other Occupation.	
	M.	F.	M.	F.	M.	F.		M.	F.	M.	F.	M.	F.
10	11	12	13	14	15	16	17	18	19	20	21	22	23
10,123	*7,739*	*294*	*73*	*4*	*1,979*	*34*	*4,948*	*2,634*	*56*	*82*	*4*	*2,161*	*11*
60	60	..	..	..	..	..	3	3	..	..	..	..	..
946	807	..	2	..	137	..	33	30	..	..	..	3	..
44	41	..	..	..	3	..	3	3	..	..	..	..	..
672	643	..	..	..	29	..	6	3	..	..	..	3	..
1	1	..	..	..	..	..	..	..	..	..	..	..	..
2,593	1,636	71	59	1	810	16	4,335	2,124	16	82	4	2,098	11
5,807	4,551	223	12	3	1,000	18	568	471	40	..	..	57	..
6,368	*6,345*	..	..	..	*23*	..	*40*	*40*	..	..	..	..	..
3,116	3,112	..	..	..	4	..	5	5	..	..	..	..	..
3,252	3,233	..	..	..	19	..	35	35	..	..	..	..	..
451	*451*	..	..	..	..	..	*126*	*121*	..	..	..	*5*	..
451	451	..	..	..	..	..	126	121	..	..	..	5	..
16,427	8,936	30	75	54	7,322	10	5,308	4,445	27	8	7	819	2
112	*100*	..	..	..	*12*	..	..	..	..	..	..	..	..
112	100	..	..	..	12	..	..	..	..	..	..	..	..
185	*175*	..	..	..	*10*	..	*31*	*25*	..	..	..	*6*	..
185	175	..	..	..	10	..	31	25	..	..	..	6	..
2,283	*1,603*	*2*	*39*	..	*633*	*6*	*768*	*717*	..	*2*	..	*49*	..
2,283	1,603	2	39	..	633	6	768	717	..	2	..	49	..
82	*55*	..	..	..	*27*	..	*19*	*12*	..	..	..	*7*	..
82	55	..	..	..	27	..	19	12	..	..	..	7	..
19	*18*	..	..	..	*1*	..	..	..	..	..	..	..	..
19	18	..	..	..	1	..	..	..	..	..	..	..	..
18	*18*	..	..	..	..	..	..	..	..	..	..	..	..
18	18	..	..	..	..	..	..	..	..	..	..	..	..
9	*9*	..	..	..	..	..	*11*	*11*	..	..	..	..	..
9	9	..	..	..	..	..	11	11	..	..	..	..	..
100	*84*	*3*	..	..	*13*	..	*33*	*2*	..	*1*	..	*30*	..
100	84	3	..	..	13	..	33	2	..	1	..	30	..
513	*496*	*6*	..	..	*11*	..	*88*	*88*	..	..	..	..	..
51	49	..	..	..	2	..	27	27	..	..	..	..	..
332	323	5	..	..	4	..	21	21	..	..	..	..	..
130	124	1	..	..	5	..	40	40	..	..	..	..	..
2,367	*1,914*	*12*	*8*	..	*430*	*3*	*1,035*	*886*	*22*	*5*	*7*	*115*	..
98	76	..	..	..	22	..	389	375	5	..	..	9	..
9	9	..	..	..	..	..	20	19	1	..	..	..	..
484	425	3	..	..	53	3	68	33	2	5	6	22	..
333	103	1	..	..	229	..	121	94	..	..	..	27	..
56	50	..	..	..	6	..	4	4	..	..	..	..	..
1,217	1,085	8	8	..	116	..	404	332	14	..	1	57	..
163	160	..	..	..	3	..	26	26	..	..	..	..	..
3	2	..	..	..	1	..	..	..	..	..	..	..	..
4	4	..	..	..	..	..	3	3	..	..	..	..	..
446	*431*	*2*	..	..	*13*	..	*115*	*111*	*3*	..	..	*1*	..
446	431	2	..	..	13	..	115	111	3	..	..	1	..
78	*75*	..	..	..	*3*	..	*54*	*3*	..	..	..	*51*	..
31	28	..	..	..	3	..	54	3	..	..	..	51	..
47	47	..	..	..	..	..	..	..	..	..	..	..	..

M. = Males; F. = Females.

TABLE X, PART I.—OCCUPATION OR MEANS
TOTALS FOR PROVINCE,

Group Number.	Occupation.	BALUCHISTAN. Total following occupation.	As Principal Occupation. M.	As Principal Occupation. F.	As Working Dependents. M.	As Working Dependents. F.	As Subsidiary to other Occupation. M.	As Subsidiary to other Occupation. F.
1	2	3	4	5	6	7	8	9
	ORDER 35. TRADE IN BUILDING MATERIALS	*4*	*4*	..	..	..	..	..
141	Trade in building materials (other than bricks, tiles and woody materials)	4	4	..	..	..	..	..
	ORDER 36. TRADE IN MEANS OF TRANSPORT	*6,141*	*329*	*2*	*1*	..	*5,808*	*1*
142	Dealers and hirers, in mechanical transport motors, cycles, etc.	43	42	..	..	..	1	..
144	Dealers and hirers of elephants, camels, horses, cattle, asses, mules, etc.	6,098	287	2	1	..	5,807	1
	ORDER 37. TRADE IN FUEL	*1,023*	*459*	*2*	*26*	*54*	*481*	*1*
145	Dealers in firewood, charcoal, coal, cowdung, etc.	1,023	459	2	26	54	481	1
	ORDER 38. TRADE IN ARTICLES OF LUXURY AND THOSE PERTAINING TO LETTERS AND THE ARTS AND SCIENCES	*66*	*66*	..	..	..	..	..
146	Dealers in precious stones, jewellery (real and imitation), clocks, optical instruments, etc.	12	12	..	..	..	..	..
147	Dealers in common bangles, bead necklaces, fans, small articles, toys, hunting and fishing tackle, flowers, etc.	7	7	..	..	..	..	..
148	Publishers, book-sellers, stationers, dealers in music, pictures, musical instruments and curiosities	47	47	..	..	..	..	..
	ORDER 39. TRADE OF OTHER SORTS	*6,135*	*5,690*	*3*	*1*	..	*440*	*1*
150	General store-keepers and shop-keepers otherwise unspecified	6,088	5,649	3	1	..	434	1
151	Itinerant traders, pedlars and hawkers (of other than food, etc.)	41	36	..	..	..	5	..
152	Other trades (including farmers of pounds, tolls and markets)	6	5	..	..	..	1	..
	CLASS C.—PUBLIC ADMINISTRATION AND LIBERAL ARTS	35,494	33,756	302	1	9	1,419	7
	SUB-CLASS VI. PUBLIC FORCE	25,994	25,858	..	..	..	135	1
	ORDER 40. ARMY	*20,129*	*20,124*	..	..	..	*5*	..
153	Army (Imperial)	19,603	19,598	..	..	..	5	..
154	Army (Indian States)	526	526	..	..	..	..	..
	ORDER 42. AIR FORCE	*161*	*161*	..	..	..	..	..
156	Air Force	161	161	..	..	..	..	..
	ORDER 43. POLICE	*5,704*	*5,573*	..	..	..	*130*	*1*
157	Police	5,691	5,566	..	..	..	124	1
158	Village watchmen	13	7	..	..	..	6	..
	SUB-CLASS VII. PUBLIC ADMINISTRATION	4,133	3,693	1	..	..	438	1
	ORDER 44. PUBLIC ADMINISTRATION	*4,133*	*3,693*	*1*	..	..	*438*	*1*
159	Service of the State	2,058	2,053	1	..	..	4	..
160	Service of Indian and Foreign States	1,163	1,161	..	..	..	2	..
161	Municipal and other local (not village) service	375	366	..	..	..	9	..
162	Village officials and servants other than watchmen	537	113	..	..	..	423	1
	SUB-CLASS VIII. PROFESSIONS AND LIBERAL ARTS	5,367	4,205	301	1	9	846	5
	ORDER 45. RELIGION	*3,272*	*2,481*	*17*	..	..	*771*	*3*
163	Priests, ministers, etc.	2,792	2,052	11	..	..	726	3
164	Monks, nuns, religious mendicants	127	125	..	..	..	2	..
165	Other religious workers	11	11	..	..	..	..	..
166	Servants on religious edifices, burial and burning grounds, pilgrim conductors, circumcisers, etc.	342	293	6	..	..	43	..
	ORDER 46. LAW	*62*	*61*	..	..	..	*1*	..
167	Lawyers of all kinds, including Qazis, Law Agents and Mukhtiars	12	12	..	..	..	..	..
168	Lawyer's clerks, petition-writers, etc.	50	49	..	..	..	1	..
	ORDER 47. MEDICINE	*900*	*655*	*217*	..	*2*	*25*	*1*
169	Registered medical practitioners including oculists	182	177	5	..	..	..	..
170	Other persons practising the healing arts without being registered	135	103	13	..	2	17	..
171	Dentists	11	9	2	..	..	..	..
172	Midwives, vaccinators, compounders, nurses, masseurs, etc.	500	295	197	..	..	7	1
173	Veterinary Surgeons	72	71	..	..	..	1	..
	ORDER 48. INSTRUCTION	*458*	*397*	*54*	..	..	*6*	*1*
174	Professors and teachers of all kinds	394	339	48	..	..	6	1
175	Clerks and servants connected with education	64	58	6	..	..	..	..

OF LIVELIHOOD.
DISTRICTS AND STATES.

DISTRICTS.							STATES.						
Total following occupation.	As Principal Occupation.		As Working Dependents.		As Subsidiary to other Occupation.		Total following occupation.	As Principal Occupation.		As Working Dependents.		As Subsidiary to other Occupation.	
	M.	F.	M.	F.	M.	F.		M.	F.	M.	F.	M.	F.
10	11	12	13	14	15	16	17	18	19	20	21	22	23
4	*4*	..	..	..	..	..	..	..	..	..	..	..	..
4	4	..	..	..	..	..	..	..	..	..	..	..	..
5,635	*288*	*2*	*1*	..	*5,344*	..	*506*	*41*	..	..	..	*464*	*1*
43	42	..	..	..	1	..	..	..	..	..	..	..	..
5,592	246	2	1	..	5,343	..	506	41	..	..	..	464	1
990	*432*	..	*26*	*54*	*478*	..	*33*	*27*	*2*	..	..	*3*	*1*
990	432	..	26	54	478	..	33	27	2	..	..	3	1
66	*66*	..	..	..	..	..	..	..	..	..	..	..	..
12	12	..	..	..	..	..	..	..	..	..	..	..	..
7	7	..	..	..	..	..	..	..	..	..	..	..	..
47	47	..	..	..	..	..	..	..	..	..	..	..	..
3,520	*3,168*	*3*	*1*	..	*347*	*1*	*2,615*	*2,522*	..	..	..	*93*	..
3,473	3,127	3	1	..	341	1	2,615	2,522	..	..	..	93	..
41	36	..	..	..	5	..	..	..	..	..	..	..	..
6	5	..	..	..	1	..	..	..	..	..	..	..	..
30,856	**29,373**	**266**	..	**7**	**1,205**	**5**	**4,638**	**4,383**	**36**	**1**	**2**	**214**	**2**
24,197	**24,061**	..	..	..	**185**	**1**	**1,797**	**1,797**	..	..	..	..	..
19,184	*19,179*	..	..	..	*5*	..	*945*	*945*	..	..	..	..	..
19,183	19,178	..	..	..	5	..	420	420	..	..	..	..	..
1	1	..	..	..	..	..	525	525	..	..	..	..	..
161	*161*	..	..	..	..	..	..	..	..	..	..	..	..
161	161	..	..	..	..	..	..	..	..	..	..	..	..
4,852	*4,721*	..	..	..	*130*	*1*	*852*	*852*	..	..	..	..	..
4,840	4,715	..	..	..	124	1	851	851	..	..	..	..	..
12	6	..	..	..	6	..	1	1	..	..	..	..	..
2,792	*2,358*	*1*	..	..	*432*	*1*	*1,341*	*1,336*	..	..	..	*6*	..
2,792	2,358	1	..	..	432	1	1,341	1,335	..	..	..	6	..
1,899	1,894	1	..	..	4	..	159	159	..	..	..	..	..
30	29	..	..	..	1	..	1,133	1,132	..	..	..	1	..
337	329	..	..	..	8	..	38	37	..	..	..	1	..
526	106	..	..	..	419	1	11	7	..	..	..	4	..
8,867	**2,954**	**265**	..	**7**	**638**	**3**	**1,500**	**1,251**	**36**	**1**	**2**	**208**	**2**
2,234	*1,634*	*11*	..	..	*586*	*3*	*1,038*	*847*	*6*	..	..	*185*	..
1,943	1,370	6	..	..	564	3	849	682	5	..	..	162	..
82	80	..	..	..	2	..	45	45	..	..	..	..	..
11	11	..	..	..	..	..	..	..	..	..	..	..	..
198	173	5	..	..	20	..	144	120	1	..	..	23	..
52	*52*	..	..	..	..	..	*10*	*9*	..	..	..	*7*	..
8	8	..	..	..	..	..	4	4	..	..	..	..	..
44	44	..	..	..	..	..	6	5	..	..	..	1	..
796	*589*	*187*	..	..	*20*	..	*104*	*66*	*30*	..	*2*	*5*	*1*
171	166	5	..	..	..	..	11	11	..	..	..	..	..
114	89	12	..	..	13	..	21	14	1	..	2	4	..
11	9	2	..	..	..	..	..	..	..	..	..	..	..
431	257	168	..	..	6	..	69	38	29	..	..	1	1
69	68	..	..	..	1	..	3	3	..	..	..	..	..
415	*355*	*54*	..	..	*6*	..	*43*	*42*	..	..	..	..	*1*
357	308	48	..	..	6	..	37	36	..	..	..	..	1
58	52	6	..	..	..	..	6	6	..	..	..	..	..

M. = Males ; F. = Females.

TABLE X, PART I.—OCCUPATION OR MEANS
TOTALS FOR PROVINCE,

Group Number.	Occupation.	BALUCHISTAN. Total following occupation.	As Principal Occupation. M.	As Principal Occupation. F.	As Working Dependents. M.	As Working Dependents. F.	As Subsidiary to other Occupation. M.	As Subsidiary to other Occupation. F.
1	2	3	4	5	6	7	8	9
	ORDER 49. LETTERS, ARTS AND SCIENCES (OTHER THAN 44)	*675*	*611*	*13*	*1*	*7*	*43*	..
176	Public scribes, stenographers, etc.	20	19	..	..	..	1	..
177	Architects, surveyors, engineers and their employees (not being State servants)	3	3	..	..	..	..	..
178	Authors, editors, journalists and photographers	37	36	..	1	..	..	..
179	Artists, sculptors and image-makers	2	2	..	..	..	..	..
180	Scientists (astronomers, botanists, etc.)	3	3	..	..	..	..	..
181	Horoscope casters, astrologers, fortunetellers, wizards, witches and mediums)	15	14	..	..	..	1	..
182	Musicians (composers and performers other than military), actors, dancers, etc.	459	402	11	..	7	39	..
183	Managers and employees of places of public entertainments, race courses, societies, clubs	126	122	2	..	..	2	..
184	Conjurors, acrobats, reciters, exhibitors of curiosities and wild animals, etc.	10	10	..	..	..	..	..
	CLASS D.—MISCELLANEOUS	**14,310**	**11,099**	**936**	**473**	**3**	**1,766**	**33**
	SUB-CLASS IX. PERSONS LIVING ON THEIR INCOME	**1,679**	**854**	**32**	..	..	**791**	**2**
	ORDER 50. PERSONS LIVING PRINCIPALLY ON THEIR INCOME	*1,679*	*854*	*32*	..	..	*791*	*2*
185	Proprietors (other than of agricultural land), fund and scholarship holders and pensioners	1,679	854	32	..	..	791	2
	SUB-CLASS X. DOMESTIC SERVICE	**7,778**	**7,184**	**303**	..	..	**284**	**7**
	ORDER 51. DOMESTIC SERVICE	*7,778*	*7,184*	*303*	..	..	*284*	*7*
186	Private motor drivers and cleaners	482	461	..	..	..	21	..
187	Other domestic service	7,296	6,723	303	..	..	263	7
	SUB-CLASS XI. INSUFFICIENTLY DESCRIBED OCCUPATIONS.	**1,102**	**883**	**4**	**3**	..	**211**	**1**
	ORDER 52. GENERAL TERMS WHICH DO NOT INDICATE A DEFINITE OCCUPATION	*1,102*	*883*	*4*	*3*	..	*211*	*1*
188	Manufacturers, businessmen and contractors otherwise unspecified	474	396	..	1	..	76	1
189	Cashiers, accountants, book keepers, clerks and other employees in unspecified offices and warehouses and shops	611	472	4	1	..	134	..
190	Mechanics otherwise unspecified	17	15	..	1	..	1	..
	SUB-CLASS XII. UNPRODUCTIVE	**3,751**	**2,178**	**597**	**470**	**3**	**480**	**23**
	ORDER 53. INMATES OF JAILS, ASYLUMS AND ALMS HOUSES	*753*	*279*	*1*	*470*	*3*	..	..
192	Inmates of jails, asylums and alms houses	753	279	1	470	3	..	..
	ORDER 54. BEGGARS, VAGRANTS, PROSTITUTES	*2,998*	*1,899*	*596*	..	..	*480*	*23*
193	Beggars and vagrants	2,846	1,882	461	..	..	480	23
194	Procurers and prostitutes	152	17	135	..	..	..	..

OF LIVELIHOOD.
DISTRICTS AND STATES.

DISTRICTS.							STATES.						
Total following occupation.	As Principal Occupation.		As Working Dependents.		As Subsidiary to other Occupation.		Total following occupation.	As Principal Occupation.		As Working Dependents.		As Subsidiary to other Occupation.	
	M.	F.	M.	F.	M.	F.		M.	F.	M.	F.	M.	F.
10	11	12	13	14	15	16	17	18	19	20	21	22	23
370	*324*	*13*	..	*7*	*26*	..	*305*	*287*	..	*1*	..	*17*	..
20	19	..	..	..	1	..	..	..	..	..	..	..	..
3	3	..	..	..	..	..	..	..	..	..	..	..	..
26	26	..	..	..	..	..	11	10	..	1	..	..	..
2	2	..	..	..	..	..	..	..	..	..	..	..	..
3	3	..	..	..	..	..	..	..	..	..	..	..	..
14	14	..	..	..	..	..	1	..	..	..	..	1	..
179	138	11	..	7	23	..	280	264	..	..	..	16	..
115	111	2	..	..	2	..	11	11	..	..	..	..	..
8	8	..	..	..	..	..	2	2	..	..	..	..	..
11,100	**8,635**	**632**	**427**	**3**	**1,372**	**31**	**3,210**	**2,464**	**304**	**46**	..	**394**	**2**
1,129	**375**	**29**	..	..	**723**	**2**	**550**	**479**	**3**	..	..	**68**	..
1,129	*375*	*29*	..	..	*723*	*2*	*550*	*479*	*3*	..	..	*68*	..
1,120	375	29	..	..	723	2	550	479	3	..	..	68	..
6,596	**6,247**	**192**	..	..	**150**	**7**	**1,182**	**937**	**111**	..	..	**134**	..
6,596	*6,247*	*192*	..	..	*150*	*7*	*1,182*	*937*	*111*	..	..	*134*	..
471	450	..	..	..	21	..	11	11	..	..	..	..	..
6,125	5,797	192	..	..	129	7	1,171	926	111	..	..	134	..
1,047	**846**	**4**	**2**	..	**194**	**1**	**55**	**37**	..	**1**	..	**17**	..
1,047	*846*	*4*	*2*	..	*194*	*1*	*55*	*37*	..	*1*	..	*17*	..
428	361	..	1	..	65	1	46	35	..	..	..	11	..
603	471	4	..	..	128	..	8	1	..	1	..	6	..
16	14	..	1	..	1	..	1	1	..	..	..	..	..
2,328	**1,167**	**407**	**425**	**3**	**305**	**21**	**1,423**	**1,011**	**190**	**45**	..	**175**	**2**
588	*159*	*1*	*425*	*3*	..	..	*165*	*120*	..	*45*	..	..	..
588	159	1	425	3	..	..	165	120	..	45	..	..	..
1,740	*1,008*	*406*	..	..	*305*	*21*	*1,258*	*891*	*190*	..	..	*175*	*2*
1,588	991	271	..	..	305	21	1,258	891	190	..	..	175	2
152	17	135	..	..	..	..	..	..	..	..	..	..	..

M. = Males; F. = Females.

TABLE X.

PART II.—DISTRIBUTION BY DISTRICTS AND STATES.

The distribution by Districts and States of non-working dependents shown in columns 8 and 9 of this Table is given below :—

District or state.	Total.	Males.	Females.
Total. ..	549,335	185,286	364,049
Quetta-Pishin ..	83,808	29,167	54,641
Loralai ..	49,819	16,996	32,823
Zhob ..	33,266	10,608	22,658
Bolan ..	1,791	585	1,206
Chagai ..	15,417	5,133	10,284
Sibi ..	96,279	33,879	62,400
Kalat ..	231,006	76,388	154,618
Las-Bela ..	37,949	12,530	25,419

TABLE X, PART II.—DISTRIBUTION BY

Baluchistan.

Group Number.	Occupation.	Total Population.	Total Earners Principal Occupation. M.	Total Earners Principal Occupation. F.	Total Working Dependents. M.	Total Working Dependents. F.	Total Non-Working Dependents. M.	Total Non-Working Dependents. F.	Total Earners with Subsidiary Occupation. M.	Total Earners with Subsidiary Occupation. F.
1	2	3	4	5	6	7	8	9	10	11
	TOTAL CLASSES A, B, C AND D	868,617	292,246	4,739	10,882	11,415	185,286	364,049	72,901	406
	CLASS A. PRODUCTION OF RAW MATERIALS	..	199,779	693	9,915	5,655	..	..	55,429	146
	SUB-CLASS I.—EXPLOITATION OF ANIMALS AND VEGETATION	..	199,231	693	9,915	5,655	..	..	55,417	146
	ORDER 1.—PASTURE AND AGRICULTURE	..	*197,003*	*687*	*9,894*	*5,636*	..	..	*55,127*	*145*
	(a) *Cultivation*	..	*172,439*	*526*	*5,725*	*4,960*	..	..	*24,200*	*64*
1	Non-cultivating proprietors taking rent in money or kind	..	11,222	291	..	..	..	..	14,459	48
2	Estate Agents and Managers of owners	..	9	..	..	..	..	..	1	..
3	Estate Agents and Managers of Government	..	2	..	..	..	..	..	..	..
4	Rent Collectors, clerks, etc.	..	15	..	..	..	..	..	..	..
5	Cultivating owners	..	104,529	30	..	..	..	..	1,635	3
6	Tenant cultivators	..	50,905	10	90	2	..	..	6,679	4
7	Agricultural labourers	..	5,807	195	5,635	4,958	..	..	1,426	9
	(b) *Cultivation of Special Crops, Fruits, etc. (Planters, Managers, Clerks and Labourers)*	..	*862*	..	*6*	*5*	..	..	*36*	..
16	Market gardeners, flower and fruit growers	..	862	..	6	5	..	..	36	..
	(c) *Forestry*	..	*464*	*36*	*340*	*55*	..	..	*134*	..
17	Forest Officers, rangers, guards, etc.	..	69	..	..	..	..	..	5	..
18	Woodcutters and Charcoal burners	..	389	35	339	55	..	..	120	..
19	Collectors of Forest produce	..	6	1	1	..	..	..	9	..
	(d) *Stock raising*	..	*23,187*	*125*	*3,823*	*616*	..	..	*30,757*	*81*
21	Cattle and buffalo breeders and keepers	..	1,130	32	203	84	..	..	2,542	1
22	Breeders of transport animals	..	1,286	8	7	..	..	..	1,781	38
23	Herds-men, shepherds and breeders of other animals	..	20,771	85	3,613	532	..	..	26,434	42
	(e) *Raising of small animals and insects*	..	*1*	..	..	..	..	..	..	..
24	Birds, Bees, etc.	..	1	..	..	..	..	..	..	..
	ORDER 2.—FISHING AND HUNTING	..	*2,228*	*6*	*21*	*19*	..	..	*290*	*1*
27	Fishing and Pearling	..	2,225	6	21	19	..	..	289	1
28	Hunting	..	3	..	..	..	..	..	1	..
	SUB-CLASS II—EXPLOITATION OF MINERALS.	..	548	..	..	..	..	..	12	..
	ORDER 3.—METALLIC MINERALS	..	*176*	..	..	..	..	..	*5*	..
34	Other metallic minerals	..	176	..	..	..	..	..	5	..
	ORDER 4.—NON-METALLIC MINERALS	..	*372*	..	..	..	..	..	*7*	..
35	Coal	..	296	..	..	..	..	..	1	..
40	Salt, salt-petre and other saline substances	..	76	..	..	..	..	..	6	..
	CLASS B. PREPARATION AND SUPPLY OF MATERIAL SUBSTANCES	..	47,891	2,809	493	5,748	..	..	14,287	220
	SUB-CLASS III—INDUSTRY	..	17,059	2,402	255	5,679	..	..	1,974	168
	ORDER 5.—TEXTILES	..	*654*	*196*	*33*	*1,213*	..	..	*233*	*41*
42	Cotton ginning, cleaning and pressing	..	8	..	..	..	..	..	2	..
43	Cotton spinning, sizing and weaving	..	223	1	..	..	..	..	38	1
44	Jute pressing, spinning and weaving	..	..	16	1	15	..	..	..	..
45	Rope, twine, string, and other fibres	..	77	10	..	..	..	..	87	4
46	Wool carding, spinning and weaving	..	273	167	32	1,198	..	..	102	32
47	Silk spinning and weaving	..	7	..	..	..	..	..	1	..
49	Dyeing, bleaching, printing, preparation and sponging of textiles	..	66	2	..	..	..	..	3	..
50	Lace, crepe, embroideries, fringes, etc., and insufficiently described textile industries	..	..	..	..	..	..	..	..	4
	ORDER 6.—HIDES, SKINS AND HARD MATERIALS FROM THE ANIMAL KINGDOM	..	*27*	*8*	*4*	*5*	..	..	..	..
51	Working in leather	..	24	8	4	5	..	..	..	..
52	Furriers and persons occupied with feathers, and bristles, brush makers	..	3	..	..	..	..	..	..	..

Quetta-Pishin.						Loralai.						Zhob.						
Total Earners Principal Occupation.		Total Working Dependents.		Total following Occupation as Subsidiary to Others.		Total Earners Principal Occupation.		Total Working Dependents.		Total following Occupation as Subsidiary to Others.		Total Earners Principal Occupation.		Total Working Dependents.		Total following Occupation as Subsidiary to Others.		Group Number.
M.	F.	M.	F.	M.	F.	M.	F.	M.	F.	M.	F.	M.	F.	M.	F.	M.	F.	
12	13	14	15	16	17	18	19	20	21	22	23	24	25	26	27	28	29	
59,229	962	1,906	1,636	11,188	43	28,212	339	2,728	4,989	11,245	60	22,545	170	1,443	539	7,028	32	
16,409	77	1,776	172	8,919	36	21,382	134	2,534	4,598	9,007	17	13,767	53	1,421	538	5,805	5	
16,327	77	1,776	172	8,918	36	21,382	134	2,534	4,598	9,007	17	13,534	53	1,421	538	5,805	5	
16,326	*77*	*1,776*	*172*	*8,917*	*36*	*21,382*	*134*	*2,534*	*4,598*	*9,007*	*17*	*13,534*	*53*	*1,421*	*538*	*5,805*	*5*	
14,823	*46*	*1,199*	*104*	*7,341*	*32*	*18,868*	*109*	*1,230*	*4,227*	*2,887*	*4*	*11,488*	*47*	*958*	*491*	*2,993*	*5*	
964	18	..	..	6,682	31	1,000	78	..	..	1,753	1	464	40	..	..	2,618	4	1
9	..	..	..	..	..	..	..	..	..	1	..	..	..	..	..	..	..	2
2	..	..	..	..	..	..	..	..	..	..	..	..	..	..	..	..	..	3
15	..	..	..	..	..	..	..	..	..	..	..	..	..	..	..	..	..	4
19,676	2	..	..	162	1	14,264	..	..	..	182	..	10,143	..	..	..	144	1	5
3,003	..	37	..	296	..	3,385	9	..	..	686	2	548	..	18	..	114	..	6
1,154	26	1,162	104	201	..	219	22	1,230	4,227	265	1	333	7	940	491	117	..	7
664	..	*6*	..	*16*	..	*45*	..	..	..	*4*	..	*34*	..	..	..	*1*	..	
664	..	6	..	16	..	45	..	..	..	4	..	34	..	..	..	1	..	16
64	..	*206*	*40*	*18*	..	*31*	*1*	*6*	..	*5*	..	*1*	..	*123*	*10*	*8*	..	
22	..	..	..	..	..	20	..	..	..	5	..	1	..	..	..	..	..	17
42	..	206	40	18	..	11	1	6	..	..	..	..	..	123	10	8	..	18
..	..	..	..	..	..	..	..	..	..	..	..	..	..	..	..	..	..	19
775	*31*	*365*	*28*	*1,542*	*4*	*2,438*	*24*	*1,298*	*371*	*6,111*	*13*	*2,011*	*6*	*340*	*37*	*2,803*	..	
171	26	..	..	..	..	14	1	..	..	531	1	13	..	..	..	1	..	21
66	..	..	..	12	..	352	..	..	..	15	..	10	..	..	..	..	..	22
538	5	365	28	1,530	4	2,072	23	1,298	371	5,565	12	1,988	6	340	37	2,802	..	23
..	..	..	..	..	..	..	..	..	..	..	..	..	..	..	..	..	..	
..	..	..	..	..	..	..	..		..	..	..	..	..	..	..	..	..	24
1	..	..	..	*1*	..	..	..	..	..	..	..	..	..	..	..	..	..	
1	..	..	..	..	..	..	..	..	..	..	..	..	..	..	..	..	..	27
..	..	..	..	1	..	..	..	..	..	..	..	..	..	..	..	..	..	28
82	..	..	..	1	..	..	..	..	..	..	..	233	..	..	..	..	..	
..	..	..	..	..	..	..	..	..	..	..	..	*175*	..	..	..	..	..	
..	..	..	..	..	..	..	..	..	..	..	..	175	..	..	..	..	..	34
82	..	..	..	*1*	..	..	..	..	..	..	..	*58*	..	..	..	..	..	
82	..	..	..	1	..	..	..	..	..	..	..	58	..	..	..	..	..	35
..	..	..	..	..	..	..	..	..	..	..	..	..	..	..	..	..	..	40
18,700	413	99	1,464	1,369	5	3,456	78	174	384	1,819	34	3,312	59	18	1	801	11	
7,638	365	21	1,412	140	4	1,201	50	122	381	503	27	1,228	44	..	1	77	4	
107	*25*	..	..	*10*	*3*	*42*	*5*	*2*	..	*43*	*1*	*157*	*1*	..	..	*25*	*4*	
8	..	..	..	2	..	..	..	..	..	..	..	..	..	..	..	..	..	42
..	..	..	..	1	1	10	..	..	..	9	..	84	..	..	..	..	..	43
..	..	..	..	..	..	..	..	..	..	..	..	..	..	..	..	..	..	44
2	..	..	..	..	..	2	..	..	..	..	..	..	..	..	..	..	..	45
67	25	..	..	7	2	18	3	2	..	34	1	63	1	..	..	24	..	46
..	..	..	..	..	..	..	..	..	..	..	..	..	..	..	..	1	..	47
30	..	..	..	..	..	12	2	..	..	..	..	10	..	..	..	..	..	49
..	..	..	..	..	..	..	..	..	..	..	..	..	..	..	..	..	4	50
16	..	..	..	..	..	*2*	..	*4*	*2*	..	..	..	..	..	..	..	..	
13	..	..	..	..	..	2	..	4	2	..	..	..	..	..	..	..	..	51
3	..	..	..	..	..	..	..	..	..	..	..	..	..	..	..	..	..	52

M = Males; F = Females.

TABLE X, PART II.—DISTRIBUTION BY

Group Number.	Occupation.	Bolan. Total Earners Principal Occupation. M.	F.	Bolan. Total Working Dependents. M.	F.	Bolan. Total following Occupation as Subsidiary to Others. M.	F.	Chagai. Total Earners Principal Occupation. M.	F.	Chagai. Total Working Dependents. M.	F.	Chagai. Total following Occupation a[illegible] Subsidiary to Others. M.	F.
1	2	30	31	32	33	34	35	36	37	38	39	40	41
	TOTAL CLASSES A, B, C AND D	2,515	13	366	3	870	..	8,554	217	34	2	1,498	[illegible]
	CLASS A. PRODUCTION OF RAW MATERIALS	318	..	..	..	332	..	4,605	25	27	2	1,272	[illegible]
	SUB-CLASS I—EXPLOITATION OF ANIMALS AND VEGETATION	269	..	..	..	332	..	4,605	25	27	2	1,272	[illegible]
	ORDER 1.—PASTURE AND AGRICULTURE ..	*269*	..	..	..	*332*	..	*4,605*	*25*	*27*	*2*	*1,872*	[illegible]
	(a) *Cultivation*	*253*	..	..	..	*327*	..	*3,092*	*14*	*2*	..	*547*	[illegible]
1	Non-cultivating proprietors taking rent in money or kind	19	..	..	..	317	..	345	13	..	..	378	[illegible]
2	Estate Agents and Managers of owners ..	..	..	..	..	..	..	..	..	..	..	..	..
3	Estate Agents and Managers of Government ..	..	..	..	..	..	..	..	..	..	..	..	..
4	Rent collectors, clerks, etc.	..	..	..	..	..	..	..	..	..	..	..	..
5	Cultivating owners	199	..	..	..	1	..	2,118	..	..	..	82	..
6	Tenant cultivators	29	..	..	..	9	..	606	..	..	..	84	..
7	Agricultural labourers	6	..	..	..	..	..	23	1	2	..	3	..
	(b) *Cultivation of Special Crops, Fruits, etc., (Planters, Managers, Clerks and Labourers).*	*10*	..	..	..	..	..	*15*	..	..	..	*1*	..
16	Market gardeners, flower and fruit growers ..	10	..	..	..	..	..	15	..	..	..	1	..
	(c) *Forestry*	..	..	..	..	..	..	*5*	..	..	..	..	..
17	Forest Officers, rangers, guards, etc. ..	..	..	..	..	..	..	..	..	..	..	..	..
18	Woodcutters and charcoal burners	..	..	..	..	..	..	5	..	..	..	..	..
19	Collectors of Forest produce	..	..	..	..	..	..	..	..	..	..	..	..
	(d) *Stock raising*	*6*	..	..	..	*5*	..	*1,493*	*11*	*25*	*2*	*724*	*3*
21	Cattle and buffalo breeders and keepers ..	..	..	..	..	3	..	6	..	..	..	8	..
22	Breeders of transport animals	..	..	..	..	..	..	158	..	..	..	89	..
23	Herds-men, shepherds and breeders of other animals	6	..	..	..	2	..	1,329	11	25	2	627	3
	(e) *Raising of small animals and insects* ..	..	..	..	..	..	..	..	..	..	..	..	..
24	Birds, bees, etc.	..	..	..	..	..	..	..	..	..	..	..	..
	ORDER 2.—FISHING AND HUNTING	..	..	..	..	..	..	..	..	..	..	..	..
27	Fishing and Pearling	..	..	..	..	..	..	..	..	..	..	..	..
28	Hunting	..	..	..	..	..	..	..	..	..	..	..	..
	SUB-CLASS II—EXPLOITATION OF MINERALS.	49	..	..	..	..	..	..	..	..	..	..	..
	ORDER 3.—METALLIC MINERALS	..	..	..	..	..	..	..	..	..	..	..	..
34	Other metallic Mineral	..	..	..	..	..	..	..	..	..	..	..	..
	ORDER 4.—NON-METALLIC MINERALS ..	*49*	..	..	..	..	..	..	..	..	..	..	..
35	Coal	49	..	..	..	..	..	..	..	..	..	..	..
40	Salt, salt-petre and other saline substances ..	..	..	..	..	..	..	..	..	..	..	..	..
	CLASS B. PREPARATION AND SUPPLY OF MATERIAL SUBSTANCES	1,698	7	..	..	5	..	2,830	184	1	..	156	13
	SUB-CLASS III—INDUSTRY	333	6	..	..	2	..	338	26	1	..	28	10
	ORDER 5.—TEXTILES	..	..	..	..	..	..	*3*	*5*	..	..	*1*	..
42	Cotton ginning, cleaning and pressing ..	..	..	..	..	..	..	..	..	..	..	..	..
43	Cotton spinning, sizing and weaving	..	..	..	..	..	..	..	..	..	..	..	..
44	Jute pressing, spinning and weaving	..	..	..	..	..	..	..	..	..	..	..	..
45	Rope twine, string and other fibres	..	..	..	..	..	..	..	..	..	..	..	..
46	Wool carding, spinning and weaving	..	..	..	..	..	..	1	5	..	..	..	..
47	Silk spinning and weaving	..	..	..	..	..	..	..	..	..	..	..	..
49	Dyeing, bleaching, printing, preparation and sponging of textiles	..	..	..	..	..	..	2	..	..	..	1	..
50	Lace, Crepe, embroideries, fringes, etc., and insufficiently described textile industries ..	..	..	..	..	..	..	..	..	..	..	..	..
	ORDER 6.—HIDES, SKINS AND HARD MATERIALS FROM THE ANIMAL KINGDOM	..	..	..	..	..	..	..	..	..	..	..	..
51	Working in leather	..	..	..	..	..	..	..	..	..	..	..	..
52	Furriers and persons occupied with feathers and bristles; brush makers	..	..	..	..	..	..	..	..	..	..	..	..

DISTRICTS AND STATES.

Sibi.						Kalat.						Las Bela.						
Total Earners Principal Occupation.		Total Working Dependents.		Total following Occupation as Subsidiary to Others.		Total Earners Principal Occupation.		Total Working Dependents.		Total following Occupation as Subsidiary to Others.		Total Earners Principal Occupation.		Total Working Dependents.		Total following Occupation as Subsidiary to Others.		Group Number.
M.	F.	M.	F.	M.	F.	M.	F.	M.	F.	M.	F.	M.	F.	M.	F.	M.	F.	
42	43	44	45	46	47	48	49	50	51	52	53	54	55	56	57	58	59	
45,699	595	405	27	16,839	133	106,341	989	1,686	1,579	19,019	64	18,651	1,454	2,314	2,640	5,714	53	
36,151	78	395	11	9,788	46	91,696	226	1,533	61	16,551	9	15,451	105	2,229	278	3,755	27	
36,051	78	395	11	9,786	46	91,612	226	1,538	61	16,546	9	15,451	105	2,229	278	3,751	27	
36,051	73	395	11	9,786	46	90,770	226	1,533	61	16,538	9	14,066	99	2,208	254	3,470	26	
34,242	70	4	3	1,864	7	80,591	194	669	36	7,382	5	9,132	46	1,663	99	859	8	
1,211	46	..	..	991	..	6,991	79	..	..	1,550	1	228	17	..	..	170	8	1
..	..	..	..	..	..	..	..	..	..	..	..	..	..	..	..	..	..	2
..	..	..	..	..	..	..	..	..	..	..	..	..	..	..	..	..	..	3
19,633	..	..	..	17	..	41,110	..	..	..	1,034	1	7,386	28	..	..	13	..	4
13,079	..	..	..	723	..	28,878	..	31	2	4,175	2	1,377	1	4	..	592	..	6
319	24	4	3	133	7	3,612	115	638	34	623	1	141	..	1,659	99	84	..	7
54	..	..	..	2	..	36	..	..	5	3	..	4	..	..	..	9	..	
54	..	..	..	2	..	36	..	..	5	3	..	4	..	..	..	9	..	16
160	..	2	5	64	..	94	..	..	..	4	..	109	35	3	..	35	..	
24	..	..	..	..	..	..	..	..	..	..	..	2	..	..	..	..	..	17
136	..	2	5	64	..	94	..	..	..	4	..	101	34	2	..	26	..	18
..	..	..	..	..	..	..	..	..	..	..	..	8	1	1	..	9	..	19
1,594	3	389	3	7,856	39	10,049	32	864	20	9,149	4	4,821	18	542	155	2,567	18	
73	..	..	..	337	..	162	..	..	..	1,509	..	691	5	208	84	153	..	21
33	..	..	..	88	35	252	7	..	..	55	..	415	1	7	..	1,522	3	22
1,488	3	389	3	7,431	4	9,635	25	864	20	7,585	4	3,715	12	332	71	892	15	23
1	..	..	..	..	..	..	..	..	..	..	..	..	..	..	..	..	..	
1	..	..	..	..	..	..	..	..	..	..	..	..	..	..	..	..	..	24
..	..	..	..	..	..	842	..	..	..	8	..	1,385	6	21	19	281	1	
..	..	..	..	..	..	839	..	..	..	8	..	1,385	6	21	19	281	1	27
..	..	..	..	..	..	3	..	..	..	..	..	..	..	..	..	..	..	28
100	..	..	..	2	..	84	..	..	..	5	..	..	..	..	..	4	..	
..	..	..	..	..	..	1	..	..	..	5	..	..	..	..	..	..	..	
..	..	..	..	..	..	1	..	..	..	5	..	..	..	..	..	..	..	34
100	..	..	..	2	..	83	..	..	..	..	..	..	..	..	..	4	..	
100	..	..	..	..	..	7	..	..	..	..	..	..	..	..	..	..	..	35
..	..	..	..	2	..	76	..	..	..	..	..	..	..	..	..	4	..	40
6,282	346	10	16	6,318	80	9,315	625	106	1,516	2,007	53	2,803	1,147	85	2,367	1,812	24	
2,024	222	10	13	394	54	3,754	572	44	1,516	660	43	543	1,117	57	2,356	170	21	
10	..	..	4	7	..	294	156	12	560	54	24	41	4	19	649	93	9	
2	..	..	..	..	..	127	..	..	..	28	..	..	1	..	..	..	..	42
..	..	..	..	..	..	..	16	1	15	..	..	..	..	..	..	..	..	43
..	..	..	..	..	..	48	10	..	..	..	..	25	..	..	..	..	..	44
..	..	..	4	7	..	119	130	11	545	26	24	5	3	19	649	87	4	45
7	..	..	..	..	..	..	..	..	..	..	..	..	..	..	..	4	5	46
..	..	..	..	..	..	..	..	..	..	..	..	..	..	..	..	..	..	47
1	..	..	..	..	..	..	..	..	..	..	..	11	..	..	..	2	..	49
..	..	..	..	..	..	..	..	..	..	..	..	..	..	..	..	..	..	50
..	..	..	..	..	..	7	8	..	..	..	..	2	..	..	3	..	..	
..	..	..	..	..	..	7	8	..	..	..	..	2	..	..	3	..	..	51
..	..	..	..	..	..	..	..	..	..	..	..	..	..	..	..	..	..	52

M = Males; F = Females.

TABLE X, PART II.—DISTRIBUTION BY

Group Number.	Occupation.	Total Population.	*Baluchistan.* Total Earners Principal Occupation. M.	F.	Total Working Dependents. M.	F.	Total Non-Working Dependents. M.	F.	Total Earners With Subsidiary Occupation. M.	F.
1	2	3	4	5	6	7	8	9	10	11
	ORDER 7.—WOOD	..	*1,498*	*1,306*	*144*	*2,516*	..	..	*483*	*100*
54	Sawyers	..	47	..	..	..	..	..	..	..
55	Carpenters, turners and joiners, etc.	..	959	..	10	..	..	..	228	..
56	Basket-makers and other industries of woody materials, including leaves and thatchers and builders working with Bamboo, reeds or similar materials	..	492	1,306	134	2,516	..	..	255	100
	ORDER 8.—METALS	..	*2,489*	..	*21*	*5*	..	..	*178*	..
58	Makers of arms, guns, etc.	..	487	..	..	..	..	..	..	..
59	Blacksmiths, other workers in iron, makers of implements	..	1,826	..	20	5	..	..	169	..
60	Workers in brass, copper and bell metal ..	..	59	..	..	..	..	..	2	..
61	Workers in other metals (except precious metals)..	..	117	..	1	..	..	..	7	..
	ORDER 9.—CERAMICS	..	*554*	*32*	..	*12*	..	..	*217*	..
63	Potters and makers of earthen-ware ..	..	220	12	..	10	..	..	22	..
64	Brick and tile makers	..	310	20	..	2	..	..	195	..
65	Other workers in Ceramics	..	24	..	..	..	..	..	..	..
	ORDER 10.—CHEMICAL PRODUCTS, PROPERLY SO CALLED AND ANALOGOUS	..	*292*	..	*1*	..	..	..	*81*	..
67	Manufacture of aerated and mineral waters and ice	..	28	..	..	..	..	..	..	..
68	Manufacture and refining of vegetable oils ..	..	63	..	..	..	..	..	73	..
70	Others	..	201	..	1	..	..	..	8	..
	ORDER 11.—FOOD INDUSTRIES	..	*1,570*	*221*	*12*	*20*	..	..	*170*	*10*
71	Rice pounders and huskers and flour grinders ..	..	151	186	..	14	..	..	56	5
72	Grain parchers, etc.	..	77	35	..	..	..	..	35	5
73	Butchers	..	430	..	..	..	..	..	71	..
75	Sweetmeat and condiment makers	..	263	..	..	..	..	..	2	..
77	Brewers and distillers	..	49	..	..	..	..	..	..	..
81	Others	..	600	..	12	6	..	..	6	..
	ORDER 12.—INDUSTRIES OF DRESS AND THE TOILET.	..	*3,324*	*209*	*26*	*1,892*	..	..	*211*	*9*
82	Boot, shoe, sandal and clog makers ..	..	1,117	1	3	..	..	..	108	..
83	Tailors, milliners, dressmakers and darners ..	..	1,099	23	16	1,480	..	..	22	2
84	Embroiderers, hat-makers and makers of other articles of wear	..	14	136	5	404	..	..	1	4
85	Washing and cleaning	..	496	48	2	8	..	..	27	3
86	Barbers, hair-dressers and wig-makers ..	..	594	1	..	..	..	..	53	..
87	Other Industries connected with the toilet ..	..	4	..	..	..	..	..	..	..
	ORDER 13.—FURNITURE INDUSTRIES ..	..	*570*	*12*	..	*3*	..	..	*9*	*2*
88	Cabinet-makers, carriage painters, etc. ..	..	569	..	..	..	..	..	9	..
89	Upholsterers, tent-makers, etc.	..	1	12	..	3	..	..	..	2
	ORDER 14.—BUILDING INDUSTRIES	..	*2,024*	*16*	*3*	..	..	..	*319*	*1*
90	Lime burners; cement workers; Excavators and well-sinkers; Stone cutters and dressers; Brick layers and masons; Builders (other than buildings made of bamboo or similar materials) painters, decorators of houses, tilers, plumbers, etc. ..	..	2,024	16	3	..	..	..	319	1
	ORDER 15.—CONSTRUCTION OF MEANS OF TRANSPORT	..	*109*	..	..	..	..	..	*3*	..
91	Persons engaged in making, assembling or repairing Motor Vehicles or Cycles	..	109	..	..	..	..	..	2	..
93	Ship, Boat, aeroplane Builders	..	..	..	..	..	..	..	1	..
	ORDER 16.—PRODUCTION AND TRANSMISSION OF PHYSICAL FORCE	..	*194*	..	..	..	..	..	..	..
94	Heat, light, electricity, motive power, etc., Gas works and electric light and power ..	..	194	..	..	..	..	..	..	..
	ORDER 17.—MISCELLANEOUS AND UN-DEFINED INDUSTRIES	..	*3,754*	*402*	*11*	*13*	..	..	*70*	..
95	Printers, Engravers, Book-binders, etc. ..	..	65	..	..	..	..	..	..	..
97	Makers of Clocks and Surgical or Scientific Instruments, etc.	..	39	..	..	..	..	..	..	..
98	Makers of Jewellery and Ornaments	..	742	..	3	..	..	..	38	..
99	Other Miscellaneous and un-defined Industries (Toy making, Taxidermy, etc.)	..	15	..	..	..	..	..	27	..
100	Scavenging	..	2,893	402	8	13	..	..	5	..

Quetta-Pishin.						Loralai.						Zhob.						
Total Earners Principal Occupation.		Total Working Dependents.		Total following Occupation as Subsidiary to Others.		Total Earners Principal Occupation.		Total Working Dependents.		Total following Occupation as Subsidiary to Others.		Total Earners Principal Occupation.		Total Working Dependents.		Total following Occupation as Subsidiary to Others.		Group Number.
M.	F.	M.	F.	M.	F.	M.	F.	M.	F.	M.	F.	M.	F.	M.	F.	M.	F.	
12	13	14	15	16	17	18	19	20	21	22	23	24	25	26	27	28	29	
151	..	..	..	*2*	..	*25*	*4*	*109*	*367*	*65*	*25*	*15*	..	..	..	*3*	..	
30	..	..	..	..	..	1	..	..	..	..	..	14	..	..	..	..	..	54
88	..	..	..	2		17	..	3	..	37	..	1		..	..	3	..	55
33	..	..	..	..	..	7	4	106	367	28	25	..	..	..	..	..	..	56
1,034	..	*5*	..	*12*	..	*192*	..	*7*	*3*	*107*	..	*118*	..	..	..	*21*	..	
480	..	..	..	..	..	..	..	..	..	..	..	3	..	..	..	..	..	58
476	..	5	..	16	..	184	..	7	3	106	..	109	..	..	..	21	..	59
45	..	..	..	2	..	3	..	..	..	..	..	5	..	..	..	..	..	60
33	..	..	..	..	..	5	..	..	..	1	..	1	..	..	..	..	..	61
67	*3*	..	..	..	..	*157*	*3*	..	..	*192*	..	*45*	*1*	..	..	..	..	
15	3	..	..	..	..	3	..	..	..	4	..	3	1	..	..	..	..	63
50	..	..	..	..	..	152	3	..	..	188	..	42	..	..	..	..	..	64
2	..	..	..	..	..	2	..	..	..	..	..	..	..	..	..	..	..	65
30	..	..	..	*5*	..	*6*	..	..	..	..	..	*162*	..	..	..	*6*	..	
20	..	..	..	..	..	6	..	..	..	..	..	..	..	..	..	..	..	67
1	.	..	..	4	..	..	..	..	..	..	..	..	..	..	..	..	..	68
9	.	..	..	1	..	..	..	..	..	..	..	162	..	..	..	6	..	70
982	..	..	..	*27*	..	*99*	*3*	..	..	*34*	*1*	*58*	..	..	..	*6*	..	
76	..	..	..	7	..	31	3	..	..	33	1	3	..	..	..	4	..	71
21	..	..	..	..	..	..	..	..	..	..	..	..	..	..	..	..	..	72
268	..	..	..	15	..	16	..	..	..	..	..	15	..	..	..	..	..	73
146	..	..	..	2	..	22	..	..	..	..	..	11	..	..	..	..	..	75
49	..	..	..	..	..	..	..	..	..	..	..	..	..	..	..	..	..	77
422	..	..	..	3	..	30	..	..	..	1	..	29	..	..	..	2	..	81
1,764	*39*	*15*	*1,410*	*19*	*1*	*207*	*7*	..	*1*	*33*	..	*217*	*17*	..	*1*	*5*	..	
394	1	..	..	16	..	73	..	..	..	12	..	49	..	..	..	..	..	82
740	12	15	1,404	2	..	72	1	..	..	1	..	79	1	..	..	5	..	83
6	1	..	6	..	..	..	..	..	..	..	..	1	15	..	1	..	..	84
327	24	..	..	1	1	27	6	..	1	17	..	37	1	..	..	..	..	85
294	1	..	..	..	..	35	..	..	..	3	..	51	..	..	..	..	..	86
3	..	..	..	..	..	..	..	..	..	..	..	..	..	..	..	..	..	87
376	..	..	..	*8*	..	*55*	..	..	..	..	..	*62*	..	..	..	*1*	..	
376	..	..	..	8	..	55	..	..	..	..	..	62	..	..	..	1	..	88
..	..	..	..	..	..	..	..	..	..	..	..	..	..	..	..	..	..	89
659	..	..	..	*36*	..	*181*	..	..	..	*16*	..	*138*	..	..	..	*7*	..	
659		..	..	36	..	181	..	..	..	16	..	138	..	..	..	7	.	90
101	..	..	..	*2*	..	*5*	..	..	..	..	..	..	..	..	..	..	..	
101	..	..	..	2	..	5	..	..	..	..	..	..	..	..	..	..	..	91
..	..	..	..	.	..	..	..	..	..	..	..	..	..	..	..	..	..	93
158	..	..	..	..	..	..	..	..	..	..	..	*4*	..	..	..	..	..	
158	..	..	..	..	..	..	..	..	..	..	..	4	..	..	..	..	..	94
2,193	*298*	*1*	*2*	*19*	..	*230*	*28*	..	*8*	*13*	..	*252*	*25*	..	..	*3*	..	
61	..	..	..	..	..	..	..	..	..	..	..	..	..	..	..	..	..	95
27	..	..	..	..	..	4	..	..	..	..	..	6	..	..	..	..	..	97
234	..	1	..	..	..	40	..	..	..	6	..	18	..	..	..	3	..	98
11	..	..	..	18	..	1	..	..	..	7	..	1	..	..	..	..	..	99
1,860	298	..	2	1	..	185	28	..	8	..	..	227	25	..	..	..	..	100

M = Males. F = Females.

Group Numbers.	Occupation.	*Bolan.* Total Earners Principal Occupation.		*Bolan.* Total Working Dependents.		*Bolan.* Total following Occupation as Subsidiary to Others.		*Chagai.* Total Earners Principal Occupation.		*Chagai.* Total Working Dependents.		*Chagai.* Total following Occupation as Subsidiary to Others.	
		M.	F.	M.	F.	M.	F.	M.	F.	M.	F.	M.	F.
1	2	30	31	32	33	34	35	36	37	38	39	40	41
	ORDER 7.—WOOD	*2*	..	..	..	*1*	..	*34*	*5*	..	..	*11*	*5*
54	Sawyers	..	..	..	..	..	..	..	..	..	..	..	..
55	Carpenters, turners and joiners, etc.	..	..	..	..	1	..	24	..	..	..	5	..
56	Basket-makers and other industries of woody materials, including leaves and thatchers and builders working with bamboo, reeds or similar materials	2	..	..	..	..	..	10	5	..	..	6	5
	ORDER 8.—METALS	*8*	..	..	..	..	..	*83*	..	..	..	..	..
58	Makers of arms, guns, etc.	..	..	..	..	..	..	..	..	..	..	..	..
59	Blacksmiths, other workers in iron, makers of implements	6	..	..	..	..	..	77	..	..	..	..	..
60	Workers in brass, copper and bell metal ..	..	..	..	..	..	..	5	..	..	..	..	..
61	Workers in other metals (except precious metals)	2	..	..	..	..	..	1	..	..	..	..	..
	ORDER 9.—CERAMICS	*3*	..	..	..	..	..	*4*	..	..	..	*1*	..
63	Potters and makers of earthenware	3	..	..	..	..	..	..	..	..	..	..	..
64	Brick and tile makers	..	..	..	..	..	..	4	..	..	..	1	..
65	Other workers in ceramics	..	..	..	..	..	..	..	..	..	..	..	..
	ORDER 10.—CHEMICAL PRODUCTS, PROPERLY SO CALLED AND ANALOGOUS	..	..	..	..	..	..	*30*	..	*1*	..	..	..
67	Manufacture of aerated and mineral waters and ice	..	..	..	..	..	..	1	..	..	..	..	..
68	Manufacture and refining of vegetable oils ..	..	..	..	..	..	..	..	..	..	..	..	..
79	Others	..	..	..	..	..	..	29	..	1	..	..	..
	ORDER 11.—FOOD INDUSTRIES	*46*	..	..	..	..	..	*10*	*8*	..	..	*10*	
71	Rice pounders and huskers and flour grinders ..	1	..	..	..	..	..	3	8	..	..	1	
72	Grain parchers, etc.	..	..	..	..	..	..	..	..	..	..	..	..
73	Butchers	12	..	..	..	..	..	3	..	..	..	9	..
75	Sweetmeat and condiment makers	18	..	..	..	..	..	2	..	..	..	..	..
77	Brewers and distillers	..	..	..	..	..	..	..	..	..	..	..	..
81	Others	15	..	..	..	..	..	2	..	..	..	..	..
	ORDER 12.—INDUSTRIES OF DRESS AND THE TOILET	*35*	..	..	..	*1*	..	*51*	*5*	..	..	*3*	
82	Boot, shoe, sandal and clog makers ..	9	..	..	..	..	..	18	..	..	..	1	..
83	Tailors, milliners, dressmakers and darners ..	13	..	..	..	1	..	20	1	..	..	..	
84	Embroiderers, hatmakers and makers of other articles of wear	..	..	..	..	..	..	..	2	..	..	..	
85	Washing and cleaning	4	..	..	..	..	..	4	2	..	..	2	..
86	Barbers, hair-dressers and wig-makers ..	9	..	..	..	..	..	9	..	..	..	..	..
87	Other industries connected with the toilet ..	..	..	..	..	..	..	..	..	..	..	..	..
	ORDER 13.—FURNITURE INDUSTRIES ..	*24*	..	..	..	..	..	*5*	..	..	..	..	..
88	Cabinet-makers, carriage painters, etc. ..	24	..	..	..	..	..	5	..	..	..	..	..
89	Upholsterers, Tent-makers, etc.	..	..	..	..	..	..	..	..	..	..	..	..
	ORDER 14.—BUILDING INDUSTRIES ..	*119*	..	..	..	..	..	*36*	..	..	..	*2*	..
90	Lime burners, cement workers; Excavators and well-sinkers; Stone cutters and dressers; Brick layers and masons; Builders (other than buildings made of bamboo or similar materials) painters, decorators of houses, tilers, plumbers, etc. ..	119	..	..	..	..	..	36	..	..	..	2	..
	ORDER 15.—CONSTRUCTION OF MEANS OF TRANSPORT	*1*	..	..	..	..	..	*1*	..	..	..	..	..
91	Persons engaged in making, assembling or repairing motor vehicles or cycles	1	..	..	..	..	..	1	..	..	..	..	..
93	Ship, boat, aeroplane builders	..	..	..	..	..	..	..	..	..	..	..	..
	ORDER 16.—PRODUCTION AND TRANSMISSION OF PHYSICAL FORCE	*6*	..	..	..	..	..	*1*	..	..	..	..	..
94	Heat, Light, electricity, motive power, etc., Gas works and electric light and power ..	6	..	..	..	..	..	1	..	..	..	..	..
	ORDER 17.—MISCELLANEOUS AND UNDEFINED INDUSTRIES	*89*	*6*	..	..	..	..	*80*	*3*	..	..	..	..
95	Printers, engravers, book-binders, etc. ..	..	..	..	..	..	..	..	..	..	..	..	..
97	Makers of clocks and surgical or scientific instruments, etc.	1	..	..	..	..	..	..	..	..	..	..	..
98	Makers of jewellery and ornaments	1	..	..	..	..	..	19	..	..	..	..	..
99	Other miscellaneous and undefined Industries (Toy making, Taxidermy, etc.)	..	..	..	..	..	..	..	..	..	..	..	..
100	Scavenging	87	6	..	..	..	..	61	3	..	..	..	..

Sibi.						Kalat.						Las Bela.						
Total Earners Principal Occupation.		Total Working Dependents.		Total following Occupation as Subsidiary to Others.		Total Earners Principal Occupation.		Total Working Dependents.		Total following Occupation as Subsidiary to Others.		Total Earners Principal Occupation.		Total Working Dependents.		Total following Occupation as Subsidiary to Others.		Group Number.
M.	F.	M.	F.	M.	F.	M.	F.	M.	F.	M.	F.	M.	F.	M.	F.	M.	F.	
42	43	44	45	46	47	48	49	50	51	52	53	54	55	56	57	58	59	
362	*137*	*2*	*5*	*220*	*52*	*786*	*130*	*8*	*503*	*154*	*9*	*123*	*1,030*	*25*	*1,641*	*27*	*9*	
2	..	..	..	..	..	..	..	..	..	..	..	..	..	..	..	..	..	54
77	..	..	..	48	..	669	..	6	..	113	..	83	..	1	..	19	..	55
283	137	2	5	172	52	117	130	2	503	41	9	40	1,030	24	1,641	8	9	56
166	..	..	..	*5*	..	*824*	..	*9*	*2*	*21*	..	*64*	..	..	..	*12*	..	
..	..	..	..	..	..	..	..	..	..	..	..	4	..	..	..	..	..	58
138	..	..	..	5	..	795	..	8	2	19	..	41	..	..	..	8	..	59
1	..	..	..	..	..	..	..	..	..	..	..	..	..	..	..	..	..	60
27	..	..	..	..	..	29	..	1	..	2	..	19	..	..	..	4	..	61
124	*25*	..	..	*2*	..	*133*	..	..	*12*	*20*	..	*21*	..	..	..	*2*	..	
45	8	..	..	..	..	131	..	..	10	18	..	20	..	..	..	..	..	63
59	17	..	..	2	..	2	..	..	2	2	..	1	..	..	..	2	..	64
20	..	..	..	..	..	..	..	..	..	..	..	..	..	..	..	..	..	65
14	..	..	..	*11*	..	*44*	..	..	..	*53*	..	*6*	..	..	..	*6*	..	
1	..	..	..	..	..	..	..	..	..	..	..	..	..	..	..	..	..	67
12	..	..	..	10	..	44	..	..	..	53	..	6	..	..	..	6	..	68
1	..	..	..	1	..	..	..	..	..	..	..	..	..	..	..	..	..	70
202	*7*	..	..	*22*	..	*143*	*170*	..	*1*	*67*	*8*	*30*	*33*	*12*	*19*	*4*	..	
16	7	..	..	8	..	19	135	..	1	3	3	2	33	..	13	..	..	71
..	..	..	..	..	..	56	35	..	..	35	5	..	..	..	..	..	..	72
53	..	..	..	14	..	60	..	..	..	29	..	3	..	..	..	4	..	73
48	..	..	..	..	..	4	..	..	..	..	..	12	..	..	..	..	..	75
..	..	..	..	..	..	..	..	..	..	..	..	..	..	..	..	..	..	77
85	..	..	..	..	..	4	..	..	..	..	..	13	..	12	6	..	..	81
294	*10*	..	*1*	*8*	*2*	*639*	*94*	*10*	*435*	*127*	*2*	*117*	*37*	*1*	*44*	*15*	..	
90	..	..	..	1	..	410	..	3	..	75	..	74	..	..	..	3	..	82
80	..	..	..	1	..	78	8	1	76	8	1	17	..	..	..	4	..	83
1	3	..	1	..	2	4	84	5	359	..	1	2	31	..	37	1	..	84
42	7	..	..	..	..	40	2	1	..	4	..	15	6	1	7	3	..	85
81	..	..	..	6	..	106	..	..	..	40	..	9	..	..	..	4	..	86
..	..	..	..	..	..	1	..	..	..	..	..	..	..	..	..	..	..	87
45	..	..	..	..	..	*3*	*12*	..	*3*	..	..	..	..	..	..	..	*2*	
44	..	..	..	..	..	3	..	..	..	..	..	..	..	..	..	..	..	88
1	..	..	..	..	..	..	12	..	3	..	..	..	..	..	..	..	2	89
486	*15*	..	..	*108*	..	*319*	..	*3*	..	*139*	..	*86*	*1*	..	..	*11*	*1*	
486	15	..	..	108	..	319	..	3	..	139	..	86	1	..	..	11	1	90
1	..	..	..	..	..	..	..	..	..	*1*	..	..	..	..	..	..	..	
1	..	..	..	..	..	..	..	..	..	..	..	..	..	..	..	..	..	91
..	..	..	..	..	..	..	..	..	..	1	..	..	..	..	..	..	..	93
22	..	..	..	..	..	*3*	..	..	..	..	..	..	..	..	..	..	..	
22	..	..	..	..	..	3	..	..	..	..	..	..	..	..	..	..	..	94
298	*28*	*8*	*3*	*11*	..	*559*	*2*	*2*	..	*24*	..	*53*	*12*	..	..	..	..	
4	..	..	..	..	..	..	..	..	..	..	..	..	..	..	..	..	..	95
1	..	..	..	..	..	..	..	..	..	..	..	..	..	..	..	..	..	97
33	..	..	..	11	..	370	..	2	..	18	..	27	..	..	..	..	..	98
1	..	..	..	..	..	1	..	..	..	2	..	..	..	..	..	..	..	99
259	28	8	3	..	..	188	2	..	..	4	..	26	12	..	..	..	..	100

M = Males. F = Females.

Group Number.	Occupation.	Total Population.	*Baluchistan.* Total Earners Principal Occupation. M.	F.	Total Working Dependents. M.	F.	Total Non-Working Dependents. M.	F.	Total Earners with Subsidiary Occupation. M.	F.
1	2	3	4	5	6	7	8	9	10	11
	SUB-CLASS IV.—TRANSPORT	..	17,451	350	155	8	..	..	4,172	45
	ORDER 18.—TRANSPORT BY AIR	..	*40*	..	..	..	..	..	..	..
101	Persons concerned with aerodromes and aeroplanes	..	40	..	..	..	..	..	..	..
	ORDER 19.—TRANSPORT BY WATER	..	*81*	..	..	..	..	..	*4*	..
102	Ship owners, boat owners and their employees, officers, mariners, etc., Shipsbrokers, boatmen and towmen	..	81	..	..	..	..	..	4	..
	ORDER 20.—TRANSPORT BY ROAD	..	*10,373*	*350*	*155*	*8*	..	..	*4,140*	*45*
105	Persons (other than labourers) employed on the construction and maintenance of roads and bridges	..	63	..	..	..	..	..	..	..
106	Labourers employed on roads and bridges	..	837	..	2	..	..	..	140	..
107	Owners, managers and employees (excluding personal servants) connected with mechanically driven Vehicles (including trams)	..	44	..	.	..	..	..	3	..
108	Owners, managers and employees (excluding personal servants) connected with other Vehicles	..	646	..	..	..	..	..	32	..
109	Palki, etc., bearers and owners	..	1	..	..	..	..	..	..	..
110	Pack elephant, camel, mule, ass and bullock owners and drivers	..	3,760	87	141	5	..	..	2,908	27
111	Porters and messengers	..	5,022	263	12	3	..	..	1,057	18
	ORDER 21.—TRANSPORT BY RAIL	..	*6,385*	..	..	..	..	..	*23*	..
112	Railway employees of all kinds other than coolies	..	3,117	..	..	..	..	..	4	..
113	Labourers employed on railway construction and maintenance and coolies and porters employed on railway premises	..	3,268	..	..	..	..	..	19	..
	ORDER 22.—POST OFFICE, TELEGRAPH AND TELEPHONE SERVICES	..	*572*	..	..	..	..	..	*5*	..
114	Post Office, Telegraph and Telephone Services	..	572	..	..	..	..	..	5	..
	SUB-CLASS V.—TRADE	..	13,881	57	83	61	..	..	8,141	12
	ORDER 23.—BANKS, ESTABLISHMENTS OF CREDIT, EXCHANGE AND INSURANCE	..	*100*	..	..	..	..	..	*12*	..
115	Bank managers, money-lenders, exchange and insurance agents, money changers and brokers and their employees	..	100	..	..	..	..	..	12	..
	ORDER 24.—BROKERAGE, COMMISSION AND EXPORT	.	*200*	..	..	..	..	..	*16*	..
116	Brokers, commission agents, commercial travellers, warehouse owners and employees	..	200	..	..	..	..	..	16	..
	ORDER 25.—TRADE IN TEXTILES	..	*2,320*	*2*	*41*	..	..	..	*682*	*6*
117	Trade in piece-goods, wool, cotton, silk, hair and other textiles	..	2,320	2	41	..	..	..	682	6
	ORDER 26.—TRADE IN SKINS, LEATHER AND FURS	..	*67*	..	..	..	..	..	*34*	..
118	Trade in Skins, leather, furs, feathers, horn, etc., and the articles made from these	..	67	..	..	..	..	..	34	..
	ORDER 27.—TRADE IN WOOD	..	*18*	..	..	..	..	..	*1*	..
119	Trade in wood (not firewood)	..	18	..	..	..	..	..	1	..
	ORDER 28.—TRADE IN METALS	..	*18*	..	..	..	..	..	..	..
123	Trade in metals, machinery, knives, tools, etc.	..	18	..		..	..	..	..	..
	ORDER 29.—TRADE IN POTTERY, BRICKS AND TILES	..	*20*	..	..	..	..	..	..	..
124	Trade in Pottery, Bricks and Tiles	..	20	.	..	..	..	..	..	..
	ORDER 30.—TRADE IN CHEMICAL PRODUCTS	.	*86*	*3*	*1*	..	..	..	*43*	..
125	Drugs, dyes, paints, petroleum, explosives, etc.	..	86	3	1	..	..	..	43	..
	ORDER 31.—HOTELS, CAFES, RESTAURANTS, ETC.	..	*584*	*6*	..	..	..	..	*11*	..
126	Vendors of wine, liquors, aerated waters and ice	..	76	..	..	..	..	..	2	..
127	Owners and Managers of Hotels, cookshops, serais, etc. (and employees)	..	314	5	..	..	..	..	4	..
128	Hawkers of drink and food stuffs	..	164	1	..	..	..	..	5	..

Quetta-Pishin.						*Loralai.*						*Zhob.*						
Total Earners Principal Occupation.		Total Working Dependents.		Total following Occupation as Subsidiary to Others.		Total Earners Principal Occupation.		Total Working Dependents.		Total following Occupation as Subsidiary to Others.		Total Earners Principal Occupation.		Total Working Dependents.		Total following Occupation as Subsidiary to Others.		Group Number.
M.	F.	M.	F.	M.	F.	M.	F.	M	F.	M.	F.	M.	F.	M.	F.	M.	F.	
12	13	14	15	16	17	18	19	20	21	22	23	24	25	26	27	28	29	
5,901	31	13	1	517	..	1,134	26	42	..	515	4	1,620	13	18	..	614	4	
40	..	..	..	..	..	..	..	..	..	..	..	..	..	..	..	..	..	
40	..	..	..	..	..	..	..	..	..	..	..	..	..	..	..	..	..	101
..	..	..	..	..	..	..	..	..	..	..	..	..	..	..	..	..	..	
..	..	..	..	..	..	..	..	..	..	..	..	..	..	..	..	..	..	102
3,598	*31*	*13*	*1*	*517*	..	*1,087*	*26*	*42*	..	*515*	*4*	*900*	*13*	*18*	..	*596*	*4*	
16	..	..	..	..	..	5	..	..	..	..	..	29	..	..	..	..	..	105
417	..	..	..	6	..	202	..	..	..	83	..	84	..	2	..	41	..	106
17	..	..	..	1	..	17	..	..	..	..	..	3	..	..	..	..	..	107
539	..	..	..	22	..	4	..	..	..	..	..	2	..	..	..	..	..	108
1	..	..	..	..	..	..	..	..	..	..	..	..	..	..	..	..	..	109
454	1	13	1	152	..	464	3	38	..	369	1	106	..	8	..	106	2	110
2,154	30	..	..	336	..	395	23	4	..	63	3	676	13	8	..	449	2	111
1,973	..	..	..	..	..	*8*	..	..	..	..	..	*671*	..	..	..	*18*	..	
1,080	..	..	..	..	..	8	..	..	..	..	..	239	..	..	..	2	..	112
893	..	..	..	..	..	..	..	..	..	..	..	432	..	..	..	16	..	113
290	..	..	..	..	..	*39*	..	..	..	..	..	*49*	..	..	..	..	..	
290	..	..	..	..	..	39	..	..	..	..	..	49	..	..	..	..	..	114
5,161	17	65	51	712	1	1,121	2	10	3	801	3	464	2	..	..	110	3	
79	..	..	..	*3*	..	*16*	..	..	..	*3*	..	*1*	..	..	..	..	..	
79	..	..	..	3	..	16	..	..	..	3	..	1	..	..	..	..	..	115
117	..	..	..	*2*	..	*12*	..	..	..	*5*	..	*6*	..	..	..	..	..	
117	..	..	..	2	..	12	..	..	..	5	..	6	..	..	..	..	..	116
1,010	*1*	*39*	..	*222*	..	*230*	*1*	..	..	*380*	*3*	*61*	..	..	..	*15*	..	
1,010	1	39	..	222	..	230	1	..	..	380	3	61	..	..	..	15	..	117
39	..	..	..	*1*	..	*3*	..	..	..	*2*	..	*2*	..	..	..	*2*	..	
39	..	..	..	1	..	3	..	..	..	2	..	2	..	..	..	2	..	118
18	..	..	..	*1*	..	..	..	..	..	..	..	..	..	..	..	..	..	
18	..	..	..	1	..	..	..	..	..	..	..	..	..	..	..	..	..	119
14	..	..	..	..	..	..	..	..	..	..	..	*1*	..	..	..	..	..	
14	..	..	..	..	..	..	..	..	..	..	..	1	..	..	..	..	..	123
8	..	..	..	..	..	..	..	..	..	..	..	..	..	..	..	..	..	
8	..	..	..	..	..	..	..	..	..	..	..	..	..	..	..	..	..	124
29	..	..	..	*1*	..	*3*	..	..	..	..	..	*5*	..	..	..	*4*	..	
29	..	..	..	1	..	3	..	..	..	..	..	5	..	..	..	4	..	125
392	*6*	..	..	*7*	..	*20*	..	..	..	*3*	..	*30*	..	..	..	..	..	
37	..	..	..	1	..	7	..	..	..	..	..	2	..	..	..	..	..	126
246	5	..	..	1	..	12	..	..	..	3	..	26	..	..	..	..	..	127
109	1	..	..	5	..	1	..	..	..	..	..	2	..	..	..	..	..	128

M = Males ; F = Females.

Group Number.	Occupation.	*Bolan.*						*Chagai.*					
		Total Earners Principal Occupation.		Total Working Dependents.		Total following Occupation as Subsidiary to Others.		Total Earners Principal Occupation.		Total Working Dependents.		Total following Occupation as Subsidiary to Others.	
		M.	F.	M.	F.	M.	F.	M.	F.	M.	F.	M.	F.
		30	31	32	33	34	35	36	37	38	39	40	41
	SUB-CLASS IV.—TRANSPORT	1,209	..	..	..	2	..	2,161	108	..	..	63	..
	ORDER 18.—TRANSPORT BY AIR ..	..	..	..	..	..	..	..	..	..	..	..	..
101	Persons concerned with aerodromes and aeroplanes	..	..	..	..	..	..	..	..	..	..	..	..
	ORDER 19.—TRANSPORT BY WATER	..	..	..	..	..	..	..	..	..	..	..	..
102	Ship owners, boat owners and their employees, officers, Mariners, etc., Shipsbrokers, boatmen and towmen	..	..	..	..	..	..	..	..	..	..	..	..
	ORDER 20.—TRANSPORT BY ROAD	*74*	..	..	..	*2*	..	*832*	*108*	..	..	*60*	..
105	Persons (other than labourers) employed on the construction and maintenance of roads and bridges	..	..	..	..	..	..	..	..	..	..	..	..
106	Labourers employed on roads and bridges ..	12	..	..	..	..	..	35	..	..	..	2	..
107	Owners, managers and employees (excluding personal servants) connected with mechanically driven vehicles (including trams)	..	..	..	..	..	..	..	..	..	..	..	..
108	Owners, managers and employees (excluding personal servants) connected with other vehicles ..	1	..	..	..	..	..	1	..	..	..	..	..
109	Palki, etc., bearers and owners	..	..	..	..	..	..	..	..	..	..	..	..
110	Pack elephant, camel, mule, ass and bullock owners and drivers	13	..	..	..	2	..	202	1	..	..	35	..
111	Porters and messengers	48	..	..	..	..	..	594	107	..	..	23	..
	ORDER 21.—TRANSPORT BY RAIL	*1,124*	..	..	..	..	.	*1,293*	..	..	..	*3*	..
112	Railway employees of all kinds other than coolies	600	..	..	..	..	..	453	..	..	..	..	..
113	Labourers employed on railway construction and maintenance and coolies and porters employed on railway premises	524	..	..	..	..	..	840	..	..	..	3	..
	ORDER 22.—POST OFFICE, TELEGRAPH AND TELEPHONE SERVICES	*11*	..	..	..	..	..	*36*	..	..	..	..	..
114	Post Office, Telegraph and Telephone Services ..	11	..	..	..	..	..	36	..	..	..	..	..
	SUB-CLASS V.—TRADE	151	1	..	..	1	..	331	..	..	..	65	3
	ORDER 23.—BANKS, ESTABLISHMENTS OF CREDIT, EXCHANGE AND INSURANCE	..	..	..	..	*1*	..	*2*	..	..	..	*7*	..
115	Bank managers, money-lenders, exchange and insurance agents, money-changers and brokers and their employees	..	..	..	..	1	..	2	..	..	..	1	..
	ORDER 24.—BROKERAGE, COMMISSION AND EXPORT.	*7*	..	..	..	..	..	*9*	..	..	..	..	..
116	Brokers, commission agents, commercial travellers, ware-house owners and employees ..	7	..	..	..	..	..	9	..	..	..	..	..
	ORDER 25.—TRADE IN TEXTILES	*33*	..	..	..	..	..	*90*	..	..	..	*15*	*3*
117	Trade in piece-goods, wool, cotton, silk hair and other Textiles	33	..	..	..	..	..	90	..	..	..	15	3
	ORDER 26.—TRADE IN SKINS, LEATHER AND FURS	..	..	..	..	..	..	1	..	..	..	..	..
118	Trade in skins, leather, furs, feathers, horn, etc., and the articles made from these	..	..	..	..	..	..	1	..	..	..	..	..
	ORDER 27.—TRADE IN WOOD	..	..	..	..	..	..	..	..	..	..	..	..
119	Trade in wood (not fire wood)	..	..	..	..	..	..	..	..	..	..	..	..
	ORDER 28.—TRADE IN METALS	..	..	..	..	..	..	..	..	..	..	..	..
123	Trade in metals, machinery, knives, tools, etc...	..	..	..	..	..	..	..	..	..	..	..	..
	ORDER 29.—TRADE IN POTTERY, BRICKS AND TILES.	..	..	..	..	..	..	..	..	..	..	..	..
124	Trade in pottery, bricks and tiles	..	..	..	..	..	..	..	..	..	..	..	..
	ORDER 30.—TRADE IN CHEMICAL PRODUCTS ..	..	..	..	..	..	..	*4*	.	..	..	*8*	..
125	Drugs, dyes, paints, petroleum, explosives, etc.	..	..	..	..	..	..	4	..	..	..	8	..
	ORDER 31.—HOTELS, CAFES, RESTAURANTS, ETC.	*13*	..	..	..	..	..	*3*	..	..	..	..	..
126	Vendors of wine, liquors, aerated waters and ice	1	..	..	..	..	..	1	..	..	..	..	..
127	Owners and managers of hotels, cook shops, Serais, etc. (and employees)	10	..	..	..	..	..	2	..	..	..	..	.
128	Hawkers of drink and food Stuffs	2	..	..	..	..	..	..	..	..	..	..	..

Sibi. Total Earners Principal Occupation. M.	F.	Total Working Dependents. M.	F.	Total following Occupation as Subsidiary to Others. M.	F.	Kalat. Total Earners Principal Occupation. M.	F.	Total Working Dependents. M.	F.	Total following Occupation as Subsidiary to Others. M.	F.	Las Bela. Total Earners Principal Occupation. M.	F.	Total Working Dependents. M.	F.	Total following Occupation as Subsidiary to Others. M.	F.	Group Number.
42	43	44	45	46	47	48	49	50	51	52	53	54	55	56	57	58	59	
2,550	116	..	3	291	26	1,815	49	60	..	879	9	1,061	7	22	4	1,291	2	
..	..	..	..	..	..	..	..	..	.	..	..	..	..	..	..	..	..	
..	..	..	..		..	..	..	..	..	..	..	..	.	..	..	..	..	101
..	..	..	..	..	..	*8*	..	..	..	..	..	*73*	.	..	..	*4*	..	
..	..	..		..	..	8	..	..	..	..	..	73	..	..	..	4	..	102
1,248	*116*	..	*3*	*289*	*26*	*1,680*	*49*	*60*	..	*874*	*9*	*954*	*7*	*22*	*4*	*1,287*	*2*	
10	..	..	..	..	..	3	..	..	..	..	..	..	..	..	..	..	..	105
57	..	..	..	5	..	30	..	..	..	3	..	..	..	..	..	..	..	106
4	..	..	..	2	..	3	..	..	..	..	..	..	..	..	..	..	..	107
96	..	..	..	7	..	3	..	..	..	3	..	..	..	..	..	..	..	108
..	..	..	..	..	..	..	..	..	..	..	..	..	..	..	..	..	..	109
397	66	..	..	146	13	1,397	9	60	..	853	9	727	7	22	4	1,245	2	110
684	50	..	3	129	13	244	40	..	..	15	..	227	..	..	..	42	..	111
1,276	..	.	..	*2*	..	*40*	..	..	..	..	..	..	..	..	..	..	..	
732	..	..	..	2	..	5	..	..	..	..	..	..	..	..	..	..	..	112
544	..	..	..	..	..	35	..	..	..	..	..	..	..	..	..	..	..	113
26	..	..	..	..	..	*87*	..	..	..	*5*	..	*34*	..	..	..	..	..	
26	..	..	..	..	..	87	..	..	..	5	..	34	..	..	..	..	..	114
1,708	8	..	..	5,633	..	3,746	4	2	..	468	1	699	23	6	7	351	1	
2	..	..	..	*4*	..	..	..	..	..	..	..	..	..	..	..	..	..	
2	..	..	..	4	..	..	..	..	..	..	..	..	..	..	..	..	..	115
24	..	..	..	*3*	..	*17*	..	..	..	*5*		*8*	..	..	..	*1*	..	
24	..	..	..	3	..	17	..	..	..	5	..	8	..	..	..	1	..	116
179	..	..	..	*1*	..	*636*	..	*1*	..	*18*	..	*81*	..	*1*	..	*31*	..	
179	..	..	..	1	..	636	..	1	..	18	..	81	..	1	..	31	..	117
10	..	..	..	*22*	..	*3*	..	..	..	*7*	..	*9*	..	..	..	..	..	
10	..	..	..	22	..	3	..	..	..	7	..	9	..	..	..	..	..	118
..	..	..	..	..	..	..	..	..	..	..	..	..	..	..	..	..	..	
..	..	..	..	..	..	..	..	..	..	..	..	..	..	..	..	..	..	119
3	..	..	..	..	..	..	..	..	..	..	..	..	..	..	..	..	..	
3	..	..	..	..	..	..	..	..	..	..	..	..	..	..	..	..	..	123
1	..	..	..	..	..	*11*	..	..	..	..	..	..	..	..	..	..	..	
1	..	..	..	..	..	11	..	..	..	..	..	..	..	..	..	..	..	124
43	*3*	..	..	..	..	*2*	..	*1*	..	*30*	..	..	..	..	..	..	..	
43	3	..	..	..	..	2	..	1	..	30	..	..	..	..	..	..	..	125
38	..	..	..	*1*	..	*69*	..	..	..	..	..	*19*	..	..	..	..	..	
1	..	..	..	1	..	25	..	..	..	..	..	2	..	..	..	..	..	126
27	..	..	..	..	..	4	..	..	..	..	..	17	..	..	..	..	..	127
10	..	..	..	..	..	40	..	..	..	..	..	..	..	..	..	..	..	128

M. = Males. F. = Females.

TABLE X, PART II.—DISTRIBUTION BY

Group Number.	Occupation.	Total Population.	Baluchistan. Total Earners Principal Occupation. M.	F.	Total Working Dependents. M.	F.	Total Non-Working Dependents. M.	F.	Total Earners with Subsidiary Occupation. M.	F.
1	2	3	4	5	6	7	8	9	10	11
	ORDER 32.—OTHER TRADE IN FOOD STUFFS	..	2,800	34	13	7	..	..	545	3
129	Grain and pulse dealers	..	451	5	..	..	..	..	31	..
130	Dealers in sweetmeats, sugar and spices	..	28	1	..	..	..	..	..	..
131	Dealers in dairy product, eggs and poultry	..	458	5	5	6	..	..	75	3
132	Dealers in animals for food	..	197	1	..	..	..	..	256	..
133	Dealers in fodder for animals	..	54	..	..	..	..	..	6	..
134	Dealers in other food stuffs	..	1,417	22	8	1	..	..	173	..
135	Dealers in tobacco	..	186	..	..	..	..	..	3	..
136	Dealers in opium	..	2	..	..	..	..	..	1	..
137	Dealers in ganja	..	7	..	..	..	..	..	..	..
	ORDER 33.—TRADE IN CLOTHING AND TOILET ARTICLES	..	*542*	*5*	..	..	..	..	*14*	..
138	Trade in ready-made clothing and other articles of dress and the toilet (hats, umbrellas, socks, ready made shoes, perfumes, etc.)	..	542	5	..	..	..	..	14	..
	ORDER 34.—TRADE IN FURNITURE	..	*78*	..	..	..	..	..	*54*	..
139	Trade in furniture, carpets, curtains and bedding	..	31	..	..	..	..	..	54	..
140	Hard-ware, cooking utensils, porcelain, crockery, glass-ware, bottles, articles for gardening, etc.	..	47	..	..	..	..	..	..	..
	ORDER 35.—TRADE IN BUILDING MATERIALS	..	*4*	..	..	..	..	..	..	..
141	Trade in building materials (other than bricks, tiles and wood materials)	..	4	..	..	..	..	..	..	..
	ORDER 36.—TRADE IN MEANS OF TRANSPORT	..	*329*	*2*	*1*	..	..	..	*5,808*	*1*
142	Dealers and hirers, in mechanical transport, motors, cycles, etc.	..	42	..	..	..	..	..	1	..
144	Dealers and hirers of elephants, camels, horses, cattle, asses, mules, etc.	..	287	2	1	..	..	..	5,807	1
	ORDER 37.—TRADE IN FUEL	..	*459*	*2*	*26*	*54*	..	..	*481*	*1*
145	Dealers in firewood, charcoal, coal, cow-dung, etc.	..	459	2	26	54	..	..	481	1
	ORDER 38.—TRADE IN ARTICLES OF LUXURY AND THOSE PERTAINING TO LETTERS AND THE ARTS AND SCIENCES	..	*66*	..	..	..	..	..	..	..
146	Dealers in precious stones, jewellery (real and imitation), clocks, optical instruments, etc.	..	12	..	..	..	..	..	..	..
147	Dealers in common bangles, bead necklaces, fans, small articles, toys, hunting and fishing tackle, flowers, etc.	..	7	..	..	..	..	..	..	..
148	Publishers, booksellers, stationers, dealers in music, pictures, musical instruments and curiosities	..	47	..	..	..	..	..	..	..
	ORDER 39.—TRADE OF OTHER SORTS	..	*5,690*	*3*	*1*	..	..	..	*440*	*1*
150	General store-keepers and shop-keepers otherwise unspecified	..	5,649	3	1	..	..	..	434	1
151	Itinerant traders, pedlars and hawkers (of other than food, etc.)	..	36	..	..	..	..	..	5	..
152	Other traders (including farmers of pounds), tools and markets	..	5	..	..	..	..	..	1	..
	CLASS C.—PUBLIC ADMINISTRATION AND LIBERAL ARTS	..	33,756	302	1	9	..	..	1,419	7
	SUB-CLASS VI—PUBLIC FORCE	..	25,858	..	..	..	..	..	135	1
	ORDER 40.—ARMY	..	*20,124*	..	..	..	..	..	*5*	..
153	Army (Imperial)	..	19,598	..	..	..	..	..	5	..
154	Army (Indian States)	..	526	..	..	..	..	..	..	..
	ORDER 42.—AIR FORCE	..	*161*	..	..	..	..	..	..	..
156	Air Force	..	161	..	..	..	..	..	..	..
	ORDER 43.—POLICE	..	*5,573*	..	..	..	..	..	*130*	*1*
157	Police	..	5,566	..	..	..	..	..	124	1
158	Village watchmen	..	7	..	..	..	..	..	6	..
	SUB-CLASS VII—PUBLIC ADMINISTRATION	..	3,693	1	..	..	..	..	438	1
	ORDER 44.—PUBLIC ADMINISTRATION	..	*3,693*	*1*	..	..	..	..	*438*	*1*
159	Service of the State	..	2,053	1	..	..	..	..	4	..
160	Service of Indian and Foreign States	..	1,161	..	..	..	..	..	2	..
161	Municipal and other local (not village) service	..	366	..	..	..	..	..	9	..
162	Village officials and servants other than watchmen	..	113	..	..	..	..	..	423	1

Quetta-Pishin.						*Loralai.*						*Zhob.*						Group Number.
Total Earners Principal Occupation.		Total Working Dependents.		Total following Occupation as Subsidiary to Others.		Total Earners Principal Occupation.		Total Working Dependents.		Total following Occupation as Subsidiary to Others.		Total Earners Principal Occupation.		Total Working Dependents.		Total following Occupation as Subsidiary to Others.		
M.	F.	M.	F.	M.	F.	M.	F.	M.	F.	M.	F.	M.	F.	M.	F.	M.	F.	
12	13	14	15	16	17	18	19	20	21	22	23	24	25	26	27	28	29	
1,088	6	7	..	54	..	420	1	1	..	104	..	82	..	..	..	56	3	
41	..	..	..	10	..	6	..	..	..	6	..	16	..	..	..	..	..	129
3	..	..	..	..	..	3	..	..	..	..	..	..	..	..	..	..	..	130
190	2	..	..	13	..	198	1	..	..	19	..	13	..	..	..	20	3	131
45	1	..	..	8	..	4	..	..	..	..	..	3	..	..	..	21	..	132
21	..	..	..	1	..	10	..	..	..	..	..	3	..	..	..	1	..	133
743	3	7	..	22	..	105	..	1	..	77	..	42	..	..	..	14	..	134
38	..	..	..	..	..	94	..	..	..	2	..	5	..	..	..	..	..	135
1	..	..	..	..	..	..	..	..	..	..	..	..	..	..	..	..	..	136
4	..	..	..	..	..	..	..	..	..	..	..	..	..	..	..	..	..	137
374	*2*	..	..	*8*	..	*17*	..	..	..	*5*	..	*25*	..	..	..	..	..	
374	2	..	..	8	..	17	..	..	..	5	..	25	..	..	..	..	..	138
68	..	..	..	..	..	*2*	..	..	..	..	..	..	..	..	..	..	..	
23	..	..	..	..	..	1	..	..	..	..	..	..	..	..	..	..	..	139
45	..	..	..	..	..	1	..	..	..	..	..	..	..	..	..	..	..	140
2	..	..	..	..	..	..	..	..	..	..	..	..	..	..	..	..	..	
2	..	..	..	..	..	..	..	..	..	..	..	..	..	..	..	..	..	141
191	..	..	..	*73*	..	*39*	..	*1*	..	*38*	..	*4*	*2*	..	..	*2*	..	
34	..	..	..	1	..	5	..	..	..	..	..	2	..	..	..	..	..	142
157	..	..	..	72	..	34	..	1	..	38	..	2	2	..	..	2	..	144
368	..	*18*	*51*	*263*	..	*13*	..	*8*	*3*	*102*	..	*2*	..	..	..	*24*	..	
368	..	18	51	263	..	13	..	8	3	102	..	2	..	..	..	24	..	145
51	..	..	..	..	..	*4*	..	..	..	..	..	*3*	..	..	..	..	..	
6	..	..	..	..	..	..	..	..	..	..	..	..	..	..	..	..	..	146
7	..	..	..	..	..	..	..	..	..	..	..	..	..	..	..	..	..	147
38	..	..	..	..	..	4	..	..	..	..	..	3	..	..	..	..	..	148
1,315	*2*	*1*	..	*77*	*1*	*342*	..	..	..	*159*	..	*242*	..	..	..	*7*	..	
1,287	2	1	..	72	1	334	..	..	..	158	..	241	..	..	..	7	..	150
28	..	..	..	5	..	3	..	..	..	..	..	1	..	..	..	..	..	151
..	..	..	..	..	..	5	..	..	..	1	..	..	..	..	..	..	..	152
18,221	212	..	..	164	..	2,801	17	..	7	303	3	5,003	6	..	..	307	1	
15,337	..	..	..	..	..	2,159	..	..	..	5	..	4,464	..	..	..	128	1	
13,556	..	..	..	..	..	*1,359*	..	..	..	..	..	*3,617*	..	..	..	*4*	..	
13,555	..	..	..	..	..	1,359	..	..	..	..	..	3,617	..	..	..	4	..	153
1	..	..	..	..	..	..	..	..	..	..	..	..	..	..	..	..	..	154
161	..	..	..	..	..	..	..	..	..	..	..	..	..	..	..	..	..	
161	..	..	..	..	..	..	..	..	..	..	..	..	..	..	..	..	..	155
1,620	..	..	..	..	..	*800*	..	..	..	*5*	..	*847*	..	..	..	*124*	*1*	
1,620	..	..	..	..	..	797	..	..	..	..	..	845	..	..	..	124	1	157
..	..	..	..	..	..	3	..	..	..	5	..	2	..	..	..	..	..	158
1,322	..	..	..	42	..	243	..	..	..	150	..	214	..	..	..	15	..	
1,322	..	..	..	*42*	..	*243*	..	..	..	*150*	..	*214*	..	..	..	*15*	..	
1,008	..	..	..	..	..	197	..	..	..	..	..	187	..	..	..	..	..	159
23	..	..	..	..	..	..	..	..	..	..	..	..	..	..	..	..	..	160
266	..	..	..	..	..	12	..	..	..	..	..	14	..	..	..	1	..	161
25	..	..	..	42	..	34	..	..	..	150	..	13	..	..	..	14	..	162

M. = Males ; F. = Females.

Group Number.	Occupation.	Bolan. Total Earners Principal Occupation. M.	F.	Total Working Dependents. M.	F.	Total following Occupation as Subsidiary to Others. M.	F.	Chagai. Total Earners Principal Occupation. M.	F.	Total Working Dependents. M.	F.	Total following Occupation as Subsidiary to Others. M.	F.
1	2	30	31	32	33	34	35	36	37	38	39	40	41
	ORDER 32.—OTHER TRADE IN FOOD STUFFS ..	*17*	..	..	..	..	..	*18*	..	..	..	*5*	..
129	Grain and pulse dealers	1	..	..	..	..	..	5	..	..	..	2	..
130	Dealers in sweetmeats, sugar and spices	..	..	..	..	..	..	1	..	..	..	..	..
131	Dealers in dairy product, eggs and poultry	2	..	..	..	..	..	1	..	..	..	..	..
132	Dealers in animals for food	..	..	..	..	..	..	..	..	..	..	..	..
133	Dealers in fodder for animals ..	..	..	..	..	..	..	..	..	..	..	..	..
134	Dealers in other food stuffs ..	13	..	..	..	..	..	4	..	..	..	2	..
135	Dealers in tobacco	1	..	..	..	..	..	1	..	..	..	..	..
136	Dealers in opium	..	..	..	..	..	..	1	..	..	..	1	..
137	Dealers in ganja	..	..	..	..	..	..	..	..	..	..	..	..
	ORDER 33.—TRADE IN CLOTHING AND TOILET ARTICLES	*2*	..	..	..	..	..	*2*	..	..	..	..	..
138	Trade in ready made clothing and other articles of dress and the toilet (hats, umbrellas, socks, ready made shoes, perfumes etc. ..	2	..	..	..	..	..	2	..	..	..	..	..
	ORDER 34.—TRADE IN FURNITURE	*1*	..	..	..	..	..	*1*	..	..	..	*1*	..
139	Trade in furniture, carpets, curtains and bedding ..	1	..	..	..	..	..	1	..	..	..	1	..
140	Hard-ware, cooking utensils, porcelain, crockery, glass-ware, bottles, articles for gardening, etc. ..	..	..	..	..	..	..	..	..	..	..	..	..
	ORDER 35.—TRADE IN BUILDING MATERIALS ..	..	..	..	..	..	..	..	..	..	..	..	..
141	Trade in building materials (other than bricks, tiles and wood materials) ..	..	..	..	..	..	..	..	..	..	..	..	..
	ORDER 36.—TRADE IN MEANS OF TRANSPORT	..	..	..	..	..	..	*8*	..	..	..	..	..
142	Dealers and hirers in mechanical transport, motors, cycles etc.	..	..	..	..	..	..	..	..	..	..	..	..
144	Dealers and hirers of elephants, camels, horses, cattle, asses, mules, etc. ..	..	..	..	..	..	..	8	..	..	..	..	..
	ORDER 37.—TRADE IN FUEL	*2*	..	..	..	..	..	*29*	..	..	..	*31*	..
145	Dealers in firewood, charcoal, coal, cow-dung, etc.	2	..	..	..	..	..	29	..	..	..	31	..
	ORDER 38.—TRADE IN ARTICLES OF LUXURY AND THOSE PERTAINING TO LETTERS AND THE ARTS AND SCIENCES	..	..	..	..	..	..	*2*	..	..	..	..	..
146	Dealers in precious stones, jewellery (real and imitation), clocks, optical instruments, etc. ..	..	..	..	..	..	..	2	..	..	..	..	..
147	Dealers in common bangles, bead necklaces, fans, small articles, toys, hunting and fishing tackle, flowers, etc. ..	..	..	..	..	..	..	..	..	..	..	..	..
148	Publishers, booksellers, stationers, dealers in music, pictures, musical instruments and curiosities ..	..	..	..	..	..	..	..	..	..	..	..	..
	ORDER 39.—TRADE OF OTHER SORTS ..	*76*	*1*	..	..	..	..	*167*	..	..	..	*4*	..
150	General storekeepers and shopkeepers otherwise unspecified	76	1	..	..	..	..	166	..	..	..	4	..
151	Itinerant traders, pedlars and hawkers (of other than food etc.)	..	..	..	..	..	..	1	..	..	..	..	..
152	Other traders (including farmers of pounds), tools and markets	..	..	..	..	..	..	..	..	..	..	..	..
	CLASS C. PUBLIC ADMINISTRATION AND LIBERAL ARTS	430	1	..	..	4	..	835	3	..	..	27	..
	SUB-CLASS VI—PUBLIC FORCE ..	251	..	..	..	..	..	654	..	..	..	1	..
	ORDER 40. ARMY	*11*	..	..	..	..	..	*338*	..	..	..	*1*	..
153	Army (Imperial)	11	..	..	..	..	..	338	..	..	..	1	..
154	Army (Indian States) ..	..	..	..	..	..	..	..	..	..	..	..	..
	ORDER 42.—AIR FORCE	..	..	..	..	..	..	..	..	..	..	..	..
156	Air Force	..	..	..	.	..	..	..	..	..	..	..	..
	ORDER 43.—POLICE	*240*	..	.	..	..	..	*316*	..	..	..	..	..
157	Police	240	..	.	..	..	..	316	..	..	..	..	..
158	Village watchmen ..	.	..	.	..	..	..	..	..	..	..	..	..
	SUB-CLASS VII—PUBLIC ADMINISTRATION	144	1	.	.	..	..	47	..	..	..	6	..
	ORDER 44.—PUBLIC ADMINISTRATION ..	*144*	*1*	..	.	..	..	*47*	..	..	..	*6*	..
159	Service of the State	142	1	..	..	..	..	37	..	..	..	1	..
160	Service of Indian and Foreign States	..	..	..	..	.	..	..	..	..	..	..	..
161	Municipal and other local (not village) service ..	1	.	.	..	..	..	4	..	..	..	1	..
162	Village officials and servants other than watchmen	1	..	..	..	..	..	6	..	..	..	4	..

Sibi						Kalat.						Las Bela.						
Total Earners Principal Occupation.		Total Working Dependents.		Total following Occupation as Subsidiary to Others.		Total Earners Principal Occupation.		Total Working Dependents.		Total following Occupation as Subsidiary to Others.		Total Earners Principal Occupation.		Total Working Dependents.		Total following Occupation as Subsidiary to Others.		Group Number.
M.	F.	M.	F.	M.	F.	M.	F.	M.	F.	M.	F.	M.	F.	M.	F.	M.	F.	
42	43	44	45	46	47	48	49	50	51	52	53	54	55	56	57	58	59	
296	5	..	..	24	..	479	2	..	..	18	..	407	20	5	7	97	.	
7	..	..	..	4	..	82	..	..	..	2	..	293	5	..	.	7	.	129
2	..	.	..	..	..	19	..	..	..	..	..	..	1	..	.	..	..	130
21	..	..	..	1	..	17	2	..	..	4	..	16	..	5	6	18	..	131
51	..	..	..	200	..	88	..	..	..	..	..	6	..	..	..	27	..	132
16	..	..	..	4	..	1	..	.	..	..	..	3	..	..	..	.	..	133
178	5	..	..	1	..	246	..	..	..	12	..	86	14	..	1	45	..	134
21	..	..	..	1	..	26	..	..	..	..	..	..	..	..	..	..	..	135
..	..	..	..	..	..	..	..	..	..	..	..	..	..	..	..	..	..	136
..	..	..	..	..	..	..	..	..	..	..	..	3	..	..	..	..	..	137
11	..	..	..	..	..	108	..	..	..	..	..	3	3	..	..	1	..	
11	..	..	..	..	..	108	..	..	..	..	..	3	3	..	..	1	..	138
3	..	..	..	2	..	2	..	..	..	51	..	1	..	..	..	.	..	
2	..	..	..	2	..	2	..	..	..	51	..	1	..	..	..	..	.	139
1	..	..	..	..	..	..	..	..	..	..	..	..	..	..	..	..	..	140
2	.	..	..	..	..	..	..	..	..	..	..	..	..	..	..	..	..	
2	..	..	..	..	..	..	..	..	..	..	..	..	..	..	..	..	..	141
46	.	..	..	5,231	..	26	..	..	..	271	..	15	..	..	..	193	1	
1	..	..	..	..	..	..	..	..	..	..	..	..	..	..	..	.	..	142
45	..	..	..	5,231	..	26	..	..	..	271	..	15	.	..	..	193	1	144
18	..	..	..	58	..	17	2	..	..	2	1	10	..	..	..	1	..	
18	..	..	..	58	..	17	2	.	..	2	1	10	.	..	.	1	..	145
6	..	..	..	..	..	.	..	..	..	..	..	..	..	.	..	..	..	
4	.	.	..	..	..	..	..	..	..	..	..	..	..	..	.	.	..	146
..	..	..	..	.	..	..	..	..	..	..	..	..	..	..	..	..	.	147
2	..	..	..	..	..	..	..	.	..	..	..	..	..	..	..	.	..	148
1,026	..	..	..	100	..	2,376	..	..	..	66	..	146	.	..	..	27	.	
1,023	..	.	..	100	..	2,376	..	..	..	66	..	146	..	..	..	27	..	150
3	..	..	..	..	..	..	..	..	..	..	..	..	..	..	.	..	..	151
..	..	..	..	..	..	..	..	..	..	..	..	..	..	..	..	..	..	152
2,083	27	..	..	400	1	3,915	88	1	2	195	2	468	3	..	..	19	..	
1,196	..	..	..	1	.	1,558	..	..	..	..	..	244	..	..	..	..	.	
298	..	..	..	..	..	832	..	..	..	..	..	113	.	..	..	..	..	
298	..	..	..	..	..	420	.	..	..	..	..	..	..	..	..	..	..	153
..	..	..	..	..	..	412	..	..	..	..	..	113	..	..	..	..	..	154
..	..	..	..	..	..	..	..	..	..	..	..	..	..	..	..	..	..	
..	..	.	..	..	..	..	..	..	..	..	..	..	..	..	..	..	..	155
898	.	..	..	1	..	721	..	..	..	..	..	131	..	..	..	..	..	
897	..	..	..	..	..	720	..	..	..	..	..	131	..	..	..	..	..	157
1	..	..	..	1	..	1	..	..	..	..	..	..	..	..	..	..	.	158
388	.	..	..	219	1	1,234	..	..	.	5	..	101	..	.	..	1	..	
388	.	..	..	219	1	1,234	..	..	..	5	..	101	..	..	..	1	..	
323	..	..	..	3	..	159	..	..	..	..	..	..	..	..	..	..	.	159
6	..	..	..	1	..	1,053	..	..	.	1	..	79	..	.	..	..	..	160
32	..	..	..	6	..	18	..	..		..	..	19	..	..	..	1	..	161
27	..	..	..	209	1	4	..	..	..	4	..	3	..	..	..	..	..	162

M. = Males ; F. = Females.

Group Number.	Occupation.	Total Population.	*Baluchistan.* Total Earners Principal Occupation.		Total Working Dependents.		Total Non-Working Dependents.		Total Earners with Subsidiary Occupation.	
			M.	F.	M.	F.	M.	F.	M.	F.
1	2	3	4	5	6	7	8	9	10	11
	SUB-CLASS VIII—PROFESSIONS AND LIBERAL ARTS	..	4,205	301	1	9	..	..	846	5
	ORDER 45.—RELIGION	..	*2,481*	*17*	..	..	..	..	*771*	*3*
163	Priests, ministers, etc.	..	2,052	11	..	..	..	..	726	3
164	Monks, nuns, religious mendicants ..	..	125	..	..	..	..	..	2	..
165	Other religious workers	..	11	..	..	..	..	..	..	..
166	Servants in religious edifices—burial and burning grounds—Pilgrim conductors, circumcisers, etc.	..	293	6	..	..	..	..	43	..
	ORDER 46.—LAW	..	*61*	..	..	..	..	..	*1*	..
167	Lawyers of all kinds, including Qazis, Law agents and Mukhtiars	..	12	..	..	..	..	..	..	..
168	Lawyers' clerks, petition-writers, etc.	..	49	..	..	..	..	..	1	..
	ORDER 47.—MEDICINE	..	*655*	*217*	..	*2*	..	..	*25*	*1*
169	Registered medical practitioners including oculists	..	177	5	..	..	..	..	..	..
170	Other persons practising the healing arts without being registered	..	103	13	..	2	..	..	17	..
171	Dentists	..	9	2	..	..	..	..	..	..
172	Midwives, vaccinators, compounders, nurses, masseurs etc.	..	295	197	..	..	..	..	7	1
173	Veterinary surgeons	..	71	..	..	..	..	..	1	..
	ORDER 48.—INSTRUCTION	..	*397*	*54*	..	..	..	..	*6*	*1*
174	Professors and teachers of all kinds	..	339	48	..	..	..	..	6	1
175	Clerks and servants connected with education ..	..	58	6	..	..	..	..	..	..
	ORDER 49.—LETTERS, ARTS AND SCIENCES (OTHER THAN 44)	..	*611*	*13*	*1*	*7*	..	..	*43*	..
176	Public scribes, stenographers, etc.	..	19	..	..	..	..	..	1	..
177	Architects, surveyors, engineers, and their employees (not being State servants)	..	3	..	..	..	..	..	..	..
178	Authors, editors, journalists and photographers	..	36	..	1	..	..	..	..	..
179	Artists, sculptors and image makers	..	2	..	..	..	..	..	..	..
180	Scientists (astronomers, botanists, etc.) ..	..	3	..	..	..	..	..	..	..
181	Horoscope casters, astrologers, fortunetellers, wizards, witches and mediums	..	14	..	..	..	..	..	1	..
182	Musicians (composers and performers other than military), actors, dancers, etc. ..	..	402	11	..	7	..	..	39	..
183	Managers and employees of places of public entertainments, racecourses, societies, clubs ..	..	122	2	..	..	..	..	2	..
184	Conjurors, acrobats, reciters, exhibitors of curiosities and wild animals, etc.	..	10	..	..	..	..	..	..	..
	CLASS D.—MISCELLANEOUS	..	11,099	936	473	3	..	..	1,766	33
	SUB-CLASS IX.—PERSONS LIVING ON THEIR INCOME	..	854	32	..	..	..	..	791	2
	ORDER 50.—PERSONS LIVING PRINCIPALLY ON THEIR INCOME	..	*854*	*32*	..	..	..	..	*791*	*2*
185	Proprietors (other than of agricultural land), fund and scholarship holders and pensioners ..	..	854	32	..	..	..	..	791	2
	SUB-CLASS X.—DOMESTIC SERVICE ..	..	7,184	303	..	..	..	..	284	7
	ORDER 51.—DOMESTIC SERVICE	..	*7,184*	*303*	..	..	..	..	*284*	*7*
186	Private motor drivers and cleaners ..	..	461	..	..	..	..	..	21	..
187	Other domestic service	..	6,723	303	..	..	..	..	263	7
	SUB-CLASS XI.—INSUFFICIENTLY DESCRIBED OCCUPATIONS	..	883	4	3	..	..	..	211	1
	ORDER 52.—GENERAL TERMS WHICH DO NOT INDICATE A DEFINITE OCCUPATION	..	*883*	*4*	*3*	..	..	..	*211*	*1*
188	Manufacturers, businessmen and contractors otherwise unspecified	..	396	..	1	..	..	..	76	1
189	Cashiers, accountants, book-keepers, clerks and other employees in unspecified offices and warehouses and shops	..	472	4	1	..	..	..	134	..
190	Mechanics otherwise unspecified ..	..	15	..	1	..	..	..	1	..
	SUB-CLASS XII.—UNPRODUCTIVE ..	..	2,178	597	470	3	..	..	480	23
	ORDER 53.—INMATES OF JAILS, ASYLUMS AND ALMS HOUSES	..	*279*	*1*	*470*	*3*	..	..	..	..
192	Inmates of jails, asylums and alms houses	..	279	1	470	3	..	..	..	..
	ORDER 54.—BEGGARS, VAGRANTS, PROSTITUTES..	..	*1,899*	*596*	..	..	..	..	*480*	*23*
193	Beggars and vagrants	..	1,882	461	..	..	..	..	480	23
194	Procurers and prostitutes	..	17	135	..	..	..	..	..	..

Quetta-Pishin.						Loralai.						Zhob.						
Total Earners Principal Occupation.		Total Working Dependents.		Total following Occupation as Subsidiary to Others.		Total Earners Principal Occupation.		Total Working Dependents.		Total following Occupation as Subsidiary to Others.		Total Earners Principal Occupation.		Total Working Dependents.		Total following Occupation as Subsidiary to Others.		Group Number.
M.	F.	M.	F.	M.	F.	M.	F.	M.	F.	M.	F.	M.	F.	M.	F.	M.	F.	
12	13	14	15	16	17	18	19	20	21	22	23	24	25	26	27	28	20	
1,562	**212**	..	..	**122**	..	**399**	**17**	..	**7**	**148**	**3**	**325**	**6**	..	..	**164**	..	
758	*7*	..	..	*112*	..	*263*	..	..	..	*139*	*3*	*223*	..	..	..	*154*	..	
580	4	..	..	104	..	233	..	..	..	135	3	205	..	..	..	154	..	163
79	..	..	..	2	..	..	..	..	..	..	..	..	..	..	..	..	..	164
..	..	..	..	..	..	..	..	..	..	..	..	11	..	..	..	..	..	166
99	3	..	..	6	..	30	..	..	..	4	..	7	..	..	..	..	..	
21	.	..	..	..	..	*10*	..	..	..	..	.	*6*	..	..	..	..	..	
6	..	..	..	..	..	..	..	..	..	..	.	..	..	..	..	..	..	167
18	..	..	..	..	..	10	..	..	..	..	..	6	..	..	..	..	..	168
345	*147*	..	..	*7*	..	*56*	*14*	..	..	*2*	..	*68*	*4*	..	..	*4*	..	
105	4	..	.	..	..	12	1	..	..	..	..	15	..	..	..	..	..	169
50	4	..	..	7	..	10	..	..	..	2	..	10	..	..	..	1	..	170
6	2	..	..	..	..	1	..	..	..	..	..	1	..	..	..	..	..	171
142	137	..	..	..	..	21	13	..	..	..	..	30	4	..	..	3	..	172
42	..	..	..	..	..	12	..	..	..	..	..	6	..	..	..	..	.	173
242	*45*	..	..	..	..	*23*	*3*	..	..	*1*	..	*26*	*2*	..	..	*5*	..	
197	41	..	..	..	..	22	2	..	..	1	..	21	2	..	..	5	..	174
45	4	..	..	..	..	1	1	..	..	..	..	5	..	..	..	..	..	175
193	*13*	..	..	*3*	..	*47*	..	..	*7*	*6*	..	*2*	..	..	..	*1*	..	
11	..	..	..	..	..	..	..	..	..	..	..	..	..	..	..	..	..	176
2	..	..	..	..	..	1	..	..	..	..	..	..	..	..	..	..	..	177
22	..	..	..	..	..	2	..	..	..	..	..	1	..	..	..	..	..	178
2	..	..	..	..	..	..	..	..	..	..	..	..	..	..	..	..	..	179
3	..	..	..	..	..	..	..	..	..	..	..	..	..	..	..	..	..	180
7	.	..	..	..	..	6	..	..	..	..	..	..	..	..	..	..	..	181
39	11	..	..	1	..	36	..	..	7	6	..	..	..	..	..	1	..	182
107	2	..	..	2	..	2	..	..	..	..	..	1	..	.	..	..	..	183
..	..	..	..	..	..	..	..	..	..	..	..	..	..	..	..	..	..	184
5,949	**261**	**81**	..	**736**	**2**	**614**	**110**	**20**	..	**116**	**6**	**494**	**52**	**4**	..	**115**	**15**	
384	**15**	..	..	**549**	..	**12**	**3**	..	..	**35**	..	**6**	..	..	..	**39**	..	
334	*15*	..	..	*549*	..	*12*	*3*	..	..	*35*	..	*6*	..	..	..	*39*	..	
334	15	..	..	549	..	12	3	..	..	35	..	6	..	..	..	39	..	185
4,619	**98**	..	..	**31**	**1**	**341**	**16**	..	..	**24**	..	**320**	**3**	..	..	**19**	**2**	
4,619	*98*	..	..	*31*	*1*	*341*	*16*	..	..	*24*	..	*320*	*3*	..	..	*19*	*2*	
270	..	..	..	5	..	73	..	..	..	8	..	58	..	..	..	8	..	186
4,343	98	..	..	26	1	268	16	..	..	16	..	262	3	..	..	11	2	187
631	..	**1**	..	**128**	**1**	**37**	..	**1**	..	**11**	..	**47**	..	..	..	**34**	..	
631	..	*1*	..	*128*	*1*	*37*	..	*1*	..	*11*	..	*47*	..	..	..	*34*	..	
270	..	1	..	6	1	17	..	..	..	11	..	27	..	..	..	33	..	188
355	..	..	..	122	..	18	..	..	..	..	..	20	..	..	..	..	..	189
6	.	..	..	..	..	2	..	1	..	..	..	..	..	..	..	1	..	190
365	**148**	**30**	..	**28**	..	**224**	**91**	**19**	..	**46**	**6**	**121**	**49**	**4**	..	**23**	**13**	
50	*1*	*30*	..	..	..	*41*	..	*19*	.	..	..	*31*	..	*4*	.	..	..	192
50	1	30	..	..	..	41	..	19	.	..	..	31	..	4	..	..	..	
315	*147*	..	..	*28*	..	*183*	*91*	..	..	*46*	*6*	*90*	*49*	..	..	*23*	*13*	
298	37	..	..	28	..	183	81	..	..	46	6	90	49	..	..	23	13	193
17	110	..	..	..	..	..	10	..	..	..	..	..	..	..	..	..	.	194

M. = Males. F. = Females.

Group Number.	Occupation.	Bolan. Total Earners Principal Occupation. M.	F.	Bolan. Total Working Dependents. M.	F.	Bolan. Total following Occupation as Subsidiary to Others. M.	F.	Chagai. Total Earners Principal Occupation. M.	F.	Chagai. Total Working Dependents. M.	F.	Chagai. Total following Occupation as Subsidiary to Others. M.	F.
1	2	30	31	32	33	34	35	36	37	38	39	40	41
	SUB-CLASS VIII—PROFESSIONS AND LIBERAL ARTS	**35**	..	..	..	**4**	..	**184**	**3**	..	..	**20**	..
	ORDER 45.—RELIGION	*15*	..	..	..	*3*	..	*103*	*1*	..	..	*20*	..
163	Priests, ministers, etc.	9	..	..	..	2	..	101	1	..	..	12	.
164	Monks, nuns, religious mendicants ..	..	..	..	..	..	..	..	..	..	..	..	..
165	Other religious workers	..	..	..	..	..	..	..	..	..	..	..	..
166	Servants in religious edifices—burial and burning grounds—Pilgrim conductors, circumcisers, etc.	6	..	..	..	1	..	2	..	..	.	8	..
	ORDER 46.—LAW	*1*	..	..	..	.	..	*2*	..	..	..	..	..
167	Lawyers of all kinds, including, Qazis, Law Agents and Mukhtiars	1	..	..	..	..	..	..	..	..	..	..	..
168	Lawyers clerks, petition-writers, etc. ..	..	..	..	..	..	..	2	..	..	..	..	..
	ORDER 47.—MEDICINES	*16*	..	..	..	..	..	*20*	*2*	..	..	.	..
169	Registered medical practitioners including oculists	7	..	..	..	..	..	5	..	..	..	..	..
170	Other persons practising the healing arts without being registered	3	..	..	..	..	.	..	..	..	..	..	..
171	Dentists	..	..	..	..	..	..	..	..	..	..	..	..
172	Midwives, vaccinators, compounders, nurses, masseurs, etc.	6	..	..	..	..	..	13	2	..	..	..	..
173	Veterinary surgeons	..	..	..	..	..	..	2	..	..	..	..	..
	ORDER 48.—INSTRUCTION	*2*	..	..	..	..	..	*8*	..	..	..	..	..
174	Professors and teachers of all kinds	2	..	..	..	..	..	8	..	..	..	..	..
175	Clerks and servants connected with education ..	..	..	..	..	..	..	..	..	..	..	..	..
	ORDER 49.—LETTERS, ARTS AND SCIENCES (OTHER THAN 44)	*1*	..	..	..	*1*	..	*1*	..	..	..	..	..
176	Public scribes, stenographers, etc.	..	..	..	..	..	..	..	..	..	..	..	..
177	Architects, surveyors, engineers, and their employees (not being State servants)	..	..	..	..	..	..	..	..	..	..	..	..
178	Authors, editors, journalists and photographers .	..	..	..	..	..	..	..	..	..	..	..	..
179	Artists, sculptors and image makers ..	..	..	..	..	..	..	..	..	..	..	..	..
180	Scientists (astronomers), botanists, etc. ..	..	..	..	..	..	..	..	..	..	..	..	..
181	Horoscope casters, astrologers, fortunetellers, wizards, witches and mediums	..	..	..	..	..	..	1	..	..	..	..	..
182	Musicians (composers and performers other than military), actors, dancers, etc. ..	..	..	..	..	1	..	..	..	..	..	..	..
183	Managers and employees of places of public entertainments, racecourses, societies, clubs, etc. ..	1	..	..	..	..	..	..	..	..	..	..	..
184	Conjurors, acrobats, reciters, exhibitor sof curiosities and wild animals, etc.	..	..	..	..	..	..	..	..	..	..	..	..
	CLASS D. MISCELLANEOUS	**79**	**5**	**366**	**3**	**29**	..	**287**	**55**	**6**	..	**43**	**2**
	SUB-CLASS IX—PERSONS LIVING ON THEIR INCOME	**1**	..	..	..	**29**	..	**3**	**9**	..	..	**21**	**1**
	ORDER 50.—PERSONS LIVING PRINCIPALLY ON THEIR INCOME	*1*	..	..	..	*29*	..	*3*	*9*	..	..	*21*	*1*
185	Proprietors (other than of agricultural land), fund and scholarship holders and pensioners ..	1	..	..	..	29	..	3	9	..	..	21	1
	SUB-CLASS X—DOMESTIC SERVICE ..	**57**	..	..	..	..	..	**164**	**29**	..	..	**7**	**1**
	ORDER 51.—DOMESTIC SERVICE	*57*	..	..	..	..	..	*164*	*29*	..	..	*7*	*1*
186	Private motor drivers and cleaners ..	2	..	..	..	..	..	9	..	..	..	..	..
187	Other domestic service	55	..	..	..	..	..	155	29	..	..	7	1
	SUB-CLASS XI—INSUFFICIENTLY DESCRIBED OCCUPATIONS	**9**	..	..	..	..	..	**11**	..	..	..	**10**	..
	ORDER 52.—GENERAL TERMS WHICH DO NOT INDICATE A DEFINITE OCCUPATION ..	*9*	..	..	..	..	..	*11*	..	..	..	*10*	..
188	Manufacturers, businessmen and contractors, otherwise unspecified	7	..	..	..	..	..	9	..	..	..	10	..
189	Cashiers, accountants, book-keepers, clerks and other employees in unspecified offices and warehouses and shops	1	..	..	..	..	..	2	..	..	..	..	..
190	Mechanics otherwise unspecified	1	..	..	..	..	..	..	..	..	..	..	..
	SUB-CLASS XII—UNPRODUCTIVE ..	**12**	**5**	**366**	**3**	..	..	**109**	**17**	**6**	..	**5**	..
	ORDER 53.—INMATES OF JAILS, ASYLUMS AND ALMS HOUSES	*5*	..	*366*	*3*	..	..	*3*	..	*6*	..	..	..
192	Inmates of jails, asylums and alms houses ..	5	..	366	3	..	..	3	..	6	..	..	..
	ORDER 54.—BEGGARS, VAGRANTS, PROSTITUTES	*7*	*5*	..	..	..	..	*106*	*17*	..	..	*5*	..
193	Beggars and vagrants	7	5	..	..	..	..	106	17	..	..	[illegible]	..
194	Procurers and prostitutes	..	..	..	..	..	..	..	..	..	..	..	..

Sibi.						*Kalat.*						*Las Bela.*						
Total Earners Principal Occupation.		Total Working Dependents.		Total following Occupation as Subsidiary to Others.		Total Earners Principal Occupation.		Total Working Dependents.		Total following Occupation as Subsidiary to Others.		Total Earners Principal Occupation.		Total Working Dependents.		Total following Occupation as Subsidiary to Others.		Group Number.
M.	F.	M.	F.	M.	F.	M.	F.	M.	F.	M.	F.	M.	F.	M.	F.	M.	F.	
42	43	44	45	46	47	48	49	50	51	52	53	54	55	56	57	58	59	
499	27	..	..	180	..	1,128	33	1	2	190	2	123	3	..	..	18	..	
272	*3*	..	..	*158*	..	*801*	*5*	..	..	*170*	..	*46*	*1*	..	..	*15*	..	
242	1	..	..	157	..	657	5	..	..	157	..	25	..	..	..	5	..	163
1	..	..	..	..	..	45	..	..	..	..	..	..	..	..	..	..	..	164
..	..	..	..	..	..	..	..	..	..	..	..	..	..	..	..	..	..	165
29	2	..	..	1	..	99	..	..	..	13	..	21	1	..	..	10	..	166
9	..	..	..	..	..	*8*	..	..	..	..	..	*1*	..	..	..	*1*	..	
1	..	..	..	..	..	4	..	..	..	..	..	..	..	..	..	..	..	167
8	..	..	..	..	..	4	..	..	..	..	..	1	..	..	..	1	..	168
84	*20*	..	..	*7*	..	*48*	*28*	..	*2*	*5*	*1*	*18*	*2*	..	..	..	..	
22	..	..	..	..	..	8	..	..	..	..	..	3	..	..	..	..	..	169
16	8	..	..	3	..	9	1	..	2	4	..	5	..	..	..	..	..	170
1	..	..	..	..	..	..	..	..	..	..	..	..	..	..	..	..	..	171
39	12	..	..	3	..	30	27	..	..	1	1	8	2	..	..	..	..	172
6	..	..	..	1	..	1	..	..	..	..	..	2	..	..	..	..	..	173
54	*4*	..	..	..	..	*36*	..	..	..	..	*1*	*6*	..	..	..	..	..	
53	3	..	..	..	..	31	..	..	..	..	1	5	..	..	..	..	..	174
1	1	..	..	..	..	5	..	..	..	..	..	1	..	..	..	..	..	175
80	..	..	..	*15*	..	*235*	..	*1*	..	*15*	..	*52*	..	..	..	*2*	..	
8	..	..	..	1	..	..	..	..	..	..	..	..	..	..	..	..	..	176
..	..	..	..	..	..	..	..	..	..	..	..	..	..	..	..	..	..	177
1	..	..	..	..	..	10	..	1	..	..	..	..	..	..	..	..	..	178
..	..	..	..	..	..	..	..	..	..	..	..	..	..	..	..	..	..	179
..	..	..	..	..	..	..	..	..	..	..	..	..	..	..	..	..	..	180
..	..	..	..	..	..	..	..	..	..	1	..	..	..	..	..	..	..	181
63	..	..	..	14	..	215	..	..	..	14	..	49	..	..	..	2	..	182
..	..	..	..	..	..	9	..	..	..	..	..	2	..	..	..	..	..	183
8	..	..	..	..	..	1	..	..	..	..	..	1	..	..	..	..	..	184
1,212	149	..	..	333	6	2,035	105	46	..	266	..	429	199	..	..	128	2	
19	2	..	..	50	1	471	..	..	..	60	..	8	3	..	..	8	..	
19	*2*	..	..	*50*	*1*	*471*	..	..	..	*60*	..	*8*	*3*	..	..	*8*	..	
19	2	..	..	50	1	471	..	..	..	60	..	8	3	..	..	8	..	185
746	46	..	..	69	3	689	6	..	..	42	..	248	105	..	..	92	..	
746	*46*	..	..	*69*	*3*	*689*	*6*	..	..	*42*	..	*248*	*105*	..	..	*92*	..	
32	..	..	..	..	..	8	..	..	..	..	..	3	..	..	..	..	..	186
714	46	..	..	69	3	681	6	..	..	42	..	245	105	..	..	92	..	187
111	4	..	..	11	..	22	..	1	..	11	..	15	..	..	..	6	..	
111	*4*	..	..	*11*	..	*22*	..	*1*	..	*11*	..	*15*	..	..	..	*6*	..	
31	..	..	..	5	..	21	..	..	..	11	..	14	..	..	..	..	..	188
75	4	..	..	6	..	1	..	1	..	..	..	..	..	..	..	6	..	189
5	..	..	..	..	..	..	..	..	..	..	..	1	..	..	..	..	..	190
336	97	..	..	203	2	853	99	45	..	153	..	158	91	..	..	22	2	
29	..	..	..	..	..	*120*	..	*45*	..	..	..	..	..	..	..	..	..	
29	..	..	..	..	..	120	..	45	..	..	..	..	..	..	..	..	..	192
307	*97*	..	..	*203*	*2*	*733*	*99*	..	..	*153*	..	*158*	*91*	..	..	*22*	*2*	
307	82	..	..	203	2	733	99	..	..	153	..	158	91	..	..	22	2	193
..	15	..	..	..	..	..	..	..	..	..	..	..	..	..	..	..	..	194

M. = Males; F. = Females.

TABLE XI.—OCCUPATION BY

PART A—OCCUPATION OF SELECTED

Caste, Tribe or Race.	Traditional Occupation.	*Population dealt with* Earners. M.	Earners. F.	Working Dependants. M.	Working Dependants. F.	Non-working Dependants. Both Sexes.	*Number of earners whose traditional Caste Occupation was returned as their* Principal means of livelihood. M.	Principal means of livelihood. F.	Subsidiary means of livelihood. M.	Subsidiary means of livelihood. F.	*Number of working dependants following the traditional Occupation of their Caste.* M.	F.	*Number of earners returning their Traditional Occupation as their Principal means of livelihood who had some Subsidiary Occupation.* M.	F.
1	2	3	4	5	6	7	8	9	10	11	12	13	14	15
							Indigenous and Semi-Indigenous							
I.—INDIGENOUS—		**283,102**	**3,500**	**10,342**	**10,835**	**502,846**	**140,723**	**304**	**25,634**	**39**	**2,491**	**323**	**44,705**	**48**
A.—Baloch ..		**68,086**	**1,234**	**2,221**	**4,830**	**149,720**	**39,312**	**69**	**8,998**	**7**	**499**	**9**	**18,848**	**17**
(i) Eastern ..		*45,209*	*150*	*1,405*	*4,386*	*99,214*	*28,267*	..	*8,143*	*2*	*221*	*3*	*16,655*	..
Bugti ..	Pillage and Plunder, Flock owners and Cultivating owners	8,212	7	14	4	22,376	7506	..	78	..	..	..	5,556	..
Dombki ..	Cultivating owners	2,338	1	3	..	4,899	1,470	..	4	..	..	..	475	..
Khetran ..	Cultivating owners, Horse breeders and Flock owners	5,062	69	572	3,746	7,713	3,287	..	1,429	2	..	..	1,804	..
Magasi ..	Cultivating owners and Horse breeders	4,552	22	253	22	8,437	1,465	..	66	..	..	..	1,008	..
Mari ..	Pillage and Plunder, Flock owners and Cultivating owners	11,330	5	454	333	23,132	7,920	..	6,504	..	221	3	5,775	..
Rind Bulodi ..	Cultivating owners and Camel breeders	2,079	8	14	12	3,596	391	..	..	..	..	..	68	..
,, Jamali ..	Cultivating owners and Camel breeders	2,144	15	2	206	4,218	933	..	22	..	..	..	374	..
,, Khosa ..	Cultivating owners and Camel breeders	1,571	2	16	..	3,030	548	..	7	..	..	..	110	..
,, Lashari ..	Cultivating owners and Camel breeders	1,929	15	51	41	5,163	1,163	..	23	..	..	..	302	..
,, Unspecified	Cultivating owners and Camel breeders	5,202	2	3	16	13,987	3,451	..	10	..	..	..	1,131	..
Umrani ..	Cultivating owners and Camel breeders	449	..	..	..	2,192	81	..	..	..	..	..	11	..
Others ..	Cultivating owners	341	4	23	6	471	52	..	..	..	..	..	41	..
(ii) Western ..		*22,827*	*1,084*	*816*	*444*	*50,506*	*11,045*	*69*	*855*	*5*	*278*	*6*	*2,193*	*17*
Buledi ..	Cultivating owners	47	..	..	..	111	4	..	..	..	..	..	..	..
Dashti ..	Cultivating owners, Camel breeders and Flock owners	331	5	..	..	660	61	..	43	1	..	..	52	..
Gichki ..	Non-cultivating owners	88	..	..	..	205	4	..	3	..	..	..	..	..
Kaudai ..	Cultivating owners	11.717	1	..	..	1,590	1	..	..	..	..	..	1	..
Rais ..	Cultivating owners	6,778	39	2	13	2,719	315	..	..	..	..	..	45	..
Rakhshani ..	Cultivating and Non-cultivating owners, Flock owners and Camel breeders	45	210	729	374	16,048	4,239	68	612	4	277	6	1,530	17
Rind ..	Cultivating owners, Camel breeders and Flock owners	9,587	93	11	9	21,355	5,284	1	162	..	1	..	177	..
Sangur ..	Cultivating owners and trade in fish ..	2,415	674	68	48	4,129	754	..	..	..	..	..	381	..
Sanjrani ..	Cultivating and Non-cultivating owners, Flock owners and Camel breeders	53	..	..	..	348	38	..	2	..	..	..	..	..
Others ..	Flock owners	1,666	62	6	..	3,341	345	..	33	..	..	..	7	..
B.—Brahui ..		**48,815**	**474**	**501**	**1,395**	**101,903**	**29,083**	**26**	**5,781**	**11**	**218**	**13**	**7,336**	**7**
(i) Original Nucleus.		*4,219*	*31*	*104*	*364*	*8,240*	*2,531*	*3*	*499*	..	*52*	*1*	*773*	..
Ahmadzai ..	Non-cultivating owners	16	..	..	..	61	1	..	..	..	..	..	..	..
Gurgnari ..	Flock owners and Cultivating owners	495	5	16	96	854	311	1	43	..	3	..	177	..
Iltazai ..	Non-cultivating Owners	54	..	1	..	147	4	..	..	..	..	..	..	..
Kalandrari ..	Cultivating owners and Flock owners	434	..	17	4	875	234	..	49	..	2	..	28	..
Kambrari ..	Cultivating Owners and Flock Owners ..	627	5	1	..	1,432	376	..	56	..	..	..	118	..
Mirwari ..	Cultivating and Non-cultivating owners and Flock owners.	634	5	..	6	1,233	360	1	142	..	..	..	140	..
Rodeni ..	Cultivating owners and Flock owners	448	3	2	1	881	197	..	97	..	1	..	93	..
Sumalari ..	Flock owners and Cultivating owners and Tenants, all kinds ..	1,511	13	67	257	2,757	1,048	1	112	..	46	1	217	..
(ii) Sarawan ..		*14,329*	*89*	*95*	*42*	*27,293*	*6,784*	*2*	*1,546*	..	*29*	*1*	*2,207*	*1*
Bangulzai ..	Cultivating owners, Camel transport and Flock owners	2,498	8	5	2	4,876	1,043	..	270	..	2	..	373	..
Kurd ..	Cultivating owners	756	46	13	4	1,411	339	..	..	..	..	..	116	..
Lahri ..	Cultivating owners and Camel transport and Flock owners ..	1,488	3	20	12	2,967	627	..	192	..	11	..	159	..
Langav ..	Camel transport, Flock owners, Cultivating owners and Tenants ..	2,274	7	4	1	4,362	1,594	..	526	..	..	..	668	..
Mamashahi ..	Cultivating owners	927	1	..	..	1,800	231	..	..	..	..	..	82	..
Raisani ..	Cultivating and Non-cultivating owners	811	6	11	18	1,870	196	..	23	..	..	..	17	..
Rustamzai ..	Cultivating and Non-cultivating owners	89	..	..	..	154	33	..	9	..	..	..	3	..
Sarparra ..	Cultivating owners and Flock owners ..	645	..	..	..	1,261	320	..	..	..	..	..	80	..
Satakzai ..	Flock owners	596	..	1	..	989	..	..	33	..	..	..	..	..
Shahwani ..	Cultivating and Non-cultivating owners, Flock owners and Camel transport	2,098	3	21	5	3,962	1,245	2	195	..	2	1	491	
Zagr Mengal ..	Cultivating and Non-cultivating owners, Flock owners and Camel transport	2,147	15	20	..	3,641	1,156	..	299	..	14	..	218	..

CASTE, TRIBE OR RACE.

CASTES, TRIBES OR RACES.

Recorded principal occupation of earners, other than traditional occupation of Caste (by Sub-Classes).

I Exploitation of Animals and Vegetation.		II Exploitation of Minerals.		III Industry.		IV Transport.		V Trade.		VI Public Force.		VII Public Administration.		VIII Professions and Liberal Arts.		IX Persons living on their income.		X Domestic Service.		XI Insufficiently described occupations.		XII Unproductive.	
M.	F.	M.	F.	M.	F.	M.	F.	M.	F.	M.	F.	M.	F.	M.	F.	M.	F.	M.	F.	M.	F.	M.	F.
16	17	18	19	20	21	22	23	24	25	26	27	28	29	30	31	32	33	34	35	36	37	38	39
RACES AND TRIBES.																							
58,839	**467**	**341**	..	**6,206**	**1,880**	**8,805**	**198**	**4,336**	**33**	**5,220**	..	**1,597**	..	**2,403**	**55**	**733**	**22**	**1,998**	**145**	**250**	..	**1,651**	**396**
23,066	**120**	**40**	..	**804**	**849**	**2,005**	**18**	**288**	**2**	**1,251**	..	**160**	..	**286**	**6**	**14**	**13**	**456**	**32**	**33**	..	**326**	**125**
14,666	*69*	*2*	..	*426*	*38*	*625*	*10*	*153*	*1*	*420*	..	*63*	..	*189*	*2*	*5*	..	*240*	*4*	*6*	..	*147*	*26*
599	3	..	..	22	3	66	..	4	..	6	..	2	..	3	..	..	..	3	..	..	..	1	1
744	..	..	..	16	..	35	..	4	..	32	..	4	..	4	..	..	..	18	..	4	..	7	1
1,466	42	..	..	142	7	18	4	7	1	37	..	4	..	56	1	..	..	8	1	..	..	37	13
2,921	2	..	..	30	16	24	2	3	..	1	..	..	..	22	..	..	..	43	..	..	..	43	2
2,718	4	..	..	43	1	176	..	68	..	217	..	5	..	60	..	1	..	89	..	..	..	33	..
1,596	1	..	..	14	6	16	..	24	..	18	..	5	..	5	..	..	..	10	1	..	..	..	..
1,151	9	..	..	12	1	9	..	2	..	14	..	1	..	4	..	..	..	13	..	..	..	5	5
944	2	2	..	10	..	38	..	9	..	9	..	4	..	6	..	1	..	..	..	..	..	..	..
668	6	..	..	11	2	38	2	..	..	19	..	7	..	6	1	1	..	3	..	1	..	12	4
1,435	..	..	..	66	2	117	..	24	..	43	..	23	..	17	..	2	..	18	..	..	..	6	..
328	..	..	..	13	..	..	..	1	..	10	..	2	..	3	..	..	..	10	..	..	..	1	..
96	..	..	..	47	..	88	2	7	..	14	..	6	..	3	..	..	..	25	2	1	..	2	..
8,400	*51*	*38*	..	*378*	*811*	*1,380*	*8*	*130*	*1*	*831*	..	*97*	..	*97*	*4*	*9*	*13*	*216*	*28*	*27*	..	*179*	*99*
43	..	..	..	..	..	..	..	..	..	..	..	..	..	..	..	..	..	..	..	..	..	..	..
217	..	..	..	..	4	28	..	1	..	7	..	1	..	3	..	..	..	4	..	..	..	9	1
72	..	..	..	..	..	3	..	..	..	5	..	2	..	..	..	..	..	..	..	..	..	2	..
670	1	..	..	10	..	3	..	1	..	17	..	1	..	2	..	..	..	2	..	..	..	10	..
725	..	16	..	10	21	49	..	12	..	30	..	4	..	3	..	..	1	12	..	1	..	1	17
1,018	46	7	..	106	53	554	7	25	..	560	..	45	..	51	2	8	2	63	9	13	..	56	23
3,703	2	10	..	112	43	179	..	45	..	125	..	19	..	19	..	..	7	34	1	1	..	56	39
1,153	2	1	..	49	663	370	..	16	..	7	..	5	..	3	1	..	..	32	1	9	..	16	7
1	..	..	..	2	..	3	..	..	..	7	..	..	..	..	..	..	..	..	..	..	..	2	..
798	..	4	..	89	27	101	1	30	1	73	..	20	..	16	1	1	3	69	17	3	..	27	12
12,963	**56**	**21**	..	**719**	**270**	**2,130**	**58**	**271**	**2**	**1,445**	..	**313**	..	**291**	**2**	**467**	**1**	**416**	**26**	**12**	..	**184**	**38**
1,133	*6*	*7*	..	*39*	*8*	*169*	*3*	*17*	..	*194*	..	*35*	..	*16*	..	*29*	*1*	*20*	*1*	..	..	*29*	*9*
4	..	..	..	1	..	4	..	1	..	..	..	..	..	..	..	5	..	..	..	..	..	..	..
151	2	1	..	2	1	15	..	2	..	4	..	2	..	1	..	..	..	2	1	..	..	4	..
49	..	..	..	..	..	1	..	..	..	..	..	..	..	..	..	..	..	..	..	..	..	..	..
179	..	..	..	10	..	5	..	..	..	1	..	..	..	2	..	1	..	..	..	..	..	2	..
210	3	2	..	3	2	20	..	1	..	5	..	1	..	3	..	..	..	4	..	..	..	2	..
234	..	..	..	8	4	15	..	2	..	..	..	..	..	8	..	..	..	1	..	..	..	6	..
163	..	..	..	5	..	31	1	1	..	10	..	16	..	..	..	22	..	..	..	..	..	3	2
143	1	4	..	10	1	78	2	10	..	174	..	16	..	2	..	1	1	13	..	..	..	12	7
4,296	*9*	*13*	..	*387*	*48*	*946*	*8*	*156*	*2*	*701*	..	*217*	..	*139*	*1*	*421*	..	*189*	*10*	*6*	..	*74*	*9*
972	5	2	..	51	..	135	..	12	..	126	..	31	..	13	..	92	..	12	2	..	..	9	1
223	..	5	..	24	43	51	..	12	..	35	..	12	..	15	1	19	..	17	..	1	..	3	2
551	..	..	..	25	..	71	2	34	..	64	..	6	..	7	..	62	..	35	1	1	..	5	..
271	3	..	..	102	..	221	2	28	..	4	..	11	..	21	..	4	..	14	1	..	..	4	1
353	..	..	..	62	..	98	1	8	..	117	..	21	..	11	..	1	..	23	..	..	..	2	..
234	1	..	..	27	..	65	2	11	2	30	..	7	..	4	..	217	..	15	1	..	..	5	..
18	..	1	..	9	..	12	..	..	..	13	..	3	..	..	..	..	..	..	..	..	..	..	..
202	..	..	..	5	..	41	..	5	..	60	..	1	..	2	..	2	..	4	..	..	..	3	..
534	..	5	..	11	..	20	..	1	..	17	..	2	..	..	..	1	..	4	..	..	..	1	..
423	..	..	..	38	..	134	1	18	..	72	..	57	..	33	..	23	..	42	..	3	..	10	..
515	..	..	..	33	5	98	..	27	..	163	..	66	..	33	..	..	..	23	5	1	..	32	5

M= Males; F= Females.

TABLE XI.—OCCUPATION BY

PART A—OCCUPATION OF SELECTED

Caste, Tribe or Race.	Traditional Occupation.	Population dealt with: Earners. M.	Earners. F.	Working Dependants. M.	Working Dependants. F.	Non-working Dependants. Both Sexes.	Number of earners whose traditional Caste Occupation was returned as their Principal means of livelihood. M.	Principal means of livelihood. F.	Subsidiary means of livelihood. M.	Subsidiary means of livelihood. F.	Number of working dependants following the traditional Occupation of their Caste. M.	F.	Number of earners returning that Traditional Occupation as their Principal means of livelihood who had some Subsidiary Occupation. M.	F.
1	2	3	4	5	6	7	8	9	10	11	12	13	14	15
(iii) Jhalawan ..		*28,673*	*348*	*302*	*989*	*64,495*	*19,522*	*21*	*3,736*	*11*	*137*	*11*	*4,315*	
Bizanjav ..	Cultivating and Non-cultivating owners and Flock owners	4,278	204	43	106	8,960	3,035	3	368	2	21	4	730	
Haruni ..	Cultivating owners and Flock owners ..	381	5	2	2	1,222	225	..	75	..	..	..	51	..
Mamasani ..	Flock owners	3,126	41	165	148	6,876	896	13	513	3	80	5	95	..
Mengal ..	Flock owners, Cultivating and Non-cultivating Owners	7,618	24	62	256	18,417	5,365	4	678	5	26	..	953	
Nichari ..	Cultivating owners and Camel Transport	603	1	1	..	1,100	483	..	14	..	..	..	67	..
Pandrani ..	Cultivating owners	348	1	3	16	695	140	..	..	..	..	..	97	..
Sajdi ..	Cultivating owners, Flock owners and Camel breeders	1,090	18	5	101	2,065	583	..	45	..	..	..	64	..
Zahri ..	Cultivating and Non-cultivating owners Flock owners and Camel breeders	11,229	54	21	360	25,160	8,795	1	2,043	1	10	2	2,258	
(iv) Miscellaneous.		*1,094*	*6*	..	..	*1,875*	*246*	..	..	..	..	..	*41*	..
Nighari ..	Cultivating owners and occupancy tenants	348	..	..	..	780	85	..	..	..	..	..	18	..
Rekizai ..	Cultivating owners	151	..	..	..	383	75	..	..	..	..	..	17	..
Others ..	Cultivating owners	595	6	..	..	712	86	..	..	..	..	..	6	..
C.—Pathan ..		**52,686**	**417**	**4,538**	**2,017**	**116,349**	**34,956**	**33**	**7,713**	**7**	**1,207**	**199**	**11,779**	
Babi ..	Cultivating owners	84	..	..	2	108	47	..	..	..	..	..	..	..
Barech ..	Cultivating owners, Flock owners and Camel breeders	555	2	11	4	1,038	83	..	10	..	4	..	36	..
Jafar ..	Cultivating owners	477	13	8	55	926	371	..	..	..	..	..	95	..
Kakar ..		27,088	186	2,145	520	59,892	18,311	6	4,502	2	638	12	6,437	..
Dawi ..	Cultivating owners	66	1	3	1	203	2	..	..	..	..	..	..	..
Dumar ..	Cultivating owners and Flock owners ..	2,134	2	446	17	4,509	1,807	..	1,185	1	310	11	1,294	..
Husain Pasenr	Cultivating owners	226	1	21	7	550	101	..	..	..	..	..	3	..
Sanzar Khel ..	Cultivating owners	14,349	115	1,142	145	30,810	10,439	4	2,739	..	276	1	3,683	..
Sargara ..	Cultivating owners	601	5	60	9	1,325	147	..	19	..	..	..	7	..
Snatia ..	Cultivating owners and Flock owners	5,875	43	214	24	13,606	3,606	2	476	1	30	..	1,248	..
Targhara ..	Cultivating owners and Flock owners	3,233	17	258	317	8,345	2,183	..	83	..	22	..	192	..
Others ..	Cultivating owners	604	2	1	..	544	26	..	..	..	..	..	10	..
Kasi ..	Non-cultivating owners and Cultivating owners	577	1	3	5	1,389	206	..	27	..	..	..	10	..
Luni ..	Cultivating and Non-cultivating owners and Flock owners ..	1,084	15	262	50	2,170	777	5	228	..	26	8	264	
Pani ..		8,730	89	612	138	18,132	6,750	21	1,030	2	287	119	1,724	..
Main Branch ..	Cultivating and Non-cultivating owners	1,394	10	3	..	2,759	896	8	19	..	..	..	155	..
Isot ..	Cultivating and Non-cultivating owners	816	1	4	..	1,734	700	..	8	..	..	..	70	..
Laun ..	Flock owners	182	2	18	1	340	129	2	5	..	9	1	72	..
Mandokhel ..	Cultivating owners and Flock owners ..	1,532	2	241	1	2,859	1,211	..	35	..	47	1	72	..
Musakhel ..	Cultivating owners and Flock owners ..	4,158	70	214	117	9,019	3,479	11	947	2	200	115	1,288	..
Zarkun ..	Cultivating owners and Flock owners ..	617	4	132	19	1,351	330	..	16	..	31	2	67	..
Unspecified ..	Cultivating owners	31	..	..	..	70	5	..	..	..	..	..	..	..
Shirani ..	Cultivating owners and Flock owners ..	2,515	20	445	513	4,923	1,659	..	505	..	52	35	502	..
Tarin ..		10,316	81	1,039	727	24,591	6,029	1	1,411	3	300	25	2,673	
Abdal Achakzai	Cultivating owners and Flock owners ..	5,656	32	699	155	13,254	3,118	1	1,387	3	300	25	1,627	
Spin Tarin ..	Cultivating owners	2,923	36	178	17	6,555	1,923	..	..	..	..	..	798	..
Tor Tarin ..	Cultivating owners	1,534	8	157	554	4,484	947	..	24	..	..	..	216	..
Unspecified ..	Cultivating owners	203	5	5	1	298	46	..	..	..	..	..	37	..
Zmarai ..	Cultivating owners	716	7	13	3	2,150	661	..	..	..	..	..	38	..
Other Pathan ..	Cultivating owners	544	3	..	..	1,030	43	..	..	..	..	..	..	..
D.—Lasi ..		**8,700**	**163**	**1,856**	**717**	**20,374**	**5,776**	**19**	**332**	..	**230**	**96**	**1,586**	
Angaria ..	Cultivating owners and Cattle breeders	1,013	15	265	179	2,494	725	2	5	..	..	..	136	..
Burra ..	Cultivating owners and Cattle breeders	971	..	279	31	2,130	629	..	17	..	..	..	112	..
Jamot ..	Cultivating and Non-cultivating owners	1,678	12	126	199	3,800	604	5	6	..	..	..	141	..
Runjha ..	Cultivating and Non-cultivating owners and Camel Transport ..	1,513	3	128	1	3,011	1,091	2	81	..	..	..	188	..
Sheikh ..	Cultivating and Non-cultivating owners and Cattle breeders and Sellers of grass and Dwarf Palm	1,160	46	237	102	2,761	849	..	83	..	42	11	300	..
Others ..	Cultivating owners, Flock owners and Cattle breeders	2,365	87	823	205	6,178	1,878	10	140	..	188	85	709	
E.—Jatt ..	Cultivating tenants and Cattle breeders	**26,606**	**331**	**168**	**922**	**49,128**	**21,471**	**13**	**2,136**	..	..	..	**4,456**	
F.—Sayyid ..	Non-cultivating owners and spiritual leaders	**5,696**	**57**	**637**	**550**	**15,086**	**728**	**19**	**414**	**1**	..	..	**198**	
G.—Other Muslims ..		**16,844**	**683**	**413**	**281**	**39,370**	**6,209**	**125**	**195**	**12**	**237**	**6**	**386**	
Darzada ..	Cultivating owners, occupancy tenants and tenants at will	2,673	122	3	5	6,536	1,435	..	..	..	..	..	23	..
Dehwar ..	Cultivating owners	1,354	14	..	6	3,443	694	..	1	..	..	..	192	..
Gadra ..	Domestic servants and Field labourers	1,650	77	236	42	5,980	54	60	13	..	207	5	..	..

CASTE, TRIBE OR RACE.

CASTES, TRIBES OR RACES.

Recorded principal occupation of earners, other than traditional occupation of Caste (by Sub-Classes).

I Exploitation of Animals and Vegetation.		II Exploitation of Minerals.		III Industry.		IV Transport.		V Trade.		VI Public Force.		VII Public Administration.		VIII Professions and Liberal Arts.		IX Persons living on their income.		X Domestic Service.		XI Insufficiently described occupations.		XII Unproductive.	
M.	F.	M.	F.	M.	F.	M.	F.	M.	F.	M.	F.	M.	F.	M.	F.	M.	F.	M.	F.	M.	F.	M.	F.
16	17	18	19	20	21	22	23	24	25	26	27	28	29	30	31	32	33	34	35	36	37	38	39
7,153	*40*	*1*	..	*230*	*214*	*820*	*46*	*79*	..	*463*	..	*50*	..	*108*	*1*	*17*	..	*146*	*11*	*5*	..	*79*	*15*
1,003	18	..	..	89	177	70	..	35	..	13	..	1	..	11	..	..	..	8	..	1	..	12	6
117	..	..	..	3	..	26	..	..	..	3	..	..	..	..	..	..	..	6	5	1	..	..	..
1,973	14	..	..	12	12	138	1	10	..	49	..	7	..	14	..	1	..	17	..	1	..	8	1
1,465	4	..	..	49	2	325	5	26	..	228	..	16	..	46	1	15	..	55	6	2	..	26	2
79	..	1	..	7	1	21	..	1	..	8	..	1	..	..	..	..	..	1	..	..	..	1	..
192	1	..	..	7	..	3	..	1	..	2	..	..	..	2	..	..	..	1	..	..	..	..	..
417	2	..	..	4	16	25	..	2	..	1	..	..	..	5	..	..	..	40	..	..	..	13	..
1,907	1	..	..	59	6	212	40	4	..	159	..	25	..	30	..	1	..	18	..	..	..	19	6
381	*1*	..	..	*63*	..	*195*	*1*	*19*	..	*87*	..	*11*	..	*28*	..	..	..	*61*	*4*	*1*	..	*2*	..
248	..	..	..	1	..	..	..	1	..	3	..	..	..	6	..	..	..	4	..	..	..	..	..
64	..	..	..	2	..	2	..	1	..	7	..	..	..	..	..	..	..	..	..	..	..	..	..
69	1	..	..	60	..	193	1	17	..	77	..	11	..	22	..	..	..	57	4	1	..	2	..
8,516	157	127	..	1,119	33	2,840	29	1,050	3	1,958	..	288	..	870	4	157	2	419	14	105	..	841	142
4	..	..	..	4	..	..	..	1	..	..	..	18	..	6	..	..	..	..	..	..	..	4	..
120	..	..	..	42	..	165	..	30	..	18	..	5	..	41	..	2	..	35	2	..	..	14	..
73	11	..	..	2	..	2	1	3	1	14	..	4	..	4	..	..	..	..	..	1	..	8	..
4,382	61	119	..	387	15	1,525	24	355	..	979	..	81	..	457	3	84	..	179	7	68	..	161	70
48	..	..	..	..	..	3	..	10	..	..	..	..	..	2	..	..	..	1	1	..	..	..	..
131	1	1	..	5	1	66	..	14	..	72	..	5	..	9	..	..	..	11	..	1	..	12	..
79	1	..	..	31	..	6	..	2	..	1	..	..	..	4	..	2	..	..	..	..	..	..	..
2,213	36	18	..	150	11	547	20	136	..	405	..	13	..	215	2	48	..	52	2	20	..	93	40
323	2	..	..	9	..	71	1	7	..	10	..	4	..	16	..	..	..	6	..	1	..	7	2
897	14	20	..	64	1	567	1	80	..	358	..	41	..	114	1	10	..	47	..	36	..	35	24
684	7	2	..	23	2	95	..	36	..	65	..	5	..	85	..	21	..	20	4	4	..	10	4
7	..	78	..	105	..	170	2	70	..	68	..	13	..	12	..	3	..	42	..	6	..	4	..
18	..	3	..	19	..	181	..	64	..	5	..	10	..	11	..	4	..	24	1	1	..	32	..
202	..	..	..	19	4	8	1	10	..	44	..	1	..	10	..	..	..	5	..	2	..	6	5
1,200	19	..	..	194	5	119	2	36	2	259	..	23	..	91	1	..	..	17	..	3	..	38	39
357	..	..	..	42	1	34	1	3	..	34	..	7	..	18	..	..	..	1	..	..	..	2	..
37	..	..	..	26	..	20	..	2	..	26	..	..	..	3	..	..	..	..	..	..	..	2	1
44	..	..	..	..	..	6	..	..	..	..	..	..	..	3	..	..	..	..	..	..	..	..	..
120	..	..	..	3	..	43	..	15	2	76	..	12	..	37	..	..	..	10	..	1	..	4	..
398	18	..	..	113	4	6	1	10	..	100	..	..	..	21	1	..	..	3	..	1	..	27	35
238	1	..	..	7	..	6	..	5	..	19	..	1	..	7	..	..	..	2	..	..	..	2	3
6	..	..	..	3	..	4	..	1	..	4	..	3	..	2	..	..	..	1	..	1	..	1	..
312	14	..	..	186	3	14	..	11	..	257	..	14	..	49	..	..	..	5	..	1	..	7	3
2,147	51	4	..	149	6	707	1	470	..	340	..	49	..	177	..	66	2	99	2	18	..	61	18
1,184	23	4	..	70	..	422	1	388	..	228	..	32	..	98	..	18	..	50	2	16	..	33	5
643	25	..	..	25	4	172	..	16	..	75	..	5	..	26	..	..	..	20	..	1	..	17	7
299	3	..	..	40	2	43	..	51	..	26	..	7	..	48	..	48	1	14	..	..	..	11	2
21	..	..	..	14	..	70	..	15	..	11	..	5	..	5	..	..	1	15	..	1	..	..	4
9	1	..	..	5	..	2	..	7	..	8	..	..	..	2	..	..	..	..	..	..	..	2	6
49	..	1	..	112	..	117	..	63	..	29	..	28	..	22	..	1	..	55	2	11	..	13	1
2,156	40	6	..	115	72	289	..	89	2	94	..	26	..	70	..	3	..	48	27	7	..	21	3
141	..	..	..	2	13	126	..	3	..	14	..	..	..	..	..	..	..	..	..	..	..	2	..
287	..	..	..	1	..	8	..	13	..	3	..	2	..	19	..	..	..	3	..	..	..	6	..
905	2	..	..	22	1	73	..	29	..	8	..	4	..	13	..	3	..	9	2	4	..	4	2
259	..	..	..	53	..	3	..	18	..	35	..	17	..	19	..	..	..	12	..	2	..	4	1
230	1	..	..	18	28	23	..	8	1	16	..	1	..	3	..	..	..	7	16	1	..	4	..
334	37	6	..	19	30	56	..	18	1	18	..	2	..	16	..	..	..	17	9	..	..	1	..
1,820	17	69	..	1,520	196	614	17	97	1	152	..	118	..	325	24	4	1	182	28	15	..	221	39
3,549	5	1	..	154	6	251	16	277	1	119	..	80	..	216	..	62	..	68	..	17	..	174	10
6,716	66	76	..	1,627	390	427	10	292	17	194	..	590	..	250	18	2	..	125	20	16	..	320	37
763	3	5	..	201	104	46	..	40	..	8	..	31	..	43	7	..	..	37	6	2	..	62	2
484	6	7	..	89	3	70	2	14	..	16	..	389	..	35	1	..	..	32	1	8	..	16	1
1,149	4	..	..	202	6	130	..	29	4	47	..	18	..	12	..	1	..	..	..	3	..	5	3

TABLE XI.—OCCUPATION BY

PART A—OCCUPATION OF SELECTED

Caste, Tribe or Race.	Traditional Occupation.	Population dealt with: Earners.		Working Dependants.		Non-working Dependants.	Number of earners whose traditional Caste Occupation was returned as their: Principal means of livelihood.		Subsidiary means of livelihood.		Number of working dependants following the traditional Occupation of their Caste.		Number of earners returning their Traditional Occupation as their Principal means of livelihood who had some Subsidiary Occupation.	
		M.	F.	M.	F.	Both Sexes.	M.	F.	M.	F.	M.	F.	M.	F.
1	2	3	4	5	6	7	8	9	10	11	12	13	14	15
Gola ..	Domestic servants and Field labourers	110	..	..	..	367	1	..	..	..	..	..	..	..
Jat ..	Camel drivers and graziers ..	1,046	202	11	159	1,818	355	20	127	13	7	..	78	7
Khoja ..	General Tradesmen and Traders in Stores	105	2	..	..	245	1	..	..	..	..	..	..	..
Langah ..	Domestic servants and Musicians ..	145	22	..	..	339	1	..	2	..	..	..	..	..
Lori ..	Blacksmiths and Domestic servants ..	1,812	12	13	6	3,810	763	..	6	..	6	..	8	..
Med ..	Fishermen and Transport by sea ..	957	55	..	4	2,025	897	2	3	..	..	..	14	..
Nakib ..	Tenants and Cultivating owners ..	2,091	50	59	43	4,911	1,223	1	26	..	..	..	39	..
Others ..		4,401	127	91	16	9,946	785	42	17	..	17	1	32	..
(a) Sorazai ..	Domestic service and Field labourers ..	3,404	91	17	4	7,648	779	42	8	..	17	1	32	..
(b) Others ..	Domestic service and Daily labourers	997	36	74	12	2,298	6	..	9	..	..	..	..	..
H.—Hindus ..	General store-keepers and shop-keepers	6,186	141	6	122	10,449	3,160	..	65	..	..	..	121	..
I.—Sikh ..	General store-keepers and shop-keepers	31	..	..	..	17	28	..	..	..	..	..	..	..
II.—SEMI-INDIGENOUS.		*8,942*	*150*	*366*	*308*	*12,156*	*775*	..	*314*	..	*53*	*5*	*208*	..
BALOCH ..		591	2	85	149	978	216	..	237	..	53	5	111	..
Buzdar ..	Flock owners and Cultivating owners ..	563	2	85	148	940	216	..	225	..	53	4	111	..
Others ..	Flock owners and Field labourers ..	28	..	..	1	38	..	..	12	..	..	1	..	..
PATHAN ..		6,558	142	273	159	9,886	547	..	77	..	..	..	97	..
Durrani ..	Non-cultivating owners	1,062	13	12	13	1,310	54	..	73	..	..	..	3	..
Ghilzai ..	Cultivating owners and Karez diggers ..	5,255	126	260	146	8,322	458	..	3	..	..	..	93	..
Others ..	Cultivating owners, Field labourers and Daily labourers	241	3	1	..	254	35	..	1	..	..	..	1	..
OTHER MUSLIMS ..		1,793	6	8	..	1,292	12	..	..	..	..	..	..	..
Hazara ..	Cultivating owners	1,786	6	8	..	1,275	12	..	..	..	..	..	..	..
Others ..	Cultivating owners and Daily labourers	7	..	..	..	17	..	..	..	..	..	..	..	..
III.—ALIENS ..	...	*3,445*	*103*	..	..	*1,855*	..	..	..	..	..	..	..	..
Europeans ..		3,344	91	..	..	1,589	..	..	..	..	..	..	..	..
Anglo-Indians ..		101	12	..	..	266	..	..	..	..	..	..	..	..

CASTE, TRIBE OR RACE.

CASTES, TRIBES OR RACES.

Recorded principal occupation of earners, other than traditional occupation of Caste (by Sub-Classes).

I Exploitation of Animals and Vegetation.		II Exploitation of Minerals.		III Industry.		IV Transport.		V Trade.		VI Public Force.		VII Public Administration.		VIII Professions and Liberal Arts.		IX Persons living on their income.		X Domestic Service.		XI Insufficiently described occupations.		XII Unproductive.	
M.	F.	M.	F.	M.	F.	M.	F.	M.	F.	M.	F.	M.	F.	M.	F.	M.	F.	M.	F.	M.	F.	M.	F.
16	17	18	19	20	21	22	23	24	25	26	27	28	29	30	31	32	33	34	35	36	37	38	39
101	..	..	..	2	..	..	..	..	..	..	..	..	..	..	..	..	..	..	..	..	..	6	..
462	7	..	..	171	175	4	..	2	..	14	..	6	..	6	..	..	..	14	..	..	..	12	..
3	..	..	..	3	2	..	..	87	..	..	..	3	..	..	..	..	..	7	..	1	..	..	..
94	1	..	..	3	2	1	..	1	..	..	..	1	..	..	..	..	..	..	..	..	..	44	19
156	2	1	..	666	3	25	..	1	..	2	..	28	..	88	2	..	..	1	..	..	..	81	5
5	..	..	..	23	31	2	..	6	9	2	..	2	..	1	..	..	..	19	13	..	..	..	..
631	31	63	..	48	16	27	..	36	..	8	..	10	..	12	..	..	..	12	..	2	..	19	2
2,868	12	..	..	219	48	122	8	76	4	97	..	102	..	53	8	1	..	3	..	..	..	75	5
2,212	..	..	..	124	37	108	8	55	4	24	..	86	..	13	..	..	..	..	..	..	..	3	..
656	12	..	..	95	11	14	..	21	..	73	..	16	..	40	8	1	..	3	..	..	..	72	5
52	6	1	..	148	64	249	50	1,977	5	12	..	75	..	95	1	24	5	284	3	45	..	64	7
1	..	..	..	..	..	..	..	..	..	..	..	2	..	..	..	..	..	..	..	..	..	..	..
2,272	*12*	*162*	..	*755*	..	*2,089*	*107*	*1,060*	*4*	*999*	..	*155*	..	*223*	*6*	*54*	..	*273*	*10*	*44*	..	*81*	*11*
321	..	..	..	12	..	5	..	2	..	14	..	6	..	9	..	..	..	3	1	..	..	3	1
308	..	..	..	5	..	1	..	2	..	11	..	6	..	9	..	..	..	2	1	..	..	3	1
13	..	..	..	7	..	4	..	..	..	3	..	..	..	..	..	..	..	1	..	..	..	..	..
1,943	12	49	..	584	..	1,763	104	921	4	210	..	109	..	183	6	17	..	136	7	24	..	72	9
138	..	7	..	17	..	171	2	158	1	69	..	63	..	87	6	12	..	58	4	18	..	20	..
1,794	12	40	..	306	..	1,557	102	740	3	110	..	43	..	86	..	4	..	71	2	6	..	40	7
11	..	2	..	61	..	35	..	28	..	31	..	3	..	10	..	1	..	12	1	..	..	12	2
8	..	113	..	159	..	321	3	137	..	775	..	40	..	31	..	37	..	134	2	20	..	6	1
8	..	113	..	158	..	316	3	137	..	775	..	39	..	31	..	37	..	134	2	20	..	6	1
..	..	..	..	1	..	5	..	..	..	..	..	1	..	..	..	..	..	..	..	..	..	..	—
2	..	*2*	..	*29*	*1*	*121*	..	*15*	*6*	*3,168*	..	*33*	..	*63*	*84*	*7*	*1*	*3*	*11*	*2*	..	..	..
2	..	2	..	23	1	55	..	12	5	3,158	..	27	..	56	75	7	1	2	9	..	..	..	..
..	..	..	..	6	..	66	..	3	1	10	..	6	..	7	9	..	..	1	2	2	..	..	..

TABLE XI.—PART B.—DISTRIBUTION OF EARNERS AND WORKING DEPENDANTS IN CERTAIN GROUPS OF OCCUPATION BY CASTE, TRIBE OR RACE.

GROUP NUMBER AND OCCUPATION.	INDIGENOUS (INCLUDING SEMI-INDIGENOUS) POPULATION BY RACES BUT EXCLUDING ALIENS.																	
	BALOCH. Earners and working Dependants.		BRAHUI. Earners and working Dependants.		PATHAN. Earners and working Dependants.		LASI. Earners and working Dependants.		JATT. Earners and working Dependants.		SAYYID. Earners and working Dependants.		OTHER MUSLIMS. Earners and working Dependants.		HINDU. Earners and working Dependants.		SIKH. Earners and working Dependants.	
	M.	F.	M.	F.	M.	F.	M.	F.	M.	F.	M.	F.	M.	F.	M.	F.	M.	F.
1	2	3	4	5	6	7	8	9	10	11	12	13	14	15	16	17	18	19
TOTAL ..	70,983	6,215	46,816	1,869	64,065	2,735	10,558	880	26,776	1,258	6,333	607	19,058	970	6,192	264	31	..
1. Non-cultivating proprietors taking rent in money or kind ..	5,361	105	2,155	16	2,349	120	155	7	199	4	447	14	402	17	27	6	1	..
5. Cultivating owners	36,223	..	19,226	..	31,853	..	4,855	9	7,145	13	2,659	..	2,506	1	12	..	..	..
6. Tenant cultivators	15,413	2	8,829	3	5,145	..	509	..	14,307	..	544	..	5,656	7	7	..	..	..
7. Agricultural labourers	1,453	3,906	1,624	38	4,088	716	1,522	83	401	10	522	168	1,785	70	..	..	..	..
16. Market gardeners, flower and fruit growers	23	7	31	..	108	..	..	..	5	..	3	..	22	..	3	..	..	..
21. Cattle and buffaloe breeders and keepers	523	5	155	..	21	1	829	84	19	..	16	..	12	..	..	..	..	..
22. Breeders of transport animals	229	1	247	..	366	..	136	..	52	..	5	..	183	7	..	..	..	..
23. Herdsmen, shepherds and breeders of other animals ..	4,983	84	9,625	39	6,034	341	1,530	52	1,237	3	282	49	360	4	2	..	..	..
34. Other metallic minerals	1	..	..	..	50	..	..	..	..	..	1	..	95	..	..	..	..	..
35. Coal	26	..	21	..	126	..	..	..	6	..	..	..	94	1	..	..	..	..
40. Salt, saltpetre and other saline substances	13	..	..	..	..	..	..	..	63	..	..	..	..	..	..	..	..	..
46. Wool carding, spinning and weaving	73	385	30	722	78	3	8	97	50	97	..	..	52	50	..	..	..	..
51. Working in Leather	1	..	..	..	4	..	..	..	5	6	..	..	4	5	..	..	..	..
55. Carpenters, turners and joiners, etc.	42	..	74	..	63	..	23	..	212	..	5	..	507	..	..	..	..	..
56. Basket makers and other industries of woody materials, including leaves and thatchers and builders working with bamboos, reeds, or similar materials.	178	1,294	44	780	22	38	21	482	197	881	2	2	137	334	..	..	..	..
59. Blacksmiths, other workers in iron, makers of implements ..	170	2	98	..	251	1	19	..	87	..	66	..	838	2	..	..	..	..
63. Potters and makers of earthen-ware	7	..	7	..	19	1	8	..	126	18	..	..	38	..	..	..	..	..
64. Brick and tile makers	5	..	9	2	184	3	..	..	9	..	2	..	5	..	..	..	..	..
67. Manufacture of aerated and mineral waters and ice ..	..	..	1	..	..	..	..	..	..	..	..	..	..	..	1	..	..	..
73. Butchers	17	..	12	..	43	..	2	..	33	..	16	..	24	..	..	..	..	..
75. Sweetmeat and condiment makers	..	..	..	..	5	..	..	..	..	..	..	..	..	..	28	..	..	..
82. Boot, shoe, sandal and clog makers	43	..	22	..	245	..	11	..	190	..	6	..	232	..	..	..	..	..
83. Tailors, milliners, dress-makers and darners	22	51	45	6	71	1,098	2	..	9	..	20	294	53	38	13	..	..	..
84. Embroiderers, hat-makers and makers of other articles of wear.	6	83	..	91	1	19	..	2	4	79	..	46	4	65	2	165	..	..
85. Washing and cleaning	..	10	5	..	5	4	5	..	39	..	..	2	9	13	..	..	..	..
91. Persons engaged in making, assembling or repairing motor vehicles or cycles.	6	..	1	..	2	..	..	..	..	..	..	..	7	..	2	..	..	..
94. Heat, light, electricity, motive power, etc., gas works and electric light and power.	..	..	2	..	1	..	..	..	..	..	..	..	2	..	..	..	..	..
95. Printers, engravers, bookbinders, etc.	..	..	4	..	2	..	..	..	..	..	..	..	1	..	..	..	..	..
98. Makers of jewellery and ornaments	61	..	19	..	34	..	8	..	83	..	1	..	191	..	73	..	..	..
101. Persons concerned with aerodromes and aeroplanes ..	..	..	..	..	1	..	..	..	..	..	..	..	4	..	..	..	..	..
105. Persons (other than labourers) employed on the construction and maintenance of roads and bridges.	..	..	1	..	11	..	..	..	..	..	..	..	6	..	..	..	..	..
106. Labourers employed on roads and bridges ..	26	..	144	..	462	1	..	..	..	..	19	..	157	..	..	..	..	..
107. Owners, managers and employees (excluding personal servants) connected with mechanically driven vehicles (including trams).	1	..	1	..	4	..	..	..	..	..	..	..	..	..	..	..	..	..

CERTAIN GROUPS OF OCCUPATION BY CASTE, TRIBE OR RACE.

110. Pack elephant, camel, mule, ass and bullock owners and drivers.	993	7	877	48	822	2	267	..	322	13	61	1	480	20	18	..	..	..
111. Porters and messengers	417	15	663	12	2,211	131	24	..	65	4	68	15	276	13	173	50	..	..
112. Railway employees of all kinds other than porters and coolies	118	..	220	..	260	..	..	..	70	..	34	..	16	..	31	..	..	..
113. Labourers employed on railway construction and maintenance and coolies and porters employed on railway premises.	398	..	411	..	764	..	..	..	132	..	58	..	47	..	10	..	..	..
114. Post Office, Telegraph and Telephone services	44	..	44	..	25	..	22	..	9	..	5	..	16	..	3	..	..	..
117. Trade in piece-goods, wool, cotton, silk, hair and other textiles.	25	..	16	..	237	2	6	..	2	..	186	..	38	..	998	..	..	..
118. Trade in skins, leather, furs, feathers, horn, etc., and the articles made from these.	4	..	3	..	16	..	4	..	2	..	1	..	6	..	..	..	..	..
123. Trade in metals, machinery, knives, tools, etc. ..	..	..	..	..	..	..	..	..	..	..	..	..	..	..	1	..	..	..
124. Trade in pottery, bricks and tiles	..	..	..	..	..	..	..	..	..	..	..	..	..	..	11	..	..	..
126. Vendors of wine, liquors, aerated waters and ice	..	..	..	..	1	..	..	..	..	..	1	..	..	..	36	..	..	..
127. Owners and managers of hotels, cookshops, sarais, etc. (and employees).	23	..	15	..	59	..	2	..	20	..	3	..	29	..	2	..	..	..
129. Grain and pulse dealers	9	..	3	..	12	..	3	..	4	..	..	..	57	..	308	5	..	..
131. Dealers in dairy product, eggs and poultry	5	2	6	..	222	..	11	4	10	1	4	2	4	..	8	..	..	..
132. Dealers in animals for food	67	..	27	..	65	..	10	..	..	..	17	1	7	..	..	..	..	..
133. Dealers in fodder for animals	2	..	16	..	26	..	..	..	4	..	1	..	..	..	5	..	..	..
138. Trade in ready-made clothing and other articles of dress and the toilet (hats, umbrellas, socks, ready-made shoes, perfumes, etc.).	2	..	9	..	102	..	..	..	..	..	3	..	43	3	121	..	..	..
139. Trade in furniture, carpets, curtains and bedding ..	1	..	2	..	1	..	..	..	..	..	4	..	2	..	..	..	..	..
144. Dealers and hirers of elephants, camels, horses, cattle, asses, mules, etc.	31	..	39	..	155	2	2	..	26	..	4	..	8	..	5	..	..	..
150. General storekeepers and shopkeepers otherwise unspecified	31	..	35	..	302	..	27	1	44	..	44	..	83	..	3,160	..	28	..
153. Army (Imperial)	4	..	127	..	54	..	..	..	10	..	14	..	712	..	..	..	..	..
154. Army (Indian States)	296	..	58	..	5	..	34	..	10	..	8	..	91	..	1	..	..	.
157. Police	960	..	1,260	..	2,100	..	60	..	131	..	97	..	165	..	10	..	..	..
159. Service of the State	62	..	76	..	230	..	..	..	28	..	34	..	45	..	9	..	..	..
160. Service of Indian and Foreign States	78	..	226	..	61	..	20	..	76	..	35	..	571	..	18	..	2	..
161. Municipal and other Local (not village) Service ..	7	..	11	..	30	..	4	..	12	..	3	..	16	..	10	..	..	..
162. Village Officials and servants other than watchmen ..	16	..	..	..	21	..	..	..	2	..	8	..	..	..	..	..	..	..
163. Priests, ministers, etc.	153	..	216	..	821	..	9	..	146	..	422	3	93	..	43	1	..	..
167. Lawyers of all kinds, including Qazis, Law Agents and Mukhtiars.	3	..	1	..	1	..	1	..	1	..	1	..	4	..	..	..	..	..
170. Other persons practising the healing arts without being registered.	8	3	..	..	8	2	3	..	4	..	4	..	1	8	4	..	..	..
172. Midwives, vaccinators, compounders, nurses, masseurs, etc.	15	4	17	2	11	5	..	..	5	22	2	..	14	10	9	..	..	..
174. Professors and teachers of all kinds	10	..	8	..	41	3	2	..	20	1	32	..	4	..	2	..	..	..
186. Private motor drivers and cleaners	12	..	27	..	89	..	6	..	..	..	12	..	23	..	12	..	..	..
187. Other domestic service	449	32	389	26	466	21	42	27	182	23	56	..	504	96	272	3	..	..
193. Beggars and vagrants	329	26	184	33	413	151	21	3	221	39	174	10	326	38	64	7	..	..
All other groups	1,455	191	1,398	51	2,776	70	335	29	731	39	321	..	1,991	168	678	27	..	..

M = Males. F = Females.

TABLE XII.

EDUCATED UNEMPLOYMENT.

1. Out of a total population of 868,617, educated unemployment was returned by 32 persons of whom 29 were aliens from other Indian Provinces and only 3 were local men. The numbers of aliens are necessarily small owing to the Census having been taken in winter when most of them move down to India.

2. Indigenous Hindus, Sikhs and Anglo-Indians and other alien classes returned no educated unemployment.

3. There was no educated unemployment in the age period 30—39.

TABLE XII.—(PART I).

EDUCATED UNEMPLOYMENT BY CLASS.

District or State.	Class.	Total Unemployment.	Aged 20—24.		Aged 25—29.	
			Unemployed for less than 1 year.	Unemployed for one year or more.	Unemployed for less than 1 year.	Unemployed for one year or more.
BALUCHISTAN		22	8	10	1	3
	I. Muslim ..	6	2	4	..	..
	(a) Indigenous ..	2	2	..	..	..
	(b) Aliens ..	4	..	4	..	..
	II. Hindus ..	12	4	5	1	2
	(a) Brahman ..	1	..	..	..	1
	(b) Depressed Hindus	..	..	..	..	..
	(c) Other Hindus ..	11	4	5	1	1
	III. Sikhs ..	4	2	1	..	1
Districts ..	..	21	7	10	1	3
States ..	..	1	1	..	..	..

Total of educated unemployed under 20 years 10
Total of educated unemployed over 40 years .. .. Nil.
Total number of educated unemployed whose fathers were soldiers .. .. .. Nil.
Total number of educated unemployed whose fathers were cultivators 8
Total number of educated unemployed whose fathers were artisans 1
Total number of educated unemployed whose fathers were menials or servants .. .. Nil.
Total number of educated unemployed who had passed the Matriculation or S. L. C. examination and who though not totally unemployed had failed to obtain employment with which they were satisfied 1

TABLE XII.—(PART II).

EDUCATED UNEMPLOYMENT BY DEGREE.

Degree.	Total Unemployment.	Aged 20—24.		Aged 25—29.	
		Unemployed for less than 1 year.	Unemployed for one year or more.	Unemployed for less than 1 year.	Unemployed for one year or more.
.C. or Matric or Senior Cambridge)	22	8	10	1	3
DISTRICTS	21	7	10	1	3
Quetta-Pishin	19	5	10	1	3
Zhob	1	1	..	..	..
Chagai	1	1	..	..	..
STATES	1	1	..	..	..
Kalat—Mekran	1	1	..	..	..

TABLE XIII

LITERACY BY RELIGION AND AGE.

This table contains figures of literates and illiterates as well as those literate in English, for each religion by certain age-periods.

2. There is a summary in the beginning which gives totals for the Province as a whole followed by details for each District and State.

3. Statistics of literacy for selected castes will be found in Table XIV.

4. All persons of five years of age and over who were able to read a letter and write an answer to it have been treated as literate and included in this table.

5. As age was not recorded in the Tribal Areas the numbers of literates censused in those areas have been shown in the table as "age-unspecified."

6. In a total population of 868,617 persons Baluchistan has only 40,775 literates of whom 31,578 are aliens from India and elsewhere and 9,197 indigenous inhabitants. The latter consist of 5,101 Muslims, 4,084 Hindus and 12 Sikhs.

7. In the Christian figures are included the following Indian Christians :—

Age.	Literate.			Illiterate.			Literate in English.		
	Persons.	Males.	Females.	Persons.	Males.	Females.	Persons.	Males.	Females.
0—5 ..	..	..	..	400	217	183	..	..	..
5—10 ..	55	28	27	262	145	117	46	20	26
10—15 ..	66	35	31	198	107	91	54	26	28
15—20 ..	78	51	27	205	118	87	53	33	20
20 and over ..	366	258	108	1,023	673	350	243	152	91
Unspecified ..	..	..	..	3	3	..	..	..	..
Total ..	565	372	193	2,091	1,263	828	396	231	165

8. The numbers of literates for the whole province in the various vernaculars are shown below :—

	Males.	Females.		Males.	Females.
Urdu ..	17,484	938	Lande Sindhi ..	1,999	23
Hindi ..	6,220	891	Sindhi ..	1,256	50
Roman Urdu ..	3,839	5	Lande Punjabi ..	1,289	5
Gurmukhi ..	2,678	812	Marathi ..	1,073	10
Persian ..	3,226	61	Arabic ..	226	58

9. Several individuals returned themselves as literates in more than one vernacular. The totals in the case of the above figures do not therefore agree with the totals for literacy in the table.

10. Persons literate in English (columns 12 to 14) are included in the figures for the total literate (columns 6 to 8).

TABLE XIII.—LITERACY BY RELIGION AND AGE.—SUMMARY FOR THE PROVINCE.

District or State.	Religion and Age.	POPULATION.									LITERATE IN ENGLISH.		
		TOTAL.			LITERATE.			ILLITERATE.					
		Persons.	Males.	Females.	Persons.	Males.	Females.	Persons.	Males.	Females.	Persons.	Males.	Females.
1	2	3	4	5	6	7	8	9	10	11	12	13	14
BALUCHISTAN.	**ALL RELIGIONS** ..	**868,617**	**488,414**	**380,203**	**40,775**	**36,835**	**3,940**	**827,842**	**451,579**	**376,263**	**11,588**	**10,063**	**1,525**
	0—5 ..	11,356	5,793	5,563	..	..	..	11,356	5,793	5,563	..	..	..
	5—10 ..	8,484	4,682	3,802	1 290	871	419	7,194	3,811	3,388	354	222	132
	10—15 ..	7,764	4,539	3,225	1,904	1,357	547	5,860	3,182	2,678	583	421	162
	15—20 ..	14,260	10,686	3,574	5,386	4,813	573	8,874	5,873	3,001	1,619	1,473	146
	20 and over ..	68,985	54,497	14,488	24,654	22,322	2,332	44,331	32,175	12,156	8,922	7,837	1,085
	Unspecified ..	757,768	408,217	349,551	7,541	7,472	69	750,227	400,745	349,482	110	110	..
	***HINDU** ..	**53,681**	**36,180**	**17,501**	**18,361**	**16,858**	**1,503**	**350,820**	**19,322**	**15,998**	**3,212**	**3,120**	**92**
	0—5 ..	4,005	2,039	1,966	..	..	..	4,005	2,039	1,966	..	..	..
	5—10 ..	2,793	1,489	1,304	536	346	190	2,257	1,143	1,114	58	53	5
	10—15 ..	2,598	1,502	1,096	842	585	257	1,756	917	839	165	154	11
	15—20 ..	5,355	4,081	1,274	2,622	2,361	261	2,733	1,720	1,013	432	413	19
	20 and over ..	23,315	18,548	4,767	11,101	10,341	760	12,214	8,207	4,007	2,546	2,489	57
	Unspecified ..	15,615	8,521	7,094	3,260	3,225	35	12,355	5,296	7,059	11	11	..
	SIKH ..	**8,425**	**6,270**	**2,155**	**4,193**	**3,669**	**524**	**4,232**	**2,601**	**1,631**	**937**	**980**	**51**
	0—5 ..	778	400	378	..	..	..	778	400	378	..	..	..
	5—10 ..	572	335	237	153	99	54	419	236	183	17	9	8
	10—15 ..	520	309	211	239	163	76	281	146	135	56	40	16
	15—20 ..	1,225	935	290	782	676	106	443	259	184	214	201	13
	20 and over ..	4,845	3,965	880	2,997	2,709	288	1,848	1,256	592	699	679	20
	Unspecified ..	485	326	159	22	22	..	463	304	159	1	1	..
	MUSLIM ..	**798,093**	**440,089**	**358,004**	**12,656**	**12,093**	**563**	**785,437**	**427,996**	**357,441**	**2,055**	**1,997**	**58**
	0—5 ..	5,676	2,886	2,790	..	..	..	5,676	2,886	2,790	..	..	..
	5—10 ..	4,455	2,502	1,953	341	284	57	4,114	2,218	1,896	32	27	5
	10—15 ..	4,129	2,453	1,676	545	460	85	3,584	1,993	1,591	106	95	11
	15—20 ..	6,806	4,992	1,814	1,326	1,228	98	5,480	3,764	1,716	353	340	13
	20 and over ..	35,362	27,889	7,473	6,185	5,896	289	29,177	21,993	7,184	1,466	1,437	29
	Unspecified ..	741,665	399,367	342,298	4,259	4,225	34	737,406	395,142	342,264	98	98	..
	CHRISTIAN ..	**8,059**	**5,637**	**2,422**	**5,369**	**4,075**	**1,294**	**2,690**	**1,562**	**1,128**	**5,198**	**3,934**	**1,264**
	0—5 ..	866	454	412	..	..	..	866	454	412	..	..	..
	5—10 ..	632	343	289	252	139	113	380	204	176	239	130	109
	10—15 ..	484	260	224	263	142	121	221	118	103	246	130	116
	15—20 ..	827	644	183	625	528	97	202	116	86	601	511	90
	20 and over ..	5,247	3,933	1,314	4,229	3,266	963	1,018	667	351	4,112	3,163	949
	Unspecified ..	3	3	..	..	..	..	3	3	..	...	..	..
	ZOROASTRIAN ..	**167**	**90**	**77**	**118**	**70**	**48**	**49**	**20**	**29**	**109**	**61**	**48**
	0—5 ..	12	5	7	..	..	..	12	5	7	..	..	..
	5—10 ..	17	6	11	6	2	4	11	4	7	6	2	4
	10—15 ..	20	9	11	14	7	7	6	2	4	9	2	7
	15—20 ..	20	10	10	19	9	10	1	1	..	15	5	10
	20 and over ..	98	60	38	79	52	27	19	8	11	79	52	27
	Unspecified ..	..	..	..	..	..	..	..	..	..	..	..	..
	JEW ..	**17**	**14**	**3**	**8**	**8**	..	**9**	**6**	**3**	**6**	**6**	..
	0—5 ..	3	2	1	..	..	..	3	2	1	..	..	..
	5—10 ..	1	..	1	..	..	..	1	..	1	..	..	..
	10—15 ..	1	1	..	..	..	..	1	1	..	..	..	..
	15—20 ..	1	1	..	1	1	..	..	..	..	1	1	..
	20 and over ..	11	10	1	7	7	..	4	3	1	5	5	..
	Unspecified ..	..	..	..	..	..	..	..	..	..	..	..	..
	BUDDHIST ..	**68**	**53**	**15**	**45**	**41**	**4**	**23**	**12**	**11**	**12**	**9**	**3**
	0—5 ..	4	2	2	..	..	..	4	2	2	..	..	..
	5—10 ..	4	1	3	..	..	..	4	1	3	..	..	..
	10—15 ..	3	..	3	..	..	..	3	..	3	..	..	..
	15—20 ..	10	9	1	9	8	1	1	1	..	3	2	1
	20 and over ..	47	41	6	36	33	3	11	8	3	9	7	2
	Unspecified ..	..	..	..	..	..	..	..	..	..	..	..	..
	JAIN ..	**32**	**20**	**12**	**15**	**14**	**1**	**17**	**6**	**11**	**2**	**2**	..
	0—5 ..	5	2	3	..	..	..	5	2	3	..	..	..
	5—10 ..	4	2	2	1	1	..	3	1	2	1	1	..
	10—15 ..	3	1	2	..	..	..	3	1	2	..	..	..
	15—20 ..	3	2	1	2	2	..	1	..	1	..	..	..
	20 and over ..	17	13	4	12	11	1	5	2	3	1	1	..
	Unspecified ..	..	..	..	..	..	..	..	..	..	..	..	..
	TRIBAL RELIGIONS ..	**32**	**25**	**7**	..	..	..	**32**	**25**	**7**	..	..	..
	0—5 ..	5	2	3	..	..	..	5	2	3	..	..	..
	5—10 ..	3	2	1	..	..	..	3	2	1	..	..	..
	10—15 ..	3	2	1	..	..	..	3	2	1	..	..	..
	15—20 ..	5	5	..	..	..	..	5	5	..	..	..	..
	20 and over ..	16	14	2	..	..	..	16	14	2	..	..	..
	Unspecified ..	..	..	..	..	..	..	..	..	..	..	..	..
	OTHERS ..	**43**	**36**	**7**	**10**	**7**	**3**	**33**	**29**	**4**	**7**	**4**	**3**
	0—5 ..	2	1	1	..	..	..	2	1	1	..	..	..
	5—10 ..	3	2	1	1	..	1	2	2	..	1	..	1
	10—15 ..	3	2	1	1	..	1	2	2	..	1	..	1
	15—20 ..	8	7	1	..	..	..	8	7	1	..	..	..
	20 and over ..	27	24	3	8	7	1	19	17	2	5	4	1
	Unspecified ..	..	..	..	..	..	..	..	..	..	..	..	..

*Hindu including Arya and Brahmo.

TABLE XIII.—LITERACY BY RELIGION AND AGE—DISTRIBUTION BY DISTRICTS AND STATES.

District or State.	Religion and Age.	POPULATION.									Literate in English.		
		Total.			Literate.			Illiterate.					
		Persons.	Males.	Females.	Persons.	Males.	Females.	Persons.	Males.	Females.	Persons.	Males.	Females.
1	2	3	4	5	6	7	8	9	10	11	12	13	14
QUETTA—PISHIN.	**ALL RELIGIONS** ..	**147,541**	**90,302**	**57,239**	**25,044**	**21,917**	**3,127**	**122,497**	**68,385**	**54,112**	**9,456**	**8,074**	**1,382**
	0—5 ..	7,566	3,821	3,745	..	..	..	7,566	3,821	3,745	..	..	..
	5—10 ..	5,786	3,190	2,596	1,049	704	345	4,737	2,486	2,251	320	196	124
	10—15 ..	5,332	3,156	2,176	1,527	1,081	446	3,805	2,075	1,730	517	362	155
	15—20 ..	9,365	7,012	2,353	3,926	3,482	444	5,439	3,530	1,909	1,349	1,214	135
	20 and over ..	43,250	33,569	9,681	17,358	15,468	1,890	25,892	18,101	7,791	7,239	6,271	968
	Unspecified	76,242	39,554	36,688	1,184	1,182	2	75,058	38,372	36,686	31	31	..
	HINDU ..	**26,718**	**19,212**	**7,506**	**10,642**	**9,541**	**1,101**	**16,076**	**9,671**	**6,405**	**2,377**	**2,308**	**74**
	0—5 ..	2,922	1,467	1,455	..	..	..	2,922	1,467	1,455	..	..	..
	5—10 ..	2,022	1,083	939	422	272	150	1,600	811	789	51	47	4
	10—15 ..	1,894	1,120	774	664	462	202	1,230	658	572	151	140	11
	15—20 ..	3,843	2,937	906	1,917	1,725	192	1,926	1,212	714	334	316	18
	20 and over ..	15,924	12,521	3,403	7,619	7,062	557	8,305	5,459	2,846	1,839	1,798	41
	Unspecified ..	113	84	29	20	20	..	93	64	29	2	2	..
	SIKH ..	**5,255**	**3,754**	**1,501**	**2,575**	**2,178**	**397**	**2,680**	**1,576**	**1,104**	**747**	**693**	**54**
	0—5 ..	583	305	278	..	..	..	583	305	278	..	..	..
	5—10 ..	445	270	175	125	84	41	320	186	134	16	8	8
	10—15 ..	406	247	159	191	135	56	215	112	103	53	37	16
	15—20 ..	751	529	222	464	382	82	287	147	140	166	153	13
	20 and over ..	3,060	2,394	666	1,793	1,575	218	1,267	819	448	512	495	17
	Unspecified ..	10	9	1	2	2	..	8	7	1	..	..	..
	MUSLIM ..	**107,945**	**62,024**	**45,921**	**6,690**	**6,294**	**396**	**101,255**	**55,730**	**45,525**	**1,367**	**1,321**	**46**
	0—5 ..	3,250	1,629	1,621	..	..	..	3,250	1,629	1,621	..	..	..
	5—10 ..	2,723	1,525	1,198	264	220	44	2,459	1,305	1,154	26	21	5
	10—15 ..	2,563	1,546	1,017	416	350	66	2,147	1,196	951	76	66	10
	15—20 ..	3,966	2,921	1,045	924	854	70	3,042	2,067	975	255	244	11
	20 and over	19,324	14,942	4,382	3,924	3,710	214	15,400	11,232	4,168	981	961	20
	Unspecified ..	76,119	39,461	36,658	1,162	1,160	2	74,957	38,301	36,656	29	29	..
	CHRISTIAN ..	**7,370**	**5,169**	**2,201**	**4,981**	**3,804**	**1,177**	**2,389**	**1,365**	**1,024**	**4,839**	**3,685**	**1,154**
	0—5 ..	787	409	378	..	..	..	787	409	378	..	..	..
	5—10 ..	570	304	266	230	125	105	340	179	161	219	117	102
	10—15 ..	440	231	209	241	127	114	199	104	95	227	117	110
	15—20 ..	777	609	168	598	509	89	179	100	79	576	494	82
	20 and over ..	4,796	3,616	1,180	3,912	3,043	869	884	573	311	3,817	2,957	860
	Unspecified ..	..	..	..	..	..	..	..	..	..	..	..	..
	OTHERS ..	**253**	**143**	**110**	**156**	**100**	**56**	**97**	**43**	**54**	**126**	**72**	**54**
	0—5 ..	24	11	13	..	..	..	24	11	13	..	..	..
	5—10 ..	26	8	18	8	3	5	18	5	13	8	3	5
	10—15 ..	29	12	17	15	7	8	14	5	9	10	2	8
	15—20 ..	28	16	12	23	12	11	5	4	1	18	7	11
	20 and over ..	146	96	50	110	78	32	36	18	18	90	60	30
	Unspecified ..	..	..	..	..	..	..	..	..	..	..	..	..
LORALAI.	**ALL RELIGIONS** ..	**86,087**	**47,936**	**38,151**	**2,746**	**2,587**	**159**	**83,341**	**45,349**	**37,992**	**500**	**474**	**26**
	0—5 ..	569	267	302	..	..	..	569	267	302	..	..	..
	5—10 ..	401	219	182	52	38	14	349	181	168	7	7	..
	10—15 ..	381	223	158	89	68	21	292	155	137	25	24	1
	15—20 ..	825	641	184	314	282	32	511	359	152	76	73	3
	20 and over ..	4,127	3,433	694	1,652	1,562	90	2,475	1,871	604	372	350	22
	Unspecified ..	79,784	43,153	36,631	639	637	2	79,145	42,516	36,629	20	20	..
	HINDU ..	**3,504**	**2,403**	**1,101**	**1,304**	**1,227**	**77**	**2,200**	**1,176**	**1,024**	**176**	**175**	**1**
	0—5 ..	220	103	117	..	..	..	220	103	117	..	..	..
	5—10 ..	145	79	66	24	17	7	121	62	59	2	2	..
	10—15 ..	144	80	64	38	29	9	106	51	55	5	5	..
	15—20	302	229	73	142	125	17	160	104	56	23	23	..
	20 and over ..	1,459	1,198	261	749	705	44	710	493	217	145	144	1
	Unspecified ..	1,234	714	520	351	351	..	883	363	520	1	1	..
	SIKH ..	**562**	**447**	**115**	**353**	**319**	**34**	**209**	**128**	**81**	**69**	**69**	..
	0—5 ..	44	20	24	..	..	..	44	20	24	..	..	..
	5—10 ..	30	15	15	10	6	4	20	9	11	1	1	..
	10—15 ..	30	16	14	17	10	7	13	6	7	2	2	..
	15—20 ..	80	65	15	54	46	8	26	19	7	12	12	..
	20 and over ..	374	328	46	271	256	15	103	72	31	53	53	..
	Unspecified ..	4	3	1	1	1	..	3	2	1	1	1	..
	MUSLIM ..	**81,812**	**44,943**	**36,869**	**988**	**967**	**21**	**80,824**	**43,976**	**36,848**	**170**	**169**	**1**
	0—5 ..	284	132	152	..	..	..	284	132	152	..	..	..
	5—10 ..	210	115	95	17	15	2	193	100	93	4	4	..
	10—15 ..	195	119	76	31	27	4	164	92	72	17	17	..
	15—20 ..	424	334	90	109	104	5	315	230	85	34	33	1
	20 and over ..	2,154	1,808	346	544	536	8	1,610	1,272	338	97	97	..
	Unspecified ..	78,545	42,435	36,110	287	285	2	78,258	42,150	36,108	18	18	..
	CHRISTIAN ..	**209**	**143**	**66**	**101**	**74**	**27**	**108**	**69**	**39**	**85**	**61**	**24**
	0—5 ..	21	12	9	..	..	..	21	12	9	..	..	..
	5—10 ..	16	10	6	1	..	1	15	10	5	..	..	..
	10—15 ..	12	8	4	3	2	1	9	6	3	1	..	1
	15—20 ..	19	13	6	9	7	2	10	6	4	7	5	2
	20 and over ..	140	99	41	88	65	23	52	34	18	77	56	21
	Unspecified ..	1	1	..	..	..	..	1	1	..	..	..	..

TABLE XIII.—LITERACY BY RELIGION AND AGE—DISTRIBUTION BY DISTRICTS AND STATES.

District or State.	Religion and Age.	POPULATION.									LITERATE IN ENGLISH.		
		TOTAL.			LITERATE.			ILLITERATE.					
		Persons.	Males.	Females.	Persons.	Males.	Females.	Persons.	Males.	Females.	Persons.	Males.	Females
1	2	3	4	5	6	7	8	9	10	11	12	13	14
ZHOB.	ALL RELIGIONS	57,963	34,596	23,367	3,672	3,521	151	54,291	31,075	23,216	499	486	13
	0—5	522	264	258	..	..	..	522	264	258	..	..	..
	5—10	381	204	177	53	38	15	328	166	162	3	2	1
	10—15	363	223	140	88	67	21	275	156	119	7	6	1
	15—20	1,518	1,356	162	671	644	27	847	712	135	68	68	..
	20 and over	6,834	6,240	594	2,697	2,610	87	4,137	3,630	507	418	407	11
	Unspecified	48,345	26,309	22,036	163	162	1	48,182	26,147	22,035	3	3	..
	HINDU	2,839	2,402	437	1,653	1,566	87	1,186	836	350	191	191	..
	0—5	163	85	78	..	..	..	163	85	78	..	..	..
	5—10	122	60	62	28	19	9	94	41	53	1	1	..
	10—15	118	67	51	50	35	15	68	32	36	2	2	..
	15—20	476	417	59	321	302	19	155	115	40	25	25	..
	20 and over	1,950	1,766	184	1,251	1,208	43	699	558	141	163	163	..
	Unspecified	10	7	3	3	2	1	7	5	2	..	..	..
	SIKH	1,134	1,089	95	821	797	24	313	242	71	74	74	..
	0—5	43	24	19	..	..	..	43	24	19	..	..	..
	5—10	25	14	11	4	2	2	21	12	9	..	..	..
	10—15	21	12	9	8	6	2	13	6	7	..	..	..
	15—20	266	253	13	203	199	4	63	54	9	17	17	..
	20 and over	779	736	43	606	590	16	173	146	27	57	57	..
	Unspecified	..	..	..	..	..	..	..	..	..	..	..	..
	MUSLIM	53,844	31,025	22,819	1,093	1,062	31	52,751	29,963	22,788	159	155	4
	0—5	313	154	159	..	..	..	313	154	159	..	..	..
	5—10	228	127	101	20	17	3	208	110	98	1	1	..
	10—15	220	142	78	29	26	3	191	116	75	4	4	..
	15—20	761	671	90	136	132	4	625	539	86	22	22	..
	20 and over	3,988	3,630	358	748	727	21	3,240	2,903	337	129	125	4
	Unspecified	48,334	26,301	22,033	160	160	..	48,174	26,141	22,033	3	3	..
	CHRISTIAN	115	99	16	78	69	9	37	30	7	75	66	9
	0—5	3	1	2	..	..	..	3	1	2	..	..	..
	5—10	6	3	3	1	..	1	5	3	2	1	..	1
	10—15	4	2	2	1	..	1	3	2	1	1	..	1
	15—20	7	7	..	4	4	..	3	3	..	4	4	..
	20 and over	94	85	9	72	65	7	22	20	2	69	62	7
	Unspecified	1	1	..	..	..	..	1	1	..	..	..	..
	OTHERS	31	31	..	27	27	..	4	4	..	..	..	..
	0—5	..	..	..	..	..	..	..	..	..	..	..	..
	5—10	..	..	..	..	..	..	..	..	..	..	..	..
	10—15	..	..	..	..	..	..	..	..	..	..	..	..
	15—20	8	8	..	7	7	..	1	1	..	..	..	..
	20 and over	23	23	..	20	20	..	3	3	..	..	..	..
	Unspecified	..	..	..	..	..	..	..	..	..	..	..	..
BOLAN.	ALL RELIGIONS	4,688	3,466	1,222	717	649	68	3,971	2,817	1,154	227	203	24
	0—5	385	197	188	..	..	..	385	197	188	..	..	..
	5—10	238	138	100	18	11	7	220	127	93	5	2	3
	10—15	200	110	90	21	13	8	179	97	82	5	3	2
	15—20	453	322	131	84	76	8	369	246	123	25	24	1
	20 and over	2,808	2,403	495	582	537	45	2,316	1,866	450	192	174	18
	Unspecified	514	296	218	12	12	..	502	284	218	..	..	..
	HINDU	1,165	908	257	384	353	31	781	555	226	114	110	4
	0—5	89	51	38	..	..	..	89	51	38	..	..	..
	5—10	56	32	24	7	5	2	49	27	22	..	..	..
	10—15	47	24	23	8	4	4	39	20	19	..	..	..
	15—20	135	96	39	37	33	4	98	63	35	10	10	..
	20 and over	828	697	131	329	308	21	499	389	110	104	100	4
	Unspecified	10	8	2	3	3	..	7	5	2	..	..	..
	SIKH	173	148	30	82	77	5	91	66	25	22	22	..
	0—5	16	11	5	..	..	..	16	11	5	..	..	..
	5—10	13	8	5	1	1	..	12	7	5	..	..	..
	10—15	10	6	4	2	2	..	8	4	4	..	..	..
	15—20	25	21	4	12	11	1	13	10	3	5	5	..
	20 and over	109	97	12	67	63	4	42	34	8	17	17	..
	Unspecified	..	..	..	..	..	..	..	..	..	..	..	..
	MUSLIM	3,229	2,333	896	200	190	10	3,029	2,143	886	45	45	..
	0—5	265	127	138	..	..	..	265	127	138	..	..	..
	5—10	156	90	66	5	3	2	151	87	64	..	..	..
	10—15	133	74	59	6	5	1	127	69	58	1	1	..
	15—20	282	197	85	32	30	2	250	167	83	7	7	..
	20 and over	1,889	1,557	332	148	143	5	1,741	1,414	327	37	37	..
	Unspecified	504	288	216	9	9	..	495	279	216	..	..	..
	CHRISTIAN	91	56	35	48	26	22	43	30	13	46	26	20
	0—5	13	7	6	..	..	..	13	7	6	..	..	..
	5—10	11	6	5	5	2	3	6	4	2	5	2	3
	10—15	8	4	4	5	2	3	3	2	1	4	2	2
	15—20	6	4	2	3	2	1	3	2	1	3	2	1
	20 and over	53	35	18	35	20	15	18	15	3	34	20	14
	Unspecified	..	..	..	..	..	..	..	..	..	..	..	..
	OTHERS	30	26	4	3	3	..	27	23	4	..	..	..
	0—5	2	1	1	..	..	..	2	1	1	..	..	..
	5—10	2	2	..	..	..	..	2	2	..	..	..	..
	10—15	2	2	..	..	..	..	2	2	..	..	..	..
	15—20	5	4	1	..	..	..	5	4	1	..	..	..
	20 and over	19	17	2	3	3	..	16	14	2	..	..	..
	Unspecified	..	..	..	..	..	..	..	..	..	..	..	..

TABLE XIII.—LITERACY BY RELIGION AND AGE—DISTRIBUTION AND STATES.

District or State.	Religion and Age.	POPULATION.											
		TOTAL.			LITERATE.			ILLITERATE.			LITERATE IN ENGLISH.		
		Persons.	Males.	Females.	Persons.	Males.	Females.	Persons.	Males.	Females.	Persons.	Males.	Females.
1	2	3	4	5	6	7	8	9	10	11	12	13	14
CHAGAI.	ALL RELIGIONS ..	24,224	13,721	10,503	801	749	52	23,423	12,972	10,451	146	142	4
	0—5 ..	654	346	308	..	..	..	654	346	308	..	..	..
	5—10	418	223	195	15	13	2	403	210	193	1	1	..
	10—15	353	180	173	23	20	3	330	160	170	1	1	..
	15—20	545	322	223	81	72	9	464	250	214	15	15	..
	20 and over	2,738	2,077	661	530	492	38	2,208	1,585	623	129	125	4
	Unspecified ..	19,516	10,573	8,943	152	152	..	19,364	10,421	8,943	..	..	..
	HINDU	1,313	891	422	374	335	39	939	556	383	66	64	2
	0—5	170	93	77	..	..	..	170	93	77	..	..	..
	5—10	120	63	57	9	7	2	111	56	55	..	..	..
	10—15	96	48	48	14	12	2	82	36	46	..	..	..
	15—20	163	101	62	53	46	7	110	55	55	7	7	..
	20 and over	762	585	177	298	270	28	464	315	149	59	57	2
	Unspecified ..	2	1	1	..	..	..	2	1	1	..	..	..
	SIKH	117	89	28	47	45	2	70	44	26	8	8	..
	0—5	16	8	8	..	..	..	16	8	8	..	..	..
	5—10	8	5	3	1	1	..	7	4	3	..	..	..
	10—15	6	4	2	2	2	..	4	2	2	..	..	..
	15—20	14	10	4	6	5	1	8	5	3	2	2	..
	20 and over	73	62	11	38	37	1	35	25	10	6	6	..
	Unspecified ..	..	..	..	..	..	..	..	..	..	..	..	..
	MUSLIM	22,769	12,722	10,047	363	355	8	22,406	12,367	10,039	60	59	1
	0—5	466	244	222	..	..	..	466	244	222	..	..	..
	5—10	286	152	134	3	3	..	283	149	134	..	..	..
	10—15	248	125	123	6	5	1	242	120	122	..	..	..
	15—20	367	210	157	21	20	1	346	190	156	5	5	..
	20 and over	1,888	1,419	469	181	175	6	1,707	1,244	463	55	54	1
	Unspecified ..	19,514	10,572	8,942	152	152	..	19,362	10,420	8,942	..	..	..
	CHRISTIAN ..	25	19	6	17	14	3	8	5	3	12	11	1
	0—5	2	1	1	..	..	..	2	1	1	..	..	..
	5—10	4	3	1	2	2	..	2	1	1	1	1	..
	10—15	3	3	..	1	1	..	2	2	..	1	1	..
	15—20	1	1	..	1	1	..	..	..	..	1	1	..
	20 and over	15	11	4	13	10	3	2	1	1	9	8	1
	Unspecified	..	..	..	..	..	..	..	..	..	..	..	..
SIBI.	ALL RELIGIONS ..	143,005	79,983	63,022	2,864	2,563	301	140,141	77,420	62,721	634	560	74
	0—5	1,478	806	672	..	..	..	1,478	806	672	..	..	..
	5—10	1,137	641	496	96	62	34	1,041	579	462	18	14	4
	10—15	1,033	593	440	145	100	45	888	493	395	28	25	3
	15—20	1,374	910	464	283	233	50	1,091	677	414	76	69	7
	20 and over	8,226	6,045	2,181	1,640	1,468	172	6,586	4,577	2,009	501	441	60
	Unspecified	129,757	70,988	58,769	700	700	..	129,057	70,288	58,769	11	11	..
	Administered Area ..	*74,533*	*40,452*	*34,081*	*602*	*602*	..	*73,931*	*39,850*	*34,081*	*10*	*10*	..
	Mari Bugti Country ..	*55,224*	*30,536*	*24,688*	*98*	*98*	..	*55,126*	*30,438*	*24,688*	*1*	*1*	..
	HINDU	5,893	3,713	2,180	1,301	1,180	121	4,592	2,533	2,059	249	239	10
	0—5	414	221	193	..	..	..	414	221	193	..	..	..
	5—10	308	162	146	42	24	18	266	138	128	4	3	1
	10—15	283	155	128	63	40	23	220	115	105	7	7	..
	15—20	411	283	128	139	120	19	272	163	109	28	27	1
	20 and over	2,247	1,667	580	772	711	61	1,475	956	519	210	202	8
	Unspecified ..	2,230	1,225	1,005	285	285	..	1,945	940	1,005	..	..	..
	Administered Area ..	*1,909*	*1,057*	*852*	*241*	*241*	..	*1,668*	*816*	*852*	..	..	..
	Mari Bugti Country ..	*321*	*168*	*153*	*44*	*44*	..	*277*	*124*	*153*	..	..	..
	SIKH	1,127	755	372	297	235	62	830	520	310	57	54	3
	0—5	76	32	44	..	..	..	76	32	44	..	..	..
	5—10	51	23	28	12	5	7	39	18	21	..	..	..
	10—15	47	24	23	19	8	11	28	16	12	..	..	..
	15—20	88	56	32	42	32	10	46	24	22	1	1	..
	20 and over ..	440	338	102	212	178	34	228	160	68	11	11	..
	Unspecified ..	425	282	143	12	12	..	413	270	143	45	42	3
	Administered Area ..	*425*	*282*	*143*	*12*	*12*	..	*413*	*270*	*143*	..	..	..
	Mari Bugti Country ..	..	..	..	..	..	..	..	..	..	..	..	..
	MUSLIM	135,710	75,342	60,368	1,124	1,061	63	134,586	74,281	60,305	189	183	6
	0—5	944	527	417	..	..	..	944	527	417	..	..	..
	5—10	749	436	313	29	23	6	720	413	307	1	1	..
	10—15	684	401	283	51	42	9	633	359	274	8	7	1
	15—20	854	557	297	92	76	16	762	481	281	27	26	1
	20 and over ..	5,377	3,940	1,437	549	517	32	4,828	3,423	1,405	142	138	4
	Unspecified	127,102	69,481	57,621	403	403	..	126,699	69,078	57,621	11	11	..
	Administered Area ..	*72,199*	*39,113*	*33,086*	*349*	*349*	..	*71,850*	*38,764*	*33,086*	*10*	*10*	..
	Mari Bugti Country ..	*54,903*	*30,358*	*24,535*	*54*	*54*	..	*54,849*	*30,314*	*24,535*	*1*	*1*	..
	CHRISTIAN ..	234	139	95	134	79	55	100	60	40	131	76	55
	0—5	39	24	15	..	..	..	39	24	15	..	..	..
	5—10	25	17	8	13	10	3	12	7	5	13	10	3
	10—15	17	12	5	12	10	2	5	2	3	12	10	2
	15—20	16	9	7	10	5	5	6	4	2	10	5	5
	20 and over ..	137	77	60	99	54	45	38	23	15	96	51	45
	Unspecified ..	..	..	..	..	..	..	..	..	..	..	..	..
	OTHERS	41	34	7	8	8	..	33	26	7	8	8	..
	0—5	5	2	3	..	..	..	5	2	3	..	..	..
	5—10	4	3	1	..	..	..	4	3	1	..	..	..
	10—15	2	1	1	..	..	..	2	1	1	..	..	..
	15—20	5	5	..	..	..	..	5	5	..	..	..	..
	20 and over ..	25	23	2	8	8	..	17	15	2	8	8	..
	Unspecified ..	..	..	..	..	..	..	..	..	..	..	..	..

TABLE XIII.—LITERACY BY RELIGION AND AGE—DISTRIBUTION BY DISTRICTS AND STATES.

District or State.	Religion and Age.	POPULATION.									LITERATE IN ENGLISH.		
		TOTAL.			LITERATE.			ILLITERATE.					
		Persons.	Males.	Females.	Persons.	Males.	Females.	Persons.	Males.	Females.	Persons.	Males.	Females.
1	2	3	4	5	6	7	8	9	10	11	12	13	14
KALAT STATE.	**ALL RELIGIONS** ..	**342,101**	**184,915**	**157,186**	**4,101**	**4,045**	**56**	**338,000**	**180,870**	**157,130**	**102**	**100**	**2**
	0—5 ..	182	92	90	..	..	..	182	92	90	..	..	..
	5—10 ..	123	67	56	7	5	2	116	62	54	..	..	..
	10—15 ..	102	54	48	11	8	3	91	46	45	..	..	..
	15—20 ..	180	123	57	27	24	3	153	99	54	10	10	..
	20 and over ..	912	730	182	195	185	10	717	545	172	71	69	2
	Unspecified ..	340,602	183,849	156,753	3,861	3,823	38	336,741	180,026	156,715	21	21	..
	Sarawan ..	*28,285*	*15,404*	*12,881*	*586*	*556*	*30*	*27,699*	*14,848*	*12,851*	*2*	*2*	..
	Jhalawan ..	*88,916*	*47,925*	*40,991*	*255*	*255*	..	*88,661*	*47,670*	*40,991*	*5*	*5*	..
	Kachhi ..	*105,805*	*57,764*	*48,041*	*2,055*	*2,049*	*6*	*103,750*	*55,715*	*48,035*	*8*	*8*	..
	Dombki Kaheri Country	*26,953*	*14,553*	*12,400*	*507*	*507*	..	*26,446*	*14,046*	*12,400*	..	..	..
	Makran ..	*67,285*	*35,700*	*31,585*	*273*	*273*	..	*67,012*	*35,427*	*31,585*	*6*	*6*	..
	Kharan ..	*23,358*	*12,503*	*10,855*	*185*	*183*	*2*	*23,173*	*12,320*	*10,853*	..	..	..
	HINDU ..	**10,806**	**5,841**	**4,965**	**2,298**	**2,251**	**47**	**8,508**	**3,590**	**4,918**	**34**	**33**	**1**
	0—5 ..	27	19	8	..	..	..	27	19	8	..	..	..
	5—10 ..	20	10	10	4	2	2	16	8	8	..	..	..
	10—15 ..	16	8	8	5	3	2	11	5	6	..	..	..
	15—20 ..	25	18	7	13	10	3	12	8	4	5	5	..
	20 and over ..	145	114	31	83	77	6	62	37	25	26	25	1
	Unspecified ..	10,573	5,672	4,901	2,193	2,159	34	8,380	3,513	4,867	3	3	..
	Sarawan ..	*635*	*334*	*301*	*87*	*57*	*30*	*548*	*277*	*271*	..	..	..
	Jhalawan ..	*191*	*155*	*36*	*31*	*31*	..	*160*	*124*	*36*	..	..	..
	Kachhi ..	*6,993*	*3,725*	*3,268*	*1,645*	*1,641*	*4*	*5,348*	*2,084*	*3,264*	*1*	*1*	..
	Dombki Kaheri Country	*2,588*	*1,309*	*1,279*	*406*	*406*	..	*2,182*	*903*	*1,279*	..	..	..
	Makran ..	*126*	*124*	*2*	*9*	*9*	..	*117*	*115*	*2*	*2*	*2*	..
	Kharan ..	*40*	*25*	*15*	*15*	*15*	..	*25*	*10*	*15*	..	..	..
	SIKH ..	**42**	**31**	**11**	**13**	**13**	..	**29**	**18**	**11**	**10**	**10**	..
	0—5 ..	..	..	..	..	..	..	..	..	..	..	..	..
	5—10 ..	..	..	..	..	..	..	..	..	..	..	..	..
	10—15 ..	..	..	..	..	..	..	..	..	..	..	..	..
	15—20 ..	1	1	..	1	1	..	..	..	..	1	1	..
	20 and over ..	10	10	..	10	10	..	..	..	..	9	9	..
	Unspecified ..	31	20	11	2	2	..	29	18	11	..	..	..
	Sarawan ..	*7*	*5*	*2*	..	..	..	*7*	*5*	*2*	..	..	..
	Jhalawan ..	..	..	..	..	..	..	..	..	..	..	..	..
	Kachhi ..	*6*	*5*	*1*	*1*	*1*	..	*5*	*4*	*1*	..	..	..
	Dombki Kaheri Country	*16*	*8*	*8*	..	..	..	*16*	*8*	*8*	..	..	..
	Makran ..	*2*	*2*	..	*1*	*1*	..	*1*	*1*	..	..	..	..
	Kharan ..	..	..	..	..	..	..	..	..	..	..	..	..
	MUSLIM ..	**331,234**	**179,027**	**152,207**	**1,778**	**1,770**	**8**	**329,456**	**177,257**	**152,199**	**46**	**46**	..
	0—5 ..	154	73	81	..	..	..	154	73	81	..	..	..
	5—10 ..	103	57	46	3	3	..	100	54	46	..	..	..
	10—15 ..	86	46	40	6	5	1	80	41	39	..	..	..
	15—20 ..	152	102	50	12	12	..	140	90	50	3	3	..
	20 and over ..	742	593	149	91	88	3	651	505	146	25	25	..
	Unspecified ..	329,997	178,156	151,841	1,666	1,662	4	328,331	176,494	151,837	18	18	..
	Sarawan ..	*27,643*	*15,065*	*12,578*	*499*	*499*	..	*27,144*	*14,566*	*12,578*	*2*	*2*	..
	Jhalawan ..	*88,725*	*47,770*	*40,955*	*224*	*224*	..	*88,501*	*47,546*	*40,955*	*5*	*5*	..
	Kachhi ..	*98,806*	*54,034*	*44,772*	*409*	*407*	*2*	*98,397*	*53,627*	*44,770*	*7*	*7*	..
	Dombki Kaheri Country	*24,349*	*13,236*	*11,113*	*101*	*101*	..	*24,248*	*13,135*	*11,113*	..	..	..
	Makran ..	*67,156*	*35,573*	*31,583*	*253*	*253*	..	*66,893*	*35,310*	*31,583*	*4*	*4*	..
	Kharan ..	*23,318*	*12,478*	*10,840*	*170*	*168*	*2*	*23,148*	*12,310*	*10,838*	..	..	..
	CHRISTIAN ..	**15**	**12**	**3**	**10**	**9**	**1**	**5**	**3**	**2**	**10**	**9**	**1**
	0—5 ..	1	..	1	..	..	..	1	..	1	..	..	..
	5—10 ..	..	..	..	..	..	..	..	..	..	..	..	..
	10—15 ..	..	..	..	..	..	..	..	..	..	..	..	..
	15—20 ..	1	1	..	..	..	..	1	1	..	..	..	..
	20 and over ..	12	10	2	10	9	1	2	1	1	10	9	1
	Unspecified ..	1	1	..	..	..	..	1	1	..	..	..	..
	Sarawan ..	..	..	..	..	..	..	..	..	..	..	..	..
	Jhalawan ..	..	..	..	..	..	..	..	..	..	..	..	..
	Kachhi ..	..	..	..	..	..	..	..	..	..	..	..	..
	Dombki Kaheri Country	..	..	..	..	..	..	..	..	..	..	..	..
	Makran ..	*1*	*1*	..	..	..	..	*1*	*1*	..	..	..	..
	Kharan ..	..	..	..	..	..	..	..	..	..	..	..	..
	OTHERS ..	**4**	**4**	..	**2**	**2**	..	**2**	**2**	..	**2**	**2**	—
	0—5 ..	..	..	..	..	..	..	..	..	..	..	..	..
	5—10 ..	..	..	..	..	..	..	..	..	..	..	..	..
	10—15 ..	..	..	..	..	..	..	..	..	..	..	..	..
	15—20 ..	1	1	..	1	1	..	..	..	..	1	1	..
	20 and over ..	3	3	..	1	1	..	2	2	..	1	1	..
	Unspecified ..	—	—	..	..	..	..	..	..	..	..	..	..

TABLE XIII.—LITERACY BY RELIGION AND AGE—DISTRIBUTION BY DISTRICTS AND STATES—(concld.)

District or State.	Religion and Age.	POPULATION.									LITERATE IN ENGLISH.		
		TOTAL.			LITERATE.			ILLITERATE.					
		Persons.	Males.	Females.	Persons.	Males.	Females.	Persons.	Males.	Females.	Persons.	Males.	Females.
1	2	3	4	5	6	7	8	9	10	11	12	13	14
LAS BELA STATE.	**ALL RELIGIONS** ..	**63,008**	**33,495**	**29,513**	**830**	**804**	**26**	**62,178**	**32,691**	**29,487**	**24**	**24**	..
	0—5	..	..	..	..	..	..	..	..	..	..	..	..
	5—10	..	..	..	..	..	..	..	..	..	..	..	..
	10—15	..	..	..	..	..	..	..	..	..	..	..	..
	15—20	..	..	..	..	..	..	..	..	..	..	..	..
	20 and over	..	..	..	..	..	..	..	..	..	..	..	..
	Unspecified ..	63,008	33,495	29,513	830	804	26	62,178	32,691	29,487	24	24	..
	HINDU ..	**1,443**	**810**	**633**	**405**	**405**	..	**1,038**	**405**	**633**	**5**	**5**	..
	0—5	..	..	..	..	..	..	..	..	..	..	..	..
	5—10	..	..	..	..	..	..	..	..	..	..	..	..
	10—15	..	..	..	..	..	..	..	..	..	..	..	..
	15—20	..	..	..	..	..	..	..	..	..	..	..	..
	20 and over	..	..	..	..	..	..	..	..	..	..	..	..
	Unspecified ..	1,443	810	633	405	405	..	1,038	405	633	5	5	..
	SIKH ..	**15**	**12**	**3**	**5**	**5**	..	**10**	**7**	**3**	..	..	..
	0—5	..	..	..	..	..	..	..	..	..	..	..	..
	5—10	..	..	..	..	..	..	..	..	..	..	..	..
	10—15	..	..	..	..	..	..	..	..	..	..	..	..
	15—20	..	..	..	..	..	..	..	..	..	..	..	..
	20 and over	..	..	..	..	..	..	..	..	..	..	..	..
	Unspecified ..	15	12	3	5	5	..	10	7	3	..	..	..
	MUSLIM ..	**61,550**	**32,673**	**28,877**	**420**	**394**	**26**	**61,130**	**32,279**	**28,851**	**19**	**19**	..
	0—5	..	..	..	..	..	..	..	..	..	..	..	..
	5—10	..	..	..	..	..	..	..	..	..	..	..	..
	10—15	..	..	..	..	..	..	..	..	..	..	..	..
	15—20	..	..	..	..	..	..	..	..	..	..	..	..
	20 and over	..	..	..	..	..	..	..	..	..	..	..	..
	Unspecified	61,550	32,673	28,877	420	394	26	61,130	32,279	28,851	19	19	..

TABLE XIV.

LITERACY BY SELECTED CASTES, TRIBES OR RACES.

The numbers of literates and illiterates shown in this table are the same as those in Imperial Table XIII. In the beginning a summary for the whole Province giving totals separately for the indigenous population and for aliens has been given. These are followed by details for Districts and States and for the various indigenous and semi-indigenous tribes and the races to which they belong. Totals for the indigenous population by races are shown below :—

Races or Tribes.	TOTAL.	LITERATE.	ILLITERATE	LITERATE IN ENGLISH.
	Persons.	Persons.	Persons.	Persons.
I. MUSLIM	765,094	6,117	758,977	445
A. Baloch	227,846	964	226,882	48
B. Brahui	152,588	1,012	151,576	43
C. Pathan	193,025	2,314	190,711	251
D. Lasi	31,812	115	31,697	..
E. Jatt	77,157	318	76,839	6
F. Sayyid	21,976	587	21,389	40
G. Other Muslims ..	60,690	807	59,883	57
II. HINDU	16,905	4,084	12,821	39
III. SIKH	48	12	36	..

TABLE XIV.—LITERACY BY SELECTED CASTES, TRIBES, OR RACES.

Caste, Tribe or Race.	Locality.	Population. Total. P.	M.	F.	Literate. P.	M.	F.	Illiterate. P.	M.	F.	Literate in English. P.	M.	F.
1	2	3	4	5	6	7	8	9	10	11	12	13	14
SUMMARY.													
TOTAL ..		868,617	488,414	380,203	40,775	36,835	3,940	827,842	451,579	376,263	11,588	10,063	1,525
I. Indigenous and Semi-Indigenous ..	..	782,047	425,147	356,900	10,213	9,966	247	771,834	415,181	356,653	484	477	7
(a) Muslim ..	..	765,094	415,937	349,157	6,117	5,987	130	758,977	409,950	349,027	445	438	7
(b) Hindu ..	..	16,905	9,175	7,730	4,084	3,968	116	12,821	5,207	7,614	39	39	..
(c) Others ..	..	48	35	13	12	11	1	36	24	12	..	..	..
II. Aliens ..	..	86,570	63,267	23,303	30,562	26,869	3,693	56,008	36,398	19,610	11,104	9,586	1,518
(a) Muslim ..	..	32,999	24,152	8,847	6,539	6,106	433	26,460	18,046	8,414	1,610	1,559	51
(b) Hindu ..	..	36,776	27,005	9,771	14,277	12,890	1,387	22,499	14,115	8,384	3,173	3,081	92
(c) Sikh ..	..	8,377	6,235	2,142	4,181	3,658	523	4,196	2,577	1,619	987	930	57
(d) Christian ..	..	8,059	5,637	2,422	5,369	4,075	1,294	2,690	1,562	1,128	5,198	3,934	1,264
(e) Others ..	..	359	238	121	196	140	56	163	98	65	136	82	54
INDIGENOUS AND SEMI-INDIGENOUS RACES AND TRIBES.													
I. MUSLIM ..	Baluchistan ..	765,094	415,937	349,157	6,117	5,987	130	758,977	409,950	349,027	445	438	7
	Districts ..	373,294	204,862	168,432	4,035	3,937	98	369,259	200,925	168,334	409	402	7
	States ..	391,800	211,075	180,725	2,082	2,050	32	389,718	209,025	180,693	36	36	..
A. Baloch ..	Baluchistan ..	227,846	123,852	103,994	964	953	11	226,882	122,899	103,983	48	48	..
	Districts ..	114,150	62,677	51,473	491	483	8	113,659	62,194	51,465	47	47	..
	States ..	113,696	61,175	52,521	473	470	3	113,223	60,705	52,518	1	1	..
(i) Eastern, Indigenous—													
Bugti ..	Baluchistan ..	30,613	16,797	13,816	45	45	..	30,568	16,752	13,816	5	5	..
	Districts ..	29,756	16,354	13,402	44	44	..	29,712	16,310	13,402	5	5	..
	States ..	857	443	414	1	1	..	856	442	414	..	..	..
Dombki ..	Baluchistan ..	7,241	3,943	3,298	38	38	..	7,203	3,905	3,298	7	7	..
	Districts ..	1,987	1,070	917	17	17	..	1,970	1,053	917	7	7	..
	States ..	5,254	2,873	2,381	21	21	..	5,233	2,852	2,381	..	..	..
Khetran ..	Baluchistan ..	17,162	8,997	8,165	70	70	..	17,092	8,927	8,165	9	9	..
	Districts ..	17,044	8,931	8,113	70	70	..	16,974	8,861	8,113	9	9	..
	States ..	118	66	52	..	..	..	118	66	52	..	..	..
Magasi ..	Baluchistan ..	13,286	7,212	6,074	34	34	..	13,252	7,178	6,074	..	..	..
	Districts ..	284	153	131	5	5	..	279	148	131	..	..	..
	States ..	13,002	7,059	5,943	29	29	..	12,973	7,030	5,943	..	..	..
Mari ..	Baluchistan ..	35,254	19,700	15,554	66	66	..	35,188	19,634	15,554	1	1	..
	Districts ..	34,304	19,223	15,081	50	50	..	34,254	19,173	15,081	1	1	..
	States ..	950	477	473	16	16	..	934	461	473	..	..	..
Rind Eastern ..	Baluchistan ..	43,322	23,688	19,634	180	179	1	43,142	23,509	19,633	11	11	..
	Districts ..	16,607	9,036	7,571	134	133	1	16,473	8,903	7,570	10	10	..
	States ..	26,715	14,652	12,063	46	46	..	26,669	14,606	12,063	1	1	..
Umrani ..	Baluchistan ..	2,641	1,433	1,208	1	1	..	2,640	1,432	1,208	..	..	..
	Districts ..	2,327	1,269	1,058	1	1	..	2,326	1,268	1,058	..	..	..
	States ..	314	164	150	..	..	..	314	164	150	..	..	..
Unspecified ..	Baluchistan ..	845	484	361	9	9	..	836	475	361	1	1	..
	Districts ..	367	246	121	7	7	..	360	239	121	1	1	..
	States ..	478	238	240	2	2	..	476	236	240	..	..	..
(ii) Western, Indigenous—													
Buledi ..	Baluchistan ..	158	84	74	..	..	..	158	84	74	..	..	..
	Districts ..	..	..	..	..	..	..	..	..	..	..	..	..
	States ..	158	84	74	..	..	..	158	84	74	..	..	..
Dashti ..	Baluchistan ..	996	543	453	8	8	..	988	535	453	..	..	..
	Districts ..	6	6	..	..	..	..	6	6	..	..	..	..
	States ..	990	537	453	8	8	..	982	529	453	..	..	..
Gichki ..	Baluchistan ..	293	142	151	24	24	..	269	118	151	..	..	..
	Districts ..	2	1	1	..	..	..	2	1	1	..	..	..
	States ..	291	141	150	24	24	..	267	117	150	..	..	..
Kaudai ..	Baluchistan ..	2,308	1,231	1,077	12	12	..	2,296	1,219	1,077	..	..	..
	Districts ..	422	232	190	..	..	..	422	232	190	..	..	..
	States ..	1,886	999	887	12	12	..	1,874	987	887	..	..	..
Rais ..	Baluchistan ..	3,951	2,068	1,883	35	35	..	3,916	2,033	1,883	..	..	..
	Districts ..	96	52	44	..	..	..	96	52	44	..	..	..
	States ..	3,855	2,016	1,839	35	35	..	3,820	1,981	1,839	..	..	..
Rakshani	Baluchistan ..	24,106	13,104	11,002	256	254	2	23,850	12,850	11,000	4	4	..
	Districts ..	6,580	3,635	2,945	91	91	..	6,489	3,544	2,945	4	4	..
	States ..	17,526	9,469	8,057	165	163	2	17,361	9,306	8,055	..	..	..

P= Persons ; M= Males ; F= Females.

TABLE XIV.—LITERACY BY SELECTED CASTES, TRIBES, OR RACES.

Caste, Tribe or Race.	Locality.	Population: Total P.	Total M.	Total F.	Literate P.	Literate M.	Literate F.	Illiterate P.	Illiterate M.	Illiterate F.	Literate in English P.	Literate in English M.	Literate in English F.
1	2	3	4	5	6	7	8	9	10	11	12	13	14
Rind Western	Baluchistan	*31,055*	*16,531*	*14,524*	*55*	*52*	*3*	*31,000*	*16,479*	*14,521*	*1*	*1*	..
	Districts	767	434	333	10	8	2	757	426	331	1	1	..
	States	30,288	16,097	14,191	45	44	1	30,243	16,053	14,190	..	..	..
Sangur	Baluchistan	*7,334*	*3,924*	*3,410*	*40*	*40*	..	*7,294*	*3,884*	*3,410*	..	..	..
	Districts	..	..	..	..	..	..	..	..	..	..	..	..
	States	7,334	3,924	3,410	40	40	..	7,294	3,884	3,410	..	..	..
Sanjrani	Baluchistan	*401*	*208*	*193*	*1*	*1*	..	*400*	*207*	*193*	..	..	..
	Districts	367	190	177	..	..	..	367	190	177	..	..	..
	States	34	18	16	1	1	..	33	17	16	..	..	..
Others	Baluchistan	*5,075*	*2,771*	*2,304*	*70*	*66*	*4*	*5,005*	*2,705*	*2,300*	*7*	*7*	..
	Districts	1,468	871	597	42	38	4	1,426	833	593	7	7	..
	States	3,607	1,900	1,707	28	28	..	3,579	1,872	1,707	..	..	..
(iii) Semi-Indigenous.													
Buzdar	Baluchistan	*1,738*	*953*	*785*	*19*	*18*	*1*	*1,719*	*935*	*784*	*2*	*2*	..
	Districts	1,699	935	764	19	18	1	1,680	917	763	2	2	..
	States	39	18	21	..	..	..	39	18	21	..	..	..
Others	Baluchistan	*67*	*39*	*28*	*1*	*1*	..	*66*	*38*	*28*	..	..	..
	Districts	67	39	28	1	1	..	66	38	28	..	..	..
B. Brahui	Baluchistan	*152,588*	*83,528*	*69,060*	*1,012*	*1,004*	*8*	*151,576*	*82,524*	*69,052*	*43*	*43*	..
	Districts	26,741	15,231	11,510	372	368	4	26,369	14,863	11,506	33	33	..
	States	125,847	68,297	57,550	640	636	4	125,207	67,661	57,546	10	10	..
(i) Original Nucleus.													
Ahmadzai	Baluchistan	*77*	*30*	*47*	*13*	*12*	*1*	*64*	*18*	*46*	*1*	*1*	..
	Districts	44	20	24	13	12	1	31	8	23	1	1	..
	States	33	10	23	..	..	..	33	10	23	..	..	..
Gurgnari	Baluchistan	*1,466*	*798*	*668*	*8*	*8*	..	*1,458*	*790*	*668*	..	..	..
	Districts	28	18	10	..	..	..	28	18	10	..	..	..
	States	1,438	780	658	8	8	..	1,430	772	658	..	..	..
Iltazai	Baluchistan	*202*	*112*	*90*	*1*	*1*	..	*201*	*111*	*90*	..	..	..
	States	202	112	90	1	1	..	201	111	90	..	..	..
Kalandrari	Baluchistan	*1,330*	*750*	*580*	*21*	*21*	..	*1,309*	*729*	*580*	..	..	..
	Districts	173	110	63	5	5	..	168	105	63	..	..	..
	States	1,157	640	517	16	16	..	1,141	624	517	..	..	..
Kambrari	Baluchistan	*2,065*	*1,142*	*923*	*19*	*19*	..	*2,046*	*1,123*	*923*	*2*	*2*	..
	Districts	547	303	244	18	18	..	529	285	244	2	2	..
	States	1,518	839	679	1	1	..	1,517	838	679	..	..	..
Mirwari	Baluchistan	*1,878*	*980*	*898*	*7*	*7*	..	*1,871*	*973*	*898*	..	..	..
	States	1,878	980	898	7	7	..	1,871	973	898	..	..	..
Rodeni	Baluchistan	*1,335*	*734*	*601*	*8*	*8*	..	*1,327*	*726*	*601*	..	..	..
	Districts	101	54	47	4	4	..	97	50	47	..	..	..
	States	1,234	680	554	4	4	..	1,230	676	554	..	..	..
Sumalari	Baluchistan	*4,605*	*2,516*	*2,089*	*52*	*52*	..	*4,553*	*2,464*	*2,089*	..	..	..
	Districts	1,790	1,010	780	20	20	..	1,770	990	780	..	..	..
	States	2,815	1,506	1,309	32	32	..	2,783	1,474	1,309	..	..	..
(ii) Sarawan.													
Bangulzai	Baluchistan	*7,389*	*4,083*	*3,306*	*54*	*53*	*1*	*7,335*	*4,030*	*3,305*	*2*	*2*	..
	Districts	2,226	1,301	925	31	31	..	2,195	1,270	925	2	2	..
	States	5,163	2,782	2,381	23	22	1	5,140	2,760	2,380	..	..	..
Kurd	Baluchistan	*2,230*	*1,235*	*995*	*26*	*26*	..	*2,204*	*1,209*	*995*	..	..	..
	Districts	542	327	215	9	9	..	533	318	215	..	..	..
	States	1,688	908	780	17	17	..	1,671	891	780	..	..	..
Lahri	Baluchistan	*4,490*	*2,528*	*1,962*	*47*	*47*	..	*4,443*	*2,481*	*1,962*	*5*	*5*	..
	Districts	1,403	808	595	30	30	..	1,373	778	595	1	1	..
	States	3,087	1,720	1,367	17	17	..	3,070	1,703	1,367	4	4	..
Langav	Baluchistan	*6,648*	*3,631*	*3,017*	*30*	*30*	..	*6,618*	*3,601*	*3,017*	*2*	*2*	..
	Districts	2,262	1,245	1,017	9	9	..	2,253	1,236	1,017	..	..	..
	States	4,386	2,386	2,000	21	21	..	4,365	2,365	2,000	2	2	..
Mamashahi	Baluchistan	*2,728*	*1,535*	*1,193*	*50*	*50*	..	*2,678*	*1,485*	*1,193*	..	..	..
	Districts	566	353	213	8	8	..	558	345	213	..	..	..
	States	2,162	1,182	980	42	42	..	2,120	1,140	980	..	..	..
Raisani	Baluchistan	*2,716*	*1,500*	*1,216*	*33*	*33*	..	*2,683*	*1,467*	*1,216*	*1*	*1*	..
	Districts	653	394	259	9	9	..	644	385	259	1	1	..
	States	2,063	1,106	957	24	24	..	2,039	1,082	957	..	..	..
Rustumzai	Baluchistan	*243*	*141*	*102*	*16*	*16*	..	*227*	*125*	*102*	*1*	*1*	..
	Districts	113	67	46	2	2	..	111	65	46	1	1	..
	States	130	74	56	14	14	..	116	60	56	..	..	..

P= Persons; M= Males; F= Females.

TABLE XIV.—LITERACY BY SELECTED CASTES, TRIBES, OR RACES.

Caste, Tribe or Race.	Locality.	Population.									Literate in English.		
		Total.			Literate.			Illiterate.					
		P.	M.	F.	P.	M.	F.	P.	M.	F.	P.	M.	F.
1	2	3	4	5	6	7	8	9	10	11	12	13	14
Sarparra ..	Baluchistan ..	1,906	1,029	877	25	25	..	1,881	1,004	877	4	4	..
	Districts ..	317	192	125	9	9	..	308	183	125	4	4	..
	States ..	1,589	837	752	16	16	..	1,573	821	752	..	..	..
Satakzai ..	Baluchistan ..	1,586	923	663	4	4	..	1,582	919	663	..	..	..
	Districts ..	179	112	67	3	3	..	176	109	67	..	..	..
	States ..	1,407	811	596	1	1	..	1,406	810	596	..	..	..
Shahwani ..	Baluchistan ..	6,089	3,362	2,727	114	113	1	5,975	3,249	2,726	4	4	..
	Districts ..	2,326	1,334	992	77	76	1	2,249	1,258	991	4	4	..
	States ..	3,763	2,028	1,735	37	37	..	3,726	1,991	1,735	..	..	..
Zagr Mengal ..	Baluchistan ..	5,823	3,177	2,646	28	28	..	5,795	3,149	2,646	..	..	..
	Districts ..	4,287	2,355	1,932	18	18	..	4,269	2,337	1,932	..	..	..
	States ..	1,536	822	714	10	10	..	1,526	812	714	..	..	..
(iii) Jhalawan.													
Bizanjav ..	Baluchistan ..	13,591	7,651	5,940	39	39	..	13,552	7,612	5,940	..	..	..
	Districts ..	110	62	48	5	5	..	105	57	48	..	..	..
	States ..	13,481	7,589	5,892	34	34	..	13,447	7,555	5,892	..	..	..
Haruni ..	Baluchistan ..	1,612	847	765	3	3	..	1,609	844	765	1	1	..
	Districts ..	130	74	56	2	2	..	128	72	56	1	1	..
	States ..	1,482	773	709	1	1	..	1,481	772	709	..	..	..
Mamasani ..	Baluchistan ..	10,356	5,602	4,754	35	34	1	10,321	5,568	4,753	1	1	..
	Districts ..	3,504	1,890	1,614	28	27	1	3,476	1,863	1,613	1	1	..
	States ..	6,852	3,712	3,140	7	7	..	6,845	3,705	3,140	..	..	..
Mengal ..	Baluchistan ..	26,377	14,344	12,033	104	103	1	26,273	14,241	12,032	12	12	..
	Districts ..	3,218	1,844	1,374	36	35	1	3,182	1,809	1,373	8	8	..
	States ..	23,159	12,500	10,659	68	68	..	23,091	12,432	10,659	4	4	..
Nichari ..	Baluchistan ..	1,705	951	754	1	1	..	1,704	950	754	1	1	..
	Districts ..	138	84	54	1	1	..	137	83	54	1	1	..
	States ..	1,567	867	700	..	..	..	1,567	867	700	..	..	..
Pandrani ..	Baluchistan ..	1,063	572	491	1	1	..	1,062	571	491	..	..	..
	Districts ..	419	227	192	1	1	..	418	226	192	..	..	..
	States ..	644	345	299	..	..	..	644	345	299	..	..	..
Sajdi ..	Baluchistan ..	3,279	1,843	1 436	16	16	..	3,263	1,827	1,436	..	..	..
	States ..	3,279	1,843	1,436	16	16	..	3,263	1,827	1,436	..	..	..
Zahri ..	Baluchistan ..	36,824	19 766	17,059	28	28	..	36,796	19,737	17,059	1	1	..
	Districts ..	625	356	269	5	5	..	620	351	269	1	1	..
	States ..	36,199	19,409	16,790	23	23	..	36,176	19,386	16,790	..	..	..
(iv) Miscellaneous.													
Nighari ..	Baluchistan ..	1,128	608	520	25	25	..	1,103	583	520	..	..	..
	Districts ..	1	1	..	..	..	..	1	1	..	..	..	..
	States ..	1,127	607	520	25	25	..	1,102	582	520	..	..	..
Rekizai ..	Baluchistan ..	534	291	243	19	19	..	515	272	243	..	..	..
	Districts ..	3	2	1	..	..	..	3	2	1	..	..	..
	States ..	531	289	242	19	19	..	512	270	242	..	..	..
Others ..	Baluchistan ..	1,313	848	465	185	182	3	1,128	666	462	5	5	..
	Districts ..	1,036	688	348	29	29	..	1,007	659	348	5	5	..
	States ..	277	160	117	156	153	3	121	7	114	..	..	..
C. Pathan ..	Baluchistan ..	193,025	105,444	87,581	2,314	2,253	61	190,711	103,191	87,520	251	245	
	Districts ..	191,500	104,593	86,907	2,222	2,161	61	189,278	102,432	86,846	246	240	
	States ..	1,525	851	674	92	92	..	1,433	759	674	5	5	..
(i) Indigenous.													
Babi ..	Baluchistan ..	194	103	91	12	12	..	182	91	91	..	..	..
	Districts ..	17	8	9	..	..	..	17	8	9	..	..	..
	States ..	177	95	82	12	12	..	165	83	82	..	..	..
Barech ..	Baluchistan ..	1,610	886	724	51	51	..	1,559	835	724	3	3	..
	Districts ..	1,497	826	671	51	51	..	1,446	775	671	3	3	..
	States ..	113	60	53	..	..	..	113	60	53	..	..	..
Jafar ..	Baluchistan ..	1,479	805	674	32	28	4	1,447	777	670	5	5	..
	Districts ..	1,479	805	674	32	28	4	1,447	777	670	5	5	..
Kakar ..	Baluchistan ..	89,831	49,237	40,594	862	861	1	88,969	48,376	40,593	40	40	..
	Districts ..	89,518	49,061	40,457	850	849	1	88,668	48,212	40,456	39	39	..
	States ..	313	176	137	12	12	..	301	164	137	1	1	..
(a) Dumar ..	Baluchistan ..	7,108	3,964	3,144	39	39	..	7,069	3,926	3,144	5	5	..
	Districts ..	7,094	3,957	3,137	39	39	..	7,055	3,918	3,137	5	5	..
	States ..	14	7	7	..	..	..	14	7	7	..	..	..
(b) Sanzarkhel ..	Baluchistan ..	46,561	25,623	20,938	267	266	1	46,294	25,357	20,937	12	12	..
	Districts ..	46,554	25,619	20,935	265	264	1	46,289	25,355	20,934	12	12	..
	States ..	7	4	3	2	2	..	5	2	3	..	..	..

P= Persons; M= Males; F= Females.

TABLE XIV.—LITERACY BY SELECTED CASTES, TRIBES, OR RACES.

Caste, Tribe or Race.	Locality.	Population.									Literate in English.		
		Total.			Literate.			Illiterate.					
		P.	M.	F.	P.	M.	F.	P.	M.	F.	P.	M.	F.
1	2	3	4	5	6	7	8	9	10	11	12	13	14
(c) Sargara ..	Baluchistan ..	2,000	1,076	924	48	48	..	1,952	1,028	924	1	1	..
	Districts ..	2,000	1,076	924	48	48	..	1,952	1,028	924	1	1	..
(d) Snatia	Baluchistan ..	19,762	10,840	8,922	288	288	..	19,474	10,552	8,922	6	6	..
	Districts ..	19,762	10,840	8,922	288	288	..	19,474	10,552	8,922	6	6	..
(e) Targhara ..	Baluchistan ..	12,170	6,380	5,790	129	129	..	12,041	6,251	5,790	5	5	..
	Districts ..	12,170	6,380	5,790	129	129	..	12,041	6,251	5,790	5	5	..
(f) Others ..	Baluchistan ..	2,230	1,354	876	91	91	..	2,139	1,263	876	11	11	..
	Districts ..	1,938	1,189	749	81	81	..	1,857	1,108	749	10	10	..
	States ..	292	165	127	10	10	..	282	155	127	1	1	..
Kasi ..	Baluchistan ..	1,975	1,055	920	155	154	1	1,820	901	919	19	19	..
	Districts ..	1,960	1,047	913	155	154	1	1,805	893	912	19	19	..
	States ..	15	8	7	..	..	..	15	8	7	..	..	..
Luni ..	Baluchistan ..	3,581	1,881	1,700	25	25	..	3,556	1,856	1,700	..	..	..
	Districts ..	3,581	1,881	1,700	25	25	..	3,556	1,856	1,700	..	..	..
Pani ..	Baluchistan ..	27,701	15,011	12,690	131	130	1	27,570	14,881	12,689	13	13	..
	Districts ..	27,536	14,927	12,609	131	130	1	27,405	14,797	12,608	13	13	..
	States ..	165	84	81	..	..	..	165	84	81	..	..	..
(a) Main Branch ..	Baluchistan ..	4,166	2,209	1,957	15	15	..	4,151	2,194	1,957	1	1	..
	Districts ..	4,001	2,125	1,876	15	15	..	3,986	2,110	1,876	1	1	..
	States ..	165	84	81	..	..	..	165	84	81	..	..	..
(b) Isot ..	Baluchistan ..	2,555	1,352	1,203	11	11	..	2,544	1,341	1,203	..	..	..
	Districts ..	2,555	1,352	1,203	11	11	..	2,544	1,341	1,203	..	..	..
(c) Mandokhel ..	Baluchistan ..	4,635	2,562	2,073	21	21	..	4,614	2,541	2,073	3	3	..
	Districts ..	4,635	2,562	2,073	21	21	..	4,614	2,541	2,073	3	3	..
(d) Musakhel ..	Baluchistan ..	13,578	7,376	6,202	56	56	..	13,522	7,320	6,202	4	4	..
	Districts ..	13,578	7,376	6,202	56	56	..	13,522	7,320	6,202	4	4	..
(e) Zarkun ..	Baluchistan ..	2,123	1,141	982	22	21	1	2,101	1,120	981	5	5	..
	Districts ..	2,123	1,141	982	22	21	1	2,101	1,120	981	5	5	..
(f) Laun ..	Baluchistan ..	543	305	238	..	..	..	543	305	238	..	..	..
	Districts ..	543	305	238	..	..	..	543	305	238	..	..	..
(g) Pani Unspecified ..	Baluchistan ..	101	66	35	6	6	..	95	60	35	..	..	..
	Districts ..	101	66	35	6	6	..	95	60	35	..	..	..
Shirani ..	Baluchistan ..	8,416	4,446	3,970	21	21	..	8,395	4,425	3,970	4	4	..
	Districts ..	8,398	4,433	3,965	21	21	..	8,377	4,412	3,965	4	4	..
	States ..	18	13	5	..	..	..	18	13	5	..	..	..
Tarin ..	Baluchistan ..	36,754	19,557	17,197	270	269	1	36,484	19,288	17,196	16	16	..
	Districts ..	36,662	19,509	17,153	267	266	1	36,395	19,243	17,152	16	16	..
	States ..	92	48	44	3	3	..	89	45	44	..	..	..
(a) Abdal Achakzai	Baluchistan ..	19,796	10,913	8,883	128	128	..	19,668	10,785	8,883	3	3	..
	Districts ..	19,791	10,912	8,879	127	127	..	19,664	10,785	8,879	3	3	..
	States ..	5	1	4	1	1	..	4	--	4	..	..	..
(b) Spin Tar ..	Baluchistan ..	9,709	5,090	4,619	34	34	..	9,675	5,056	4,619	5	5	..
	Districts ..	9,708	5,089	4,619	34	34	..	9,674	5,055	4,619	5	5	..
	States ..	1	1	..	..	..	..	1	1	..	..	..	..
(c) Tor Tarin ..	Baluchistan ..	6,737	3,229	3,508	81	80	1	6,656	3,149	3,507	2	2	..
	Districts ..	6,669	3,191	3,478	81	80	1	6,588	3,111	3,477	2	2	..
	States ..	68	38	30	..	..	..	68	38	30	..	..	..
(d) Others ..	Baluchistan ..	512	325	187	27	27	..	485	298	187	6	6	..
	Districts ..	494	317	177	25	25	..	469	292	177	6	6	..
	States ..	18	8	10	2	2	..	16	6	10	..	..	..
Zmarai ..	Baluchistan ..	2,889	1,526	1,363	18	18	..	2,871	1,508	1,363	..	..	..
	Districts ..	2,889	1,526	1,363	18	18	..	2,871	1,508	1,363	..	..	..
Others Pathans ..	Baluchistan ..	1,577	965	612	178	164	14	1,399	801	598	35	35	..
	Districts ..	1,274	796	478	150	136	14	1,124	660	464	32	32	..
	States ..	303	169	134	28	28	.	275	141	134	3	3	..
(ii) Semi-Indigenous.													
Durrani ..	Baluchistan ..	2,410	1,541	869	282	250	32	2,128	1,291	837	83	79	4
	Districts ..	2,224	1,428	796	260	228	32	1,964	1,200	764	83	79	4
	States ..	186	113	73	22	22	..	164	91	73	..	..	..
Ghilzai ..	Baluchistan ..	14,109	8,102	6,007	230	224	6	13,879	7,878	6,001	23	21	2
	Districts ..	13,970	8,021	5,949	218	212	6	13,752	7,809	5,943	22	20	2
	States ..	139	81	58	12	12	..	127	69	58	1	1	..
Other Pathans ..	Baluchistan ..	499	329	170	47	46	1	452	283	169	10	10	..
	Districts ..	495	325	170	44	43	1	451	282	169	10	10	..
	States ..	4	4	..	3	3	..	1	1	..	..	..	..

P= Persons ; M= Males ; F= Females.

TABLE XIV.—LITERACY BY SELECTED CASTES, TRIBES, OR RACES.

CASTE, TRIBE OR RACE.	LOCALITY.	POPULATION.									LITERATE IN ENGLISH.		
		TOTAL.			LITERATE.			ILLITERATE.					
		P.	M.	F.	P.	M.	F.	P.	M.	F.	P.	M.	F.
1	2	3	4	5	6	7	8	9	10	11	12	13	14
D. Lasi ..	Baluchistan ..	31,812	16,635	15,177	115	115	..	31,697	16,520	15,177	..	..	..
	Districts ..	44	25	19	..	..	..	44	25	19	..	..	..
	States ..	31,768	16,610	15,158	115	115	..	31,653	16,495	15,158	..	..	..
E. Jatt ..	Baluchistan ..	77,157	42,227	34,930	318	318	..	76,839	41,909	34,930	6	6	..
	Districts ..	14,704	8,267	6,437	79	79	..	14,625	8,188	6,437	4	4	..
	States ..	62,453	33,960	28,493	239	239	..	62,214	33,721	28,493	2	2	..
F. Sayyid ..	Baluchistan ..	21,976	11,127	10,849	587	578	9	21,389	10,549	10,840	40	40	..
	Districts ..	18,070	9,075	8,995	365	358	7	17,705	8,717	8,988	33	33	..
	States ..	3,906	2,052	1,854	222	220	2	3,684	1,832	1,852	7	7	..
G. Other Muslims ..	Baluchistan ..	60,690	33,124	27,566	807	766	41	59,883	32,358	27,525	57	56	1
	Districts ..	8,085	4,994	3,091	506	488	18	7,579	4,506	3,073	46	45	1
	States ..	52,605	28,130	24,475	301	278	23	52,304	27,852	24,452	11	11	..
(i) INDIGENOUS.													
Darzada ..	Baluchistan ..	9,339	4,831	4,608	60	60	..	9,279	4,771	4,508	..	..	..
	Districts ..	29	18	11	..	..	..	29	18	11	..	..	..
	States ..	9,310	4,813	4,497	60	60	..	9,250	4,753	4,497	..	..	..
Dehwar ..	Baluchistan ..	5,317	2,934	2,383	69	68	1	5,248	2,866	2,382	1	1	
	Districts ..	517	315	202	16	15	1	501	300	201	1	1	
	States ..	4,800	2,619	2,181	53	53	..	4,747	2,566	2,181	..	..	..
Gadra ..	Baluchistan ..	7,935	4,539	3,396	..	..	..	7,935	4,539	3,396	..	..	..
	States ..	7,935	4,539	3,396	..	..	..	7,935	4,539	3,396	..	..	..
Gola ..	Baluchistan ..	477	264	213	..	..	..	477	264	213	..	..	..
	States ..	477	264	213	..	..	..	477	264	213	..	..	..
Jat ..	Baluchistan ..	3,236	1,798	1,438	1	1	..	3,235	1,797	1,438	1	1	..
	Districts ..	1,651	911	740	..	..	..	1,651	911	740	..	..	..
	States ..	1,585	887	698	1	1	..	1,584	886	698	1	1	..
Khoja ..	Baluchistan ..	352	177	175	135	111	24	217	66	151	15	15	..
	Districts ..	13	8	5	7	6	1	6	2	4	6	6	..
	States ..	339	169	170	128	105	23	211	64	147	9	9	..
Langah ..	Baluchistan ..	506	255	251	5	5	..	501	250	251	..	..	..
	Districts ..	125	63	62	5	5	..	120	58	62	..	..	..
	States ..	381	192	189	..	..	..	381	192	189	..	..	..
Lori ..	Baluchistan ..	5,653	3,044	2,609	8	8	..	5,645	3,036	2,609	1	1	..
	Districts ..	1,040	560	480	4	4	..	1,036	556	480	1	1	..
	States ..	4,613	2,484	2,129	4	4	..	4,609	2,480	2,129	..	..	..
Med ..	Baluchistan ..	3,041	1,566	1,475	..	..	..	3,041	1,566	1,475	..	..	..
	States ..	3,041	1,566	1,475	..	..	..	3,041	1,566	1,475	..	..	..
Nakib ..	Baluchistan ..	7,154	3,814	3 340	8	8	..	7,146	3,806	3,340	..	..	..
	Districts ..	137	94	43	1	1	..	136	93	43	..	..	..
	States ..	7 017	3,720	3,297	7	7	..	7,010	3,713	3,297	..	..	..
Others ..	Baluchistan ..	14,581	7,660	6,921	84	79	5	14,497	7,581	6,916	9	9	..
	Districts ..	1,481	790	691	37	32	5	1,444	758	686	8	8	..
	States ..	13,100	6,870	6,230	47	47	..	13,053	6,823	6,230	1	1	..
(a) Sorozai ..	Baluchistan ..	11,164	5,829	5,335	21	17	4	11,143	5,812	5,331	..	..	..
	Districts ..	785	404	381	16	12	4	769	392	377	..	..	..
	States ..	10,379	5,425	4,954	5	5	..	10,374	5,420	4,954	..	..	..
(b) Others ..	Baluchistan ..	3,417	1,831	1,586	63	62	1	3,354	1,769	1,585	9	9	..
	Districts ..	696	386	310	21	20	1	675	366	309	8	8	..
	States ..	2,721	1,445	1,276	42	42	..	2,679	1,403	1,276	1	1	..
(ii) SEMI-INDIGENOUS.													
Hazara ..	Baluchistan ..	3,075	2,226	849	437	426	11	2,638	1,800	838	30	29	1
	Districts ..	3,068	2,219	849	436	425	11	2,632	1,794	838	30	29	1
	States ..	7	7	..	1	1	..	6	6	..	..	..	..
Others ..	Baluchistan ..	24	16	8	..	..	..	24	16	8	..	..	..
	Districts ..	24	16	8	..	..	..	24	16	8	..	..	..
II. HINDUS, INDIGENOUS.	Baluchistan ..	16,905	9,175	7,730	4,084	3,968	116	12,821	5,207	7,614	39	39	..
	Districts ..	5,136	2,883	2,253	1,502	1,420	82	3,634	1,463	2,171	32	32	..
	States ..	11,769	6,292	5,477	2,582	2,548	34	9,187	3,744	5,443	7	7	..
Arora ..	Baluchistan ..	16,359	8,825	7,534	3,884	3,777	107	12,475	5,048	7,427	35	35	..
	Districts ..	4,770	2,652	2,118	1,364	1,291	73	3,406	1,361	2,045	30	30	..
	States ..	11,589	6,173	5,416	2,520	2,486	34	9,069	3,687	5,382	5	5	..
Others ..	Baluchistan ..	546	350	196	200	191	9	346	159	187	4	4	..
	Districts ..	366	231	135	138	129	9	228	102	126	2	2	..
	States ..	180	119	61	62	62	..	118	57	61	2	2	..
III. SIKH, INDIGENOUS	Baluchistan ..	48	35	13	12	11	1	36	24	12	..	..	..
	Districts ..	31	26	5	11	10	1	20	16	4	..	..	..
	States ..	17	9	8	1	1	..	16	8	8	..	..	..

P= Persons; M= Males; F= Females.

TABLE XV.

PART I.—LANGUAGE.

The principal languages spoken in the Province are shown below :—

Language.	Total.	Males.	Females.
TOTAL POPULATION ..	868,617	488,414	380,203
A. VERNACULARS OF INDIA	858,035	480,871	377,164
I. Vernaculars of Baluchistan	779,260	423,745	355,515
Balochi ..	266,957	144,436	122,521
Dehwari (Local Persian)	5,233	2,842	2,391
Pashto ..	207,181	113,295	93,886
Lahnda or Western Punjabi.	27,283	14,359	12,924
Sindhi ..	143,210	77,960	65,250
Unspecified (Jattki or Jagdali and Jatki).	1,800	1,041	759
Brahui ..	127,479	69,746	57,733
Lorichini ..	117	66	51
II. Vernaculars of other parts of India.	78,775	57,126	21,649
B. VERNACULARS OF OTHER ASIATIC COUNTRIES AND AFRICA.	5,079	3,479	1,600
C. EUROPEAN LANGUAGES.	5,503	4,064	1,439

Details under each of these main heads are given in the body of the table.

2. Lahnda or Western Punjabi includes Jafiri or Jafarki, Khetrani and Siraiki which are dialects of Western Punjabi spoken by certain indigenous classes.

3. Sindhi spoken by indigenous residents represents Jattki-Sindhi and Lasi-Sindhi which are dialects of Sindhi spoken in Sind.

Language.	Baluchistan. Persons.	Males.	Females.	Districts. Quetta-Pishin. M.	F.	Loralai. M.	F.	Zhob. M.	F.	Bolan. M.	F.	Chagai. M.	F.	Sibi. Administered area. M.	F.	Sibi. Mari Bugti Country. M.	F.
1	2	3	4	5	6	7	8	9	10	11	12	13	14	15	16	17	18
TOTAL ..	868,617	488,414	380,203	90,302	57,289	47,936	38,151	34,596	28,867	3,466	1,222	13,721	10,503	49,447	38,334	30,586	24,688
A. Vernaculars of India.	*858,035*	*480,871*	*377,164*	*83,861*	*54,586*	*47,707*	*38,077*	*34,237*	*28,328*	*3,379*	*1,178*	*13,646*	*10,456*	*49,166*	*38,201*	*30,536*	*24,688*
I. Of Baluchistan	779,260	423,745	355,515	47,059	40,216	43,932	36,931	28,685	22,401	1,481	529	12,130	9,851	42,910	35,011	30,384	24,551
Eranian Branch ..	*479,371*	*260,573*	*218,798*	*42,391*	*36,783*	*33,438*	*27,508*	*28,537*	*22,391*	*648*	*281*	*7,476*	*6,109*	*23,335*	*20,152*	*30,114*	*24,330*
Eastern Group ..	*479,371*	*260,573*	*218,798*	*42,391*	*36,783*	*33,438*	*27,508*	*28,537*	*22,391*	*648*	*281*	*7,476*	*6,109*	*23,335*	*20,152*	*30,114*	*24,330*
Balochi ..	266,957	144,436	122,521	1,046	849	2,565	1,997	38	26	461	252	6,061	5,153	12,815	11,390	30,111	24,330
Dehwari (Local Persian).	5,233	2,842	2,391	51	51	..	..	..	..	1	..	..	..	2	1	..	..
Pashto ..	207,181	113,295	93,886	41,294	35,883	30,873	25,511	28,499	22,365	186	29	1,415	956	10,518	8,761	3	..
Outer Sub-Branch	172,293	93,360	78,933	20	12	10,202	9,233	7	5	36	1	69	50	15,638	11,862	270	221
North-Western Group.																	
(i) Lahnda or Western Punjabi.	*27,283*	*14,359*	*12,924*	*1*	*1*	*10,142*	*9,206*	*6*	*5*	..	..	..	..	*1,598*	*1,287*	..	..
Jafiri (Jafarki)	1,670	880	790	1	1	874	783	2	5	..	..	..	..	278	259	..	..
Khetrani ..	18,232	9,550	8,682	..	..	9,268	8,423	4	..	..	..	..	..	1,317	1,027	..	..
Siraiki ..	7,381	3,929	3,452	..	..	..	..	..	..	..	..	..	..	3	1	..	..
(ii) Sindhi-Branch	*143,210*	*77,960*	*65,250*	*11*	*4*	..	..	*1*	..	*3*	*1*	*5*	*2*	*13,947*	*10,540*	..	..
Jattki Sindhi ..	97,412	53,745	43,667	11	4	..	..	1	..	3	1	5	2	13,947	10,540	..	..
Lasi ..	45,798	24,215	21,583	..	..	..	..	..	..	..	..	..	..	..	..	..	..
(iii) Unspecified	*1,800*	*1,041*	*759*	*8*	*7*	*60*	*27*	..	..	*33*	..	*64*	*48*	*88*	*35*	*270*	*221*
Jattki or Jagdali	775	470	305	8	7	23	8	..	..	33	..	64	48	72	21	270	221
Jatki ..	1,025	571	454	..	..	37	19	..	..	..	..	..	..	16	14	..	..
Dravidian Family	*127,479*	*69,746*	*57,733*	*4,646*	*3,417*	*292*	*190*	*141*	*5*	*797*	*247*	*4,585*	*3,692*	*3,911*	*2,976*	..	..
North-Western Language. Brahui ..	127,479	69,746	57,733	4,646	3,417	292	190	141	5	797	247	4,585	3,692	3,911	2,976	..	..
Unclassed Language.	*117*	*66*	*51*	*2*	*4*	..	..	..	..	..	..	..	..	*31*	*21*	..	..
Lorichini ..	117	66	51	2	4	..	..	..	..	..	..	..	..	31	21	..	..
II. Of other Parts of India.	78,775	57,126	21,649	36,302	14,370	8,775	1,146	5,552	927	1,398	649	1,516	605	6,256	3,190	152	127
Tibeto-Himalayan Branch.	*597*	*595*	*2*	*16*	*2*	*7*	..	*572*	..	..	..	..	..	..	..	..	..
Tibetan Group	*29*	*29*	..	*16*	..	*7*	..	*6*	..	..	..	..	..	..	..	..	..
Tibetan ..	21	21	..	14	..	7	..	..	..	..	..	..	..	..	..	..	..
Sharpa Bhotia	6	6	..	..	..	..	..	6	..	..	..	..	..	..	..	..	..
Sikkim Bhotia	2	2	..	2	..	..	..	..	..	..	..	..	..	..	..	..	..
Pronominalized Himalayan Group.	*488*	*488*	..	..	..	..	..	*488*	..	..	..	..	..	..	..	..	..
Kiranti ..	488	488	..	..	..	..	..	488	..	..	..	..	..	..	..	..	..
(a) Limbu ..	262	262	..	..	..	..	..	262	..	..	..	..	..	..	..	..	..
(b) Rai or Jimdar.	226	226	..	..	..	..	..	226	..	..	..	..	..	..	..	..	..
Non-Pronominalized Himalayan Group ..	*80*	*78*	*2*	..	*2*	..	..	*78*	..	..	..	..	..	..	..	..	..
Gurang ..	16	16	..	..	..	..	..	16	..	..	..	..	..	..	..	..	..
Sanwar ..	38	38	..	..	..	..	..	38	..	..	..	..	..	..	..	..	..
Magari ..	24	24	..	..	..	..	..	24	..	..	..	..	..	..	..	..	..
Rong or Lepcha	2	..	2	..	2	..	..	..	..	..	..	..	..	..	..	..	..
Dravidian Family	214	134	80	122	72	3	1	5	5	..	..	2	..	2	2	..	..
Dravida Group	*172*	*103*	*69*	*96*	*63*	*2*	*1*	*3*	*5*	..	..	*2*	..	..	..	..	..
Tamil ..	150	89	61	83	55	2	1	3	5	..	..	1	..	..	..	..	..
Malayalam ..	12	8	4	8	4	..	..	..	..	..	..	..	..	..	..	..	..
Kanarese ..	10	6	4	5	4	..	..	..	..	..	..	1	..	..	..	..	..
Andhra Language. Telugu ..	*42*	*31*	*11*	*26*	*9*	*1*	..	*2*	..	..	..	..	..	*2*	*2*	..	..
Aryan Sub-Family. Dard Group ..	201	133	68	102	58	14	1	5	1	..	..	2	1	10	7	..	..
Kashmiri ..	201	133	68	102	58	14	1	5	1	..	..	2	1	10	7	..	..
(i) Outer Sub-Branch.	32,068	22,742	9,326	12,909	5,015	1,732	595	2,103	466	938	423	734	305	3,396	1,980	65	48
North-Western Group. ..	*31,093*	*21,909*	*9,184*	*12,131*	*4,894*	*1,708*	*582*	*2,093*	*460*	*935*	*423*	*731*	*305*	*3,382*	*1,978*	*65*	*48*

STATES.															
KALAT.														LAS-BELA.	
TOTAL KALAT.		SARAWAN.		JHALAWAN.		KACHHI.		DOMBKI-KAHERI COUNTRY.		MAKRAN.		KHARAN.			
M. 19	F. 20	M. 21	F. 22	M. 23	F. 24	M. 25	F. 26	M. 27	F. 28	M. 29	F. 30	M. 31	F. 32	M. 33	F. 34
184,915	157,186	15,545	12,919	47,987	40,991	57,844	48,042	14,558	12,400	36,488	31,979	12,503	10,855	33,495	29,513
184,848	*157,140*	*15,499*	*12,884*	*47,987*	*40,991*	*57,834*	*48,032*	*14,553*	*12,400*	*36,472*	*31,978*	*12,503*	*10,855*	*33,491*	*29,510*
183,886	156,625	15,027	12,536	47,776	40,950	57,708	47,994	14,550	12,392	36,297	31,918	12,478	10,840	33,328	29,400
87,650	*75,161*	*5,327*	*4,750*	*10,435*	*8,343*	*19,946*	*16,536*	*3,409*	*2,857*	*36,055*	*31,835*	*12,478*	*10,840*	*6,984*	*6,083*
87,650	75,161	5,327	4,750	10,435	8,343	19,946	16,536	3,409	2,857	36,055	31,835	12,478	10,840	6,984	6,083
84,364	72,444	2,153	2,118	10,413	8,328	19,912	16,501	3,401	2,849	36,017	31,812	12,468	10,836	6,975	6,080
2,788	2,339	2,776	2,325	..	..	12	14	..	..	..	..	..	..	..	..
498	378	398	307	22	15	22	21	8	8	38	23	10	4	9	3
43,118	36,101	..	..	823	627	32,072	26,748	10,210	8,722	13	4	..	..	24,005	21,448
2,612	*2,425*	..	..	*2*	*2*	*2,507*	*2,334*	*100*	*85*	*3*	*4*	..	..	..	..
..	..	..	..	..	..	..	..	..	..	..	..	..	..	..	..
..	..	..	..	..	..	..	..	..	..	..	..	..	..	..	..
2,612	2,425	..	..	2	2	2,507	2,334	100	85	3	4	..	..	..	..
39,988	*33,255*	..	..	*821*	*625*	*29,047*	*23,993*	*10,110*	*8,637*	*10*	...	..	..	*24,005*	*21,448*
39,778	33,120	..	..	621	490	29,047	23,993	10,110	8,637	..	..	..	..	..	..
210	135	..	..	200	135	..	..	..	..	10	..	..	..	24,005	21,448
518	*421*	..	..	..	..	*518*	*421*	..	..	..	..	..	..	..	..
..	..	..	..	..	..	..	..	..	..	..	..	..	..	..	..
518	421	..	..	..	..	518	421	..	..	..	..	..	..	..	..
53,035	*45,337*	*9,700*	*7,786*	*36,518*	*31,980*	*5,657*	*4,684*	*931*	*813*	*229*	*74*	..	..	*2,339*	*1,869*
53,035	45,337	9,700	7,786	36,518	31,980	5,657	4,684	931	813	229	74	..	..	2,339	1,869
33	26	..	..	..	..	33	26	..	..	..	..	..	..	..	..
33	26	..	..	..	..	33	26	..	..	..	..	..	..	..	..
1,012	*515*	*472*	*348*	*211*	*41*	*126*	*38*	*3*	*8*	*175*	*65*	*25*	*15*	*163*	*110*
..	..	..	..	..	..	..	..	..	..	..	..	..	..	..	..
..	..	..	..	..	..	..	..	..	..	..	..	..	..	..	..
..	..	..	..	..	..	..	..	..	..	..	..	..	..	..	..
..	..	..	..	..	..	..	..	..	..	..	..	..	..	..	..
..	..	..	..	..	..	..	..	..	..	..	..	..	..	..	..
..	..	..	..	..	..	..	..	..	..	..	..	..	..	..	..
..	..	..	..	..	..	..	..	..	..	..	..	..	..	..	..
..	..	..	..	..	..	..	..	..	..	..	..	..	..	..	..
..	..	..	..	..	..	..	..	..	..	..	..	..	..	..	..
..	..	..	..	..	..	..	..	..	..	..	..	..	..	..	..
..	..	..	..	..	..	..	..	..	..	..	..	..	..	..	..
..	..	..	..	..	..	..	..	..	..	..	..	..	..	..	..
..	..	..	..	..	..	..	..	..	..	..	..	..	..	..	..
..	..	..	..	..	..	..	..	..	..	..	..	..	..	..	..
..	..	..	..	..	..	..	..	..	..	..	..	..	..	..	..
..	..	..	..	..	..	..	..	..	..	..	..	..	..	..	..
..	..	..	..	..	..	..	..	..	..	..	..	..	..	..	..
	..	..	..	..	..	..	..	..	..	..	..	..	..	..	..
..	..	..	..	..	..	..	..	..	..	..	..	..	..	..	..
..	..	..	..	..	..	..	..	..	..	..	..	..	..	..	..
..	..	..	..	..	..	..	..	..	..	..	..	..	..	..	..
802	456	407	338	188	36	68	26	3	8	111	33	25	15	63	33
801	*456*	*407*	*338*	*188*	*36*	*68*	*26*	*3*	*8*	*110*	*33*	*25*	*15*	*63*	*33*

M = Males; F = Females

Language.	Baluchistan.			Districts.													
				Quetta-Pishin.		Loralai.		Zhob.		Bolan.		Chagai.		Sibi.			
														Administered area.		Mari Bugti Country.	
	Persons.	Males.	Females.	M.	F.	M.	F.	M.	F.	M.	F.	M.	F.	M.	F.	M.	F.
1	2	3	4	5	6	7	8	9	10	11	12	13	14	15	16	17	18
Lahnda or Western Punjabi.	23,071	16,576	6,495	9,780	4,063	1,581	508	2,040	444	663	342	485	157	1,729	837	..	..
Sindhi ..	8,022	5,333	2,689	2,351	831	127	74	53	16	272	61	246	148	1,653	1,141	65	48
SOUTHERN GROUP	*882*	*770*	*112*	*735*	*100*	*16*	*8*	*6*	*2*	*3*	..	*1*	..	*8*	*2*	..	..
Marathi ..	789	697	92	672	81	16	8	2	2	1	..	..	..	6	1	..	..
Kankani ..	93	73	20	63	19	..	..	4	..	2	..	1	..	2	1	..	..
EASTERN GROUP.																	
Bengali ..	93	63	30	43	21	8	5	4	4	..	..	2	..	6	..	..	..
(ii) Mediate Sub-Branch.	*39*	*26*	*13*	*21*	*7*	..	..	*3*	*6*	..	..	..	..	..	..	*2*	..
MEDIATE GROUP.																	
Eastern Hindi	39	26	13	21	7	..	..	3	6	..	..	..	..	..	..	2	..
(iii) Inner Sub-Branch. ..	*45,656*	*33,496*	*12,160*	*23,632*	*9,216*	*2,019*	*549*	*2,864*	*449*	*960*	*226*	*778*	*299*	*2,848*	*1,201*	*85*	*89*
CENTRAL GROUP	*37,755*	*27,210*	*10,545*	*18,716*	*7,668*	*1,620*	*542*	*2,375*	*441*	*829*	*213*	*657*	*278*	*2,655*	*1,183*	*85*	*89*
Western Hindi	17,092	12,630	4,462	9,209	3,288	860	315	594	116	471	76	176	82	1,126	452	85	89
(a) Hindi	464	342	122	253	32	..	..	1	..	3	..	..	..	2	2	83	88
(b) Hindustani	16,628	12,288	4,340	8,956	3,256	860	315	593	116	468	76	176	82	1,124	450	2	1
Rajasthani ..	530	325	205	52	24	..	..	1	1	..	..	93	34	177	142	..	..
Gujrati ..	618	408	210	356	206	14	..	13	..	..	..	1	..	21	4	..	..
Punjabi ..	19,515	13,847	5,668	9,099	4,150	746	227	1,767	324	358	137	387	162	1,331	585	..	..
PAHARI GROUP ..	*7,901*	*6,286*	*1,615*	*4,916*	*1,548*	*399*	*7*	*489*	*8*	*131*	*13*	*121*	*21*	*193*	*18*	..	..
Central Pahari	3,169	2,903	266	1,707	206	371	6	432	5	131	13	121	21	104	15	..	..
Eastern Pahari	4,653	3,309	1,344	3,185	1,341	18	..	51	2	..	..	..	..	55	1	..	..
Khaskura or Naipali.																	
Western Pahari	25	24	1	24	1	..	..	..	..	..	..	..	..	..	..	..	..
Pahari (unspecified).	54	50	4	..	..	10	1	6	1	..	..	..	..	34	2	..	..
B. Vernaculars of other Asiatic Countries and Africa.	*5,079*	*3,479*	*1,600*	*2,648*	*1,341*	*165*	*47*	*297*	*28*	*43*	*13*	*64*	*43*	*198*	*80*	..	..
Eranian Branch	*5,021*	*3,445*	*1,576*	*2,620*	*1,319*	*165*	*47*	*296*	*28*	*43*	*13*	*64*	*43*	*195*	*78*	..	..
PERSIAN GROUP.																	
Persian ..	5,020	3,444	1,576	2,620	1,319	165	47	296	28	43	13	64	43	195	78	..	..
ARMENIAN GROUP.																	
Armenian ..	1	1	..	..	..	..	..	..	..	..	..	..	..	..	..	..	..
Chinese Branch ..	40	21	19	21	19	..	..	..	..	..	..	..	..	..	..	..	..
CHINESE GROUP.																	
Chinese ..	40	21	19	21	19	..	..	..	..	..	..	..	..	..	..	..	..
Semitic Family ..	*10*	*6*	*4*	*2*	*2*	..	..	*1*	..	..	..	..	..	*2*	*2*	..	..
Arabic ..	9	5	4	2	2	..	..	1	..	..	..	..	..	2	2	..	..
Hebrew ..	1	1	..	..	..	..	..	..	..	..	..	..	..	..	..	..	..
Mongolian Family	*7*	*6*	*1*	*5*	*1*	..	..	..	..	..	..	..	..	*1*	..	..	..
URAL ALTAIC GROUP																	
Turkish ..	7	6	1	5	1	..	..	..	..	..	..	..	..	1	..	..	..
Malayo-Polynesian Family.	*1*	*1*	..	..	..	..	..	..	..	..	..	..	..	..	..	..	..
MALAYAN GROUP.																	
Javanese ..	1	1	..	..	..	..	..	..	..	..	..	..	..	..	..	..	..
C. European Languages.	*5,503*	*4,064*	*1,439*	*3,793*	*1,312*	*64*	*27*	*62*	*11*	*44*	*31*	*11*	*4*	*83*	*53*	..	..
Indo-European Family.	5,508	4,064	1,489	3,798	1,312	64	27	62	11	44	31	11	4	83	53	..	..
Romanic Group ..	*68*	*51*	*17*	*42*	*10*	..	..	..	..	..	..	..	..	*9*	*7*	..	..
Italian ..	1	1	..	1	..	..	..	..	..	..	..	..	..	..	..	..	..
French ..	9	4	5	4	5	..	..	..	..	..	..	..	..	..	..	..	..
Spanish ..	3	3	..	3	..	..	..	..	..	..	..	..	..	..	..	..	..
Portuguese ..	55	43	12	34	5	..	..	..	..	..	..	..	..	9	7	..	..
Celtic Group ..	*60*	*46*	*14*	*46*	*14*	..	..	..	..	..	..	..	..	..	..	..	..
Welsh ..	9	9	..	9	..	..	..	..	..	..	..	..	..	..	..	..	..
Scotch ..	35	28	7	28	7	..	..	..	..	..	..	..	..	..	..	..	..
Irish ..	16	9	7	9	7	..	..	..	..	..	..	..	..	..	..	..	..
Teutonic Group ..	*5,375*	*3,967*	*1,408*	*3,707*	*1,288*	*64*	*27*	*62*	*11*	*44*	*31*	*11*	*4*	*74*	*46*	..	..
English ..	5,369	3,965	1,404	3,703	1,284	64	27	62	11	44	31	11	4	74	46	..	..
Danish ..	2	1	1	1	1	..	..	..	..	..	..	..	..	..	..	..	..
German ..	4	1	3	1	3	..	..	..	..	..	..	..	..	..	..	..	..

STATES.															
KALAT.														LAS-BELA.	
TOTAL KALAT.		SARAWAN.		JHALAWAN.		KACHHI.		DOMBKI-KAHERI COUNTRY.		MAKRAN.		KHARAN.			
M. 19	F. 20	M. 21	F. 22	M. 23	F. 24	M. 25	F. 26	M. 27	F. 28	M. 29	F. 30	M. 31	F. 32	M. 33	F. 34
235	86	64	18	48	3	68	26	3	8	52	31	..	..	63	38
566	370	343	315	140	33	..	..	..	..	58	7	25	15	..	..
1	..	..	..	..	..	..	..	..	..	*1*	..	..	..	..	..
..	..	..	..	..	..	..	..	..	..	..	..	..	..	..	..
1	..	..	..	..	..	..	..	..	..	1	..	..	..	..	..
..	..	..	..	..	..	..	..	..	..	..	..	..	..	..	..
..	..	..	..	..	..	..	..	..	..	..	..	..	..	..	..
..	..	..	..	..	..	..	..	..	..	..	..	..	..	..	..
210	*59*	*65*	*15*	*23*	*5*	*58*	*12*	..	..	*64*	*27*	..	..	*100*	*72*
173	*59*	*59*	*15*	*18*	*5*	*34*	*12*	..	..	*62*	*27*	..	..	*100*	*72*
58	14	22	3	3	..	14	5	..	..	19	6	..	..	51	30
..	..	..	..	..	..	..	..	..	..	..	..	..	..	..	..
58	14	22	3	3	..	14	5	..	..	19	6	..	..	51	30
2	4	2	4	..	..	..	..	..	..	..	..	..	..	..	..
2	..	..	..	..	..	1	..	..	..	1	..	..	..	1	..
111	41	35	8	15	5	19	7	..	..	42	21	..	..	48	42
37	..	*6*	..	*5*	..	*24*	..	..	..	*2*	..	..	..	..	..
37	..	6	..	5	..	24	..	..	..	2	..	..	..	..	..
..	..	..	..	..	..	..	..	..	..	..	..	..	..	..	..
..	..	..	..	..	..	..	..	..	..	..	..	..	..	..	..
..	..	..	..	..	..	..	..	..	..	..	..	..	..	..	..
60	*45*	*46*	*35*	..	..	*10*	*10*	..	..	*4*	..	..	..	*4*	*3*
58	*45*	*46*	*35*	..	..	*10*	*10*	..	..	*2*	..	..	..	*4*	*3*
57	45	46	35	..	..	10	10	..	..	1	..	..	..	4	3
1	..	..	..	..	..	..	..	..	..	1	..	..	..	..	..
..	..	..	..	..	..	..	..	..	..	..	..	..	..	..	..
..	..	..	..	..	..	..	..	..	..	..	..	..	..	..	..
1	..	..	..	..	..	..	..	..	..	*1*	..	..	..	..	..
..	..	..	..	..	..	..	..	..	..	..	..	..	..	..	..
1	..	..	..	..	..	..	..	..	..	1	..	..	..	..	..
..	..	..	..	..	..	..	..	..	..	..	..	..	..	..	..
..	..	..	..	..	..	..	..	..	..	..	..	..	..	..	..
1	..	..	..	..	..	..	..	..	..	*1*	..	..	..	..	..
1	..	..	..	..	..	..	..	..	..	1	..	..	..	..	..
7	*1*	..	..	..	..	..	..	..	..	*7*	*1*	..	..	..	..
7	1	..	..	..	..	..	..	..	..	7	1	..	..	..	..
..	..	..	..	..	..	..	..	..	..	..	..	..	..	..	..
..	..	..	..	..	..	..	..	..	..	..	..	..	..	..	..
..	..	..	..	..	..	..	..	..	..	..	..	..	..	..	..
..	..	..	..	..	..	..	..	..	..	..	..	..	..	..	..
..	..	..	..	..	..	..	..	..	..	..	..	..	..	..	..
..	..	..	..	..	..	..	..	..	..	..	..	..	..	..	..
..	..	..	..	..	..	..	..	..	..	..	..	..	..	..	..
..	..	..	..	..	..	..	..	..	..	..	..	..	..	..	..
..	..	..	..	..	..	..	..	..	..	..	..	..	..	..	..
..	..	..	..	..	..	..	..	..	..	..	..	..	..	..	..
7	*1*	..	..	..	..	..	..	..	..	*7*	*1*	..	..	..	..
7	1	..	..	..	..	..	..	..	..	7	1	..	..	..	..
..	..	..	..	..	..	..	..	..	..	..	..	..	..	..	..
..	..	..	..	..	..	..	..	..	..	..	..	..	..	..	..

M = Males; F = Females.

TABLE XV.

PART II.—BILINGUALISM.

This part of Table XV. gives for speakers of each mother tongue the numbers speaking other local languages of Baluchistan in addition to their mother tongues. Languages of other parts of India or foreign countries are not shown with the exception of Western Hindi (which represents Urdu, Hindostani and Hindi), Persian and Sindhi. The numbers speaking these languages are likely to increase in future and they have therefore been shown separately.

TABLE XV.—(PART II)

Area of Bilingualism	Mother-Tongue	Number of Persons speaking Mother-Tongue P.	M.	F.	Number of Persons speaking — Local — Balochi P.	M.	F.	Dehwari (Local Persian) P.	M.	F.	Pashto P.	M.	F.	Lahnda (or Western Punjabi) P.	M.	F.
1	2	3	4	5	6	7	8	9	10	11	12	13	14	15	16	17
BALUCHISTAN.	TOTAL ..	**809,277**	**445,086**	**364,191**	**15,571**	**11,363**	**4,208**	**2,938**	**1,796**	**1,142**	**7,995**	**6,451**	**1,544**	**2,952**	**1,877**	**1,075**
Local	Balochi ..	266,957	144,436	122,521	..	..	..	941	551	390	1,542	1,243	299	2,290	1,482	808
	Dehwari or Local Persian ..	5,233	2,842	2,391	..	..	..	..	..	..	11	6	5	..	..	..
	Pashto ..	207,181	113,295	93,886	1,185	777	408	184	108	76	..	..	..	211	133	78
	Lahnda or Western Punjabi ..	27,283	14,359	12,924	3,350	2,834	516	..	..	..	1,190	945	245	..	..	..
	Unspecified Jagdali and Jatki ..	1,800	1,041	759	81	56	25	..	..	..	54	48	6	41	26	15
	Sindhi (Jattki and Lasi) ..	143,210	77,960	65,250	3,821	2,949	872	..	..	..	305	207	98	356	197	159
	Brahui ..	127,479	69,746	57,733	6,592	4,325	2,267	1,795	1,126	669	2,663	2,078	585	51	37	14
Non-Local	Sindhi ..	8,022	5,333	2,689	435	349	86	14	9	5	813	772	41	..	..	..
	Western Hindi ..	17,092	12,630	4,462	18	18	..	..	..	..	230	214	16	..	..	..
	Persian ..	5,020	3,444	1,576	89	55	34	4	2	2	1,187	938	249	3	2	1
DISTRICTS.	TOTAL ..	**404,949**	**227,219**	**177,730**	**9,790**	**7,216**	**2,574**	..	..	..	**7,646**	**6,212**	**1,434**	**2,762**	**1,756**	**1,006**
Local	Balochi ..	97,094	53,097	43,997	..	..	..	..	..	..	1,514	1,225	289	2,208	1,425	783
	Dehwari ..	106	54	52	..	..	..	..	..	..	3	2	1	..	..	..
	Pashto ..	206,293	112,788	93,505	1,148	751	397	..	..	..	..	..	..	211	188	78
	Lahnda or Western Punjabi ..	22,246	11,747	10,499	3,248	2,767	481	..	..	..	1,189	944	245	..	..	..
	Unspecified Jagdali and Jatki ..	861	523	338	48	35	13	..	..	..	54	48	6	16	11	5
	Sindhi (Jattki and Lasi)	24,514	13,967	10,547	1,109	892	217	..	..	..	182	123	59	302	165	137
	Brahui ..	24,899	14,372	10,527	3,849	2,479	1,370	..	..	..	2,478	1,950	528	22	20	2
Non-Local	Sindhi ..	7,086	4,767	2,319	294	232	62	..	..	..	813	772	41	..	..	..
	Western Hindi ..	16,939	12,521	4,418	12	12	..	..	..	..	230	214	16	..	..	..
	Persian ..	4,911	3,383	1,528	82	48	34	..	..	..	1,183	934	249	3	2	1
QUETTA-PISHIN DISTRICT.	TOTAL ..	**106,887**	**61,237**	**45,650**	**245**	**183**	**62**	..	..	..	**3,319**	**2,755**	**564**	**17**	**10**	**7**
Local	Balochi ..	1,895	1,046	849	..	..	..	..	..	..	299	226	73	6	2	4
	Dehwari or Local Persian ..	102	51	51	..	..	..	..	..	..	1	1	..	..	..	..
	Pashto ..	77,177	41,294	35,883	108	90	18	..	..	..	..	..	..	2	2	..
	Lahnda or Western Punjabi ..	2	1	1	..	..	..	..	..	..	..	..	..	..	..	..
	Unspecified Jagdali and Jatki ..	15	8	7	..	..	..	..	..	..	1	1	..	..	..	..
	Sindhi (Jattki and Lasi) ..	15	11	4	..	..	..	..	..	..	..	..	..	..	..	..
	Brahui ..	8,063	4,646	3,417	89	58	31	..	..	..	1,498	1,230	268	7	5	2
Non-Local	Sindhi ..	3,182	2,351	831	15	15	..	..	..	..	530	506	24	..	..	..
	Western Hindi ..	12,497	9,209	3,288	3	3	..	..	..	..	156	148	8	..	..	..
	Persian ..	3,939	2,620	1,319	30	17	13	..	..	..	834	643	191	2	1	1
Pishin Tahsil.	TOTAL ..	**51,699**	**26,564**	**25,135**	**8**	**5**	**3**	..	..	..	**288**	**244**	**39**	..	..	—
Local	Balochi ..	189	111	78	..	..	..	..	..	..	73	46	27	..	..	..
	Pashto ..	50,225	25,428	24,797	5	2	3	..	..	..	..	..	..	..	..	..
	Sindhi (Jattki and Lasi)	12	9	3	..	..	..	..	..	..	..	..	..	..	..	..
	Brahui ..	263	186	77	2	2	..	..	..	..	57	50	7	..	..	..
Non-Local	Sindhi ..	324	216	108	..	..	..	..	..	..	106	104	2	..	..	..
	Western Hindi ..	619	562	57	..	..	..	..	..	..	6	6	..	..	..	..
	Persian ..	67	52	15	1	1	..	..	..	..	41	38	3	..	..	..
Chaman Sub-Division.	TOTAL ..	**14,098**	**8,331**	**5,767**	**6**	**6**	..	..	..	..	**279**	**252**	**27**	..	..	..
Local	Balochi ..	2	1	1	..	..	..	..	..	..	1	1	..	..	..	..
	Pashto ..	12,898	7,427	5,471	..	..	..	..	..	..	..	..	..	..	..	..
	Brahui ..	19	18	1	6	6	..	..	..	..	2	2	..	..	..	..
Non-Local	Sindhi ..	475	340	135	..	..	..	..	..	..	166	153	13	..	..	..
	Western Hindi ..	590	454	136	..	..	..	..	..	..	31	29	2	..	..	..
	Persian ..	114	91	23	..	..	..	..	..	..	79	67	12	..	..	..
Quetta Tahsil.	TOTAL ..	**41,090**	**26,342**	**14,748**	**231**	**172**	**59**	..	..	..	**2,757**	**2,259**	**498**	**17**	**10**	**7**
Local	Balochi ..	1,704	934	770	..	..	..	..	..	..	225	179	46	6	2	4
	Dehwari or Local Persian ..	102	51	51	..	..	..	..	..	..	1	1	..	..	..	..
	Pashto ..	14,054	8,439	5,615	103	88	15	..	..	..	..	..	..	2	2	..
	Lahnda or Western Punjabi ..	2	1	1	..	..	..	..	..	..	..	..	..	..	..	..
	Unspecified Jagdali and Jatki ..	15	8	7	..	..	..	..	..	..	1	1	..	..	..	..
	Sindhi (Jattki and Lasi)	3	2	1	..	..	..	..	..	..	..	..	..	..	..	..
	Brahui ..	7,781	4,442	3,339	81	50	31	..	..	..	1,439	1,178	261	7	5	2
Non-Local	Sindhi ..	2,383	1,795	588	15	15	..	..	..	..	253	249	9	..	..	..
	Western Hindi ..	11,288	8,193	3,095	3	3	..	..	..	..	119	113	6	..	..	..
	Persian ..	3,758	2,477	1,281	29	16	13	..	..	..	714	538	176	2	1	1

BILINGUALISM.

SUBSIDIARY LANGUAGES.

Local.									Non-Local.									All other mother-tongues not specified in column 2.		
Unspecified Jagdali and Jatki.			*Sindhi (Jatki and Lasi).*			*Brahui.*			*Sindhi.*			*Western Hindi.*			*Persian.*					
P.	M.	F.	P.	M.	F.	P.	M.	F.	P.	M.	F.	P.	M.	F.	P.	M.	F.	P.	M.	F.
18	19	20	21	22	23	24	25	26	27	28	29	30	31	32	33	34	35	36	37	38
1,488	**1,018**	**420**	**30,105**	**18,315**	**11,790**	**24,753**	**15,299**	**9,454**	**929**	**697**	**232**	**16,251**	**14,634**	**1,617**	**3,388**	**2,948**	**440**	**59,340**	**43,328**	**16,012**
154	152	2	23,552	13,935	9,617	16,904	9,993	6,911	381	276	105	1,532	1,269	263	295	245	50	..	..	..
..	..	..	3	3	..	2,305	1,250	1,055	5	2	3	163	120	43	4	2	2	..	..	..
1,060	691	369	116	84	32	2,399	1,632	767	72	64	8	6,986	6,511	475	1,914	1,725	189	..	..	..
104	72	32	1,271	661	610	97	71	26	5	4	1	40	37	3	3	3	..	..	..	..
..	..	..	734	410	324	98	75	23	15	13	2	89	72	17	..	..	..	..	..	..
..	..	..	..	..	..	2,328	1,812	516	93	52	41	168	163	5	148	113	35	..	..	..
90	87	3	4,377	3,176	1,201	..	..	..	294	230	64	2,946	2,696	250	684	546	138	..	..	..
26	16	10	13	12	1	488	368	120	..	..	..	2,239	2,013	226	204	192	12	..	..	..
4	..	4	26	21	5	11	11	..	46	40	6	..	..	..	136	122	14	..	..	..
..	..	..	13	13	..	123	87	36	18	16	2	2,088	1,753	335	..	..	..	..	..	..
1,419	**1,005**	**414**	**11,694**	**6,602**	**5,092**	**7,139**	**4,464**	**2,675**	**674**	**549**	**125**	**14,976**	**13,585**	**1,391**	**2,880**	**2,541**	**339**	**58,559**	**42,785**	**15,774**
154	152	2	9,291	5,039	4,252	4,384	2,524	1,860	216	172	44	1,358	1,117	241	186	140	46	..	..	..
..	..	..	..	..	..	4	4	..	..	..	..	22	19	3	..	..	..	..	..	..
1,060	691	369	94	68	26	2,192	1,505	687	72	64	8	6,902	6,439	463	1,880	1,699	181	..	..	..
85	59	26	317	177	140	5	3	2	5	4	1	34	31	3	2	2	..	..	..	..
..	..	..	1	1	..	49	38	11	15	13	2	83	70	13	..	..	..	..	..	..
..	..	..	..	..	..	198	132	66	74	41	33	28	26	2	3	3	..	..	..	..
90	87	3	1,967	1,295	672	..	..	..	229	200	29	2,368	2,242	126	525	429	96	..	..	..
26	16	10	13	12	1	193	170	23	..	..	..	2,101	1,892	209	150	148	2	..	..	..
4	..	4	4	3	1	9	9	..	45	39	6	..	..	..	134	120	14	..	..	..
..	..	..	7	7	..	105	79	26	18	16	2	2,080	1,749	331	..	..	..	..	..	..
51	**40**	**11**	**136**	**107**	**29**	**1,125**	**910**	**215**	**166**	**147**	**19**	**10,904**	**10,035**	**869**	**2,013**	**1,757**	**256**	**40,654**	**29,065**	**11,589**
..	..	..	11	10	1	146	82	64	13	9	4	541	495	46	108	78	30	..	..	..
..	..	..	..	..	..	4	4	..	..	..	..	22	19	3	..	..	..	..	..	..
7	6	1	12	12	..	823	696	127	51	45	6	5,348	5,019	329	1,284	1,128	156	..	..	..
..	..	..	..	..	..	..	..	..	..	..	..	2	1	1	..	..	..	..	..	..
..	..	..	..	..	..	..	..	..	..	..	..	5	5	..	..	..	..	..	..	..
..	..	..	..	..	..	1	1	..	..	..	..	1	1	..	1	1	..	..	..	..
21	21	..	107	79	28	..	..	..	74	72	2	1,603	1,518	85	374	314	60	..	..	..
23	13	10	..	..	..	68	65	3	..	..	..	1,608	1,493	115	141	139	2	..	..	..
..	..	..	..	..	..	5	5	..	13	8	5	..	..	..	105	97	8	..	..	..
..	..	..	6	6	..	78	57	21	15	13	2	1,774	1,484	290	..	..	..	..	..	..
..	**..**	**..**	**34**	**27**	**7**	**21**	**20**	**1**	**16**	**14**	**2**	**1,731**	**1,707**	**24**	**211**	**210**	**1**	**1,676**	**1,256**	**420**
..	..	..	1	1	..	8	8	..	2	2	..	18	18	..	4	4	..	..	..	..
..	..	..	4	4	..	11	10	1	7	7	..	1,512	1,490	22	196	195	1	..	..	..
..	..	..	..	..	..	..	..	..	..	..	..	..	..	..	..	..	..	..	..	..
..	..	..	24	17	7	..	..	..	2	1	1	107	107	..	4	4	..	..	..	..
..	..	..	..	..	..	..	..	..	..	..	..	74	72	2	6	6	..	..	..	..
..	..	..	..	..	..	..	..	..	..	..	..	..	..	..	1	1	..	..	..	..
..	..	..	5	5	..	2	2	..	5	4	1	20	20	..	..	..	..	..	..	..
3	**3**	**..**	**..**	**..**	**..**	**1**	**1**	**..**	**29**	**24**	**5**	**551**	**537**	**14**	**200**	**194**	**6**	**3,419**	**2,624**	**795**
..	..	..	..	..	..	..	..	..	..	..	..	..	..	..	2	1	1	..	..	..
..	..	..	..	..	..	1	1	..	22	17	5	380	370	10	130	127	3	..	..	..
3	3	..	..	..	..	..	..	..	5	5	..	15	15	..	4	4	..	..	..	..
..	..	..	..	..	..	..	..	..	..	..	..	131	130	1	60	58	2	..	..	..
..	..	..	..	..	..	..	..	..	2	2	..	..	..	..	4	4	..	..	..	..
..	..	..	..	..	..	..	..	..	..	..	..	25	22	3	..	..	..	..	..	..
46	**37**	**11**	**102**	**80**	**22**	**1,108**	**889**	**214**	**121**	**109**	**12**	**8,622**	**7,791**	**831**	**1,609**	**1,358**	**249**	**35,559**	**25,185**	**10,374**
..	..	..	10	9	1	138	74	64	11	7	4	523	477	46	102	73	29	..	..	..
..	..	..	..	..	..	4	4	..	..	..	..	22	19	3	..	..	..	..	..	..
7	6	1	8	8	..	811	685	126	22	21	1	3,456	3,159	297	958	806	152	..	..	..
..	..	..	..	..	..	..	..	..	..	..	..	2	1	1	..	..	..	..	..	..
..	..	..	..	..	..	..	..	..	..	..	..	5	5	..	..	..	..	..	..	..
..	..	..	..	..	..	1	1	..	..	..	..	1	1	..	1	1	..	..	..	..
18	18	..	83	62	21	..	..	..	67	66	1	1,461	1,396	85	366	306	60	..	..	..
23	13	10	..	..	..	68	65	3	..	..	..	1,403	1,291	112	75	75	..	..	..	..
..	..	..	..	..	..	5	5	..	11	6	5	..	..	..	100	92	8	..	..	..
..	..	..	1	1	..	76	55	21	10	9	1	1,729	1,442	287	..	..	..	..	..	..

P = Persons ; M = Males ; F = Females.

TABLE XV.—(PART II)

1 Area of Bilingualism.		Mother-Tongue.	Number of Persons speaking Mother-Tongue. P.	M.	F.	Number of Persons Speaking — Local. Balochi. P.	M.	F.	Dehwari (Local Persian). P.	M.	F.	Pashto. P.	M.	F.	Lahnda (or Western Punjabi). P.	M.	F.
		2	3	4	5	6	7	8	9	10	11	12	13	14	15	16	17
Loralai District.		TOTAL ..	82,451	45,084	37,367	3,467	2,912	555	..	..	..	1,990	1,591	399	699	557	142
	Local.	Balochi ..	4,562	2,565	1,997	..	..	..	..	..	..	527	385	142	580	480	100
	Local.	Pashto ..	56,384	30,873	25,511	371	236	135	..	..	..	..	..	..	95	58	37
	Local.	Lahnda or Western Punjabi ..	19,348	10,142	9,206	2,986	2,592	394	..	..	..	1,112	899	213	..	..	..
	Local.	Unspecified Jagdali and Jatki ..	87	60	27	13	8	5	..	..	..	32	27	5	16	11	5
	Local.	Brahui ..	482	292	190	81	67	14	..	..	..	139	118	21	7	7	..
	Non-Local.	Sindhi ..	201	127	74	15	8	7	..	..	..	58	51	7	..	..	..
	Non-Local.	Western Hindi ..	1,175	860	315	..	..	..	..	..	..	18	15	3	..	..	..
	Non-Local.	Persian ..	212	165	47	1	1	..	..	..	..	104	96	8	1	1	..
Duki Tahsil.		TOTAL ..	17,799	9,635	8,164	366	228	138	..	..	..	784	520	264	52	33	19
	Local.	Balochi ..	439	252	187	..	..	..	..	..	..	302	187	115	2	2	..
	Local.	Pashto ..	16,531	8,885	7,646	334	206	128	..	..	..	..	..	..	47	28	19
	Local.	Lahnda or Western Punjabi	450	251	199	11	7	4	..	..	..	333	200	133	..	..	..
	Local.	Unspecified Jagdali and Jatki ..	11	9	2	1	1	..	..	..	..	6	6	..	2	2	..
	Local.	Brahui ..	232	132	100	18	12	6	..	..	..	79	70	9	1	1	..
	Non-Local.	Sindhi ..	40	20	20	2	2	..	..	..	..	21	14	7	..	..	..
	Non-Local.	Western Hindi ..	29	19	10	..	..	..	..	..	..	5	5	..	..	..	..
	Non-Local.	Persian ..	67	67	..	..	..	..	..	..	..	38	38	..	..	..	..
Bori Tahsil.		TOTAL ..	15,650	9,140	6,510	70	62	8	..	..	..	163	142	21	9	9	..
	Local.	Balochi ..	184	114	70	..	..	..	..	..	..	26	21	5	2	2	..
	Local.	Pashto ..	13,889	7,900	5,989	5	5	..	..	..	..	..	..	..	..	..	..
	Local.	Lahnda or Western Punjabi ..	17	16	1	..	..	..	..	..	..	6	5	1	..	..	..
	Local.	Unspecified Jagdali and Jatki ..	19	14	5	..	..	..	..	..	..	11	11	..	..	..	..
	Local.	Brahui ..	242	155	87	63	55	8	..	..	..	52	43	9	6	6	..
	Non-Local.	Sindhi ..	115	76	39	1	1	..	..	..	..	25	25	..	..	..	..
	Non-Local.	Western Hindi ..	1,110	815	295	..	..	..	..	..	..	6	4	2	..	..	..
	Non-Local.	Persian ..	74	50	24	1	1	..	..	..	..	37	33	4	1	1	..
Sanjawi Sub-Tahsil.		TOTAL ..	6,238	3,451	2,787	1	1	..	.	.	..	49	36	13	..	..	..
	Local.	Balochi ..	26	15	11	..	..	..	..	..	..	8	4	4	..	..	..
	Local.	Pashto ..	6,104	3,367	2,737	..	..	..	..	..	..	..	..	..	..	..	..
	Local.	Lahnda or Western Punjabi ..	18	11	7	..	..	..	..	..	..	10	7	3	..	..	..
	Local.	Brahui ..	8	5	3	..	..	..	..	..	..	8	5	3	..	..	..
	Non-Local.	Sindhi ..	18	16	2	1	1	..	..	..	..	11	11	..	..	..	..
	Non-Local.	Western Hindi ..	21	14	7	..	..	..	..	..	..	6	5	1	..	..	..
	Non-Local.	Persian ..	43	23	20	..	..	..	..	..	..	6	4	2	..	..	..
Barkhan Tahsil.		TOTAL ..	20,148	10,691	9,457	2,604	2,313	291	..	..	..	562	548	14	550	447	103
	Local.	Balochi ..	2,671	1,520	1,151	..	..	..	..	..	..	94	93	1	527	430	97
	Local.	Pashto ..	190	126	64	10	10	..	..	..	..	..	..	..	10	9	1
	Local.	Lahnda or Western Punjabi ..	17,197	8,985	8,212	2,583	2,297	286	..	..	..	442	436	6	..	..	..
	Local.	Unspecified Jagdali and Jatki ..	49	31	18	11	6	5	..	..	..	11	6	5	13	8	5
	Non-Local.	Sindhi ..	11	5	6	..	..	..	..	..	..	1	1	..	..	..	..
	Non-Local.	Western Hindi ..	13	10	3	..	..	..	..	..	..	1	1	..	..	..	..
	Non-Local.	Persian ..	17	14	3	..	..	..	..	..	..	13	11	2	..	..	..
Musakhel Tahsil.		TOTAL ..	22,616	12,167	10,449	426	308	118	..	..	..	432	345	87	88	68	20
	Local.	Balochi ..	1,242	664	578	..	..	..	..	..	..	97	80	17	49	46	3
	Local.	Pashto ..	19,670	10,595	9,075	22	15	7	..	..	..	..	..	..	38	21	17
	Local.	Lahnda or Western Punjabi ..	1,666	879	787	392	288	104	..	..	..	321	251	70	..	..	..
	Local.	Unspecified Jagdali and Jatki ..	8	6	2	1	1	..	..		..	4	4	..	1	1	..
	Non-Local.	Sindhi ..	17	10	7	11	4	7	..	..	..	..	..	..	..	..	..
	Non-Local.	Western Hindi ..	2	2	..	..	..	..	..	..	..	..	..	..	..	..	..
	Non-Local.	Persian ..	11	11	..	..	..	..	..	..	..	10	10	..	..	..	..
Zhob District.		TOTAL ..	52,189	29,628	22,561	12	9	3	..	..	..	292	275	17	..	..	..
	Local.	Balochi ..	64	38	26	..	..	..	..	..	..	12	9	3	..	..	..
	Local.	Pashto ..	50,864	28,499	22,365	9	6	3	..	..	..	..	..	..	..	..	..
	Local.	Lahnda or Western Punjabi ..	11	6	5	..	..	..	..	..	..	1	1	..	..	..	..
	Local.	Sindhi (Jattki and Lasi)	1	1	..	..	..	..	..	..	..	1	1	..	..	..	..
	Local.	Brahui ..	146	141	5	1	1	..	..	..	..	103	163		..	..	..
	Non-Local.	Sindhi ..	69	53	16	..	..	..	..	..	..	5	5	..	..	..	..
	Non-Local.	Western Hindi ..	710	594	116	..	..	..	..	..	..	39	36	3	..	..	..
	Non-Local.	Persian ..	324	296	28	2	2	..	..	..	..	131	120	11	..	..	..

BILINGUALISM.

SUBSIDIARY LANGUAGES.																		All other mother-tongues not specified in column 2.		
LOCAL.									NON-LOCAL.											
Unspecified Jagdali and Jatki.			*Sindhi (Jatki and Lasi).*			*Brahui.*			*Sindhi.*			*Western Hindi.*			*Persian.*					
P.	M.	F.	P.	M.	F.	P.	M.	F.	P.	M.	F.	P.	M.	F.	P.	M.	F.	P.	M.	F.
18	19	20	21	22	23	24	25	26	27	28	29	30	31	32	33	34	35	36	37	38
1,283	888	395	19	18	1	423	251	172	12	12	..	614	571	43	390	375	15	3,636	2,852	784
148	147	1	4	4	..	35	32	3	..	..	..	27	27	..	5	3	2	..	..	..
1,050	682	368	8	8	..	388	219	169	3	3	..	328	303	25	354	349	5	..	..	..
85	59	26	..	..	..	..	..	..	..	..	..	22	21	1	1	1	..	..	..	..
..	..	..	1	1	..	..	..	..	5	5	..	4	4	..	..	..	..	..	..	..
..	..	..	..	..	..	..	..	..	2	2	..	96	87	9	20	14	6	..	..	..
..	..	..	6	5	1	..	..	..	..	..	..	40	35	5	1	1	..	..	..	..
..	..	..	..	..	..	..	..	..	2	2	..	..	..	..	9	7	2	..	..	..
..	..	..	..	..	..	..	..	..	..	..	..	97	94	3	..	..	..	..	..	..
89	89	..	..	..	..	..	..	..	1	1	..	76	76	..	194	194	..	199	136	63
1	1	..	..	..	..	..	..	..	..	..	..	3	3	..	..	..	..	..	..	..
88	88	..	..	..	..	..	..	..	1	1	..	31	31	..	194	194	..	..	..	..
..	..	..	..	..	..	..	..	..	..	..	..	..	..	..	..	..	..	..	..	..
..	..	..	..	..	..	..	..	..	..	..	..	3	3	..	..	..	..	..	..	..
..	..	..	..	..	..	..	..	..	..	..	..	1	1	..	..	..	..	..	..	..
..	..	..	..	..	..	..	..	..	..	..	..	..	..	..	..	..	..	..	..	..
..	..	..	..	..	..	..	..	..	..	..	..	..	..	..	..	..	..	..	..	..
..	..	..	..	..	..	..	..	..	..	..	..	38	38	..	..	..	..	..	..	..
148	147	1	17	16	1	35	32	3	8	8	..	442	401	41	163	150	13	2,882	2,324	558
74	73	1	4	4	..	35	32	3	..	..	..	23	23	..	..	..	..	..	..	..
74	74	..	6	6	..	..	..	..	..	..	..	257	232	25	134	129	5	..	..	..
..	..	..	..	..	..	..	..	..	..	..	..	4	4	..	..	..	..	..	..	..
..	..	..	1	1	..	..	..	..	5	5	..	..	..	..	..	..	..	..	..	..
..	..	..	..	..	..	..	..	..	2	2	..	94	85	9	20	14	6	..	..	..
..	..	..	6	5	1	..	..	..	..	..	..	34	29	5	1	1	..	..	..	..
..	..	..	..	..	..	..	..	..	1	1	..	..	..	..	8	6	2	..	..	..
..	..	..	..	..	..	..	..	..	..	..	..	30	28	2	..	..	..	..	..	..
..	..	..	1	1	..	..	..	..	3	3	..	37	36	1	15	13	2	75	50	25
..	..	..	..	..	..	..	..	..	..	..	..	1	1	..	4	2	2	..	..	..
..	..	..	1	1	..	..	..	..	2	2	..	22	22	..	9	9	..	..	..	..
..	..	..	..	..	..	..	..	..	..	..	..	2	2	..	1	1	..	..	..	..
..	..	..	..	..	..	..	..	..	..	..	..	1	1	..	..	..	..	..	..	..
..	..	..	..	..	..	..	..	..	..	..	..	6	6	..	..	..	..	..	..	..
..	..	..	..	..	..	..	..	..	1	1	..	..	..	..	1	1	..	..	..	..
..	..	..	..	..	..	..	..	..	..	..	..	5	4	1	..	..	..	..	..	..
1	1	..	1	1	..	..	..	..	..	..	..	40	39	1	5	5	..	286	210	76
..	..	..	..	..	..	..	..	..	..	..	..	..	..	..	..	..	..	..	..	..
..	..	..	1	1	..	..	..	..	..	..	..	10	10	..	5	5	..	..	..	..
1	1	..	..	..	..			..	..	..	..	15	14	1	..	..	..	..	..	..
..	..	..	..	..	..	..	..	..	..	..	..	1	1	..	..	..	..	..	..	..
..	..	..	..	..	..	..	..	..	..	..	..	..	..	..	..	..	..	..	..	..
..	..	..	..	..	..	..	..	..	..	..	..	..	..	..	..	..	..	..	..	..
..	..	..	..	..	..	..	..	..	..	..	..	14	14	..	..	..	..	..	..	..
1,045	651	394	..	..	..	388	219	169	..	..	..	19	19	..	13	13	..	194	132	62
73	73	..	..	..	..	..	..	..	..	..	..	..	..	..	1	1	..	..	..	..
888	520	368	..	..	..	388	219	169	..	..	..	8	8	..	12	12	..	..	..	..
84	58	26	..	..	..	..	..	..	..	..	..	1	1	..	..	..	..	..	..	..
..	..	..	..	..	..	..	..	..	..	..	..	..	..	..	..	..	..	..	..	..
..	..	..	..	..	..	..	..	..	..	..	..	..	..	..	..	..	..	..	..	..
..	..	..	..	..	..	..	..	..	..	..	..	..	..	..	..	..	..	..	..	..
..	..	..	..	..	..	..	..	..	..	..	..	10	10	..	..	..	..	..	..	..
..	..	..	3	3	..	88	87	1	5	4	1	1,046	1,005	41	188	182	6	5,774	4,968	806
..	..	..	..	..	..	2	1	1	3	2	1	6	6	..	..	..	..	..	..	..
..	..	..	3	3	..	84	84	..	1	1	..	795	762	33	161	155	6	..	..	..
..	..	..	..	..	..	1	1	..	..	..	..	..	..	..	1	1	..	..	..	..
..	..	..	..	..	..	..	..	..	..	..	..	..	..	..	..	..	..	..	..	..
..	..	..	..	..	..	..	..	..	..	..	..	121	121	..	17	17	..	..	..	..
..	..	..	..	..	..	..	..	..	..	..	..	21	21	..	..	..	..	..	..	..
..	..	..	..	..	..	..	..	..	1	1	..	..	..	..	9	9	..	..	..	..
..	..	..	..	..	..	1	1	..	..	..	..	103	95	8	..	..	..	..	..	..

P = Persons; M = Males; F = Females.

TABLE XV.—(PART II

Area of Bilingualism	Mother-Tongue	Number of Persons speaking Mother-Tongue P.	M.	F.	Balochi P.	M.	F.	Dehwari (Local Persian) P.	M.	F.	Pashto P.	M.	F.	Lahnda (or Western Punjabi) P.	M.	F.
		NUMBER OF PERSONS SPEAKING — Local														
1	2	3	4	5	6	7	8	9	10	11	12	13	14	15	16	17
Fort Sandeman Tahsil	TOTAL	28,380	16,124	12,256	6	6	..	..	..	..	226	213	13	..	..	..
Local	Balochi	43	26	17	..	..	..	..	..	..	5	4	1	..	..	..
	Pashto	27,420	15,307	12,113	5	5	..	..	..	..	..	..	..	..	..	..
	Lahnda or Western Punjabi	4	4	..	..	..	..	..	..	..	..	..	..	..	..	..
	Brahui	119	119	..	..	..	..	..	..	..	91	91	..	..	..	..
Non-Local	Sindhi	55	42	13	..	..	..	..	..	..	2	2	..	..	..	..
	Western Hindi	574	483	91	..	..	..	..	..	..	32	29	3	..	..	..
	Persian	165	143	22	1	1	..	..	..	..	96	87	9	..	..	..
Hindubagh Tahsil	TOTAL	10,899	6,147	4,752	4	1	3	..	..	..	25	23	2	..	..	..
Local	Balochi	2	1	1	..	..	..	..	..	..	1	..	1	..	..	..
	Pashto	10,679	5,947	4,732	3	..	3	..	..	..	..	..	..	..	..	..
	Lahnda or Western Punjabi	7	2	5	..	..	..	..	..	..	1	1	..	..	..	..
	Sindhi (Jattki and Lasi)	1	1	..	..	..	..	..	..	..	1	1	..	..	..	..
	Brahui	10	6	4	..	..	..	..	..	..	1	1	..	..	..	..
Non-Local	Sindhi	3	3	..	..	..	..	..	..	..	..	..	..	..	..	..
	Western Hindi	72	64	8	..	..	..	..	..	..	2	2	..	..	..	..
	Persian	125	123	2	1	1	..	..	..	..	19	18	1	..	..	..
Killa Saifullah Tahsil	TOTAL	12,910	7,357	5,553	2	2	..	..	..	..	41	39	2	..	..	..
Local	Balochi	19	11	8	..	..	..	..	..	..	6	5	1	..	..	..
	Pashto	12,765	7,245	5.520	1	1	..	..	..	..	..	..	..	..	..	..
	Brahui	17	16	1	1	1	..	..	..	..	11	11	..	..	..	..
Non-Local	Sindhi	11	8	3	..	..	..	..	..	..	3	3	..	..	..	..
	Western Hindi	64	47	17	..	..	..	..	..	..	5	5	..	..	..	..
	Persian	34	30	4	..	..	..	..	..	..	16	15	1	..	..	..
Bolan District	TOTAL	2,946	2,267	679	226	151	75	..	..	..	63	53	10	..	..	..
Local	Balochi	713	461	252	..	..	..	..	..	..	25	23	2	..	..	..
	Dehwari or Local Persian	1	1	..	..	..	..	..	..	..	..	..	..	..	..	..
	Pashto	215	186	29	6	6	..	..	..	..	..	..	..	..	..	..
	Unspecified Jagdali and Jatki	33	33	..	..	..	..	..	..	..	4	4	..	..	..	..
	Sindhi (Jattki and Lasi)	4	3	1	4	3	1	..	..	..	..	..	..	..	..	..
	Brahui	1,044	797	247	204	132	72	..	..	..	23	19	4	..	..	..
Non-Local	Sindhi	333	272	61	10	8	2	..	..	..	1	..	1	..	..	..
	Western Hindi	547	471	76	2	2	..	..	..	..	..	..	..	..	..	..
	Persian	56	43	13	..	..	..	..	..	..	10	7	3	..	..	..
Chagai District	TOTAL	22,740	12,616	10,124	3,195	2,007	1,188	..	..	..	777	518	259	60	50	10
Local	Balochi	11,214	6,061	5,153	..	..	..	..	..	..	76	60	16	57	47	10
	Pashto	2,371	1,415	956	167	113	54	..	..	..	..	..	..	..	..	..
	Unspecified Jagdali and Jatki	112	64	48	35	27	8	..	..	..	14	13	1	..	..	..
	Sindhi (Jattki and Lasi)	7	5	2	2	1	1	..	..	..	..	..	..	..	..	..
	Brahui	8,277	4,585	3,692	2,821	1,728	1,093	..	..	..	575	354	221	3	3	..
Non-Local	Sindhi	394	246	148	121	107	14	..	..	..	59	53	6	..	..	..
	Western Hindi	258	176	82	6	6	..	..	..	..	3	3	..	..	..	..
	Persian	107	64	43	43	25	18	..	..	..	50	35	15	..	..	..
Nushki Tahsil	TOTAL	10,446	5,754	4,692	2,048	1,299	749	..	..	..	207	177	30	..	..	..
Local	Balochi	3,983	2,161	1,822	..	..	..	..	..	..	14	13	1	..	..	..
	Pashto	454	247	207	91	60	31	..	..	..	..	..	..	..	..	..
	Unspecified Jagdali and Jatki	112	64	48	35	27	8	..	..	..	14	13	1	..	..	..
	Sindhi (Jattki and Lasi)	7	5	2	2	1	1	..	..	..	..	..	..	..	..	..
	Brahui	5,526	3,054	2,472	1,850	1,156	694	..	..	..	117	101	16	..	..	..
Non-Local	Sindhi	220	137	83	50	43	7	..	..	..	35	32	3	..	..	..
	Western Hindi	73	45	28	1	1	..	..	..	..	1	1	..	..	..	..
	Persian	71	41	30	19	11	8	..	..	..	26	17	9	..	..	..
Dalbandin & Western Sanjrani	TOTAL	10,092	5,544	4,548	1,138	699	439	..	..	..	145	113	32	59	49	10
Local	Balochi	7,210	3,887	3,323	..	..	..	..	..	..	60	45	15	56	46	10
	Pashto	272	155	117	74	51	23	..	..	..	..	..	..	..	..	..
	Brahui	2,216	1,240	976	964	565	399	..	..	..	35	27	8	3	3	..
Non-Local	Sindhi	174	109	65	71	64	7	..	..	..	24	21	3	..	..	..
	Western Hindi	184	130	54	5	5	..	..	..	..	2	2	..	..	..	..
	Persian	36	23	13	24	14	10	..	..	..	24	18	6	..	..	..
Shorarud Sub-Tahsil	TOTAL	2,202	1,318	884	9	9	..	..	..	..	425	228	197	1	1	..
Local	Balochi	21	13	8	..	..	..	..	..	..	2	2	..	1	1	..
	Pashto	1,645	1,013	632	2	2	..	..	..	..	..	..	..	..	..	..
	Brahui	535	291	244	7	7	..	..	..	..	423	226	197	..	..	..
Non-Local	Western Hindi	1	1	..	..	..	..	..	..	..	..	..	..	..	..	..

BILINGUALISM.

SUBSIDIARY LANGUAGES.																				
LOCAL.									NON-LOCAL.									*All other mother-tongues not specified in columns 2.*		
Unspecified Jagdali and Jatki.			*Sindhi (Jattki and Lasi).*			*Brahui.*			*Sindhi.*			*Western Hindi.*			*Persian.*					
P.	M.	F.	P.	M.	F.	P.	M.	F.	P.	M.	F.	P.	M.	F.	P.	M.	F.	P.	M.	F.
18	19	20	21	22	23	24	25	26	27	28	29	30	31	32	33	34	35	36	37	38
..	..	..	..	..	..	5	4	1	1	1	..	857	825	32	124	121	3	4,609	3,987	622
..	..	..	..	..	..	2	1	1	..	..	..	2	2	..	..	..	..	..	..	..
..	..	..	..	..	..	3	3	..	..	..	..	634	608	26	101	98	3	..	..	..
..	..	..	..	..	..	..	..	..	..	..	..	..	..	..	..	..	..	..	..	..
..	..	..	..	..	..	..	..	..	..	..	..	113	113	..	17	17	..	..	..	..
..	..	..	..	..	..	..	..	..	..	..	..	19	19	..	..	..	..	..	..	..
..	..	..	..	..	..	..	..	..	1	1	..	..	..	..	6	6	..	..	..	..
..	..	..	..	..	..	..	..	..	..	..	..	89	83	6	..	..	..	..	..	..
..	..	..	3	3	..	88	88	..	..	..	..	124	121	3	46	46	..	681	577	104
..	..	..	..	..	..	..	..	..	..	..	..	..	..	..	..	..	..	..	..	..
..	..	..	3	3	..	81	81	..	..	..	..	118	115	3	43	43	..	..	..	..
..	..	..	..	..	..	1	1	..	..	..	..	..	..	..	1	1	..	..	..	..
..	..	..	..	..	..	..	..	..	..	..	..	..	..	..	..	..	..	..	..	..
..	..	..	..	..	..	..	..	..	..	..	..	..	..	..	..	..	..	..	..	..
..	..	..	..	..	..	..	..	..	..	..	..	..	..	..	..	..	..	..	..	..
..	..	..	..	..	..	..	..	..	..	..	..	..	..	..	2	2	..	..	..	..
..	..	..	..	..	..	1	1	..	..	..	..	6	6	..	..	..	..	..	..	..
..	..	..	..	..	..	..	..	..	4	3	1	65	59	6	18	15	3	484	404	80
..	..	..	..	..	..	..	..	..	3	2	1	4	4	..	..	..	..	..	..	..
..	..	..	..	..	..	..	..	..	1	1	..	43	39	4	17	14	3	..	..	..
..	..	..	..	..	..	..	..	..	..	..	..	8	8	..	..	..	..	..	..	..
..	..	..	..	..	..	..	..	..	..	..	..	2	2	..	..	..	..	..	..	..
..	..	..	..	..	..	..	..	..	..	..	..	..	..	..	1	1	..	..	..	..
..	..	..	..	..	..	..	..	..	..	..	..	8	6	2	..	..	..	..	..	..
..	..	..	87	83	4	443	276	167	37	29	8	260	246	14	32	28	4	1,742	1,199	543
..	..	..	31	31	..	412	247	165	20	18	2	46	42	4	5	5	..	..	..	..
..	..	..	..	..	..	..	..	..	..	..	..	..	..	..	..	..	..	..	..	..
..	..	..	..	..	..	5	5	..	6	4	2	39	36	3	11	7	4	..	..	..
..	..	..	..	..	..	4	4	..	..	..	..	7	7	..	..	..	..	..	..	..
..	..	..	..	..	..	4	3	1	..	..	..	..	..	..	..	..	..	..	..	..
..	..	..	56	52	4	..	..	..	11	7	4	133	130	3	16	16	..	..	..	..
..	..	..	..	..	..	13	13	..	..	..	..	24	20	4	..	..	..	..	..	..
..	..	..	..	..	..	2	2	..	..	..	..	..	..	..	..	..	..	..	..	..
..	..	..	..	..	..	3	2	1	..	..	..	11	11	..	..	..	..	..	..	..
3	3	..	66	57	9	4,585	2,597	1,988	30	21	9	672	575	97	135	107	28	1,484	1,105	379
..	..	..	36	29	7	3,585	2,004	1,581	7	2	5	240	199	41	49	37	12	..	..	..
..	..	..	2	1	1	840	464	376	..	..	..	54	45	9	38	29	9	..	..	..
..	..	..	..	..	..	43	32	11	5	3	2	45	33	12	..	..	..	..	..	..
..	..	..	..	..	..	..	..	..	..	..	..	1	1	..	..	..	..	..	..	..
..	..	..	21	20	1	..	..	..	16	14	2	189	171	18	38	31	7	..	..	..
3	3	..	7	7	..	102	83	19	..	..	..	116	103	13	8	8	..	..	..	..
..	..	..	..	..	..	1	1	..	1	1	..	..	..	..	2	2	..	..	..	..
..	..	..	..	..	..	14	13	1	1	1	..	27	23	4	..	..	..	..	..	..
3	3	..	13	12	1	3,083	1,700	1,383	15	13	2	215	193	22	28	27	1	274	262	112
..	..	..	..	..	..	2,763	1,494	1,269	..	..	..	..	..	..	..	..	..	..	..	..
..	..	..	2	1	1	184	101	83	..	..	..	15	14	1	7	6	1	..	..	..
..	..	..	..	..	..	43	32	11	5	3	2	45	33	12	..	..	..	..	..	..
..	..	..	..	..	..	..	..	..	..	..	..	1	1	..	..	..	..	..	..	..
..	..	..	5	5	..	..	..	..	10	10	..	95	94	1	17	17	..	..	..	..
3	3	..	6	6	..	85	66	19	..	..	..	52	44	8	4	4	..	..	..	..
..	..	..	..	..	..	1	1	..	..	..	..	..	..	..	..	..	..	..	..	..
..	..	..	..	..	..	7	6	1	..	..	..	7	7	..	..	..	..	..	..	..
..	..	..	53	45	8	925	577	348	7	5	2	373	305	68	96	71	25	1,093	830	263
..	..	..	36	29	7	817	506	311	..	..	..	182	148	34	38	28	10	..	..	..
..	..	..	..	..	..	84	47	37	..	..	..	31	23	8	31	23	8	..	..	..
..	..	..	16	15	1	..	..	..	5	3	2	76	59	17	21	14	7	..	..	..
..	..	..	1	1	..	17	17	..	..	..	..	64	59	5	4	4	..	..	..	..
..	..	..	..	..	..	..	..	..	1	1	..	..	..	..	2	2	..	..	..	..
..	..	..	..	..	..	7	7	..	1	1	..	20	16	4	..	..	..	..	..	..
..	..	..	..	..	..	577	320	257	8	3	5	84	77	7	11	9	2	17	13	4
..	..	..	..	..	..	5	4	1	7	2	5	58	51	7	11	9	2	..	..	..
..	..	..	..	..	..	572	316	256	..	..	..	8	8	..	..	..	..	..	..	..
..	..	..	..	..	..	..	..	..	1	1	..	18	18	..	..	..	..	..	..	..
..	..	..	..	..	..	..	..	..	..	..	..	..	..	..	..	..	..	..	..	..

P = Persons; M = Males; F = Females.

TABLE XV.—(PART II)

1—Area of Bilingualism.	Mother-Tongue.	Number of Persons speaking Mother-Tongue.			Number of Persons speaking — Local. — Balochi.			Dehwari (Local Persian).			Pashto.			Lahnda (or Western Punjabi).		
		P.	M.	F.	P.	M.	F.	P.	M.	F.	P.	M.	F.	P.	M.	F.
1	2	3	4	5	6	7	8	9	10	11	12	13	14	15	16	17
Sibi District.	TOTAL	137,736	76,387	61,349	2,645	1,954	691	..	..	..	1,205	1,020	185	1,986	1,139	847
Local.	Balochi	78,646	42,926	35,720	..	..	..	..	..	..	575	522	53	1,565	896	669
	Dehwari or Local Persian.	3	2	1	..	..	..	..	..	..	2	1	1	..	..	..
	Pashto	19,282	10,521	8,761	487	300	187	..	..	..	..	..	..	114	73	41
	Lahnda or Western Punjabi.	2,885	1,598	1,287	262	175	87	..	..	..	76	44	32	..	..	..
	Unspecified Jagdali and Jatki.	614	358	256	..	..	..	..	..	..	3	3	..	..	..	..
	Sindhi (Jattki and Lasi)	24,487	13,947	10,540	1,103	888	215	..	..	..	181	122	59	302	165	137
	Brahui	6,887	3,911	2,976	653	493	160	..	..	..	140	126	14	5	5	..
Non-Local.	Sindhi	2,907	1,718	1,189	133	94	39	..	..	..	160	157	3	..	..	..
	Western Hindi	1,752	1,211	541	1	1	..	..	..	..	14	12	2	..	..	..
	Persian	273	195	78	6	3	3	..	..	..	54	33	21	..	..	..
Sibi Tahsil.	TOTAL	23,836	13,469	10,367	885	689	196	..	..	..	664	505	159	33	22	11
Local.	Balochi	4,115	2,229	1,886	..	..	..	..	..	..	190	145	45	19	11	8
	Pashto	4,168	2,334	1,834	111	71	40	..	..	..	..	..	..	12	9	3
	Lahnda or Western Punjabi.	655	387	268	23	13	10	..	..	..	72	41	31	..	..	..
	Unspecified Jagdali and Jatki.	117	82	35	..	..	..	..	..	..	3	3	..	..	..	..
	Sindhi (Jattki and Lasi)	8,699	4,826	3,873	534	440	94	..	..	..	162	103	59	2	2	..
	Brahui	2,597	1,503	1,094	180	136	44	..	..	..	90	85	5	..	..	..
Non-Local.	Sindhi	2,015	1,062	953	30	25	5	..	..	..	96	95	1	..	..	..
	Western Hindi	1,235	879	356	1	1	..	..	..	..	10	8	2	..	..	..
	Persian	235	167	68	6	3	3	..	..	..	41	25	16	..	..	..
Shahrig Tahsil.	TOTAL	17,259	9,475	7,784	29	29	..	..	..	..	359	350	9	9	4	5
Local.	Balochi	2,354	1,366	988	..	..	..	..	..	..	272	271	1	4	2	2
	Dehwari or Local Persian.	3	2	1	..	..	..	..	..	..	2	1	1	..	..	..
	Pashto	14,479	7,821	6,658	4	4	..	..	..	..	..	..	..	5	2	3
	Lahnda or Western Punjabi.	4	3	1	..	..	..	..	..	..	4	3	1	..	..	..
	Sindhi (Jattki and Lasi).	30	23	7	..	..	..	..	..	..	19	19	..	..	..	..
	Brahui	71	53	18	..	..	..	..	..	..	29	28	1	..	..	..
Non-Local.	Sindhi	131	90	41	25	25	..	..	..	..	19	19	..	..	..	..
	Western Hindi	163	98	65	..	..	..	..	..	..	4	4	..	..	..	..
	Persian	24	19	5	..	..	..	..	..	..	10	5	5	..	..	..
Nasirabad Tahsil.	TOTAL	36,014	19,937	16,077	1,114	879	235	..	..	..	67	59	8	1,835	1,045	790
Local.	Balochi	13,407	6,834	6,573	..	..	..	..	..	..	..	..	..	1,530	877	653
	Pashto	59	41	18	12	7	5	..	..	..	..	..	..	..	..	..
	Lahnda or Western Punjabi.	1,786	983	803	104	93	11	..	..	..	..	..	..	..	..	..
	Unspecified Jagdali and Jatki.	6	6	..	..	..	..	..	..	..	..	..	..	..	..	..
	Sindhi (Jattki and Lasi)	15 758	9,098	6,660	569	448	121	..	..	..	..	..	..	300	163	137
	Brahui	4,170	2,324	1,846	425	327	98	..	..	..	21	13	8	5	5	..
Non-Local.	Sindhi	643	498	145	4	4	..	..	..	..	43	43	..	..	..	..
	Western Hindi	171	144	27	..	..	..	..	..	..	..	..	..	..	..	..
	Persian	14	9	5	..	..	..	..	..	..	3	3	..	..	..	..
Kohlu Sub-Tahsil.	TOTAL	5,405	2,972	2,433	543	317	226	..	..	..	115	106	9	109	68	41
Local.	Balochi	4,329	2,386	1,943	..	..	..	..	..	..	113	106	7	12	6	6
	Pashto	573	322	251	360	218	142	..	..	..	..	..	..	97	62	35
	Lahnda or Western Punjabi.	440	225	215	135	69	66	..	..	..	..	..	..	..	..	..
	Brahui	49	31	18	48	30	18	..	..	..	..	..	..	..	..	..
Non-Local.	Sindhi	5	3	2	..	..	..	..	..	..	2	..	2	..	..	..
	Western Hindi	9	5	4	..	..	..	..	..	..	..	..	..	..	..	..
Mari Country.	TOTAL	24,856	13,878	10,980	74	40	34	..	..	..	..	..	..	..	..	..
Local.	Balochi	24,728	13,805	10,923	..	..	..	..	..	..	..	..	..	..	..	..
	Unspecified Jagdali and Jatki.	14	6	8	..	..	..	..	..	..	..	..	..	..	..	..
Non-Local.	Sindhi	113	65	48	74	40	34	..	..	..	..	..	..	..	..	..
	Western Hindi	3	2	1	..	..	..	..	..	..	..	..	..	..	..	..
Bugti Country.	TOTAL	30,364	16,656	13,708	..	..	..	..	..	..	..	..	..	..	..	..
Local.	Balochi	29,713	16,306	13,407	..	..	..	..	..	..	..	..	..	..	..	..
	Pashto	3	3	..	..	..	..	..	..	..	..	..	..	..	..	..
	Unspecified Jagdali and Jatki.	477	264	213	..	..	..	..	..	..	..	..	..	..	..	..
Non-Local.	Western Hindi	171	83	88	..	..	..	..	..	..	..	..	..	..	..	..
States.	TOTAL	4,04,328	217,867	186,461	5,781	4,147	1,634	2,938	1,796	1,142	349	239	110	190	121	69
Local.	Balochi	169,863	91,339	78,524	..	..	..	941	551	390	28	18	10	82	57	25
	Dehwari or Local Persian.	5,127	2,788	2,339	..	..	..	..	..	..	8	4	4	..	..	..
	Pashto	888	507	381	37	26	11	184	108	76	..	..	..	..	..	..
	Lahnda or Western Punjabi.	5,037	2,612	2,425	102	67	35	..	..	..	1	1	..	..	..	..
	Unspecified Jagdali and Jatki.	939	518	421	33	21	12	..	..	..	..	..	..	25	15	10
	Sindhi (Jattki and Lasi)	118,696	63,993	54,703	2,712	2,057	655	..	..	..	123	84	39	54	32	22
	Brahui	102,580	55,374	47,206	2,743	1,846	897	1,795	1,126	669	185	128	57	29	17	12
Non-Local.	Sindhi	936	566	370	141	117	24	14	9	5	..	..	..	..	..	..
	Western Hindi	153	109	44	6	6	..	..	..	..	..	..	..	..	..	..
	Persian	109	61	48	7	7	..	4	2	2	4	4	..	..	..	..

BILINGUALISM.

SUBSIDIARY LANGUAGES.																		All other mother-tongues not specified in column 2.		
Local.									Non-Local.											
Unspecified Jagdali and Jatki.			*Sindhi (Jatki and Lasi).*			*Brahui.*			*Sindhi.*			*Western Hindi.*			*Persian.*					
P.	M.	F.	P.	M.	F.	P.	M.	F.	P.	M.	F.	P.	M.	F.	P.	M.	F.	P.	M.	F.
18	19	20	21	22	23	24	25	26	27	28	29	30	31	32	33	34	35	36	37	38
82	74	8	11,383	6,334	5,049	475	343	132	424	336	88	1,480	1,153	327	122	92	30	5,269	3,596	1,673
6	5	1	9,209	4,965	4,244	204	158	46	173	141	32	498	348	150	19	17	2	..	..	..
..	..	..		..	..	..	..	..	..	..	..	..	..	..	..	..	..	..	..	..
3	3	..	69	44	25	52	37	15	11	11	..	338	274	64	32	31	1	..	..	..
..	..	..	317	177	140	4	2	2	5	4	1	10	9	1	..	..	..	..	..	..
..	..	..	..	..	..	2	2	..	5	5	..	22	21	1	..	..	..	..	..	..
..	..	..	..	..	..	193	128	65	74	41	33	26	24	2	2	2	..	..	..	..
69	66	3	1,783	1,144	639	..	..	..	126	105	21	226	215	11	60	37	23	..	..	..
..	..	..	..	..	..	10	9	1	..	..	..	292	220	72	..	..	..	..	..	..
4	..	4	4	3	1	1	1	..	28	27	1	..	..	..	9	5	4	..	..	..
..	..	..	1	1	..	9	6	3	2	2	..	68	42	26	..	..	..	..	..	..
71	68	3	2,535	1,320	1,215	434	314	120	183	155	28	1,239	932	307	117	87	30	3,671	2,354	1,317
..	..	..	2,092	1,039	1,053	181	142	39	99	75	24	484	335	149	18	16	2	..	..	..
2	2	..	59	37	22	49	34	15	10	10	..	165	116	49	28	27	1	..	..	..
..	..	..	..	..	..	4	2	2	2	2	..	7	7	..	..	..	..	..	..	..
..	..	..	..	..	..	1	1	..	5	5	..	22	21	1	..	..	..	..	..	..
..	..	..	..	..	..	185	123	62	..	..	..	26	24	2	2	2	..	..	..	..
69	66	3	384	244	140	..	..	..	58	55	3	208	197	11	60	37	23	..	..	..
..	..	..	..	..	..	8	7	1	..	..	..	266	194	72	..	..	..	..	..	..
..	..	..	..	..	..	1	1	..	8	7	1	..	..	..	9	5	4	..	..	..
..	..	..	..	..	..	5	4	1	1	1	..	61	38	23	..	..	..	..	..	..
7	6	1	12	11	1	8	7	1	5	4	1	204	188	16	3	3	..	918	718	200
6	5	1	10	10	..	5	4	1	4	3	1	8	8	..	..	..	..	..	..	..
..	..	..	..	..	..	..	..	..	..	..	..	..	..	..	..	..	..	..	..	..
1	1	..	..	..	..	3	3	..	..	..	..	159	144	15	3	3	..	..	..	..
..	..	..	..	..	..	..	..	..	1	1	..	3	2	1	..	..	..	..	..	..
..	..	..	..	..	..	..	..	..	..	..	..	..	..	..	..	..	..	..	..	..
..	..	..	..	..	..	..	..	..	..	..	..	18	18	..	..	..	..	..	..	..
..	..	..	..	..	..	..	..	..	..	..	..	16	16	..	..	..	..	..	..	..
..	..	..	2	1	1	..	..	..	..	..	..	..	..	..	..	..	..	..	..	..
..	..	..	..	..	..	..	..	..	..	..	..	..	..	..	..	..	..	..	..	..
4	..	4	8,834	5,002	3,832	23	16	7	236	177	59	30	26	4	1	1	..	620	478	142
..	..	..	7,105	3,915	3,190	8	6	2	70	63	7	5	4	1	1	1	..	..	..	..
..	..	..	10	7	3	..	..	..	1	1	..	8	8	..	..	..	..	..	..	..
..	..	..	317	177	140	..	..	..	2	1	1	..	..	..	..	..	..	..	..	..
..	..	..	..	..	..	1	1	..	..	..	..	..	..	...	..	..	..	..	..	..
..	..	..	..	..	..	8	5	3	74	41	33	..	..	..	..	..	..	..	..	..
..	..	..	1,399	900	499	..	..	..	68	50	18	..	..	..	..	..	..	..	..	..
..	..	..	..	..	..	2	2	..	..	..	..	10	10	..	..	..	..	..	..	..
4	..	4	2	2	..	..	..	..	20	20	..	..	..	..	..	..	..	..	..	..
..	..	..	1	1	..	4	2	2	1	1	..	7	4	3	..	..	..	..	..	..
..	..	..	2	1	1	10	6	4	..	..	..	7	7	..	1	1	..	58	44	14
..	..	..	2	1	1	10	6	4	..	..	..	1	1	..	..	..	..	..	..	..
..	..	..	..	..	..		..	..	..	..	..	6	6	..	1	1	..	..	..	..
..	..	..	..	..	..	..	..	..	..	..	..	..	..	..	..	..	..	..	..	..
..	..	..	..	..	..	..	..	..	..	..	..	..	..	..	..	..	..	..	..	..
..	..	..	..	..	..	..	..	..	..	..	..	..	..	..	..	..	..	..	..	..
..	..	..	..	..	..	..	..	..	..	..	..	..	..	..	..	..	..	..	..	..
..	..	..	..	..	..	..	..	..	..	..	..	..	..	..	..	..	..	2	2	..
..	..	..	..	..	..	..	..	..	..	..	..	..	..	..	..	..	..	..	..	..
..	..	..	..	..	..	..	..	..	..	..	..	..	..	..	..	..	..	..	..	..
..	..	..	..	..	..	..	..	..	..	..	..	..	..	..	..	..	..	..	..	..
..	..	..	..	..	..	..	..	..	..	..	..	..	..	..	..	..	..	..	..	..
..	..	..	..	..	..	..	..	..	..	..	..	..	..	..	..	..	..	..	..	..
..	..	..	..	..	..	..	..	..	..	..	..	..	..	..	..	..	..	..	..	..
..	..	..	..	..	..	..	..	..	..	..	..	..	..	..	..	..	..	..	..	..
..	..	..	..	..	..	..	..	..	..	..	..	..	..	..	..	..	..	..	..	..
..	..	..	..	..	..	..	..	..	..	..	..	..	..	..	..	..	..	..	..	..
19	13	6	18,411	11,713	6,698	17,614	10,835	6,779	255	148	107	1,275	1,049	226	508	407	101	781	543	238
..	..	..	14,261	8,896	5,365	12,520	7,469	5,051	165	104	61	174	152	22	109	105	4	..	..	..
..	..	..	3	3	..	2,301	1,246	1,055	5	2	3	141	101	40	4	2	2	..	..	..
..	..	..	22	16	6	207	127	80	..	..	..	84	72	12	34	26	8	..	..	..
19	13	6	954	484	470	92	68	24	..	..	..	6	6		1	1	..	..	..	..
..	..	..	733	409	324	49	37	12	..	..	..	6	2	4	..	..	..	..	..	..
..	..	..	..	..	..	2,130	1,680	450	19	11	8	140	137	3	145	110	35	..	..	..
..	..	..	2,410	1,881	529	..	..	..	65	30	35	578	454	124	159	117	42	..	..	..
..	..	..	..	..	..	295	198	97	..	..	..	138	121	17	54	44	10	..	..	..
..	..	..	22	18	4	2	2	..	1	1	..	..	..	..	2	2	..	..	..	..
..	..	..	6	6	..	18	8	10	..	..	..	8	4	4	..	..	..	..	..	..

P. = Persons; M. = Males; F. = Females.

TABLE XV.—(PART II

Area of Bilingualism.	Mother-Tongue.	Number of Persons speaking Mother-Tongue.			Number of Persons speaking — Local. — Balochi.			Dehwari (Local Persian).			Pashto.			Lahnda (or Western Punjabi).		
		P.	M.	F.	P.	M.	F.	P.	M.	F.	P.	M.	F.	P.	M.	F.
1	2	3	4	5	6	7	8	9	10	11	12	13	14	15	16	17
Kalat State.	TOTAL ..	341,512	184,484	157,028	5,339	3,879	1,460	2,938	1,796	1,142	348	238	110	190	121	69
	Local. Balochi ..	156,808	84,344	72,444	..	..	..	941	551	390	28	18	10	82	57	25
	Dehwari or Local Persian ..	5,127	2,788	2,339	..	..	..	..	..	..	8	4	4	..	..	..
	Pashto ..	876	498	378	37	26	11	184	108	76	..	..	..	..	..	..
	Lahnda or Western Punjabi.	5,037	2,612	2,425	102	67	35	..	..	..	1	1	..	..	..	..
	Unspecified Jagdali and Jatki.	939	518	421	33	21	12	..	..	..	..	..	..	25	15	10
	Sindhi (Jattki and Lasi)	73,243	39,988	33,255	2,270	1,789	481	..	..	..	123	84	39	54	32	22
	Brahui ..	98,372	53,035	45,337	2,743	1,846	897	1,795	1,126	669	185	128	57	29	17	12
	Non-Local. Sindhi ..	936	566	370	141	117	24	14	9	5	..	..	..	..	..	..
	Western Hindi ..	72	58	14	6	6	..	..	..	..	..	..	..	..	..	..
	Persian ..	102	57	45	7	7	..	4	2	2	3	3	..	..	..	..
Sarawan.	TOTAL ..	28,327	15,438	12,889	846	546	300	2,935	1,793	1,142	171	110	61	..	..	..
	Local. Balochi ..	4,271	2,153	2,118	..	..	..	941	551	390	..	..	..	..	..	..
	Dehwari or Local Persian.	5,101	2,776	2,325	..	..	..	..	..	..	8	4	4	..	..	..
	Pashto ..	705	398	307	5	3	2	184	108	76	..	..	..	..	..	..
	Brahui ..	17,486	9,700	7,786	818	528	290	1,792	1,123	669	163	106	57	..	..	..
	Non-Local. Sindhi ..	658	343	315	23	15	8	14	9	5	..	..	..	..	..	..
	Western Hindi ..	25	22	3	..	..	..	..	..	..	..	..	..	..	..	..
	Persian ..	81	46	35	..	..	..	4	2	2	..	..	..	..	..	..
Jhalawan.	TOTAL ..	88,902	47,919	40,983	965	544	421	3	3	..	2	2	..	1	1	..
	Local. Balochi ..	18,741	10,413	8,328	..	..	..	..	..	..	..	..	..	..	..	..
	Pashto ..	37	22	15	7	5	2	..	..	..	..	..	..	..	..	..
	Lahnda or Western Punjabi.	4	2	2	..	..	..	..	..	..	..	..	..	..	..	..
	Sindhi (Jattki and Lasi)	1,446	821	625	1	1	..	..	..	..	..	..	..	..	..	..
	Brahui ..	68,498	36,518	31,980	927	515	412	3	3	..	2	2	..	1	1	..
	Non-Local. Sindhi ..	173	140	33	30	23	7	..	..	..	..	..	..	..	..	..
	Western Hindi ..	3	3	..	..	..	..	..	..	..	..	..	..	..	..	..
Kachh.	TOTAL ..	105,632	57,699	47,933	1,564	1,240	324	..	..	..	20	16	4	189	120	69
	Local. Balochi ..	36,413	19,912	16,501	..	..	..	..	..	..	6	3	3	82	57	25
	Dehwari or Local Persian.	26	12	14	..	..	..	..	..	..	..	..	..	..	..	..
	Pashto ..	43	22	21	11	8	3	..	..	..	..	..	..	..	..	..
	Lahnda or Western Punjabi.	4,841	2,507	2,334	63	42	21	..	..	..	1	1	..	..	..	..
	Unspecified Jagdali and Jatki.	939	518	421	33	21	12	..	..	..	..	..	..	25	15	10
	Sindhi (Jattki and Lasi)	53,040	29,047	23,993	946	796	150	..	..	..	6	5	1	54	32	22
	Brahui	10,341	5,657	4,684	504	366	138	..	..	..	4	4	..	28	16	12
	Non-Local. Western Hindi ..	19	14	5	..	..	..	..	..	..	..	..	..	..	..	..
	Persian ..	20	10	10	7	7	..	..	..	..	3	3	..	..	..	..
Dombki-Kaheri Country.	TOTAL ..	26,942	14,550	12,392	1,705	1,322	383	..	..	..	133	95	38	..	..	..
	Local. Balochi ..	6,250	3,401	2,849	..	..	..	..	..	..	..	..	..	..	..	..
	Pashto ..	16	8	8	2	2	..	..	..	..	..	..	..	..	..	..
	Lahnda or Western Punjabi.	185	100	85	39	25	14	..	..	..	..	..	..	..	..	..
	Sindhi (Jattki and Lasi)	18,747	10,110	8,637	1,323	992	331	..	..	..	117	79	38	..	..	..
	Brahui ..	1,744	931	813	341	303	38	..	..	..	16	16	..	..	..	..
Makran.	TOTAL ..	68,301	36,375	31,926	213	194	19	..	..	..	5	1	4	..	..	..
	Local. Balochi ..	67,829	36,017	31,812	..	..	..	..	..	..	5	1	4	..	..	..
	Pashto ..	61	38	23	..	..	..	..	..	..	..	..	..	..	..	..
	Landha or Western Punjabi.	7	3	4	..	..	..	..	..	..	..	..	..	..	..	..
	Sindhi (Jattki and Lasi)	10	10	..	..	..	..	..	..	..	..	..	..	..	..	..
	Brahui ..	303	229	74	153	134	19	..	..	..	..	..	..	..	..	..
	Non-Local. Sindhi ..	65	58	7	54	54	..	..	..	..	..	..	..	..	..	..
	Western Hindi ..	25	19	6	6	6	..	..	..	..	..	..	..	..	..	..
	Persian ..	1	1	..	..	..	..	..	..	..	..	..	..	..	..	..
Kharan.	TOTAL ..	23,358	12,503	10,855	46	33	13	..	..	..	17	14	3	..	..	..
	Local. Balochi ..	23,304	12,468	10,836	..	..	..	..	..	..	17	14	3	..	..	..
	Pashto ..	14	10	4	12	8	4	..	..	..	..	..	..	..	..	..
	Non-Local. Sindhi ..	40	25	15	34	25	9	..	..	..	..	..	..	..	..	..
Las-Bela State.	TOTAL ..	62,816	33,333	29,483	442	268	174	..	..	..	1	1	..	..	..	..
	Local. Balochi ..	13,055	6,975	6,080	..	..	..	..	..	..	..	..	..	..	..	..
	Pashto ..	12	9	3	..	..	..	..	..	..	..	..	..	..	..	..
	Sindhi (Jattki and Lasi)	45,453	24,005	21,448	442	268	174	..	..	..	..	..	..	..	..	..
	Brahui ..	4,208	2,339	1,869	..	..	..	..	..	..	..	..	..	..	..	..
	Non-Local. Western Hindi ..	81	51	30	..	..	..	..	..	..	..	..	..	..	..	..
	Persian ..	7	4	3	..	..	..	..	..	..	1	1	..	..	..	..

BILINGUALISM.

SUBSIDIARY LANGUAGES.																				
LOCAL.									NON-LOCAL.									*All other mother-tongues not specified in column 2.*		
Unspecified Jagdali and Jatki.			*Sindhi (Jatki and Lasi).*			*Brahui.*			*Sindhi.*			*Western Hindi.*			*Persian.*					
P.	M.	F.	P.	M.	F.	P.	M.	F.	P.	M.	F.	P.	M.	F.	P.	M.	F.	P.	M.	F.
18	19	20	21	22	23	24	25	26	27	28	29	30	31	32	33	34	35	36	37	38
19	13	6	16,542	10,361	6,181	17,316	10,654	6,662	255	148	107	1,275	1,049	226	508	407	101	569	431	156
..	..	..	13,324	8,304	5,020	12,274	7,324	4,950	165	104	61	174	152	22	109	105	4	..	..	..
..	..	..	3	3	..	2,301	1,246	1,055	5	2	3	141	101	40	4	2	2	..	..	..
..	..	..	12	9	3	207	127	80	..	..	..	84	72	12	34	26	8	..	..	..
19	13	6	954	484	470	92	68	24	..	..	..	6	6	..	1	1	..	..	..	..
..	..	..	733	409	324	49	37	12	..	..	..	6	2	4	..	..	..	..	..	..
..	..	..	..	..	..	2,078	1,644	434	19	11	8	140	137	3	145	110	35	..	..	..
..	..	..	1,506	1,142	364	..	..	..	65	30	35	578	454	124	159	117	42	..	..	..
..	..	..	..	..	..	295	198	97	..	..	..	138	121	17	54	44	10	..	..	..
..	..	..	7	7	..	2	2	..	1	1	..	..	..	..	2	2	..	..	..	..
..	..	..	3	3	..	18	8	10	..	..	..	8	4	4	..	..	..	..	..	..
..	..	..	..	..	..	3,576	1,946	1,630	1	1	..	809	608	201	179	128	51	137	107	30
..	..	..	..	..	..	872	458	414	..	..	..	52	43	9	..	..	..	..	..	..
..	..	..	..	..	..	2,298	1,243	1,055	..	..	..	139	99	40	4	2	2	..	..	..
..	..	..	..	..	..	201	121	80	..	..	..	64	52	12	21	13	8	..	..	..
..	..	..	..	..	..	..	..	..	1	1	..	484	361	123	98	67	31	..	..	..
..	..	..	..	..	..	194	123	71	..	..	..	65	52	13	54	44	10	..	..	..
..	..	..	..	..	..	..	..	..	..	..	..	..	..	..	2	2	..	..	..	..
..	..	..	..	..	..	11	1	10	..	..	..	5	1	4	..	..	..	..	..	..
..	..	..	..	..	..	1,781	985	796	195	109	86	52	52	..	26	18	8	76	68	8
..	..	..	..	..	..	1,640	888	752	132	81	51	..	..	..	..	..	..	..	..	..
..	..	..	..	..	..	..	..	..	..	..	..	6	6	..	3	3	..	..	..	..
..	..	..	..	..	..	3	1	2	..	..	..	..	..	..	..	..	..	..	..	..
..	..	..	..	..	..	56	33	23	..	..	..	..	..	..	..	..	..	..	..	..
..	..	..	..	..	..	..	..	..	62	27	35	35	35	..	23	15	8	..	..	..
..	..	..	..	..	..	82	63	19	..	..	..	11	11	..	..	..	..	..	..	..
..	..	..	..	..	..	..	..	..	1	1	..	..	..	..	..	..	..	..	..	..
19	13	6	14,313	8,540	5,773	3,932	3,204	728	47	27	20	184	167	17	134	117	17	204	145	59
..	..	..	11,566	6,871	4,695	2,381	1,827	554	22	13	9	41	31	10	11	10	1	..	..	..
..	..	..	3	3	..	3	3	..	5	2	3	2	2	..	..	..	..	..	..	..
..	..	..	11	8	3	4	4	..	..	..	..	8	8	..	4	4	..	..	..	..
19	13	6	914	458	456	89	67	22	..	..	..	5	5	..	1	1	..	..	..	..
..	..	..	733	409	324	49	37	12	..	..	..	6	2	4	..	..	..	..	..	..
..	..	..	..	..	..	1,398	1,258	140	19	11	8	96	93	3	83	70	13	..	..	..
..	..	..	1,076	781	295	..	..	..	1	1	..	23	23	..	35	32	3	..	..	..
..	..	..	7	7	..	2	2	..	..	..	..	..	..	..	..	..	..	..	..	..
..	..	..	3	3	..	6	6	..	..	..	..	3	3	..	..	..	..	..	..	..
..	..	..	2,229	1,821	408	660	388	272	..	..	..	72	71	1	69	47	22	11	3	8
..	..	..	1,758	1,433	325	34	33	1	..	..	..	6	5	1	..	..	..	..	..	..
..	..	..	1	1	..	2	2	..	..	..	..	3	3	..	5	5	..	..	..	..
..	..	..	40	26	14	..	..	..	..	..	..	..	..	..	..	..	..	..	..	..
..	..	..	..	..	..	624	353	271	..	..	..	43	43	..	62	40	22	..	..	..
..	..	..	430	361	69	..	..	..	..	..	..	20	20	..	2	2	..	..	..	..
..	..	..	..	..	..	36	35	1	1	1	..	121	120	1	40	40	..	161	108	53
..	..	..	..	..	..	35	34	1	..	..	..	57	57	..	38	38	..	..	..	..
..	..	..	..	..	..	..	..	..	..	..	..	3	3	..	1	1	..	..	..	..
..	..	..	..	..	..	..	..	..	..	..	..	1	1	..	..	..	..	..	..	..
..	..	..	..	..	..	..	..	..	..	..	..	1	1	..	..	..	..	..	..	..
..	..	..	..	..	..	..	..	..	1	1	..	16	15	1	1	1	..	..	..	..
..	..	..	..	..	..	..	..	..	..	..	..	53	53	..	..	..	..	..	..	..
..	..	..	..	..	..	..	..	..	..	..	..	..	..	..	..	..	..	..	..	..
..	..	..	..	..	..	1	1	..	..	..	..	..	..	..	..	..	..	..	..	..
..	..	..	..	..	..	7,331	4,096	3,235	11	10	1	27	21	6	60	57	3	..	..	..
..	..	..	..	..	..	7,312	4,084	3,228	11	10	1	18	16	2	60	57	3	..	..	..
..	..	..	..	..	..	..	..	..	..	..	..	..	..	..	..	..	..	..	..	..
..	..	..	..	..	..	19	12	7	..	..	..	9	5	4	..	..	..	..	..	..
..	..	..	1,869	1,352	517	298	181	117	..	..	..	..	..	..	..	..	..	192	112	80
..	..	..	937	592	345	246	145	101	..	..	..	..	..	..	..	..	..	..	..	..
..	..	..	10	7	3	..	..	..	..	..	..	..	..	..	..	..	..	..	..	..
..	..	..	..	..	..	52	36	16	..	..	..	..	..	..	..	..	..	..	..	..
..	..	..	904	739	165	..	..	..	..	..	..	..	..	..	..	..	..	..	..	..
..	..	..	15	11	4	..	..	..	..	..	..	..	..	..	..	..	..	..	..	..
..	..	..	3	3	..	..	..	..	..	..	..	..	..	..	..	..	..	..	..	..

P. = Persons; M. = Males; F. = Females.

TABLE XVI

RELIGION.

1. The total population of the Province by religions is given below :—

Religion.		Total.	Males.	Females.
Muslim	..	798,093	440,089	358,004
Hindu	..	53,681	36,180	17,501
Sikh	..	8,425	6,270	2,155
Christian	..	8,059	5,637	2,422
Jain	..	32	20	12
Buddhist	..	68	53	15
Zoroastrian	..	167	90	77
Jew	..	17	14	3
Tribal	..	32	25	7
Others	..	43	36	7

2. Details of "others" under various religions are given below :—

Sects.		TOTAL.			DISTRICTS.			STATES.		
		Total.	Males.	Females.	Total.	Males.	Females.	Total.	Males.	Females.
					HINDUS.					
Chuhras	..	4,533	3,155	1,378	4,512	3,136	1,376	21	19	2
Others	..	140	94	46	116	79	37	24	15	9
					SIKHS.					
Chuhras	..	134	77	57	134	77	57	..	..	..
Others	..	67	51	16	52	44	8	15	7	8
					MUSLIMS.					
Ahmadi	..	122	81	41	117	77	40	5	4	1
Ahl-i-Hadis	..	108	78	30	107	77	30	1	1	..
Chuhras	..	546	329	217	314	193	121	232	136	96
Others	..	11	7	4	..	..	..	11	7	4
					OTHERS.					
Chuhras	..	36	32	4	34	30	4	2	2	..
Indefinite belief	..	7	4	3	7	4	3	..	..	..

3. Columns 48—50 overleaf under Christians consist of the following sects :—

District or State.			ROMAN-SYRIAN.		OTHER SYRIAN.		ROMAN-CATHOLIC.		OTHERS.		TOTAL.	
			M.	F.	M.	F.	M.	F.	M.	F.	M.	F.
BALUCHISTAN	..	..	..	..	1	..	1,025	486	4,611	1,936	5,637	2,422
DISTRICTS	..	..	..	..	..	..	1,017	465	4,608	1,934	5,625	2,419
Quetta-Pishin	..	..	..	..	..	..	889	409	4,280	1,792	5,169	2,201
Loralai	..	..	..	..	..	..	40	15	103	51	143	66
Zhob	..	..	..	..	..	..	15	9	84	7	99	16
Bolan	..	..	..	..	..	..	16	14	40	21	56	35
Chagai	..	..	..	..	..	..	2	..	17	6	19	6
Sibi	..	..	..	..	..	..	55	38	84	57	139	95
STATES	..	..	..	..	1	..	8	1	3	2	12	3
Kalat	..	..	..	..	1	..	8	1	3	2	12	3

4. Columns 54—56 of the table, "Tribal Religion," include Bhils only whose tribal names were entered in place of religion in Column 4 of the Census Schedule.

TABLE XVI.—RELIGION.

Province, State or Agency.	POPULATION.			HINDU.														SIKH.									Jain.			Buddhist.			Zoroastrian.		
				Brahmanic.		Arya.		Brahmo.		Others.		Total Hindu.			Kesdhari.		Sahjdhari.		Others.		Total Sikh.														
	P.	M.	F.	M.	F.	M.	F.	M.	F.	M.	F.	P.	M.	F.	M.	F.	M.	F.	M.	F.	P.	M.	F.	P.	M.	F.	P.	M.	F.	P.	M.	F.			
1	2	3	4	5	6	7	8	9	10	11	12	13	14	15	16	17	18	19	20	21	22	23	24	25	26	27	28	29	30	31	32	33			
BALUCHISTAN	*868,617*	*488,414*	*380,203*	*30,282*	*14,663*	*2,642*	*1,414*	*7*	..	*3,249*	*1,424*	*53,681*	*36,180*	*17,501*	*5,634*	*1,855*	*508*	*227*	*128*	*73*	*8,425*	*6,270*	*2,155*	*32*	*20*	*12*	*68*	*53*	*15*	*167*	*90*	*77*			
DISTRICTS	**463,508**	**270,004**	**193,504**	**23,722**	**9,099**	**2,587**	**1,391**	**5**	..	**3,215**	**1,413**	**41,432**	**29,529**	**11,903**	**5,598**	**1,849**	**508**	**227**	**121**	**65**	**8,368**	**6,227**	**2,141**	**32**	**20**	**12**	**68**	**53**	**15**	**167**	**90**	**77**			
Quetta-Pishin	147,541	90,302	57,239	14,953	5,422	1,952	1,055	2	..	2,305	1,029	26,718	19,212	7,506	3,500	1,382	164	63	90	56	5,255	3,754	1,501	32	20	12	40	25	15	161	84	77			
Loralai	86,087	47,936	38,151	2,088	959	110	56	..	..	205	86	3,504	2,403	1,101	407	94	36	21	4	..	562	447	115	..	..	..	..	..	..	..	..	..			
Zhob	57,963	34,596	23,367	2,069	307	158	96	1	..	174	34	2,839	2,402	437	998	81	22	6	19	8	1,134	1,039	95	..	..	..	27	27	..	..	..	..			
Bolan	4,688	3,466	1,222	748	182	92	38	..	..	68	37	1,165	908	257	138	30	2	..	3	..	173	143	30	..	..	..	..	..	..	..	..	..			
Chagai	24,224	13,721	10,503	712	329	60	26	..	..	119	67	1,313	891	422	86	28	2	..	1	..	117	89	28	..	..	..	..	..	..	..	..	..			
Sibi	143,005	79,983	63,022	3,152	1,900	215	120	2	..	344	160	5,893	3,713	2,180	469	234	282	137	4	1	1,127	755	372	..	..	..	1	1	..	6	6	..			
Administered area ..	*87,781*	*49,447*	*38,334*	*3,002*	*1,764*	*215*	*120*	*2*	..	*326*	*143*	*5,572*	*3,545*	*2,027*	*469*	*234*	*282*	*137*	*4*	*1*	*1,127*	*755*	*372*	..	..	..	*1*	*1*	..	*6*	*6*	..			
Mari-Bugti Country ..	*55,224*	*30,536*	*24,688*	*150*	*136*	..	..	..	..	*18*	*17*	*321*	*168*	*153*	..	..	..	..	..	..	..	..	..	..	..	..	..	..	..	..	..	..			
STATES	**405,109**	**218,410**	**186,699**	**6,560**	**5,584**	**55**	**23**	**2**	..	**34**	**11**	**12,249**	**6,651**	**5,598**	**36**	**6**	..	..	**7**	**8**	**57**	**48**	**14**	..	..	..	..	..	..	..	..	..			
Kalat	342,101	184,915	157,186	5,757	4,933	49	21	2	..	33	11	10,806	5,841	4,965	24	3	..	..	7	8	42	31	11	..	..	..	..	..	..	..	..	..			
Sarawan	*28,464*	*15,545*	*12,919*	*378*	*329*	*9*	*3*	*2*	..	*7*	*1*	*729*	*396*	*333*	*8*	*2*	..	..	..	..	*10*	*8*	*2*	..	..	..	..	..	..	..	..	..			
Jhalawan	*88,978*	*47,987*	*40,991*	*161*	*36*	..	..	..	..	..	..	*197*	*161*	*36*	*1*	..	..	..	..	..	*1*	*1*	..	..	..	..	..	..	..	..	..	..			
Kachhi	*105,886*	*57,844*	*48,042*	*3,736*	*3,259*	..	..	..	..	*15*	*9*	*7,019*	*3,751*	*3,268*	*11*	*1*	..	..	..	..	*12*	*11*	*1*	..	..	..	..	..	..	..	..	..			
Dombki-Kaheri Country ..	*26,953*	*14,553*	*12,400*	*1,309*	*1,279*	..	..	..	..	..	..	*2,588*	*1,309*	*1,279*	*1*	..	..	..	*7*	*8*	*16*	*8*	*8*	..	..	..	..	..	..	..	..	..			
Makran	*68,462*	*36,483*	*31,979*	*148*	*15*	*40*	*18*	..	..	*11*	*1*	*233*	*199*	*34*	*3*	..	..	..	..	..	*3*	*3*	..	..	..	..	..	..	..	..	..	..			
Kharan	*23,358*	*12,503*	*10,855*	*25*	*15*	..	..	..	..	..	..	*40*	*25*	*15*	..	..	..	..	..	..	..	..	..	..	..	..	..	..	..	..	..	..			
Las-Bela	63,008	33,495	29,513	803	631	6	2	..	..	1	..	1,443	810	633	12	3	..	..	..	..	15	12	3	..	..	..	..	..	..	..	..	..			

TABLE XVI.—RELIGION.—(*concld.*)

Province, Districts and States.	Population.			Muslim.											Christian.			Jew.			Tribal.			Others.		
				Sunni.		Shia.		Zikri.		Others.		Total Muslim.														
	P.	M.	F.	M.	F.	M.	F.	M.	F.	M.	F.	P.	M.	F.	P.	M.	F.	P.	M.	F.	P.	M.	F.	P.	M.	F.
1	34	35	36	37	38	39	40	41	42	43	44	45	46	47	48	49	50	51	52	53	54	55	56	57	58	59
BALUCHISTAN	868,617	468,414	380,203	422,654	344,460	3,888	2,073	13,052	11,179	495	292	798,093	440,089	358,004	8,059	5,637	2,422	17	14	3	32	25	7	43	36	7
DISTRICTS	463,508	270,004	193,504	224,922	175,319	3,120	1,410	..	..	347	191	405,309	228,389	176,920	8,044	5,625	2,419	15	12	3	32	25	7	41	34	7
Quetta-Pishin	147,541	90,302	57,239	59,427	44,630	2,407	1,192	..	..	190	99	107,945	62,024	45,921	7,370	5,169	2,201	15	12	3	..	..	..	5	2	3
Loralai	86,087	47,936	38,151	44,759	36,819	167	44	..	..	17	6	81,812	44,943	36,869	209	143	66	..	..	..	..	..	..	..	..	..
Zhob	57,963	34,596	23,367	30,662	22,761	311	41	..	..	52	17	53,844	31,025	22,819	115	99	16	..	..	..	..	..	..	4	4	..
Bolan	4,688	3,466	1,222	2,254	871	69	21	..	..	10	4	3,229	2,333	896	91	56	35	..	..	..	..	..	..	30	26	4
Chagai	24,224	13,721	10,503	12,684	10,021	34	22	..	..	4	4	22,769	12,722	10,047	25	19	6	..	..	..	..	..	..	..	..	..
Sibi	143,005	79,983	63,022	75,136	60,217	132	90	..	..	74	61	135,710	75,342	60,368	234	139	95	..	..	..	32	25	7	2	2	..
Administered Area	87,781	49,447	38,334	44,768	35,682	132	90	..	..	74	61	80 807	44,974	35,833	234	139	95	..	..	..	32	25	7	2	2	..
Mari-Bugti Country	55,224	30,536	24,688	30,368	24,535	..	..	..	..	..	..	54,903	30,368	24,535	..	..	..	..	..	..	..	..	..	..	..	..
STATES	405,109	218,410	186,699	197,732	169,141	768	663	13,052	11,179	148	101	392,784	211,700	181,084	15	12	3	2	2	..	..	..	..	2	2	..
Kalat	342,101	184,915	157,186	168,745	143,703	596	499	9,557	7,913	129	92	331,234	179,027	152,207	15	12	3	2	2	..	..	..	..	2	2	..
Sarawan	28,464	15,545	12,919	15,128	12,582	6	..	..	..	6	..	27,722	15,140	12,582	3	1	2	..	..	..	..	..	..	..	..	..
Jhalawan	88,978	47,987	40,991	45,535	39,099	1	..	2,287	1,854	2	2	88,780	47,825	40,955	..	..	..	..	..	..	..	..	..	..	..	..
Kachhi	105,886	57,844	48,042	53,955	44,676	21	18	..	..	103	79	98,852	54,079	44,773	1	1	..	..	..	..	..	..	..	2	2	..
Dombki-Kaheri Country ..	26,953	14,553	12,400	12,663	10,628	564	478	..	..	9	7	24,349	13,236	11,113	..	..	..	..	..	..	..	..	..	..	..	..
Makran	68,462	36,483	31,979	29,188	26,050	4	3	7,068	5,887	9	4	68,213	36,269	31,944	11	10	1	2	2	..	..	..	..	..	..	..
Kharan	23,358	12,503	10,855	12,276	10,668	..	..	202	172	..	..	23,318	12,478	10,840	..	..	..	..	..	..	..	..	..	..	..	..
Las-Bela	63,008	33,495	29,513	28,987	25,438	172	164	3,496	3,266	19	9	61,550	32,673	28,877	..	..	..	..	..	..	..	..	..	..	..	..

TABLE XVII.

RACE, TRIBE OR CASTE.

1. The total population of Baluchistan is 868,617 persons distributed as under :—

	Total.	Males.	Females.
Indigenous ..	760,125	411,941	348,184
Semi-indigenous ..	21,922	13,206	8,716
Aliens ..	86,570	63,267	23,303
Total ..	868,617	488,414	380,203

2. The distribution of the above population by various races is shown below :—

	Persons.	Males.	Females.
BALOCH ..	229,473	124,848	104,625
(a) Indigenous ..	226,041	122,860	103,181
(b) Semi-indigenous ..	1,805	992	813
(c) Aliens ..	1,627	996	631
BRAHUI ..	152,588	83,528	69,060
(a) Indigenous ..	152,588	83,528	69,060
PATHAN	198,606	109,661	88,945
(a) Indigenous ..	176,007	95,472	80,535
(b) Semi-indigenous ..	17,018	9,972	7,046
(c) Aliens ..	5,581	4,217	1,364
LASI ..	31,812	16,635	15,177
(a) Indigenous ..	31,812	16,635	15,177
JATT ..	82,689	46,273	36,416
(a) Indigenous ..	77,157	42,227	34,930
(b) Aliens ..	5,532	4,046	1,486
SAYYID ..	23,655	12,277	11,378
(a) Indigenous ..	21,976	11,127	10,849
(c) Aliens ..	1,679	1,150	529
OTHER MUSLIMS ..	79,270	46,867	32,403
(a) Indigenous ..	57,591	30,862	26,709
(b) Semi-indigenous ..	3,099	2,242	857
(c) Aliens ..	18,580	13,743	4,837
HINDUS ..	53,681	36,180	17,501
(a) Indigenous ..	16,905	9,175	7,730
(c) Aliens ..	36,776	27,005	9,771
SIKHS ..	8,425	6,270	2,155
(a) Indigenous ..	48	35	13
(c) Aliens ..	8,377	6,235	2,142
OTHER ALIENS ..	8,418	5,875	2,543
(a) Europeans ..	5,024	3,802	1,222
(b) Anglo-Indians ..	379	200	179
(c) Indian Christians ..	2,656	1,635	1,021
(d) Others ..	359	238	121

3. All indigenous tribes have been shown as in 1911 and 1921. As regards aliens those tribes and castes whose strength was 2 *per mille* or more have been shown separately in the body of the table. Tribes or castes of local importance representing less than 2 *per mille* have also been shown.

4. Depressed classes are found only among alien Hindus who are immigrants from other Indian Provinces. The total strength of such depressed classes is 7,346 persons. Details are shown below :—

District or State.	Persons.	Males.	Females.
Total ..	7,346	5,131	2,215
Quetta-Pishin ..	5,245	3,638	1,607
Loralai ..	396	288	108
Zhob ..	249	209	40
Bolan ..	244	179	65
Chagai ..	183	120	63
Sibi ..	992	667	325
Kalat ..	36	29	7
Las-Bela ..	1	1	..

5. Variations in the numerical strength of the various castes, tribes and races since 1911 are shown in Imperial Table XVIII.

TABLE XVII.—RACE,

Caste, Tribe, Race or Nationality.	Baluchistan.			Districts. Quetta-Pishin.		Loralai.		Zhob.		Bolan.		Chagai.		Sibi. Administered area.		Sibi. Mari-Bugti Country.	
	P.	M.	F.	M.	F.	M.	F.	M.	F.	M.	F.	M.	F.	M.	F.	M.	F.
1	2	3	4	5	6	7	8	9	10	11	12	13	14	15	16	17	18
SUM-																	
TOTAL ..	868,617	488,414	380,203	90,302	57,239	47,936	38,151	34,596	23,367	3,466	1,222	13,721	10,503	49,447	38,334	30,536	24,688
A. INDIGENOUS ..	760,125	411,941	348,184	44,033	38,791	37,538	31,799	27,274	22,107	1,708	693	11,586	9,536	42,396	34,739	30,253	24,461
B. SEMI-INDIGENOUS ..	21,922	13,206	8,716	4,478	2,489	5,708	4,666	939	238	100	26	731	391	1,023	753	4	1
C. ALIENS ..	86,570	63,267	23,303	41,791	15,959	4,690	1,686	6,383	1,022	1,658	503	1,404	576	6,028	2,842	279	226
DETAILS BY RACES, TRIBES,																	
A. Indigenous Total.	**760,125**	**411,941**	**348,184**	**44,033**	**38,791**	**37,538**	**31,799**	**27,274**	**22,107**	**1,708**	**693**	**11,586**	**9,536**	**42,396**	**34,739**	**30,253**	**24,461**
Muslim Indigenous.	**743,172**	**402,731**	**340,441**	**43,472**	**38,384**	**36,839**	**31,255**	**27,266**	**22,106**	**1,600**	**660**	**11,315**	**9,366**	**41,275**	**33,767**	**30,112**	**24,330**
Baloch ..	**226,041**	**122,860**	**103,181**	**757**	**488**	**9,823**	**8,741**	**56**	**25**	**452**	**198**	**4,449**	**3,682**	**16,253**	**13,393**	**29,913**	**24,154**
(i) Eastern ..	*150,364*	*82,254*	*68,110*	*440*	*306*	*9,796*	*8,724*	*39*	*19*	*280*	*137*	*6*	*8*	*15,808*	*13,046*	*29,913*	*24,154*
Bugti ..	30,613	16,797	13,816	33	32	28	15	..	..	14	..	4	5	117	73	16,158	13,277
Dombki ..	7,241	3,943	3,298	3	..	2	..	..	..	25	12	..	..	1,040	905	..	..
Khetran ..	17,162	8,997	8,165	..	..	8,649	7,888	4	..	26	..	..	..	252	225	..	..
Magasi ..	13,286	7,212	6,074	3	3	..	..	..	..	1	..	..	..	149	128	..	..
Mari ..	35,254	19,700	15,554	58	30	994	737	15	11	19	3	..	..	4,392	3,430	13,745	10,870
Rind Buledi ..	5,709	3,093	2,616	96	74	83	61	..	..	8	5	..	..	2,496	2,102	..	..
,, Jamali ..	6,585	3,557	3,028	1	1	..	..	2	2	2	..	..	..	2,345	2,007	..	..
,, Khosa ..	4,619	2,535	2,084	39	25	1	..	5	5	31	4	..	..	1,998	1,694	6	3
,, Lashari ..	7,199	3,808	3,391	13	12	16	9	..	..	34	17	2	3	491	458	..	..
,, Un-specified	19,210	10,695	8,515	84	59	22	14	3	..	120	96	..	..	1,137	923	1	2
Umrani ..	2,641	1,433	1,208	..	..	1	..	..	..	..	..	..	..	1,268	1,058	..	..
Baloch Unspecified. ..	845	484	381	110	70	..	..	10	1	..	..	..	..	123	48	3	2
(ii) Western ..	*75,677*	*40,606*	*35,071*	*317*	*182*	*27*	*17*	*17*	*6*	*172*	*61*	*4,443*	*3,674*	*445*	*347*	..	..
Buledi ..	158	84	74	..	..	..	..	..	..	..	..	..	..	..	..	..	..
Dashti ..	936	543	453	..	..	..	..	..	..	6	..	..	..	..	..	..	..
Gichki ..	293	142	151	1	..	..	..	..	..	..	1	..	..	..	..	..	..
Kaudai ..	2,308	1,231	1,077	..	..	..	..	..	..	..	..	232	190	..	..	..	..
Rais ..	3,951	2,038	1,883	..	..	..	..	..	..	16	12	35	30	1	2	..	..
Rakhshani ..	24,106	13,104	11,002	60	30	6	4	11	6	18	6	3,321	2,736	219	163	..	..
Rind ..	31,055	16,531	14,524	22	17	..	..	1	..	35	14	346	275	30	27	..	..
Sangur ..	7,334	3,924	3,410	..	..	..	..	..	..	..	..	..	..	..	..	..	..
Sanjrani ..	401	208	193	..	..	..	..	..	..	..	..	190	177	..	..	..	..
Others ..	5,075	2,771	2,304	234	135	21	13	5	..	97	28	319	266	195	155	..	..
Brahui ..	**152,588**	**83,528**	**69,060**	**4,583**	**3,459**	**366**	**250**	**181**	**4**	**676**	**330**	**5,240**	**4,263**	**4,235**	**3,204**	..	..
(i) Original Nucleus.	*12,958*	*7,062*	*5,896*	*341*	*219*	*72*	*52*	*18*	*2*	*142*	*103*	*524*	*438*	*418*	*354*	..	..
Ahmadzai ..	77	30	47	6	4	..	..	..	..	..	..	..	..	14	20	..	..
Gurgnari ..	1,466	798	668	1	..	..	..	..	..	5	..	12	10	..	..	..	..
Iltazai ..	202	112	90	..	..	..	..	..	..	..	..	..	..	..	..	..	..
Kalandrari ..	1,330	750	580	26	12	62	40	..	..	2	..	20	11	..	..	..	..
Kambrari ..	2,065	1,142	923	188	147	..	..	..	..	4	..	62	57	49	40	..	..
Mirwari ..	1,878	980	898	..	..	..	..	..	..	..	..	..	..	..	..	..	..
Rodeni ..	1,335	734	601	18	16	..	..	..	..	5	..	23	24	8	7	..	..
Sumalari ..	4,605	2,516	2,089	102	40	10	12	18	2	126	103	407	336	347	287	..	..
(ii) Sarawan ..	*41,846*	*23,144*	*18,704*	*3,267*	*2,569*	*205*	*123*	*51*	*1*	*412*	*169*	*2,347*	*1,885*	*2,206*	*1,639*	..	..
Bangulzai ..	7,389	4,083	3,306	360	241	55	45	16	..	114	60	5	2	751	577	..	..
Kurd ..	2,230	1,235	995	189	127	..	..	..	..	82	48	11	10	45	30	..	..
Lahri ..	4,490	2,528	1,962	344	276	13	8	2	..	22	9	15	5	412	297	..	..
Langav ..	6,648	3,631	3,017	610	530	34	23	1	..	12	2	168	125	420	337	..	..
Mamashahi ..	2,728	1,535	1,193	212	143	10	..	6	..	32	10	23	11	70	49	..	..
Raisani ..	2,716	1,500	1,216	208	174	5	5	1	1	48	9	5	2	127	68	..	..
Rustumzai ..	243	141	102	41	35	..	..	..	..	6	5	19	5	1	1	..	..
Sarparra ..	1,906	1,029	877	54	44	8	..	23	..	21	5	71	70	15	6	..	..
Satakzai ..	1,586	923	663	57	42	1	..	..	..	35	8	..	..	19	17	..	..
Shahwani ..	6,089	3,362	2,727	1,104	891	54	26	2	..	37	13	33	17	104	45	..	..
Zagr Mengal ..	5,823	3,177	2,646	88	66	25	16	..	..	3	..	1,997	1,638	242	212	..	..
(iii) Jhalawan ..	*94,807*	*51,575*	*43,232*	*647*	*483*	*57*	*47*	*5*	..	*102*	*53*	*2,287*	*1,895*	*1,439*	*1,129*	..	..
Bizanjav ..	13,591	7,631	5,940	3	4	..	..	..	..	..	..	50	42	9	2	..	..
Haruni ..	1,612	847	765	27	19	..	..	..	..	1	3	39	31	7	3	..	..
Mamasani ..	10,356	5,602	4,754	35	27	..	..	..	..	8	2	1,766	1,527	81	58	..	..
Mengal ..	26,377	14,344	12,033	399	285	56	47	5	..	68	39	406	275	910	728	..	..
Nichari ..	1,705	951	754	34	19	..	..	..	..	11	7	15	15	24	13	..	..
Pandrani ..	1,063	572	491	..	..	..	..	..	..	..	..	..	..	227	192	..	..
Sajdi ..	3,279	1,843	1,436	..	..	..	..	..	..	..	..	..	..	..	..	..	..
Zahri ..	36,824	19,765	17,059	149	129	1	..	..	..	14	2	11	5	181	133	..	..
(iv) Miscellaneous	*2,975*	*1,747*	*1,228*	*328*	*188*	*32*	*28*	*57*	*1*	*20*	*5*	*82*	*45*	*172*	*82*	..	..
Nighari ..	1,128	608	520	1	..	..	..	..	..	..	..	..	..	..	..	..	..
Rekizai ..	534	291	243	..	..	..	..	..	..	..	..	..	..	2	1	..	..
Others ..	1,313	848	465	327	188	32	28	57	1	20	5	82	45	170	81	..	..

P = Persons ; M = Males ; F = Females.

TRIBE OR CASTE.

STATES.																
Total Kalat.		Sarawan.		Jhalawan.		Kachhi		Dombki-Kaheri Country.		Makran.		Kharan.		Lasbela.		Caste, Tribe, Race or Nationality.
M.	F.	M.	F.	M.	F.	M.	F.	M.	F.	M.	F.	M.	F.	M.	F.	
19	20	21	22	23	24	25	26	27	28	29	30	31	32	33	34	35
MARY.																
184,915	157,186	15,545	12,919	47,987	40,991	57,844	48,042	14,553	12,400	36,483	31,979	12,503	10,855	33,495	29,513	TOTAL.
183,314	156,636	15,199	12,766	47,758	40,934	57,536	47,844	14,536	12,380	36,311	31,888	12,474	10,824	33,339	29,422	A. INDIGENOUS.
222	152	122	62	18	15	24	28	5	5	24	11	29	31	1	..	B. SEMI-INDIGENOUS.
879	398	224	91	211	42	284	170	12	15	148	80	..	..	155	91	C. ALIENS.
AND CASTES.																
183,314	156,636	15,199	12,766	47,758	40,934	57,536	47,844	14,536	12,380	36,311	31,888	12,474	10,824	33,339	29,422	A. Indigenous Total.
178,291	151,769	14,869	12,460	47,735	40,980	53,832	44,593	13,220	11,098	36,186	31,884	12,449	10,809	32,561	28,804	Muslim Indigenous.
57,716	49,445	483	374	938	839	20,865	17,374	3,501	2,941	24,026	21,117	7,903	6,800	3,441	3,056	Baloch.
25,092	*20,973*	*392*	*296*	*459*	*458*	*20,739*	*17,275*	*3,501*	*2,941*	*1*	*3*	..	..	*880*	*743*	(i) Eastern.
443	414	..	..	..	..	440	409	3	5	..	..	..	..	..	..	Bugti
2,873	2,381	..	..	..	..	..	..	2,873	2,381	..	..	..	..	..	..	Dombki
66	52	..	..	..	..	66	52	..	..	..	..	..	..	..	..	Khetran.
7,059	5,943	16	9	182	151	6,773	5,715	88	68	..	..	..	..	..	..	Magasi
402	400	8	10	186	225	200	155	8	10	..	..	..	..	75	73	Mari
410	374	1	2	..	..	282	257	127	115	..	..	..	..	..	..	Rind Buledi.
736	666	..	..	71	69	500	443	165	154	..	..	..	..	471	352	" Jamali
455	353	..	..	8	5	447	348	..	..	..	..	..	..	..	..	" Khosa.
3,156	2,819	2	..	3	2	3,151	2,817	..	..	..	..	..	..	96	78	" Lashari.
9,328	7,421	360	271	9	6	8,780	6,988	179	156	..	..	..	..	..	..	" Unspecified.
164	150	5	4	..	..	100	91	58	52	1	3	..	..	..	..	Umrani
..	..	..	..	..	..	..	..	..	..	..	..	..	..	238	240	Baloch Unspecified..
32,624	*28,472*	*91*	*78*	*479*	*381*	*126*	*99*	..	..	*24,025*	*21,114*	*7,903*	*6,800*	*2,561*	*2,312*	(ii) Western.
84	74	..	..	..	..	..	..	..	..	84	74	..	..	..	..	Buledi.
537	453	..	..	8	5	..	..	..	..	529	448	..	..	..	..	Dashti.
141	150	..	..	1	7	..	..	..	..	136	134	4	9	..	..	Gichki.
999	887	..	..	21	15	18	10	..	..	960	862	..	..	..	..	Kaudai.
2,016	1,839	..	..	9	9	..	..	..	..	1,921	1,748	86	82	..	..	Rais.
9,440	8,036	91	78	414	328	49	39	..	..	1,101	903	7,785	6,688	29	21	Rakhshani.
15,540	13,711	..	..	20	15	52	45	..	..	15,443	13,631	25	20	557	480	Rind.
1,949	1,599	..	..	4	1	..	..	..	..	1,945	1,598	..	..	1,975	1,811	Sangur.
18	16	..	..	..	..	..	..	..	..	18	16	..	..	..	..	Sanjrani.
1,900	1,707	..	..	2	1	7	5	..	..	1,888	1,700	3	1	..	..	Others.
63,711	53,859	10,427	8,564	40,814	34,781	6,445	5,353	931	813	2,994	2,871	2,300	1,977	4,586	3,691	Brahui.
5,166	*4,421*	*590*	*528*	*2,979*	*2,550*	*381*	*351*	*110*	*92*	*753*	*604*	*353*	*296*	*381*	*307*	(i) Original Nucleus.
10	23	10	23	..	..	..	..	..	..	..	..	..	..	..	..	Ahmadzai.
462	405	15	18	330	292	6	10	..	..	63	49	48	36	318	253	Gurgnari.
112	90	..	..	101	72	11	18	..	..	..	..	..	..	..	..	Iltazi.
640	517	129	104	429	350	7	5	..	..	72	54	3	4	..	..	Kalandrari.
836	674	94	71	566	453	90	76	..	..	48	38	38	36	3	5	Kambrari.
924	852	6	6	529	474	3	3	..	..	381	364	5	5	56	46	Mirwari.
680	554	127	120	185	148	196	172	34	23	117	76	21	15	..	..	Rodeni.
1,502	1,306	209	186	839	761	68	67	76	69	72	23	238	200	4	3	Sumalari.
14,517	*12,184*	*7,721*	*6,348*	*1,336*	*1,218*	*4,483*	*3,735*	*665*	*599*	*212*	*192*	*100*	*92*	*139*	*134*	(ii) Sarawan.
2,782	2,381	380	308	39	31	1,941	1,668	416	367	4	4	2	3	..	..	Bangulzai.
783	658	203	174	170	170	261	186	42	33	89	79	18	16	125	122	Kurd.
1,720	1,367	328	257	420	370	942	713	30	27	..	..	..	..	..	..	Lahri.
2,386	2,000	2,135	1,802	175	124	10	10	31	30	10	9	25	25	..	..	Langav.
1,182	980	986	810	27	19	132	115	18	14	19	22	..	..	..	..	Mamashahi.
1,106	957	481	390	28	32	570	504	21	23	6	8	..	..	..	..	Raisani.
74	56	44	26	..	..	30	30	..	..	..	..	..	..	..	..	Rustumzai.
837	752	778	693	..	..	59	59	..	..	..	..	..	..	..	..	Sarparra.
811	596	705	531	..	..	106	65	..	..	..	..	..	..	..	..	Satakzai.
2,028	1,735	1,242	992	193	200	412	364	52	63	76	70	53	46	..	..	Shahwani.
808	702	439	365	284	272	20	21	55	42	8	..	2	2	14	12	Zagr Mengal.
42,979	*36,379*	*2,113*	*1,688*	*35,400*	*30,244*	*1,553*	*1,246*	*156*	*122*	*1,910*	*1,490*	*1,847*	*1,589*	*4,059*	*3,246*	(iii) Jhalawan.
5,622	4,351	2	..	4,693	3,590	10	4	..	..	894	731	23	26	1,967	1,541	Bizanjav.
773	709	65	49	544	516	..	..	..	..	138	121	26	23	..	..	Haruni.
3,683	3,101	172	156	1,772	1,464	60	32	35	39	7	5	1,637	1,405	29	39	Mamasani.
11,452	9,795	544	415	9,967	8,660	492	379	82	57	264	193	103	91	1,048	864	Mengal.
867	700	731	579	..	..	136	121	..	..	..	..	..	..	..	..	Nichari.
345	299	26	19	156	138	163	142	..	..	..	..	..	..	..	..	Pandrani.
1,741	1,341	..	..	1,242	949	..	..	..	..	451	354	48	38	102	95	Sajdi.
18,496	16,083	573	470	17,026	14,927	692	568	39	26	156	86	10	6	913	707	Zahri.
1,049	*875*	*3*	..	*899*	*769*	*28*	*21*	..	..	*119*	*85*	..	..	*7*	*4*	(iv) Miscellaneous.
607	520	..	..	599	517	8	3	..	..	..	..	..	..	..	..	Nighari.
289	242	..	..	289	242	..	..	..	..	..	..	..	..	..	..	Rakizai.
153	113	3	..	11	10	20	18	..	..	119	85	..	..	7	4	Others.

P = Persons; M = Males; F = Females.

Caste, Tribe Race or Nationality.	Baluchistan.			Districts. Quetta-Pishin.		Loralai.		Zhob.		Bolan.		Chagai.		Sibi. Administered area.		Sibi. Mari-Bugti Country.	
	P.	M.	F.	M.	F.	M.	F.	M.	F.	M.	F.	M.	F.	M.	F.	M.	F.
1	2	3	4	5	6	7	8	9	10	11	12	13	14	15	16	17	18
athan Indigenous	**176,007**	**95,472**	**80,585**	**33,243**	**28,957**	**24,583**	**20,514**	**26,462**	**21,560**	**150**	**18**	**810**	**283**	**10,070**	**8,660**	**1**	..
abi ..	194	103	91	..	..	..	..	..	..	..	..	8	9	..	..	..	..
arech ..	1,610	886	724	533	412	30	26	3	3	7	1	204	198	49	31	..	..
afar ..	1,479	805	674	3	3	790	663	4	2	..	..	..	..	8	6	..	..
Kakar ..	89,831	49,237	40,594	17,105	15,125	9,184	7,253	19,305	15,419	61	3	25	16	3,380	2,641	1	..
Dawi ..	*274*	*150*	*124*	*150*	*124*	..	..	..	..	..	..	..	..	..	..	..	..
Dumar ..	*7,108*	*3,964*	*3,144*	*258*	*217*	*3,136*	*2,546*	*23*	*22*	*4*	..	..	..	*586*	*352*	..	..
Husain Pasenr	*805*	*414*	*391*	*398*	*383*	*14*	*7*	*2*	*1*	..	..	..	..	..	..	..	..
Sanzar Khel ..	*46,561*	*25,623*	*20,938*	*3,273*	*3,177*	*5,613*	*4,332*	*16,403*	*13,226*	*43*	*3*	*4*	*1*	*288*	*196*	..	..
Sargara ..	*2,000*	*1,076*	*924*	*707*	*591*	*95*	*100*	*264*	*225*	*2*	..	*7*	*7*	*1*	*1*	..	..
Snatia ..	*19,762*	*10,840*	*8,922*	*5,563*	*4,687*	*294*	*242*	*2,469*	*1,930*	*5*	..	..	..	*2,509*	*2,063*	..	..
Targhara ..	*12,170*	*6,380*	*5,790*	*6,332*	*5,763*	*32*	*26*	*12*	*1*	*2*	..	..	..	*2*	..	..	..
Others ..	*1,151*	*790*	*361*	*424*	*183*	..	..	*132*	*14*	*5*	..	*14*	*8*	*49*	*29*	*1*	..
Kasi ..	1,975	1,055	920	1,015	893	1	1	6	4	2	..	..	..	23	15	..	..
Luni ..	3,581	1,881	1,700	1	2	1,815	1,636	..	..	1	..	..	..	64	62	..	..
Pani ..	27,701	15,011	12,690	52	40	9,648	8,224	2,791	2,228	26	..	..	..	2,410	2,117	..	..
Main Branch ..	*4,166*	*2,209*	*1,957*	*22*	*29*	*285*	*203*	*14*	*10*	*5*	..	..	..	*1,799*	*1,634*	..	..
Isot ..	*2,555*	*1,352*	*1,203*	..	..	*1,294*	*1,158*	*3*	..	*2*	..	..	..	*53*	*45*	..	..
Laun ..	*543*	*305*	*238*	..	..	*12*	*10*	*234*	*168*	..	..	..	..	*59*	*60*	..	..
Mandokhel ..	*4,635*	*2,562*	*2,073*	*14*	*8*	*22*	*19*	*2,524*	*2,044*	*1*	..	..	..	*1*	*2*	..	..
Musakhel ..	*13,578*	*7,376*	*6,202*	*6*	*1*	*7,308*	*6,167*	*12*	*5*	*7*	..	..	..	*43*	*29*	..	..
Zarkun ..	*2,123*	*1,141*	*982*	*5*	*2*	*726*	*667*	*4*	*1*	*11*	..	..	..	*395*	*312*	..	..
Unspecified ..	*101*	*66*	*35*	*5*	..	*1*	..	..	..	..	..	..	..	*60*	*35*	..	..
Shirani ..	8,416	4,446	3,970	50	32	26	26	4,329	3,891	2	..	2	..	24	16	..	..
Tarin ..	36,754	19,557	17,197	14,003	12,169	1,549	1,316	11	6	24	2	6	4	3,916	3,656	..	..
Abdal Achakzai	*19,796*	*10,913*	*8,883*	*10,870*	*8,869*	*7*	*2*	*3*	*5*	*18*	..	*1*	..	*13*	*3*	..	..
Spin Tarin ..	*9,709*	*5,090*	*4,619*	*89*	*44*	*1,231*	*1,034*	*2*	..	..	..	*1*	..	*3,766*	*3,541*	..	..
Tor Tarin ..	*6,737*	*3,229*	*3,508*	*2,892*	*3,206*	*296*	*270*	..	..	..	..	..	..	*3*	*2*	..	..
Unspecified ..	*512*	*325*	*187*	*152*	*59*	*15*	*10*	*6*	*1*	*6*	*2*	*4*	*4*	*134*	*110*	..	..
Zmarai ..	2,889	1,526	1,363	..	..	1,526	1,363	..	..	..	..	..	..	..	..	..	..
Other Pathans ..	1,577	965	612	481	281	14	6	13	7	27	12	65	56	196	116	..	..
Lasi ..	**31,812**	**16,635**	**15,177**	**8**	**4**	..	..	..	..	..	..	..	..	**17**	**15**	..	..
Angaria ..	3,966	2,116	1,850	..	..	..	..	..	..	..	..	..	..	..	..	..	..
Burra ..	3,411	1,895	1,516	..	..	..	..	..	..	..	..	..	..	..	..	..	..
Jamot ..	5,815	3,050	2,765	8	4	..	..	..	..	..	..	..	..	16	15	..	..
Runjha ..	4,656	2,387	2,269	..	..	..	..	..	..	..	..	..	..	..	..	..	..
Sheikh ..	4,306	2,270	2,036	..	..	..	..	..	..	..	..	..	..	..	..	..	..
Mangia ..	2,661	1,393	1,268	..	..	..	..	..	..	..	..	..	..	..	..	..	..
Shahok ..	1,315	727	588	..	..	..	..	..	..	..	..	..	..	..	..	..	..
Mondra ..	3,231	1,724	1,507	..	..	..	..	..	..	..	..	..	..	..	..	..	..
Gonga ..	2,443	1,065	1,378	..	..	..	..	..	..	..	..	..	..	..	..	..	..
Unspecified ..	8	8	..	..	..	..	..	..	..	..	..	..	..	1	..	..	..
Jatt Indigenous	**77,157**	**42,227**	**34,930**	**46**	**37**	**18**	**19**	**1**	..	**225**	**79**	**19**	**2**	**7,958**	**6,800**	..	..
Sayyid Indigenous	**21,976**	**11,127**	**10,849**	**4,337**	**5,078**	**1,985**	**1,669**	**580**	**489**	**45**	**15**	**867**	**694**	**1,218**	**1,013**	**48**	**37**
Bukhari ..	11,784	5,585	6,199	3,282	4,227	962	773	32	30	12	1	87	84	544	483	27	26
Chishti ..	1,837	928	909	111	115	159	147	1	..	1	..	..	..	318	277	..	..
Gharshin ..	1,015	542	473	195	149	253	245	94	79	..	..	..	..	..	..	..	..
Kaheri ..	1,215	652	563	78	69	3	4	..	..	..	..	66	72	..	..	..	..
Mashwani ..	1,040	593	447	46	34	2	..	..	..	5	..	493	375	..	..	..	..
Taran ..	1,220	672	548	231	178	128	129	17	15	..	..	..	..	286	216	..	..
Ustrana ..	638	356	282	10	10	339	265	..	..	..	..	..	..	7	7	..	..
Others ..	3,227	1,799	1,428	384	296	139	106	436	365	27	14	221	163	63	30	16	11
Other Muslims ..	**57,591**	**30,882**	**26,709**	**498**	**361**	**64**	**62**	**36**	**28**	**52**	**20**	**430**	**442**	**1,524**	**1,182**	**155**	**139**
Darzada ..	9,339	4,831	4,508	..	..	..	..	..	..	10	5	..	..	8	6	..	..
Dehwar ..	5,317	2,934	2,383	231	163	..	..	1	..	11	1	11	9	61	29	..	..
Gadra ..	7,935	4,539	3,396	..	..	..	..	..	..	..	..	..	..	..	..	..	..
Gola ..	477	264	213	..	..	..	..	..	..	..	..	..	..	..	..	..	..
Jat ..	3,236	1,798	1,438	28	30	12	12	..	..	..	..	..	..	871	698	..	..
Khoja ..	352	177	175	8	5	..	..	..	..	..	..	..	..	..	..	..	..
Langah ..	506	255	251	..	..	..	..	..	..	..	..	..	..	63	62	..	..
Lori ..	5,653	3,044	2,609	91	66	36	36	15	12	11	6	75	80	332	280	..	..
Med ..	3,041	1,566	1,475	..	..	..	..	..	..	..	..	..	..	..	..	..	..
Nakib ..	7,154	3,814	3,340	..	..	..	..	..	..	..	..	..	..	94	43	..	..
Others ..	14,581	7,660	6,921	140	97	16	14	20	16	20	8	344	353	95	64	155	139
(a) Sorozai ..	11,164	5,829	5,335	67	45	..	..	2	..	18	8	312	326	5	2	..	..
(b) Others ..	3,417	1,831	1,586	73	52	16	14	18	16	2	..	32	27	90	62	155	139
Hindu Indigenous	**16,905**	**9,175**	**7,730**	**561**	**407**	**699**	**544**	**8**	**1**	**108**	**33**	**268**	**169**	**1,098**	**968**	**141**	**131**
Arora ..	16,359	8,825	7,534	512	361	658	521	8	1	82	27	204	142	1,047	935	141	131
Brahman ..	157	97	60	8	13	23	15	..	..	..	..	27	8	1	..	..	..
Khatri ..	259	166	93	37	27	18	8	..	..	19	1	25	15	44	26	..	..
Others ..	130	87	43	4	6	..	..	..	..	7	5	12	4	6	7	..	..
Sikh Indigenous ..	**48**	**35**	**13**	..	..	..	..	..	..	..	..	**3**	**1**	**23**	**4**	..	..
B. Total Semi-Indigenous ..	**21,922**	**13,206**	**8,716**	**4,478**	**3,489**	**5,708**	**4,666**	**989**	**288**	**100**	**26**	**731**	**391**	**1,028**	**758**	**4**	**1**
Muslim Semi-Indigenous—																	
Baloch ..	*1,805*	*992*	*813*	*3*	*5*	*888*	*764*	*26*	*13*	*22*	..	*7*	*2*	*28*	*8*	..	..
Buzdar ..	1,738	953	785	2	2	869	740	26	13	22	..	7	2	9	7	..	..
Others	67	39	28	1	3	19	24	..	..	..	..	..	..	19	1	..	..

P = Persons; M = Males; F = Females.

STATES.																
TOTAL KALAT.		SARAWAN.		JHALAWAN.		KACHHI.		DOMBKI-KAHERI COUNTRY.		MAKRAN.		KHARAN.		LASBELA.		CASTE, TRIBE RACE OR NATIONALITY.
M.	F.	M.	F.	M.	F.	M.	F.	M.	F.	M.	F.	M.	F.	M.	F.	
19	20	21	22	23	24	25	26	27	28	29	30	31	32	33	34	35
644	540	394	253	25	32	154	129	132	94	17	11	22	21	9	8	**Pathan Indigenous.**
95	82	76	64	13	12	6	6	..	..	..	..	..	..	..	..	Babi.
60	53	27	20	..	..	19	16	..	..	..	..	14	17	..	..	Barech.
..	..	..	..	..	..	..	..	..	..	..	..	..	..	..	..	Jafar.
167	134	32	34	1	..	7	10	172	90	..	..	..	..	9	3	Kakar.
..	..	..	..	..	..	..	..	..	..	..	..	..	..	..	..	*Dawi.*
7	*7*	*1*	..	*1*	..	*5*	*7*	..	..	..	..	..	..	..	..	*Dumar.*
..	..	..	..	..	..	..	..	..	..	..	..	..	..	..	..	*Husain Pasenr.*
4	*3*	*4*	*3*	..	..	..	..	..	..	..	..	..	..	..	..	*Sanzar Khel.*
..	..	..	..	..	..	..	..	..	..	..	..	..	..	..	..	*Sargara.*
..	..	..	..	..	..	..	..	..	..	..	..	..	..	..	..	*Snatia.*
..	..	..	..	..	..	..	..	..	..	..	..	..	..	..	..	*Targhara.*
156	*124*	*27*	*31*	..	..	*2*	*3*	*127*	*90*	..	..	..	..	*9*	*3*	*Others.*
8	7	8	7	..	..	..	..	..	..	..	..	..	..	..	..	Kasi.
..	..	..	..	..	..	..	..	..	..	..	..	..	..	..	..	Luni.
84	81	70	71	..	..	14	10	..	..	..	..	..	..	..	..	Pani.
84	*81*	*70*	*71*	..	..	*14*	*10*	..	..	..	..	..	..	..	..	*Main Branch.*
..	..	..	..	..	..	..	..	..	..	..	..	..	..	..	..	*Isot.*
..	..	..	..	..	..	..	..	..	..	..	..	..	..	..	..	*Laun.*
..	..	..	..	..	..	..	..	..	..	..	..	..	..	..	..	*Mandokhel.*
..	..	..	..	..	..	..	..	..	..	..	..	..	..	..	..	*Musakhel.*
..	..	..	..	..	..	..	..	..	..	..	..	..	..	..	..	*Zarkun.*
..	..	..	..	..	..	..	..	..	..	..	..	..	..	..	..	*Unspecified.*
13	5	12	5	..	..	..	..	..	..	..	..	1	..	..	..	Shirani.
48	44	2	..	..	..	45	40	..	..	1	4	..	..	..	..	Tarin.
1	*4*	..	..	..	..	..	..	..	..	*1*	*4*	..	..	..	..	*Abdal Achakzai.*
1	..	*1*	..	..	..	..	..	..	..	..	..	..	..	..	..	*Spin Tarin.*
38	*30*	..	..	..	..	*38*	*30*	..	..	..	..	..	..	..	..	*Tor Tarin.*
8	*10*	*1*	..	..	..	*7*	*10*	..	..	..	..	..	..	..	..	*Unspecified.*
..	..	..	..	..	..	..	..	..	..	..	..	..	..	..	..	Zmarai.
169	134	67	52	11	20	63	47	5	4	16	7	7	4	..	..	Other Pathans.
522	371	..	..	306	202	..	..	..	..	216	169	..	..	16,068	14,787	**Lasi.**
3	1	..	..	3	1	..	..	..	..	..	..	..	..	2,113	1,849	Angaria.
8	6	..	..	8	6	..	..	..	..	..	..	..	..	1,887	1,510	Burra.
391	277	..	..	184	108	..	..	..	..	207	169	..	..	2,635	2,469	Jamot.
21	18	..	..	21	18	..	..	..	..	..	..	..	..	2,366	2,251	Runjha.
26	19	..	..	24	19	..	..	..	..	2	..	..	..	2,244	2,017	Sheikh
59	47	..	..	59	47	..	..	..	..	..	..	..	..	1,334	1,221	Mangia.
7	3	..	..	7	3	..	..	..	..	..	..	..	..	720	585	Shahok.
..	..	..	..	..	..	..	..	..	..	..	..	..	..	1,724	1,507	Mondra.
..	..	..	..	..	..	..	..	..	..	..	..	..	..	1,065	1,378	Gonga.
7	..	..	..	..	..	..	..	..	..	7	..	..	..	..	..	Unspecified.
31,831	26,299	61	42	3	4	24,282	20,004	7,483	6,246	2	1	..	..	2,129	2,194	**Jatt Indigenious.**
1,885	1,692	366	334	142	134	661	602	579	512	57	45	80	65	167	162	**Sayyid Indigenous.**
502	441	171	129	12	17	237	203	54	72	28	20	..	..	137	134	Bukhari.
338	370	120	142	21	28	155	157	28	29	14	14	..	..	..	..	Chishti.
..	..	..	..	..	..	..	..	..	..	..	..	..	..	..	..	Gharshin.
505	418	19	15	23	17	..	..	462	385	1	1	..	..	..	..	Kaheri.
47	38	44	38	3	..	..	..	..	..	..	..	..	..	..	..	Mashwani.
10	10	10	10	..	..	..	..	..	..	..	..	..	..	..	..	Taran.
..	..	..	..	..	..	..	..	..	..	..	..	..	..	..	..	Ustrana.
483	415	2	..	83	72	269	242	35	26	14	10	80	65	30	28	Others.
21,982	19,563	3,288	2,893	5,707	4,928	1,425	1,181	504	465	8,874	8,170	2,144	1,946	6,141	4,918	**Other Muslims.**
4,780	4,474	..	..	32	33	13	12	..	..	4,666	4,353	69	76	33	23	Darzada.
2,619	2,181	2,444	2,010	116	106	20	26	..	..	8	7	31	32	..	..	Dehwar.
30	19	..	..	30	19	..	..	..	..	..	..	..	..	4,509	3,377	Gadra.
264	213	..	..	..	..	..	..	264	213	..	..	..	..	..	..	Gola.
887	698	..	..	..	..	638	495	246	203	3	..	..	..	..	..	Jat.
..	..	..	..	..	..	..	..	..	..	..	..	..	..	169	170	Khoja.
139	139	..	..	..	..	8	8	32	21	99	110	..	..	53	50	Langah.
2,481	2,129	245	186	1,426	1,279	175	141	6	6	483	402	146	115	8	..	Lori.
374	331	1	..	..	..	..	..	..	..	373	331	..	..	1,192	1,144	Med.
3,711	3,297	..	..	1,293	1,056	122	98	..	..	1,728	1,601	568	542	9	..	Nakib.
6,697	6,082	548	697	2,810	2,445	449	351	46	42	1,514	1,366	1,330	1,181	173	148	Others.
5,252	4,806	548	697	2,792	2,431	373	284	45	39	1,494	1,355	..	..	173	148	(a) Sorozai.
1,445	1,276	..	..	18	14	76	67	1	3	20	11	1,330	1,181	..	..	(b) Others.
5,514	4,859	330	306	28	4	3,704	3,251	1,309	1,279	128	4	25	15	778	618	**Hindu Indigenous.**
5,395	4,798	327	306	28	4	3,614	3,197	1,287	1,272	119	4	25	15	778	618	Arora.
38	24	1	..	..	..	36	24	..	..	1	..	..	..	..	..	Brahman.
23	16	..	..	..	..	8	9	12	7	3	..	..	..	..	..	Khatri.
58	21	2	..	..	..	46	21	10	..	..	..	..	..	..	..	Others.
9	8	..	..	..	..	..	..	7	8	2	..	..	..	..	..	**Sikh Indigenous.**
222	152	122	62	18	15	24	26	5	5	24	11	29	31	1	..	**B. Total Semi-indigenous.**
																Muslim Semi-indigenous—
18	*21*	..	..	..	..	*14*	*19*	..	..	*4*	*2*	..	..	..	..	*Baloch.*
18	21	..	..	..	..	14	19	..	..	4	2	..	..	..	..	Buzdar.
..	..	..	..	..	..	..	..	..	..	..	..	..	..	..	..	Others.

P = Persons ; M = Males ; F = Females.

Caste, Tribe, Race or Nationality.	Baluchistan.			Districts. Quetta Pishin.		Loralai.		Zhob.		Bolan.		Chagai.		Sibi. Administered area.		Sibi. Mari-Bugti Country.	
	P.	M.	F.	M.	F.	M.	F.	M.	F.	M.	F.	M.	F.	M.	F.	M.	F.
1	2	3	4	5	6	7	8	9	10	11	12	13	14	15	16	17	18
Pathan ..	*17,018*	*9,972*	*7,046*	*2,706*	*1,701*	*4,632*	*3,867*	*643*	*203*	*57*	*25*	*702*	*376*	*980*	*742*	*4*	*1*
Durrani ..	2,410	1,541	869	1,080	600	80	38	76	23	6	7	93	65	91	62	2	1
Ghilzai ..	14,109	8,102	6,007	1,489	987	4,532	3,822	547	178	28	9	589	297	834	656	2	..
Others ..	499	329	170	137	114	70	7	20	2	23	9	20	14	55	24	..	..
Other Muslims ..	*3,099*	*2,242*	*857*	*1,769*	*783*	*138*	*35*	*270*	*22*	*21*	*1*	*22*	*13*	*15*	*3*	..	..
Hazara ..	3,075	2,226	849	1,755	775	138	35	270	22	20	1	22	13	14	3	..	..
Others ..	24	16	8	14	8	..	..	..	..	1	..	..	..	1	..	..	..
C. Aliens ..	**86,570**	**63,267**	**23,303**	**41,791**	**15,959**	**4,690**	**1,686**	**6,383**	**1,022**	**1,658**	**503**	**1,404**	**576**	**6,028**	**2,842**	**279**	**226**
Muslim (Aliens) ..	*32,999*	*24,152*	*8,847*	*14,074*	*5,048*	*2,396*	*948*	*2,820*	*475*	*633*	*210*	*676*	*290*	*2,676*	*1,318*	*252*	*204*
Baloch ..	1,627	996	631	90	40	668	473	80	26	40	9	6	4	48	26	..	..
Pathan ..	5,581	4,217	1,364	2,539	927	424	111	824	86	68	44	41	28	309	161	..	..
Jatt ..	5,532	4,046	1,486	2,132	614	220	57	267	52	102	39	179	50	878	465	252	204
Sayyid ..	1,679	1,150	529	656	301	74	19	108	39	16	4	22	6	192	107	..	..
Rajput ..	5,305	4,257	1,048	2,582	662	363	68	538	45	129	30	128	54	391	158	..	..
Sheikh ..	5,077	3,390	1,687	2,607	1,327	193	59	142	65	53	22	63	27	261	136	..	..
Awan ..	1,959	1,569	390	851	222	150	45	306	44	81	17	46	13	121	41	..	..
Chuhras ..	546	329	217	83	46	12	6	29	15	3	2	1	..	65	52	..	..
Others ..	5,693	4,198	1,495	2,554	909	292	110	526	103	141	43	190	108	411	167	..	..
Hindu (Aliens) ..	*36,776*	*27,005*	*9,771*	*18,651*	*7,099*	*1,704*	*557*	*2,394*	*436*	*800*	*224*	*623*	*253*	*2,447*	*1,059*	*27*	*22*
Arora ..	7,157	4,862	2,295	3,007	1,460	307	108	395	167	128	52	133	76	718	370	1	2
Gorkha ..	5,029	3,691	1,338	3,016	1,338	11	..	589	..	21	..	..	..	54	..	..	..
(a) Rai ..	2,103	1,603	500	1,289	500	..	..	261	..	..	..	..	..	53	..	..	..
(b) Limbu ..	1,579	1,151	428	974	428	..	..	176	..	..	..	..	..	1	..	..	..
(c) Gurung ..	185	121	64	88	64	2	..	31	..	..	..	..	..	..	..	..	..
(d) Magar ..	62	35	27	24	27	..	..	11	..	..	..	..	..	..	..	..	..
(e) Rana ..	19	19	..	19	..	..	..	..	..	..	..	..	..	..	..	..	..
(f) Unspecified	81	71	10	36	10	..	..	14	..	21	..	..	..	..	..	..	..
(g) Others ..	1,000	691	309	586	309	9	..	96	..	..	..	..	..	..	..	..	..
Khatri ..	4,263	2,978	1,285	2,085	898	182	86	253	107	105	45	75	29	251	107	..	..
Rajput ..	3,937	3,373	564	2,164	336	198	64	372	19	160	21	181	36	267	83	..	..
Brahman ..	3,546	2,790	756	1,594	505	445	40	270	47	117	28	61	20	232	85	6	3
Arya ..	1,725	1,086	639	844	489	75	50	79	47	12	2	22	11	37	30	..	..
Others ..	11,119	8,225	2,894	5,941	2,073	486	209	436	49	257	73	151	81	388	384	20	17
(a) Depressed Classes ..	*7,346*	*5,131*	*2,215*	*3,638*	*1,607*	*288*	*108*	*209*	*40*	*179*	*65*	*120*	*63*	*649*	*308*	*18*	*17*
1. Chuhras ..	4,533	3,155	1,378	2,285	1,015	196	86	173	34	65	37	81	44	318	143	18	17
2. Dhobi	749	453	296	390	267	9	10	15	6	6	2	..	..	31	11	..	..
3. Kori ..	477	349	128	234	84	2	..	..	..	66	16	5	5	42	23	..	..
4. Moochi ..	388	289	99	227	88	24	4	12	..	..	..	1	3	23	2	..	..
5. Pasi ..	228	193	35	131	15	2	1	..	..	18	3	8	2	34	14	..	..
6. Nat ..	227	122	105	..	..	..	..	..	..	..	..	..	..	122	105	..	..
7. Jaiswara	205	136	69	131	69	4	..	1	..	..	..	..	..	..	..	..	..
8. Nai ..	125	110	15	85	9	1	..	4	..	2	2	1	1	16	3	..	..
9. Kurmi ..	109	93	16	49	8	5	1	..	..	10	2	..	..	23	2	..	..
10. Kumbhar	71	60	11	10	1	21	3	1	..	6	1	5	2	17	4	..	..
11. Kabirpanthi.	56	35	21	30	21	3	..	2	..	..	..	..	..	..	..	..	..
12. Gadarya	46	36	10	26	9	..	..		..	4	1	..	..	6	..	..	..
13. Jullaha ..	31	24	7	2	1	6	..	..	..	..	..	15	6	1	..	..	..
14. Kohli ..	28	20	8	15	8	..	..	..	..	..	..	..	..	5	..	..	..
15. Chamar ..	22	19	3	..	..	13	3	1	..	..	..	3	..	2	..	..	..
16. Teli ..	21	17	4	6	3	2	..	..	..	..	..	1	..	8	1	..	..
17. Khatik ..	19	10	9	7	8	..	..	..	..	2	1	..	..	1	..	..	..
18. Shudar ..	7	7	..	7	..	..	..		..	..	..	..	..	..	..	..	..
19. Ramdasi	3	2	1	2	1	..	..		..	..	..	..	..	..	..	..	..
20. Ghasia ..	1	1	..	1	..	..	..	..	..	..	..	..	..	..	..	..	..
(b) Others (Hindus).	*3,773*	*3,094*	*679*	*2,303*	*466*	*198*	*101*	*227*	*9*	*78*	*8*	*31*	*18*	*229*	*76*	*2*	..
Sikh ..	*8,377*	*6,235*	*2,142*	*3,754*	*1,501*	*447*	*115*	*1,039*	*95*	*143*	*30*	*86*	*27*	*732*	*368*	..	..
Jatt ..	2,612	2,228	384	985	254	184	16	770	5	77	20	12	4	199	85	..	..
Sikh Unspecified ..	2,070	1,373	697	868	480	95	48	89	38	8	2	57	22	226	101	..	..
Chuhras ..	134	77	57	54	48	2	..	18	8	..	..	..	..	3	1	..	..
Others ..	3,561	2,557	1,004	1,847	719	166	51	162	44	58	8	17	1	304	181	..	..
Miscellaneous (Aliens) ..	*8,418*	*5,875*	*2,543*	*6,312*	*2,311*	*143*	*66*	*130*	*16*	*82*	*39*	*19*	*6*	*173*	*102*	..	..
(1) Christians.																	
Europeans ..	5,024	3,802	1,222	3,602	1,136	62	25	62	11	13	12	2	..	56	37	..	..
Anglo-Indians	379	200	179	145	141	..	2	..	..	13	11	8	4	31	21	..	..
Indian Christians.	2,656	1,635	1,021	1,422	924	81	39	37	5	30	12	9	2	52	37	..	..
(2) Others ..	359	238	121	148	110	..	..	31	..	26	4	..	..	34	7	..	..
(a) Jain ..	32	20	12	27	12	..	..	..	..	..	..	..	..	..	..	..	..
(b) Buddhist ..	68	53	15	25	15	..	..	27	..	..	..	..	..	1	..	..	..
(c) Zoroastrian	167	90	77	84	77	..	..	..	..	..	..	..	..	6	..	..	..
(d) Jew ..	17	14	3	12	3	..	..	..	..	..	..	..	..	..	..	..	..
(e) Tribal ..	32	25	7	..	..	..	..	..	..	..	..	..	..	25	7	..	..
(f) Others ..	43	36	7	2	3	..	..	4	..	26	4	..	..	2	..	..	..

P = Persons; M = Males; F = Females.

TRIBE OR CASTE.

STATES.																
Total Kalat.		Sarawan.		Jhalawan.		Kachhi.		Dombki-Kaheri Country.		Makran.		Kharan.		Las Bela.		Caste, Tribe, Race or Nationality.
M.	F.	M.	F.	M.	F.	M.	F.	M.	F.	M.	F.	M.	F.	M.	F.	
19	20	21	22	23	24	25	26	27	28	29	30	31	32	33	34	35
198	*131*	*116*	*62*	*18*	*15*	*10*	*9*	*5*	*5*	*20*	*9*	*29*	*31*	..	..	*Pathan.*
113	73	81	50	8	9	1	2	5	5	16	7	2	..	..	..	Durrani.
81	58	35	12	6	6	9	7	..	..	4	2	27	31	..	..	Ghilzai.
4	..	..	..	4	..	..	..	..	..	..	..	..	..	..	..	Others.
6	..	*6*	..	..	..	..	..	..	..	..	..	..	..	*1*	..	*Other Muslims.*
6	..	6	..	..	..	..	..	..	..	..	..	..	..	1	..	Hazara.
..	..	..	..	..	..	..	..	..	..	..	..	..	..	..	..	Others.
879	**398**	**224**	**91**	**211**	**42**	**284**	**170**	**12**	**15**	**146**	**90**	..	..	**155**	**91**	**C. Aliens.**
514	*286*	*149*	*60*	*72*	*10*	*223*	*152*	*11*	*15*	*59*	*49*	..	..	*111*	*73*	*Muslim (Aliens).*
64	53	..	..	..	..	64	53	..	..	..	..	..	..	..	..	Baloch.
12	7	..	..	7	1	..	..	..	..	5	6	..	..	..	..	Pathan.
16	5	9	..	3	2	..	..	..	..	4	3	..	..	..	..	Jatt.
54	29	38	22	3	..	3	1	..	..	10	6	..	..	28	24	Sayyid.
130	23	50	4	39	..	32	6	1	6	8	7	..	..	16	8	Rajput.
48	35	30	25	4	..	10	7	..	..	4	3	..	..	23	16	Sheikh.
13	8	2	..	2	..	2	..	1	2	6	6	..	..	1	..	Awan.
120	88	6	..	2	2	103	79	9	7	..	..	..	..	16	8	Chuhras.
57	38	14	9	12	5	9	6	..	..	22	18	..	..	27	17	Others.
327	*106*	*66*	*27*	*138*	*32*	*47*	*17*	..	..	*76*	*30*	..	..	*32*	*15*	*Hindu (Aliens).*
173	60	16	7	132	32	16	17	..	..	9	4	..	..	..	..	Arora.
..	..	..	..	..	..	..	..	..	..	..	..	..	..	..	..	Gorkha.
..	..	..	..	..	..	..	..	..	..	..	..	..	..	..	..	(a) Rai.
..	..	..	..	..	..	..	..	..	..	..	..	..	..	..	..	(b) Limbu.
	..	..	..	..	..	..	..	..	..	..	..	..	..	..	..	(c) Gurung.
..	..	..	..	..	..	..	..	..	..	..	..	..	..	..	..	(d) Magar.
..	..	..	..	..	..	..	..	..	..	..	..	..	..	..	..	(e) Rana.
..	..	..	..	..	..	..	..	..	..	..	..	..	..	..	..	(f) Unspecified.
..	..	..	..	..	..	..	..	..	..	..	..	..	..	..	..	(g) Others.
23	12	1	..	..	..	3	..	..	..	19	12	..	..	4	1	Khatri.
31	2	4	..	4	..	14	..	..	..	9	2	..	..	..	..	Rajput.
38	14	22	12	2	..	7	..	..	..	7	2	..	..	27	14	Brahman.
17	10	2	3	..	..	1	..	..	..	14	7	..	..	..	..	Arya.
45	8	21	5	..	..	6	..	..	..	18	3	..	..	1	..	Others.
29	*7*	*13*	*4*	..	..	..	..	..	..	*16*	*3*	..	..	*1*	..	(a) Depressed Classes.
18	2	7	1	..	..	..	..	..	..	11	1	..	..	1	..	1. Chuhras.
2	..	..	..	..	..	..	..	..	..	2	..	..	..	..	..	2. Dhobi.
..	..	..	..	..	..	..	..	..	..	..	..	..	..	..	..	3. Kori.
2	2	..	..	..	..	..	..	..	..	2	2	..	..	..	..	4. Mochi.
..	..	..	..	..	..	..	..	..	..	..	..	..	..	..	..	5. Pasi.
..	..	..	..	..	..	..	..	..	..	..	..	..	..	..	..	6. Nat.
..	..	..	..	..	..	..	..	..	..	..	..	..	..	..	..	7. Jaiswara.
1	..	..	..	..	..	..	..	..	..	1	..	..	..	..	..	8. Nai.
6	3	6	3	..	..	..	..	..	..	..	..	..	..	..	..	9. Kurmi.
..	..	..	..	..	..	..	..	..	..	..	..	..	..	..	..	10. Kumbhar.
..	..	..	..	..	..	..	..	..	..	..	..	..	..	..	..	11. Kabirpanthi.
..	..	..	..	..	..	..	..	..	..	..	..	..	..	..	..	12. Gadarya.
..	..	..	..	..	..	..	..	..	..	..	..	..	..	..	..	13. Jullaha.
..	..	..	..	..	..	..	..	..	..	..	..	..	..	..	..	14. Kohli.
..	..	..	..	..	..	..	..	..	..	..	..	..	..	..	..	15. Chamar
..	..	..	..	..	..	..	..	..	..	..	..	..	..	..	..	16. Teli.
..	..	..	..	..	..	..	..	..	..	..	..	..	..	..	..	17. Khatik.
..	..	..	..	..	..	..	..	..	..	..	..	..	..	..	..	18. Shudar.
..	..	..	..	..	..	..	..	..	..	..	..	..	..	..	..	19. Ramdasi.
..	..	..	..	..	..	..	..	..	..	..	..	..	..	..	..	20. Ghasia.
16	*1*	*8*	*1*	..	..	*6*	..	..	..	*2*	..	..	..	..	..	(b) Others. (Hindus).
22	*3*	*8*	*2*	*1*	..	*11*	*1*	*1*	..	*1*	..	..	..	*12*	*3*	*Sikh.*
1	..	1	..	..	..	..	..	..	..	..	..	..	..	..	..	Jatt.
18	3	5	2	1	..	11	1	1	..	..	..	..	..	12	3	Sikh Unspecified.
..	..	..	..	..	..	..	..	..	..	..	..	..	..	..	..	Chubras.
3	..	2	..	..	..	..	..	..	..	1	..	..	..	..	..	Others.
16	*3*	*1*	*2*	..	..	*3*	..	..	..	*12*	*1*	..	..	..	..	*Miscellaneous (Aliens).*
																(1) Christians.
5	1	..	..	..	..	..	..	..	..	5	1	..	..	..	..	Europeans.
3	..	..	..	..	..	..	..	..	..	3	..	..	..	..	..	Anglo-Indians.
4	2	1	2	..	..	1	..	..	..	2	..	..	..	..	..	Indian Christians.
4	..	..	..	..	..	2	..	..	..	2	..	..	..	..	..	(2) Others.
..	..	..	..	..	..	..	..	..	..	..	..	..	..	..	..	(a) Jain.
..	..	..	..	..	..	..	..	..	..	..	..	..	..	..	..	(b) Buddhist.
..	..	..	..	..	..	..	..	..	..	..	..	..	..	..	..	(c) Zoroastrian.
2	..	..	..	..	..	..	..	..	..	2	..	..	..	..	..	(d) Jew.
..	..	..	..	..	..	..	..	..	..	..	..	..	..	..	..	(e) Tribal.
2	..	..	..	..	..	2	..	..	..	..	..	..	..	..	..	(f) Others.

P = Persons; M = Males; F = Females.

TABLE XVIII.

VARIATION OF POPULATION OF SELECTED TRIBES.

Variations are shown for 1911, 1921 and 1931 only. Complete figures for previous Censuses are not available.

2. Owing to complete figures not being available for previous Censuses, it has not been found possible to readjust tribal figures in accordance with territorial transfers.

3. The variations in the numbers of various races since 1911 are summarised in the sub-joined table :—

Race.	Persons.			Remarks.
	1911.	1921.	1931.	
Total ..	834,703	799,625	868,617	
Baloch ..	172,473	176,336	229,473	
Brahui ..	167,787	159,734	152,588	
Pathan ..	214,517	192,164	198,606	
Lasi ..	27,779	23,212	31,812	
Jatt ..	78,400	66,982	82,689	
Sayyid ..	22,183	21,542	23,655	
Other Muslims ..	99,509	93,507	79,270	
Hindu ..	37,602	51,348	53,681	
Sikh ..	8,390	7,741	8,425	
Other Aliens ..	6,063	7,059	8,418	
(1) Christian :— ..	5,085	6,693	8,059	
(a) European ..	4,210	4,751	5,024	
(b) Anglo-Indian ..	123	234	379	
(c) Indian ..	752	1,708	2,656	
(2) Others :— ..	978	366	359	
(a) Jain ..	10	17	32	
(b) Buddhist ..	16	160	68	
(c) Zoroastrian ..	170	165	167	
(d) Jew ..	57	19	17	
(e) Tribal ..	..	..	32	
(f) Others ..	725	5	43	

TABLE XVIII.—VARIATION OF POPULATION OF SELECTED TRIBES.

Tribe and Locality.	Persons			Variation Increase (+) Decrease (—)		Net Variation 1911 to 1931 Increase + Decrease —	Males.			Females.		
	1931	1921	1911	1921 to 1931	1911 to 1921		1931	1921	1911	1931	1921	1911
1	2	3	4	5	6	7	8	9	10	11	12	13
					SUMMARY.							
BALUCHISTAN ..	868,617	799,625	834,703	+68,992	−35,078	+33,914	488,414	461,000	466,419	380,203	338,625	368,284
DISTRICTS ..	463,508	420,648	414,412	+42,860	+6,236	+49,096	270,004	255,014	239,181	193,504	165,634	175,231
STATES ..	405,109	378,977	420,291	+26,132	−41,314	−15,182	218,410	205,986	227,238	186,699	172,991	193,053
(a) Indigenous ..	760,125	703,944	752,394	+56,181	−48,450	+7,731	411,941	385,999	407,763	348,184	317,945	344,631
Districts ..	356,914	326,676	335,795	+30,238	−9,119	+21,119	194,788	181,178	182,870	162,126	145,498	152,925
States ..	403,211	377,268	416,599	+25,943	−39,331	−13,388	217,153	204,821	224,893	186,058	172,447	191,706
(b) Semi-Indigenous ..	21,922	18,658	*29,515	+3,264	−10,857	−7,593	13,206	11,805	17,989	8,716	6,853	11,526
Districts ..	21,547	18,138	28,170	+3,409	−10,032	−6,623	12,983	11,490	17,239	8,564	6,648	10,931
States ..	375	520	1,345	−145	−825	−970	223	315	750	152	205	595
(c) Aliens ..	86,570	77,023	*52,794	+9,547	+24,229	+33,776	63,267	63,196	40,667	23,303	13,827	12,127
Districts ..	85,047	75,834	50,447	+9,213	+25,387	+34,600	62,233	62,346	39,072	22,814	13,488	11,375
States ..	1,523	1,189	2,347	+334	−1,158	−824	1,034	850	1,595	489	339	752
					RACES AND TRIBES.							
A. Baloch Total ..	229,473	176,336	172,473	+53,137	+3,863	+57,000	124,848	97,375	93,819	104,625	78,961	78,654
Districts ..	115,660	88,707	83,677	+26,953	+5,030	+31,983	63,609	49,744	45,962	52,051	38,963	37,715
States ..	113,813	87,629	88,796	+26,184	−1,167	+25,017	61,239	47,631	47,857	52,574	39,998	40,939
(i) INDIGENOUS BALOCH	226,041	173,395	169,190	+52,646	+4,205	+56,851	122,860	95,563	91,959	103,181	77,832	77,231
Districts ..	112,384	85,780	81,210	+26,604	+4,570	+31,174	61,703	47,942	44,532	50,681	37,838	36,678
States ..	113,657	87,615	87,980	+26,042	−365	+25,677	61,157	47,621	47,427	52,500	39,994	40,553
Bugti ..	30,613	22,737	19,370	+7,876	+3,367	+11,243	16,797	12,928	10,893	13,816	9,809	8,477
Districts ..	29,756	22,676	19,257	+7,080	+3,419	+10,499	16,354	12,894	10,830	13,402	9,782	8,427
States ..	857	61	113	+796	−52	+744	443	34	63	414	27	50
Dombki ..	7,241	6,046	5,913	+1,195	+133	+1,328	3,943	3,309	3,220	3,298	2,737	2,693
Districts ..	1,987	1,926	1,849	+61	+77	+138	1,070	1,032	989	917	894	860
States ..	5,254	4,120	4,064	+1,134	+56	+1,190	2,873	2,277	2,231	2,381	1,843	1,833
Khetran ..	17,162	17,123	14,153	+39	+2,970	+3,009	8,997	9,018	7,372	8,165	8,105	6,781
Districts ..	17,044	17,123	14,153	−79	+2,970	+2,891	8,931	9,018	7,372	8,113	8,105	6,781
States ..	118	..	..	+118	..	+118	66	..	..	52	..	..
Magasi ..	13,286	8,282	17,777	+5,004	−9,495	−4,491	7,212	4,589	9,772	6,074	3,693	8,005
Districts ..	284	125	1,060	+159	−935	−776	153	78	582	131	47	478
States ..	13,002	8,157	16,717	+4,845	−8,560	−3,715	7,059	4,511	9,190	5,943	3,646	7,527
Mari ..	35,254	22,601	22,233	+12,653	+368	+13,021	19,700	13,127	12,508	15,554	9,474	9,725
Districts ..	34,304	22,321	21,473	+11,983	+848	+12,831	19,223	12,964	12,080	15,081	9,357	9,393
States ..	950	280	760	+670	−480	+190	477	163	428	473	117	332
Rind Eastern ..	43,322	30,736	31,267	+12,586	−531	+12,055	23,688	17,144	16,938	19,634	13,592	14,329
Districts ..	16,607	14,294	15,121	+2,313	−827	+1,486	9,036	7,940	8,153	7,571	6,354	6,968
States ..	26,715	16,442	16,146	+10,273	+296	+10,569	14,652	9,204	8,785	12,063	7,238	7,361
Umrani ..	2,641	1,104	989	+1,537	+115	+1,652	1,433	594	520	1,208	510	469
Districts ..	2,327	1,072	988	+1,255	+84	+1,339	1,260	576	519	1,058	496	469
States ..	314	32	1	+282	+31	+313	164	18	1	150	14	..
Baloch Eastern Unspecified	845	376	217	+469	+159	+628	484	257	128	361	119	89
Districts ..	367	363	214	+4	+149	+153	246	249	125	121	114	89
States ..	478	13	3	+465	+10	+475	238	8	3	240	5	..
Buledi ..	158	1,289	1,340	−1,131	−51	−1,182	84	696	723	74	593	617
Districts ..	..	..	..	..	..	..	..	..	..	..	..	..
States ..	158	1,289	1,340	−1,131	−51	−1,182	84	696	723	74	593	617
Dashti ..	996	4,474	1,149	−3,478	+3,325	−153	543	2,359	640	453	2,115	509
Districts ..	6	..	25	+6	−25	−19	6	..	18	..	..	7
States ..	990	4,474	1,124	−3,484	+3,350	−134	537	2,359	622	453	2,115	502
Gichki ..	293	575	554	−282	+21	−261	142	294	269	151	281	285
Districts ..	2	6	3	−4	+3	−1	1	4	1	1	2	2
States ..	291	569	551	−278	+18	−260	141	290	268	150	279	283
Kaudai ..	2,308	1,694	1,132	+614	+562	+1,176	1,231	911	607	1,077	783	525
Districts ..	422	4	..	+418	+4	+422	232	4	..	190	..	..
States ..	1,886	1,690	1,132	+196	+558	+754	999	907	607	887	783	525
Rais ..	3,951	5,696	4,147	−1,745	+1,549	−196	2,068	2,986	2,187	1,883	2,710	1,960
Districts ..	96	..	..	+96	..	+96	52	..	..	44	..	..
States ..	3,855	5,696	4,147	−1,841	+1,549	−292	2,016	2,986	2,187	1,839	2,710	1,960
Rakhshani ..	24,106	21,677	20,068	+2,429	+1,609	+4,038	13,104	11,757	10,810	11,002	9,920	9,258
Districts ..	6,580	4,681	6,690	+1,899	−2,009	−110	3,635	2,532	3,647	2,945	2,149	3,043
States ..	17,526	16,996	13,378	+530	+3,618	+4,148	9,469	9,225	7,163	8,057	7,771	6,215

*These figures differ by 4,104 from those shown in the Census Report for 1911, owing to the fact that Hazaras numbering 4,104, were classed as Trans-Indus aliens in 1911, but have now been included under "Semi-Indigenous" for purposes of comparison.

TABLE XVIII.—VARIATION OF POPULATION OF SELECTED TRIBES—*contd.*

Tribe and Locality.	Persons.			Variation Increase (+) Decrease (−)		Net Variation 1911 to 1931 Increase + Decrease −	Males.			Females.		
	1931	1921	1911	1921 to 1931	1911 to 1921		1931	1921	1911	1931	1921	1911
1	2	3	4	5	6	7	8	9	10	11	12	13
Rind Western	31,055	17,136	14,561	+13,919	+2,575	+16,494	16,531	9,198	7,669	14,524	7,938	6,892
Districts	767	83	79	+684	+4	+688	434	44	43	333	39	36
States	30,288	17,053	14,482	+13,235	+2,571	+15,806	16,097	9,154	7,626	14,191	7,899	6,856
Sangur	7,334	4,336	5,798	+2,998	−1,462	+1,536	3,924	2,362	3,049	3,410	1,974	2,749
Districts	..	..	..	..	..	..	..	..	..	..	..	..
States	7,334	4,336	5,798	+2,998	−1,462	+1,536	3,924	2,362	3,049	3,410	1,974	2,749
Sanjrani	401	481	121	−80	+360	+280	208	252	62	193	229	59
Districts	367	481	121	−114	+360	+246	190	252	62	177	229	59
States	34	..	..	+34	..	+34	18	..	..	16	..	..
Others	5,075	7,032	8,401	−1,957	−1,369	−3,326	2,771	3,782	4,592	2,304	3,250	3,809
Districts	1,468	625	177	+843	+448	+1,291	871	355	111	597	270	66
States	3,607	6,407	8,224	−2,800	−1,817	−4,617	1,900	3,427	4,481	1,707	2,980	3,743
(ii) SEMI-INDIGENOUS BALOCH. ..	1,805	2,578	3,094	−773	−516	−1,289	992	1,497	1,720	813	1,081	1,374
(iii) ALIEN BALOCH ..	1,627	363	189	+1,264	+174	+1,438	996	315	140	631	48	49
B. Brahui Total ..	152,588	159,734	167,787	−7,146	−8,053	−15,199	83,528	88,961	93,095	69,060	70,773	74,692
Districts	26,741	22,005	21,189	+4,736	+816	+5,552	15,231	12,794	12,003	11,510	9,211	9,186
States	125,847	137,729	146,598	−11,882	−8,869	−20,751	68,297	76,167	81,092	57,550	61,562	65,506
Ahmadzai	77	119	25	−42	+94	+52	30	48	15	47	71	10
Districts	44	84	9	−40	+75	+35	20	29	8	24	55	1
States	33	35	16	−2	+19	+17	10	19	7	23	16	9
Bangulzai	7,389	10,281	11,595	−2,892	−1,314	−4,206	4,083	5,881	6,377	3,306	4,400	5,218
Districts	2,226	2,132	2,082	+94	+50	+144	1,301	1,310	1,182	925	822	900
States	5,163	8,149	9,513	−2,986	−1,364	−4,350	2,782	4,571	5,195	2,381	3,578	4,318
Bizanjav	13,591	9,923	10,858	+3,668	−935	+2,733	7,651	5,416	5,906	5,940	4,507	4,952
Districts	110	..	67	+110	−67	+43	62	..	37	48	..	30
States	13,481	9,923	10,791	+3,558	−868	+2,690	7,589	5,416	5,869	5,892	4,507	4,922
Gurgnari	1,466	1,391	2,041	+75	−650	−575	798	737	1,124	668	654	917
Districts	28	6	64	+22	−58	−36	18	6	41	10	..	23
States	1,438	1,385	1,977	+53	−592	−539	780	731	1,083	658	654	894
Haruni	1,612	1,114	1,248	+498	−134	+364	847	605	674	765	509	574
Districts	130	134	159	−4	−25	−29	74	80	85	56	54	74
States	1,482	980	1,089	+502	−109	+393	773	525	589	709	455	500
Iltazai	202	451	156	−249	+295	+46	112	259	85	90	192	71
Districts	..	..	..	..	..	..	..	..	..	..	..	..
States	202	451	156	−249	+295	+46	112	259	85	90	192	71
Kalandrari	1,330	4,532	2,012	−3,202	+2,520	−682	760	2,361	1,138	580	2,171	874
Districts	173	162	126	+11	+36	+47	110	90	75	63	72	51
States	1,157	4,370	1,886	−3,213	+2,484	−729	640	2,271	1,063	517	2,099	823
Kambrari	2,065	2,414	3,095	−349	−681	−1,030	1,142	1,331	1,679	923	1,083	1,416
Districts	547	405	479	+142	−74	+68	303	229	267	244	176	212
States	1,518	2,009	2,616	−491	−607	−1,098	839	1,102	1,412	679	907	1,204
Kurd	2,230	2,982	3,476	−752	−494	−1,246	1,235	1,719	1,928	995	1,263	1,548
Districts	542	478	567	+64	−89	−25	327	286	324	215	192	243
States	1,688	2,504	2,909	−816	−405	−1,221	908	1,433	1,604	780	1,071	1,305
Lahri	4,490	5,572	5,839	−1,082	−267	−1,349	2,528	3,218	3,314	1,962	2,354	2,525
Districts	1,403	1,238	1,239	+165	−1	+164	808	706	697	595	532	542
States	3,087	4,334	4,600	−1,247	−266	−1,513	1,720	2,512	2,617	1,367	1,822	1,983
Langav	6,648	9,301	10,979	−2,653	−1,678	−4,331	3,631	5,193	6,007	3,017	4,108	4,972
Districts	2,262	1,856	1,862	+406	−6	+400	1,245	1,064	1,057	1,017	792	805
States	4,386	7,445	9,117	−3,059	−1,672	−4,731	2,386	4,129	4,950	2,000	3,316	4,167
Mamasani	10,356	14,845	13,489	−4,489	+1,356	−3,133	5,602	8,179	7,474	4,754	6,666	6,015
Districts	3,504	3,388	2,629	+116	+759	+875	1,890	1,899	1,471	1,614	1,489	1,158
States	6,852	11,457	10,860	−4,605	+597	−4,008	3,712	6,280	6,003	3,140	5,177	4,857
Mamashahi	2,728	2,790	3,866	−62	−1,076	−1,138	1,535	1,562	2,143	1,193	1,228	1,723
Districts	566	419	474	+147	−55	+92	353	272	284	213	147	190
States	2,162	2,371	3,392	−209	−1,021	−1,230	1,182	1,290	1,859	980	1,081	1,533
Mengal	26,377	24,021	26,805	+2,356	−2,784	−428	14,344	13,295	15,199	12,033	10,726	11,606
Districts	3,218	1,971	2,143	+1,247	−172	+1,075	1,844	1,158	1,256	1,374	813	887
States	23,159	22,050	24,662	+1,109	−2,612	−1,503	12,500	12,137	13,943	10,659	9,913	10,719
Mirwari	1,878	2,590	2,654	−712	−64	−776	980	1,409	1,450	898	1,181	1,204
Districts	..	7	..	−7	+7	..	..	5	..	..	2	..
States	1,878	2,583	2,654	−705	−71	−776	980	1,404	1,450	898	1,179	1,204
Nichari	1,705	1,885	3,641	−180	−1,756	−1,936	951	1,087	2,060	754	798	1,631
Districts	138	162	162	−24	..	−24	84	92	115	54	70	47
States	1,567	1,723	3,479	−156	−1,756	−1,912	867	995	1,945	700	728	1,584

TABLE XVIII.—VARIATION OF POPULATION OF SELECTED TRIBES—*contd.*

Tribe and Locality.	Persons.			Variation Increase (+) Decrease (—)		Net Variation 1911 to 1931 Increase + Decrease —	Males.			Females.		
	1931	1921	1911	1921 to 1931	1911 to 1921		1931	1921	1911	1931	1921	1911
1	2	3	4	5	6	7	8	9	10	11	12	13
Nighari	1,128	1,502	1,311	—374	+191	—183	608	843	718	520	659	593
Districts	1	..	..	+1	..	+1	1	..	..	..	..	..
States	1,127	1,502	1,311	—375	+191	—184	607	843	718	520	659	593
Pandrani	1,063	1,488	2,007	—425	—519	—944	572	825	1,115	491	663	892
Districts	419	462	618	—43	—156	—199	227	245	345	192	217	273
States	644	1,026	1,389	—382	—363	—745	345	580	770	299	446	619
Raisani	2,716	2,618	1,977	+98	+641	+739	1,500	1,438	1,093	1,216	1,180	884
Districts	653	407	402	+246	+5	+251	394	244	231	259	163	171
States	2,063	2,211	1,575	—148	+636	+488	1,106	1,194	862	957	1,017	713
Rekizai	534	653	611	—119	+42	—77	291	369	336	243	284	275
Districts	3	..	9	+3	—9	—6	2	..	5	1	..	4
States	531	653	602	—122	+51	—71	289	369	331	242	284	271
Rodeni	1,335	1,788	1,325	—453	+463	+10	734	991	724	601	797	601
Districts	101	165	140	—64	+25	—39	54	105	80	47	60	60
States	1,234	1,623	1,185	—389	+438	+49	680	886	644	554	737	541
Rustumzai	243	636	656	—393	—20	—413	141	352	341	102	284	315
Districts	113	85	114	+28	—29	—1	67	48	54	46	37	60
States	130	551	542	—421	+9	—412	74	304	287	56	247	255
Sajdi	3,279	4,137	4,011	—858	+126	—732	1,843	2,319	2,239	1,436	1,818	1,772
Districts	..	1	2	—1	—1	—2	..	1	1	..	..	1
States	3,279	4,136	4,009	—857	+127	—730	1,843	2,318	2,238	1,436	1,818	1,771
Sumalari	4,605	4,671	3,739	—66	+932	+866	2,516	2,610	2,087	2,089	2,061	1,652
Districts	1,790	943	1,023	+847	—80	+767	1,010	555	558	780	388	465
States	2,815	3,728	2,716	—913	+1,012	+99	1,506	2,055	1,529	1,309	1,673	1,187
Sarparra	1,906	2,112	2,212	—206	—100	—306	1,029	1,167	1,213	877	945	999
Districts	317	269	334	+48	—65	—17	192	164	213	125	105	121
States	1,589	1,843	1,878	—254	—35	—289	837	1,003	1,000	752	840	878
Satakzai	1,586	1,588	1,278	—2	+310	+308	923	922	715	663	666	563
Districts	179	90	105	+89	—15	+74	112	57	59	67	33	46
States	1,407	1,498	1,173	—91	+325	+234	811	865	656	596	633	517
Shahwani	6,089	8,163	8,770	—2,074	—607	—2,681	3,362	4,633	4,894	2,727	3,530	3,876
Districts	2,326	1,861	1,989	+465	—128	+337	1,334	1,062	1,098	992	799	891
States	3,763	6,302	6,781	—2,539	—479	—3,018	2,028	3,571	3,796	1,735	2,731	2,985
Zagr Mengal	5,823	5,914	4,722	—91	+1,192	+1,101	3,177	3,296	2,590	2,646	2,618	2,132
Districts	4,287	4,116	3,157	+171	+959	+1,130	2,355	2,294	1,728	1,932	1,822	1,429
States	1,536	1,798	1,565	—262	+233	—29	822	1,002	862	714	796	703
Zahri	36,824	29,359	32,649	+7,465	—3,290	+4,175	19,765	16,279	18,030	17,059	13,080	14,619
Districts	625	684	1,135	—59	—451	—510	356	392	650	269	292	485
States	36,199	28,675	31,514	+7,524	—2,839	+4,685	19,409	15,887	17,380	16,790	12,788	14,134
Others	1,313	894	740	+419	+154	+573	848	617	427	465	277	313
Districts	1,036	480	99	+556	+381	+937	688	401	82	348	79	17
States	277	414	641	—137	—227	—364	160	216	345	117	198	296
C. Pathan Total	198,606	192,164	214,517	+6,442	—22,353	—15,911	109,661	108,401	118,582	88,945	83,763	95,935
Districts	197,062	189,486	212,608	+7,576	—23,122	—15,546	108,798	106,889	117,518	88,264	82,597	95,090
States	1,544	2,678	1,909	—1,134	+769	—365	863	1,512	1,064	681	1,166	845
(i) INDIGENOUS PATHANS	176,007	174,061	188,093	+1,946	—14,032	—12,086	95,472	95,889	102,148	80,535	78,172	85,945
Districts	174,811	171,982	186,627	+2,829	—14,645	—11,816	94,819	94,752	101,346	79,992	77,230	85,281
States	1,196	2,079	1,466	—883	+613	—270	653	1,137	802	543	942	664
Babi	194	..	323	+194	—323	—129	103	..	173	91	..	150
Districts	17	..	162	+17	—162	—145	8	..	86	9	..	76
States	177	..	161	+177	—161	+16	95	..	87	82	..	74
Barech	1,610	1,550	854	+60	+696	+756	886	907	480	724	643	374
Districts	1,497	1,144	736	+353	+408	+761	826	688	413	671	456	323
States	113	406	118	—293	+288	—5	60	219	67	53	187	51
Jafar	1,479	1,355	1,286	+124	+69	+193	805	733	690	674	622	596
Districts	1,479	1,355	1,286	+124	+69	+193	805	733	690	674	622	596
States	..	..	..	..	..	..	..	..	..	..	..	..
Kakar	89,831	92,600	105,073	—2,769	—12,473	—15,242	49,237	51,951	57,752	40,594	40,649	47,321
Districts	89,518	92,478	105,000	—2,960	—12,522	—15,482	49,061	51,873	57,709	40,457	40,605	47,291
States	313	122	73	+191	+49	+240	176	78	43	137	44	30
(a) Dawi	274	..	284	+274	—284	—10	150	..	156	124	..	128
Districts	274	..	281	+274	—281	—7	150	..	154	124	..	127
States	..	..	3	..	—3	—3	..	..	2	..	..	1
(b) Dumar	7,108	7,741	7,755	—633	—14	—647	3,964	4,336	4,267	3,144	3,405	3,488
Districts	7,094	7,741	7,729	—647	+12	—635	3,957	4,336	4,251	3,137	3,405	3,478
States	14	..	26	+14	—26	—12	7	..	16	7	..	10

TABLE XVIII.—VARIATION OF POPULATION OF SELECTED TRIBES—*contd.*

Tribe and Locality.	Persons.			Variation Increase (+) Decrease (−)		Net Variation 1911 to 1931 Increase + Decrease −	Males.			Females.		
	1931	1921	1911	1921 to 1931	1911 to 1921		1931	1921	1911	1931	1921	1911
1	2	3	4	5	6	7	8	9	10	11	12	13
(c) Husain Pasenr ..	805	..	492	+805	−492	+313	414	..	274	391	..	218
Districts ..	805	..	492	+805	−492	+313	414	..	274	391	..	218
States ..	..	..	..	..	..	..	..	..	..	..	..	..
(d) Sanzarkhel ..	46,561	46,438	56,032	+123	−9,594	−9,471	25,623	25,845	30,644	20,938	20,593	25,388
Districts ..	46,554	46,381	56,019	+173	−9,638	−9,465	25,619	25,809	30,636	20,935	20,572	25,383
States ..	7	57	13	−50	+44	−6	4	36	8	3	21	5
(e) Sargara ..	2,000	2,352	2,343	−352	+9	−343	1,076	1,294	1,265	924	1,058	1,078
Districts ..	2,000	2,352	2,343	−352	+9	−343	1,076	1,294	1,265	924	1,058	1,078
States ..	..	..	..	..	..	..	..	..	..	..	..	..
(f) Snatia ..	19,762	22,519	23,349	−2,757	−830	−3,587	10,840	12,775	12,945	8,922	9,744	10,404
Districts ..	19,762	22,503	23,340	−2,741	−837	−3,578	10,840	12,759	12,941	8,922	9,744	10,399
States ..	..	16	9	−16	+7	−9	..	16	4	..	..	5
(g) Targhara ..	12,170	12,021	14,089	+149	−2,068	−1,919	6,380	6,702	7,770	5,790	5,319	6,319
Districts ..	12,170	12,021	14,088	+149	−2,067	−1,918	6,380	6,702	7,769	5,790	5,319	6,319
States ..	..	..	1	..	−1	−1	..	..	1	..	..	..
(h) Others ..	1,151	1,529	729	−378	+800	+422	790	999	431	361	530	298
Districts ..	859	1,480	708	−621	+772	+151	625	973	419	234	507	289
States ..	292	49	21	+243	+28	+271	165	26	12	127	23	9
Kasi	1,975	1,295	1,337	+680	−42	+638	1,055	673	705	920	622	632
Districts	1,960	1,276	1,304	+684	−28	+656	1,047	661	685	913	615	619
States	15	19	33	−4	−14	−18	8	12	20	7	7	13
Luni	3,581	3,187	2,816	+394	+371	+765	1,881	1,683	1,496	1,700	1,504	1,320
Districts	3,581	3,187	2,805	+394	+382	+776	1,881	1,683	1,490	1,700	1,504	1,315
States	..	..	11	..	−11	−11	..	..	6	..	..	5
Pani	27,701	27,727	28,675	−26	−948	−974	15,011	15,065	15,245	12,690	12,662	13,430
Districts	27,536	27,120	27,963	+416	−843	−427	14,927	14,741	14,866	12,609	12,379	13,097
States	165	607	712	−442	−105	−547	84	324	379	81	283	333
(a) Main Branch ..	4,166	4,972	6,714	−806	−1,742	−2,548	2,209	2,657	3,496	1,957	2,315	3,218
Districts ..	4,001	4,370	6,030	−369	−1,660	−2,029	2,125	2,335	3,133	1,876	2,035	2,897
States ..	165	602	684	−437	−82	−519	84	322	363	81	280	321
(b) Isot ..	2,555	2,601	2,812	−46	−211	−257	1,352	1,410	1,515	1,203	1,191	1,297
Districts ..	2,555	2,601	2,812	−46	−211	−257	1,352	1,410	1,515	1,203	1,191	1,297
States ..	..	..	..	..	..	..	..	..	..	..	..	..
(c) Laun ..	543	1,081	..	−538	+1,081	+543	305	602	..	238	479	..
Districts ..	543	1,081	..	−538	+1,081	+543	305	602	..	238	479	..
States ..	..	..	..	..	..	..	..	..	..	..	..	..
(d) Mandokhel ..	4,635	3,870	4,944	+765	−1,074	−309	2,562	2,179	2,653	2,073	1,691	2,291
Districts ..	4,635	3,865	4,944	+770	−1,079	−309	2,562	2,177	2,653	2,073	1,688	2,291
States ..	..	5	..	−5	+5	..	..	2	..	..	3	..
(e) Musakhel ..	13,578	13,146	12,202	+433	+943	+1,376	7,376	7,136	6,533	6,202	6,009	5,669
Districts ..	13,578	13,145	12,174	+433	+971	+1,404	7,376	7,136	6,517	6,202	6,009	5,657
States ..	..	..	28	..	−28	−28	..	..	16	..	..	12
(f) Zarkun ..	2,123	2,017	2,003	+106	+14	+120	1,141	1,055	1,048	982	962	955
Districts ..	2,123	2,017	2,003	+106	+14	+120	1,141	1,055	1,048	982	962	955
States ..	..	..	..	..	..	..	..	..	..	..	..	..
(g) Unspecified ..	101	41	..	+60	+41	+101	66	26	..	35	15	..
Districts ..	101	41	..	+60	+41	+101	66	26	..	35	15	..
States ..	..	..	..	..	..	..	..	..	..	..	..	..
Shirani	8,416	7,297	8,552	+1,119	−1,255	−136	4,446	3,871	4,538	3,970	3,426	4,014
Districts	8,398	7,251	8,438	+1,147	−1,187	−40	4,433	3,846	4,475	3,965	3,405	3,963
States	18	46	114	−28	−68	−96	13	25	63	5	21	51
Tarin	36,754	36,010	37,411	+744	−1,401	−657	19,557	19,270	20,077	17,197	16,740	17,334
Districts	36,662	35,567	37,366	+1,095	−1,799	−704	19,509	19,046	20,053	17,153	16,521	17,313
States	92	443	45	−351	+398	+47	48	224	24	44	219	21
(a) Abdal Achakzai ..	19,796	19,146	20,272	+650	−1,126	−476	10,913	10,250	11,199	8,883	8,896	9,073
Districts ..	19,791	19,129	20,251	+662	−1,122	−460	10,912	10,244	11,189	8,879	8,885	9,062
States ..	5	17	21	−12	−4	−16	1	6	10	4	11	11
(b) Spin Tarin ..	9,709	9,613	5,134	+96	+4,479	+4,575	5,090	5,233	2,713	4,619	4,380	2,421
Districts ..	9,708	9,480	5,123	+228	+4,357	+4,585	5,089	5,175	2,706	4,619	4,305	2,417
States ..	1	133	11	−132	+122	−10	1	58	7	..	75	4
(c) Tor Tarin ..	6,737	7,023	11,890	−286	−4,867	−5,153	3,229	3,643	6,086	3,508	3,380	5,804
Districts ..	6,669	6,879	11,877	−210	−4,998	−5,208	3,191	3,572	6,079	3,478	3,307	5,798
States ..	68	144	13	−76	+131	+55	38	71	7	30	73	6
(d) Unspecified ..	512	228	115	+284	+113	+397	325	144	79	187	84	36
Districts ..	494	79	115	+415	−36	+379	317	55	79	177	24	36
States ..	18	149	..	−131	+149	+18	8	89	..	10	60	..

TABLE XVIII.—VARIATION OF POPULATION OF SELECTED TRIBES—*contd.*

Tribe and Locality.	Persons.			Variation Increase (+) Decrease (—)		Net Variation 1911 to 1931 Increase + Decrease—	Males.			Females.		
	1931	1921	1911	1921 to 1931	1911 to 1921		1931	1921	1911	1931	1921	1911
1	2	3	4	5	6	7	8	9	10	11	12	13
Zmarai	2,889	1,700	1,228	+1,189	+472	+1,661	1,526	931	694	1,363	769	534
Districts	2,889	1,700	1,228	+1,189	+472	+1,661	1,526	931	694	1,363	769	534
States	..	..	..	..	..	..	..	..	..	..	..	..
Other Pathans ..	1,577	1,340	538	+237	+302	+1,039	965	805	298	612	535	240
Districts	1,274	904	339	+370	+565	+935	796	550	185	478	354	154
States	303	436	199	—133	+237	+104	169	255	113	134	181	86
(ii) SEMI-INDIGENOUS PATHANS.	17,018	13,467	22,317	+3,551	—8,850	—5,299	9,972	8,477	13,047	7,046	4,990	9,270
(iii) ALIEN PATHANS ..	5,581	4,636	4,107	+945	+529	+1,474	4,217	4,035	3,387	1,364	601	720
D. Lasi	31,812	23,212	27,779	+8,600	—4,567	+4,033	16,635	12,365	14,857	15,177	10,847	12,922
Districts	44	5	..	+39	+5	+44	25	2	..	19	3	..
States	31,768	23,207	27,779	+8,561	—4,572	+3,989	16,610	12,363	14,857	15,158	10,844	12,922
E. Jatt	82,689	66,982	78,400	+15,707	—11,418	+4,289	46,273	38,459	42,673	36,416	28,523	35,727
Districts	20,215	18,520	13,397	+1,695	+5,123	+6,818	12,297	11,671	7,467	7,918	6,849	5,930
States	62,474	48,462	65,003	+14,012	—16,541	—2,529	33,976	26,788	35,206	28,498	21,674	29,797
(i) INDIGENOUS JATT ..	77,157	63,191	78,397	+13,966	—15,206	—1,240	42,227	35,095	42,670	34,930	28,096	35,727
Districts	14,704	14,805	13,394	—101	+1,411	+1,310	8,267	8,353	7,464	6,437	6,452	5,930
States	62,453	48,386	65,003	+14,067	—16,617	—2,550	33,960	26,742	35,206	28,493	21,644	29,797
(ii) ALIEN JATTS ..	5,532	3,791	3	+1,741	+3,788	+5,529	4,046	3,364	3	1,486	427	..
Districts	5,511	3,715	3	+1,796	+3,712	+5,508	4,030	3,318	3	1,481	397	..
States	21	76	..	—55	+76	+21	16	46	..	5	30	..
F. Sayyid	23,655	21,542	22,183	+2,113	—641	+1,472	12,277	11,565	11,662	11,378	9,977	10,521
Districts	19,614	17,927	18,408	+1,687	—481	+1,206	10,143	9,653	9,671	9,471	8,274	8,737
States	4,041	3,615	3,775	+426	—160	+266	2,134	1,912	1,991	1,907	1,703	1,784
(i) INDIGENOUS SAYYIDS	21,976	20,265	[illegible]	+1,711	—1,081	+680	11,127	10,567	11,008	10,849	9,698	10,288
Districts	18,070	16,713	17,522	+1,357	—809	+548	9,075	8,695	9,018	8,995	8,018	8,504
States	3,906	3,552	3,774	+354	—222	+132	2,052	1,872	1,990	1,854	1,680	1,784
(ii) ALIEN SAYYIDS ..	1,679	1,277	887	+402	+390	+792	1,150	998	654	529	279	233
Districts	1,544	1,214	886	+330	+328	+658	1,068	958	653	476	256	233
States	135	63	1	+72	+62	+134	82	40	1	53	23	..
G. Other Muslims ..	79,270	93,507	99,509	—14,237	—6,002	—20,239	46,867	55,064	56,162	32,403	38,443	43,347
Districts	25,973	30,632	28,077	—4,659	+2,555	—2,104	18,286	22,487	19,207	7,687	8,145	8,870
States	53,297	62,875	71,432	—9,578	—8,557	—18,135	28,581	32,577	36,955	24,716	30,298	34,477
(i) INDIGENOUS ..	57,591	71,766	82,068	—14,175	—10,302	—24,477	30,882	37,363	42,467	26,709	34,403	39,601
Districts	4,993	9,290	11,230	—4,297	—1,940	—6,237	2,759	5,047	5,916	2,234	4,243	5,314
States	52,598	62,476	70,838	—9,878	—8,362	—18,240	28,123	32,316	36,551	24,475	30,160	34,287
Darzada	9,339	10,685	10,257	—1,346	+428	—918	4,831	5,525	5,215	4,508	5,160	5,042
Districts	29	258	109	—229	+149	—80	18	165	67	11	93	42
States	9,310	10,427	10,148	—1,117	+279	—838	4,813	5,360	5,148	4,497	5,067	5,000
Dehwar	5,317	5,455	7,326	—138	—1,871	—2,009	2,934	3,027	4,009	2,383	2,428	3,317
Districts	517	413	584	+104	—171	—67	315	249	338	202	164	246
States	4,800	5,042	6,742	—242	—1,700	—1,942	2,619	2,778	3,671	2,181	2,264	3,071
Gadra	7,935	6,958	7,201	+977	—243	+734	4,539	3,550	3,716	3,396	3,408	3,485
Districts	..	..	..	..	..	..	..	..	..	..	..	..
States	7,935	6,958	7,201	+977	—243	+734	4,539	3,550	3,716	3,396	3,408	3,485
Gola	477	172	834	+305	—662	—357	264	94	462	213	78	372
Districts	..	..	151	..	—151	—151	..	..	84	..	..	67
States	477	172	683	+305	—511	—206	264	94	378	213	78	305
Jat	3,236	3,726	5,680	—490	—1,954	—2,444	1,798	2,046	3,151	1,438	1,680	2,529
Districts	1,651	1,748	2,735	—97	—987	—1,084	911	983	1,532	740	765	1,203
States	1,585	1,978	2,945	—393	—967	—1,360	887	1,063	1,619	698	915	1,326
Khoja	352	311	367	+41	—56	—15	177	151	185	175	160	182
Districts	13	..	..	+13	..	+13	8	..	..	5	..	..
States	339	311	367	+28	—56	—28	169	151	185	170	160	182
Langah	506	1,371	570	—865	+801	—64	255	787	308	251	634	262
Districts	125	..	..	+125	..	+125	63	..	..	62	..	..
States	381	1,371	570	—990	+801	—189	192	787	308	189	634	262
Lori	5,658	6,890	10,936	—1,237	—4,046	—5,283	3,044	3,744	5,912	2,609	3,146	5,024
Districts	1,040	919	3,103	+121	—2,184	—2,063	560	497	1,672	480	422	1,431
States	4,618	5,971	7,833	—1,353	—1,862	—3,220	2,484	3,247	4,240	2,129	2,724	3,593

TABLE XVIII.—VARIATION OF POPULATION OF SELECTED TRIBES—*concld.*

Tribe and Locality.	Persons. 1931	Persons. 1921	Persons. 1911	Variation Increase (+) Decrease (—) 1921 to 1931	Variation Increase (+) Decrease (—) 1911 to 1921	Net Variation 1911 to 1931 Increase + Decrease —	Males. 1931	Males. 1921	Males. 1911	Females. 1931	Females. 1921	Females. 1911
1	2	3	4	5	6	7	8	9	10	11	12	13
Mad	*3,041*	*1,628*	*2,494*	*+1,413*	*—866*	*+547*	*1,566*	*840*	*1,259*	*1,475*	*788*	*1,235*
Districts	..	..	..	..	..	..	..	..	..	..	..	..
States	3,041	1,628	2,494	+1,413	—866	+547	1,566	840	1,259	1,475	788	1,235
Nakib	*7,154*	*5,577*	*6,536*	*+1,577*	*—959*	*+618*	*3,814*	*2,895*	*3,444*	*3,340*	*2,682*	*3,092*
Districts	137	2	56	+135	—54	+81	94	2	36	43	..	20
States	7,017	5,575	6,480	+1,442	—905	+537	3,720	2,893	3,408	3,297	2,682	3,072
Sorozai	*11,164*	*24,888*	*27,982*	*—13,724*	*—3,094*	*—16,818*	*5,829*	*12,468*	*13,778*	*5,335*	*12,420*	*14,204*
Districts	785	3,245	3,599	—2,460	—354	—2,814	404	1,610	1,690	381	1,635	1,909
States	10,379	21,643	24,383	—11,264	—2,740	—14,004	5,425	10,858	12,088	4,954	10,785	12,295
Others	*3,417*	*4,105*	*1,885*	*—688*	*+2,220*	*+1,532*	*1,831*	*2,286*	*1,028*	*1,586*	*1,819*	*857*
Districts	696	2,705	893	—2,009	+1,812	—197	386	1,541	497	310	1,164	396
States	2,721	1,400	992	+1,321	+408	+1,729	1,445	745	531	1,276	655	461
(ii) SEMI-INDIGENOUS ..	3,099	2,613	4,104	+486	—1,491	—1,005	2,242	1,831	3,222	857	782	882
Districts	3,092	2,598	3,884	+494	—1,286	—792	2,235	1,824	3,077	857	774	807
States	7	15	220	—8	—205	—213	7	7	145	..	8	75
Hazara	*3,075*	*1,997*	*2,454*	*+1,078*	*—457*	*+621*	*2,226*	*1,435*	*2,015*	*849*	*562*	*439*
Districts	3,068	1,996	2,453	+1,072	—457	+615	2,219	1,434	2,014	849	562	439
States	7	1	1	+6	..	+6	7	1	1	..	..	..
Others	*24*	*616*	*1,650*	*—592*	*—1,034*	*—1,626*	*16*	*396*	*1,207*	*8*	*220*	*443*
Districts	24	602	1,431	—578	—829	—1,407	16	390	1,063	8	212	368
States	..	14	219	—14	—205	—219	..	6	144	..	8	75
(iii) ALIENS	18,580	19,123	13,337	—546	+5,791	+5,243	13,743	15,870	10,473	4,837	3,258	2,864
Districts	17,888	18,744	12,963	—856	+5,781	+4,925	13,292	15,616	10,214	4,596	3,128	2,749
States	692	384	374	+308	+10	+318	451	254	259	241	130	115
H. Hindus	53,681	51,343	37,602	+2,333	+13,746	+16,079	36,180	37,001	25,008	17,501	14,347	12,594
Districts	41,432	38,673	25,764	+2,754	+12,914	+15,668	29,529	30,058	18,470	11,903	8,620	7,294
States	12,249	12,670	11,838	—421	+832	+411	6,651	6,943	6,538	5,598	5,727	5,300
(i) INDIGENOUS HINDUS	16,905	17,479	14,985	—574	+2,494	+1,920	9,175	9,663	8,122	7,730	7,816	6,863
Districts	5,136	5,269	4,565	—133	+704	+571	2,883	3,066	2,553	2,253	2,203	2,012
States	11,769	12,210	10,420	—441	+1,790	+1,349	6,292	6,597	5,569	5,477	5,613	4,851
(ii) ALIEN HINDUS ..	36,776	33,869	22,617	+2,907	+11,252	+14,159	27,005	27,338	16,886	9,771	6,531	5,731
Districts	36,296	33,409	21,199	+2,887	+12,210	+15,097	26,646	26,992	15,917	9,650	6,417	5,282
States	480	460	1,418	+20	—958	—938	359	346	969	121	114	449
I—Sikh	8,425	7,741	8,390	+684	—649	+35	6,270	6,308	6,017	2,155	1,433	2,373
Districts	8,368	7,645	5,290	+723	+2,355	+3,078	6,227	6,231	4,393	2,141	1,414	897
States	57	96	3,100	—39	—3,004	—3,043	43	77	1,624	14	19	1,476
(i) INDIGENOUS SIKHS..	43	841	2,799	—798	—1,958	—2,751	35	533	1,437	13	308	1,362
Districts	31	827	58	—796	+769	—27	23	527	38	5	300	20
States	17	14	2,741	+3	—2,727	—2,724	9	6	1,399	8	8	1,342
(ii) ALIEN SIKHS ..	8,377	6,900	5,591	+1,477	+1,309	+2,786	6,235	5,775	4,580	2,142	1,125	1,011
Districts	8,337	6,818	5,232	+1,519	+1,586	+3,105	6,201	5,704	4,355	2,136	1,114	877
States	40	82	359	—42	—277	—319	34	71	225	6	11	134
J—Christians	8,039	6,693	5,085	+1,366	+1,608	+2,974	5,637	5,214	3,941	2,422	1,479	1,144
Districts	8,044	6,678	5,030	+1,363	+1,648	+3,014	5,625	5,199	3,892	2,419	1,479	1,138
States	15	15	55	..	—40	—40	12	15	49	3	..	6
(a) European ..	*5,024*	*4,751*	*4,210*	*+273*	*+541*	*+814*	*3,802*	*3,966*	*3,382*	*1,222*	*785*	*828*
Districts ..	5,018	4,746	4,190	+272	+556	+828	3,797	3,961	3,366	1,221	785	824
States ..	6	5	20	+1	—15	—14	5	5	16	1	..	4
(b) Anglo-Indian ..	*379*	*234*	*123*	*+145*	*+111*	*+256*	*200*	*129*	*64*	*179*	*105*	*59*
Districts ..	376	229	118	+147	+111	+258	197	124	59	179	105	59
States ..	3	5	5	—2	..	—2	3	5	5	..	..	..
(c) Indian Christian ..	*2,656*	*1,708*	*752*	*+948*	*+956*	*+1,904*	*1,635*	*1,119*	*495*	*1,021*	*589*	*257*
Districts ..	2,650	1,703	722	+947	+981	+1,928	1,631	1,114	467	1,019	589	255
States ..	6	5	30	+1	—25	—24	4	5	28	2	..	2
K—Other Aliens ..	356	366	978	—7	—612	—619	238	287	603	121	79	375
Districts	355	365	972	—10	—607	—617	234	286	598	121	79	374
States	4	1	6	+3	—5	—2	4	1	5	..	..	1

TABLE XIX.—EUROPEANS AND ALLIED RACES AND ANGLO-INDIANS BY RACE AND AGE.

(a) Europeans and Allied Races including Armenians.

District or State.	TOTAL (Columns 5—32.) All Ages.			BRITISH SUBJECTS. All Ages.			0—13		14—16		17—23		24—33		34—43		44—53		54 and over.		OTHERS. All Ages.			24—33		34—43		44—53		54 and over.	
	Total.	M.	F.	Total.	M.	F.	M.	F.	M.	F.	M.	F.	M.	F.	M.	F.	M.	F.	M.	F.	T.	M.	F.	M.	F.	M.	F.	M.	F.	M.	F.
1	2	3	4	5	6	7	8	9	10	11	12	13	14	15	16	17	18	19	20	21	22	23	24	25	26	27	28	29	30	31	32
BALUCHISTAN	5,034	3,803	1,226	5,014	3,795	1,219	415	382	28	27	903	80	1,826	369	447	259	147	79	29	23	20	13	7	2	3	8	1	1	3	2	..
Districts	5,028	3,803	1,225	5,010	3,792	1,218	415	382	28	27	903	80	1,824	368	446	259	147	79	29	23	18	11	7	2	3	6	1	1	3	2	..
Quetta-Pishin	4,747	3,607	1,140	4,731	3,597	1,134	387	358	27	26	877	76	1,756	343	402	240	122	70	26	21	16	10	6	2	3	5	1	1	2	2	..
Loralai	87	62	25	87	62	25	5	4	..	1	10	1	26	10	11	6	8	2	2	1	..	..	..	..	..	..	..	..	..	..	..
Zhob	73	62	11	73	62	11	1	4	..	..	8	..	28	3	22	3	3	1	..	..	..	..	..	..	..	..	..	..	..	..	..
Bolan	25	13	12	25	13	12	2	5	..	..	2	..	3	4	1	3	5	..	..	..	..	..	..	..	..	..	..	..	..	..	..
Chagai	2	2	..	2	2	..	..	..	..	..	..	..	1	..	..	..	1	..	..	..	..	..	..	..	..	..	..	..	..	..	..
Sibi	94	57	37	92	56	36	20	11	1	..	6	3	10	8	10	7	8	6	1	1	2	1	1	..	..	1	..	..	1	..	..
States	6	5	1	4	3	1	..	..	..	..	..	..	2	1	1	..	..	..	..	..	2	2	..	..	..	2	..	..	..	..	..
Kalat	6	5	1	4	3	1	..	..	..	..	..	..	2	1	1	..	..	..	..	..	2	2	..	..	..	2	..	..	..	..	..
Sarawan	..	..	..	..	..	..	..	..	..	..	..	..	..	..	..	..	..	..	..	..	..	..	..	..	..	..	..	..	..	..	..
Jhalawan	..	..	..	..	..	..	..	..	..	..	..	..	..	..	..	..	..	..	..	..	..	..	..	..	..	..	..	..	..	..	..
Kachhi	1	1	..	..	..	..	..	..	..	..	..	..	..	..	..	..	..	..	..	..	1	1	..	..	..	1	..	..	..	..	..
Dombki-Kaheri Country	..	..	..	..	..	..	..	..	..	..	..	..	..	..	..	..	..	..	..	..	..	..	..	..	..	..	..	..	..	..	..
Makran	5	4	1	4	3	1	..	..	..	..	..	..	2	1	1	..	..	..	..	..	1	1	..	..	..	1	..	..	..	..	..
Kharan	..	..	..	..	..	..	..	..	..	..	..	..	..	..	..	..	..	..	..	..	..	..	..	..	..	..	..	..	..	..	..
Las-Bela	..	..	..	..	..	..	..	..	..	..	..	..	..	..	..	..	..	..	..	..	..	..	..	..	..	..	..	..	..	..	..

(b) ANGLO-INDIANS.

District or State.	All Ages.			0—3		4—6		7—13		14—16		17—19		20—29		30—39		40—49		50—59		60—69		70 and over.	
	Total.	M.	F.	M.	F.	M	F.	M.	F.	M.	F.	M.	F.	M.	F.	M.	F	M.	F.	M.	F.	M.	F.	M.	F.
1	2	3	4	5	6	7	8	9	10	11	12	13	14	15	16	17	18	19	20	21	22	23	24	25	26
BALUCHISTAN.	379	200	179	21	21	24	17	41	37	18	9	4	5	25	36	41	30	24	16	6	5	1	2	..	1
Districts	376	197	179	21	21	24	17	41	37	18	9	4	5	23	36	40	30	24	16	6	5	1	2	..	1
Quetta-Pishin	286	145	141	15	17	18	9	24	32	13	8	3	3	17	29	27	23	22	12	5	4	1	2	..	1
Loralai	2	..	2	..	..	..	..	..	1	..	..	..	..	..	..	..	..	..	1	..	..	..	..	..	..
Zhob	..	..	..	..	..	..	..	..	..	..	..	..	..	..	..	..	..	..	..	..	..	..	..	..	..
Bolan	24	13	11	1	1	2	2	3	3	..	..	1	1	2	1	4	3	..	..	..	..	..	..	..	..
Chagai	12	8	4	..	1	..	1	4	..	..	..	..	..	..	1	3	..	1	1	..	..	..	..	..	..
Sibi	52	31	21	5	2	4	5	10	1	..	1	..	1	4	5	6	4	1	1	1	1	..	..	..	..
States	3	3	..	..	..	..	..	..	..	..	..	..	..	2	..	1	..	..	..	..	..	..	..	..	..
Kalat	3	3	..	..	..	..	..	..	..	..	..	..	..	2	..	1	..	..	..	..	..	..	..	..	..
Sarawan	..	..	..	..	..	..	..	..	..	..	..	..	..	..	..	..	..	..	..	..	..	..	..	..	..
Jhalawan	..	..	..	..	..	..	..	..	..	..	..	..	..	..	..	..	..	..	..	..	..	..	..	..	..
Kachhi	..	..	..	..	..	..	..	..	..	..	..	..	..	..	..	..	..	..	..	..	..	..	..	..	..
Dombki-Kaheri Country	..	..	..	..	..	..	..	..	..	..	..	..	..	..	..	..	..	..	..	..	..	..	..	..	..
Makran	3	3	..	..	..	..	..	..	..	..	..	..	..	2	..	1	..	..	..	..	..	..	..	..	..
Kharan	..	..	..	..	..	..	..	..	..	..	..	..	..	..	..	..	..	..	..	..	..	..	..	..	..
Las-Bela	..	..	..	..	..	..	..	..	..	..	..	..	..	..	..	..	..	..	..	..	..	..	..	..	..

NOTE.—The difference of 10 persons (6 males and 4 females) among Europeans shown in this table and in table XVII is made up as under—

Religion.	Nationality.	Males.	Females.
Indefinite Beliefs.	British.	3	3
Jew.	British.	2	0
Muslim.	German.	1	1
	Total	6	4

TABLE XX.

SUMMARY FIGURES FOR DISTRICTS AND STATES.

The number of persons per square mile for the indigenous population living in Tribal Areas, and in the Regular Areas consisting of Towns and Cantonments and Railway premises, is shown below :—

Tribal Areas (population 757,768 persons.)

Districts and States.	Area.	Population.	No. of Persons per square mile.
DISTRICTS.			
Quetta-Pishin	4,756	76,242	16
Loralai	7,521	79,784	11
Zhob	10,225	48,345	5
Bolan	344	514	1
Chagai	20,016	19,516	1
Sibi	11,175	129,757	12
Total ..	54,037	354,158	7
STATES.			
Kalat	73,269	340,602	5
Sarawan	5,229	28,285	5
Jhalawan	20,795	88,916	4
Kachhi	4,060	105,805	26
Dombki-Kaheri Country	1,359	26,953	20
Makran	23,261	67,285	3
Kharan	18,565	23,358	1
Las-Bela	7,132	63,008	9
Total ..	80,401	403,610	5

Regular Areas (population 110,849 persons.)

Districts and States.	Area.	Population.	No. of Persons per square mile.
DISTRICTS.			
Quetta-Pishin	50	71,299	1426
Loralai	4	6,303	1576
Zhob	90	9,618	107
Bolan	15	4,174	278
Chagai	20	4,708	235
Sibi	12	13,248	1,104
Total ..	191	109,350	573
STATES.			
Kalat	9	1,499	167
Sarawan	1	179	179
Jhalawan	..	62	..
Kachhi	..	81	..
Dombki-Kaheri Country	..	..	..
Makran	8	1,177	147
Kharan	..	..	..
Las-Bela	..	..	..
Total ..	9	1,499	167

2. Figures of population in column 6 differ from those given in the corresponding table for 1921 in the case of Sibi and Shahrig Tahsils and the Mari Country within the Sibi District and in that of Bolan owing to internal and inter-district transfers, as shown on the fly-leaf of Imperial Table II.

TABLE XX.—SUMMARY FIGURES FOR DISTRICTS AND STATES.

DISTRICT OR STATE.	AREA IN SQUARE MILES.	POPULATION (1931.)			POPULATION.	PERCENTAGE OF VARIATION.		NUMBER OF PERSONS PER SQUARE MILE.		DISTRIBUTION BY RELIGION.											
										HINDU.		MUSLIM.		SIKH.		CHRISTIAN.		TRIBAL.		OTHERS.	
		Persons.	Males.	Females.	1921	1921-1931	1911-1921	in 1931-1921		M.	F.	M.	F.	M.	F.	M.	F.	M.	F.	M.	F.
1	2	3	4	5	6	7	8	9	10	11	12	13	14	15	16	17	18	19	20	21	22
BALUCHISTAN ..	*134,638*	*868,617*	*488,414*	*380,203*	*799,625*	+8·6	−4·2	*6*	*6*	*36,180*	*17,501*	*440,089*	*358,004*	*6,270*	*2,155*	*5,637*	*2,422*	*25*	*7*	*213*	*114*
DISTRICTS ..	**54,228**	**463,508**	**270,004**	**193,504**	**420,648**	+10·2	+1·5	**9**	**8**	**29,529**	**11,908**	**228,389**	**176,920**	**6,227**	**2,141**	**5,625**	**2,449**	**25**	**7**	**209**	114
Quetta-Pishin ..	4,806	147,541	90,302	57,239	135,809	+8·6	+8·2	31	28	19,212	7,506	62,024	45,921	3,754	1,501	5,169	2,201	..	..	143	110
Loralai ..	7,525	86,087	47,936	38,151	82,473	+4·4	+2·1	11	11	2,403	1,101	44,943	36,869	447	115	143	66	..	..	..	..
Zhob ..	10,315	57,963	34,596	23,367	56,668	+2·3	−19·5	6	5	2,402	437	31,025	22,819	1,039	95	99	16	..	..	31	..
Bolan ..	359	4,688	3,466	1,222	4,874	−3·8	+69·2	13	14	908	257	2,333	896	143	30	56	35	..	..	26	4
Chagai ..	20,036	24,224	13,721	10,503	22,616	+7·1	+22·7	1	1	891	422	12,722	10,047	89	28	19	6	..	..	..	..
Sibi ..	11,187	143,005	79,983	63,022	118,208	+21·0	+1·5	13	11	3,713	2,180	75,342	60,368	755	372	139	95	25	7	9	..
Administered Area ..	*3,907*	*87,781*	*49,447*	*38,334*	*80,249*	*+9·4*	*−·5*	*22*	*21*	*3,545*	*2,027*	*44,974*	*35,833*	*755*	*372*	*139*	*95*	*25*	*7*	*9*	..
Mari-Bugti Country ..	*7,280*	*55,224*	*30,536*	*24,688*	*37,959*	*+45·5*	*+6·2*	*8*	*5*	*168*	*153*	*30,368*	*24,535*	..	..	..	..	..	..	..	..
STATES ..	**80,410**	**405,109**	**218,410**	**186,699**	**378,977**	+6·9	−9·8	**5**	**5**	**6,651**	**5,596**	**211,700**	**181,084**	**43**	**14**	**12**	**3**	..	..	**4**	..
Kalat ..	73,278	342,101	184,915	157,186	328,281	+4·2	−8·6	5	4	5,841	4,965	179,027	152,207	31	11	12	3	..	..	4	..
Sarawan ..	*5,230*	*28,464*	*15,545*	*12,919*	*54,262*	*−47·5*	*−14·9*	*5*	*10*	*396*	*333*	*15,140*	*12,582*	*8*	*2*	*1*	*2*	..	..	..	..
Jhalawan ..	*20,795*	*88,978*	*47,987*	*40,991*	*79,710*	*+11·6*	*−5·6*	*4*	*4*	*161*	*36*	*47,825*	*40,955*	*1*	..	..	..	..	..	..	..
Kachhi ..	*4,060*	*105,886*	*57,844*	*48,042*	*75,153*	*+40·9*	*−19·0*	*26*	*19*	*3,751*	*3,268*	*54,079*	*44,773*	*11*	*1*	*1*	..	..	..	*2*	..
Dombki-Kaheri Country	*1,359*	*26,953*	*14,553*	*12,400*	*19,558*	*+37·8*	*−16·9*	*20*	*14*	*1,309*	*1,279*	*13,236*	*11,113*	*8*	*8*	..	..	..	..	..	..
Makran ..	*23,269*	*68,462*	*36,483*	*31,979*	*71,860*	*−4·7*	*−·1*	*3*	*3*	*199*	*34*	*36,269*	*31,944*	*3*	..	*10*	*1*	..	..	*2*	..
Kharan ..	*18,565*	*23,358*	*12,503*	*10,855*	*27,738*	*−15·8*	*+22·4*	*1*	*1*	*25*	*15*	*12,478*	*10,840*	..	..	..	..	..	..	..	..
Las-Bela ..	7,132	63,008	33,495	29,513	50,696	+24·3	−17·2	9	7	810	633	32,673	28,877	12	3	..	..	..	..	..	..

M=Males; F=Females.

PROVINCIAL TABLE I.

AREA AND POPULATION BY POLITICAL AGENCIES AND OTHER LOCAL AREAS.

The number of persons per square mile for the indigenous population living in Tribal Areas (Total population 757,768 persons) and in the Regular Areas (Total population 110,849 persons) consisting of Towns and Cantonments and Railway premises is shown below :—

Tribal Areas (Total population 757,768 persons).

Districts and States.	Area.	Population.	No. of Persons per square mile.
DISTRICTS.			
Quetta-Pishin	4,756	76,242	16
Loralai	7,521	79,784	11
Zhob	10,225	48,345	5
Bolan	344	514	1
Chagai	20,016	19,516	1
Sibi	11,175	129,757	12
Total ..	54,037	354,158	7
STATES.			
Kalat	73,269	340,602	5
Sarawan	5,229	28,285	5
Jhalawan	20,795	88,916	4
Kachhi	4,060	105,805	26
Dombki-Kaheri Country	1,359	26,953	20
Makran	23,261	67,285	3
Kharan	18,565	23,358	1
Las-Bela	7,132	63,008	9
Total ..	80,401	403,610	5

Regular Areas (Total population 110,849 persons).

Districts and States.	Area.	Population.	No. of Persons per square mile.
DISTRICTS.			
Quetta-Pishin	50	71,299	1,426
Loralai	4	6,303	1,576
Zhob	90	9,618	107
Bolan	15	4,174	278
Chagai	20	4,708	235
Sibi	12	13,248	1,104
Total ..	191	109,350	573
STATES.			
Kalat	9	1,499	167
Sarawan	1	179	179
Jhalawan	..	62	..
Kachhi	..	81	..
Dombki-Kaheri Country	..	..	..
Makran	8	1,177	147
Kharan	..	..	..
Las-Bela	..	..	..
Total ..	9	1,499	167

2. Figures of population in column 9 differ from those given in the corresponding table for 1921 in the case of Sibi and Shahrig Tahsils and the Mari Country within the Sibi District and in that of Bolan owing to internal and Inter-district transfers, as shown on fly-leaf of Imperial Table II.

PROVINCIAL TABLE I.—AREA AND POPULATION BY POLITICAL AGENCIES AND OTHER LOCAL AREAS.

Political Agency, Tahsil, etc.	Area in square miles.	Number of Towns.	Number of Villages.	Number of occupied Houses.	Population 1931. Persons.	Population 1931. Males.	Population 1931. Females.	Population 1921 (both Sexes.)	Percentage of Variation. 1921 to 1931.	Percentage of Variation. 1911 to 1921.	Number of Persons per square mile.
1	2	3	4	5	6	7	8	9	10	11	12
BALUCHISTAN ..	*134,638*	*17*	*3,501*	*166,644*	*868,617*	*488,414*	*380,203*	*799,625*	+8·6	—4·2	6
1. Quetta-Pishin Agency	**4,806**	**6**	**376**	**28,172**	**147,541**	**90,302**	**57,239**	**135,809**	**+8·6**	**+3·2**	**31**
Pishin Tahsil ..	3,052	2	275	11,055	53,375	27,820	25,555	49,981	+6·8	—7·2	17
Chaman Tahsil ..	1,206	2	53	3,137	17,517	10,955	6,562	17,605	—·5	+2·0	15
Quetta Tahsil ..	548	2	48	13,980	76,649	51,527	25,122	68,223	+12·4	+24·0	140
2. Loralai Agency ..	**7,525**	**2**	**429**	**16,402**	**86,087**	**47,936**	**38,151**	**82,478**	**+4·4**	**+2·1**	**11**
Duki Tahsil ..	1,888	..	74	3,415	17,998	9,771	8,227	15,806	+13·9	—8·2	11
Bori Tahsil ..	1,671	2	125	3,598	18,532	11,464	7,068	17,767	+4·3	+2·7	11
Sanjawi Sub-Tahsil.	676	..	40	1,260	6,313	3,501	2,812	8,895	—29·0	+17·5	9
Barkhan Tahsil ..	1,309	..	120	3,661	20,434	10,901	9,533	18,129	+12·7	+·9	16
Musakhel Tahsil	2,181	..	70	4,468	22,810	12,299	10,511	21,876	+4·3	+5·6	10
3. Zhob Agency ..	**10,315**	**2**	**251**	**12,675**	**57,963**	**34,596**	**23,367**	**56,568**	**+2·3**	**—19·5**	**6**
Fort Sandeman Tahsil.	6,458	2	114	6,543	32,989	20,111	12,878	31,612	+4·4	—21·3	5
Hindubagh Tahsil	1,459	..	79	2,573	11,580	6,724	4,856	13,162	—12·0	+6·4	8
Killa Saifullah Tahsil.	2,398	..	58	3,557	13,394	7,761	5,633	11,894	+12·6	—39·3	6
4. Chagai Agency ..	**20,036**	..	**72**	**6,187**	**24,224**	**13,721**	**10,503**	**22,618**	**+7·1**	**+22·7**	**1**
Nushki Tahsil ..	2,361	..	23	2,665	10,820	6,016	4,804	9,905	+9·2	+22·0	5
Dalbandin including Western Sanjrani.	17,261	..	45	3,019	11,185	6,374	4,811	11,438	—2·2	+39·0	1
Shorarud Sub-Tahsil.	414	..	4	503	2,219	1,331	888	1,273	+74·3	—38·8	5
5. Sibi Agency ..	**11,187**	**1**	**269**	**25,045**	**143,005**	**79,983**	**63,022**	**118,208**	**+21·0**	**+1·5**	**13**
Sibi Tahsil ..	1,148	1	33	6,138	27,507	15,823	11,684	22,440	+22·5	—3·3	24
Shahrig Tahsil ..	1,576	..	93	3,852	18,177	10,193	7,984	20,186	—10·0	+3·2	12
Nasirabad Tahsil	821	..	91	6,551	36,634	20,415	16,219	30,456	+20·3	—8·2	45
Kohlu Sub-Tahsil	362	..	25	1,006	5,463	3,016	2,447	7,167	—23·8	+52·1	15
Mari Country ..	3,404	..	17	3,235	24,860	13,880	10,980	14,501	+71·4	—3·7	7
Bugti Country ..	3,876	..	10	4,260	30,364	16,656	13,708	23,458	+29·4	+13·6	8
6. Kalat Agency ..	**80,769**	**6**	**2,104**	**78,163**	**409,797**	**221,876**	**187,921**	**383,851**	**+6·8**	**—9·2**	**5**
(a) **Bolan** ..	*359*	*1*	28	*1,635*	*4,688*	*3,466*	*1,222*	*4,374*	—3·8	+69·2	13
(b) **Kalat** ..	*73,278*	4	*1,797*	*65,007*	*342,101*	*184,915*	*157,186*	*328,281*	+4·2	—8·6	5
Sarawan ..	5,230	2	186	6,281	28,464	15,545	12,919	54,262	—47·5	—14·9	5
Jhalawan ..	20,795	..	475	14,139	88,978	47,987	40,991	79,710	+11·6	—5·6	4
Kachhi ..	4,060	..	589	18,255	105,886	57,844	48,042	75,153	+40·9	—19·0	26
Dombki-Kaheri Country.	1,359	..	123	4,592	26,953	14,553	12,400	19,558	+37·8	—16·9	20
Makran ..	23,269	2	305	15,484	68,462	36,483	31,979	71,860	—4·7	—·1	3
Kharan ..	18,565	..	119	6,276	23,358	12,503	10,855	27,738	—15·8	+22·4	1
(c) **Las-Bela** ..	7,132	1	279	11,521	63,008	33,495	29,513	50,696	+24·3	—17·2	9

PROVINCIAL TABLE II.

POPULATION OF POLITICAL AGENCIES BY RELIGION AND LITERACY.

" Others " in this table include :—

RELIGION.	DISTRICT OR STATE.	TAHSIL.	POPULATION.			LITERATE.	
			Persons.	Males.	Females.	Males.	Females.
		Total ..	359	238	121	140	56
Jain ..	Quetta-Pishin ..	Quetta ..	32	20	12	14	1
Buddhist ..	Quetta-Pishin ..	Quetta ..	40	25	15	14	4
	Zhob ..	Fort Sandeman	27	27	..	27	..
	Sibi ..	Sibi ..	1	1	..	..	..
Zoroastrian ..	Quetta-Pishin ..	Quetta ..	160	83	77	63	48
	Quetta-Pishin ..	Chaman ..	1	1	..	1	..
	Sibi ..	Sibi ..	6	6	..	6	..
Jew ..	Quetta-Pishin ..	Quetta ..	12	9	3	6	..
	Quetta-Pishin ..	Chaman ..	3	3	..	..	..
	Kalat State ..	Makran ..	2	2	..	2	..
Tribal ..	Sibi ..	Nasirabad ..	32	25	7	..	..
Others ..	Quetta-Pishin ..	Quetta ..	5	2	3	2	3
	Zhob ..	Fort Sandeman	4	4	..	..	..
	Bolan ..	Bolan ..	30	26	4	3	..
	Sibi ..	Sibi ..	2	2	..	2	..
	Kalat State ..	Kachhi ..	2	2	..	..	..

PROVINCIAL TABLE II.—POPULATION OF POLITICAL AGENCIES BY RELIGION AND LITERACY.

Political Agency, Tahsil, etc.	Muslims. No. of Persons. M.	Muslims. No. of Persons. F.	Muslims. No. of Literates. M.	Muslims. No. of Literates. F.	Hindus. Brahman. No. of Persons. M.	Brahman. No. of Persons. F.	Brahman. No. of Literates. M.	Brahman. No. of Literates. F.	Other Hindus. No. of Persons. M.	Other Hindus. No. of Persons. F.	Other Hindus. No. of Literates. M.	Other Hindus. No. of Literates. F.	Depressed Classes. No. of Persons. M.	Depressed Classes. No. of Persons. F.	Depressed Classes. No. of Literates. M.	Depressed Classes. No. of Literates. F.
1	2	3	4	5	6	7	8	9	10	11	12	13	14	15	16	17
BALUCHISTAN	440,039	358,004	12,093	563	2,887	816	1,664	150	28,162	14,470	14,699	1,345	5,131	2,215	495	8
I. Quetta-Pishin Agency	62,024	45,921	6,294	396	1,602	518	858	98	13,972	5,381	8,334	997	3,638	1,607	349	6
Pishin Tahsil (B. B.)	26,547	25,151	940	15	97	20	42	1	851	248	518	16	126	45	7	..
Chaman Sub-division (B. B.)	8,330	5,636	373	8	67	20	30	4	1,978	694	1,290	50	222	60	29	..
Quetta Tahsil (A. T.)	27,147	15,134	4,981	373	1,438	478	786	93	11,143	4,439	6,526	931	3,290	1,502	313	6
II. Loralai Agency	44,943	36,869	967	21	468	55	369	13	1,647	938	806	64	288	108	52	..
Duki Tahsil (B. B.)	9,512	8,079	104	1	13	8	10	1	211	126	64	1	10	6	..	..
Bori Tahsil (A. T.)	9,309	6,322	620	16	428	34	348	12	925	464	421	57	271	95	50	..
Sanjawi Sub-Tahsil (A. T.)	3,452	2,791	48	2	1	1	..	..	37	10	21	..	4	4	..	..
Barkhan Tahsil (A. T.)	10,454	9,206	90	..	25	12	10	..	399	301	264	6	..	..	..	..
Musakhel Tahsil (A. T.)	12,216	10,471	105	2	1	..	1	..	75	37	36	..	3	3	2	..
III. Zhob Agency	31,025	22,819	1,062	31	270	47	176	8	1,923	350	1,354	77	209	40	36	2
Fort Sandeman Tahsil (A. T.)	17,260	12,457	790	26	187	41	118	8	1,674	271	1,210	64	156	31	22	..
Hindubagh Tahsil (A. T.)	6,227	4,787	149	2	27	4	20	..	128	31	71	4	38	9	11	2
Killa Saifullah Tahsil (A. T.)	7,538	5,575	123	3	56	2	38	..	121	48	73	9	15	..	3	..
IV. Chagai Agency	12,722	10,047	355	8	88	28	36	4	683	331	292	35	120	63	7	..
Nushki Tahsil (A. T.)	5,622	4,583	125	..	25	13	8	1	290	171	136	9	34	30	3	..
Dalbandin Tahsil including Western Sanjrani (A. T.)	5,771	4,576	179	8	63	15	28	3	393	160	156	26	85	33	4	..
Shorarud Sub-Tahsil (B. B.)	1,329	888	51	..	..	..	..	..	..	..	..	..	1	..	..	..
V. Sibi Agency	75,292	60,368	1,061	63	239	88	117	20	2,807	1,767	1,022	101	667	325	41	..
Sibi Tahsil (B. B.)	13,262	10,025	591	53	162	62	82	17	1,515	1,097	514	88	491	236	35	..
Shahrig Tahsil (B. B.)	9,762	7,813	156	3	38	14	20	3	247	96	146	9	64	26	4	..
Nasirabad Tahsil (A. T.)	18,965	15,566	236	7	31	9	13	..	878	427	311	1	89	42	2	..
Kohlu Sub-Tahsil (A. T.)	2,935	2,429	24	..	2	..	2	..	23	14	7	3	5	4	..	..
Mari Country (T. A.)	13,712	10,827	28	..	6	3	..	..	144	133	44	..	18	17	..	..
Bugti Country (T. A.)	16,656	13,708	26	..	..	..	..	..	..	..	..	..	..	..	..	..
VI. Kalat Agency	214,033	181,980	2,354	44	220	80	108	7	7,130	5,703	2,891	71	209	72	10	..
Bolan (A. T.)	2,333	896	190	10	117	28	76	5	612	164	269	26	179	65	8	..
Kalat (I. S.)	179,027	152,207	1,770	8	76	38	32	2	5,736	4,920	2,217	45	29	7	2	..
Sarawan (I. S.)	15,140	12,582	516	..	23	12	7	1	360	317	93	33	13	4	1	..
Jhalawan (I. S.)	47,825	40,955	240	..	2	..	2	..	159	36	34	..	..	..	..	..
Kachhi (I. S.)	54,079	44,773	426	2	43	24	19	..	3,708	3,244	1,635	4	..	..	..	..
Dombki-Kaheri Country (I. S.)	13,236	11,113	101	..	..	..	..	..	1,309	1,279	406	..	..	..	..	..
Makran (I. S.)	36,269	31,944	319	4	8	2	4	1	175	29	34	8	16	3	1	..
Kharan (I. S.)	12,478	10,840	168	2	..	..	..	..	25	15	15	..	..	..	..	..
Las-Bela (I. S.)	32,673	28,877	394	26	27	14	..	..	782	619	405	..	1	..	..	..

Political Agency, Tahsil, etc.	Sikhs. No. of Persons. M.	Sikhs. No. of Persons. F.	Sikhs. No. of Literates. M.	Sikhs. No. of Literates. F.	Christians. No. of Persons. M.	Christians. No. of Persons. F.	Christians. No. of Literates. M.	Christians. No. of Literates. F.	Others. No. of Persons. M.	Others. No. of Persons. F.	Others. No. of Literates. M.	Others. No. of Literates. F.	* No. of Literates. M.	* No. of Literates. F.	Literate in English. M.	Literate in English. F.
1	18	19	20	21	22	23	24	25	26	27	28	29	30	31	32	33
BALUCHISTAN	6,270	2,155	3,669	524	5,637	2,422	4,075	1,294	238	121	140	56	36,835	3,940	10,063	1,526
I. Quetta-Pishin Agency	3,754	1,501	2,178	397	5,169	2,201	3,804	1,177	143	110	100	56	21,917	3,127	8,074	1,383
Pishin Tahsil (B. B.)	129	63	65	9	70	28	39	7	..	..	..	..	1,611	48	195	10
Chaman Sub-division (B. B.)	210	50	154	17	144	102	39	22	4	..	1	..	1,916	101	211	23
Quetta Tahsil (A. T.)	3,415	1,388	1,959	371	4,955	2,071	3,726	1,148	139	110	99	56	18,390	2,978	7,668	1,350
II. Loralai Agency	447	115	319	34	143	66	74	27	..	..	..	..	2,587	159	474	26
Duki Tahsil (B. B.)	14	3	5	1	11	5	..	..	..	..	..	..	183	4	14	..
Bori Tahsil (A. T.)	408	99	297	29	123	54	74	27	..	..	..	..	1,810	141	422	25
Sanjawi Sub-Tahsil (A. T.)	7	6	3	..	..	..	..	..	..	..	..	..	72	2	16	1
Barkhan Tahsil (A. T.)	14	7	11	4	9	7	..	..	..	..	..	..	375	10	13	..
Musakhel Tahsil (A. T.)	4	..	3	..	..	..	..	..	..	..	..	..	147	2	9	..
III. Zhob Agency	1,039	95	797	24	99	16	69	9	31	..	27	..	3,521	151	486	13
Fort Sandeman Tahsil (A. T.)	730	64	582	17	73	14	57	9	31	..	27	..	2,806	124	381	12
Hindubagh Tahsil (A. T.)	286	23	203	6	18	2	11	..	..	..	..	..	465	14	64	..
Killa Saifullah Tahsil (A. T.)	23	8	12	1	8	..	1	..	..	..	..	..	250	13	41	1
IV. Chagai Agency	89	28	45	2	19	6	14	3	..	..	..	..	749	52	142	4
Nushki Tahsil (A. T.)	38	6	17	1	7	1	4	..	..	..	..	..	293	11	43	..
Dalbandin Tahsil including Western Sanjrani (A. T.)	50	22	27	1	12	5	10	3	..	..	..	..	404	41	95	4
Shorarud Sub-Tahsil (B. B.)	1	..	1	..	..	..	..	..	..	..	..	..	52	..	4	..
V. Sibi Agency	755	372	235	62	139	95	79	55	34	7	8	..	2,563	301	560	74
Sibi Tahsil (B. B.)	261	175	123	45	123	89	71	51	9	..	8	..	1,424	254	428	67
Shahrig Tahsil (B. B.)	68	29	37	9	14	6	7	4	..	..	..	..	370	28	66	5
Nasirabad Tahsil (A. T.)	425	168	75	8	2	..	1	..	25	7	..	..	638	16	62	2
Kohlu Sub-Tahsil (A. T.)	1	..	..	..	..	..	..	..	..	..	..	..	33	3	3	..
Mari Country (T. A.)	..	..	..	..	..	..	..	..	..	..	..	..	72	..	..	..
Bugti Country (T. A.)	..	..	..	..	..	..	..	..	..	..	..	..	26	..	1	..
VI. Kalat Agency	186	44	95	5	68	38	35	23	30	4	5	..	5,498	150	327	26
Bolan (A. T.)	143	30	77	5	56	35	26	22	26	4	3	..	649	68	203	24
Kalat (I. S.)	31	11	13	..	12	3	9	1	4	..	2	..	4,045	56	100	2
Sarawan (I. S.)	8	2	3	..	1	2	..	..	..	..	..	..	620	34	13	1
Jhalawan (I. S.)	1	..	1	..	..	..	..	..	..	..	..	..	277	..	15	..
Kachhi (I. S.)	11	1	7	..	1	..	1	..	2	..	..	..	2,068	6	26	..
Dombki-Kaheri Country (I. S.)	8	8	..	..	..	..	..	..	..	..	..	..	507	..	..	..
Makran (I. S.)	3	..	2	..	10	1	8	1	2	..	2	..	370	14	46	1
Kharan (I. S.)	..	..	..	..	..	..	..	..	..	..	..	..	183	2	..	..
Las-Bela (I. S.)	12	3	5	..	..	..	..	..	..	..	..	..	804	26	24	..

Abbreviations used in Column 1.
B. B.=British Baluchistan. | T. A.=Tribal Area.
A. T.=Agency Territory. | I. S.=Indian States.

M.=Males.
F.=Females.

* The figures in columns 30 and 31 are inclusive of those in columns 32 and 33.